Accounting and Finance

Fifth Edition

Accounting and Finance

Understanding and Practice

Fifth Edition

Danny Leiwy, Robert Perks, Neeta Shah

McGraw Hill

Accounting and Finance: Understanding and Practice, Fifth Edition
Danny Leiwy, Robert Perks, Neeta Shah
ISBN-13 9781526850164
ISBN-10 1526850168

Published by McGraw-Hill Education (UK) Limited
Unit 4, Foundation Park,
Roxborough Way
Maidenhead, SL6 3UD
Telephone: +44 (0) 1628 502 500
Website: www.mheducation.co.uk

British Library Cataloguing in Publication Data
A catalogue record for this book is available from the British Library

Portfolio Manager: Felicity Baines
Content Developers: Maggie du Randt and Umeeka Raichura
Production Manager: Ben King
Marketing Manager: Ros Letellier

ISBN-13 9781526850164
ISBN-10 1526850168
eISBN-13 9781526850157

G11221 ACL 2025

Dedication

To Malki
Kate and Menachem
Jonny and Natalie
and
David and Jo

Brief Table of Contents

About the Authors xi
Preface xii
Acknowledgements xiii
Guided Tour xiv

Part 1 Introduction to Financial Accounting 1

1 The Statement of Financial Position (Balance Sheet) and What it Tells Us 6
2 The Income Statement (Profit and Loss Account) 31
3 The Development of Financial Reporting 54
4 Ratios and Interpretation: A Straightforward Introduction 78
5 How the Stock Market Assesses Company Performance 106
6 Cash Flow Statements: IAS 7 Understanding and Preparation 129
7 Advanced Interpretation of Company and Group Accounts 162
8 Current Issues in Financial Reporting 189
9 Bookkeeping to Trial Balance 221
10 Trial Balance to Final Accounts 252

Part 2 Financial Management 292

11 Financing a Business 293
12 Management of Working Capital 314

Part 3 Introduction to Management Accounting 334

13 Introduction to Management Accounting 335
14 Investment Appraisal 350
15 Budgetary Planning and Control 383
16 Absorption Costing 405
17 Marginal Costing and Decision-making 423
18 Standard Costing and Variance Analysis 442
19 Sustainability and Accounting 461

Answers to Self-testing Questions 476
Answers to Chapter 4 Activities 533
Glossary 538
Index 546

The following additional material is available online:
Chapter 20: Incomplete Records
Appendix: Developments in Management Accounting

Detailed Table of Contents

About the Authors xi
Preface xii
Acknowledgements xiii
Guided Tour xiv

Part 1 Introduction to Financial Accounting 1

Introduction 1
What Is Accounting? 1
Private Business - Accountability 2
Users of Accounting Information 3

1 The Statement of Financial Position (Balance Sheet) and What it Tells Us 6

1.1 Introduction 6
1.2 An Individual's Statement of Financial Position (Balance Sheet) 7
1.3 A Company's Statement of Financial Position (Balance Sheet) 8
1.4 Short- and Long-term Classification 11
1.5 Statement of Financial Position: Financial Strengths and Weaknesses 12
1.6 Depreciation and Statement of Financial Position 'Values' 14
1.7 Statements of Financial Position and Profit 15
1.8 A Company's Published Statement of Financial Position 17
1.9 Role and Limitations of Statements of Financial Position 20
1.10 Financial Accounting and Management Accounting 22

2 The Income Statement (Profit and Loss Account) 31

2.1 Introduction 31
2.2 Terminology and Format 32
2.3 Reasons for Measuring Profit 34
2.4 What Is Included as Revenues (or Income) 36
2.5 What Is Included as Expenses 37
2.6 A Company's Published Income Statement 41
2.7 Income Statement Detailed Items 43
2.8 Subjective Measurement and Creativity Problems 45
2.9 Role and Limitations of Income Statements 46

3 The Development of Financial Reporting 54

3.1 Introduction 55
3.2 Functions of Profit Measurement 55
3.3 Setting Accounting Standards 58
3.4 Concepts and Principles 60
3.5 The Statement of Financial Position Approach: Definition and Measurement of Assets and Liabilities 62
3.6 The Income Statement Approach: Definition and Measurement of Revenues and Expenses 68
3.7 Adjusting Financial Statements for Price Changes 72

4 **Ratios and Interpretation: A Straightforward Introduction 78**
4.1 Introduction 78
4.2 Financial Strength/Solvency 80
4.3 Profitability 84
4.4 Stock Market Ratios 89
4.5 Working Capital Management 91
4.6 Financial Structure/Gearing 92
4.7 Limitations and Comparisons 92
4.8 Ratios Ready Reference 94

5 **How the Stock Market Assesses Company Performance 106**
5.1 Introduction 107
5.2 Investing in Shares 107
5.3 What Influences Share Prices? 108
5.4 Accounting Information and Share Prices 110
5.5 The *Financial Times* 112
5.6 Price/Earnings (P/E) Ratios 114
5.7 Dividend Yield 116
5.8 Dividend Cover 118
5.9 Net Asset (or Statement of Financial Position) Value 119
5.10 Cash Flow 120
5.11 Other Indicators/Predictors of Performance 121
5.12 A Further Illustration 122

6 **Cash Flow Statements: IAS 7 Understanding and Preparation 129**
6.1 Introduction 129
6.2 The Accruals Concept 130
6.3 Cash Flow Statements 132
6.4 Interpreting Cash Flow Statements 137
6.5 Format for Cash Flow Statements 141
6.6 How to Prepare a Cash Flow Statement 147

7 **Advanced Interpretation of Company and Group Accounts 162**
7.1 Introduction 163
7.2 Calculating Ratios from Published Accounts 163
7.3 Consolidated (Group) Financial Statements 169
7.4 Solvency and Predicting Financial Distress 174
7.5 Selective Performance 177
7.6 Other Information from Annual Reports 180

8 **Current Issues in Financial Reporting 189**
8.1 Introduction 190
8.2 What Is Creative Accounting? 190
8.3 Some Problem Areas 195
8.4 How to Curtail Creative Accounting 202
8.5 Social and Environmental Reporting 206

9 **Bookkeeping to Trial Balance 221**
9.1 Introduction 222
9.2 Bookkeeping in Practice 231
9.3 Bookkeeping Systems 239

10 Trial Balance to Final Accounts 252
10.1 Introduction 252
10.2 Sole Traders 253
10.3 Companies 264
10.4 Partnerships 274

Part 2 Financial Management 292

11 Financing a Business 293
11.1 Introduction 293
11.2 Share Capital 295
11.3 Borrowing 299
11.4 Retained Profits 303
11.5 Other Sources of Finance 306

12 Management of Working Capital 314
12.1 Introduction 314
12.2 Definition and Importance of Working Capital 315
12.3 Economic Order Quantity (EOQ) 325

Part 3 Introduction to Management Accounting 334

13 Introduction to Management Accounting 335
13.1 Introduction 335
13.2 The Origins of Management Accounting 336
13.3 Management Accounting and Financial Accounting 337
13.4 Budgetary Control 339
13.5 Manufacturing Accounts 340
13.6 Absorption and Marginal Costing 342
13.7 Standard Costing and Variance Analysis 343
13.8 Developments in Management Accounting 343

14 Investment Appraisal 350
14.1 Introduction 351
14.2 Investment 351
14.3 Methods of Investment Appraisal 352
14.4 Cost of Capital 368
14.5 Uncertainty and Risk 373

15 Budgetary Planning and Control 383
15.1 Introduction 383
15.2 Budgets and Budgetary Control 384
15.3 Implementing Budgetary Control 387
15.4 Cash Budgets 390
15.5 Advantages of Operating Budgetary Control Systems 392
15.6 Problems of Budgetary Control in Practice 394
15.7 Zero-based and Rolling Budgets 396
15.8 Planning and Programming Budgeting Systems (PPBS) 399

16 Absorption Costing 405
16.1 Introduction 405
16.2 Role and Origins of Costing Systems 406
16.3 Classification of Costs 407

16.4 Direct Materials and Pricing 408
16.5 Direct Labour 409
16.6 Direct Expenses 410
16.7 Production Overheads 410
16.8 Allocation, Apportionment and Absorption 412
16.9 Evaluation of Absorption Costing 413
16.10 Activity-based Costing 414

17 Marginal Costing and Decision-making 423

17.1 Introduction 423
17.2 Marginal Costing Presentation and Contribution 424
17.3 Separating Fixed and Variable Costs 426
17.4 Break-even Analysis 427
17.5 Break-even Charts and Profit/Volume Graphs 430
17.6 Marginal Costing and Decision-making 431
17.7 Advantages of Marginal Costing 431
17.8 Limitations of Marginal Costing 436

18 Standard Costing and Variance Analysis 442

18.1 Introduction 442
18.2 Direct Material Variances 444
18.3 Direct Labour Variances 445
18.4 Variable Overhead Variances 447
18.5 Fixed Overhead Variances 448
18.6 Sales Margin Variances 449
18.7 Summary of Variances 450
18.8 Another Approach 451
18.9 Evaluation 453

19 Sustainability and Accounting 461

19.1 Introduction 461
19.2 Why Is Sustainability Important? 462
19.3 Integrated Reporting (IR) Framework 463
19.4 International Sustainability Standards Board Issues - IFRS S1 and IFRS S2 465
19.5 Value Chain for Sustainable Businesses 466
19.6 Climate Change Risks and the Associated Financial Implications 466
19.7 Recommendations of the Task Force on Climate-related Financial Disclosures (TCFD) 467
19.8 UN SDGs and their Significance for Organizations 469

Answers to Self-testing Questions 476
Answers to Chapter 4 Activities 533
Glossary 538
Index 546

The following additional material is available online:

Chapter 20: Incomplete Records
Appendix: Developments in Management Accounting

About the Authors

The late **Danny Leiwy** taught at the London School of Economics and Political Science and on the University of London's International Programme at City University, London. He was a Senior Teaching Fellow at the School of Oriental and African Studies (SOAS), University of London. Danny also practiced as a Chartered Accountant. He was a Principal Lecturer in Accounting and Tax at the University of Westminster for 30 years, teaching at both undergraduate and postgraduate level.

Robert Perks formerly taught Accounting and Finance at the International Business School on the Isle of Man. Robert also held chairs at the following universities: Queen's University, Belfast, Middlesex University, Aberdeen University, Birkbeck College University of London and University of Westminster.

Neeta Shah is a senior lecturer in Accounting and Finance at the University of Westminster. She is a Fellow of the Association of Chartered Certified Accountants and has an MBA from the University of Warwick. She completed her PhD in corporate governance at the Royal Holloway University of London. Shah and Napier's article, 'Governors and Directors', was presented with the Robert W. Gibson Manuscript Award in 2019. She has taught at both undergraduate and postgraduate levels in financial accounting, management accounting and taxation. Her research interests include accounting education, corporate governance, financial accounting, financialization and pensions.

Preface

This book is intended to help readers understand accounting and to see how it can be used in practice, particularly in the interpretation and management of company finances. It should appeal to future managers, rather than to those who simply want to become accountants. It is intended to be 'user-friendly' for those who are put off by conventional presentations of the subject based on arcane rules and procedures. Non-specialist accounting students, for whom figures are sometimes a painful necessity, will probably find that this is as good as it gets with accounting textbooks.

It is an introductory text, which is particularly suitable for degree courses in management and business studies, including MBAs and other postgraduate degree programmes. It is suitable for year-long introductory accounting modules or semester-long modules on financial accounting and management accounting. The approach is analytical, critical and evaluative, amply illustrated with real-world examples, and for those modules that include the preparation of accounts, there is an extended section on bookkeeping and the preparation of financial accounts at the end of **Part 1** (**Chapters 9** and **10**).

The book is divided into three parts and begins with financial accounting (**Chapters 1–10**) and then moves on to financial management (**Chapters 11** and **12**) and then to management accounting (**Chapters 13–20**). Readers may be interested in the application of published financial reports in relation to the stock market (**Chapter 5**), financing a business (**Chapter 11**), investment appraisal (**Chapter 14**), or current issues in the rapidly developing area on financial accounting (**Chapters 3** and **8**). This 5th edition provides an introduction with an explanation of the characteristics of a limited liability company that result in the need for public disclosure to various stakeholders of every company's financial accounts. This edition includes a chapter on sustainability (**Chapter 19**), which is a growing area for research. The production of accounts from incomplete records (**Chapter 20**) has been kept as an online chapter, and some more advanced management accounting developments, such as backflush accounting and balanced scorecards, are briefly explained in an online **Appendix**.

Interpretation of accounts is a problem for many students and a simplified 'ready reference' guide to accounting 'ratios' is now provided in **Chapter 4**, with more advanced issues dealt with in a separate chapter (**Chapter 7**). After covering the basics of statements of financial position and income statements (**Chapters 1** and **2**), the book is designed so that any chapter can be studied in almost any order according to the readers' particular interests or the requirements of a course.

Ample resources are provided to enable readers to understand and apply financial accounting. Self-testing questions (numerical, theoretical and analytical) are included in each chapter, with answers at the end of the book. Assessment questions are provided without answers. Discussion questions and group activities are included to encourage readers to become involved in exploring important questions, and these can be related to current issues in the press by analysing the 'Accounting in context' illustrations. There is also an extensive **Glossary**.

All companies produce annual reports and accounts that include a great deal of valuable information if only managers, analysts, financial journalists, economists, bankers and everyone with an interest in business and management would take the time and trouble to understand them. This book is intended to help. Similarly, students who produce projects and dissertations, and politicians and journalists who analyse particular companies and industries, can benefit from the thorough understanding of published financial statements that this book provides. In the main, it explains financial accounting as an important resource that has valuable applications and gives an understanding of management accounting techniques used widely in businesses everywhere; but its approach is also critical, and it encourages readers to think about important issues and to reach their own conclusions.

Neeta Shah

Acknowledgements

Author's acknowledgements

First, I would like to thank the previous authors who wrote the earlier editions of this book.

Additionally, my thanks go to Felicity Baines, Maggie du Randt and Ben King at McGraw Hill for advising me at all stages and ensuring that the chapters were written in a timely manner.

Publisher's acknowledgements

Our thanks go to the following reviewers for their comments at various stages in the text's development:

Jock Anderson, Queen Margaret University
Stuart Cooper, Aston University
Siobhan Goggin, University of Lincoln
Louise Gracia, University of Warwick
Lindsey Hamilton, University of Keele
Qile He, University of Bedfordshire
Andreas Hoepner, University of St Andrews
Elisavet Mantzari, University of Westminster
Paul Marambos, University of Hertfordshire
Jim O'Hare, University of Leicester
Mohammad Rajjaque, University of Sheffield
Ane Ripoll-Zarraga, University of Keele
Deirdre Ruddy, National University of Ireland, Galway
Sheeja Sivaprasad, University of Westminster
Anne Stafford, University of Manchester
Grigorios Theodosopoulos, University of Hertfordshire

Every effort has been made to trace and acknowledge ownership of copyright and to clear permission for material reproduced in this book. The publishers will be pleased to make suitable arrangements to clear permission with any copyright holders who it has not been possible to contact.

Neeta Shah

Guided Tour

Chapter contents

A brief list of key chapter contents is highlighted at the start of each chapter.

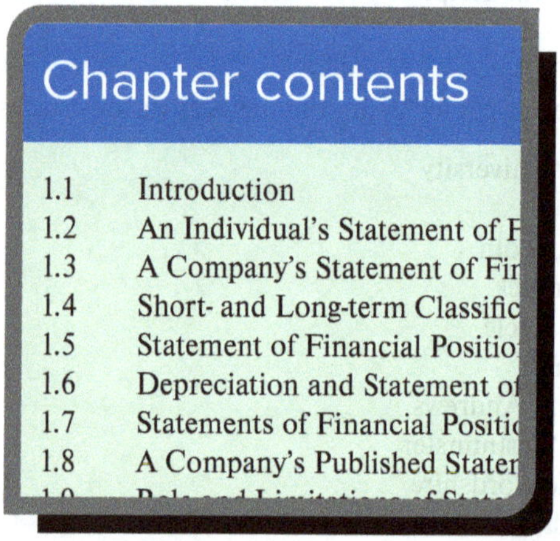
Chapter contents

1.1 Introduction
1.2 An Individual's Statement of F
1.3 A Company's Statement of Fir
1.4 Short- and Long-term Classific
1.5 Statement of Financial Positio
1.6 Depreciation and Statement of
1.7 Statements of Financial Positic
1.8 A Company's Published Stater

Learning objectives

Each chapter opens with a list of learning objectives, summarizing what you will learn from that chapter.

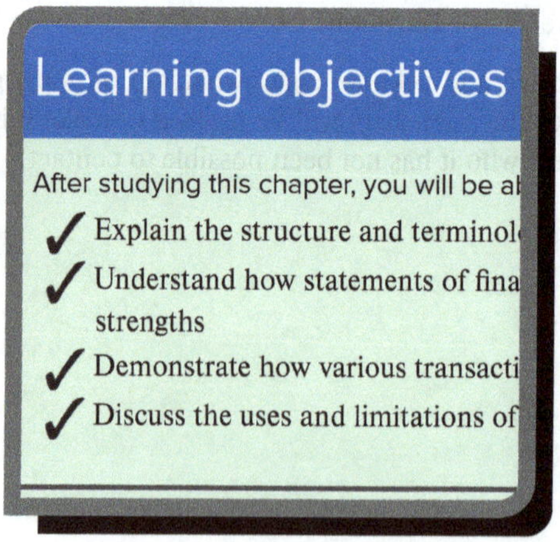
Learning objectives

After studying this chapter, you will be al
✓ Explain the structure and terminol
✓ Understand how statements of fina strengths
✓ Demonstrate how various transacti
✓ Discuss the uses and limitations of

Introduction

Each chapter opens with an introduction, which sets the scene and introduces you to the issues that will be addressed in the chapter.

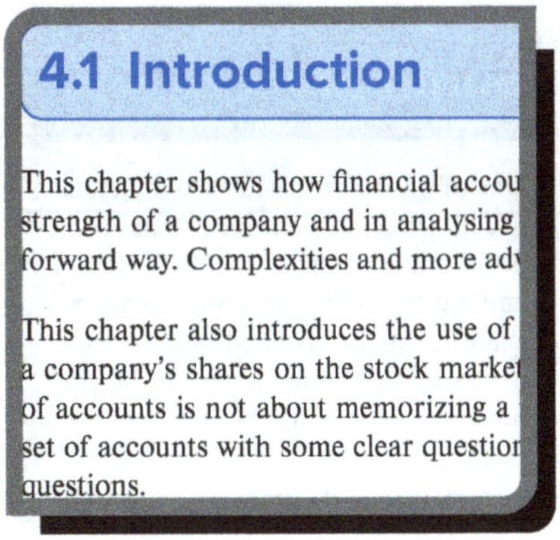

4.1 Introduction

This chapter shows how financial accou
strength of a company and in analysing
forward way. Complexities and more adv

This chapter also introduces the use of
a company's shares on the stock market
of accounts is not about memorizing a
set of accounts with some clear questior
questions.

Illustrations

Figures, tables and statements of financial position illustrate and summarize important concepts, helping you apply theory to accounting practice.

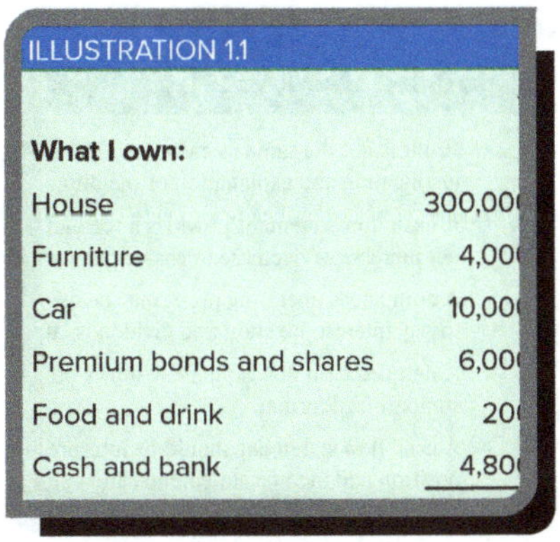

ILLUSTRATION 1.1

What I own:

House	300,00
Furniture	4,00
Car	10,00
Premium bonds and shares	6,00
Food and drink	20
Cash and bank	4,80

Examples

The chapters contain varied examples, including real-life accounting situations and worked problems which bring accounting to life.

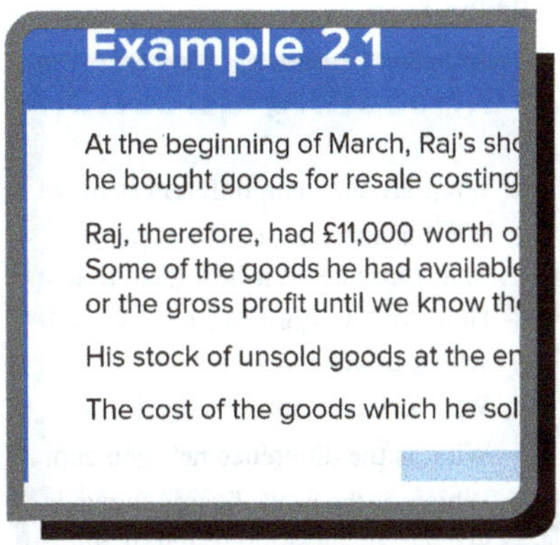

Example 2.1

At the beginning of March, Raj's sh
he bought goods for resale costing

Raj, therefore, had £11,000 worth o
Some of the goods he had availabl
or the gross profit until we know th

His stock of unsold goods at the er

The cost of the goods which he sol

Summary

This briefly reviews and reinforces the main topics you will have covered in each chapter to ensure you have acquired a solid understanding of the key topics.

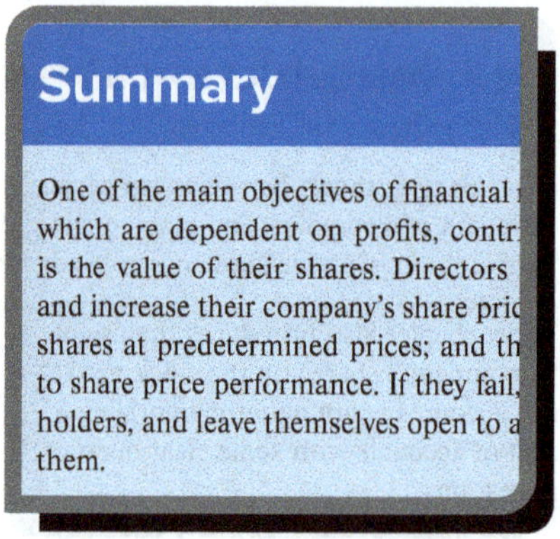

Summary

One of the main objectives of financial
which are dependent on profits, contr
is the value of their shares. Directors
and increase their company's share pric
shares at predetermined prices; and th
to share price performance. If they fail,
holders, and leave themselves open to a
them.

Review of key points

These bullet points at the end of each chapter are ideal for revising accounting concepts.

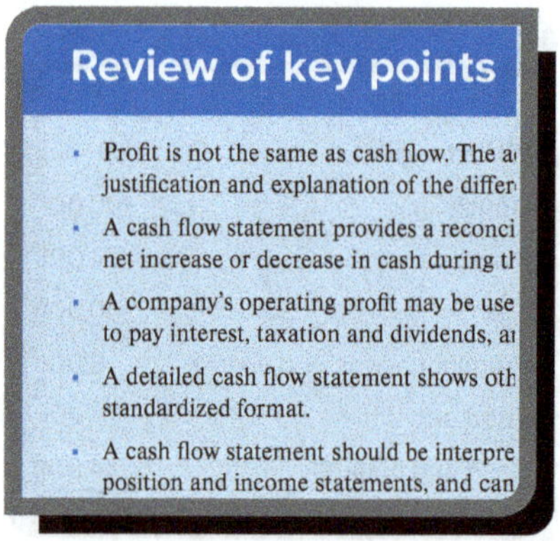

Review of key points

- Profit is not the same as cash flow. The a
justification and explanation of the differ
- A cash flow statement provides a reconci
net increase or decrease in cash during th
- A company's operating profit may be use
to pay interest, taxation and dividends, a
- A detailed cash flow statement shows oth
standardized format.
- A cash flow statement should be interpre
position and income statements, and can

Self-testing questions

These questions encourage you to review and apply the knowledge you have acquired from each chapter. Answers are provided at the back of the book.

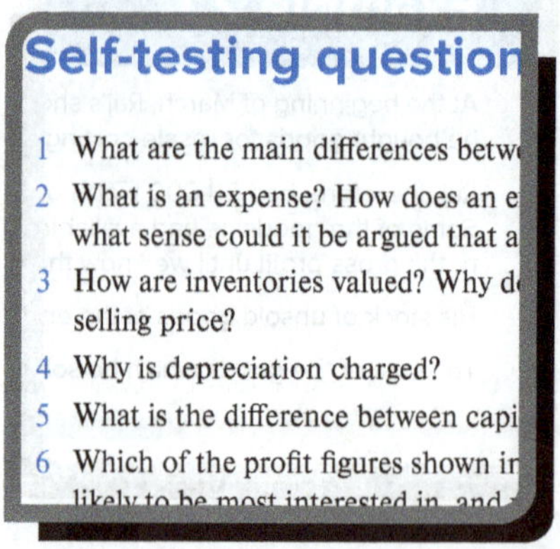

Self-testing question

1 What are the main differences betw
2 What is an expense? How does an e
what sense could it be argued that a
3 How are inventories valued? Why d
selling price?
4 Why is depreciation charged?
5 What is the difference between capi
6 Which of the profit figures shown ir

Assessment questions

This section provides a multitude of questions you may be asked in an exam. They can be used as helpful revision questions or to check progress as you cover the topics throughout the text.

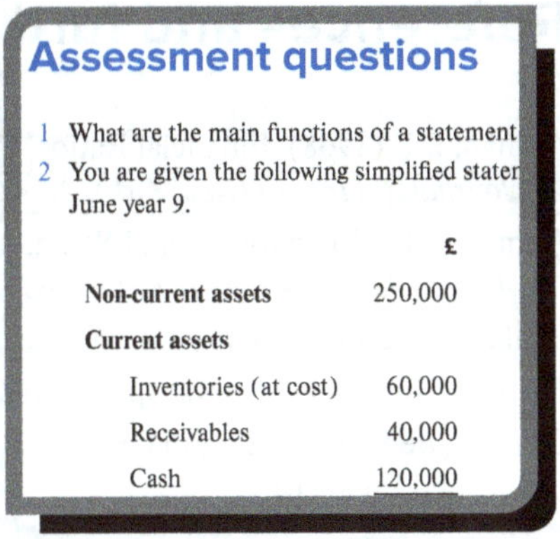

Assessment questions

1 What are the main functions of a statement

2 You are given the following simplified stater
June year 9.

	£
Non-current assets	250,000
Current assets	
Inventories (at cost)	60,000
Receivables	40,000
Cash	120,000

Group activities and discussion questions

These questions are ideal for sparking debate in class and also help readers think around the topic.

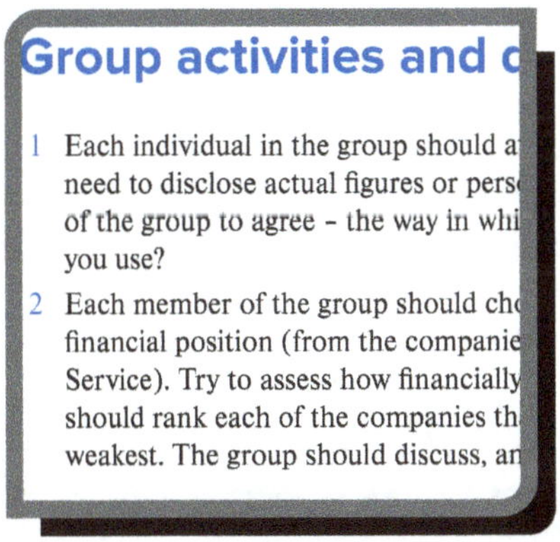

Group activities and d

1 Each individual in the group should a
need to disclose actual figures or pers
of the group to agree – the way in whi
you use?

2 Each member of the group should ch
financial position (from the companie
Service). Try to assess how financially
should rank each of the companies th
weakest. The group should discuss, an

Accounting in context

Each chapter ends with an article from the media that aims to illustrate the main themes of the chapter, allowing you to appreciate how the theory applies to real life.

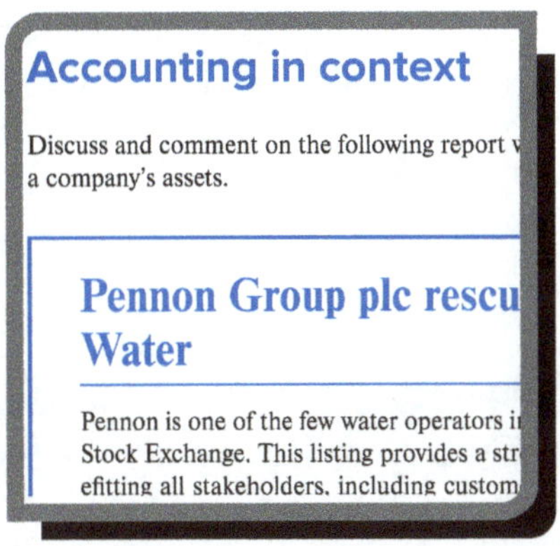

Accounting in context

Discuss and comment on the following report v
a company's assets.

Pennon Group plc rescu
Water

Pennon is one of the few water operators i
Stock Exchange. This listing provides a str
efitting all stakeholders, including custom

References and further reading

A list of references from the chapter, plus useful websites, which can be used for further research.

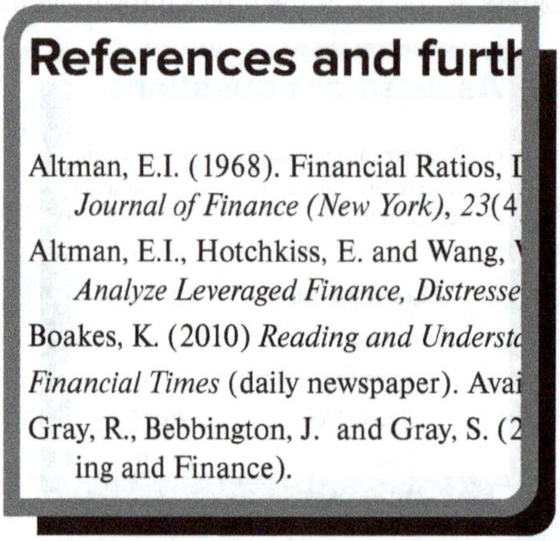
References and furth

Altman, E.I. (1968). Financial Ratios, I
Journal of Finance (New York), 23(4

Altman, E.I., Hotchkiss, E. and Wang,
Analyze Leveraged Finance, Distresse

Boakes, K. (2010) *Reading and Underst*

Financial Times (daily newspaper). Avai

Gray, R., Bebbington, J. and Gray, S. (2
ing and Finance).

Connect® for Accounting

We have a wide selection of resources on hand to help students gain valuable practice during their course. By applying what they have learned to real world scenarios and consistently testing their knowledge of the subject matter, these tools help prepare them for the real world of accounting.

Assignable Case Studies

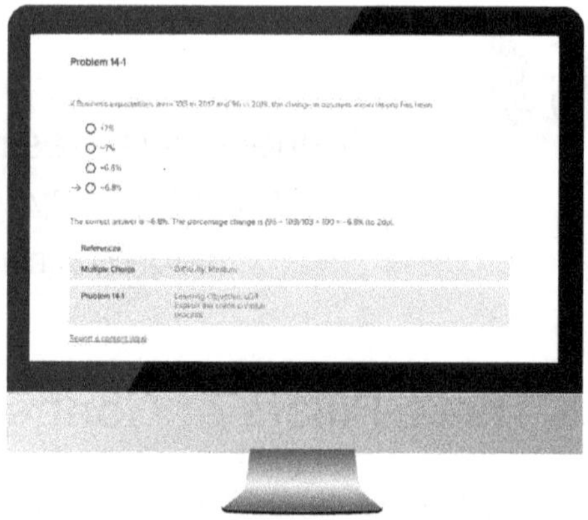

Students will develop strong analytical skills studying a series of case studies from innovative companies. Each case study is accompanied by questions which test the students application on theory and concept.

Assignable within Connect, these case studies keep the subject matter current and allow for students to obtain real-world practice during their study.

PowerPoints

Engage students with the textbook content during lectures with the powerpoint versions of each chapter, complete with learning objectives, figures and exercises.

Test Bank

Build your own question banks relating to end-of-chapter material and featuring video case content to both test student knowledge and ability, and ensure engagement with existing real world cases.

Instructor Manual

Equip yourself with your very own instructor manual of solutions, broken down chapter by chapter, to provide quick support and ease when navigating end of chapter questions.

Part 1

Introduction to Financial Accounting

Introduction

Contents

What Is Accounting?
Private Business - Accountability
Users of Accounting Information

What Is Accounting?

A conventional definition of accounting is the process of producing financial information about a business that will enable those with rights to that information to make informed economic decisions. An 'economic decision' relates to how scarce resources should be best used. For example, an investor, who is an example of someone with rights to information about a business, will need to assess whether or not to invest their money in Company A or Company B. A bank will need information to help decide whether or not to lend money to that business.

The process of accounting, like any process, has many stages. First, the transactions of the business are **recorded**. Then, these transactions are **classified**. Payments from the bank account of the business might be for buying inventory, the goods it buys in order to sell them, or perhaps to pay the wages of the employees of the business. Then, assets, expenses, liabilities, profits and sales will be **measured**. Businesses, such as Marks and Spencer Group plc or BP plc, are owned and financed by shareholders. Shareholders are investors (for example, individuals, companies or large institutional investors) who have purchased a share of the business but are not involved in running the business, and the directors of such companies have been appointed by the shareholders to run their business. However, directors cannot just run away with the shareholders' money; they are made accountable to the shareholders by the requirement to produce annual reports and accounts. In a sense these documents are the 'election address' of directors, who hope to present themselves in a good light so that they will be re-elected. These directors are the stewards of these investments. The notion of **stewardship** is that the directors are accountable to the shareholders for how their investment has been managed. The resources of the business must be *monitored and controlled* to ensure the resources of the business are effectively and efficiently used. The resources and performance and the risks attached to the business need to be *evaluated*. And periodically, the accounting information showing, for example, the assets and liabilities and sales revenue, expenses and profits, are **communicated** to those with rights to that information.

Private Business – Accountability

In this book, we are mainly focused upon accounting of privately owned, for-profit businesses. Such organizations come in different legal structures. Firstly, a *sole trader* is a business organization with a single owner with no legal structure separate from the owner. In fact, there are no legal formalities involved in forming such a business. A simple example would be if I start buying and selling goods on eBay. I am obliged to inform the tax authorities that I am self-employed and am in business. If, for another example, I am in business as a builder anyone owed money by the business can, if the business is unable to pay them, recover the sum owed from me as the sole trader of the business. That is because there is no legal distinction between the business and the owner. Hence if the nature of the business is risky, like that of a builder, running a business as a sole trader is very worrying because any activity such as building a wall which could fall on a passer-by could lead to the builder being sued for not only the assets of the business but all their personal assets too.

Secondly, a *partnership* is a business much like a sole trader but with more than one owner. Again, partnerships can be formed with no legal formalities. Here the resources and skills of more than one owner are available to the business but in much the same way as the entire personal 'fortune' of a sole trader is at risk and can be at the mercy of any creditors of the business - that is, anyone owed money by the business for whatever reason - exactly the same situation applies in a partnership. The partners are liable 'jointly and severally' for the debts of the business, that is, the personal fortunes of *all* the partners are available to the creditors of a partnership in the event that there are insufficient funds to pay any creditors.

Thirdly, a *limited liability company*, however, has, as a lawyer would put it, 'a separate legal personality' from those that own it. A company is formed by a legal process, filling in forms submitted to Companies House, an Executive Agency of the Department for Business, Innovation and Skills (BIS). And since these accounts have to be 'filed' at Companies House, and are available for 'public inspection' so all creditors and anyone else interested in the company's 'annual report' can download the accounts via the Companies House website, www.companieshouse.gov.uk. Unincorporated businesses (sole traders and partnerships) are not required by law to produce financial statements, but most find it useful to do so.

The primary distinction between a sole trader and a limited company is that a sole trader and their business are not recognized as separate legal entities. While this presents certain benefits, it also entails some drawbacks. If you are a sole trader, the absence of legal separation implies that you could be held accountable for all company liabilities. This means that there is little protection from debt or legal problems, and you would be responsible for any failings of the business.

On the other hand, a limited company is seen as a distinct legal entity from its proprietors and can have one or more stakeholders and shareholders. The liability of people involved in the company is limited and linked to their ownership in the enterprise. A limited company can still be owned by a single proprietor, much like how a sole trader works. However, even in this scenario, the owner and the business are viewed as separate entities in the eyes of the law. One of the most notable advantages of a limited company is the legal separation between individuals and the business. Since the owner(s) of a limited company are not responsible for company liabilities, there is no obligation to use personal funds to address any debt issues.

A *limited liability partnership* (LLP) is in most respects a cross between a partnership and a limited liability company and is most commonly used by accountants and lawyers. Each partner is only liable for debts arising from their own activities but the LLP is also required to submit its accounts to Companies House.

Users of Accounting Information

Businesses, particularly companies, produce statements of financial position, income statements and detailed financial reports, because in addition to the legal requirement to do so, they are assumed to be useful to a range of 'users'. Published financial statements are supposed to meet the information needs of a variety of different 'users'. The main groups of users, and their information needs, are summarized below.

1 Shareholders, including potential shareholders, who are considering buying or selling shares in the company. They are interested in such things as the value of the company, the profits, dividends and cash flows that it has generated in recent periods, what its performance is likely to be in future periods and its financial position and survival prospects.
Directors are also accountable to shareholders, and annual financial reports fulfil a 'stewardship' role, showing how well the directors have acted as 'stewards' of their money.

2 Creditors and suppliers including potential creditors. They are interested in the company's cash flows and ability to meet their liabilities in general and to pay their creditors on time.

3 Lenders, both short (for example, banks in relation to overdrafts) and long term (for example, debenture holders and those considering lending), have similar information needs to other creditors. They want to know about the company's ability to repay the loans, and their future prospects. They are interested in financial position (statements of financial position), performance (income statements) and cash generation (cash flow statements).

4 Employees, and potential employees, want to know about the future prospects of the company, whether the company will survive and prosper and be able to pay wages and salaries and provide expanding career prospects in the future. They are also interested in companies' pension schemes, and whether they are viable or in deficit. When going for an interview with a company, applicants are well advised to find out all they can about their potential employer's business and their proposed developments.

5 Customers may be interested in the financial position and prospects of a company, although this is a bit unlikely in relation to most consumer goods. If a government or large company is considering entering into a substantial or long-term contract they will want to know if proposed contractors are reputable, and in a strong enough financial position to meet the commitments that are being considered.

6 Government and public sector bodies are interested in companies in various ways. They gather information about businesses in relation to a whole range of public policy concerns, including employment levels and policies, research and development, investment and growth, their impact on the balance of payments, pricing and inflation, mergers, takeovers and competition policy, and environmental and public health. Wherever politicians see a public policy impact, or evidence of voters' concerns, they are likely to want to know what companies are doing, and to consider gathering more information, and implementing additional regulations.

7 In the UK, HM Revenue and Customs (HMRC) are responsible for collecting corporation tax, income tax, value added tax, and customs and excise duties, which they do on the basis of specific forms and information requirements. But as part of their general checking and control procedures they are likely to be interested in the published accounts of companies, and to investigate any apparent discrepancies.

8 Managers and directors of companies are likely to be interested in the annual financial statements and even more interested in monthly statements. But financial accounting information is primarily designed for people outside the business. Managers should have access to specially produced internal

management accounting information on a regular basis. But there are many small companies that produce little management accounting information other than monthly income statements, statements of financial position and cash flow statements that are relied on by managers and directors.

9 Financial analysts and advisers come in all shapes and sizes, and have many different information needs. Some may be advising the companies about raising additional finance, or on a potential takeover bid. More generally, there are investment analysts who carry out fundamental analysis of the financial information about a company and produce recommendations for those considering buying or selling shares in the company. They are interested in the financial position and performance, and still more interested in its future prospects. They may attempt to value a company based on the future cash flows that it is expected to generate, and in assessing whether or not the current share price represents good value in relation to future prospects.

10 Competitors usually like to compare their own results with those of their rivals, perhaps to gloat where they are doing better, and to learn what they can in order to improve their own performance. They are interested in how much their competitors are expanding, their profit margins and in how the different segments of the business are performing.

11 The public, special interest groups and students may want a very wide range of information about a company, much of which can be found in annual reports and accounts. There are environmental lobby groups, animal welfare groups, local people interested in possible building expansion, trade unions acting on behalf of employees, people concerned with health, safety and accidents and many others. The internet is usually the first port of call for students undertaking projects; but they should not overlook the company's annual report and accounts, which is the company's official information, intended mainly for investors, and includes much more than students usually expect.

The information needs of some of these groups should not be taken too seriously because they are in a position to get most of what they want to meet their specific needs directly from the company. These groups include governments, HMRC, managers and directors. Lenders such as bankers demand and are usually given much more information than is included in published financial statements, including forecast information, monthly breakdowns and cash budgets. Similarly, financial advisers are likely to be given most available information if they are acting for the company concerned (but not if they are acting for competitors!).

In some cases the information that particular groups want is so detailed and specific that it would be impractical to include it in a general purpose annual report. Expansion plans at a supermarket site, safety records at a particular factory and employment prospects at a particular location may all be matters of interest locally, but it would be impractical to expand annual reports to include all the detail that some groups might want in respect of a particular location. Annual reports are necessarily 'general purpose'. Many of the supposed information needs of the various groups are a matter for legitimate public concern, but perhaps it should be governments who act on behalf of the public and obtain appropriate information; it is unrealistic to expect everything to be included in a company's annual report and accounts.

A major problem with the information needs of the various groups is that most want to know what is going to happen in the future. Shareholders, creditors, lenders and employees all want to know what the company's future prospects are. Will they be able to meet their liabilities? Will shares be a good investment? Will the company thrive, and provide good career prospects? These are all legitimate questions, but financial statements deal almost entirely with what has already happened. Many users are concerned to assess the value of published, historic financial information by assessing the extent to which it provides an effective basis for future forecasts, and there are increasing pressures for companies to publish additional forecast information. Some see the role of financial statements as being to provide a basis for predicting future cash flows.[1]

As it is not possible for a company to publish exactly the information that everyone wants, the emphasis is on statements of financial position, income statements and cash flow statements that are primarily designed for the benefit of shareholders and creditors.

[1] Cash flows are, of course, different from profits. These differences are explained in Chapter 6.

It may be assumed that, by focusing on the interests that investors have in the financial performance and position of a company, the needs of a wide range of users will be met. The income statement, statement of financial position and cash flow statement are assumed to meet most information requirements of general users of financial statements. This is a bit like a truism: the statements that are available are the ones that are used and so must be the statements that users want. These three statements - the income statement, the statement of financial position and the cash flow statement - are introduced in **Chapter 2**, **Chapter 1** and **Chapter 6**, respectively.

Chapter 1

The Statement of Financial Position (Balance Sheet) and What it Tells Us

Chapter contents

1.1 Introduction
1.2 An Individual's Statement of Financial Position (Balance Sheet)
1.3 A Company's Statement of Financial Position (Balance Sheet)
1.4 Short- and Long-term Classification
1.5 Statement of Financial Position: Financial Strengths and Weaknesses
1.6 Depreciation and Statement of Financial Position 'Values'
1.7 Statements of Financial Position and Profit
1.8 A Company's Published Statement of Financial Position
1.9 Role and Limitations of Statements of Financial Position
1.10 Financial Accounting and Management Accounting

Learning objectives

After studying this chapter, you will be able to:

- ✓ Explain the structure and terminology of a statement of financial position
- ✓ Understand how statements of financial position can indicate financial weaknesses and strengths
- ✓ Demonstrate how various transactions and profits affect the statement of financial position
- ✓ Discuss the uses and limitations of the statement of financial position

1.1 Introduction

The term 'balance sheet' is widely used, although most people have never seen one and have little idea of what it shows. First, it should be noted that the balance sheet is more commonly called a 'statement of financial position'. This chapter provides a gentle introduction to statements of financial position by showing how individuals can prepare their own personal statement of financial position and how similar these are to a company's statement of financial position. Second, it also gives some indication of the usefulness of financial position statements: they can indicate what an individual or company is worth (but with severe limitations). They also show what liabilities there are, which can help to predict future bankruptcy. In summary the statement of financial position provides the users with information of the assets, liabilities and equity.

1.2 An Individual's Statement of Financial Position (Balance Sheet)

If you want to know how much you are worth as an individual you would probably start by drawing up a list of everything that you own, and then try to put a value on each item. After working for a few years, you might own a house, some furniture, a car, some premium bonds and shares in a listed company that you intend to keep on a long-term basis, and perhaps some short-term investments. You might also have a good stock of food and wine in the kitchen as well as some money in the bank. But you may have debts: a mortgage owed to your bank or building society, an overdraft, money you owe on your credit card, and bills not yet paid for such things as electricity, gas, telephone and council tax.

It is easy to produce a list of what you own, and a list of what you owe. You can then deduct what you owe from what you own to show your 'net worth'. An example is given in **Illustration 1.1**.

ILLUSTRATION 1.1

	£
What I own:	
House	300,000
Furniture	4,000
Car	10,000
Premium bonds and shares	6,000
Food and drink	200
Cash and bank	4,800
Total	325,000
What I owe:	
Mortgage	222,000
Bills (gas and electricity, etc.)	1,000
Credit card	2,000
Total	225,000
What I am worth	**100,000**

We can summarize this as:

What I own *minus* what I owe = what I am worth

If you are a full-time student, this might be more difficult. It may be that the most valuable things that you own are items such as books, clothes, a smartphone, a laptop and video games. You may have paid a lot for them, but their value now is open to question - especially if you suddenly need to sell them. They would cost a lot to replace, and if they were all stolen you would probably claim quite a high value for them if they were insured. But if you try to sell them, their second-hand value would probably be very disappointing: it is likely to be only a small fraction of what you paid for them. Worse still, you may well have a student loan or an overdraft and owe other amounts of money, which means that your net worth is zero or even negative - that is, you owe more than you own. But it is all worth it, you tell yourself, because all the time you are spending money on your education, that is an investment, and what you are really worth is your future earning power. If you go to your bank wanting to borrow money, they will be much more interested in your future earning power than they are in a pile of second-hand clothes and a laptop. Three main problems arise in trying to establish what any individual or business is worth:

1. What items are we going to list? Are we going to include a five-year-old computer, video games, all the food in the kitchen, educational qualifications and our children? We might think of these as being some of the best things we have, but we would probably exclude them. We need some basis, or principle, for deciding what to include and what to exclude.
2. How do we establish what particular items are worth? We attempt this in several different ways; for example, by looking at what they originally cost, what the second-hand value is, or what it would cost to replace them.
3. What is our future earning power worth? Whether we look at an individual or a company, in many cases the money that they can earn in the future is worth a lot more than a collection of bits and pieces that they own. If you want to borrow money, you could tell your bank that you expect to earn at least £1 million during your working life and ask to borrow the £1 million now. The bank's response is likely to be short and not very sweet.

You can, of course, make up your own rules, and decide that you are worth £100,000. But if you want to compare your own wealth with someone else's, then you need to agree on how the calculation is to be made. Are you going to show your house at the amount you paid for it, or at the market value now? Are you going to show your car at the amount you paid for it, or allow for the fact that it has depreciated since you bought it? If you attempt any comparisons like this, you will soon find that you need some agreed rules on what to include and the basis of valuation to be used. This is where you will need accounting principles.

It is difficult to know what something is really worth until you sell it. I might boast that my house is worth £500,000, but we might agree that it is more objective to show it at cost, and it cost £300,000 a few years ago. The accounting principle would be to list everything that we own and show everything at the original cost price.

Deciding what principle to adopt for furniture and for a car is more difficult. They have only a limited life, and are likely to depreciate over time as we 'use them up'. We could decide that a car has a five-year life and write it down by one-fifth each year.

1.3 A Company's Statement of Financial Position (Balance Sheet)

A company's statement of financial position is very much like an individual's statement of financial position, except that a standard layout is used, and specific terminology is applied.

The layout and terminology probably look quite confusing at first and it may be hard to believe that **Illustration 1.2** really is the same statement of financial position as **Illustration 1.1**. By using standardized terminology and presentation, accountants say that they are making it easier to compare one company with another. You might think that they are just making it more complicated so that it is 'impenetrable' to non-accountants. But professionals can no longer hide behind their terminology, conventions and so-called 'expertise'. These days many patients question their doctor's recommendations (perhaps by looking things up on the internet and becoming instantly more 'expert' than the doctor). Similarly, you are learning to question accountants (and other management 'experts'), and now is the time to make sure that you understand the basic terminology of financial statements.

ILLUSTRATION 1.2

Statement of financial position of A Company as at 31 December year 1	
	£
Non-current assets	
Freehold land and buildings (at cost)	300,000
Furniture (at cost)	4,000
Vehicles (at cost)	10,000
Investments	6,000
	320,000
Current assets	
Inventories	200
Cash and bank	4,800
	5,000
Total assets	325,000
Equity and liabilities	
Liabilities	
Current liabilities	
Trade payables	1,000
Short-term borrowings	2,000
	3,000
Non-current liabilities	
Mortgage	222,000
Total liabilities	225,000
Equity	
Share capital and reserves	100,000
Total equity and liabilities	325,000

The terminology used on the statement of financial positions has become more standardized since the widespread application of International Accounting Standards (IASs) in 2006. **Illustrations 1.2** and **1.3** are both consistent with international accounting standards; the first is in the format illustrated in International Accounting Standard 1 (IAS 1). The second one also complies with the standard, and is also fairly conventional. Unfortunately, we have to be able to cope with statements of financial position presented in different ways.[1]

[1] That is the price of international 'standardization', prior to which there was a standardized UK form of statement of financial position which, unfortunately, differed from that of other countries.

ILLUSTRATION 1.3

A Company statement of financial position as at 31 December year 1		
	£	£
Assets		
Non-current assets		
Freehold land and buildings (at cost)	300,000	
Furniture (at cost)	4,000	
Vehicles (at cost)	10,000	
Total of tangible assets	314,000	
Financial assets (investments)	6,000	320,000
Current assets		
Inventories	200	
Cash and bank	4,800	5,000
Total assets		325,000
Current liabilities		
Trade payables	1,000	
Credit card	2,000	3,000
Non-current liabilities		
Mortgage		222,000
Equity		
Share capital and reserves		100,000
Total liabilities and equity		325,000

In accountant's terms, what a company controls and what it owes are called *assets* and *liabilities*, and the statement showing assets and liabilities (and *net assets,* or *net worth*, or *equity*, or *capital*) is called a *statement of financial position* – formerly a 'balance sheet'. Note some companies still use the term balance sheet (e.g. J. Sainsbury plc Annual Report 2023, p. 128). The idea is that it 'balances'; the total of assets used to be shown on the one side, and the total of liabilities and equity on the other side: the two sides balance in this horizontal presentation or the account form. But nowadays, it is usual to show one 'side' at the top and the other 'side' underneath in a vertical presentation or the report form.

In everyday English, we have seen that what I am worth is the total of what I own, minus the total of what I owe. In accountancy terms, we would say that the statement of financial position value of a company is the total of assets minus liabilities. We could call this capital, 'equity', net assets or net worth. Accountants sometimes talk about the 'statement of financial position (or balance sheet) equation' that has three items (assets, liabilities and equity), which can be arranged in different ways, as follows:

(a) assets = liabilities *plus* equity

This shows the total of assets, and then how they were financed: partly with other people's money, and partly with the owners' equity;

or

(b) assets *minus* liabilities = equity

This emphasizes the amount of equity.

It is easy enough to establish the 'statement of financial position value' of a company, or its 'net asset value', or 'equity', or 'net worth'. In **Illustration 1.2** it would be £100,000. It is much more difficult to establish what a company is really worth, because of the same three problems already identified:

1. What items are we going to include on the list?
2. How do we establish what particular items are worth?
3. What is the future earning power of the company as a whole worth?

These problems are addressed more fully later in the book.

1.4 Short- and Long-term Classification

The usual formats for statements of financial position make it relatively straightforward to compare one company with another. Both assets and liabilities are classified as being long or short term. Any asset or liability that is intended to be around for more than a year is long term. Similarly, any asset or liability that changes within a year is short term.

Assets

An **asset** is a resource controlled by a business as a result of past events and from which future economic benefits are expected.

Long-term assets are called 'non-current assets'. They are still often referred to as 'fixed assets', although there is nothing fixed about them: they include cars and aeroplanes just as much as they include land and buildings. The main categories within the non-current assets section of a statement of financial position are:

1. *Intangible assets* - for example: goodwill; patents; trademarks; licences.
2. *Property, plant and equipment (tangible fixed assets)* - for example: land and buildings; plant, machinery and equipment; vehicles; furniture, fixtures and fittings.
3. *Financial assets or investments* - items such as shares in other companies or loans that have been made.

We can say that things like vehicles or furniture are *usually* classed as non-current assets, but that is not always the case. If a business intends to use them for a period of years, then they are non-current. But if someone is in business to buy and sell vehicles, or furniture, then any items held short term, awaiting sale, are not fixed assets. Stocks of goods held for sale are labelled as 'inventories' and shown as current assets.

The same arguments apply with investments. Any surplus funds invested in shares, or loaned to someone or another business, might be intended to be long term, and so are 'non-current'. Or they might be intended to be short term, and so are shown as current assets.

Current assets are short term. They include cash and any assets intended to become cash within a year. They include:

1. *Inventories (or stocks)* - merchandise, production supplies, materials, work in progress and finished goods.
2. *Trade receivables (or debtors)* - money owed to the business by customers and others.[2]
3. *Investments* - (those that are not fixed assets).

---

[2] And even prepayments, and accrued income if you want to be technical!

4 *Prepayments* - expenses such as rent or insurance, paid before the statement of financial position date from which the benefits will arise in the following accounting year.

5 *Cash.*[3]

Current assets are short term, and constantly circulating. They are all cash, or cash equivalents, or things that are expected to become cash within a year. We intend that all our inventories will be sold; even raw materials and components will be incorporated into finished goods that are sold. Investments that are shown as current assets are assumed to be temporary, and so will be sold and converted into cash. The amounts shown for receivables should be received from debtors within a few months.

Liabilities

Liabilities are also categorized as current and non-current (short and long term).

A **liability** is a present obligation arising from past transactions that are expected to be paid in the future.

1 Current liabilities are creditors where the amount is due to be paid within a year. They include:
   - most ordinary trade payables (creditors for goods and services who have not yet been paid);
   - corporation taxation payable;
   - accrued charges - expenses, such as electricity, which are paid in arrears and for which no invoice has been received at the statement of financial position date;
   - bank overdrafts.

The statements of financial position shown in **Illustrations 1.2** and **1.3** clearly show current and non-current assets and liabilities separately from each other.

2 Non-current liabilities include long-term borrowings such as mortgages and debentures.

The distinction between what is short term and what is long term is important in assessing the financial strength or solvency of a business in assessing whether or not it is likely to go bust!

Equity

Equity is the assets less the liabilities and is the owners' interest in the business. In a company it will include:

1 Share capital - the book (or par) value of the shares subscribed for.

2 Share premium - any excess paid into the company on the issue of shares in excess of the book (or par) value of the shares.

3 Retained profits - profits after tax made by the business not yet distributed to the owners as a 'dividend'.

4 Other reserves, such as a revaluation reserve.

1.5 Statement of Financial Position: Financial Strengths and Weaknesses

A statement of financial position may suggest that a business is financially strong, although it does not prove it. It can also show signs of weakness - and we ignore these at our peril. Accountants are often criticized

[3] Cash includes money in the bank, and petty cash in hand. Obviously the two are quite distinct and a bookkeeper needs to account for them separately. But for the sake of simplicity, in interpreting statements of financial position, the two can be lumped together.

when a company gets into financial difficulty because they did not warn in big red letters, 'This company is dodgy. Avoid it like the plague.' But, in most cases, the signs of financial difficulty are there for all to see long before a much-publicized collapse, if only the trouble is taken to try to understand the statement of financial position.

Companies collapse in one way or another, for example, when they cannot pay what they are required to pay, that is, when they are unable to meet their financial liabilities. Many factors may contribute to this situation: poor management, poor marketing, poor planning, trying to do too much with too little money, bad luck, dodgy customers, changes in the world economy and so on. There is usually someone or something to blame. But, in the end, either a company can pay its bills or it cannot. The statement of financial position gives a pretty good guide to what amounts are due to be paid - and the resources available for paying them.

Although there may be question marks about the reliability of some figures in published accounts, the liabilities[4] figures are among the most reliable. A company needs to have sufficient funds readily available to meet its liabilities when they fall due. A company's 'current liabilities' are shown clearly on the statement of financial position. The important question is: does the company have sufficient short-term assets to be able to pay its short-term liabilities as they fall due?

A company's current assets include money in the bank, receivables[5] that are due to become money in the bank within a few months, and inventories, or stocks of goods that the company plans to sell and convert into money in the bank within a matter of months. If a company has a lot more current assets than current liabilities, it should be able to pay its current liabilities when they fall due. If their current assets are two or three times as much as their current liabilities, then they appear to be fairly strong; or in the terminology of accounting, they have a high current ratio.

In **Illustrations 1.1, 1.2 and 1.3**, current assets are £5,000, and short-term liabilities are £3,000. The current ratio is 1.67 : 1.[6] This is not particularly high, but it looks as if there is enough cash and near cash available in the short term to be able to pay the short-term liabilities as they fall due.

Although all current assets should become cash within a matter of months, this is more difficult with some items than others. Not all inventories (or stocks of goods) are easily and quickly turned into cash. A half-baked loaf will probably be finished and sold for cash within a matter of hours. A half-built house in an area where no one wants to live could remain unsold for a long time. If most of a company's 'current assets' are actually inventories, its ability to pay trade payables and other creditors quickly may be less than its current ratio suggests. A useful approach to assessing a company's ability to pay its short-term liabilities is to exclude inventories from current assets and to assess the company's 'liquidity' by comparing its 'liquid assets' with its current liabilities. This is known as the liquidity ratio, or acid test, or quick assets ratio.

Long-term liabilities are also important - a company or individual can go bankrupt because of the weight of long-term creditors. It is difficult to say how much debt is too much - some people, and some companies, seem to manage with huge amounts of debt,[7] whereas others (like a number of airlines or even governments) collapse. An individual who has lots of money can afford to borrow lots of money. Similarly, a company with a large amount of equity or shareholders' funds (the company's 'own' money), can afford to borrow more money than a company with very little equity. In **Illustrations 1.1, 1.2 and 1.3**, the amount of equity is £100,000, so it would seem reasonable to borrow another £100,000. If a business is financed half by borrowing and half from its own shareholders' equity (or funds), then the borrowing is high, but probably not excessive. But in these illustrations, the borrowing is much more than the equity. If we add together all the long-term funds (shareholders' funds plus long-term creditors = £322,000), then we can see that the assets of

[4] There are occasions when accountants and directors omit liabilities completely, or hide them as some form of 'off statement of financial position finance'. These 'creative accounting' issues are addressed in **Chapter 8**.

[5] Receivables are also known as debtors; these are customers who have not yet paid for the goods and services with which they have been supplied.

[6] £5,000 ÷ £3,000 = 1.67.

[7] At the year-end of 2022, GlaxoSmithKline had long-term borrowings of £17,035m; shareholders' equity amounted to £10,096m. This is most unusual!

the business are mainly[8] financed by borrowing. In accounting terminology, such a company is 'high geared', which usually means high risk.

But high gearing, or high amounts of long-term debt, does not particularly matter if the individual or company has a substantial amount of income with which to pay the interest and to repay the creditors (or borrow more!) when repayment is due. Individuals who have to pay mortgage interest of £20,000 a year should have no problems if their annual income is £100,000 a year or more. Someone who has to pay £20,000 a year mortgage interest from an annual income of £25,000 is likely to have real problems! It is worth comparing the amount of interest that has to be paid each year, with the income available to pay that interest. If the interest is covered, say, five times by the income, then it is probably alright. But if the interest is covered only 1.25 times by the available income, then there are likely to be problems.

In assessing the financial strength of a company, or how likely it is to go bankrupt, it is worth calculating the current ratio, the liquidity ratio, the capital gearing ratio and the interest times cover.

1.6 Depreciation and Statement of Financial Position 'Values'

Before looking at the published statement of financial position of a real company, it is useful to know that all assets are not simply shown at cost. Some non-current assets, particularly land and buildings, are revalued from time to time. Most property,[9] plant and equipment ('tangible non-current assets') are depreciated each year.

If you buy a car for £10,000, you might decide that you will keep it for four years and expect that at the end of the four years, you will be able to sell it for £2,000. This is a plan or an accounting policy. After one year, you can show the car as being £8,000; after two years, it would be £6,000, and so on. This does not mean that the car is 'worth' £8,000 after one year. What we need to do is to show three things:

1 The car cost £10,000.
2 After one year, the cumulative depreciation is £2,000 (after two years, it would be £4,000; after three years, it would be £6,000).
3 After one year the net book[10] value of the car would be £8,000 (after two years it would be £6,000; after three years it would be £4,000).

It is important that *all three* of the above can be found on the statement of financial position, or in notes to the statement of financial position: the cost of an asset, the cumulative depreciation and the net book value. As the above example shows, the net book value is not an attempt to show what the asset is really worth now. We decided to write off the initial cost of the car down to an estimated trade-in value when we have finished with it and to charge the same amount of depreciation each year[11] for four years. A published statement of financial position does not, of course, show individual assets; totals for groups of similar assets are shown.

In **Illustrations 1.1, 1.2 and 1.3** depreciation has been ignored to simplify it. The car is shown at £10,000. If we decided that a depreciation charge, or expense, of £2,000 is appropriate, there would be *two effects* on the statement of financial position: (i) the car (assets) would be reduced by £2,000; and (ii) the equity would be reduced by £2,000. The basic balance sheet equation, shown below, would still balance.

[8] £222,000 of £322,000 is almost 69 per cent.

[9] Yes, even property.

[10] The amount shown in the 'books' of the company, or its statement of financial position value.

[11] Depreciation does not have to be on a 'straight line' or 'equal annual instalments' basis. Businesses can choose to charge more depreciation in the early years by using a 'diminishing balance' basis.

Assets − liabilities = equity

Illustration 1.4 shows how the statement of financial position changes as a result of charging expenses, earning income and making a profit.

ILLUSTRATION 1.4

Statement of financial position of A. Reader Company Ltd as at 31 December				
		Year 1		Year 2
	£	£	£	£
Non-current assets				
Tangible assets:				
Freehold land and buildings (at cost)	300,000		300,000	
Furniture (at cost less depreciation)	4,000		3,200	
Vehicles (at cost less depreciation)	10,000		8,000	
	314,000		311,200	
Investments	6,000	320,000	6,000	317,200
Current assets				
Inventories	200		9,000	
Trade receivables	–		20,000	
Cash and bank	4,800		5,000	
		5,000		34,000
Total assets		325,000		351,200
Current liabilities				
Trade payables		3,000		4,200
Non-current liabilities				
Mortgage		222,000		222,000
Total liabilities		225,000		226,200
Equity				
Capital and reserves		100,000		100,000
Retained earnings for year 2				?
		325,000		351,200

1.7 Statements of Financial Position and Profit

A successful individual or business is likely to show an increase in capital or equity or net worth each year.

Expenses, such as depreciation, decrease both assets and equity. Most expenses reduce the asset of cash when they are paid.[12] If they have not yet been paid, then there is an increase in liabilities – shown as payables

[12] Depreciation is an expense that reduces the non-current asset; it does not reduce the cash – it is not paid as it is a non-cash expense.

(which has the same effect as a reduction in assets). Whether expenses are paid out in cash or not, the effect of all expenses is to reduce equity.

Revenues, mainly from sales, increase assets and increase equity. If they come in the form of cash, then the asset of cash is increased. If the customers have not yet paid, then the increase in assets shows up as an increase in receivables.[13] Whether they are received in the form of cash or not, the effect of all revenues is to increase equity.

In a successful business revenues should be greater than expenses. This means that profit is earned; the net effect is to increase equity. Profit is added to equity.

If we take the statement of financial position at the end of one year, and compare it with the statement of financial position at the end of the next year, we can get a fairly good idea of the amount of profit that was made in the period between the two dates. All we do is compare the figure for equity (or net assets, or shareholders' funds) on the most recent statement of financial position with the equivalent figure a year ago. This is shown in **Illustration 1.4**. The profit has shown up in additional inventory, receivables and cash: they have increased by £29,000. But non-current (or fixed) assets have gone down by £2,800 (depreciation), and there are additional liabilities of £1,200; the total effect of these is an increase in net assets of £25,000. That £25,000 should be added to equity: until the question mark has been replaced by £25,000 of 'retained earnings', the statement of financial position will not balance.

Without more evidence, we cannot always be sure that the increase in net assets is the profit for the year, for three main reasons:

1. It could be that the amount of equity has increased because shareholders have put more money into the business; there has been a new issue of shares. Any extra coming in from the issue of shares does not count as profit, and so should be deducted from the increase in equity shown on the statement of financial position to arrive at the profit figure for the year.
2. All the profits that have been made do not necessarily stay within the business. Most companies pay out dividends. They can make a substantial profit, and pay most of it out as dividends. Dividends do not reduce profits, but they do mean that the whole of the profit for the year does not increase equity. If we are to calculate the amount of profit for the year using the statement of financial position, dividends must be added to the amount of retained profit for the year to arrive at the total profit for the year.
3. Sometimes the amount shown for equity has increased because the company has revalued its assets. An increase in the value of assets does not count as profit. In **Illustration 1.4**, if the company had wanted to revalue its land and buildings from £300,000 to £350,000, there would be two effects: (i) the amount for the asset would increase by £50,000, and (ii) the amount of equity would have increased by £50,000. This has not happened in **Illustration 1.4**.

If there has been an increase in the amount shown for equity from one year to the next, this is an indication of profit; but adjustments may need to be made for the three items listed above to arrive at the correct profit figure for the year.

A statement of financial position is not the most convenient way of calculating profit, but it can be done! Profit for the year is the increase in equity during the year, minus any additional shares that have been issued, plus any dividends that have been distributed to shareholders, minus any amounts resulting from the revaluation of assets.

Some may argue that even an increase in asset values should count as profit. But the traditional accountant would not be impressed with such an 'all-inclusive' view of profit.

[13] Or debtors.

1.8 A Company's Published Statement of Financial Position

A recently published statement of the financial position of the Marks and Spencer Group plc for the year ended 1 April 2023 (slightly simplified) is shown in **Illustration 1.5**. It provides useful indications in relation to several aspects of a company, especially when comparing one year with another.

1 *Size and growth:*[14] The book value of the Marks and Spencer Group net assets decreased from £2917.9m in 2022 to £2814.9m in 2023, a decrease of 3.5 per cent. There has been a decrease in current assets and non-current assets.

2 *How the business is financed:* The balance sheet equation, assets *equals* liabilities *plus* equity, shows that a business finances its assets partly with other people's money (liabilities), and partly with the owners' money (equity). The Marks and Spencer Group's decrease in total assets of £345.6m (3.7 per cent decrease) has been financed by an increase in current liabilities of £335.6m (14.2 per cent increase), which has been offset by a decrease in long-term liabilities of £578.2m (13.9 per cent decrease) and decrease in equity of £103.0m (3.5 per cent decrease). No additional shares were issued.

3 *Profits:* Comparing statements of financial positions of two different dates does not show the amount of profit (or loss) made in the intervening period unless a few adjustments are made, as explained above. It does not show what dividends were paid. However, Marks and Spencer Group did not pay any dividends in both years.

4 *Solvency:* Statements of financial position show the amount of liabilities and give some indication of whether or not these are excessive. This can be done in two stages, as follows.

ILLUSTRATION 1.5 Marks and Spencer Group plc

	1 April 2023 £m	2 April 2022 £m
Non-current assets		
Intangible assets	163.1	192.5
Property, plant and equipment	5,203.7	4,902.3
Other	1,576.0	2,166.3
	6,942.8	7,261.1
Current assets		
Inventories	764.4	706.1
Trade and other receivables	280.6	217.1
Other	42.1	61.2
Cash and cash equivalents	1,067.9	1,197.9
	2,155.0	2,182.3
Total assets	9,097.8	9,443.4
Equity and liabilities		
Current liabilities		
Trade and other payables	2,048.8	1,960.9
Borrowings	444.0	247.2

[14] In assessing size and growth it is useful also to look at sales revenue, profits and market capitalization.

	1 April 2023 £m	2 April 2022 £m
Current tax liabilities	38.5	34.0
Provisions	44.0	53.6
Other	131.1	75.5
	2,706.4	2,370.8
Non-current liabilities		
Retirement benefit deficit	4.6	5.7
Trade and other payables	181.3	188.2
Long-term borrowings	3,184.0	3,561.0
Other non-current liabilities	58.9	120.8
Provisions for liabilities	75.4	91.8
Deferred tax liabilities	72.3	187.2
	3,576.5	4,154.7
Total liabilities	6,282.9	6,525.5
Equity		
Share capital	19.8	19.7
Share premium	910.7	910.6
Capital redemption reserve	2,680.4	2,680.4
Other reserves	−6,639.5	−6,594.9
Retained earnings	5,839.1	5,897.9
Total shareholders' equity	2,810.5	2,913.7
Non-controlling interests in equity	4.4	4.2
Total equity	2,814.9	2,917.9
Total liabilities and equity	9,097.8	9,443.8

Current liabilities

Are these excessive in relation to current assets? The amounts are as follows:

	2023 £m	2022 £m
Current assets	2,155.0	2,182.3
Current liabilities	2,706.4	2,370.8

Current liabilities are amounts that have to be paid out in the short term. Current assets include cash and items that should become cash within a year. As the Marks and Spencer Group has more current liabilities than current assets, there could be a problem in paying those liabilities as they fall due. This is often expressed as the *current ratio*, which is the ratio of current assets to current liabilities, which is:

$$2023 : \frac{2,155.0}{2,706.4} = 0.80 : 1 \qquad 2022 : \frac{2,182.3}{2,370.8} = 0.92 : 1$$

The ratio fell slightly in 2023 but is still in line with similar retailers.

With some current assets, such as inventories, it could take many months before they are turned into cash, although not in clothing retailers, perhaps. Liquidity can be assessed by taking only 'quick assets' and comparing them with current liabilities. This is the 'acid test'. If inventories are excluded from current assets, the *liquidity ratio* is calculated as follows:

	2023 £m	2022 £m
Current assets excluding inventories	1,390.6	1476.2
Current liabilities	2,706.4	2,370.8
Liquidity ratio	0.51 : 1	0.62 : 1

The liquidity ratio has fallen in 2023, but even though there are not enough current assets to pay the current liabilities, this is still in line with similar businesses, so it would not be considered a problem in this case.

Non-current liabilities

The Marks and Spencer Group's statement of financial position shows that borrowings within non-current liabilities (or '*debt*', *D*) are significant, amounting to £3,184m. The total shareholders' equity ('E' or shareholders' funds) amounted to over £2,673.5m in 2023. This can be expressed as a *gearing ratio* for each year by asking the question: what proportion of long-term finance was borrowed (as opposed to being part of shareholders' funds)? This can be expressed as: what is D as a proportion of D + E?

	2023 £m	2022 £m
D Long-term borrowings	3,184.0	2,673.5
E Equity	2,810.5	2,913.7
D + E Total long-term finance	5,994.5	6,474.7
D / (D+E)	53%	55%

The gearing is relatively high, meaning that the company is significantly dependent on long-term borrowings, but this is in line with other retailers. Many companies have gearing ratios of 40 per cent or more without any problems. Marks and Spencer Group might be regarded as being highly geared, so riskier - as the ratio is over 50 per cent in both years - but, again, this depends on the business sector in which the company operates.

In assessing whether there is too much borrowing, it is important to see how much interest the company has to pay and if its operating profits are high enough to ensure that the interest is amply covered by the earnings available to pay it.

The published annual reports of companies show much more detail than the simplified statement of financial positions included in this chapter, which can look frighteningly complex. A great deal of additional information is shown in notes to the accounts. In studying statements of financial position, it is important to have a few clear questions in mind, to concentrate on the larger figures, and to avoid becoming lost in detail that is hard to understand.

1.9 Role and Limitations of Statements of Financial Position

Statements of financial position can be useful in a number of ways:

1 We saw that the statement of financial position, or a statement of assets and liabilities, can be useful in showing what a person or business is worth. But there are problems in establishing agreed rules as to exactly which assets (and perhaps even which liabilities) should be included, and in determining the basis upon which they should be valued. There is also the problem that the value of a business as a whole is likely to be different from the value of all of its assets (less liabilities) added together. The real value of a business (or an individual) might depend more on the income that it can generate (as a whole entity) in the future than on whatever amounts might be shown for individual assets and liabilities.

2 We also saw that, in listing the various liabilities that have to be paid, short and long term, we can get an idea of the financial strength of a business. If its liabilities are too high, and it cannot pay them, it is likely to get into serious financial difficulties, and perhaps go out of business. Statements of financial position can give a good indication of whether liabilities are too high, or whether the business is reasonably strong. The statement of financial position is the basis for assessing the financial position of a company.

3 We can also measure profit using the statement of financial position. There are easier ways of measuring profit, but it is useful to calculate it in two different ways so that one checks the other. The statement of financial position approach to measuring profit is one of the two main approaches, and one that may increase in importance.

4 Statements of financial position play an important role in 'stewardship'. Shareholders put their money into a company; directors and managers are the 'stewards' of that money; and shareholders want to know what has happened to their money. The statement of financial position shows what money has been put in by the shareholders, and what retained profits have been added to it; this amount is shown as equity (or shareholders' funds). Examination of the statement of financial position, the assets and liabilities, shows what that money is now financing or, if you like, what has happened to it.

5 In order to produce a statement of financial position it is necessary to produce a listing of all the company's assets and liabilities. This can be useful in keeping track of various assets, and ensuring that all are being put to good use and are earning their keep. When a company gets into financial difficulties it sometimes seems that they manage to find assets that they had previously forgotten about, or done nothing with. There may be investments that are not much use; sports and social facilities that are hardly used; receivables (debtors) who have been neglected and have got away with not paying for too long (perhaps because of a half-forgotten dispute); a workshop developing a new product that made little progress; machinery, or components and raw materials that were specially bought for a new product that was quietly abandoned; too many premises or branches; an expensive head office in the city centre; a training centre, kitchens, computer workshops and maintenance facilities that should have been sold or redeployed when these activities were outsourced.

   Many companies do not even know what assets they own, or how many laptops have 'walked' out of the door, and they do not even have an up-to-date non-current assets register. The process of producing listings of assets in order to compile a statement of financial position can be a useful housekeeping exercise.

6 In addition to providing a basis for assessing the financial *position* of a company, the statement of financial position also provides a basis for assessing the financial *performance* of a company. The shareholders of a company are likely to be concerned about performance in terms of profitability. They are not concerned merely with the amount of profit the company makes; they are concerned with how much profit the company makes in relation to the amount of capital employed. A profit of £1m may look

good for a company with capital employed of £5m; it would look pathetic in relation to capital employed of £100m. It is the statement of financial position that shows the amount of capital employed. The ratio of profit to capital employed is a key ratio in assessing and improving a company's financial performance.

7 Financial accounting is a whole system, and the statement of financial position is an essential part of it in checking, balancing and controlling other parts of the system. If a company's statement of financial position does not balance, there is definitely something wrong! Accountants are only (or nearly!) human, and inevitably some mistakes are made with figures. The financial accounting system is designed to show up errors, and to find where they occurred. An accounting system can also show up fraud and theft. When a statement of financial position does balance, we cannot be sure that there is no fraud or error. If it does not balance, we can be sure that something is wrong; and if we do make a mistake, it will probably show up during the accounting processes before producing a statement of financial position.[15]

But we should not expect too much from statements of financial position. They were never properly designed to achieve anything very useful. When double-entry bookkeeping first became widely used, the statement of financial position was just a matter of bookkeeping convenience. It was not even necessary to produce one every year. Until the eighteenth century a statement of financial position was often not produced until the ledger was full; then a statement of financial position was a summary of the assets and liabilities that were transferred to the new ledger. Any remaining old balances, mostly revenues and expenses, were written off. The balances shown on the statement of financial position are items that are continuing, but they tend to be shown at the cost price when they are first entered in the business's books.

By the end of the nineteenth century the production of statements of financial position on an annual basis became normal. It became a requirement for companies to publish annual statements of financial position; and during the twentieth century legislation became increasingly specific about what should be shown on a statement of financial position. Towards the end of the twentieth century accounting standards laid down more detailed requirements, and since 2006 large companies have been following IASs in the same way as in many other countries.

The main limitations of statements of financial position have already been referred to:

1 What items are we going to include?
2 How do we establish the value of particular items?
3 The value of a company as a whole is likely to be very different from the total net value of the individual assets and liabilities.

Sometimes it is very difficult to decide whether or not an item should appear on the statement of financial position. If a company running a number of hotels buys an additional hotel, that is clearly an extra non-current asset that would be shown on the statement of financial position, and the amount shown would be the amount paid for it. If such a company pays for routine cleaning of a hotel, there is no additional asset, and the amount paid should not appear on the statement of financial position as an additional asset. A payment for cleaning will reduce assets (cash) and also reduce equity. Routine redecoration, like cleaning, is an expense that does not appear on the statement of financial position. Improvements, such as installing double-glazing, an extension or additional bathrooms, are 'capital expenditure': the amounts are added to non-current assets on the statement of financial position. Sometimes the boundary between 'capital expenditure' (which appears on the statement of financial position, and does not reduce equity) and 'revenue expenditure' (which does not appear on the statement of financial position, and does reduce equity) is not clear and there may be scope for creative accounting.

Where there is a lack of clear principles to determine what should be included on a statement of financial position, and the basis or valuation that is to be used for the various items, the value of statements of financial position is restricted. A series of official Financial Reporting Standards (FRSs) in the UK and

---

[15] Mistakes usually show up in the trial balance - if it does not balance!

International Financial Reporting Standards (IFRSs) have been produced to deal with this problem, and the development of financial accounting has steadily encouraged users to expect more from statements of financial position. It would be difficult for them to satisfy all the different expectations that interested parties might have. But we cannot even begin to assess a company's financial position and performance without a good understanding of the statements of financial position.

1.10 Financial Accounting and Management Accounting

Financial accounting is mainly concerned with producing financial statements for shareholders, creditors and others who are outside the organization concerned. The main financial statements are the statement of financial position, the income statement and the cash flow statement. In published accounts these are supported by substantial additional information, notes and explanations. The Companies Act, and official accounting standards, regulate the information that is published. Within the company a sophisticated bookkeeping system is required to record all the transactions that form the basis of these financial statements. Bookkeeping systems are explained in **Chapter 9**. In large-scale businesses managers do not rely very much on published financial accounting information; they have access to much more detailed and relevant management accounting information.

Management accounting is concerned with producing information for managers who are concerned with planning, decision-making and control. Management accounting information is not usually published, and it is designed to meet the needs of the managers of the organization concerned; it does not have to comply with official regulations. The subject of management accounting is introduced in **Chapter 13**, where it is clearly distinguished from financial accounting.

Summary

A statement of financial position shows the assets and liabilities of a company, and can provide useful information about a company's financial position. Solvency ratios can give an indication of whether a company is likely to become insolvent. Assets are not usually shown at their current value, and care is needed in using the statements of financial position as an indication of the value of a company. A business as a whole, as a going concern, is usually worth much more than the total of its net assets.

Review of key points

- A statement of financial position shows what a company controls (assets) and what it owes (liabilities).
- By deducting liabilities from assets, we arrive at the figure for 'equity' or 'capital' or 'net assets'.
- Assets and liabilities are classified as being long (non-current) or short-term (current). UK statements of financial position usually begin with non-current assets, followed by current assets. The second part of the statement of financial position shows how the assets were financed: by liabilities (current and non-current) and by equity.

- A successful business is usually worth more than the statement of financial position figure for its net assets.
- A statement of financial position shows how a company is financed and may indicate if a company has excessive liabilities.
- Comparing this year's statement of financial position with last year's can provide a basis for calculating profit.
- The main financial accounting statements are published; management accounting information differs and is internal to the organization.

Self-testing questions

1 Which of the following are shown on a statement of financial position: assets; expenses; liabilities; sales revenue; share capital; profit for the year?

2 What is the difference between a non-current asset and a current asset?

3 Give examples of non-current assets. In what circumstances would some of the items you have listed be current assets?

4 Arrange the three main elements of the statement of financial position (assets, liabilities, equity) as an equation.

5 A statement of financial position appears to show what a business is worth. What are the main problems with this statement?

6 You are given the following simplified statement of financial position of the Sandin Castle Company:

	£	£
Non-current assets		50,000
Current assets		
Inventories (at cost)	24,000	
Trade receivables	12,000	
Cash	9,000	
		45,000
Total assets		95,000
Current liabilities		
Trade payables		22,000
Equity		
Share capital	50,000	
Retained earnings	23,000	
		73,000
		95,000

a Calculate the current ratio.

b Calculate the liquidity ratio.

c After preparing the statement of financial position, the company sells inventories, which had cost £4,000, for £8,000, which it immediately receives in cash. Show how the statement of financial position would appear after this transaction.

d How does the above transaction affect the current ratio and the liquidity ratio?

7 You are given the following simplified[16] statements of financial position of the Windysand Company as at 31 December.

Simplified statements of financial position of the Windysand Company as at 31 December

	Year 1	Year 2
	£	£
Non-current assets	320,000	350,000
Current assets	5,000	45,000
Total assets	325,000	395,000
Non-current liabilities	222,000	202,000
Current liabilities	3,000	10,000
	225,000	212,000
Equity	100,000	183,000
	325,000	395,000

a How much profit does it at first seem that the company made during year 2?

b How would your answer to (a) be affected if you found out that the company had paid £10,000 in dividends; that additional shares with a value of £20,000 had been issued; and that non-current assets had been revalued upwards by £30,000?

8 You are given the following simplified statements of financial position of two very similar companies, Domer Castle Company and Warmer Castle Company as at 31 December year 1.

	Domer Castle Company	Warmer Castle Company
	£	£
Non-current assets		
Tangible assets		
Freehold premises (at cost)	300,000	100,000
Furniture (at cost less depreciation)	4,000	80,000
Vehicles (at cost less depreciation)	10,000	90,000
	-	44,000
Investments	314,000	314,000
Current assets		
Inventories	8,000	9,000
Receivables	12,000	10,000

[16] The order of items on this statement of financial position follows the illustration given in IAS 1; it differs from the order given in the Marks and Spencer Group's published statement of financial position. We have to be prepared for statements of financial position that show items in a different order.

	Domer Castle Company	Warmer Castle Company
	£	£
Cash	14,000	5,000
	34,000	34,000
Total assets	348,000	348,000
Current liabilities		
Trade payables	17,000	17,000
Non-current liabilities		
10% debentures	100,000	200,000
Total liabilities	117,000	217,000
Equity		
Share capital	100,000	100,000
Retained earnings	131,000	31,000
	231,000	131,000
Total liabilities and equity	348,000	348,000

During year 1 the operating profit (earnings before interest and taxation) of the Domer Castle Company amounted to £31,000. The operating profit of the Warmer Castle Company amounted to £32,000.

Which of the two companies appears to be financially weakest, and why? You should calculate the current ratio, the liquidity ratio, the capital gearing ratio and the number of times interest is covered by operating profit.

9 You are given the following simplified statement of financial position of the Stonefolk Company as at 31 March year 4.

	£
Non-current assets	158,000
Current assets	
Inventories (at cost)	110,000
Receivables	120,000
Cash	20,000
	250,000
Total assets	408,000
Current liabilities	
Trade payables	120,000
Equity	
Share capital	250,000
Retained earnings	38,000
	288,000
Total equity and liabilities	408,000

a The following transactions took place in April year 4. Show how each would affect the statement of financial position. (Each transaction must affect two or more figures, and the statement of financial position must continue to balance.)

i A building, which had cost £80,000, was sold for £100,000, which was immediately received in cash.

ii Inventories, which had cost £30,000, were sold to Mr Spliff for £80,000. Mr Spliff agreed to pay for the goods by the end of May year 4.

iii The company paid £40,000 of the amount that it owed to creditors, which is shown on the statement of financial position as 'payables'.

b Show how the statement of financial position would appear after these transactions have been recorded.

Assessment questions

1 What are the main functions of a statement of financial position?

2 You are given the following simplified statement of financial position of the Hackin Company as at 30 June year 9.

	£
Non-current assets	250,000
Current assets	
Inventories (at cost)	60,000
Receivables	40,000
Cash	120,000
	220,000
Total assets	470,000
Current liabilities	
Payables	100,000
Equity	
Share capital	250,000
Retained earnings	120,000
	370,000
Total equity and liabilities	470,000

a Calculate the company's current ratio and liquidity ratio.

b The following transactions take place during July year 9:

i New plant and equipment are bought for £80,000, and payment is made in cash.

ii Additional inventories of goods are bought for £15,000; it is agreed that they will be paid for in August.

Prepare a revised statement of financial position after these transactions have been recorded.

c How do these transactions affect the current ratio and the liquidity ratio?

3 You are given the following simplified statements of financial position of the Fourpine Company as at 31 December.

	Year 1	Year 2
	£	£
Non-current assets	520,000	450,000
Current assets	45,000	55,000
Total assets	565,000	505,000
Equity		
Share capital	300,000	310,000
Retained earnings	35,000	60,000
	335,000	370,000
Non-current liabilities	200,000	100,000
Current liabilities	30,000	35,000
Total equity and liabilities	565,000	505,000

a How much profit does it at first seem that the company made during year 2?

b How would your answer to (a) be affected if you found out that the company had paid £25,000 in dividends?

4 You are given the following simplified statements of financial position of the Port Andrew Company and the Port Edward Company as at 31 December year 1.

	Port Andrew Ltd	Port Edward Ltd
	£	£
Non-current assets		
Tangible assets		
Freehold premises (at cost)	100,000	200,000
Plant (at cost less depreciation)	200,000	100,000
Vehicles (at cost less depreciation)	100,000	100,000
	400,000	400,000
Investments	200,000	30,000
	600,000	430,000
Current assets		
Inventories	70,000	40,000
Receivables	50,000	90,000
Cash	10,000	60,000
	130,000	190,000
Total assets	730,000	620,000
Current liabilities		
Trade payables	70,000	80,000

	Port Andrew Ltd	Port Edward Ltd
	£	£
Non-current liabilities		
10% debentures	300,000	100,000
Total liabilities	370,000	180,000
Equity		
Share capital	300,000	300,000
Retained earnings	60,000	140,000
	360,000	440,000
Total equity and liabilities	730,000	620,000

During year 1 the operating profit of the Port Andrew Company amounted to £61,000. The operating profit of the Port Edward Company amounted to £40,000.

Which of the two companies appears to be the financially weaker, and why? You should calculate the current ratio, the liquidity ratio, the capital gearing ratio and the interest times cover.

5 You are given the following simplified statement of financial position of the Whiting Company as at 31 August year 6.

	£	£
Non-current assets		350,000
Current assets		
Inventories (at cost)	90,000	
Trade receivables	80,000	
Cash	30,000	200,000
Total assets		550,000
Current liabilities		
Trade payables		130,000
Equity		
Share capital	380,000	
Retained earnings	40,000	420,000
Total equity and liabilities		550,000

a The following transactions took place in September year 6. Show how each would affect the statement of financial position. (Each transaction must affect two figures, and the statement of financial position must continue to balance.)

i A new machine costing £10,000 was purchased and paid for in cash.

ii Inventories, which had cost £50,000, were sold to Mrs Fish for £90,000 and paid for immediately in cash.

iii £30,000 was received from debtors, which were shown as 'receivables' on the statement of financial position.

b Show how the statement of financial position would appear after these transactions have been recorded.

Group activities and discussion questions

1 Each individual in the group should attempt to answer the question 'How much am I worth?' There is no need to disclose actual figures or personal information. The objective is to determine - and for members of the group to agree - the way in which the question would be answered. What principles or rules would you use?

2 Each member of the group should choose two listed companies, and obtain their published statement of financial position (from the companies' websites or by using the *Financial Times* Annual Reports Service). Try to assess how financially strong each company is (or is it likely to collapse?). The group should rank each of the companies that members have examined from the strongest financially, to the weakest. The group should discuss, and try to agree, criteria to form the basis for this assessment.

3 Is it possible to calculate the value of a company? If not, why not? If so, how?

4 Which of the following should be included as assets on a company's statement of financial position: money that is owed to the company; the cost of an advertising campaign; machinery that is over 20 years old but which is still used occasionally; key employees who have a high market value; money paid as 'commission' to a government minister in Wayawayaland that has helped to secure a lucrative contract; brand names; money receivable under a contract that was signed yesterday and that will be earned next year; machinery that the company does not own, but for which they have signed a five-year lease.

Accounting in context

Discuss and comment on the following report with particular reference to the nature and accounting value of a company's assets.

Pennon Group plc rescues Sutton and East Surrey Water

Pennon is one of the few water operators in the UK that has a stock exchange listing on the London Stock Exchange. This listing provides a strong platform for sustainable investment and growth, benefitting all stakeholders, including customers and employees. The balance sheet and level of financial transparency provided by the stock exchange listing add to the overall financial stability of the company.

Pennon has recently stepped in to rescue Sutton and East Surrey Water (SES), a private supplier to some of England's most affluent areas, by acquiring 100 per cent share capital from its holding company, Sumisho Osaka Gas Water UK Limited. Sutton and East Surrey Water has been facing financial troubles for some time and has even received a monetary injection from its Japanese owners. The SES acquisition complements Pennon's existing water portfolio. To fund the takeover, Pennon has raised £180m from its investors, Sumitomo Corporation, and Osaka Gas will receive £89m for their shares. The remaining funds from Pennon's investment will be used to decrease SES's debts, which have been rising rapidly. The post-equity placing will have no material impact on the group gearing, which will be maintained between 55 per cent and 65 per cent in accordance with Ofwat.

Ofwat has pointed out that SES's financial metrics have been under pressure due to high inflation rates and operational issues. The company acknowledges that it will need further funding to support its capital programme and increase its financial resilience. SES is highly indebted, lost £31m in the previous year and announced a 'strategic review' to find a buyer. SES, although financially struggling, has paid out over £8m despite calls from Ofwat to cease such payments.

S&P, the rating agency, has recently rated SES with a low credit rating of BBB (negative outlook). The agency cites the company's inflation-linked debt accretion and operating margins as the primary reasons for the low rating.

Last year, Sumitomo and Osaka Gas pledged to inject £22m into Sutton and East Surrey Water by the end of this financial year in March. It is understood that £14m of this has already been invested and is included in Pennon's £89m consideration. The Japanese owners, who bought the company for £164m in 2013, will receive a poor return on their investment, although they have already recovered some of their money through past dividends.

In essence, SES exemplifies the state of the privatized industry in England. Owned by foreign investors who treat it as a cash cow to pay dividends, the company has been burdened with an excessive amount of debt to ensure that shareholders receive free cash. Consequently, SES are facing significant financial challenges due to high levels of operational cost inflation and interest rates that haven't been seen in a generation. It has pushed the company into a financial spiral and has put it on an insolvency alert watchlist with its regulator.

Despite the need to invest in the infrastructure, foreign investors have continued to take dividends, but now they are unwilling to reinvest in a public utility that should benefit the community. Furthermore, SES's poor performance has negatively affected its customers. In the last year, it missed four out of five water quality key performance indicators, which include supply interruptions and mains repairs. This failure has resulted in fines from Ofwat, exacerbating its financial crisis.

Adding insult to injury, the CEO of SES, who manages just 345 people, receives a salary of over £500,000 per annum, of which nearly half comes from bonuses.

Sources: R. Lea, Pennon buys debt-ridden water supplier in £380m deal, *The Times*, 11 January 2024.

https://www.pennon-group.co.uk/sites/default/files/attachments/pdf/presentation-pennon-acquisition-of-ses-10-jan-2024.pdf

References and further reading

IASB (2018) Conceptual Framework for Financial Reporting. London, UK: International Accounting Standards Board. https://www.ifrs.org/content/dam/ifrs/publications/pdf-standards/english/2021/issued/part-a/conceptual-framework-for-financial-reporting.pdf

International Accounting Standard 1 (2003, amended 2012) *Presentation of Financial Statements*. IASB.

Melville, A. (2011) *International Financial Reporting* (3rd edn.). Harlow: FT Prentice Hall.

Wood, F. and Sangster, A. (2012) *Business Accounting* (vol. 1) (12th edn.). Harlow: FT Prentice Hall.

https://corporate.marksandspencer.com/investors/our-performance-updates/2023-annual-report

www.frc.org.uk (gives details of the Financial Reporting Council and arrangements for accounting standards in the British Isles)

www.ifrs.org (gives details of international financial reporting standards)

Chapter 2

The Income Statement (Profit and Loss Account)

Chapter contents

2.1 Introduction
2.2 Terminology and Format
2.3 Reasons for Measuring Profit
2.4 What Is Included as Revenues (or Income)
2.5 What Is Included as Expenses
2.6 A Company's Published Income Statement
2.7 Income Statement Detailed Items
2.8 Subjective Measurement and Creativity Problems
2.9 Role and Limitations of Income Statements

Learning objectives

After studying this chapter, you will be able to:

- ✓ Explain the structure and terminology of simple income statements
- ✓ Understand that there are different reasons for measuring profit and different views of what profit is
- ✓ Describe the main categories of expenses
- ✓ Assess some possibilities for 'creative accounting' in measuring profit
- ✓ Discuss the role and limitations of income statements

2.1 Introduction

In **Chapter 1** we saw that the amount of profit a company makes during a year can be calculated by comparing the statement of financial position at the beginning of the year with the statement of financial position at the end of the year. Some additional information may be needed, and it is not the easiest way of calculating profit.

Income statements (or profit and loss accounts) provide more straightforward presentations of profit figures. But even a brief examination of the published income statement of a company shows a complex assortment of different profit figures, and it can be difficult to know where to start.

At first sight, the notion of profit seems very straightforward. If you buy something for £6 and sell it for £10, you have made a profit of £4. But accountants would say this is 'gross profit', the first of the profit figures shown on an income statement. We need to deduct expenses before we arrive at operating profit. There are more deductions, and profit is shown both before and after tax.

To begin with, we need to be clear about (a) terminology, and (b) the usual formats for presenting the information. Most people are clear that they want to know the profit figures, but they are much less clear about exactly what profit means, and what the profit figures are to be used for. If we are clear about the function(s) of profit figures, we can then see what principles for measuring profit are appropriate.

2.2 Terminology and Format

Income statements show profit for the year[1] and the term 'income statement' has now generally replaced the term 'profit and loss account', following international accounting standards (IAS).

An income statement shows the calculation on the basis that expenses are deducted from revenues.

Revenues *minus* expenses = profit

'Revenues', 'turnover' and 'sales' are much the same thing, and are shown on an income statement along with any 'other income'.[2] The words 'expenses' and 'costs' mean much the same thing, but payments (of cash) are quite different. Hence, if you have never studied accounting before, some of the accounting terminology may be confusing.

One thing we need to be very clear about is that the word 'receipts' has nothing to do with income or profit; it means receipts of cash. Similarly, the word 'payments' has nothing to do with expenses or profit measurement; it means payments of cash. The differences between receipts and payments of cash, and profit are essential to an understanding of financial accounts. They are dealt with in **Chapter 6**.

The standard format appearing in IAS 1 is shown in **Illustration 2.1**.

ILLUSTRATION 2.1

Income statement of IAS1 Company Ltd for the year ended 31 December year 3

	£000
Revenue	100
Cost of sales	60
Gross profit	40
Other income	2
Distribution costs	(12)
Administration expenses	(9)

[1] An income statement can be for a year, a month or any period you like. A statement of financial position is never for a period – it is always 'as at' a given date.

[2] It is easier to think of 'income' as being revenues for the period, before expenses are deducted; but, unfortunately, some accountants use the word 'income' to mean profit. Accounting terminology can be very confusing!

Income statement of IAS1 Company Ltd for the year ended 31 December year 3	
	£000
Other expenses	(2)
Financing costs	(3)
Profit before taxation	16
Tax on profit for year	(4)
Profit for the year	12
Statement of changes in equity of IAS1 Company Ltd for the year ended 31 December year 3	
Balance at 31 December year 2	500
Add Profit for the year	12
Deduct Dividends for the year	(5)
Balance as at 31 December year 3	507

Another commonly seen format of the income statement, a variation of the IAS 1 format in **Illustration 2.1**, can be seen in **Illustration 2.2** in which profit is presented in four main stages.

ILLUSTRATION 2.2

Income statement of Simple Company Ltd for the year ended 31 December year 3	
	£000
Revenue	100
Cost of sales	60
Gross profit	40
Distribution costs	(12)
Administration expenses	(9)
Operating profit	19
Financing costs	(3)
Profit before taxation	16
Tax on profit for year	(4)
Profit for the year (i.e. after taxation)	12
Statement of changes in equity of Simple Company Ltd for the year ended 31 December year 3	
Balance at 31 December year 2	500
Add Profit for the year	12
Deduct Dividends for the year	(5)
Balance as at 31 December year 3	507

First, there is 'gross profit', which is the difference between the sales figure and *the cost of the goods that have been sold.*[3] This phrase, more simply expressed as the *cost of sales*, is very important in profit measurement.

[3] It excludes the cost of goods that have not been sold (closing inventory or closing stock), which is carried forward to be treated as an expense in the following period.

Second, there is 'operating profit', which is arrived at after deducting the main categories of expenses, which are distribution costs and administrative expenses. Operating profit is an important figure: it shows how much profit has been made from the normal operations of the business before deducting any interest payable. Operating profit is not shown explicitly in the IAS 1 format in **Illustration 2.1** but can be computed by the reader.

Third, there is 'profit before taxation', which is arrived at after bringing in interest receivable and interest payable - usually shown as 'finance costs'.

Fourth, there is 'profit after taxation', which obviously comes after deducting the company's tax charge for the year, and is the net amount that has been earned for the shareholders.

Each of the above four versions of profit may be useful in assessing different aspects of a company's performance. The fourth figure shows the profit available after taxation, which is the basis for determining the amount of dividends to be paid to shareholders.

The dividend[4] for the year is shown on a separate 'Statement of changes in equity for the year'. As we saw in **Chapter 1**, we can compare the statement of financial position at the beginning of the year with the statement of financial position at the end of the year to show the amount by which 'equity' has changed: it is increased by the amount of profit earned during the year; it is reduced by the amount of dividends to be paid for the year; and it may be changed by other items such as a revaluation of assets. The 'Statement of changes in equity for the year' shows these items and anything else that has changed the amount of equity during the year.

Although company income statements can be almost infinitely complex, it is also possible to have relatively simple versions, as shown in **Illustrations 2.1** and **2.2**. Each of the different profit figures has its uses, but the two marked with asterisks are perhaps the most important in assessing the overall performance of a company. It is useful to compare the profit figures for the current year with those of previous years to see what improvement (if any) there has been. It is also useful to compare the profit figures with the amount of resources invested in the company to see if a reasonable return has been achieved.

The income statement emphasizes what profit has been earned for the shareholders. The final figures on a published income statement show the 'earnings per share' (EPS). This is the total amount of profit after tax that the company has earned during the year, divided by the number of shares that the company has. This figure is widely used as a measure of a company's success. Not all of the EPS is paid out to shareholders as dividends: the total earnings for the year can be compared with the dividends for the year on the statement of changes in equity. In **Illustration 2.2** the Simple Company Ltd made profits of £12,000 during the year; £5,000 of this was paid to shareholders as dividends; the remaining £7,000 was retained in the business.

An income statement might show a substantial increase in profits, but this does not necessarily mean that the shareholders are going to be better off. If profits have increased by 50 per cent, but the number of shares has doubled, then the EPS will be reduced. EPS is sometimes seen as being the most important figure in assessing company performance. Shareholders expect to see it increase year after year, and some companies even aim for 'double-digit' growth in EPS - they want it to increase by at least 10 per cent each year. Not many companies have managed to achieve this for more than a very few years.

2.3 Reasons for Measuring Profit

There are many good reasons for measuring profit. It is a symbol of success for companies and their managers. A company that shows steadily increasing profits is likely to go from strength to strength. A company that shows losses or falling profits is likely to find itself in difficulties.

4 The dividend for the year is the amount paid to shareholders; it is usually part of the profit (after tax) for the year. The remaining profits are 'retained' within the business.

More specifically, the main reasons for measuring profit, or functions that profit measurement may serve, are as follows:

1. It is a measure of *performance*. Shareholders want to know how well the directors and managers of a company are doing, running the company for its owners (the shareholders).
2. It is a guide to dividend policy. A company chooses how much profit is paid out as dividends. Occasionally, a company pays out more dividends than it earns in profits, but it can only do that for a short time. A company must earn profits if it is to continue paying dividends. There is a Companies Act requirement that dividends should be paid only when sufficient accumulated realized, retained earnings are used to justify them.
3. Directors and managers may have a direct interest in such a performance for their own reasons: they are often shareholders themselves and may have some sort of performance-related pay, meaning they get extra salaries or bonuses[5] if profits achieve specified levels.
4. It is a measure of the *efficiency* of a company. Efficiency is about the relationship between inputs and outputs. Maximizing efficiency means minimizing the cost per unit of output or maximizing the outputs per £ of cost. For a company, the inputs are shown as costs, outputs are shown as sales, and the difference between sales and costs is shown as profit. Maximizing profits, therefore, maximizes efficiency.
5. It is a measure of the *effectiveness* of a company. Effectiveness is about the relationship between outputs and objectives. An effective organization (or individual) is one that achieves what it intends to do. If we assume that companies intend to maximize profits, then maximizing profits maximizes effectiveness.
6. It is a guide to the financial strength of a company. A profitable company is more likely to survive and be able to pay its liabilities when they fall due than one which is loss-making.
7. It is a basis for taxation. The government lays down various rules for taxation purposes (e.g. what rate of depreciation or 'writing-down allowance' should be used), which means that the profit figure shown in a company's published accounts may be quite different from the figure used in calculating the amount of corporation tax payable.
8. It is relevant in pricing decisions. In most circumstances, prices are determined more by what the market will bear, and the company has to find ways of keeping costs below the market price (and/or ways of pushing up what the market will bear). In some circumstances (e.g. in public utilities that were previously publicly owned), there might be official restrictions on price increases that are related to profits.
9. Employees have an interest in profits. They may believe that a profitable company is the best guarantee of long-term employment. They may also believe that good profits present an opportunity for pressing for increases in wages and salaries.
10. Profits are sometimes seen as being the key to a successful economy and a successful country. Most profitable companies find it easier to raise capital at the lowest cost, and so resources in the country flow into the most profitable companies, which are also the most efficient and effective. The least profitable companies find it hardest to raise additional capital and pay more for it, so the least efficient and effective companies tend to decline.

Some of the above may be questionable or political, and you are, of course, free to take very different views. You may believe that profit is a measure of the success of the strong in exploiting the weak, that big business makes too much profit, that more should go to the workers, that profit fails to measure social costs, and all of the above ignores issues such as health and safety, child labour, damage to the environment and non-sustainable development. If you wish, you can take the view that profits are a 'bad thing'. It is probably a 'good thing' if this book encourages you to think about these issues!

---

[5] Or they may have share options. Or they may be 'fat cats' who get good bonuses even when the company does badly. Or their bonuses may depend on the share price achieving a particular level. Or they may have share options that are valuable only when the share price achieves particular levels. As directors are supposed to be accountable to shareholders, it is worth considering the effectiveness of accountability arrangements; these are discussed later.

It is, however, worth being explicit about the general assumptions that seem to lie behind the measuring and reporting of profit. Many different people and groups in society are likely to favour companies making good and increasing profits for many different reasons. In some circumstances, governments may try to restrict the amount of profit that monopolies (or near-monopolies) are allowed to make. But increasing profits are generally favoured by shareholders, managers (and the Treasury, who are usually happy to rake in more in taxation), the company's bankers and professional advisers (whose fees seem to keep going up), the financial press, many employees and anyone else who can jump on the gravy train. There is enormous pressure on managers to perform and to produce profits. And if they cannot, they are liable to be replaced by others, sometimes by managers who can produce profits out of thin air,[6] like magicians. There are always some who can make use of creative accounting techniques for their own advantage. But, like magicians, such managers do not want to be watched too closely, and the more successful ones move on rapidly to other companies to display their tricks and illusions.

Given that profit figures are likely to be used for many different purposes, it is not surprising that there are different approaches to profit measurement. The principles of profit measurement could be based mainly on comparing statements of financial position values from one period to the next. They can also be based on the income statement, and how revenues and income are defined and measured.

2.4 What Is Included as Revenues (or Income)?

The income statement begins with the figure for revenue, which could also be called sales or turnover. It includes all the sales made during the period, not just of goods, but, depending on what kind of business it is, also of services, and it can include other items such as rents receivable. The turnover figure is shown net of such things as value added tax.

It includes all sales made during a period, even if the money for those sales is not received until a later period. This principle is important. It means that a rapidly expanding business might be making very good sales each month and good profits, but the amount owed by receivables (debtors) will increase each month. The cash that comes into the business lags behind the profits that are being earned. This could mean a rapidly expanding and profitable business has much less money than the sales figures suggest.

It is also important because it is sometimes not clear exactly when a sale has been made. It could be that a sale is initially agreed upon by phone; a few days later, an order is received; then a few weeks later, the goods are completed and ready for dispatch; then, a few days later, the goods are received by the purchaser; then the seller sends out the invoice. Payment for the goods is probably not made for another month or two. There is a need for a transparent accounting principle that determines the exact point, or the critical event, at which a sale is recognized. In practice, an accounting system usually recognizes a sale when the invoice is sent out, signifying ownership of goods has been transferred from seller to buyer or that services have been delivered. But it is easy to see that temptations can arise to recognize sales at an earlier date. When sales are below target, perhaps in the last month of the year, and managers see their bonuses disappearing or even their jobs, it is not difficult to create a few extra sales by bringing some forward or sending invoices out early; they can be reversed the following month. It is a bit like a shop assistant borrowing from the till, with the intention of paying back before the final reckoning comes: you can get away with it for a while, but eventually, it will catch up with you. You can bring forward your revenues one year, but you cannot bring them forward more and more each year.

Other items of income are included in published income statements, such as profits on sales of non-current assets, investment income, interest receivable, various 'exceptional items' and any share of profits from associated companies.

[6] Such 'creative accounting' is examined in **Chapter 8**.

2.5 What Is Included as Expenses?

There are more problems with defining and measuring expenses and no shortage of accounting standards or principles attempting to deal with them. Expenses are recognized in accordance with the *accruals concept*, which means that it is not the amount of cash paid out during a period that is counted; it is the amount incurred in earning the revenue that is recognized during the period. This is also about *matching*: after recognizing the turnover for a period, we match against it expenses incurred in earning that turnover. This is particularly important with the cost of sales and with depreciation.

Cost of sales

The first expense on the income statement is the cost of sales or the cost of goods sold. This means that if you buy 100 items but sell only 70 of them, only the 70 count in the cost of sales. The other 30 are 'closing inventory' (stocks remaining at the end of the period) and are carried forward as a current asset in the statement of financial position to be treated as an expense in the following period (see **Example 2.1**).

As the calculation of gross profit (or any other profit) depends on the closing inventory figure, determining how this is determined is important. If, in **Example 2.1**, Raj had made a mistake, and his closing inventory figure was £3,000, then his cost of sales would be only £8,000, and the gross profit would be £7,000.

Example 2.1

At the beginning of March, Raj's shop had an inventory of goods amounting to £1,000. During March, he bought goods for resale costing £10,000.[7] His sales figure for March was £15,000.

Raj, therefore, had £11,000 worth of goods available for sale. But that is not the cost of sales figure. Some of the goods he had available for sale were not sold, and we cannot calculate the cost of sales or the gross profit until we know the closing inventory figure.

His stock of unsold goods at the end of March was £2,000.

The cost of the goods which he sold can now be calculated as follows:

	£
Opening inventory	1,000
Add Purchases	10,000
Cost of goods available for sale	11,000
Deduct Closing inventory	2,000
Cost of goods sold (or cost of sales)	9,000

The cost of sales figure is then compared with the sales figure, and the difference, £6,000, is the gross profit.

[7] That is what he bought during March. He probably did not pay for them until April. But actual payments of cash, and receipts of cash, are quite distinct from revenues and expenses, that are used in profit measurement.

	£
Sales	15,000
Cost of sales	9,000
Gross profit	6,000

If Raj's actual closing inventory figure was only £1,500, then his gross profit would be only £5,500. If a higher closing inventory figure is shown, then the profit figure will be higher, and the assets[8] and equity figures on the statement of financial position will be higher. If a lower closing inventory figure is shown, then the profit figure will be lower, and the assets and equity figures on the statement of financial position will be lower. This has important consequences: if Raj overstated his closing inventory figure by £1m, his income statement and statement of financial position would look better by £1m. We need some clear rules and principles for determining closing inventory figures. The general rule is that the inventory of goods is shown at cost price.[9]

In a retail business, it is relatively easy to establish the cost price of goods. Whereas in a manufacturing business, it is more difficult because we need to establish the cost of manufacturing the goods, which involves some difficult decisions in allocating overheads.

The cost of sales figure includes only the costs of buying or producing goods and services. It includes an appropriate share of production overheads, including the costs of running the factory or other production facilities (including rent, lighting, heating, depreciation and maintenance of machinery, and factory supervision costs). The cost of sales does not include the general administration costs of the business or the selling and distribution costs.

Gross profit ratio

In examining the income statement of a business, analysts usually calculate the gross profit ratio. This expresses gross profit as a percentage of sales as follows:

$$\frac{£6,000}{£15,000} = 40\%$$

Mark-up

The cost of the goods that Raj sold was £9,000. He marked them up by £6,000 and sold them for £15,000. The mark-up can be expressed as a percentage as follows:

$$\frac{£6,000}{£9,000} = 66⅔\%$$

It is important to distinguish percentage mark-ups from gross profit percentages, and it is worth playing with a few calculations to become familiar with them. A 25 per cent mark-up becomes a 20 per cent gross profit ratio (e.g. buy for £80, sell for £100). A 33⅓ per cent gross profit ratio comes from a 50 per cent mark-up (e.g. buy for £100, sell for £150).

---

8 Closing inventory is shown as a current asset on the statement of financial position.

9 Or, more precisely, closing inventories are shown at the lower of cost or the net realizable value.

Depreciation

Figures for depreciation are less obvious on a published income statement; they are usually included under several headings, with the detail hidden away in the notes to the accounts. When a business buys a non-current asset (a fixed asset), such as a piece of machinery, it is not immediately treated as an expense. The asset is shown on the statement of financial position; the business decides how long the asset's useful life is expected to be; and the figure is written down, or depreciated, each year. If machinery is purchased for £12,000 and is expected to have a useful economic life of four years, that is, to produce revenue for four years, the cost of £12,000 will be written off as an expense over the four years in accordance with the accruals, or matching principle. On the day it is purchased, it is an asset expected to produce future benefits for four years. After one year, one-quarter of its benefits have arisen, and the depreciation expense will be £3,000, leaving a net book value in the statement of financial position of £9,000, reflecting, at that point, that there are three years of expected benefits remaining. Depreciation is an expense in calculating profit that sounds straightforward enough. But it causes problems for students of accounting because:

1. They often think that expenses are paid out in cash, but depreciation is not paid out in cash. The non-current asset has already been bought, and the cash has already flowed out. Depreciation is a bookkeeping entry, not a flow of cash. Profit is always calculated *after* charging the depreciation expense. If we want to know what cash flow a business generates, we have to add depreciation back onto profit. Some people say a business's cash flow is its profit plus depreciation, which is roughly correct. Some even see depreciation as being an inflow of cash, but that is completely wrong: depreciation is something that, in calculating profit, we treat as if it had been paid out as cash (but it hasn't), so we add it back to profit to indicate the cash that has been generated during the period.
2. They see depreciation as part of a process of valuing assets, which it is not. The objective is to write down the cost of a non-current asset, year by year, as the fixed asset's useful life is being used up. Usually,[10] this results in asset figures being shown on the statement of financial position that are closer to current values, but that is incidental. The main point is to charge the amount of the non current asset that has been 'used up' as an expense in calculating profit.
3. They think a provision for depreciation is a pool of money that can be used to replace non-current assets when they come to the end of their lives. But there is no money in a provision (or in 'reserves'). If you want to know what money (or cash and bank) is in a business, you must look in current assets. The provision for depreciation is a bookkeeping entry, not an allocation of cash. It reduces profits, and as companies usually relate dividend decisions to the level of profits, the fact that depreciation is charged may limit the amount of dividends paid out - a way of achieving 'capital maintenance'.

Even for sophisticated users of accounts, there are problems with depreciation. Different companies have different depreciation policies, and we never know how long a non-current asset will last, how long we will keep it, or how much it will be sold for when we have finished with it. We might buy a car for £10,000, plan to keep it for four years, and then sell it for £2,000. But that might change; we might keep it much longer or sell it much earlier, and the amount we sell it for might be much more or less than we planned.

The easiest approach to depreciation is to use the 'straight-line' method. If we buy a car for £10,000 and plan to sell it for £2,000 after four years, then the total amount to be depreciated is £8,000, which works out at £2,000 a year for four years.

Another depreciation method that is slightly more complicated but still reasonably popular is the 'diminishing balance' method.[11] If we charged 33 per cent[12] per annum on this basis, the figures would be as follows:

[10] But not always. Companies are expected to depreciate buildings as their effective lives are 'used up', even if they are increasing in value.

[11] Also known as the reducing balance method.

[12] Thirty-three per cent. Not 33⅓ per cent - that would give a different answer.

	£
Initial cost of car	10,000
Year 1 depreciation 33% of £10,000	3,300
Balance at end of year 1	6,700
Year 2 depreciation 33% of £6,700	2,211
Balance at end of year 2	4,489
Year 3 depreciation 33% of £4,489	1,481
Balance at end of year 3	3,008
Year 4 depreciation 33% of £3,008	993
Balance at end of year 4	2,015

This method of depreciation results in higher depreciation in the early years and lower depreciation in the later years than depreciation calculated using the straight-line basis. Occasionally, depreciation is calculated in more obscure ways. A vehicle could be depreciated in relation to the number of miles it does each year.

If a company suddenly changed its policy and planned to keep its vehicles (or ships, or aeroplanes, or machinery) for twice as long as it had previously planned, that could halve its depreciation charges and produce a very significant increase in profits. Such a change in policy and its financial effects would have to be disclosed in a note to the financial statements. But there is inevitably some scope for individual judgement or manipulation as there is no certainty in non-current assets' future lives or residual values.

Depreciation figures and policies should be disclosed fully in the notes to the financial statements, but they do not usually appear on the face of a published income statement. The three main categories of expenses (cost of sales, distribution costs, and administration expenses) may all include some depreciation as there may be non-current assets involved in producing the goods and services, in selling and distributing them, and in the administration of the business.

Impairment of goodwill

When one company buys another business, the amount of money it pays is partly for the net assets of the business and partly for its 'goodwill', a term that covers a multitude of attributes of a business that enable it to earn profits. If a company buys a business with excellent prospects, it may pay a lot for 'goodwill', and the goodwill amount must be shown on the statement of financial position as a non-current asset; and, as with other non-current assets, it is likely to be 'used up' over a number of years. Traditionally, accountants would 'amortize' goodwill in much the same way as they depreciate other non-current assets. But it is difficult to know how long this goodwill will last, so deciding whether it should be written off over 5 or 20 years or some other period is difficult. What happens now is that any goodwill appearing on the statement of financial position will be assessed each year. This valuation is known as the 'impairment test'; the company assesses how much goodwill has been impaired or used up during the year. An impairment charge is then made, which is, in effect, depreciation or amortization of goodwill.

Goodwill and its amortization are controversial areas in accounting. The traditional view was that if goodwill is an asset and its value is dubious, it should be written off immediately. A more current view is that provided the business is well run, goodwill should last indefinitely, and there is no need to amortize it each year - especially as this can lead to massive reductions in reported profits. The present requirement is that goodwill should be subject to an annual impairment test and then written down accordingly. A business may decide that it has been impaired very little during the year or not at all. Some subjectivity is inevitable, and the door is wide open for creative accounting. Companies are not allowed to *increase* the amount they show for goodwill. Regardless of the requirements of financial reporting standards, many companies and investment analysts choose to emphasize profit figures that have not been charged with goodwill impairment.

Classification and disclosure of expenses

A business can produce an income statement showing as much detail as it wishes - with separate figures for wages and salaries, repairs and maintenance, cleaning, rent and rates, lighting and heating, insurance, telephones, stationery, postage, newspapers, directors' fees, auditors' fees, lawyers' fees and many other things. But, the published accounts of companies are in standardized formats, such as the one shown in **Illustration 2.1**, which group most expenses under the general headings 'cost of sales', 'distribution costs' and 'administrative expenses'. The income statements included in the published annual reports and accounts of companies probably look more complicated, but the basics are the same, as shown in **Illustration 2.1**.

Suppose you plough through the notes to the accounts and the directors' report. In that case, you will find lots more detail and further analysis of expenses, including wages and salaries, directors' remuneration, costs of hiring plant and machinery, auditors' remuneration, depreciation and amortization, and charitable and political donations. Other items disclosed include exceptional items such as profits or losses on disposals, the results of discontinued operations and new acquisitions, and an analysis of results classified as different segments for the various activities of the company and the geographical areas in which it operates.

As long as an expense is clearly recognized as such, which heading it is included under is less important. The chief executive may spend part of their time dealing with production issues (arguably part of the cost of sales), distribution issues and administration. But there is no need to bother allocating the costs of employing the CEO to these different headings, and treating the whole cost as administrative expenses is acceptable. Gross profit ratios[13] may be important, but it is sometimes difficult to be clear about which expenses have been included in the cost of sales.

2.6 A Company's Published Income Statement

The income statement for Marks and Spencer Group plc is shown in **Illustration 2.3**. It is called a 'group income statement' because it includes the results of subsidiary companies that the Marks and Spencer Group plc controls.

ILLUSTRATION 2.3

Group income statement of Marks and Spencer Group plc for the 52 weeks ended 1 April 2023

	Notes	**52 weeks ended 1 April 2023 £m**	**53 weeks ended 2 April 2022 £m**
Revenue	2, 3	11,931.3	10,885.1
Cost of sales	3	(7,786.7)	(7,130.3)
Gross profit		4,144.6	3,754.8
Selling and administration expenses		(3,609.2)	(3,244.1)
Other operating income		23.2	80.1
Other adjustments	3	−43.5	−18.6
Operating profit		515.1	572.2

13 Gross profit expressed as a percentage of sales revenue.

Group income statement of Marks and Spencer Group plc for the 52 weeks ended 1 April 2023

	Notes	52 weeks ended 1 April 2023 £m	53 weeks ended 2 April 2022 £m
Finance income	6	166.1	33.9
Finance expenses	6	(205.5)	(214.4)
Profit before tax	4	475.7	391.7
Income tax expense		(111.2)	(82.7)
Profit for the period		364.5	309.0
Attributable to			
Equity shareholders of the company		363.4	306.6
Non-controlling interests		1.1	2.4
Profit for the period		364.5	309.0
Earnings per share			
Basic	8	18.5p	15.7p
Diluted	8	17.9p	15.1p

Group statement of changes in equity of Marks and Spencer Group plc (simplified extract) for the 52 weeks ended 1 April 2023

	£m
Balance at beginning of the year 2 April 2022	5,897.9
Add Profit for the period	383.4
Deduct Actuarial gains/losses on retirement benefit scheme	(622.8)
Add Other items	180.6
Deduct Dividends	(0.0)
Balance at end of the year 1 April 2023	5,839.1

The main feature to note, from the shareholders' point of view, is that the 'profit for the period' has increased from £309.0m to £364.5m, an increase of 18 per cent. Although sales revenue has increased by 9.6 per cent (from £10,885.1m to £11,931.3m), the cost of goods sold has increased by 9.2 per cent, the selling and distribution costs (which Marks and Spencer have chosen to combine) have risen by 11.3 per cent; while the finance income has risen by 390 per cent, the finance expenses have fallen by 4.2 per cent; and taxation has only increased by 34.5 per cent. The statement of financial position (shown as **Illustration 1.5**) shows that equity has decreased from £2,810.5m to £2,913.7m (a decrease of 3.5 per cent). Shareholders would be quite happy to see an increase in sales, but they might be even happier to see an increase in the income for the period resulting from the finance income. However, the company's measurement of retirement benefits schemes amounted to a loss of £622.8m, and these factors have caused a substantial decrease of £58.8m in group retained profits, which amounts to a 1.0 per cent decrease, and we also see a decrease in shareholders' equity of 3.5 per cent.

The main categories of expenses shown are:

- Cost of sales
- Selling and administration costs
- Finance expenses.

Finance expenses relate to interest payable by the company. The Marks and Spencer Group's borrowings are relatively low - in the most recent year, they paid more interest than they received (finance expense is greater than finance income). In **Chapter 1**, we saw that some companies are very dependent on borrowings; interest costs can be high in relation to profits, and such companies may be at risk if they are unable to pay their liabilities as they fall due. The Marks and Spencer Group gearing ratio for 2023 is relatively high at 56 per cent (3576.5/(3576.5+2814.9), but this has no real risk in relation to borrowings.

We can see that total profits have increased and that most of the various categories of expenses have increased. This is not surprising as the business has expanded: total revenues have thus increased. It is worth examining whether or not expenses have increased faster than revenues; whether expenses seem to be carefully controlled, or whether they are rocketing upwards even faster than turnover. The main expenses are expressed as a percentage of sales, including the cost of sales. It is more usual to express gross profit as a percentage of sales; both are shown as follows:

Ratio	2023	2022	Percentage change
Cost of sales/revenue	7,786.7/11,931.3	7130.3/10,885.1	
	65.3%	65.5%	−0.4%
Gross profit/revenue	4,144.7/11,931.3	3,754.8/10,885.1	
	34.7%	34.5%	+0.7%
Selling and administration expenses/revenue	3,609.2/11,931.3	3244.1/10,885.1	
	30.2%	29.8%	+1.5

The gross profit ratio seems fairly high. It would be interesting to compare it with other clothing retailers. The selling and administration expenses have increased as a percentage of sales. From the notes to the accounts other information about expenses, and some explanation of the increases, can be found.

2.7 Income Statement Detailed Items

Examining a company's published income statement usually reveals more complexities than have been outlined so far. These can be seen in the accounts of most listed companies, that is, those whose shares are traded on a stock exchange. You can download the accounts of such a company from its website. The annual report of Marks and Spencer Group plc can be found at corporate.marksandspencer.com/investors/our-performance-updates/2024-annual-report.

Company or group

Most large companies that are listed on the stock market own a number of subsidiary companies. It is most useful to look at the group results that include all the results of the subsidiary companies.

Non-controlling interests

A company often owns only, say, 90 per cent of a subsidiary company, but the income statement includes 100 per cent of the results of all the subsidiaries. At the end of the income statement, after profit for the period has been calculated, an item for 'non-controlling interests', formerly known as 'minority interests', is shown.

This is the part of the group's profit that belongs to shareholders outside the group (e.g. 10 per cent of the shareholders of a subsidiary company). The amount of profit remaining (after deducting the non-controlling or minority interest) belongs to the shareholders of the parent company.

Associates and joint ventures

A company (e.g. Parent Co) may invest in other companies (e.g. Associate Co) but own only between, say, 20 per cent and 49 per cent of Associate Co's shares. Parent Co is likely to have significant influence over Associate Co. But Parent Co does not include 100 per cent of Associate Co's profits in its income statement. Instead, Parent Co includes, say, 20 per cent to 50 per cent, according to the proportion owned.

Dividends receivable

A company (e.g. Parent Co) may have only a small shareholding in another company (e.g. Investment Co) as an investment. If Parent Co has no significant influence over Investment Co, then Investment Co is not part of the group, and the group's income statement does not include a share of Investment Co's profits. Instead, the group income statement includes dividends (not profits) from such companies.

Acquisitions, discontinued operations and continuing operations

Large companies often sell off parts of the business and buy new businesses. If you want to assess the future performance of a business, it is not much use doing so on the basis of information that includes parts of the business that have been closed down or disposed of. If you want to assess the past performance of a business, it is not much use comparing last year's figures with this year's figures if there has been a major acquisition; in that case, we would expect to see a significant increase in this year's figures. To make meaningful comparisons, we need to separate the figures for new acquisitions from continuing operations, and we need to separate the figures for operations that have been discontinued or disposed of.

Income statements provide the information under the three headings (acquisitions, discontinued operations and continuing operations) for sales and operating profit.

Segmental reporting

Many large companies combine together a number of different businesses, perhaps with very different products or with very different geographical areas. International Accounting Standard (IAS) 14 requires companies to disclose their revenues, profits and capital employed for each major geographical and business segment. This can be very useful if you are trying to forecast a company's future performance and you believe that one area of business is going to perform better than another in the future. It can also be useful in assessing whether the management of one company has been as successful as others in dealing with areas of growth, and areas of decline and in assessing different prospects for growth or levels of risk in different activities or different geographical regions. The Marks and Spencer Group accounts show segmental analysis in terms of 'UK Clothing and Home' and 'UK Food', geographical segments - 'International' - and finally, 'Ocado'.

Exceptional items

A company's results are sometimes affected by 'one-off' exceptional items such as a profit on selling part of the business or some assets, inventories being written down, some write-offs to reflect the impairment of non-current assets or the costs of redundancies and reorganization. These are usually shown as a separate item on the income statement, with more detail shown in the notes. The profit for the year and the basic EPS are shown after deducting (or crediting) all exceptional items. However, companies sometimes show a second EPS figure that may exclude any bad news that they have managed to label as 'exceptional items'.

2.8 Subjective Measurement and Creativity Problems

Creative accounting is an important subject in its own right, but even an introductory look at income statements reveals several areas where subjective judgements are required and where there may be scope for creative accounting.

Capital expenditure and revenue expenditure

Capital expenditure adds to the amount for non-current assets (sometimes called fixed assets) that are shown on the statement of financial position as 'property, plant and equipment' under the heading 'non-current assets'. The statement of financial position shows the amount of assets that the company owns at the year end. In an expanding company, this usually increases each year because the company buys additional non-current assets during the year. 'Capital expenditure' is the term used for purchasing additional non-current assets; its effect on profit figures is delayed and spread over a number of years as depreciation. The net effect of capital expenditure and depreciation is shown on the statement of financial position, and more detail is shown in the notes to the accounts. Revenue expenditure appears on the income statement, not the statement of financial position, and is an immediate charge against profit. Buying a new car, premises, or machinery is a capital expenditure. Maintaining them and the costs of using them are revenue expenditures.

The important distinction between capital expenditure and revenue expenditure is usually clear, but there are some grey areas and sometimes there may be a temptation to 'capitalize'[14] expenditure that is more like revenue expenditure and should be treated as an expense immediately. If a company can make most of its 'repairs and maintenance' expenditures look more like improvements and additions to non-current assets, they can avoid charging them as expenses on the income statement, boost profits and show higher asset figures on the statement of financial position.

There are areas, such as research and development, where companies can capitalize large amounts of development expenditure in this way. It is also possible, when constructing a non-current asset (perhaps building a new hotel), to treat the cost of interest during the period of construction as part of the capital expenditure rather than revenue expenditure.

Depreciation

There is inevitably scope for differences of view on the lives of non-current assets, likely values at the end of their lives and in choosing what method of depreciation to use.

Valuation of inventories

The value of inventories at the end of the year affects profits: if closing inventories are overstated, then profits and assets are overstated. Although the general rule is that inventories are shown at cost price (or

[14] Treat it as adding to non-current assets.

net realizable value if it is lower), there may be some room for manoeuvre, especially when the company has itself manufactured the unsold items. There are important rules to determine which costs should be included in the cost of production and which costs should be treated as expenses immediately. There is also a grey area in assessing 'net realizable value'. If an item costs £100 to make or buy, it should continue to be included in the accounts at that price until it seems that it can only be sold for a lower figure. It is possible for a company to be too optimistic in assessing net realizable values or to be too pessimistic; either approach can lead to unrealistic profit figures.

Timing

The rules on when sales should be recognized are not very clear, and there is sometimes scope for bringing forward the recognition of sales and, so, boosting the sales figure for the year.

2.9 Role and Limitations of Income Statements

The main role of the income statement is to set out the profit that a business has made during the period and its component parts. The old term 'profit and loss account' may still be preferred because it shows the profits and losses from the various activities undertaken by the company. There are many good reasons for measuring profit, as set out in **Section 2.3**.

The income statement also has a role in indicating how and where profits might be increased. Comparing this year's results with last year's is a useful monitoring exercise. Most businesses expect their sales figure to grow each year, with an increase in the cost of sales and an increase in gross profit. But they also hope to at least maintain their operating margins: that gross profit as a proportion of sales will be maintained or increased. The same kind of analysis should be applied to the main categories of expenses. As sales increase, expenses might also be expected to increase. But management should be monitoring the various expenses as a proportion of sales, and trying to ensure that expenses, as a percentage of sales, do not increase. Sometimes, as a matter of policy, a company might decide to increase particular items of expense (e.g. spending more on marketing). But, more generally, a company should expect some economies of scale as it expands and monitor the results to see if each category of expense really is declining as a proportion of sales.

The information shown in the income statement can be useful in comparing this year's results with last year's as part of the financial control.[15] It can also be useful in comparing one company's results with another. Of course, a large supermarket chain makes more profits than a small one. Still, a detailed analysis of the income statement, looking at the various expenses as a proportion of sales, can show where one company is doing better than another and where there is room for improvement.

In comparing companies with each other, we need to look carefully for explanations of differences in performance. One company might lease all its premises and equipment while another owns them. One might have very old non-current assets and, therefore, very low depreciation charges, while another has much newer non-current assets. One company might be financed wholly by shareholders' funds and so have no interest charges. In contrast, another is largely financed by borrowing (i.e. it has high gearing), and so it has high 'finance expenses' (interest charges). There might also be different accounting policies, and where there is scope for 'creative accounting', it may be difficult to make meaningful comparisons between one company and another. Among the functions of the International Financial Reporting Standards (IFRSs) and International Accounting Standards (IASs), referred to in **Chapter 1**, are to aid comparisons between different companies and different countries and to minimize the scope for manipulation and creative accounting.

[15] The exercise is often carried out comparing budgeted (or planned) income statements with the actual results achieved.

It is also important to realize that profits are not the same as cash flow. A company might do very well in selling equipment and civil engineering products to what the Americans call 'rogue states', but there could be massive delays in receiving the money from these sales, which rather takes the shine off the performance. Income statements should be interpreted together with cash flow statements. Indeed, the main published financial accounting statements should be taken as a whole. Making profits is not enough. Profits need to be sufficient when compared with the amount of money invested in the business to justify that investment. Companies need to make a good return on capital employed (ROCE), and assessing the performance of a company requires the use of figures both from the income statement and from the statement of financial position.

Summary

An income statement (previously known as a profit and loss account) shows the profit for a period, typically a year. Profit is based on the difference between revenue (or sales or turnover) and the costs incurred in earning those sales. Profit figures are useful in many different ways, and care is needed in interpreting the information. Profit is calculated after charging the cost of sales (which requires a value to be put on closing inventories) and depreciation; these are examples of expenses where there is an element of subjectivity.

IASs permit a variety of different ways of presenting statements of financial position and income statements, provided the same information is disclosed (sometimes on the face of statements; sometimes in the notes to the accounts). **Illustration 2.1** is the most popular way of presenting income statements in the UK, but with additional items, many look much more complex.

Review of key points

- The income statement (or profit and loss account) shows the profit for a period by deducting from sales (and any other revenues) the costs incurred in earning those revenues.
- It is useful to measure profit as an indication of a company's performance and as a basis for dividend decisions.
- Profit figures are also useful to a range of different groups in society.
- There is some subjectivity in profit measurement, for example, in depreciation and in valuing closing inventories.
- Profit figures are most useful when they are used in making comparisons.
- Profit is different from cash flow.

Self-testing questions

1 What are the main differences between a statement of financial position and an income statement?

2 What is an expense? How does an expense differ from an asset? Can an asset become an expense? In what sense could it be argued that an asset is an expense waiting to happen?

3 How are inventories valued? Why does it matter? Would it be a good idea to show inventories at the selling price?

4 Why is depreciation charged?

5 What is the difference between capital expenditure and revenue expenditure?

6 Which of the profit figures shown in a simplified income statement (**Illustration 2.2**) are shareholders likely to be most interested in, and why?

7 The Kingsdun Company buys a delivery van for £25,000 and a boring machine for £25,000. They decided that the delivery van should be depreciated at 25 per cent per annum on a diminishing balance basis and that the boring machine should be depreciated at 10 per cent per annum on a straight-line basis. Calculate the depreciation charge for each of the first four years of the assets' lives and the net book value of each at the end of year 4.

8 The Dargate Retailing Company sells a range of different products, some with modest gross profit margins and some with much higher gross profit margins. For example, they buy Fargs for £100 each, apply a 25 per cent mark-up, and sell them for £125 each; the gross profit on Fargs is, therefore, 20 per cent (£25 gross profit is 20 per cent of the selling price). Employees often confuse percentage mark-ups with percentage gross profit. To avoid confusion, you are asked to produce a definitive list showing the cost, mark-up percentage, selling price and gross profit percentage of each product by completing the gaps in the table below:

Product	**Cost price** £	**Mark-up** %	**Selling price** £	**Gross profit** %
Fargs	100	25	125	20
Gargs	100	10	(i)	9.09
Hargs	50	(ii)	100	(iii)
Jargs	40	(iv)	80	(v)
Kargs	80	(vi)	(vii)	33⅓
Largs	(viii)	20	60	16⅔
Margs	(ix)	30	40	(x)
Nargs	(xii)	(xiii)	50	10
Pargs	75	(xiv)	(xv)	25

9 Banterbury Company Ltd

Income statement of the Banterbury Company Ltd for the year ended 31 December		
	Year 3	**Year 4**
	£000	£000
Revenue	100	120
Cost of sales	(60)	(73)
Gross profit	40	47
Distribution costs	(12)	(14)
Administration expenses	(9)	(12)

Income statement of the Banterbury Company Ltd for the year ended 31 December		
	Year 3	Year 4
Operating profit	9	21
Finance expenses	(3)	(3)
Profit before taxation	16	18
Taxation	(4)	(3)
Profit for the year	12	15
Statement of changes in equity of Banterbury Company Ltd for the year ended 31 December		
	£000	£000
Balance at beginning of year	93	100
Profit for the year	12	15
Dividends paid	(5)	(6)
Balance at end of year	100	109

The chair of the company boasts that sales, profits and dividends are at record levels and that the amount of shareholders' funds in the business has increased to £109,000 at the end of year 4.

Critically assess the performance of the company.

Assessment questions

1 The Broadstores Company:

Income statement of Broadstores Company for the year ended 31 December

	Year 7	Year 8
	£000	£000
Revenue	200	220
Cost of sales	(120)	(131)
Gross profit	80	89
Distribution costs	(22)	(24)
Administration expenses	(40)	(41)
Operating profit	18	24
Finance expenses	(10)	(18)
Profit before taxation	8	6
Tax on profit for year	(3)	(2)
Profit after tax for the year	5	4

Statement of changes in equity of Broadstores Company for the year ended 31 December

	£000	£000
Balance at beginning of year	50	51
Profit for the year	5	4
Dividends paid	(4)	0
Balance at end of year	51	55

The chair of the company states that the management of the company has performed well in a very difficult economic climate and that increased profits have been retained within the business to finance profitable expansion.

A shareholder at the company's annual general meeting claims that the reduction in profits and the absence of dividends prove that the management of the company is a disaster.

You are required to assess the evidence for each point of view.

2 The Billygate Company operates with a 40 per cent mark-up on the goods that it buys. What is its gross profit ratio?

The Sillygate Company operates with a 40 per cent gross profit margin. What percentage mark-up does it use?

3 Roger, a graduate of the University of South East England, has been running a business called 'SuperSoftService' since he completed his information technology (IT) degree six years ago. He sells software and prides himself on providing fast delivery using his sports car. He has an extensive stock of software, catering for the latest developments as well as meeting the demand for software for old operating systems - he still can supply most things for Windows 95 and makes the occasional sale of old software.

About half of his sales are on a cash basis, and about half are on credit. He sells on credit only to friends, graduates, and people he knows, and he has no experience of bad debts.

The business is very profitable and is almost entirely financed by borrowing from his father. However, his father is concerned that Roger keeps borrowing more and more money to keep the business afloat.

His summarized financial statements are shown as follows:

Income statement of SuperSoftService for the year ended 31 December year 6

Revenue		£100,000
Cost of goods sold		
Opening inventories	60,000	
Purchases	40,000	
	100,000	
Less Closing inventories	(80,000)	20,000
Gross profit		80,000
Administration and distribution expenses		(50,000)
Net profit		30,000
Drawings for personal expenditure		(29,000)
Retained profit for year		1,000

Statement of financial position of SuperSoftService as at 31 December year 6

Non-current assets		
Car at cost 1 January year 1		£18,000
Less Provision for depreciation		(9,000)
		9,000
Current assets		
Inventories at cost	80,000	
Receivables	80,000	
		160,000
Total assets		169,000
Current liabilities		
Payables	3,000	
Overdraft	3,000	6,000
Loan from father		150,000
Equity		
Roger's capital	6,000	
Roger's retained earnings	7,000	13,000
		169,000

a Comment on the financial position and performance of the business.
b How 'real' are the profits?

4 The Depreciation Company

The directors of the Depreciation Company are deciding on their accounting policy for the depreciation of their non-current assets.

They have just purchased some new assets that cost £200,000 and which they expect to sell after five years for £20,000.

a Calculate the depreciation expense in the income statement and the figures that will appear in the statement of financial position of the company assuming:
   i They adopt the straight-line basis of depreciation
   ii They adopt the diminishing basis at 30 per cent

b Advise the directors which method is the more appropriate and why.

5 The Chinese Motor Company

The Chinese Motor Company runs a UK branch and a China branch. Both branches run three departments for sales, car servicing and the sale of parts.

Advise the management of the company:

a why the users of the company's financial statements would find a segmental report useful
b what information it should contain
c how this information would improve the users' decision-making process

Group activities and discussion questions

1 Profit figures are wanted by various groups of people for different purposes, and it is not possible to define and measure profits in such a way as to meet all of those different needs. Discuss.

2 Attempt a definition of 'profit'. You can use other books. Can all members of the group agree on the definition? Is the definition clear and robust enough to provide a basis for measuring profits in all businesses? You could have a formal debate with two people arguing in favour of a particular definition of profit, and two could argue against that definition. Or two could argue that it is possible to produce a workable definition, and two could argue that it is not.

3 Last year, a company's statement of financial position showed freehold land and buildings at cost, the amount being £4m. This year, the properties have been revalued at £7m. Is the company £3m better off? Have they made £3m profit?

4 Why do companies aim to earn profits? Should all organizations attempt to earn profits? If you think that some organizations should not attempt to earn profits, on what basis would you decide which should earn profits and which should not?

5 Do companies have too much freedom to determine the methods and rates of depreciation that they use for their published accounts? Where governments specify methods and rates of depreciation to be used to calculate profits for taxation purposes, should companies be required to use those same rates in their published accounts?

6 You are a shareholder in a listed company. You are told that last year the company's net profit after tax increased from £100m to £130m and that the management of the company is therefore performing extremely well.

   a What additional information would you want in order to assess the effectiveness of management? (Produce a list, and only look at (b) once you have done that!)

   b Obtain the published annual report and accounts of a listed company. How much of what you wanted to know does it tell you?

7 Examine Marks and Spencer Group's results since 2022. Has the expansion of the company been successful in leading to a big enough increase in profits?

8 Compare the gross profit ratios of a number of different retailers. Are the differences very substantial? How do you explain or justify such differences?

Accounting in context

Discuss and comment on the following report based on an article from the press with particular reference to the importance of turnover, operating profit and expenses in assessing the effectiveness of an organization and its future prospects.

Watches of Switzerland

The luxury watch specialist, Watches of Switzerland (WOSG), is a UK retailer, and the company first listed on the London Stock Exchange in June 2019 with an initial public offering of its ordinary shares at £2.70 per share and realizing a market capitalization of £647m. The company gave a profits warning in January 2024, attributed to volatile trading performance during and after the holiday season, which has resulted in a significant drop in their share price. In August,

WOSG's share price had already fallen by 20 per cent after Rolex announced its purchase of the Swiss Retailer Bucherrer, raising concerns that Rolex would set up its own retail outlet, affecting WOSG's market share.

Despite Rolex being crucial to WOSG, holding 10 per cent of the global Rolex market share, the drop in share price may have been overdone as nothing fundamental had changed. WOSG's half-year results show 5 per cent growth in the US with adjusted cash profits of £73m. However, the adjusted margin is 9.6 per cent, down 170 basis points, which is a 15 per cent decline from the previous year. WOSG's Chief Executive, Brian Duffy, has reported that customers have been spending more on other luxury categories, such as fashion and travel, which is expected to continue for the rest of the financial year.

The warning has caused a significant decline in WOSG's shares over a 12-month period, from a high of £10.70 to a low of £4.75, and has dropped further to £3.83 (closing price on 24 January, 2024). The company now expects revenue for the financial year to be between £1.53bn and £1.55bn, down from previous guidance of £1.65bn to £1.7bn. Additionally, the operating margin, previously expected to be in line with last year's 10.7 per cent, is now predicted to be between 8.7 and 8.9 per cent. The decline in profits was due to higher costs and £3.1m impairment charges over property, plant, and equipment.

It is worth noting that the shares trade at 12 times forward earnings, compared to a 5-year average of 18 times. Also, the company has not paid any dividends in the last 10 years. Therefore, the dividend yield is zero.

Sources: https://uk.advfn.com/stock-market/london/watches-of-switzerland-WOSG/dividends

Investors' Chronicle, 15–28 December 2023, p. 70.

L. Onita and R. Oliver (2024) Watches of Switzerland Knocked by Rapid Slowdown in Luxury Spending. *Financial Times,* 19 January.

Isabella Fish (2024) Troubled Times as Watches of Switzerland Sounds Alarm. *The Times,* 19 January.

Roula Khalaf (2024) What the Watches of Switzerland Warning Says about Rolex Demand. *Financial Times,* 18 January, https://www.ft.com/content/0fc667c3-719a-4b5b-b1c3-b07d45fa804f

https://www.thewosgroupplc.com/group/history/

https://www.thewosgroupplc.com/investors/ipo/

References and further reading

Doupnik, T.S., Finn, M. and Gotti, G. (2024) *International Accounting* (6th edn.), International student edition. New York: McGraw Hill.

International Accounting Standard 1 (2003, amended 2012) *Presentation of Financial Statements.* IFRC.

Melville, A. (2022) *International Financial Reporting* (8th edn.). Harlow: Pearson Education Limited.

http://annualreport.marksandspencer.com/ (gives the Marks and Spencer Group accounts in full)

www.ifrc.org (gives details of international financial reporting standards)

Chapter 3

The Development of Financial Reporting

Chapter contents

3.1 Introduction
3.2 Functions of Profit Measurement
3.3 Setting Accounting Standards
3.4 Concepts and Principles
3.5 The Statement of Financial Position Approach: Definition and Measurement of Assets and Liabilities
3.6 The Income Statement Approach: Definition and Measurement of Revenues and Expenses
3.7 Adjusting Financial Statements for Price Changes

Learning objectives

After studying this chapter, you will be able to:

- ✓ Understand the different ways in which profit is seen to be important
- ✓ Appreciate and critically assess the role of accounting standards
- ✓ Evaluate the various attempts to base accounting on a number of concepts
- ✓ Understand the two main ways of approaching profit measurement
- ✓ Define assets and liabilities and understand some measurement difficulties
- ✓ Define revenues and expenses and understand some measurement difficulties
- ✓ Understand the effects of price changes on financial statements
- ✓ Appreciate different ways of adjusting for price changes

3.1 Introduction

Most people are familiar with the idea of profit and may have assumptions about the usefulness of profit figures. Some, even journalists, seem to assume that there is a single agreed definition of 'profit' and that the rules for measuring it are clear, unambiguous, uncontroversial/generally accepted.

This chapter explores the importance of profit figures by outlining the various functions that they are expected to serve. The role of accounting standards in improving financial reporting is explored, and the idea of generally accepted principles and concepts as a basis for financial accounting is examined.

Two main approaches to measuring profit are then explored: one based on the statement of financial position and the amounts shown for assets and liabilities (as indicated in **Chapter 1**), the second based on the income statement and the amounts shown for income and expenses (as indicated in **Chapter 2**).

Finally, the effects of inflation on financial statements and possible methods of dealing with them are examined.

3.2 Functions of Profit Measurement

Annual financial statements contain a great deal of financial and other information that is of interest to different users, but profit figures are central. The widespread belief that profit is important is based on the idea that it tells us something useful. Profit figures may be useful in many different ways:

1. *As a guide to dividend decisions.* The more profit a company makes, the more it can pay out as dividends. The idea of capital maintenance is important: dividends are paid out of profits, not out of shareholders' capital. Profits must be calculated after making provision for depreciation so that, as the useful life of assets declines, the amount of shareholders' funds invested in assets does not. Charging depreciation ensures that an equivalent amount stays within the business, whether in the form of cash or other net assets and is not paid out as dividends.

   When companies decide how much of their profits to pay out as dividends, they consider other factors, not just the current year's profit. In some years, even if profits are very low, they may maintain, or even increase, dividends. But they cannot do this indefinitely. In the long run, profits are the main guide to dividend decisions. The Companies Act limits the amount a company can distribute as dividends to the total of accumulated, realized profits, less accumulated losses.

   Measuring the amount of profit available for distribution as dividends may also be seen as measuring how much can be consumed during a period without reducing the amount of capital at the beginning of the year; that is, without 'living off capital'.

2. *To indicate cash generated.* Many people talk about making money as if it is the same as making profits. The differences between cash flow and profit are central to financial accounting and are explained and illustrated in **Chapter 6**. To some extent, we could argue that it is mainly a matter of timing: in the end, all profits should eventually show up as cash. Profits may be tied up in inventories and receivables, but in due course, the inventories are sold, and customers (should) pay up. But profits may also be tied up in additional non-current assets and used up in other ways (such as paying off long-term debt or reducing the company's share capital). Although we can say that profits do generate cash, there is no reason to expect profits will still be around as cash at any given time.

   The Companies Act requirement that dividends should be paid only out of *realized* profits goes along with the idea that profits turn up as cash and are 'available'. Profits are realized when a sale is made.

Unrealized profits, such as those that result from revaluing buildings and other non-current assets, are not available for distribution as dividends until the assets are sold and the profits are realized.

The idea that profits are 'available' for dividends does not mean that there is a pool of cash. It is one of the hardest things for non-accountants to understand: reserves or retained earnings are not cash. The fact that reserves are not usually available as cash is shown in **Example 3.1**.

Example 3.1

The Quirkar company was established on 1 January, year 1, with £10,000 capital. The business bought and sold second-hand cars. All profits generated were either paid out as dividends, or used to increase the stocks of cars. At the end of year 3, the company's statement of financial position was as follows:

	£
Inventories of cars	100,000
Share capital	10,000
Retained earnings	90,000
	100,000

The company has made £90,000 profit,[1] but none of it is 'available' to pay out dividends because, as the profit and cash flow were generated, it was all paid out, and more cars were bought. Legally, £90,000 is 'available' to pay out as dividends, but in cash terms, there is nothing available - only cars.

Although the idea of using profit figures to indicate the amount of cash that a company has generated may have some popular appeal, it must be rejected as misleading, impracticable and simply wrong. It is more useful to examine cash flow statements to see what has happened to the profits that have been generated.

3 *To indicate how (un)successful the management of the company is.* Companies are expected to make profits. Shareholders elect directors to run the company for them. If the directors manage the company successfully, they will make a lot of profit for the shareholders. If they do not make decent profits, then they are failing and should be got rid of. This might be a bit simplistic, but it is essentially what companies are about.

A more sophisticated version would be that the financial management of companies aims to maximize shareholder wealth; shareholder wealth is made up of dividends and the value of the shares; maximizing profits is likely to maximize dividends and share price. It is easy to make a lot of profit if the company has a lot of capital employed; profits as a proportion of capital employed are, therefore, most important.

It is difficult to maximize shareholders' wealth for very long without good and increasing profits. We should not be surprised if we find that directors sometimes try to manipulate profit figures to make their performance look better. Some naïve economists seem to believe that there are such things as 'correct' profit figures, and if we have proper accounting and auditing standards, directors would not be able to indulge in such creative accounting. But, as will become increasingly clear, there are no 'correct' profit figures; there are many difficult areas in profit measurement; and profit figures in practice are, at least in part, the result of negotiation rather than 'economic reality' (whatever that is!).

[1] It probably made much more, some of which was paid out as dividends; the £90,000 is retained earnings, after paying out dividends.

4 *As a basis for taxation.* Governments expect companies to pay corporation tax on their profits and, therefore, have an interest in the way in which profits are measured. In the UK, HM Revenue and Customs lays down rules for profit measurement for taxation purposes, and these rules are, to some extent, different from those used for financial reporting.

In some countries, companies are required to use published profit figures as the basis for taxation, but this view is not generally favoured.

5 *To guide investors in deciding to buy or sell a company's shares.* The main users of financial accounts are supposed to be investors, particularly (a) those who are thinking of buying shares in the company and (b) those who already have shares in the company and are deciding whether to sell or retain them. These investors want to know about future performance and hope that the profits of the last few years will provide the appropriate guidance. The priority is, therefore, to find profit figures that have a predictive value. One way of forecasting future profits is to analyse previous years' profits in terms of various elements, some of which are likely to continue along with known trends, some of which are one-off, some of which are coming to an end. In recent years, official segmental disclosure requirements have specified increasingly detailed analyses of the various elements of profit, as shown in **Chapter 7**.

6 *To guide creditors.* Creditors may be more interested in the statement of financial position to calculate current ratios, liquidity ratios and gearing ratios. But, in assessing a company's ability to pay amounts due to creditors, it is not just the assets available at the statement of financial position date that matter; it is also the company's ability to generate assets, particularly in the form of profits. If a company is making losses, the security that creditors see in assets can soon disappear.

Investors and creditors are mainly interested in the future cash flows that the company will generate and, therefore, the principles for profit measurement should be selected to provide the best basis for prediction. Perhaps the companies themselves should provide more predictions.

Profit figures are used as a survival indicator. A company that makes profits is more likely to survive than one that makes losses. Various sophisticated versions of 'Z-Scores' have been developed to predict corporate failure that incorporates measures of working capital, debt and equity, but the biggest single element is usually some measure of profitability.

7 *To indicate economic efficiency.* Efficiency is concerned with the relationship between inputs and outputs. An organization that maximizes the ratio of outputs to inputs is maximizing efficiency. There are, of course, difficulties in defining the inputs and outputs that should be counted and how to measure them. In a company, the simplest approach is to say that the main output is sales or revenues, and the main input is costs. The difference between sales and costs is profit. Maximizing profit, therefore, maximizes efficiency. Efficiency can be increased by (a) increasing sales, (b) reducing costs, (c) increasing sales and costs but increasing sales by more than the increase in costs, or (d) reducing sales and costs but reducing costs more than the reduction in sales. This is all very simplistic, and the overall approach could ignore many inefficiencies. It also ignores costs to society and costs to employees and other interested parties. This idea does, however, underlie much of our thinking: a profitable company is efficient; an unprofitable company is inefficient. In organizations that are not primarily intended to make profits, it is more difficult to assess efficiency.

A profitable company is also assumed to be an effective company. Effectiveness is concerned with the relationship between outputs and objectives. An effective organization is one that achieves its objectives. If we assume that profitability is a primary objective of companies, then it is also a measure of effectiveness.

Profits are also assumed to be concerned with efficiency in the economy as a whole, particularly the allocation of resources in the economy. The most profitable companies will attract investment and resources most easily; companies that are not profitable will have difficulty in finding funds for investment. Investment in the economy, therefore, goes to the most profitable and, so, the most efficient organizations.

This idea is also rather simplistic, but in attempting to understand what goes on in the economy and how it is justified, these arguments about efficiency and effectiveness should not be ignored.

8 *To indicate anything you like.* Profit figures seem to be quoted in many different contexts to indicate a wide variety of different matters of concern to individuals, groups or society. Employees and their representatives are likely to look at profits as an indicator of how much companies can afford to pay out in wage increases or as an argument against closures and redundancies. Socialists may see profits as an indicator of how much companies exploit others. Profits are also relevant in any government-imposed price controls, for example, with privatized utility companies. Such companies are usually allowed to make a reasonable return on capital but are not expected to use their near-monopoly positions to make excessive profits.

Different profit figures seem to be required for different purposes. It is reasonable to expect financial statements to identify different versions of profit to meet the needs of the various users of financial statements.

3.3 Setting Accounting Standards

Profit figures themselves are important, and they are the product of all the other figures in statements of financial position and income statements. Financial statements themselves are important to a range of users who need to have confidence that the figures shown represent 'economic reality' and are not just the opinions of some optimistic directors or accountants. Governments have long recognized that directors should not be allowed to produce financial statements in their own individual ways, and a series of Companies Acts has prescribed the information that they are required to publish. Companies Acts tend not to be very specific with accounting rules, and company directors have sometimes been tempted to produce annual reports that seem more intended to present their companies' performance in a flattering light than to hold the directors to account. The problems of such 'creative accounting' are addressed in **Chapter 8**.

There is an ongoing debate regarding whether governments possess the necessary expertise to establish intricate accounting regulations, especially since the financial sector is constantly evolving, making it difficult for governments to respond promptly to emerging issues. As a result, the responsibility of creating accounting standards has predominantly been entrusted to the accountancy profession.

Accounting standards first came into being following the establishment of the Accounting Standards Steering Committee in 1969. They were intended to provide guidance additional to the requirements of the Companies Acts by specifying additional definitions and rules for measurement and disclosure and to narrow the areas of difference and variety in accounting practice. A series of accounting scandals in the 1960s and early 1970s had shown that different accountants could come up with very different profit figures, based on the same data, because there was so much flexibility in accounting.

The professional accountancy bodies set up the Accounting Standards Steering Committee that promulgated a series of 'accounting standards', or Statements of Standard Accounting Practice (SSAPs). Twenty-five SSAPs were produced. They started as Exposure Drafts (EDs) for consultation, and, when agreed by the main professional accountancy bodies, they became authoritative statements. They did much to clarify definitions and alternatives and to improve disclosure practices. However, too often they allowed more than one treatment and there was no effective enforcement mechanism. By the 1980s, they were losing credibility as 'creative accounting' became well known.

A new accounting standards regime was established in 1990. The Accounting Standards Board (ASB) produced Financial Reporting Exposure Drafts (FREDs), which, after consultation, became Financial Reporting Standards (FRSs). It worked under the supervision of the Financial Reporting Council alongside the Financial Reporting Review Panel (FRRP). Overall, the new arrangements worked better than the old

Accounting Standards Committee. The FRSs (together with the SSAPs that they adopted) had more legal backing, and auditors are required to state if they have been followed; the number of permitted alternatives is being reduced; and the FRRP developed an enforcement role.

The ASB was essentially British. Other countries developed their own standards, and by the beginning of the twenty-first century, two main approaches had been established: the US Financial Accounting Standards Board (FASB), and the International Accounting Standards Board (IASB). There is often a need for a reconciliation statement where companies are following the requirements of both regimes. The two bodies signed a Memorandum of Understanding (MOU) in 2006 to develop a convergence programme with the intention of developing good quality accounting standards for all companies in the world's capital markets.

The International Accounting Standards Committee was formed in 1973 and issued 41 International Accounting Standards (IASs). It was reconstituted as the IASB from 2001, which now issues International Financial Reporting Standards (IFRSs). These are increasingly like the US FASB's accounting standards as we move towards international harmonization. By 2017 the IASB had issued 17 IFRSs, which are:

- IFRS 1 First-time adoption of IFRSs
- IFRS 2 Share-based Payment
- IFRS 3 Business Combinations
- IFRS 4 Insurance Contracts
- IFRS 5 Non-current Assets Held for Sale and Discontinued Operations
- IFRS 6 Exploration for and Evaluation of Mineral Resources
- IFRS 7 Financial Instruments: Disclosures
- IFRS 8 Operating Segments
- IFRS 9 Financial Instruments
- IFRS 10 Consolidated Financial Statements
- IFRS 11 Joint Arrangements
- IFRS 12 Disclosure of Interests in Other Entities
- IFRS 13 Fair Value Measurement
- IFRS 14 Regulatory Deferral Accounts
- IFRS 15 Revenue from Contracts with Customers
- IFRS 16 Leases
- IFRS 17 Insurance Contracts

The IASB has also adopted the IASs that remain extant.

It is easy to criticize accounting standards, especially in their early years. Many were imprecise or permitted different treatments. Some were revised or withdrawn or reissued in a different form. There was a lack of enforcement mechanisms. Difficult issues and decisions were avoided. And there was no consistent theoretical framework to support them. Often, it seemed that standard-setters were like firefighters rushing from one problem to the next without a clear overall strategy.

Over the years they have steadily become more professional and effective, tackling difficult issues, reducing the number of permissible different treatments, and with widespread general acceptance and more effective enforcement. Their standards have also become increasingly complex and voluminous, and there is still a tendency for issues not to be 'finally' resolved. The requirement for truly international standards requires extensive discussion and agreement. It sometimes seems that drafts are passed from one group to another and then revised and reissued almost indefinitely.

3.4 Concepts and Principles

The idea of a 'conceptual framework' that underlies all accounting standards is appealing and various attempts have been made to produce such documents, culminating in the *Framework for the Preparation and Presentation of Financial Statements* (1989).[2] Such statements usually begin by defining the objectives of financial reporting (to help users make economic decisions), sometimes listing who the users are. The Accounting Standards Steering Committee published a discussion paper titled *The Corporate Report* (1975).[3] The objective of the *Corporate Report* is to satisfy the needs of the users. The users are defined as those who have reasonable rights to information about an organization's resources and performance. Section 1.9 of the *Corporate Report* identifies several user groups: investors, employees, financial analysts and advisers, customers, suppliers, competitors, government, and the public. The report emphasized that financial statements are 'general purpose' and may not serve the needs of particular individuals. It is useful to try to define general purpose information needs, and the usual conclusion is that a statement of financial position and income statement are required. The difficult part is establishing how the items on these statements (i.e. assets, liabilities, revenues, expenses) should be defined and measured.

If the reporting entity is to fulfil the objectives of the corporate report and the needs of the users of this information, certain characteristics should be present, which are listed below:

- Relevance
- Understandability
- Reliability
- Completeness
- Objective
- Timely
- Comparability

A number of accounting principles underpin the preparation of financial statements in addition to the qualitative characteristics. The most important ones and with general acceptability include:

1. *Going concern*. This assumes that the business will continue in operational existence for the foreseeable future and that there is no intention to liquidate the business or to curtail it significantly. It was used to justify showing assets at cost (adjusted for such things as depreciation) rather than attempting to show them at the amount for which they could be sold at the statement of financial position date.
2. *Accruals*. Revenues and costs are recognized as they are earned or incurred, not as money is received or paid; they are matched with one another and dealt with in the income statement of the period to which they relate. Profit measurement is based on accruals and matching, not on receipts and payments of cash. This is used to justify a whole range of accounting adjustments, including accruals and prepayments, capitalization of fixed assets, annual depreciation charges, and carrying forward the cost of unsold inventories to be treated as an expense when they are sold.
3. *Consistency*. The accounting treatment of like items within each accounting period and from one period to the next is consistent. This means, for example, that it is not acceptable to depreciate some vehicles but not others or to change depreciation policies from one year to the next (unless full details are disclosed).
4. *Prudence*. Revenues and profits are not anticipated but are recognized only when realized as cash (or other assets, the ultimate cash realization of which can be assessed with reasonable certainty);[4] provision

[2] *The IASB's Framework* (1989) is comparable with the British ASB's *Statement of Principles for Financial Reporting* (1999).

[3] *The Corporate Report*, Accounting Standards Steering Committee (1975).

[4] It is acceptable to recognize sales before the money has been received from customers, provided it is reasonably certain how much cash will be received.

is made for all known liabilities (expenses and losses) whether the amount of these is known with certainty or is the best estimate. This conservatism is intended to ensure that profits, assets and income are not overstated and that expenses and liabilities are not understated. The assumption is that the financial position of a business should be *at least* as good as the financial statements show.

A fifth concept, 'separate valuation', is usually added because it was specifically referred to in the 1985 Companies Act along with the other four. It requires that the amount for each item included in the financial statements should be determined separately. One item should not be offset against another, and (for example) a fleet of vehicles should not be valued as a whole - the amount for each vehicle should be determined separately and then added together.

Over the years, a whole range of other concepts, doctrines, principles, postulates and statements of the obvious and pieces of nonsense have been added. *The Corporate Report* stated that financial statements should be relevant, understandable, reliable, complete, objective, timely and comparable. The entity concept is widely accepted; it means only that financial statements are produced for a business entity that is separate from the owners or managers. The materiality concept suggests that minor items will not affect a 'true and fair view', so that, for example, there is no need to capitalize and depreciate a pencil sharpener, although conceptually it might last for several years. The historical cost concept suggests that items are shown in accounts at their original cost (adjusted for such things as depreciation), not at a current market value (although market values are given for some assets). Duality indicates that every transaction must have two aspects so that it can be recorded twice in a double-entry system, as a debit and as a credit. Disclosure suggests that all information that is likely to be relevant to the needs of users should be disclosed. Verifiability suggests that items should be included only where there is verifiable evidence (such as documents) of their existence. Objectivity and neutrality suggest that those responsible for producing financial statements should not be biased in favour of a particular point of view. Money measurement indicates that items in financial statements are given monetary values. Substance over form suggests that financial statements should show the economic reality of an item rather than its legal form. Odd writers have suggested that financial accounting is based on other conventions, such as the arithmetic convention, which seems to be a statement of the obvious and the assumption that the value of the pound is constant, which is nonsense.

Even the old Accounting Standards Committee recognized contradictions within their own four fundamental concepts and argued that the prudence concept should prevail over the accruals concept. Other 'concepts' indicated above do not form any coherent framework or basis for accounting.

The (British) ASB's *Statement of Principles for Financial Reporting* (December 1999) refers to Objectives and Constraints rather than Concepts. In producing financial accounting statements, the most appropriate accounting policies are those that meet four objectives:

1 *Relevance* - to the needs of users in predicting the future or confirming the present or past.
2 *Reliability* - which means that accounting information should represent faithfully the substance of the underlying transactions; is neutral (there is no deliberate or systematic bias); is free from material error; is complete within the bounds of materiality; and, where conditions are uncertain, judgements and estimates have been made with a degree of caution.

   There is something of a conflict between these two: the more relevant information is for decision-making, the less reliable it is likely to be (perhaps because it is based on forecasts) and the more reliable it is (e.g. historical cost), the less relevant it is for decision-makers.
3 *Comparability* - which means that the financial statements of one entity can usefully be compared with those of another; this requires a combination of disclosure and consistency and is likely to need adjustment to the published figures since companies adopt different accounting policies, such as the method or date of depreciation.
4 *Understandability* - suggests that users should be able to understand financial statements (provided they have a reasonable knowledge of business, economics and accounting; and a willingness to study the information diligently).

The idea of prudence has been downgraded from being a fundamental accounting concept to being only part of reliability and applying only in conditions of uncertainty; it means only that a degree of caution should be used in making judgements and estimates. The idea of general prudence has gone; it has been dismissed as being likely to result in systematic bias in financial statements. Similarly, consistency has been downgraded to being part of comparability. The accruals concept continues to be central to financial accounting. With regard to the going concern concept, companies are now required to disclose information where there may be uncertainties about its continuance as a going concern.

The idea of understandability may be rather optimistic: the published financial statements of companies are now generally more complex and more difficult to understand than ever before.

With the FASB and the IASB increasingly working together, a revised conceptual framework was issued in 2010 and a further revision in 2018. The IASB published the conceptual framework for financial reporting in 2018. The main purpose of the conceptual framework is to enable the development of new accounting standards and the review of the existing standards by setting out the underlying concepts and promoting harmonization by reducing the number of permitted alternative accounting treatments.

The conceptual framework has established the qualitative characteristics into two groups as follows: fundamental and enhancing characteristics.

Fundamental characteristics:

- Relevance
- Faithful representation. Faithful representation replaces reliability. It means that the accounting measures and descriptions used in financial reports should correspond with the economic phenomena that they are supposed to represent.

Enhancing characteristics:

- Comparability
- Timeliness
- Understandability
- Verifiability.

These are subject to two 'pervasive constraints': (i) materiality and (ii) benefits that justify costs.[5]

3.5 The Statement of Financial Position Approach: Definition and Measurement of Assets and Liabilities

There are two basic approaches to profit measurement. One is based on the statement of financial position (**Chapter 1**); the second is the income statement approach (**Chapter 2**). Conventional accounting practice uses both at the same time, and both (should!) produce the same profit figure.

In the first approach, the *statement of financial position* would take priority. The emphasis would be on the correct definition and valuation of assets and liabilities. Any increase in a company's net asset value would be the profit figure.[6] This is an 'all-inclusive' version of profit. The emphasis of financial accounting would change from being mainly the recording and summarizing of transactions (at cost price) to being mainly concerned

[5] It is usually possible to produce 'better' information but the benefit of so doing should be greater than the costs of producing it.

[6] Except that any additional share capital has to be deducted, and any dividends have to be added back.

with the valuation of assets and liabilities. The income statement would be downgraded but would provide some detailed breakdown of the elements that have made up the overall gain.

Profit would be calculated as the increase in net assets during a period (after deducting any additional share capital subscribed and adding back any dividends paid), as shown in **Illustration 3.1**.

ILLUSTRATION 3.1

	£m
Net assets at 1 January year 4	35
Net assets at 31 December year 4	45
Increase during the year	10
Minus proceeds of share issue	(5)
Plus dividends paid	7
Profit for year	12

Assets: definition

It is easiest to think of a company's assets as being anything that they own. They may be short term (current assets such as inventories, receivables, money in cash or in the bank), or they may be long term, intended for use for more than a year (non-current assets such as land and buildings, plant and machinery, furniture and fittings, and vehicles). Most are tangible, but there are also intangible assets (such as goodwill, patents and trademarks). A company may also own financial assets (such as shares in another company or debentures).

However, a company's statement of financial position should include all assets that it controls, even if it does not own them. 'An asset is a resource controlled by the enterprise as a result of past events and from which future economic benefits are expected to flow to the enterprise.'[7] The *Conceptual Framework* has revised this definition as: 'A present economic resource controlled by the entity as a result of past events'.[8] This definition includes items such as machinery that are leased, not owned. The definition should be borne in mind when considering problem assets.

Assets: measurement

An accounting system records transactions, that is, what things cost. Traditionally, items are shown on a statement of financial position at the amount recorded in the books, which, at least to begin with, is the cost price. But many users of financial statements want to know that 'prudent' asset values have been used and that the assets are worth *at least* as much as the statement of financial position shows. As machinery and vehicles get older, their value is 'used up', and depreciation is charged. The statement of financial position shows non-current assets at net book value (which is usually cost minus the depreciation accumulated over a number of years).

Similarly, inventories are originally recorded at cost price. But if a business buys an item of inventory for £100 (perhaps intending to sell it for £150), and if it remains unsold for a long period, it may deteriorate or become out of date, and its resale value may fall to (say) £70. It would be misleading to continue to show such an item at a cost of £100; it has to be written down to £70. The rule for inventories is that they should be shown at the *lower* of cost and net realizable value.

---

7 *Framework for the Preparation and Presentation of Financial Statements* (IASB, 1989).

8 *Conceptual Framework for Financial Reporting* (IASB, 2018).

Sometimes companies are required to revalue assets; sometimes they choose to do so. If a company bought a building many years ago for £100,000, it is probably misleading to continue to show it at cost (or at cost minus depreciation) if its market value has increased to £1m or more. If companies understate the value of their assets on their statements of financial position, there is also the possibility that they will attract unwelcome takeover bids. A company's statement of financial position may show total net assets as being £10m, but if they are really worth £25m, another company may try to buy the company for (say) £15m to do an 'asset stripping' operation and sell off the assets for a substantial profit. With listed companies, the market value on the stock market (or 'market capitalization') is likely to be much higher[9] than the statement of financial position shows. But with unlisted companies, statement of financial position figures may be an important determinant of what a company is seen to be worth.

When it is decided to 'revalue' assets, it is necessary to determine the basis for such a valuation, and there are many possibilities. Often, some 'market price' is preferred to historical cost figures, but there are different versions of market price: buying prices ('input' values) may be very different from selling prices ('output' or 'exit' values), and the selling price of an asset in the normal course of business is likely to be much higher than in a forced sale (liquidation values).

If there is a 'true' value of an asset, it is the amount that a willing buyer is willing to pay to a willing seller. This was the historical cost at the time the original transaction took place. Later, we may say that the value to the business of an asset is what the business can make from that asset, which is based on the future cash flows that the asset is expected to generate. The net present value of the future cash flows that an asset (or a business) is expected to generate is its 'economic value'. If the asset is an item of inventory that the business expects to sell, then the value to the business of that item is its net realizable value - the amount for which it can be sold. The final part of this chapter deals with 'value to the business' (or 'deprival value') and with the idea of 'fair value'.

One approach is to say that the value of an asset depends on whether you are going to buy it, sell it or use it. If you are going to buy it, it is the *replacement cost* that matters. If you are going to sell it, it is the *net realizable value* that matters. If you are going to use it, it is the *value in use* that matters; this is sometimes referred to as the *economic value* or the *net present value of the future cash flows* that the item will produce.

The idea of *deprival value* was popular during the current cost accounting debates. This is the lower of replacement cost and recoverable amount. The recoverable amount is the higher of value in use and net realizable value. The idea is that if you were deprived of an asset, what value would you have lost? If you would replace it, the deprival value is the replacement cost. But if it is not worth replacing (because the replacement cost is too high), the deprival value is what the business could have recovered from the asset, either by using it or by selling it.

More recently, the idea of *fair value*, which is really market price, has found favour. It is examined in the final part of this chapter.

Problem assets

Goodwill

Goodwill arises in financial statements when one company buys another business. Suppose a business has a statement of financial position value of £10m. In that case, it is unlikely that the owners will sell it for only £10m, especially if the business has a good profit record. The agreed price might be £15m, which leaves an accounting problem. The company has paid £15m but has acquired only £10m of net assets; an extra £5m has been paid for something which they hope is worth £5m and which is labelled on the statement of financial position as 'goodwill'.

9 Unless the company is doing very badly.

There are many different reasons why a company might pay to acquire a business's goodwill: the company might have a good profit record, reputation, trained workforce, specialist manufacturing capacity, established customer base, particular products and brand names, and assets that are underused or undervalued. Perhaps it has unused borrowing capacity. Perhaps the acquiring company paid too much. Goodwill is an intangible asset and sometimes one of doubtful value. In the past, prudent accountants have written it off, sometimes as quickly as possible.[10] It is no longer allowed to amortize goodwill systematically in the same way that a non-current asset is depreciated.

In the past, a lot of 'goodwill' arose when the assets of an acquired business were undervalued. Now, when a business is acquired, its assets should be restated at 'fair value'. Where fair value is above book value, the amount of apparent goodwill is reduced. IFRS 3 also requires that different intangible assets should, where possible, be separately identified and accounted for and not be included in 'goodwill'. The standard provides a long list of such assets, including patented technology, software, trade secrets, franchise agreements, trademarks, literary and musical works, videos and television programmes, construction permits, broadcasting rights, customer contracts and relationships.

Under IFRS 3, goodwill recognised in a business combination, is an asset representing the future economic benefits of acquiring other assets in a business combination that are not individually identified and separately recognised. It should be shown as an asset on the statement of financial position, initially at cost, which is the excess of the consideration paid for the business acquired, plus any non-controlling interest over the net fair value of the identifiable assets[11] acquired. It must then be tested for impairment, with an annual impairment charge if appropriate. This supersedes systematic annual amortization charges.

It is sometimes argued that a business is creating goodwill all the time by developing and advertising products, recruiting and training employees, making profits and in many other ways. This 'internally generated' goodwill is not recognized in financial accounting. Goodwill is recognized only where it is the result of a transaction, buying another business.

Development costs and other intangibles

The days have gone when a company (like Rolls-Royce) could spend a lot of money on research and development, treat it as capital expenditure (creating a non-current asset), and continue to show profits while getting into serious financial difficulties. Accounting standards require that all research expenditure is charged as an expense and not capitalized. The position with development expenditure is more complex because sometimes it really is creating an asset.

For any 'intangible' to be recognized as an asset, there must be the probability of it generating future economic benefits, and these must be capable of being measured reliably. With development expenditure, it should be recognized as an asset and shown on the statement of financial position (rather than being written off immediately in the income statement) if the following apply: it is technically feasible and will produce something that will be used or sold, and that the business has sufficient resources to be able to complete the development and obtain the economic benefits.

If development costs are capitalized, they must subsequently be amortized or subject to impairment reviews.

IAS 38 is clear that other internally generated intangible assets such as brands, customer lists, mastheads and publishing titles should not be capitalized.

Human assets

It is sometimes argued that a company's employees are its most important asset and should be recognized in some way or valued on the statement of financial position. There may be circumstances in which some

[10] By deducting it from retained earnings.
[11] Minus liabilities.

contracts of employment may be recognized as an asset, but these are unusual. IAS 38 recognizes some employment contracts as intangible assets, where these are beneficial to the employer because their pricing is below market level. It is also possible to recognize the cost of buying professional footballers. But these are very much the exception, and the idea of widespread recognition of employees as assets for accounting purposes is unlikely.

Capitalized interest

There is no doubt that creating a new non-current asset (such as a building) is capital expenditure, even if the company itself does the work and creates it. When it takes a long time to construct an asset, substantial borrowing costs are often incurred during the construction process. If a company bought such an asset from a builder, the price would have to cover the interest costs incurred by the builder. Where the company constructs assets for itself, the interest costs during construction may be regarded as part of the cost of the building and capitalized (rather than treated as an expense). IAS 23 defines conditions for such treatment and specifies information to be disclosed. It attempts, however, to remove the discretionary element by defining when capitalization should take place.

Liabilities: definition

It is easiest to think of a company's liabilities as being anything that it owes to people outside the company. They may be short term (current liabilities such as trade payables and overdrafts), or they may be long term, that the company does not have to pay for more than a year (non-current liabilities such as loans and debentures). There are also liabilities for taxation, which may be current or non-current. It is usually not difficult to list the amounts that a company owes.

The IASB[12] defines a liability as a 'present obligation of the enterprise arising from past events, the settlement of which is expected to result in an outflow from the enterprise of resources embodying economic benefits'. An outflow of economic benefits usually means a payment. The important part is that the liability is a *present* obligation, meaning that the obligation must exist at the statement of financial position date; this may restrict the use of vague 'provisions' if they may or may not require the payment of an unknown amount at an unknown future date. The *Conceptual Framework* has a shorter definition for liability as a 'present obligation of the entity to transfer an economic resource as a result of past events'.[13]

Liabilities: measurement

With most liabilities, there are no problems in determining the amount owed.

If a liability is not due to be paid for some years, it may be appropriate to 'discount'.[14] If, for example, a company owes £10m that is due to be paid four years in the future, and the appropriate discount rate is 10 per cent, the amount could be shown on the statement of financial position at its 'present value', which would be (£10 × 0.683 =) £6.83m.

Problem liabilities

There can, however, be problems in dealing with some items, such as provisions and deferred tax.

---

[12] *Framework for the Preparation and Presentation of Financial Statements* (IASB, 1989).

[13] *Conceptual Framework for Financial Reporting* (IASB, 2018).

[14] Using the principles of discounted cash flow method, as explained in **Chapter 13**.

Provisions

The term 'provision' is sometimes used for amounts deducted from assets, such as provision for bad debts or provision for depreciation on non-current assets. There is likely to be some subjectivity in determining the amounts of such 'provisions', but otherwise, it should be straightforward. The amounts relate to assets, not liabilities; the amount of the asset could be reduced to zero, but we should not have 'negative assets'. Provisions as liabilities are more problematic. The Companies Act 1985 defined provisions as 'amounts retained as reasonably necessary to cover any liability or loss which is either likely or certain to be incurred'. This gives companies a fair amount of freedom to reduce profits in one year[15] and create a provision against which expenses can be charged in a subsequent year (without reducing profits in that year). This could be seen as an application of 'prudence'. It could also be used for 'income smoothing', and is discussed in **Chapter 8**.

Provisions were often created for future reorganizations, redundancies, legal liabilities, decommissioning costs, and future costs and losses of various sorts.

The more recent, stricter definition of liabilities refers to a 'present obligation', which would exclude current *proposals* to incur liabilities or losses in future periods. IAS 37 defined a provision as 'a liability of uncertain timing or amount'. The definition assumes that an outflow of resources is probable and that a reliable estimate of the amount can be made. The obligation may be legal or 'constructive', which allows provisions to be made where there are no legal commitments but where the company has, by its actions and announcements, committed itself to a course of action.

The accounting standard-setters are in a difficult position. If they allow too much freedom in creating, increasing and reducing provisions, they leave the door open to creative accounting. But if they are too strict in not allowing provisions, there would often be cases where companies knew of some likely bad news and kept quiet about it. A prudent set of financial statements would disclose all potential liabilities, including 'contingent liabilities'.

Warranties

Companies may make specific provisions for the cost of guarantees or warranties and other after-sales services that they are expected to provide. This may appear on a statement of financial position as a provision or it may not be separately disclosed. Sometimes companies deduct appropriate provisions from the figure for sales; sometimes it is included in a more general provision.

Contingent liabilities

Contingent liabilities can arise as a result of legal action. The company may have to pay out a lot of money as a result of losing a case; the result may not yet have been determined. A contingent liability is a possible obligation whose existence will be confirmed only by the occurrence of an uncertain future event, or it can be where a transfer of economic benefits is not probable, or the amount cannot yet be measured reliably. Contingent liabilities should not be shown on a statement of financial position. They should be disclosed as a note to the accounts (unless it is only a remote possibility).

In assessing the solvency or creditworthiness of a company, it is worth looking not only at the actual liabilities shown on the statement of financial position but also at the contingent liabilities; there may be a risk of substantial payments having to be made.

---

[15] By debiting the income statement with the 'expense' of the provision, and creating a credit balance, which is shown as a provision on the statement of financial position.

Deferred taxation

Deferred taxation arises because the rules for calculating profit for inclusion in annual reports and accounts are different from the rules for taxation purposes. Depreciation allowances for taxation purposes ('writing-down allowances') are typically quite high in the early years of a fixed asset's life; these high allowances reduce taxable profits, which means that the amount of corporation tax payable is much reduced in the first years after substantial acquisitions of fixed assets. Profits for tax purposes are much lower than the profits reported in the annual accounts, which would make the tax charge look peculiarly low and might mislead shareholders by exaggerating the after-tax profits available for dividends.

As the non-current assets get towards the end of their lives (and if there have been few additional purchases of non-current assets), the position reverses: allowances for tax purposes are smaller; the amount of tax payable is larger; and this might mislead shareholders by showing low after-tax profit being available for dividends.

Deferred taxation is a bit like a taxation equalization account. In the early years after acquisitions of fixed assets, the tax actually payable is low, but a higher charge against profits is made; this extra 'deferred taxation' is not yet payable but is shown as if it is a liability. After a few years, it may reverse: the tax actually payable is higher, but only a modest 'equalized' charge is made against profits; the extra is charged against the balance for deferred taxation that was built up for that purpose in the early years of the non-current asset's life.

In many cases, the amount shown as a long-term liability for deferred taxation will never actually be paid. If a company continues to invest in additional non-current assets, the writing-down allowances on the new non-current assets will likely have the effect of building up the credit balance on the deferred taxation account faster than it is used up by the smaller writing-down allowances on the older non-current assets. The old Accounting Standards Committee experimented with a 'partial provision' for deferred taxation, based on the idea that provisions should be made only for amounts that it was reasonably probable would become payable. But this was rather subjective and not consistent with international practice.

IAS 12 requires full provision for deferred taxation for all[16] timing differences. The effect can be to build up a substantial provision on the statement of financial position that might never actually become a liability. This makes the interpretation of financial statements and the calculation of accounting ratios rather difficult. Some people simply ignore it: they exclude it from capital employed and from liabilities, but this can lead to inconsistent ratios that never properly add up or reconcile.

Deferred taxation is normally shown as a non-current liability, identified separately from other liabilities. As in so many areas of interpretation of financial statements, there may be no definitive 'right' answer. The important thing is to treat it in a consistent way in comparing one company with another and comparing one year with another.

3.6 The Income Statement Approach: Definition and Measurement of Revenues and Expenses

In the second approach, the *income statement* takes priority. The emphasis is on reporting revenues, and carefully determining the costs that should be matched against those revenues in order to determine the amount of profit. The statement of financial position is a statement of left-over balances with no attempt to show them as the current *value* of assets and liabilities. Depreciation is necessary for profit measurement: the cost of an asset is spread over its estimated useful life; there is no pretence that the remaining balance represents the current value of the asset.

16 There are some limited exceptions.

Profit may be defined as sales and any other revenues earned during a period minus the costs incurred in earning those sales and revenues. This seems straightforward enough. Sales are relatively easy to identify, and most costs are obvious. Both are shown on an income statement, as seen in **Chapter 2**.

Determining exactly which costs should be 'matched' against the revenues of a period is, in most cases, done with little difficulty, although it does mean dealing with asset values or 'unexpired costs'.

If a company buys goods for £100 and sells half of them for £120, it has made a £70 profit. The cost of goods was £100, but half of the costs are 'unexpired' or unsold: those inventories are still there to be shown as assets on the statement of financial position. The gross profit requires the 'cost of goods sold' to be deducted from sales.

Accountants have traditionally been prudent in valuing closing inventories. They may be difficult to sell, and they may eventually have to be sold for less than the cost price of £50. The net realizable value of seasonal, perishable and fashionable items can rapidly fall below cost price. When the net realizable value of the inventories is less than the cost price, the closing inventory must be written down. In the above example, if the net realizable value of the closing inventory, which had cost £50, was only £35, then the cost of goods sold[17] would be £65, and the gross profit would be £55. If the closing inventory value falls by £15, then profit falls by £15.

There are also problems in the treatment of non-current assets and calculating depreciation based on estimates of how long the asset's useful life will be and what its scrap value will be at the end of its life. With receivables, it is necessary to assess what provisions for bad debts are appropriate, and estimates in relation to other assets and unexpired costs[18] may be needed.

The income statement approach to profit measurement is the most popular. Businesses and accounting systems record revenues that have been earned and the costs incurred, and profit is the difference between the two. Unfortunately, it is not possible to measure profit in this way without considering the amounts to be shown for various assets (e.g. closing inventories and as a result of depreciation).

Revenues, income and gains

It is easiest to think of a company's revenues as being anything that is credited to the income statement. They may be normal sales revenues, including professional fees earned, and various other income such as rent, interest and dividends receivable, or from sources such as royalties. IAS 1 is fairly permissive, but most income statements have separate headings for (1) revenue (from sales), (2) other income and (3) finance income.

Normally, income statements include only income that has been *realized*. This means that a transaction has taken place, and an item has been sold. It may be that inventories that had originally cost £100 are worth £150 at the year-end, but that 'gain' of £50 is not included in the income statement until the items have been sold. Similarly, if a building costs £1m, but at the statement of financial position date is revalued at £1.5m, that gain of £0.5m is not realized until the building is sold.

Revenues are normal sales; income comes from other sources; both are recognized when 'realized'. Other 'gains' of various kinds may or may not be realized and may or may not be recognized.

[17] Cost of goods sold, or cost of sales, is opening inventory (zero), plus purchases (£100), minus closing inventory (£35) = £65.

[18] Sometimes the benefit from paying for something (such as advertising, or development expenditure) may extend over several periods and it is necessary to determine how much of it is to be treated as an expense in the current period, and how much should be carried forward as an unexpired cost, or asset, to future periods.

Statement of changes in equity

The IASB adopts an 'all-inclusive' (or statement of financial position) approach to the definition of income: 'Income increases in economic benefits during the accounting period in question in the form of inflows or enhancements of assets or decreases of liabilities that result in increases in equity, other than those relating to contributions from equity participants.' They include increases in the value of assets as 'income', but these would not normally be included as 'revenue' on the income statement. Here, the US FASB approach is useful: it defines revenues as being from 'delivering or producing goods, rendering services, or other activities that constitute the entity's ongoing major central operations'. Other gains (which are part of an all-inclusive concept of income but are not included as revenues on the income statement) are shown on the 'Statement of Changes in Equity', which is required by IAS 1.

During the year, the total amount for equity can change because:

1 Additional shares are issued or redeemed
2 Profits or losses are made (as shown on the income statement)
3 Dividends are paid
4 A variety of other gains and losses are made, including those resulting from the revaluation of property and available-for-sale investments.

An example of a Statement of Changes in Equity is shown in **Chapter 2 (Illustration 2.1)**.

Revenue recognition

There is sometimes a problem in determining the date on which a sale takes place and, thus, when revenue is recognized. Suppose a company's year-end is 31 December, and a substantial order is received on 28 December year 1, but the goods are not dispatched until 3 January year 2. In this case, it can make an important difference to year 1 results if the sale is included in that year. Accounting systems usually record a sale as taking place when the invoice is issued, but that may not be the 'critical event' in determining when a sale should be recognized. Where management is under pressure to improve financial results in the short term, they might be tempted to amend their accounting systems to record sales at as early a date as possible. For example, IFRS 15 now allows an entity to recognize revenue from the customer in exchange for the transfer of promised goods or services for an amount that reflects the consideration to which the entity expects to be entitled.[19]

Expenses

Expenses are the costs incurred in earning the revenue that is recognized during a period and which are shown on the income statement. Thus, 'cost of sales' is the correct expense figure, not purchases. The cost of acquiring a machine (or other non-current asset) is not recognized when the machine is bought or paid for; it is spread over the asset's life as it is used up and recognized as depreciation.

There may be other losses or 'impairments', which look a bit like expenses but which are not recognized on the income statement. Where these are recognized, they are shown on the Statement of Changes in Equity.

The IASB adopts a wider, or all-inclusive, definition of expenses. They are 'decreases in economic benefits during the accounting period in the form of outflows or depletions of assets or incurrences of liabilities that result in decreases in equity, other than those relating to distributions to equity participants'. This would include all decreases in the value of assets, some of which are not normally recognized in financial accounting.

[19] Prior to IFRS 15, there were two separate standards for revenue recognition: IAS 18 Revenue and IAS 11 Construction Contracts.

Problem areas

There are a number of problem areas with expenses, including the following:

1 *Depreciation.* The expense charged for depreciation of a particular asset depends on assumptions about its future life, pattern of usage and final salvage value. As these cannot be predicted with certainty, there is inevitably some subjectivity in determining depreciation charges. There are also different methods of calculating depreciation (see **Example 3.2**).

Example 3.2

The Adle Company buys a new machine for £256,000 and intends to use it for five years, after which it is expected to have a residual value of £36,000. Calculate the amount of depreciation using:

a the straight-line method, and

b the reducing (or diminishing balance) method at 25 per cent per annum.

a £256,000 − £36,000 = £220,000 ÷ 5 = £44,000 per annum

b	Year 1	25% of £256,000	=	£64,000	leaving net book value	£192,000
	Year 2	25% of £192,000	=	£48,000	leaving net book value	£144,000
	Year 3	25% of £144,000	=	£36,000	leaving net book value	£108,000
	Year 4	25% of £108,000	=	£27,000	leaving net book value	£81,000
	Year 5	25% of £81,000	=	£20,250	leaving net book value	£60,750

2 *Impairment of goodwill.* Most large, listed companies are really groups of companies with a number of subsidiaries. When a subsidiary company is first acquired, it is usually the case that the price paid to acquire the business is higher than the statement of financial position value of the net assets acquired. If the statement of financial position of a successful company shows a net asset value of £10m, the owners of the company are unlikely to be willing to sell it for as little as £10m. They will expect an extra payment for the goodwill of the company. Perhaps the agreed price will be £22m, of which £12m is paid for goodwill. Goodwill is an intangible non-current asset and, like other non-current assets, it should be written off as it is used up.

The treatment of goodwill has varied over time, and the amounts involved have tended to increase. It used to be regarded as being very questionable and was typically written off immediately by deducting it from retained earnings; it did not pass through the income statement. That was a problem when the amount of goodwill was greater than the amount of retained earnings! In the last few decades of the twentieth century, the usual policy was to recognize goodwill as a non-current asset but to amortize it systematically as an expense via the income statement over its expected useful life (which could be 10 years or 20 or more years).

Now, IAS 36 requires that there should be an annual impairment review of goodwill, although it is recognized that goodwill does not generate cash flows separately from the assets with which it is associated. The impairment review is of a cash-generating unit, and any impairment is recognized as an expense in the income statement. This, of course, leaves open the possibility that a company will decide that there has been no impairment, so no charge is required.

3 *Capitalization of interest.* There is no doubt that creating a new non-current asset is capital expenditure, even if the company creates their own new non-current assets. When it takes a long time to construct an

asset, substantial borrowing costs are often incurred during the construction process. If a company bought such an asset from a builder, the price paid would have to cover the interest costs incurred by the builder. But, if the company constructs the asset itself, it may regard the interest cost as being part of the cost of the building (a non-current asset) rather than an expense. The idea of capitalizing interest may be controversial, but it is permitted in the circumstances specified by IAS 23, provided appropriate disclosures are made.

4 *Share options.* Some companies have chosen to give part or all of their employees' remuneration in the form of options to buy shares rather than in cash. This was popular during the dotcom boom, when companies were expanding rapidly, and their share prices were increasing, but they found it difficult to pay the high levels of remuneration that some key employees expected. If a company's shares are trading at £2 each, an option to buy 100,000 of them at £2.50 would at first not be attractive. But if the company's share price increased to, say, £12.50, the employee could make £1m by buying the 100,000 shares at £2.50 and then selling them at £12.50. That is more attractive than most salaries!

At first, that seems to be a cost-free way of paying employees generously. But there is a cost to the original shareholders: suddenly they own a smaller proportion of the company. The standard-setters require that this cost must be recognized and specified how to do this in IFRS 2 Share-based Payments.

3.7 Adjusting Financial Statements for Price Changes

The problem

Both statements of financial position and income statements are affected by changing prices, and the resultant profit figures need to be interpreted with care. During a period of rising prices, profits are usually overstated, and there are a number of problems with using conventional financial statements based on historical costs (see **Illustration 3.2**).

- The cost of sales is understated. If a business buys oil for £120 a barrel and sells it for £130 a barrel a month later, it seems to have made a profit of £10. But if, during that month, the cost of replacing that oil increases from £120 to £129, the business is not much better off. It has made a 'holding gain' of £9, but its 'operating gain' or profit is only £1.
- Depreciation is understated. If a business buys a machine for £100,000, which is expected to last for 10 years, it seems reasonable to charge £10,000 a year depreciation. But if, at the end of 10 years, it comes to replace the machine, it might cost a lot more - perhaps £200,000. Depreciation based on historical cost was much lower than it would be using current costs, and in that sense, profits have been overstated.
- Excessive dividends might be paid if profits are overstated. This would reduce the company's capital in real terms.
- Excessive taxation might be paid if it is based on overstated profits, which would reduce the company's capital in real terms.[20]
- Liquidity problems are likely to arise if a company pays excessive dividends and taxation and needs to finance the extra cost of replacing various[21] assets.
- Statement of financial position values of assets are understated during a period of rising prices, especially freehold property.

[20] HMRC's rules for measuring profits for corporation tax purposes are different, and in some ways more realistic than conventional accounting.

[21] Including receivables, which are likely to increase in line with inflation; the resulting extra amount of debt has to be financed.

- Return on capital employed is overstated; this is true if profits are overstated and asset values are understated.
- It is wrong to add together items on a statement of financial position that are expressed in different units of currency. Obviously, dollars are not added to euros. But, on a statement of financial position, items expressed in £s of 20 years ago are added to items expressed in £s of this year, although the value of the currency has changed significantly in the meantime.
- Gains from borrowing. When a business borrows money, the interest payable is correctly recorded as an expense. But if the borrowed money is used to purchase a tangible asset (such as freehold property), the gain on that asset (as prices increase) is not recorded.

ILLUSTRATION 3.2

	Historical cost	Current values
Profit for year, £	12,000	8,000
Net assets, £	100,000	133,333
Return on capital employed	12%	6%

Some of these problems have to do with the measurement of profit, some with assets, and others to do with the consequences, and some are inherent in the nature of accounting. It would be difficult to devise a satisfactory system of accounting that would solve all the problems.

Possible solutions

Various piecemeal and *ad hoc* solutions have been suggested, such as being careful about dividends (i.e. do not pay out all profits as dividends; some need to be retained to finance the increased cost of assets); revaluing fixed assets and increasing depreciation accordingly; and using last in first out (LIFO) (so that cost of sales is based on recent prices).[22]

An important principle in finding a solution is 'capital maintenance'. Profit is the amount that a business can afford to pay out as dividends without making itself less 'well off'. If a business starts a year with equity of £1m (using the statement of financial position approach to measuring profit and ends the year with equity of £1.2m, we may say that it has made £0.2m profit, it can pay out £0.2m as dividends, and it will have maintained its capital at £1m. This is true in historical cost terms, but in real terms (allowing for inflation), the value of the capital will be less.

If a business starts the year with equity of £1m, and there is 5 per cent inflation, at the end of the year, it needs £1.05m to maintain capital in 'real terms', and it can pay only £0.15m as dividends, not £0.2m. Current purchasing power (CPP) accounting is designed to maintain capital in real terms. It adjusts all items in the financial statements to reflect inflation, that is, changes in the general price level.

A different approach is to deal with the effects of *specific* price changes on the entity rather than general inflation. There are various ways[23] of doing this, but the best known is intended to maintain the *operating capability* (capital) of the business based on changes in the prices of the actual assets that the business uses. The best known method of doing this is current cost accounting, applying four adjustments to the income statement, and showing items on the statement of financial position at current cost. Profit is calculated in the usual way, and then the following adjustments are applied:

1. Cost of sales adjustment that reduces profit by calculating the cost of financing the increase in inventories required by price increases.

[22] In a period of rising prices, LIFO gives more realistic profit figures than FIFO; but LIFO statement of financial position figures for inventories are more unrealistic.

[23] ASC SSAP16 Current Cost Accounting (1979).

2 Depreciation adjustment that reduces profit by calculating the additional depreciation required to finance the increase in the cost of non-current assets.

3 Monetary working capital adjustment that reduces profit by calculating the cost of financing the increase in receivables[24] required by price increases.

During a period of rising prices, the total of the first three adjustments will reduce historical cost profits, as if equity shareholders provide the whole of the additional finance required. To the extent that a business is financed by borrowing:

4 A gearing adjustment that reduces the effect of the other three adjustments is applied.

In the current cost accounting statement of financial position, items are shown at their 'value to the business' or 'deprival value', which is often their replacement cost.[25] These figures are more realistic than historical cost (adjusted in various ways), but there may be more subjectivity. They are more relevant to the needs of users but perhaps less reliable than good old historical costs.

There has been extensive discussion about which theoretical system for financial accounting would be better than traditional accounting based on historical cost. Several different systems may be theoretically superior, but there is a lack of agreement on which, and with inflation falling to low levels, the problem no longer seems urgent, and making major changes does not seem to be a priority.

Fair value

The idea of 'fair value' is currently fashionable among standard-setters and some academics, together with an 'all-inclusive' concept of profit. This means that if all items on the statement of financial position are stated at 'fair value', an increase in equity is regarded as profit.[26] One problem with this approach is that it would include in profit any increase in the value of assets - even if they are not sold (see **Example 3.3**).

Example 3.3

Two companies, A Ltd and B Ltd, each buy an identical asset for £100,000 during Year 1. Immediately before the year end, A Ltd sells the asset at its market value of £125,000. B Ltd retains the asset, and a few months later, the asset falls in value to £90,000.

Each company reports a profit of £25,000 for Year 1. For A Ltd, it is a realized profit. B Ltd missed an opportunity and subsequently suffered an unrealized loss.

Another problem is defining and measuring 'fair value'. It has long been recognized that 'pure' historical cost (although 'fair' at the time of the transaction) may be very different from 'fair value' at the statement of financial position date. Accounting standards already require that a number of items are shown on the statement of financial position at fair value, including pension assets and liabilities, some other financial assets and liabilities such as derivatives, assets acquired as a result of a business combination, assets that have been revalued, perhaps because of impaired value, investment properties and provisions.

In establishing 'fair value' based on market values, there is often a difference between buying prices (entry values or replacement cost) and selling prices (exit values, or net realizable value), and it is the latter that seems to be favoured by standard-setters. It is likely that we will continue with statements of financial position showing a mixture of cost-based and 'fair value' figures.

24 Net receivables (receivables minus payables), or, more strictly, net monetary working capital. Where payables are greater than receivables, the adjustment would *increase* profits (offsetting the cost of sales adjustment because additional inventories are financed by payables).

25 If replacement cost is higher than 'deprival value', then economic value (net present value of future cash flows), or net realizable value, is used, whichever of the two is higher.

26 After allowing for any dividends paid and any additional equity capital.

However fair or accurate the measurement of assets and liabilities may be, the total of the amounts shown for individual assets and liabilities will not be the same as the value of the firm (or its market capitalization).

Summary

Published financial statements are designed to give useful economic information to users of accounts to enable them to make informed decisions in relation to the business. On the whole, the level and detail of disclosure arise from regulation, including the Companies Act and accounting standards. It is easy to criticize accounting standard-setters for not yet coming up with a 'final solution' to all the problems of profit definition measurement and definitions that have universal acceptance. Progress has been made in developing theoretical frameworks and the setting of underlying assumptions and definitions. This has resulted in standards that narrow the differences in accounting practice, define terms and methods, and increase the level of information disclosed. The statement of financial position and the income statement approaches to the calculation of profit are contrasted. In times of inflation, accounts under the historical cost convention have serious difficulties, but every inflation-adjusted method of accounting has serious inadequacies.

Review of key points

- Many different groups in society may use published financial statements, but the principal users are investors and creditors.
- Profit figures are assumed to be useful in various ways, including making investment decisions, assessing creditworthiness and evaluating the effectiveness of management.
- It is difficult to establish a theoretical basis for profit measurement and financial reporting.
- There are different approaches to profit measurement based mainly on the statement of financial position or on the income statement.
- Definitions have been established for assets, liabilities, revenues and expenses, but some items still present difficulties.
- Financial statements can be seriously affected by inflation, and various methods have been developed to tackle this.

Self-testing questions

1. Who are the main users of financial accounting information, and what are their information needs?
2. Define assets and liabilities.
3. Why are 'provisions' a problem?
4. What is 'goodwill', and how does it arise?
5. Why do we not have 'pure' historical cost accounting?

6 Distinguish between 'revenues', 'income' and 'gains'.
7 Why is 'profit' seen as being important?

Assessment questions

1 What is 'profit'?
2 Explain the meaning of 'relevance' and 'reliability' in financial reporting.
3 Explain the main methods of measuring (or valuing) assets.
4 Define revenues and expenses. What other sorts of gain are there?
5 What are the tests for recognizing an intangible asset?
6 Is profit usually overstated when historical cost accounting is used? Explain.

Group activities and discussion questions

1 To what extent is it possible for published financial statements to meet the needs of different user groups?
2 Does financial accounting have any fundamental accounting concepts? Is it more helpful to establish objectives and constraints?
3 Financial statements are part of the process of making the directors of companies accountable to their shareholders. How accountable do you think they really are?
4 Examine the idea of accountability in relation to an organization with which you are familiar (e.g. a university, a church, a football club, a national government).
5 Why is it challenging to define and measure profit?

Accounting in context

Discuss and comment on the following article. What are contingent liabilities and why are they such an important factor to consider when assessing published accounts? Can you identify other examples of contingent liabilities from other companies you are interested in?

Auditchain Protocol, a Web3 protocol, that uses AI to analyse financial statements

By Darren Parkin

According to the Supreme Court of the United States, every digital asset except Bitcoin is considered a security or investment contract. The US Securities and Exchange Commission (SEC) delegates the enforcement of securities laws to various gatekeepers such as banks, broker-dealers, law firms, and PCAOB-registered accounting firms. These gatekeepers want to control the crypto industry and are using the SEC and its public budget to do so.

There are concerns that the SEC is not capable of properly regulating crypto assets, as they may not fully understand the technology. Additionally, regulatory specifications for financial and operational disclosure leave a lot to be desired. Financial statements are often unreliable, and a large amount of accounting and reporting data is missing, inconsistent, or incorrect.

The Auditchain Protocol is a Web3 protocol that uses AI to analyse financial statements and detect deficiencies in internal controls over financial reporting. The protocol was able to detect disclosure deficiencies of the already fragile Silvergate Bank before they failed. However, there are concerns that if financial disclosure is not reliable or usable, then how can the SEC properly regulate a new 'thing' when they struggle to regulate the old thing?

Source: City AM Online, 4 July 2023, https://www.cityam.com/the-hypocrisy-of-crypto-regulation-oblivious-or-nefarious/

References and further reading

Chambers, R.J. (1963) Why Bother with Postulates? *Journal of Accounting Research*, 1(1): 3–15.

Dennis, I. (2018) What Is a Conceptual Framework for Financial Reporting? *Accounting in Europe*, 15(3): 374–401, DOI: 10.1080/17449480.2018.1496269.

Elliott, B. and Elliott, J. (2022) *Financial Accounting and Reporting* (20th edn.). Upper Saddle River, NJ: Pearson Education.

IASB (2018) *Conceptual Framework for Financial Reporting*. https://www.accaglobal.com/gb/en/student/exam-support-resources/professional-exams-study-resources/strategic-business-reporting/technical-articles/conceptual-framework.html

Macve, R. (2010) The Case for Deprival Value. *Abacus*, 46: 111–119. https://doi.org/10.1111/j.1467-6281.2010.00310.x

https://www.icaew.com/library/research-guides/uk-accounting-standards

https://www.ifrs.org/content/dam/ifrs/project/goodwill-and-impairment/goodwill-and-impairment-dp-march-2020.pdf

https://www.ifrs.org/issued-standards/list-of-standards/conceptual-framework/

https://www.ifrs.org/issued-standards/list-of-standards/ias-37-provisions-contingent-liabilities-and-contingent-assets/

www.annualreport.marksandspencer.com/ (gives the Marks and Spencer Group accounts in full)

www.ifrs.org (gives details of international financial reporting standards)

Chapter 4

Ratios and Interpretation: A Straightforward Introduction

Chapter contents

4.1 Introduction
4.2 Financial Strength/Solvency
4.3 Profitability
4.4 Stock Market Ratios
4.5 Working Capital Management
4.6 Financial Structure/Gearing
4.7 Limitations and Comparisons
4.8 Ratios Ready Reference

Learning objectives

After studying this chapter, you will be able to:

✓ Calculate and interpret four solvency ratios from a company's published financial statements

✓ Calculate and interpret four overall profitability ratios; three dealing with the profitability of sales, and five dealing with the utilization of assets

✓ Calculate and interpret four stock market ratios

✓ Understand the role of working capital management and apply relevant ratios

✓ Appreciate the importance of financial structure and apply relevant ratios

✓ Understand the limitations of ratio analysis and the importance of suitable bases for comparison

4.1 Introduction

This chapter shows how financial accounts provide information that can be useful in assessing the financial strength of a company and in analysing and improving its performance in terms of profitability in a straightforward way. Complexities and more advanced aspects of interpretation are dealt with in **Chapter 11**.

This chapter also introduces the use of financial accounting information in interpreting the performance of a company's shares on the stock market. These issues are dealt with more fully in **Chapter 5**. Interpretation of accounts is not about memorizing a number of ratios and then calculating them. It is about examining a set of accounts with some clear questions in mind and then carefully arranging the evidence to answer those questions.

Presentation of 'ratios'

Accounting 'ratios' are presented in a number of conventional ways, most of which are percentages or some other measures, rather than 'ratios' in the strict sense of the word:

- *Ratios.* The current ratio and quick (or acid test) ratio are presented as ratios in the form 1.8: 1.
- *Percentages.* Many so-called ratios are really expressed as percentages. A dividend yield might be 3.5 per cent. Return on capital employed (ROCE) might be 12 per cent. The gross profit ratio is also expressed as a percentage (e.g. 25 per cent).
- *Number of times.* Dividend cover is expressed as a number of times, for example, 2.2 times. Interest cover and asset turnover ratios are also expressed as, for example, 6 times, 1.9 times. The 'price/earnings ratio' (P/E) (e.g. 16) is the share price divided by earnings per share, indicating that the share price is a number of times earnings (per share).
- *Number of days.* The trade receivables (trade debtors) 'ratio' is often shown as being, for example, 36 days,[1] being the average time customers take to pay for the goods sold to them. Similarly, the inventory (stock) turnover ratio is often expressed as the number of days, on average, goods are in stock before being sold. The trade payables (trade creditors) ratio is often shown as being the average period taken to pay trade payables.
- *Sum of money.* Earnings per share are expressed as a sum of money (e.g. 10p).

There are three main groups of questions in interpreting financial statements and a number of related ones:

1. *Financial strength/solvency.* Is the business likely to survive? Can it pay its liabilities as they fall due? Is it financially strong? Is there too much debt?
2. *Profitability.* Is the business sufficiently profitable? Is it making the best use of the resources available to it? How can profitability be increased?
3. *Stock market.* How are the company's shares performing on the stock market? Are they likely to be a good investment?

The chapter demonstrates how ratios can be used to tackle each of these questions in relation to Druisdale plc for year 5. Readers are invited to calculate and interpret the equivalent ratios for year 6. (The answers are provided at the end of the book.)

Other related questions include different aspects of profitability, working capital management, financial structure and cash flows. This chapter introduces most of these issues. Cash flows are dealt with in **Chapter 6**. Stock market ratios are dealt with more fully in **Chapter 5**. More advanced interpretations of financial statements and some complexities are dealt with in **Chapter 11**.

The final part of the chapter provides an overview of ratio analysis, followed by a 'ratios ready reference' section.

[1] Alternatively, it could also be expressed as sales divided by trade receivables, giving perhaps 10 times per annum.

4.2 Financial Strength/Solvency

A statement of financial position shows what a company owns or controls (assets) and what it owes (liabilities). Unless the company is a complete disaster, it should have more assets than liabilities, and the excess of assets over liabilities is called 'equity'. If someone owns a house worth £200,000 and has a mortgage of £120,000, their 'equity' in that house is £80,000.

A business can collapse in many different ways: bankruptcy of the owner, liquidation, receivership, winding up, reorganization and takeover. Many different reasons are put forward to explain what went wrong, including bad management and bad luck. But, in the end, a company collapses if it is unable to pay its liabilities as they fall due. Statements of financial position show liabilities clearly, and it is worth trying to assess if those liabilities are excessive - if the company owes so much that it is likely to get into financial difficulties and become insolvent.

The statement of financial position clearly separates short-term assets and liabilities from long-term assets and liabilities, and the assessment can be done in two stages: short term and long term.

Short term

The key question is: can a company meet its short-term liabilities as they fall due? Current liabilities are clearly shown on statements of financial position. If a company has current liabilities of £1m and they have £2m in the bank, then there should not be a problem. There are companies with so much money in the bank that they do not know what to do with it, but that is not the norm. Even if a company does not have lots of money in the bank, it is worth looking at its current assets as a whole. Current assets include cash and things like inventories and receivables that are expected to become cash within a matter of months. If a company has a lot more current assets than current liabilities, then it looks reasonably strong.

If we look at the Druisdale plc statement of financial position at the end of year 5 (**Example 4.1**), we can see that current liabilities amount to £60m. If all their current assets are turned into cash, there should not be a problem: current assets amount to £120m. Current assets are twice as much as current liabilities - a ratio of 2:1. This relationship between current assets and current liabilities is called the current ratio.

In some businesses, inventories are not easily or quickly converted into cash. In looking at what money is immediately available with which to pay current liabilities, we should, perhaps, exclude inventories. Some inventories, such as stocks of food in a supermarket, should be sold and converted into cash within a few weeks. Other inventories may take a long time to be converted into cash; for example, raw materials and components that have not yet been incorporated into saleable products or partly built houses - perhaps where demand is currently slack. In Druisdale plc, in year 5, there is £20m of cash and £40m of trade receivables that should become cash within a month or so. In other words, 'liquid assets' of £60m (excluding inventories) are just enough to meet current liabilities of £60m as they become due. This is a quick (or acid test) ratio of 1:1.

On the year 6 statement of financial position, there are not enough liquid assets (£60m) to meet the current liabilities (£80m). The quick ratio has gone down to 0.75:1. Their liquidity position has deteriorated, and problems could arise.

Long term

A company is likely to find itself in financial difficulties if it has too much debt, whether it is short or long term. One way of assessing if debt is too high is to compare it with equity. If someone has a mortgage (debt) of £120,000, it is probably not serious if the house is worth £200,000 - there is £80,000 of the owner's equity.

It is still less of a problem if the house is worth £500,000: the owner's equity would amount to £380,000. The more equity there is in relation to the total value of the house, the less risky the borrowing is. The more borrowing there is in relation to the total value of the house, the riskier the borrowing is.

Example 4.1

Statement of financial position of Druisdale plc as at 31 December

	Year 5 £m	Year 6 £m
Assets		
Non-current assets		
Property, plant and equipment	180	200
Current assets		
Inventories	60	60
Trade receivables	40	50
Cash	20	10
	120	120
Total assets	300	320
Liabilities and equity		
Current liabilities		
Trade payables	60	80
Non-current liabilities		
Long-term borrowing	60	40
Total liabilities	120	120
Equity		
Share capital	100	100
Retained earnings	80	100
Total equity	180	200
Total liabilities and equity	300	320

Income statement of Druisdale plc for the year ended 31 December

	Year 5 £m	Year 6 £m
Revenue	300	350
Cost of sales	(200)	(230)
Gross profit	100	120

Income statement of Druisdale plc for the year ended 31 December

	Year 5 £m	Year 6 £m
Distribution costs	(15)	(20)
Administrative expenses	(25)	(31)
Operating profit	60	69
Finance costs	(5)	(4)
Profit before tax	55	65
Income tax expense	(15)	(15)
Profit for the period	40	50

Statement of changes in equity of Druisdale plc for the year ended 31 December

	£m	£m
Balance at the beginning of year	165	180
Profit for the period	40	50
Dividends	(25)	(30)
Balance at end at the end of year	180	200

Additional information

Druisdale plc's share capital consists of 100 million ordinary shares with a nominal value of £1 each. Assume that the share price on 31 December for years 5 and 6 was £5.60 and £7.50, respectively.

It is also necessary to look at an individual's or a company's ability to service the loan. If interest of 8 per cent per annum is payable on a loan of £120,000, the cost of the loan is £9,600[2] per annum. If an individual or company earns only £10,000 a year, they are going to have problems paying the interest. If they earn £30,000 a year, we can say that the interest is 'covered' just over three times, which might be satisfactory. It would be much more comfortable if the income available to pay the interest was £96,000 a year: we could say that the interest is covered 10 times since a future reduction of income will not seriously jeopardize the likelihood of being able to pay the interest.

Statements of financial position show the relationship between equity and long-term borrowings. At the end of year 5 Druisdale plc's equity amounted to £180m; their long-term borrowings were £60m. We could say that as long as equity is a lot more than borrowings, the position is satisfactory. Or we could present a 'gearing ratio' that relates debt (long-term borrowings) to equity. The total amount of long-term funding available to Druisdale is (180 + 60 =) £240m. Of this total, £60m is borrowed: the gearing ratio is therefore 25 per cent.[3]

Druisdale should have little difficulty in servicing their loan. The income statement for year 5 shows 'finance costs' of £5m. The profit available to provide that interest amounted to £60m. We could arrive at this figure simply by taking profit before tax and adding back the interest. Or we could use the 'operating profit' figure (which is the same), which is gross profit minus operating costs for distribution and administration (100 − 15 − 25 =) £60m. Interest is covered 12 times,[4] which should be very safe.

[2] 8% × £120,000 = £9,600.

[3] 60 ÷ 240 × 100 = 25%.

[4] 60 ÷ 5 = 12.

An overall view

The approach so far has been to calculate four widely used 'ratios' for year 5, which are as follows:

		Year 5
1	*Current ratio* (or working capital ratio)	2 : 1
2	*Quick* (or acid test ratio)	1 : 1
3	*Capital gearing ratio*	25%
4	*Interest cover*	12 times

Activity 4.1

Complete the following table for Druisdale plc by inserting the figures for year 6 and comment on the changes that have taken place.[5]

Ratio	Year 5		Year 6	Comment
1 Current ratio	120 : 60	2 : 1		
2 Quick ratio	60 : 60	1 : 1		
3 Gearing ratio	60/240	25%		
4 Interest cover	60/5	12 times		

This conventional approach separates short-term liabilities from long-term liabilities. It may also be important to look at the total of all liabilities in forming an assessment of a company's financial strength and survival prospects.

Example 4.2

Ratio	Tesco plc	GlaxoSmithKline
Current ratio	0.76 : 1	0.91 : 1
Quick ratio	0.61 : 1	0.68 : 1
Capital gearing ratio	57%	73%
Interest cover	4.7 times	7.5 times

It is not sensible to state what is acceptable or benchmark levels for these ratios since what would be considered acceptable in one industry might be thought to be far too high or too low in another. In **Example 4.2**, we can see two highly regarded companies in different sectors with different results (using their annual financial statements for 2022), and in order to assess these ratios, the only sensible approach is to compare Tesco plc with another supermarket group and GlaxoSmithKline (now called GSK plc) with another pharmaceutical and biotechnology company.

[5] A completed table is provided at the end of the book.

If the current ratio and quick ratio are lower than other similar companies, that tends to indicate that the company is not liquid enough. If, however, these ratios are higher than similar companies, that indicates that the company is not using its liquid resources in an effective way.

If the gearing ratio is higher than similar companies, it indicates that the company's borrowing begins to look a little risky, while if it is much lower than similar companies, it indicates the company is risk averse. Companies with very reliable income, such as property companies, often have very high gearing (with loans secured on property and the rental income receivable from it). Companies in the motor trade cannot afford a high level of gearing since their profits tend to fluctuate with the economic cycle.

The interest cover of 12 times looks fairly safe in **Activity 4.1.** Cover of much less than 5 begins to look risky since a downturn in the company's profit would put its ability to service its loans in doubt.

The above comments need to be interpreted with care, and what is satisfactory depends on the type of business. It is also useful to look at trends rather than at just a single year.

In assessing the financial strength of a company, there are many other factors to take into consideration; indications of many of these can be found in the financial accounting statements. The statement of financial position alone will not tell us all we want to know. We also have to look at the income statement in order to calculate interest cover. Profit is by no means a guarantee of survival, but creditors of a profitable company are likely to be much more secure than creditors of a loss-making company. A company that is making profits is much more likely to survive than one that is making losses.

Suppliers are interested in whether or not they are likely to be paid on time. A calculation of the average time it takes to pay trade payables (creditors) is provided in ratio 16.

In terms of survival, cash flow matters more than profit or any of the above ratios. As long as a company is generating lots of cash, it can pay its liabilities and survive. The calculation and interpretation of these ratios and the evaluation of solvency are considered more fully in **Chapter 7** and **Chapter 11**.

4.3 Profitability

Profitability is examined here in three sections:

- Overall profitability
- Profitability of sales
- Utilization of assets

Overall profitability

An income statement shows how much profit a company has made for the shareholders in a given period. Druisdale plc's profit after finance costs and taxation for year 5 was £40m (but before deducting dividends, which are shown in the Statement of Changes to Equity). Shareholders may reasonably ask: was that enough? Should the company be more profitable?

Druisdale's statement of financial position shows the total equity as being £180m at the end of year 5. If the shareholders' funds had been put into a deposit account at a bank, they might have been paid about 4 per cent per annum interest, with virtually no risk. Shareholders would expect a company to earn a much better return than that[6] in view of the risk inherent in investing in companies. A return of 4 per cent per annum on £180m

[6] Even if much of the profit or income earned is retained in the business and not paid out to shareholders as dividends.

would produce £7.2m profit a year. As Druisdale earned £40m in year 5, the shareholders may be satisfied. The return earned for them is as follows:

5 *Return on shareholders' funds*

$$\frac{\text{Profit for the year}}{\text{Equity at year end}} \times 100 \quad \frac{£40}{£180} \times 100 = 22.2\%$$

It is important to consider the *total* of shareholders' funds (£180m), not just the share capital (£100m). This ratio considers the shareholders' point of view. The ratio measures the return on *shareholders' capital employed or the return on equity.*[7]

In assessing management, however, we should consider all the funds for which they are responsible more generally and look at the return on *total long-term capital.* The return of total long-term capital employed, ROCE, is often regarded as being the most important, or key, or primary ratio, particularly in measuring profitability. Where there is a good and increasing ROCE, we can conclude that the management of the company is using its resources effectively. The statement of financial position at the end of year 5 shows that, in addition to shareholders' funds of £180m, the company had long-term borrowings of £60m. Profit is earned for the shareholders; interest is the return to lenders. If we are going to calculate a return on total long-term capital, we must include interest, in addition to profit, as being part of the return; that is, the return before remunerating either of the suppliers of capital, lenders or shareholders. In year 5, the profit was £40m, and the finance cost (presumably interest) was £5m. Rather than just adding the two together, it is easier to consider the return before taxation; sometimes the figure is described as earnings before interest and taxation (EBIT) or as operating profit.

6 *Return on total long-term capital employed*

Profit (£40m) + tax expense (£15m) + finance cost (£5m) = £60m

Or:

Gross profit (£100m) - distribution costs (£15m) - administrative expenses (£25m) = £60m

Total capital employed is equity (£180m) + long-term borrowings (£60m) = £240m operating profit

$$\frac{\text{Operating profit or EBIT}}{\text{Equity+long-term borrowings}} \times 100 \quad \frac{£60\text{m}}{£240\text{m}} \times 100 = 25\%$$

We might consider that any return on capital employed (ROCE) of more than about 10 per cent is satisfactory; anything over 20 per cent is good. As is the case with most ratios, this figure is most useful when making comparisons with previous periods (or other companies). It is important to ensure that all ratios are calculated in the same way when making comparisons, but it is particularly relevant with ROCE as there are several different ways of doing it.

Directors and shareholders often want to see an increase in the ROCE, and there are two[8] ways of achieving this: either by increasing the numerator, that is, the return, or by decreasing the denominator, that is, the capital employed.

- Increasing the return, or profit, in relation to the amount of capital employed. This can be done by reducing costs and, or increasing sales. The important thing is to increase the difference between costs and sales; in other words, to increase profit as a percentage of sales. This is assessed in ratio 7, and considered in more detail using ratios 9–11.
- Reducing the amount of capital employed (in relation to the amount of sales) or increasing the amount of sales (in relation to the amount of capital employed. This means making more intensive use of assets

[7] When there are preference shares the return on equity (ordinary shareholders' funds) will be different from the return on total shareholders' funds (ordinary shareholders' funds plus preference shares).

[8] Perhaps *only* two.

or capital employed or increasing 'asset turnover'. This is assessed in ratio 8 and considered in more detail using ratios 12–16.

7 *Operating profit*[9] *as a percentage of sales*

In year 5, Druisdale's operating profit as a percentage of sales was:

$$\frac{\text{Operating profit}}{\text{Sales}} \times 100 \qquad \times 100 = 20\% \; \frac{£60\text{m}}{£300\text{m}}$$

8 *Asset turnover*

In year 5, Druisdale's asset turnover may be measured by relating the sales figure to net operating assets.[10]

Non-current assets plus current assets minus current liabilities (£180m + £120m − £60m) = £240m

or:

Equity plus long-term borrowings (£180m + £60m) = £240m

The £240m may be shown as Non-CA + CA − CL

Sales revenue £300m

$$\text{Asset turnover} = \frac{\text{Sales}}{\text{Non-CA+CA} - \text{CL}} \quad \frac{£300\text{m}}{£240\text{m}} = 1.25 \text{ times}$$

The last three ratios considered can be related together as follows:

6	Return on total long-term capital employed	£60m/£240m	25%
7	Operating profit as a percentage of sales	£60m/£300m	20%
8	Asset turnover:	25 ÷ 20 = 1.25	1.25 times

Activity 4.2

Complete the following table for Druisdale plc by inserting the figures for year 6, and commenting on the changes that have taken place.[11] Check the relationship between ratios 6, 7 and 8.

Ratio	Year 5		Year 6	Comment
5 Return on shareholders' capital employed	40/180	22.2%		
6 Return on total long-term capital employed	60/240	25%		
7 Operating profit as a percentage of sales	60/300	20%		
8 Asset turnover	300/240 or 25/20	1.25 times		

When these four ratios have been calculated for each of the two years, it will be clear whether profitability has increased and why.

In order to increase its profitability, it is necessary to consider (a) the profitability of sales (and analyse costs) and (b) the utilization of capital employed or asset turnover (and analyse 'activity ratios').

9 Profit before interest and taxes or before deducting finance charges.

10 Net operating assets may be defined as total assets (current plus non-current) minus current liabilities. This should be equal to equity plus non-current liabilities.

11 A completed table is provided at the end of the book.

Profitability of sales

Any costs can be expressed as a percentage of sales. The first cost on an income statement is the cost of sales, but it is more usual to express gross profit as a percentage of sales. If the cost of sales is two-thirds of sales, then gross profit is one-third of sales. The figures for Druisdale plc for year 5 are as follows:

9 *Gross profit ratio*

$$\frac{\text{Gross profit}}{\text{Sales}} \times 100 \quad \frac{£100\text{m}}{£300\text{m}} \times 100 = 33\tfrac{1}{3}\%$$

It may be more useful to express the cost of raw materials or labour as a percentage of sales. But the most readily available costs from published accounts are distribution costs and administrative expenses. The ratios for Druisdale plc for year 5 are shown below. A decline in gross margin might indicate that the company is operating in a more competitive market and, perhaps, cannot pass on its purchase price increases in a similar proportion to its customers. This could occur, for example, if the pound sterling has fallen on imported goods but the company finds it is unable to increase its selling prices. Or perhaps the company's sales mix has altered, and it is selling a higher proportion of its sales in products with a lower margin.

10 *Distribution costs as a percentage of sales*

$$\frac{\text{Distribution costs}}{\text{Sales}} \times 100 \quad \frac{£15\text{m}}{£300\text{m}} \times 100 = 5\%$$

11 *Administrative expenses as a percentage of sales*

$$\frac{\text{Administrative expenses}}{\text{Sales}} \times 100 \quad \frac{£25\text{m}}{£300\text{m}} \times 100 = 8\tfrac{1}{3}\%$$

Whether or not these ratios are satisfactory depends on the business; the figures mean little except by comparison.

Activity 4.3

Complete the following table for Druisdale plc by inserting the figures for year 6, and commenting on the changes that have taken place.[12]

Ratio	Year 5		Year 6	Comment
9 Gross profit ratio	100/300	33⅓%		
10 Distribution costs as a % of sales	15/300	5%		
11 Administrative expenses as a % of sales	25/300	8⅓%		

Utilization of assets

Where there is a problem with the asset turnover ratio (number 8 above), there is a need to improve the utilization of assets. The first step is to see whether the problem lies with non-current assets or with current assets.[13] This can be done by comparing one year with the next, as demonstrated in **Activity 4.4**.

12 *Sales/non-current assets*

$$\frac{\text{Sales}}{\text{Non-current assets}} \quad \frac{300\text{m}}{180\text{m}} = 1.67 \text{ times}$$

[12] A completed table is provided at the end of the book.

[13] The problem might also lie with current liabilities. Increasing current liabilities can increase profitability (it reduces the amount of capital employed), but it might make solvency ratios look weaker.

If it is established that there is a problem with fixed assets (there are too many fixed assets in relation to the amount of sales), further analysis can be done by comparing different categories of fixed assets with sales.

13 *Sales/current assets*

$$\frac{\text{Sales}}{\text{Current assets}} \quad \frac{300\text{m}}{120\text{m}} = 2.5 \text{ times}$$

If it is established that there is a problem with current assets (there are too many current assets in relation to the amount of sales), further analysis can be done by comparing different items of current assets and current liabilities with sales. The most widely used ratios are in relation to inventories, receivables and payables. These may be measured in terms of the number of times the item is 'turned over' in a year (e.g. inventory turnover ratio). However, it is preferable to express each of inventory, trade receivables and trade payables as a number of days.

14 *Inventory (stock) turnover ratio*

The stock or inventory figure taken from the statement of financial position is shown at cost price (not selling price) and so must be compared with the cost of sales figure (not the sales revenue figure). The inventories are divided by cost of sales to give a proportion of a year (365 days):

$$\frac{\text{Inventories}}{\text{Cost of sales}} \times 365 \quad \frac{60\text{m}}{200\text{m}} \times 365 = 110 \text{ days}$$

This figure seems rather high, but it does depend on the type of business. A supermarket would probably have only a few weeks' inventory on hand at any one time: for example, Tesco plc had 14.77 days' inventory in 2023, while GSK plc (previously known as GlaxoSmithKline) had 234 days' inventory in 2023. Generally, the quicker the inventory is sold, the better.

15 *Trade receivables (debtors) ratio*

The trade debtors or trade receivables figure taken from the statement of financial position is shown at the selling price (that is, the amount that the customer owes, not the cost price) and so must be compared with the sales revenue figure (not the cost of sales figure). Again, it is expressed as a proportion of a year:

$$\frac{\text{Trade receivables}}{\text{Sales revenue}} \times 365 \quad \frac{40\text{m}}{300\text{m}} \times 365 = 49 \text{ days}$$

If all sales are on credit, and customers are expected to settle their accounts by the end of the month following the month in which the sale takes place, perhaps 49 days is reasonable.

If some or all sales are on a cash basis (as is the case with most retailers), much lower trade receivable days would be expected. If possible, credit sales should be separated from cash sales, and the trade receivable (or debtor's) figure should be compared only with the credit sales figure. Generally, a company intends to collect their trade receivables quickly, and this can be encouraged, for example, by offering discounts for prompt payment.

16 *Trade payables (creditors) ratio*

The trade creditors, or trade payables, figure taken from the statement of financial position is shown at cost price (that is, the amount owed to suppliers) and so must be compared with the cost of sales figure in the same way as with the inventory turnover ratio above:

$$\frac{\text{Trade payables}}{\text{Cost of sales}} \times 365 \quad \frac{60\text{m}}{200\text{m}} \times 365 = 100 \text{ days}$$

On the statement of financial position of Druisdale plc, it happens that the amount for inventories is the same as the amount for payables, and so the two payment periods are the same.

We do not necessarily know what is included in payables. Ideally, we should compare like with like, and payables for raw material purchases would be compared with the amount of raw material purchases. As always, we have to use the best information available, and even relatively crude measures can provide valuable information, such as: is the company taking longer to pay its trade payables than it did a year ago? On the face of it, one might think that paying one's suppliers more slowly than in the previous year would be better, and although it is in terms of the effect on the bank balance, paying slowly implies we are not taking advantage of any prompt payment discounts, it is likely to put our relationships with our suppliers under strain and might be because we do not have the bank facility to pay and could be an indication that we are in serious financial difficulties.

Activity 4.4

Complete the following table for Druisdale by inserting the figures for year 6, and comment on the changes that have taken place.[14]

Ratio	Year 5		Year 6	Comment
12 Sales/non-current assets	300/180	1.67 times		
13 Sales/current assets	300/120	2.5 times		
14 Inventory turnover ratio	60 ÷ 200 × 365	110 days		
15 Trade receivables ratio	40 ÷ 300 × 365	49 days		
16 Trade payables ratio	60 ÷ 200 × 365	110 days		

4.4 Stock Market Ratios

Investors can compare the share price of a company with information from that company's financial statements to assess how expensive the share is in relation to the last known level of earnings (income), dividends and underlying asset values.

17 *Price/earnings (P/E) ratio*

'Earnings per share' is a widely used measure and is calculated by dividing the profit for the period by the number of shares that the company has. This shows how much profit was earned for each share. The amount of profit that Druisdale plc earned for its shareholders in year 5, after deducting all expenses and taxation, was £40m. The company had a share capital of £100m, with a nominal value of £1 share.

$$\text{Earnings per share} = \frac{\text{Profit for the year}}{\text{Number of shares}} \quad \frac{£40\text{m}}{£100\text{m}} = 40\text{p per share}$$

Investors in that company might think that earnings per share will continue at 40p for the foreseeable future and be willing to pay five or ten times as much as that for each share; that would result in the share price being £2 or £4. If shareholders are optimistic that future earnings will increase substantially, they might be willing to pay more than 10 times as much as the earnings per share figure. At the end of year 5, investors were paying £5.60 for each share, so they must have been reasonably optimistic.

$$\text{P/E ratio} = \frac{\text{Share price} \quad £5.60}{\text{Earnings per share} \quad 40\text{p}} = 14$$

14 A completed table is provided at the end of the book.

A P/E ratio of 14 means that the amount investors are willing to pay for shares is 14 times the last known earnings per share figure. That is not particularly high. If shareholders are very optimistic about the future of a company, they would be prepared to pay much more for the shares, and P/E ratios of 20 or 30 are not unusual. A high P/E ratio suggests that investors are optimistic about the future prospects of the company. However, a P/E of 14 times for Druisdale should be compared to another company in the same industry, and if the average P/E of the same industry is, for example, 26 times, then the company with the P/E of 14 times is underpriced relative to the industry.

18 *Dividend yield*

Investors are interested not only in the amount of profit that has been earned for them but also in how much dividend is being paid. Companies usually pay out only a part of their profits as dividends. Druisdale plc paid out dividends of £25m in year 5 (as shown on the statement of changes in equity). This amounts to 25p per share (there are 100 million shares).

$$\text{Dividend per share} = \frac{\text{Total dividends}}{\text{Number of shares}} \quad \frac{£25\text{m}}{100\text{m}} = 25\text{p per share}$$

This may seem like only a modest return for shareholders. They had to pay £5.60, and at that time, the last known dividend per share was 25p. The dividend yield is calculated by expressing the dividend per share as a percentage of the share price.

$$\text{Dividend yield} = \frac{\text{Dividend per share}}{\text{Share price}} \times 100 \quad \frac{£0.25}{£5.60} = 4.5\%$$

Investors hope for higher dividends in the future and pay a lot more for shares where substantial growth is expected. If Druisdale's share price doubled (to £11.20), the dividend yield would halve (to about 2.25%).

19 *Dividend cover*

Some companies pay out a higher proportion of their profits than others. If a company pays out only a quarter of its profits as dividends, it is more likely to be able to maintain dividend levels in the future than a company that pays out most or all of its profits as dividends. Investors may want to know to what extent their dividends are 'covered' by earnings.[15]

Dividend cover[16] can be measured on a 'per share' basis or in total for the company.

$$\frac{\text{Earning per share}}{\text{Dividend per share}} \quad \text{or} \quad \frac{\text{Total profit for the period}}{\text{Total dividends}}$$

$$\frac{40\text{p}}{25\text{p}} \quad \text{or} \quad \frac{£40\text{m}}{£25\text{m}}$$

$$\text{Dividend cover} = 1.6 \text{ times}$$

Companies typically pay out about half of their profits as dividends; on average, dividend cover is around 2 (i.e. dividends are covered twice by profits). Shareholders who buy shares for income will be inclined to invest in companies with a low dividend cover, while shareholders motivated by higher future share price growth will prefer to invest in companies with a high dividend cover.

20 *Net assets per share* (or statement of financial position value per share)

Investors may be interested in the asset value underlying the share price. The statement of financial position of Druisdale at the end of year 5 shows net assets as being £180m. This may be calculated in two different ways, each giving the same answer:

---

[15] Just as debenture holders may want to know to what extent their interest is 'covered' by operating profits, which are available to pay that interest (ratio 4).

[16] Here it is assumed that there are no preference shares.

1 Non-current assets, plus current assets, minus non-current liabilities, minus current liabilities. £180m + £120m − £60m − £60m = £180m.

2 Total equity = £180m. Obviously, it is easier to do it this way, but it is worth making the point that (i) above, which is usually called 'net assets', is equal to total equity.

The amount of net assets per share is calculated as:

$$\frac{\text{Net assets}}{\text{Number of shares}} \quad \frac{180\text{m}}{100\text{m}} = £1.80$$

The value of the shares on the stock market at the time, at £5.60, was much higher. This is usually the case with a successful company: it is worth significantly more than the statement of financial position indicates.

Activity 4.5

Complete the following table for Druisdale plc by inserting the figures for year 6 and commenting on the changes that have taken place.[17]

Ratio	Year 5		Year 6	Comment
17 Price/earnings ratio	£5.60 ÷ 40p	14		
18 Dividend yield	25p ÷ £5.60 × 100	4.5%		
19 Dividend cover	40/25	1.6 times		
20 Net assets per share	£180/100	£1.80		

4.5 Working Capital Management

Working capital management is concerned with balancing two contradictory pressures:

1 There is a need to ensure that there are sufficient funds to pay liabilities as they fall due. Having large sums of money in the bank, and plenty of money due from trade receivables (plus additional money tied up in inventories) should reassure creditors. If creditors are paid rapidly, the figure for creditors is minimized, and that contributes to maximizing the amount of working capital. The larger the amount of working capital, the more creditors are reassured about the company's solvency.

2 The need to ensure the profitable use of capital employed. Having large sums of money tied up in current assets undermines profitability (by increasing capital employed). Similarly, minimizing the amount of creditors undermines profitability (also by increasing capital employed). The smaller the amount of working capital, the greater the profitability is likely to be.

The first of these is about maximizing solvency, and the usual ratios for assessing this are dealt with above.

1 Current ratio: are there enough current assets to cover current liabilities?

2 Quick ratio: are there enough liquid assets to cover current liabilities?

16 Trade payables ratio: how long does it take to pay creditors? Are we paying them too slowly/too quickly?

[17] A completed table is provided at the end of the book.

The second is about maximizing profitability, particularly in the utilization of assets (ratio 8, asset turnover). More specifically the main ratios are:

13 Sales/current assets ratio: are current assets excessive in relation to turnover?

14 Inventory turnover ratio: is inventory excessive in relation to turnover?[18]

15 Trade receivables ratio: are customers taking too long to pay?

16 Trade payables ratio: are we paying suppliers too quickly to maximize profitability?

Working capital management is considered more fully in **Chapter 12**.

4.6 Financial Structure/Gearing

The way in which a business is financed is often called *financial structure*. It is particularly concerned with the balance between equity (shareholders' funds) and debt (long-term borrowing). This is also called capital gearing, and is introduced previously as ratio number:

3 *Capital gearing ratio: is there too much borrowing in relation to the amount of equity?*

From the point of view of creditors, the lower the gearing (the lower the amount of borrowing), the greater is their security. Low gearing may be seen as an aspect of solvency or financial strength. High gearing suggests high risk.

However, high gearing can be advantageous in maximising profitability. A company may be able to borrow money at modest interest rates, perhaps 6 per cent per annum; it may then be able to invest that money in the business to earn a return[19] of more than, say, 10 per cent. In that situation, increasing borrowings will increase profits. But this can be a risky strategy and companies usually seek to avoid excessive borrowings.[20]

Capital gearing is considered more fully in **Chapter 11**.

4.7 Limitations and Comparisons

A systematic use of ratios can provide valuable insights into a company's financial position and performance. It is better to have some clear questions in mind than to simply read through the financial statements as presented by the company. Annual reports often emphasize the favourable aspects of a company's performance, and some systematic investigation is required to arrive at a more balanced view. Financial statements provide substantial and increasing amounts of detail, but they can still leave important questions unanswered. A detailed ratio analysis is likely to indicate areas for further investigation at least as much as it produces full and final answers.

Bases for comparison

To help users of financial statements identify and assess changes and trends, financial statements also provide comparative information for at least one preceding reporting period (Conceptual Framework, 2018, s3.5). The figures and ratios from an analysis of financial statements are meaningful only by comparison with something.

[18] More specifically, inventory in relation to cost of sales.

[19] Ratio 6: Return on total long-term capital employed. The return is measured before deducting the cost of interest.

[20] Profit before deducting tax and interest, or EBIT, or gross profit minus operating expenses.

Therefore, the easiest thing, in all companies' accounts, is to compare this year's results with last year's; they are presented side by side for that very purpose. We can immediately see whether a company's financial position and performance are improving or deteriorating, as a whole, and in detail, using many different figures and approaches. The following comparisons may be used:

- With previous years for the same company. Published financial statements always show one previous year, but a comparison over a number of years is more valuable. Listed companies show five years of figures
- With other (similar) companies
- With other divisions or branches within the same company
- With stock market or sector averages
- With market levels; a return on shareholders' funds may be compared with the general level of interest rates
- With policy: a company may have a policy of requiring credit customers to pay within 45 days
- With budgeted or planned results. This can indicate the success of management in implementing their plans and achieving the intended results.

Limitations of ratio analysis

The main limitations of ratio analysis are as follows:

- What basis for comparison should be used? To know that a company's inventory turnover ratio is 64 days does not mean much, except by comparison. Is it better or worse than last year? Or than planned? Or than a similar company? Inventory turnover of more than a few weeks would be unacceptable for a fresh food business but might be quite good in a gift shop.
- Comparisons may be limited where companies have different accounting policies. Some companies may capitalize on software or development expenditures, whereas others write them off as expenses immediately. There may be differences in approaches to the depreciation of non-current assets. Some companies' accounting policies are more prudent than others, and some may indulge in 'creative accounting'.
- Comparisons may be limited where companies have different financing policies. Some companies rely more aggressively on overdrafts and short-term borrowing, others rely more conservatively on long-term borrowing, and others have little or no borrowing. Some companies own most of their non-current assets; others lease them (which show up in the financial statements); others used to lease them as operating leases under IAS 17 (which do not show up in the financial statements). However, IFRS 16, which supersedes IAS 17, eliminates the classification of leases as either operating leases or finance leases for a lessee. Some companies spend substantially on non-current assets every year; others have major expenditures only every three, five, or ten years. Some companies sell on a cash-only basis; others sell partly or mainly on credit. Ratio analysis shows many of these differences, but care is needed in interpretation, for example, where a company changes its policy in a particular year (e.g. reducing short-term debt by issuing shares or debentures).
- Comparisons may be limited where companies have different policies to achieve growth. Where internal growth is pursued, there may be substantial investments in non-current assets in a particular year that do not earn their keep at first. Where external growth is pursued, substantial amounts may be paid for goodwill in acquiring other companies, with a subsequent charge for impairment; and there may be substantial one-off benefits from rationalization (e.g. closing down operations in some locations where there is duplication).

- Comparisons may be limited where companies have different operating policies. Some companies do most of their manufacturing in the UK (and so have substantial amounts of non-current assets); others subcontract their manufacturing, perhaps to overseas companies, and so have less money tied up in non-current assets. Some companies produce only for specific orders, or in batches, while others have mass production of standard items: this is likely to affect profit margins and stock levels.
- Comparisons may be limited where companies have different accounting dates, especially in seasonal businesses. Retailers with a year end a few weeks before Christmas are likely to have substantial inventories and trade payables shown on their statements of financial position and perhaps some short-term liquidity problems. The statement of the financial position of a retailer a few weeks after Christmas is likely to show lower inventory levels and more liquid resources.
- Results may be influenced substantially in particular years by 'exceptional items', such as losses incurred in closing down a production facility, or profits made in selling particular non-current assets (especially land and buildings).
- Statements of financial position show the position only on a given date. They are not necessarily typical for the whole year. Some companies indulge in 'window dressing' to try to make the position look better at the year end when the financial statements are published.
- Statements of financial position are usually based on historical cost, and the amounts shown for assets are not necessarily their current values. Some non-current assets are revalued from time to time, and in comparing results with different companies, we cannot always be sure that we are comparing like with like. The amount shown for 'equity' on a statement of financial position does not usually reflect the current value of the assets; nor does it indicate the market value of the equity (the 'market capitalization') on the stock market.
- Most of the information included in financial statements is for the business as a whole and so most ratios are an average for the business. Some parts of it are likely to be performing much better than others. Companies produce some 'disaggregated' or 'segmental' information about different parts of the business, but this is rather limited.
- Financial statements do not normally show the effects of inflation. A company's sales and profits may increase every year, but a 3 per cent increase is not an indication of success if the inflation rate is 4 per cent.
- Financial statements and their analysis are based on information relating to the past; much of it is inevitably out of date. And the past is not necessarily a guide to the future.
- Ratio analysis is usually limited to the information that companies are required to show in their published annual reports. There is likely to be a great deal of other information, financial and non-financial, that would be important in evaluating the financial position and performance of a company.

4.8 Ratios Ready Reference

The ratios in **Examples 4.3** and **4.4** are illustrated, taking the figures from the financial statements of Garwick Ltd for year 7. **Activity 4.6** lists these ratios and invites readers to calculate the equivalent ratios for year 8 and comment on them. A solution is provided at the end of the book.

Example 4.3

Statement of financial position of Garwick Ltd as at 31 December	Year 7 £000	Year 8 £000
Assets		
Non-current assets		
Property, plant and equipment	50	60
Current assets		
Inventories	10	13
Trade receivables	14	16
Cash	18	1
	42	30
Total assets	92	90
Liabilities and equity		
Current liabilities		
Trade payables	17	20
Non-current liabilities		
Long-term borrowing	40	30
Total liabilities	57	50
Equity		
Share capital	20	20
Retained earnings	15	20
Total equity	35	40
Total liabilities and equity	92	90

Example 4.4

Income statement of Garwick Ltd for the year ended 31 December	Year 7 £000	Year 8 £000
Revenue	101	110
Cost of sales	(70)	(74)
Gross profit	31	36

Income statement of Garwick Ltd for the year ended 31 December	Year 7 £000	Year 8 £000
Distribution costs	(7)	(7)
Administrative expenses	(5)	(6)
Operating profit	19	23
Finance costs	(4)	(3)
Profit before tax	15	20
Income tax expense	(4)	(5)
Profit for the period	11	15

Statement of changes in equity of Garwick Ltd for the year ended 31 December		
Balance at the beginning of year	32	35
Profit for the period	11	15
Dividends	(8)	(10)
Balance at the end of year	35	40

Additional information

Garwick Ltd's share capital consists of 100,000 ordinary shares with a nominal value of 20p each. Although the company is too small to be listed on a stock market, for this question, assume that the share price on 31 December year 7 was £1.87, and on 31 December year 8, it was £2.85.

Four financial strength/solvency ratios

1 Current ratio (or working capital ratio)

Current assets : Current liabilities
£42,000 : £17,000
2.47 : 1

2 Quick ratio (or acid test)

Current assets excluding inventories : Current liabilities
£32,000 : £17,000
1.88 : 1

3 Capital gearing ratio (financial gearing or leverage)

$$\frac{\text{Long-term borrowings}}{\text{Equity plus long-term borrowings}} \times 100$$

$$\frac{\pounds 40{,}000}{\pounds 40{,}000 + \pounds 35{,}000} \times 100 = 53.3\%$$

4 Interest times cover

$$\frac{\text{Profit before deducting interest}}{\text{Interest}} \quad \frac{£19{,}000}{£4{,}000} = 4.75 \text{ times}$$

Four overall profitability ratios

5 Return on shareholders' funds

$$\frac{\text{Profit for the period}}{\text{Total equity}} \times 100 \quad \frac{£11{,}000}{£35{,}000} \times 100 = 31.4\%$$

6 Return on total long-term capital employed

$$\frac{\text{Operating profit*}}{\text{Total equity plus long-term borrowings}} \times 100 \quad \times 100 = 25.3\% \ \frac{£19{,}000}{£75{,}000}$$

* Profit before deducting tax and interest, or EBIT, or gross profit minus operating expenses.

7 Operating profit as a percentage of sales (or profit/sales ratio)

$$\frac{\text{Operating profit}}{\text{Sales}} \times 100 \quad \frac{£19{,}000}{£101{,}000} \times 100 = 18.8\%$$

8 Asset turnover

$$\frac{\text{Sales}}{\text{Operating assets*}} \quad = 1.35 \text{ times} \ \frac{£101{,}000}{£75{,}000}$$

* Non-current assets plus current assets minus current liabilities. This is the same as equity plus non-current liabilities.

Three profitability of sales ratios

9 Gross profit ratio

$$\frac{\text{Gross profit}}{\text{Sales}} \times 100 \quad \frac{£31{,}000}{£101{,}000} \times 100 = 30.7\%$$

10 Distribution costs as a percentage of sales

$$\frac{\text{Distribution costs}}{\text{Sales}} \times 100 \quad \frac{£7{,}000}{£101{,}000} \times 100 = 6.9\%$$

11 Administrative expenses as a percentage of sales

$$\frac{\text{Administrative expenses}}{\text{Sales}} \times 100 \quad \frac{£5{,}000}{£101{,}000} \times 100 = 5\%$$

Five utilization of assets ratios

12 Sales/non-current assets

$$\frac{\text{Sales}}{\text{Non-current assets}} \quad \frac{£101{,}000}{£50{,}000} = 2.02 \text{ times}$$

13 Sales/current assets

$$\frac{\text{Sales}}{\text{Current assets}} \quad \frac{£101{,}000}{£42{,}000} = 2.4 \text{ times}$$

14 Inventory turnover ratio

$$\frac{\text{Inventories}}{\text{Cost of sales}} \times 365 \qquad \frac{\pounds10{,}000}{\pounds70{,}000} \times 365 = 52.1 \text{ days}$$

15 Trade receivables ratio

$$\frac{\text{Trade receivables}}{\text{Sales}} \times 365 \qquad \frac{\pounds14{,}000}{\pounds101{,}000} \times 365 = 50.6 \text{ days}$$

16 Trade payables ratio

$$\frac{\text{Trade payables}}{\text{Cost of sales}} \times 365 \qquad \frac{\pounds17{,}000}{\pounds70{,}000} \times 365 = 88.6 \text{ days}$$

Four stock market ratios

17 Price/earnings ratio (P/E ratio)

$$\frac{\text{Share price}}{\text{Earnings per share}} \qquad P/E = 17\ \frac{\pounds1.87}{\pounds0.11}$$

18 Dividend yield

$$\frac{\text{Dividend}}{\text{Share price}} \times 100 \qquad \frac{8p}{\pounds1.87} \times 100 = 4.3\%$$

19 Dividend cover

$$\frac{\text{Earnings per share}}{\text{Dividend per share}} \text{ or } \frac{\text{Profit for the period}}{\text{Dividends for the period}}$$

$$\frac{11}{8} \text{ or } \frac{\pounds11{,}000}{\pounds8{,}000} = 1.4\% \text{ times}$$

20 Net assets per share (statement of financial position value per share)

$$\frac{\text{Total equity}}{\text{Number of shares}} = \pounds0.35 \text{ per share } \frac{\pounds35{,}000}{100{,}000}$$

Activity 4.6

Calculate the ratios for Garwick Ltd for year 8 and comment on them.

Ratio	Year 7	Year 8	Comment
1 Current ratio	2.47 : 1		
2 Quick ratio	1.88 : 1		
3 Capital gearing ratio	53.3%		
4 Interest cover	4.75 times		
5 Return on shareholders' funds	31.4%		
6 Return on total long-term capital employed	25.3%		
7 Operating profit as a percentage of sales	18.8%		
8 Asset turnover	1.35 times		

Ratio	Year 7	Year 8	Comment
9 Gross profit ratio	30.7%		
10 Distribution costs as a percentage of sales	6.9%		
11 Administrative expenses as a percentage of sales	5%		
12 Sales/non-current assets	2.02 times		
13 Sales/current assets	2.4 times		
14 Inventory turnover ratio	52 days		
15 Trade receivables ratio	51 days		
16 Trade payables ratio	89 days		
17 Price/earnings ratio	17		
18 Dividend yield	4.3%		
19 Dividend cover	1.4 times		
20 Net assets per share	£0.35		

Summary

There are a number of conventional ratios that can be calculated from statements of financial position and income statements that give a good indication of a company's solvency and profitability. Care is needed in selecting and interpreting the most appropriate figures, and the exercise is more useful if comparisons are made over a number of years. Companies need to be solvent to survive. But profitability is also important and is best indicated using figures for ROCE. Careful analysis of gross profit, operating profit and various costs as a percentage of sales can indicate where improvements may be made. But utilization of assets is also an essential part of profitability: there should not be excessive assets in relation to the amount of sales generated. Ratio analysis also provides useful insights into the management of working capital and financial structure. Accounting ratios often raise as many questions as they answer but are a valuable tool of analysis, particularly in making comparisons, provided their limitations are recognized.

There is no limit to the number of ratios that can be calculated. This chapter has concentrated on a few key questions and a total of 20 widely used ratios that help answer those questions.

Review of key points

- The ratio calculations and their evaluation are broadly categorized as: profitability, liquidity, efficiency, financial gearing (or leverage) and stock market ratios.
- There are two main ways of calculating ROCE; each can be used to assess a company's profitability and how it might be improved.
- One side of ROCE can be used to assess all costs as a proportion of sales.

- The second side of ROCE can be used to assess the utilization of each group of assets by relating them to sales.
- The current ratio, quick ratio, capital gearing ratio and interest cover can be used to assess a company's solvency, but care is needed in calculating and interpreting them.
- Stock market ratios can be used to assess how expensive shares are in relation to the most recent levels of earnings, dividends and net asset values.
- The chapter is based on 20 widely used ratios and provides opportunities to practise calculating and interpreting them.
- Accounting ratios are most useful when used in making comparisons, but care is needed in comparing different types of business and in realizing the limitations of the figures.
- Published financial statements often contain a lot of detail that is hard to understand; it is important to be clear about key questions, to select the most appropriate figures and to focus on those.

Self-testing questions

1 Describe how to calculate:
   a current ratio;
   b quick ratio;
   c capital gearing ratio;
   d interest cover.

2 Why are inventories excluded from current assets when calculating the quick ratio?

3 How is the return on ordinary shareholders' capital employed calculated?

4 If debentures are included as part of capital employed, what figure is used for 'return'? How and why does it differ from the 'return' figure used for calculating the return on ordinary shareholders' capital employed?

5 If a company's gross profit ratio has increased, what does that tell us about the volume of sales and selling prices?

6 You are given the following statement of financial position information about the Nikkigra Company. You are required to comment on the financial position and performance of the company, making use of appropriate ratios.

Statement of financial position of Nikkigra as at 31 December

	Year 1 £000	Year 2 £000
Assets		
Non-current assets		
Property, plant and equipment	1,000	900
Current assets		
Inventories	1,200	1,000
Trade receivables	600	500
Cash	68	600
	1,868	2,100

Statement of financial position of Nikkigra as at 31 December

	Year 1 £000	Year 2 £000
Total assets	2,868	3,000
Liabilities and equity		
Current liabilities		
Trade payables	294	451
Taxation	60	65
Interest payable	80	84
	434	600
Non-current liabilities		
10% debentures	1,000	900
Total liabilities	1,434	1,500
Equity		
Ordinary 50p shares	1,000	1,000
Retained earnings	434	500
Total equity	1,434	1,500
Total liabilities and equity	2,868	3,000

Income statement of Nikkigra for the year ended 31 December

	Year 1	Year 2
Revenue	3,600	3,780
Cost of sales	3,225	3,396
Gross profit	375	384
Distribution costs	(50)	(48)
Administrative expenses	(30)	(31)
Operating profit	295	305
Finance costs: interest	(100)	(90)
Profit before tax	195	215
Income tax expense	(60)	(65)
Profit for the period	135	150

Statement of changes in equity of Nikkigra for the year ended 31 December

	Year 1	Year 2
Balance at beginning of year	1,379	1,434
Profit for the period	135	150
Dividends	(80)	(84)
Balance at end of year	1,434	1,500

Assessment questions

1 Why would you expect retailers to have lower current ratios than manufacturers?

2 What information (in addition to the current ratio, quick ratio, capital gearing ratio and interest cover) would you want to assess a company's solvency?

3 Accounting ratios are said to be most useful when making comparisons. If you had a set of ratios for a company, what comparisons would you make?

4 What are the main limitations of accounting ratios?

5 How could a company increase its profitability when sales are falling (assuming that it is unable to increase sales)?

6 You are given the following statement of financial position information about Jackdan Ltd. You are required to comment on the financial position and performance of the company, making use of appropriate ratios.

Statement of financial position of Jackdan Ltd as at 31 December

	Year 1 £000	Year 2 £000
Assets		
Non-current assets		
Property, plant and equipment	300	330
Current assets		
Inventories	70	90
Trade receivables	50	70
Cash	30	40
	150	200
Total assets	450	530
Liabilities and equity		
Current liabilities		
Trade payables	38	45
Taxation	32	40
Interest payable	30	35
	100	120
Non-current liabilities		
8% debentures	100	150
Total liabilities	200	270
Equity		
Ordinary 50p shares	200	200
Retained earnings	50	60
Total equity	250	260
Total liabilities and equity	450	530

Income statement of Jackdan Ltd for the year ended 31 December

	Year 1 £000	Year 2 £000
Revenue	492	550
Cost of sales	(369)	(410)
Gross profit	123	140
Distribution costs	(12)	(12)
Administrative expenses	(10)	(9)
Operating profit	101	119
Finance costs: interest	(8)	(12)
Profit before tax	93	107
Income tax expense	(32)	(40)
Profit for the period	61	67

Statement of changes in equity of Jackdan Ltd for the year ended 31 December

Balance at beginning of year	239	250
Profit for the period	61	67
Dividends	(50)	(57)
Balance at end of year	250	260

Group activities and discussion questions

1 Which is more important: increasing return on capital employed (ROCE) or increasing earnings per share (EPS), and why? Can a company increase its EPS year after year, although its ROCE is steadily falling?

2 In what circumstances can a substantial improvement in a company's position result in a reduction in its ROCE?

3 In what circumstances can a steady increase in a company's ROCE be a symptom of a company being in decline?

4 Many companies' profitability is lower than it should be because they have too much money tied up in assets. They should aim to have a zero level of assets. This would lead to a ROCE of infinity. Discuss the practicability of these suggestions.

5 Most efforts to reduce the amount of funds tied up in assets are wasted because one type of asset is turned into another: inventories and surplus buildings become receivables and cash. The total capital employed and the total profitability are unaffected. Discuss the validity of these statements.

6 The Executive Service Company has high levels of inventory and impressive premises; their sales/net assets ratio is 1 : 1. The QuickValue Service Company has low levels of inventory and back-street premises; their sales/net assets ratio is 2 : 1. Does that mean that the QuickValue Service Company is more profitable?

Making use of the above scenario, discuss the idea that the use of ratios shows the effects of companies choosing to do business in different ways and that ratios do not indicate how businesses should be run.

Accounting in context

Discuss and comment on the following report. Why must ratio analysis be considered in the context of the company's sector, wider issues affecting that sector and the company's main competitors?

Diploma plc, a UK-based company listed on the FTSE 100

At the end of September 2023, Diploma had a market capitalization of £4.46bn with an EPS of £0.88. The market price during the year had a low of £22.22 to a high of £30.34 per share and organic revenue growth of 8 per cent.

Diploma plc, a UK-based company listed on the FTSE 100, boasts a highly diversified portfolio across three key segments: Controls, Seals, and Life Sciences. Its Life Sciences Sector is dedicated to supplying healthcare markets, while its Seals Sector serves customers in the realm of heavy mobile machinery and specialized industrial equipment. Finally, the Controls Sector provides advanced technical applications to a range of industries.

The key to Diploma's successful business model is increasing sales growth ahead of costs, inflating margins in the process. In 2023, the adjusted operating margin increased to 19.7 per cent from 18.9 per cent, with an average over five years of 18 per cent.

Over the past decade, adjusted earnings have grown at a compound annual rate of nearly 14 per cent. Basic earnings per share is 90.8p (2022: 76.1p). Diluted earnings per share is 90.4p (2022: 75.9p).

The organic revenue growth of the company decreased to 8 per cent last year as the initial surge after COVID-19 began to fade. This year, the growth rate is expected to further decrease to 5 per cent. The company is not relying on price inflation to drive growth. In Q4 of the previous year, the organic revenue growth was 7 per cent, which included 5 per cent from volumes and 2 per cent from inflation. The company's shares are currently trading at 24 times forward earnings, which is not cheap according to the conventional London market standards, but is in line with the long-running average.

The company's impressive track record of making smart acquisitions may convince investors that it has the potential to continue inflating its margins in the future. Acquisitions typically contribute to half of the total revenue growth. During the year, the company has also completed 10 bolt-on acquisitions for £33m, at an average earnings before interest and tax (EBIT) multiple of under 5x and which generated a 20 per cent return on capital employed.

Since 30 September 2022, Diploma plc have acquired 12 high-quality businesses for a total of £280m. Organic growth of 8 per cent was driven by strong volumes. Acquisitions, net of a small disposal, contributed 8 per cent to reported revenue while foreign exchange translation added a further 3 per cent.

In 2023, Diploma plc reported a dividend of 0.57 GBP, which represents a 5.02 per cent increase over last year.

In 2023, Diploma plc increased its cash reserves by 49.64 per cent, or £20.70m. The company earned £189.20m from its operations for a cash flow margin of 15.76 per cent. In addition, the company generated £107.50m cash from financing while £270.90m was spent on investing; together with a £235m equity-raising this has helped to cut the financial gearing ratio from 40 per cent to 33.3 per cent.

ADVICE - To buy the shares of Diploma plc or hold as there is potential for more margin growth.

Sources:

https://www.diplomaplc.com/media/dg113jzb/diploma_2023-annual-report.pdf

https://www.diplomaplc.com/media/ec0levkn/diploma-plc-fy-2023-presentation.pdf

https://markets.ft.com/data/equities/tearsheet/profile?s=DPLM:LSE

E. Powell (2023) Diploma Market Cap £4.46bn Organic Revenue Growth 8%, *The Times*, 21 November.

References and further reading

Lewis, R., Pendrill, D. and Simon, D. (2004) *Advanced Financial Accounting* (7th edn.). Harlow: FT Prentice Hall.

McKenzie, W. (2010) *Financial Times Guide to Using and Interpreting Company Accounts* (4th edn.). Harlow: FT Prentice Hall.

Melville, A. (2017) *International Financial Reporting* (6th edn.). Harlow: Pearson.

Sugden, A., Gee, P. and Holmes, G. (2008) *Interpreting Company Reports and Accounts* (10th edn.). Harlow: FT Prentice Hall.

www.cifc.co.uk (select: benchmarking and interfirm comparison; a standardised basis for using ratios to compare different firms).

Chapter 5

How the Stock Market Assesses Company Performance

Chapter contents

5.1 Introduction
5.2 Investing in Shares
5.3 What Influences Share Prices?
5.4 Accounting Information and Share Prices
5.5 The *Financial Times*
5.6 Price/Earnings (P/E) Ratios
5.7 Dividend Yield
5.8 Dividend Cover
5.9 Net Asset (or Statement of Financial Position) Value
5.10 Cash Flow
5.11 Other Indicators/Predictors of Performance
5.12 A Further Illustration

Learning objectives

After studying this chapter you will be able to:

- ✓ Discuss various factors that influence share prices
- ✓ Understand the main information shown by the *Financial Times* London Share Service
- ✓ Calculate and interpret P/E ratios, dividend yield and dividend cover
- ✓ Explain why cash flows may influence share prices
- ✓ Understand the relationship between share prices and statement of financial position values
- ✓ Critically assess the possible influence of a variety of other factors on share prices

5.1 Introduction

The performance of companies' shares on the stock market is part of our everyday news agenda, but it isn't easy to be sure about what really influences share prices and why it is important. Share prices are determined by supply and demand for a company's shares, much like any other commodity on an open market. These are influenced by a number of factors, and the information revealed in financial accounts is perhaps the most important. It is easy to see which companies are doing well, but by the time this is obvious, their shares are usually already quite expensive; for example, Diploma plc's closing share price on 23 January 2024 was £32.96 whereas this share price was as low as £0.90 in 2009. Similarly, by the time a company's performance is obviously poor, the share price has already fallen. Unfortunately, this chapter cannot teach you how to 'beat the market', but it does a lot to explain what happens.

5.2 Investing in Shares

When we talk about investing in shares, we usually mean buying shares that are listed on the London Stock Exchange (LSE) or other leading international stock markets such as the New York Stock Exchange (NYSE), Euronext (pan-European), Nasdaq, Shanghai Stock Exchange and Toronto Stock Exchange. Currently, there are 60 major stock exchanges that vary in size, measured as market capitalization and trading volume. At the start of 2022, there were 5.5m private companies in the UK, most of them very small, typically with only about two shareholders; their shares are not available on any stock market. There are also many public companies, some quite large, which are also not listed on stock markets. Friends or family may invite you to buy shares in an unlisted company; you may set up your own company, and you may inherit some shares. But unless the company is a listed one, buying and selling the shares is usually difficult because there is no ready market.

The shares in listed companies are bought and sold frequently, sometimes every few minutes or seconds, on the stock market, and it is easy to buy and sell them. If you want to buy or sell shares in listed companies, you need to have a stockbroker; you could ask your bank to act for you, or you could register with a stockbroker who arranges for you to deal directly on the Internet. In the bull[1] market of the 1990s, many private individuals became 'day traders', buying and selling shares on the same day and making more profit than they could earn by working for a living. It is not difficult to make profits when share prices are rising.

Companies do not buy and sell shares themselves except when issuing additional shares, such as when there is a rights issue, as explained in **Chapter 15**. If you go to Marks & Spencer or Tesco and ask to buy some shares, you will be referred elsewhere. Shares are already in existence and, in effect, are bought and sold by investors (companies, institutions and individuals) via an established stock market, such as the London Stock Exchange. The price or current value of the shares is not calculated or determined by the company or individual. It constantly changes as a result of supply and demand for a particular company's shares. If demand for a share is very high, the price will be marked up; this will encourage some investors to sell their shares so that others can buy. When the price goes up too high, demand for the company's shares will slacken, and an equilibrium is reached. If a company's shares are not in demand, the price will fall until some investors decide that the shares have become good value.

Sometimes, there are exaggerated short-term effects on share prices. If there is a rumour that there will soon be a takeover bid for a particular company, demand for those shares might increase rapidly until the situation is resolved. When a company has some bad news, or there is bad news from comparable companies, there might be a sudden, exaggerated decrease in the share price, which may prove to be only temporary.

[1] A bull market is when share prices are rising; a bear market is when share prices are falling.

5.3 What Influences Share Prices?

Many different factors influence share prices. Some factors might relate to the company alone, such as those listed above, while others have nothing directly to do with the company itself but have more to do with general sentiments about investing and the economy. Such factors include expectations about interest rates, growth or recession in the economy, and exchange rates. To some extent, stock markets in different countries move in line with each other, and it often seems that the UK stock market follows that of the USA.

The most widely used measure of share price performance is the FTSE 100 ('Footsie'). This is the *Financial Times* index[2] of the share prices of the 100 largest companies, based on their market capitalization. The FTSE 250 covers the next 250 largest companies, and the FTSE All Share is the index for all listed companies. The constituent companies of the index change slightly on a regular basis as the value of their shares changes or when two of the companies in the list of 100 merges, leaving a vacancy. **From the first launch of the FTSE 100 in 1984, the price return from 1984 to 2022 was 645 per cent, with the total return over double that, at 1515 per cent.** But on an annualized basis, it shows a price return of 5.4 per cent and a total return of 7.48 per cent. By January 2024, the FTSE 100 was observed trading at 7486, giving a 1-year return of -6.57 per cent. The FTSE 100 is inexpensive, not only in absolute terms but also from a historical perspective. For example, the average PE multiple on Nasdaq is three times that of the FTSE 100; companies such as Shell are trading at nearly 29 per cent discount to its competitor ExxonMobil.

Since 2016, the UK market has experienced a significant decrease in its value as investors have become increasingly cautious about the impact of Brexit and political instability. Both domestic and international investors have reduced their investments in the UK, leading to a decrease in the overall market exposure. This trend has been more pronounced in the mid and small-cap sectors, where companies have seen their valuations shrink.

The FTSE 100 is widely used, and some 'tracker' investment funds simply buy shares in the companies that make up the index; the performance of these funds is often better than funds where the managers use their own expertise to select the best investments. Inclusion, or non-inclusion, in the index can affect a company's share price. It may be partly a matter of prestige and status. It is also a result of increased demand for shares that are going into the index; the managers of tracker funds have to buy them. When companies are about to be removed from the index (because of a relative fall in their market capitalization), the share price is hit by the need for tracker funds to sell those shares.

Investing in the stock market can be tricky, and various factors often influence a company's share price. One key factor is the performance of other companies in the same industry. For example, if one retailer reports poor financial results, it is likely that other retailers will also experience a decline in their stock prices. Similarly, in 2011, bank shares were negatively impacted by the recession and the Greek economy's collapse. However, bank shares managed to recover later that year. It is important to keep in mind that certain sectors may become more or less popular with investors over time, so it is essential to stay informed and make informed investment decisions.

Various factors affect a company's share price, some of which are related to the company itself. The company's solvency and profitability fundamentals, as well as its growth, are important. Additionally, the perceived quality of management can also have an impact on share prices. If a company has gone through a rough patch, the CEO may lose trust and credibility, sometimes leading to their replacement. A new CEO's appointment can lead to a rise in the company's share price and the CEO's popularity due to investors anticipating improved performance. Other factors that affect share prices include the company's reputation, as well as both actual and supposed takeover bids. Additionally, rumours, speculation, scandal and gossip can also influence share prices.

[2] The index is calculated by taking the average share prices of the 100 largest companies on the LSE. The index is 'weighted' so that the largest companies have most influence on the index.

Investing in shares involves a certain level of risk as it is impossible to predict the future of share prices. There are two types of risks when it comes to investing in shares. The first one is systematic risk, which is associated with the overall market conditions. The second one is unsystematic risk, which is linked to the performance of individual companies. However, it is possible to minimize unsystematic risk by creating a balanced portfolio of shares from different companies.

There may be individuals who really understand how the various factors operate and affect share prices. If such individuals exist, they are likely to keep their advice to themselves, act on it and become extremely rich. When you read advice from investment analysts, bankers and other 'professionals', you may be tempted to believe them. But you might also wonder why they are giving you this advice or selling it to you so cheaply. Why do they not simply take their own advice and make more money that way?

There are a number of possible explanations for this:

- Investment analysts are fair-minded individuals, solely interested in pursuing the truth, with no interest in making money for themselves and with more interest in helping others to make money.
- They do not really know. Like journalists, they are just writing for a living and putting out any credible stories for which they get paid.
- For some reason, they want you to follow their advice and buy and sell shares when they suggest that you should.

There are infamous tales of financial journalists who offered to share tips with readers. They would choose a company with a credible story about its future prospects; then they would buy themselves a few thousand shares at the current price, say £1 each. Then, they would recommend readers of the *Daily Whatsit* to buy the shares at £1 each. Once such a recommendation is published (unless it is total rubbish), the share price is likely to go up immediately - even prior to publication. By the time the poor readers of the *Daily Whatsit* get their shares, the price has gone up to, say, £1.10, and they are likely to stay at this increased level for at least a few days. The journalists then sell their shares at, say, £1.10, having made a nice little profit. They can then boast to readers that the share price increased as they predicted it would. Financial journalists may be influential enough to cause temporary price increases, but readers receive the advice too late to act on it. Some might argue that the market is too 'efficient' for individuals to influence share prices. But if we are talking about a major investment bank or the chief executive of the company concerned, what they say and what is reported in the financial press may have a significant effect on share prices.

At any one time, there are likely to be hundreds or thousands of theories around about which shares are going to do particularly well in the future. Some of those theories will prove to be correct, while most will be quietly forgotten.

Most investors want to buy shares when they are cheap and sell them when they are expensive. If you think that the true value of a particular share is £2, and you can buy it for £1.80, then it seems 'cheap', and you might buy some. If, soon after buying them, you still think that they are worth £2 each, but the market price has risen to £2.20, it seems 'dear', and you would make a decent profit by selling. The problem is determining what a share is really worth.

Unfortunately, there is no 'true value' with which the market price of shares can be compared. It does not mean much to say that a share with a market value of £2.50 is cheaper than a share with a market value of £3. We can, however, say that a share price is expensive or cheap in relation to key information such as the amount of earnings, dividends or net assets per share.

5.4 Accounting Information and Share Prices

Investors and investment analysts make their investment decisions and recommendations using financial accounting information, and whatever other relevant and/or credible information they are able to find. Share prices reflect the information that is available to investors, and financial accounting information is central to this. Share prices may be influenced by any information that a company discloses, but the most important figures are probably:

- The profits earned by a company;
- The dividends paid out by the company;
- The net asset (or statement of financial position) value of the company;
- The cash flows generated by the company.

Each of these can be related to the most recent share price that gives an indication of whether a share is 'expensive' or 'cheap' in relation to that information. Investors are guided by the most recent figures for each of these; predictions are also sometimes available, which is what investors really need but predictions have varying degrees of credibility and should be compared with the actual results when they become available.

Profits

From the shareholder's point of view, the most relevant profit is the amount that was earned for them in the most recent financial year. It is the figure after all expenses, including interest and any exceptional items, have been deducted, and after charging taxation for the year. It usually has a straightforward label such as 'profit for the year', and that is the amount that has been earned for the shareholders during the year. Some of it is paid out, or distributed, as dividends; the rest remains in the business and becomes part of the retained earnings shown on the statement of financial position.

If there are preference shareholders, then part of the profit earned for the year belongs to them; preference dividends have to be deducted from profits for the year to arrive at the amount earned for ordinary shareholders. The key difference between the ordinary shareholders and the preferred shareholders is that the latter has no voting rights, while the former does.

There is a relationship between the value of a company, and the amount of profits that the company earns. If a company earns £1m a year, the company might be worth, say, £10m or £15m. The relationship is called the 'price[3]/earnings ratio', which, in this example, would be 10 or 15. It can be calculated by relating the company's *total* earnings for the year to the *total* market value for all of its shares.[4] Alternatively, it can be calculated by relating the earnings *per share* to the market price *per share*.

Dividends

Some shareholders, particularly those like the elderly who buy shares for income, are more interested in the dividends that a company actually pays out than in how much profit the company makes. If a shareholder needs the income, profits are all very well, but it is the cash dividend that the shareholder actually receives that helps to pay the bills.

[3] The 'price' is the price of one share: in this example it is worth 10 or 15 times the amount of profits earned per share.

[4] The total market value of all the shares is called the market capitalization.

Companies usually declare dividends in pence per share, perhaps 4p per share. This means that the shareholders receive a 4p dividend for each share that they own. The amount varies from year to year, and companies usually try to increase it a little each year.

A company usually pays a dividend twice a year: an 'interim' dividend in the year and a 'final' dividend early in the following year. But the dividends can be paid annually or quarterly. The shareholders are most interested in the total amount for the year. A shareholder who owns 1,000 shares in a company and a company has announced a 5 pence dividend would receive a payment of £50. A company may also pay a much larger one-off dividend called a 'special dividend' to its shareholders.

Dividend yield

Dividend yield measures the relationship between the value of a company's shares and the amount of dividend paid. If a company pays a dividend of 4p per share and each share is worth, say, £1, then the 'dividend yield' is 4 per cent (4p/100p expressed as a per cent). If the share price increased to £2, the dividend yield would fall to 2 per cent. The dividend yield is usually calculated by showing the most recent annual dividend per share (interim plus final) as a percentage of the current share price. The same dividend yield figure would be produced if the company's total dividends for the year are expressed as a percentage of the company's market capitalization.

Dividend times cover

There is also an important relationship between the amount of profits a company earns and the amount that they choose to pay out as a dividend. If a company pays out a lot less than half of its profits as dividends, then the dividend looks reasonably secure: the dividend is well covered by profits. If a company pays out nearly all its profits as dividends, then the dividend looks less secure. Analysts divide the profit by the dividend and say, for example, that the dividend is covered 1.6 times by profits. If a company earned £100m profits, and paid out £62.5m as dividends, then the dividend is covered 1.6[5] times by profits.

Dividend cover[6] can be calculated using earnings and dividend figures for the company as a whole or on a per share basis. Shareholders who invest in shares because they are particularly interested in dividends will be attracted to those with a relatively low dividend cover, while those shareholders who are more interested in long-term growth in share price would be more attracted to companies distributing a smaller proportion of their profits as a dividend, which therefore have a relatively high dividend cover.

Net asset (or statement of financial position) value

A company's statement of financial position clearly shows the amount for equity or shareholders' funds, which is the same as the amount for 'net assets'. Net assets are calculated as the difference between total assets and total liabilities. But the total value of the company's shares on the stock market is likely to be very different from what the statement of financial position shows. Share prices result from the interplay of supply and demand for shares, rather than from recording financial transactions within the business. If a company's prospects are seen to be very good, there is a strong demand for the shares, and the share price tends to increase. Generally, with a successful company, the market price of the shares is much higher than the net asset value per share (based on statement of financial position values).

---

[5] £62.5 × 1.6 = £100m.

[6] Dividend cover should not be confused with interest cover.

Cash flows

Many analysts do not rely on profit information alone, but also analyse the company's cash flow statement, and are likely to have more confidence in a company that has healthy cash flows.

5.5 The *Financial Times*

The *Financial Times* shows key figures and ratios with respect to each listed company on the LSE[7] on a daily basis. On Tuesdays to Saturdays, the P/E ratio and the dividend yield are shown for each company, together with various other information (see **Illustration 5.1**, which provides information from the banking sector).

ILLUSTRATION 5.1

			52 weeks				
1	2	3	4	5	6	7	8
Stock	Closing price (pence) on previous day	Change in price (pence) since previous day	High	Low	Dividend yield (Y/d) %	P/E	Volume in 000s
Barclays '✠'	147.34	+0.56	198.86	128.12	5.23	4.36	28,479.04
HSBC '✠'	604.90	+6.10	665.60	512.30	5.38	6.41	147,760.87
LlydsBkg '✠'	42.16	−0.91	54.33	39.42	5.98	4.48	34,178.63
Natwest Group '✠'	217.60	+3.70	310.00	168.00	7.12	4.47	24,352.02

Source: Adapted from *Financial Times* Share Service, Thursday 25 January 2024.

1 Name of company, usually abbreviated.
2 Share price at the close of business on the previous day (average or the closing mid-price).[8]
3 The amount by which the share price changed during the previous day.
4 The highest the share price has been during the previous 52 weeks.
5 The lowest the share price has been during the previous 52 weeks.
6 Shows the percentage return on the shares. It is calculated as the latest known dividend per share expressed as a percentage of the share price.
7 Price earning ratio (P/E): expresses the relationship between the share price and the latest known profit, or earnings, per share. The dividend yield and P/E ratio move in opposite directions: if the share price increases, as the dividend remains constant, the dividend yield falls; and at the same time, as earnings per share remain constant, the P/E ratio increases.
8 Volume: the number of shares traded on the previous day in thousands.
9 Various notes. For example, the '✠' symbol indicates that the company is among the FT Global 500 companies. A '†' symbol indicates that the interim dividend has been increased or resumed since the previous year. A heart symbol indicates that the stock is not officially registered in the UK.

[7] Comparable information is shown on preceding pages for many other shares and markets in the world.
[8] There is always a 'spread' between the buying price and selling price: the mid-point is shown.

All the above four banking companies' shares are among the top 100 companies of the FTSE 100 index and included in the FT500 index of the world's largest companies. We can access the latest annual report of companies in the *Financial Times* Share Service or via the company's website.

On the day that the figures in **Illustration 5.1** were published,[9] the average yield for the FTSE 100 companies was 3.97 per cent, dividend cover was 2.43 times, and the average P/E ratio was 10.38.

In **Illustration 5.1**, we can see that Barclays, Lloyds, and the Natwest Group have very similar P/E ratios. However, all four banks have rather lower P/E ratios than the stock market average. Barclays' P/E ratio is lower than the other three companies, indicating a lower expectation in the market in the future than of the other three companies. It makes sense to use the P/E ratio to compare similar companies in the same industrial sector.

On Mondays, as there was no previous day's trading, the *Financial Times* provides some different information, mainly market capitalization, as shown in **Illustration 5.2**.

ILLUSTRATION 5.2

1	2	3	4	5	6	7	8
Stock	Closing price on Friday in pence	+/- Week	High – 52 weeks	Low – 52 weeks	Dividend yield %	P/E	Market capitalization, £m
Barclays '✠'	142.28	-8.44	198.86	128.12	5.41	4.21	27,265.32
HSBC '✠'	609.50	-4.60	665.60	512.30	5.34	6.46	147,123.89
LlydsBkg '✠'	41.40	-0.92	54.33	39.42	6.09	4.40	33,249.88
Natwest '✠' Group	210.7	-10.2	308.55	168.00	7.36	4.33	27,722.17

Source: Adapted from *Financial Times* Market Data, Monday 12 February 2024.

1 Name of company as above.
2 Price at the close of business on the previous Friday.
3 The weekly percentage change in the share price during the previous week.
4 The highest the share price has been during the previous 52 weeks.
5 The lowest the share price has been during the previous 52 weeks.
6 Shows the dividend yield. Note that in **Illustrations 5.1** and **5.2** the dividend yield is different as it is calculated as the ratio of dividends over the share price.
7 The P/E ratio is the market price of the share divided by the earnings per share for the past 12-month trading period.
8 Market capitalization: the share price multiplied by the number of shares that the company has in issue.
9 Previously, there used to be a column for the date when the share became 'ex-dividend'. This is no longer shown for company information.

On the date that these figures were published,[10] the average dividend cover among FTSE 100 companies was 1.90 and dividend yield was 3.95 per cent.

[9] The FT extracts are from Thursday 25 January 2024.
[10] The FT extracts are from Monday 12 February 2024.

In **Illustration 5.2**, we can see that Natwest Group shares had the biggest increase during the week, and the dividend yield was the highest. What matters is the dividend yield: the dividend as a percentage of the share price. On this measure, Natwest Group looks the best since its dividend yield, at 7.36 per cent, is much higher than the other three companies.

The dividend cover indicates how safe the dividend is. The *Financial Times* Share Service does not provide dividend cover for individual companies, but it does provide dividend cover for the FTSE actuaries' share indices, such as the FTSE 100.

Market capitalization is a measure of a company's size. It is the current share price multiplied by the number of shares in issue. Using this measure, we can see that the four banks in **Illustration 5.2** are different in size. HSBC is the largest of the four banks, whereas Barclays, Lloyds, and Natwest Group are companies of approximately similar size. Other measures of a company's size include turnover, net assets value (statement of financial position), profits, and number of employees.

When a company declares a dividend, it is payable to all who own the shares on a particular date. Anyone buying the shares after that date will not receive the company's most recent proposed dividend. If the dividend is, say, 20p per share, we can expect the share price to drop by 20p on the day that it becomes ex-dividend. It is important to know the date that a share becomes ex-dividend (and the amount of the dividend) if we are to make sense of share price movements.

For information about net asset values and cash flows, it is necessary to look at the annual report and accounts; alternatively, information produced by investment analysts and in the financial press can be examined.

5.6 Price/Earnings (P/E) Ratios

Calculating the P/E ratio

The price/earnings (P/E) ratio is perhaps the most widely used stock market indicator. It shows clearly the relationship between the last known EPS figure and the most recent share price. **Example 5.1** shows how the P/E ratio can be calculated on a per share basis (note g) or for the company as a whole (note e).

What the P/E ratio can tell us

In **Example 5.1**, Cronky plc has a P/E ratio of 15. If we pay 300p for a share, and the company's earnings are 20p per share each year, the share will have paid for itself[11] in 15 years. That seems rather a long time for an investment to pay for itself. But the position with Voddy plc is even worse: it would take 20 years. These figures are not unusual. Currently, the average P/E ratio on the London Stock Market is about 10.38. This could mean that most shares are hopelessly overpriced. It is more likely to mean that investors expect EPS to increase significantly in the coming years. The share price looks high in relation to the previous year's earnings but (hopefully) not in relation to future earnings.

If share prices seem high, it is because demand for them is high, and if demand is high, it is usually because investors are optimistic about the future prospects of the company. Investors in Voddy plc do not assume that the EPS will remain at 16p for the next 20 years: they expect or demand *growth* in EPS.

[11] In terms of profit that the company earns, not in terms of dividends that the company pays out.

Example 5.1

		Cronky plc	Voddy plc
a	Number of ordinary shares	1,000,000	1,000,000
b	Current share price	£3.00	£3.20
c	Market capitalization (a × b)	£2,000,000	£3,200,000
d	Total profits after taxation attributable to ordinary shareholders	£200,000	£160,000
e	P/E ratio (c ÷ d)	15	20
f	EPS (d ÷ a)	£0.20	£0.16
g	P/E ratio (b ÷ f)	10	20

If earnings grow at a constant rate of 10 per cent per annum, they will double in less than eight years. If they grow at 15 per cent per annum, they will double in just less than five years. Not many companies manage to maintain such rates of growth in earnings, but they may be needed to justify high share prices, that is, to justify high P/E ratios. We can assume that, generally, a high P/E ratio means that investors are expecting high rates of growth, although they may, of course, be disappointed. In recent years, many share prices have been very high, with high P/E ratios, particularly in biotechnology, media and telecommunications, together with computing and anything vaguely connected with the dot-com bubble. However, many such companies failed to deliver the rapid growth in earnings that was needed to justify the high P/E ratios, and many high share prices crashed. Many investors jumped on the bandwagon of high P/E ratios, only to be disappointed. In recent years, more modest P/E ratios and more realistic expectations of growth were the order of the day and several years of steadily increasing share prices followed until the collapse in early 2009.

We can get a feel for P/E ratios by looking at the sectors with high P/Es table in the *Financial Times*. It gives the average for the London Stock Market as a whole, the average for the top 100 companies (the FTSE 100) and the average for about 35 different sectors. Currently, the average P/E ratio for the FTSE 100 is 10.38. Sectors with high P/Es included oil equipment, personal goods, technology, hardware and equipment and equity investment. Sectors with low P/Es included mining, automobiles and parts, mobile communications and electricity utilities.

We can generalize that high P/E ratios are associated with expectations of high rates of growth. If the average P/E is 10.38, then any company with a P/E of much more than about 15 is expected to deliver high rates of growth if investors are not to be disappointed. A company with a P/E of less than about 6 is expected to produce less growth in EPS.

Most companies have a P/E of between about 5 and 20. However, care is needed in interpreting these, especially if the P/E is unusually high or low. Sometimes, P/E ratios are abnormally high - so high as to be meaningless. In **Example 5.2**, Sudndip plc had four very successful years. Profit increased each year by more than 10 per cent and at an increasing rate. This raised expectations, and the P/E ratio went up from 12 to 18 during the period. Then, in year 5, earnings collapsed; EPS were minute. We could be fairly sure that the share price would collapse, too. Maybe it would go down to £1 or even to 80p. But with a tiny EPS figure, even at 80p, the P/E ratio would still be 160, which is so far out of the normal range as to be misleading. It still means that the share price is very high in relation to the latest EPS, but the explanation has more to do with exceptionally low earnings than it has to do with a high share price.

Example 5.2

Sudndip plc has 10 million ordinary shares in issue. Their total profits, after tax and EPS, are shown below. The share price and P/E ratio shortly after the results were published are also shown.

	Year 1	Year 2	Year 3	Year 4	Year 5
Net profit after tax	£1m	£1.1m	£1.25m	£1.45m	£50,000
EPS	£0.10	£0.11	£0.125	£0.145	£ 0.005
Share price	£1.20	£1.43	£1.87½	£2.61	
P/E ratio	12	13	15	18	

The drop in earnings shown in **Example 5.2** is rather extreme, but it is often the case that a high P/E ratio signifies that the previous year's earnings were unusually low and better results are expected soon.

Although International Financial Reporting Standards (IFRSs) lay down clear rules on how EPS should be calculated, it is not always clear which EPS figures have been used in calculating the P/E ratio, particularly in the financial press. Unusual P/E ratios are often the result of unusual earnings figures, such as exceptional profits or losses on the sale of a subsidiary or charges for the impairment of goodwill. Companies often produce two different EPS figures, choosing to exclude particular items for one of them. In the financial press, P/E ratios are sometimes quoted based on future forecast earnings that may be referred to as prospective or forward P/E ratios.

5.7 Dividend Yield

Calculating the dividend yield

The dividend yield is another widely used stock market indicator. It shows clearly the relationship between the last known amount of annual dividend and the most recent share price. It can be calculated on a 'per share' basis by dividing the most recent annual dividend by the most recent share price.[12] Alternatively, it can be calculated for the company as a whole by dividing the company's total dividends payable for the most recent year[13] by its 'market capitalization' (the most recent share price multiplied by the number of shares that the company has in issue).[14]

The calculation for the two companies is shown in **Example 5.3**.

In this example, Cronky has a significantly higher dividend yield than Voddy, but care is needed in interpreting this. It does not mean that Cronky's dividends are higher than Voddy's; both companies are paying the same dividend per share, that is, 10p. Cronky's higher dividend yield means that it has a lower share price than Voddy. A high dividend yield means that the share price is low (in relation to dividends); a low dividend yield means that the share price is high in relation to dividends. It is noted that share prices are not constant and

[12] And multiplying by 100 to express it as a percentage.
[13] After deducting any preference dividends.
[14] And multiplying by 100 to express it as a percentage.

fluctuate on a daily basis, which in turn will affect the dividend yield; for example, a rise in share price will cause the dividend yield to fall and vice versa.

Example 5.3

		Cronky plc	Voddy plc
a	Number of ordinary shares	1,000,000	1,000,000
b	Current share price	£2.00	£3.20
c	Market capitalization (a × b)	£2,000,000	£3,200,000
d	Total ordinary dividends	£100,000	£100,000
e	Dividend yield (d ÷ c × 100)	5%	3.1%
f	Dividend per share (d ÷ a)	£0.10	£0.10
g	Dividend yield (f ÷ b × 100)	5%	3.1%

What the dividend yield can tell us

In the 1990s, little attention was given to low dividend yields. The average dividend yield on shares was only around 2 per cent at a time when it was possible to get 5 per cent or more from a bank or building society deposit account. Dividend yields looked very low, partly because share prices were very high. Although interest rates can vary, there is no 'growth' in the amount of interest paid on deposit accounts. But the hope and expectation is that dividends will increase, year after year, and in the majority of companies, they still do. If someone invests £100 in shares, and the only dividend they get is £2, that is a yield of 2 per cent, but it doesn't look very good. However, the following year it might be £2.15, then £2.35 the next year, then £2.55; and, after a number of years (hopefully before the investor retires!), the dividend might look very respectable in relation to the original £100 invested, with every prospect that it will continue to increase, at least in line with inflation. With a successful investment, the share price also increases, which means that the dividend yield still looks low: it is the *amount* of dividend that the investor hopes to see increasing each year, not the dividend yield.

It is 'normal' for the average yield on shares to be lower than interest rates on deposit accounts because investors expect there to be growth in dividends on ordinary shares.

Low dividend yields are mainly the result of high share prices, and low dividend yields go hand in hand with high P/E ratios. Shares that are expected to deliver rapid and sustained growth have high prices and, therefore, high P/E ratios and, therefore, low dividend yields. It might be a rational strategy for investors to choose companies with high dividend yields, provided they can be sure that the dividends will continue to be high. We do not know what future dividends will be, and it might be that with the economic growth expected to be minimal, there is no guarantee that present levels of dividends will continue. An investor interested in dividend income could look up the FTSE All-World High Dividend Yield Index, which comprises stocks that contribute higher than average dividend yields and are based on the FTSE All-World Index, which is part of the FTSE Global Equity Index Series.

The Bank of England database shows that interest rates were as low as 0.5 per cent in 2014, stayed below 1 per cent until the end of April 2022 and have slowly increased to 5.25 per cent since the beginning of August 2023. Although the average dividend yield on FTSE 100 shares is only 3.73 per cent in the year 2023,[15] one

[15] https://www.dividenddata.co.uk/ftse-index-yield.py

might expect future earnings and, therefore, dividends to fall. Many individual and institutional investors are attracted to 'good value' shares with a reasonable dividend yield. It is possible to get some guidance on how sound such an investment might be by looking at the company's record over a number of years (profits and dividends) and by looking at their cash flow statements.

5.8 Dividend Cover

The easiest and most widely used indicator of how likely it is that a company's dividend will be maintained and increased is 'dividend cover'. This is the relationship between profits and dividends. If a company pays out only a small proportion of its profits as dividends, then the dividend looks reasonably secure: even if profits fall in the following year, there should still be more than enough to pay the same level of dividend.

Dividend cover is calculated by dividing EPS by dividend per share. It can also be calculated by dividing the total profits attributable to ordinary shareholders by the total amount of ordinary dividends payable for the year.

The calculations for Cronky plc and Voddy plc are shown in **Example 5.4**.

On this basis, Cronky's dividend looks more secure than Voddy's. We must expect profits to fluctuate from time to time. Cronky can afford a bigger percentage reduction in profits before the dividend looks threatened than can Voddy. If each company suffered a 40 per cent reduction in profits, the EPS would be:

	Cronky plc	Voddy plc
Earnings per share	£0.12	£0.096

If each company continued with a 10p per share dividend, the dividend cover would be:

Dividend cover	1.2 times	0.96 times

Although it is acceptable for a company to pay out more in dividends than it earns in profits from time to time, perhaps when there is an unusually bad year, clearly, this can only continue for a short time. A dividend that is not well covered by profits looks insecure. Many companies try to maintain the amount of dividend that they pay, even in years when profits are lower; their dividend cover then looks weaker.

Example 5.4

		Cronky plc	Voddy plc
a	Total profits after taxation attributable to ordinary shareholders	£200,000	£160,000
b	Total ordinary dividends	£100,000	£100,000
c	Dividend cover (a ÷ b)	2 times	1.6 times
d	EPS	£0.20	£0.16
e	Dividend per share	£0.10	£0.10
f	Dividend cover (d ÷ e)	2 times	1.6 times

5.9 Net Asset (or Statement of Financial Position) Value

It is easy to calculate the net asset value of a company, or the value of its equity, from the statement of financial position. It is simply the total figure for equity, including share capital, all retained earnings and reserves. The amount for preference shares (if there are any) should be deducted because we are usually assessing only the value of the ordinary shareholders' funds.

This amount can be compared with the company's 'market capitalization' - the total value of all the company's shares, using the most recent share price. The comparison can be made using these total figures for the company as a whole. Alternatively, it can be made on a per share basis, comparing the net asset value per share with the share price.

In most cases, the market value of a company is much higher than the net asset value shown on the statement of financial position. This is for two main reasons:

1. Statement of financial position values may be understated, often being based on historical cost (HC) rather than current values and some assets are not shown on the statement of financial position - human assets, skills, brands and any 'internally generated'[16] goodwill.
2. Share prices are determined by supply and demand for the shares, and the statement of financial position usually has a minor influence on demand for shares. The major influence is expectations of future profits and dividends and expectations that the share price will rise in the future.

Some traditional manufacturing companies may have huge amounts of assets, and their market capitalization may not be very much more than their net asset value. Many modern companies have relatively small amounts of tangible assets, and their value lies in their skills, expertise, reputation, brands and other intangibles not shown on the statement of financial position. Such companies might easily be worth 5 or 10 times their net asset values, especially at the height of a bubble!

The *Financial Times* does not regularly publish net asset values - which might be taken as an indication that they are not seen as being particularly important. They can easily be calculated from a company's statement of financial position, and usually feature in reports by investment analysts, and are published by journals such as the *Investors Chronicle*. Some examples are shown in **Illustration 5.3**.

ILLUSTRATION 5.3

Company	Sector	Share price (pence)	Net asset value per share	Intangibles included in net asset value per share
Barclays	Banking	159	378	430
AngloAmerican	Mining	3,237	1,520	1,690
GlaxoSmithKline	Pharmaceutical and biotechnology	1,379	157	12,138
BT	Telecommunications	122	8	146
Prudential	Insurance	994	268	510
WPP	Advertising	877	−581	344

Source: FAME 31.12.2022; https://www.londonstockexchange.com/

[16] When a company buys another business, any amount paid for 'goodwill' has to be capitalized and shown as a non-current asset. But when a company generates its own goodwill, this is not shown on a statement of financial position.

In a successful company, it is normal for the market price of the share to be higher than the net asset value per share. In many companies, a large part of the net assets consists of 'intangible assets' (mainly the amounts paid for goodwill when another company is taken over). If such intangible assets are excluded, then the tangible assets of a company may be very low indeed compared with the share price.

In a minority of cases, the net asset value of a company falls below its market capitalization. If the difference is substantial, this might invite an asset-stripping takeover bid: it may be possible to buy up the company at a bargain price and then sell off all the separate parts of it at a profit. Investment analysts often assess the market value - not just the statement of financial position value - of the separate parts of a business, and when this falls below the market capitalization, there are danger signs for management: another management team may be able to take over and do a better job for the shareholders.

In some cases, such as property companies, the market capitalization is usually significantly less than the market value of the underlying assets. In part, this may be because the statement of financial position shows properties at fairly full current valuations, and it may not be easy to sell the properties at those prices. It may also be because it is difficult to generate much growth in profits: rental income is relatively stable and safe but does not produce 'double-digit' growth in profits.

5.10 Cash Flow

Cash flow may be a better indicator of a company's performance than profit. A company that generates substantial profits on paper but cannot back them up with cash flows raises serious questions. A company that makes profits year after year but has to keep raising more money (by borrowing or making rights issues) may be unpopular with investors. Cash flow statements explain how and why a company's cash flow differs from its profit, as explained in **Chapter 6**.

The first question is: does the company generate cash from its normal operations? If it does not, it is necessary to figure out why not.

The second question has to do with expansion. Is the company investing in more non-current assets and buying other businesses? This is clearly shown on the cash flow statement. Such expansion may require additional borrowing or the issue of more shares. Amounts invested in expansion can be compared with the amounts raised as additional share capital and borrowings. It is a dangerous sign if the company is raising lots more capital without any evident increase in profitable investment. It is more healthy if a company is investing in additional capacity, and this is partly financed from operating cash flows and not totally dependent on raising additional funds.

Cash flow statements show three categories of cash flow:

1. *Cash generated from operating activities.* Investors expect to see a positive figure here, even after financing any increases in working capital.
2. *Cash flow from investing activities.* Investors expect to see a negative figure here, with the company investing in additional non-current assets and perhaps buying up other businesses.
3. *Cash flow from financing activities.* Investors want to know about the company's financing, how any expansion has been financed, and whether the company has been increasing or reducing borrowings.

Some analysts emphasize profit plus depreciation and amortization as being the key figure. The cash flow from the operations figure is perhaps the most useful and readily available. Others look for 'free cash flow' that can be deduced from somewhere in the middle of the cash flow statement by estimating how much of the amount paid for additional non-current assets is essential and how much is for expansion.

5.11 Other Indicators/Predictors of Performance

There is no shortage of investment analysts, experts and charlatans giving advice on how to pick winners when investing in the stock market. Most accountants are more cautious, but not all! It is difficult to be clear about who is an expert, who is a charlatan, and who is advising investing in particular shares for self-interest.

The UK stock exchange is often considered a 'heritage' stock market due to its high concentration of traditional industries such as banking, consumer staples, energy and mining. Unfortunately, the UK has underperformed the world index over the last twenty years. In addition to this, regulation, government apathy, and Brexit have not been helpful.

However, it is worth noting that the UK's corporate governance and accounting transparency are generally best-in-class. Companies in the FTSE are often global businesses with broad exposure to growth markets. Additionally, in 2023, there are 753 companies in the Alternative Investment Markets (AIM),[17] many of which are overlooked and under-researched. Despite these positives, the UK market trades at a significant discount, both to the rest of the world and to its own history. The FTSE All-Share has a net market capitalization of £2,357,595 and a dividend yield of 3.8 per cent, valued at just ten times next year's earnings.[18]

All financial accounting information can be analysed with a view to guiding investment decisions. Many different ratios can be calculated, and an examination of trends over a number of years can be revealing.

The relationship between a company's turnover figure and its market capitalization is one of many ratios that might be worth following. The idea is that if a company's market capitalization is higher than its turnover, the shares are overpriced. If a company's turnover is much higher than its market capitalization, the shares are of good value. The theory is that if a company has a high level of sales (in relation to share price), profits will follow. The hardest thing is to achieve a high level of turnover. If the present management cannot make good profits from a high level of sales, potentially future management will. This may be no more than a hypothesis. It would probably turn out to be a good basis for investment in some companies in some years but not for other companies in other years. This is probably true for most decision rules that are supposed to form the basis for investment decisions.

Earnings before interest, taxes, depreciation and amortization

Earnings before interest, taxes, depreciation and amortization (EBITDA) is a financial metric used to determine a company's operating profitability. It is calculated by adding back non-cash accounting charges (depreciation and amortization) to net income and disregarding interest paid on debt financing and income taxes. This makes it an ideal measure for assessing a company's operating cash flow and comparing the profitability of companies with different capital structures.[19]

EBITDA has been useful in various circumstances, such as leverage buyouts and private business valuations. EBITDA is an important metric in leveraged transactions such as leveraged buyouts, where the amount of debt financing provided by lenders is often based on a ratio of debt to EBITDA. In loan agreements, EBITDA is used in financial covenants. The calculation of EBITDA may vary depending on how it is to be used. A business's valuation is often calculated as a multiple of EBITDA, with the applicable multiple determined based on the company's industry. This allows for comparing the valuations of companies in the same industry but with different capital structures.

---

17 *Source:* London Stock Exchange.

18 FTSE Russell as at 29 March 2024.

19 EBITDA information from https://uk.practicallaw.thomsonreuters.com/0-577-2465

The more fully past data are analysed, the more models that appear to predict future share prices can be developed. It is easy to find past data which, if analysed in a particular way, would have predicted share prices. But we cannot assume that such relationships will hold good in the future. In choosing between different accounting policies, accountants often favour those policies that seem to have the most predictive value, but we can know only those that would have had the most predictive value in the past. Markets are constantly changing. Companies and activities that did well in recent years, such as banks and the insurance sector, have proved to be the worst in the 'credit crunch'. Past performance is no guide to the future.

The same arguments apply to technical analysis: it is difficult to believe that graphs of share prices over time show patterns that enable us to predict future share prices.

Although financial accounting cannot give us all the answers that we might like, the information that it provides is central in making investment decisions and monitoring how successful those decisions turn out to be.

5.12 A Further Illustration

The main stock market ratios are shown in **Illustration 5.4**. The figures suggest a typical, average company, and may be used to make comparisons with other companies and to see how the ratios have been calculated. The P/E ratio, the dividend cover and the dividend yield may all be calculated using figures for the company as a whole, or on a per share basis.

ILLUSTRATION 5.4

	Stoutmouth plc
Share capital (25p shares)	£ 5,000,000
Retained earnings	£31,000,000
	£36,000,000
Net profit after tax for year	£6,400,000
Dividends for year	£4,000,000
Number of shares	20,000,000
Market price of shares	£5.44
Market capitalization	£108,800,000
EPS	£0.32
Dividend per share	£0.20
P/E ratio	17
Dividend times cover	1.6 times
Dividend yield	3.7%
Net assets per share	£1.80

The figures for Stoutmouth plc are in many ways typical of a listed company. At the beginning of 2024, the average P/E ratio of the 100 largest companies quoted on the LSE was 10.38; the average dividend yield was 3.97 per cent; and the average times cover for dividends was 2.43. The market capitalization of each of the companies in the largest 100 is between £0.5 and £100b. But the market capitalization of most listed companies is nearer to that of Stoutmouth plc.

Summary

One of the main objectives of financial management is to maximize shareholders' wealth. Dividends, which are dependent on profits, contribute to this. But the main element of shareholders' wealth is the value of their shares. Directors and chief executives are usually well motivated to maintain and increase their company's share price: they own shares themselves; they may have options to buy shares at predetermined prices; and their remuneration may include substantial incentives related to share price performance. If they fail, and the share price languishes, they risk the wrath of shareholders, and leave themselves open to a hostile takeover bid with a new management team replacing them.

Accounting measures of solvency and profitability are central to the performance of share prices. If a company is seen as having excessive debt, the share price will suffer. Profitability is essential to maintaining and increasing share prices, although more attention seems to be paid to EPS than to return on capital employed (ROCE). Growth, and expectations of future growth in sales, profits and dividends make a major contribution to increases in share prices. Sometimes it seems that expectations of share price increases are the main cause of share price increases. Share prices are influenced by expectations, rumours and many other factors that are difficult to define and measure, particularly in the short term. In the long run, sound finances and growth in EPS are likely to be the main contributors to increasing share prices.

Review of key points

- Many different factors influence share prices.
- A company's P/E ratio, dividend yield and dividend cover are widely used measures of share price performance.
- Growth and expectations of growth of sales and profits help to boost share prices.
- Many influences on share prices are difficult to quantify.
- Company directors and shareholders have an interest in maintaining and increasing share prices.
- Claims to be able to predict share prices should be treated with caution.
- Financial accounting information helps to explain changes in share prices.

Self-testing questions

1 Explain the meaning, calculation and significance of each of the following:
   a price earnings (P/E) ratio;
   b dividend yield;
   c dividend times cover.

2 Is a company's statement of financial position value (net asset value) likely to be higher or lower than its market value? Explain.

3 If a company currently has a dividend yield of 10 per cent, does that mean that someone investing £100 today will receive £10 dividend in the coming year? Explain.

4 You are given the following information about two companies. You are required to fill in the missing items for Beermouth plc.

	Alemouth plc	Beermouth plc
Share capital (20p shares)	£1,600,000	£ 2,000,000
Retained earnings	£3,200,000	£18,000,000
	£4,800,000	£20,000,000
Net profit after tax for year	£3,520,000	£1,200,000
Dividends for year	£3,200,000	£800,000
Number of shares	8,000,000	10,000,000
Market price of shares	£4.40	£1.80
Market capitalization	£35,200,000	£18,000,000
EPS	£0.44	£0.12
Dividend per share	£0.40	£0.08
P/E ratio	10	-
Dividend times cover	1.1 times	-
Dividend yield	9.09%	-
Net assets per share	£0.60	-

5 Comment on the dividend yield of Alemouth plc.

6 Comment on the relationship between the net assets per share of Beermouth plc and its share price (or on the relationship of the total shareholders' funds to the market capitalization).

Assessment questions

1 What is the level of the FTSE 100 today? What is the average P/E ratio of the top 100 companies? What is their dividend yield and dividend cover? Assume the information for some of the measures of the FTSE 100:

	Index	P/E	Dividend yield (%)	Dividend cover
16 September 2015	4299	17.6	3.3	1.72
19 June 2018	5597	12.8	3.4	2.30
8 May 2021	4462	9.8	4.8	2.13
7 November 2023	5527	9.9	3.4	2.93

What do you think are the main causes of the changes

a between September 2015 and June 2018?

b between June 2018 and May 2021?

c since May 2021?

2 You are given the following information about two companies, partly extracted from their most recent statement of financial position and income statement and partly taken from the financial press. You are required to fill in the missing items for Drinkmouth plc.

	Cidermouth plc	**Drinkmouth plc**
Share capital (20p shares)	£ 4,000,000	£1,200,000
Retained earnings	£14,000,000	£2,400,000
	£18,000,000	£3,600.000
Net profit after tax for year	£3,400,000	£1,800,000
Dividends for year	£2,000,000	£ 900,000
Number of shares	20,000,000	6,000,000
Market price of shares	£3.40	-
Market capitalization	£68,000,000	£45,000,000
EPS	£0.17	£0.30
Dividend per share	£0.10	-
P/E ratio	20	25
Dividend times cover	1.7 times	-
Dividend yield	2.9%	2.0%
Net assets per share	£0.90	-

3 You are given the following information about Swin Gin plc:

	Year 1	**Year 2**	**Year 3**	**Year 4**	**Year 5***	**Year 6**	**Year 7**
EPS	£0.50	£0.55	£0.62	£0.01	£1.20	£ 0.83	£ 0.90
Share price	£6.00	£7.70	£9.92	£6.00	£7.20	£12.45	£15.30

(after publication of results for the year)
* In year 5, the company sold its head office building in London, making a profit that amounted to 45p per share.

You are required to calculate the P/E ratio for each year and comment on how the market appears to have reacted to changes in EPS.

4 Assess the usefulness of P/E ratios and suggest how they might be misleading.

5 Select a recent takeover bid (e.g. Kraft and Cadbury). Assess the various factors that determined the price that was eventually agreed upon for the company that was taken over.

Group activities and discussion questions

1 Look at the shares listing in the *Financial Times*. What is an average P/E ratio? Select some companies with high P/E ratios. Do they seem to have anything in common? How useful are the P/E ratios given for different sectors in the 'FTSE Actuaries Share Indices'? Select some companies with low P/E ratios. Do they seem to have anything in common?

2 Look at the shares listing in the *Financial Times*. What is an average dividend yield? Select some companies with high dividend yields. Do they seem to have anything in common? How useful are the dividend yields given for different sectors in the 'FTSE Actuaries Share Indices'? Select some companies with low dividend yields. Do they seem to have anything in common?

3 Each member of the group selects one or two companies in which they believe the shares are likely to increase in price during a selected period. A long period may be preferable, but in a 10-week module, the selection could be made in week 3; the shares monitored for 6 weeks, and the 'final' results assessed in week 8.

Each member of the group is required to give a justification for selecting a particular share in week 3. Then, in week 8, each member should present an explanation of what has happened to their company's share price.

There would be a competitive element (who would have made the most money?). There should also be an assessment of the quality of the presentations; this assessment could be done partly or wholly by the students themselves.

4 Each group forms one or more hypotheses about how to select companies where the increase in share prices is expected to be higher than the average for the FTSE 100 companies. Examples might include (with variations) such things as:

a companies with a dividend yield of between 4 per cent and 5 per cent where the cover is not less than 2

b companies where sales have increased by more than 20 per cent per annum (over a given number of years), but profits have not (yet) increased

c companies where profits have increased by more than 10 per cent since last year, but the share price is lower.

This exercise might be more fun if it is done live. But it is difficult to complete it during the 10 weeks of a typical module. It is easier to do it historically. The decision rules are selected first; then, they are applied to a sample of companies.

Some competition between different groups can produce interesting results. The results produced by the winners might need careful scrutiny.

5 Each group chooses three different sectors (e.g. pharmaceuticals and biotech, construction and materials, travel and leisure, and retailers). The key stock market indicators are found for each sector and compared with the average for the FTSE. These are shown in the *Financial Times* as 'FTSE Actuaries Share Indices'. Suggest factors that make each sector different from the FTSE average.

Accounting in context

Discuss and comment on the following report based on articles from the press with reference to why movements in share price should be judged in the light of movements in the market as a whole and what factors affect the move in share price.

BP CEOs

A company's board of directors has fiduciary duties to its shareholders, which includes ensuring a clear succession plan exists should the chief executive resign unexpectedly or passes away. In rare cases, the chair may need to fire a chief executive.

BP, a UK oil major, has been plagued by CEO turnover since 2007, with John Browne, Tony Hayward and Bernard Looney all leaving their positions. Looney left in September 2023, after a less than 4-year tenure as a CEO, leaving the company in need of a clear succession plan. However, reports suggest that BP is considering external candidates for the role, which may indicate that the company's chair, Helge Lund, is being complacent.

BP has a history of making quick replacements, as evidenced by their appointment of Bob Dudley on the same day that Hayward resigned due to the *Deepwater Horizon* oil spill. This is not uncommon in other energy companies. For example, TotalEnergies Gas and Power (Total), the second biggest French listed company, on the untimely death in an air crash in 2014 of Christophe de Margarie who held the dual role of chair and CEO, within 36 hours Patrick Pouyanné became the new CEO and Thierry Desmarest was appointed as chair. The roles of the CEO and chair were split in line with good corporate governance.

As for BP, there are several candidates being considered for the position of CEO at BP. Among the internal candidates are Murray Auchincloss (current interim chief executive), Emma Delaney, and Carole Howle - all of whom have been with BP for a long time. It seems that candidates with more experience in the fossil fuel industry are being given priority over those with a focus on low-carbon alternatives.

It seems that the chair may not have given much thought to succession planning, perhaps due to Looney's status as a highly regarded figure. However, it is important for a board to keep in mind that even the most charismatic leader can be brought down by a significant flaw. In this particular case, Looney's failure to be transparent about previous relationships with employees ultimately led to his downfall.

BP's share price has been underperforming compared to the MSCI Europe Energy index, and rivals such as Shell and TotalEnergies have a 12 per cent valuation premium compared to BP's 3.2 times enterprise value to EBITDA. The Brent oil price has dropped by 14 per cent since mid-September, making matters worse. TotalEnergies' CEO Patrick Pouyanné advocates a green agenda without getting involved in public controversies, and BP needs a new CEO with similar credentials to steer the company in the right direction.

Sources: Financial Times, 21 December 2023, https://www.ft.com/content/96f6a271-a1aa-4904-b8d5-675950775c22

https://www.theguardian.com/business/2023/dec/13/bp-to-claw-back-32m-from-bernard-looney-after-dismissal-as-ceo

https://www.opec.org/opec_web/en/press_room/2933.htm

References and further reading

Arnold, G. (2020) *The Financial Times Guide to Investing: The Definitive Companion to Investment and the Financial Markets* (4th edn.). Harlow: FT Prentice-Hall.

Boakes, K. (2010) *Reading and Understanding the Financial Times*. Harlow: FT Prentice Hall.

Brealey, R.A., Myers, S.C., Allen, F. and Edmans, A. (2023) *Principles of Corporate Finance* (14th edn.). Maidenhead: McGraw Hill.

Financial Times (daily newspaper). Available online at www.ft.com.

Hillier, D., Ross, S.A., Westerfield, R., Jaffe, J.F. and Jordan, B.D. (2021) *Corporate Finance* (4th European edn.). Maidenhead: McGraw-Hill Education.

Investors' Chronicle (weekly magazine).

Lumby, S. and Jones, C.M. (2019) *Corporate Finance: Theory and Practice* (10th edn.). Boston, MA: Cengage Learning.

McKenzie, W. (2010) *Financial Times Guide to Using and Interpreting Company Accounts* (4th edn.). Harlow: FT Prentice Hall.

Vernimmen, P. et al. (2011) *Corporate Finance: Theory and Practice* (3rd edn.). Chichester: Wiley.

Watson, D., Head, A., Chan, D. and Watson, D. (2023) *Corporate Finance: Principles and Practice* (9th edn.). Harlow: Pearson.

https://www.bankofengland.co.uk/boeapps/database/Bank-Rate.asp

https://www.gov.uk/government/statistics/business-population-estimates-2022/business-population-estimates-for-the-uk-and-regions-2022-statistical-release-html#uk-countries-and-the-regions

https://www.ifrs.org/content/dam/ifrs/meetings/2021/october/iasb/ap21d-operating-profit-or-loss-before-depreciation-and-amortisation.pdf

https://www.londonstockexchange.com/

Chapter 6

Cash Flow Statements: IAS 7 Understanding and Preparation

Chapter contents

6.1 Introduction
6.2 The Accruals Concept
6.3 Cash Flow Statements
6.4 Interpreting Cash Flow Statements
6.5 Format for Cash Flow Statements
6.6 How to Prepare a Cash Flow Statement

Learning objectives

After studying this chapter you will be able to:

✓ Understand the differences between cash flow and profit
✓ Explain the accruals concept
✓ Understand and interpret cash flow statements
✓ Compare the statement of financial position at the beginning of the year with that at the end and explain how the amount of cash has changed during the year
✓ Produce cash flow statements in a format suitable for publication

6.1 Introduction

This chapter begins by explaining the difference between *cash flow* and *profit*. The terms 'profit' and 'cash' are used synonymously by many users of the financial accounts. Here, it is recognized that making money means making profits and generating cash. A successful company generates lots of cash. An unsuccessful company runs out of cash. If a company's success was judged by the amount of cash generated, the accountant's job would be very easy: there would be no need to do more than record all receipts and payments, and to report on a regular basis which one is higher. The analyst's job would also be easy: the company that generates most cash is most successful. There would be no problems of credibility or subjectivity, or manipulation of asset values and exaggeration of profits. Everything could be easily checked by looking at the company's bank statement.

But generating lots of cash is not necessarily a sign of success. Few of us would be impressed by a company that massively increased its cash balances simply by selling off assets and borrowing lots of money. A company that succeeds in generating large amounts of cash is not necessarily a successful company.

Similarly, a successful company might pay out far more cash than it receives. A profitable company might be paying out substantial sums of cash to buy assets that are going to increase future profit; the company performs well, even though it is using up lots of cash.

The distinctions between cash flow and profit are not easily understood, but are vital to an understanding of financial accounting - and to the survival of a business. This chapter begins by explaining the theoretical difference, as in the accruals concept. Cash flow statements are then explained and interpreted. The final section explains how to produce cash flow statements in a form suitable for publication in accordance with IAS 7 Cash Flow Statements.

6.2 The Accruals Concept

Statements of financial position and income statements are based on the *accruals concept,* which means that profit is the difference between the revenues earned during a period (regardless of when the money is received), and the costs incurred in earning those revenues (regardless of when cash is paid out).

The accruals concept has long been regarded as a *fundamental accounting concept.*[1] The Conceptual Framework for Financial Reporting 2018 s1.17 states that accrual accounting records the impact of transactions, events and circumstances of an entity's economic resources and claims in the periods they occur, regardless of when cash is received or paid out. By accruing revenues and costs and matching them as closely as possible, a company can obtain a more precise understanding of its financial standing, enabling an evaluation of its past and future performance. They are dealt with in the income statement of the period to which they relate, which is often not in the period when cash is received or paid.

The profit figure for a particular period is therefore likely to be very different from the amount of cash generated in that period. A naïve, non-accountant might think that the profit is the difference between the receipts and payment of cash. But they would be seriously mistaken.

Financial accounting is based on the accruals concept, which means that for a particular period:

Profit = Revenues earned less Costs incurred in earning those revenues

The words are important. Receipts and payments apply to cash. Revenues or income and costs or expenses apply to profit calculation.

The accruals concept is applied throughout financial accounting. Gross profit is the difference between sales and the cost of goods sold. In calculating profit, it is the amount of sales revenue earned during a period that matters, not when the money is received. The cost of goods sold uses the purchase figure, which is the total amount purchased during the period, regardless of when they are paid for. The cost of goods sold figure also adjusts for inventories. The expense *cost of sales* is based on the cost of the goods which were actually sold during the period. Unsold inventories from one year become a cost for the following year as they are included in the cost of sales as opening inventory. Closing inventory remaining at the end of one period is the opening inventory of unsold goods at the beginning of the next year.

---

[1] SSAP 2 specified four fundamental accounting concepts: going concern; accruals; consistency; and prudence (or conservatism).

Any payment made to buy non-current assets that is made this year (or which it is agreed will be paid in another year) is not an expense for this year. In this case, the cost is spread out over the life of the non-current asset and is charged as depreciation each year. The timing of cash paid out for buying non-current assets is very different from the timing of the depreciation expense that is charged in calculating profit.

It is important to be clear that:

1 Not all payments of cash are expenses; some payments are not a charge against profits
2 Not all receipts of cash are revenues; some receipts do not add to profits
3 Not all expenses are payments of cash; some expenses are charged against profits, although no payment of cash is required in the year that the expense is charged
4 Not all revenues are receipts of cash; some revenues are added to profits, although there is no receipt of cash in the year that credit is taken for the revenue.

There are examples of each of the above four differences. But, in interpreting financial statements, it is important to look for the big differences. Substantial inflows of cash are likely to come from borrowings, issuing share capital and selling off assets;[2] none of these count as revenues for the purpose of calculating profit. Substantial outflows of cash are usually for buying non-current assets; but such payments are not charges against profit for the year. The biggest expense, which is not paid in cash, is depreciation and that can easily cause confusion!

Some of the examples of differences are relatively minor timing differences. But they are all important in explaining the difference between cash flow and profit. And, in some circumstances, 'minor' items can become very significant.

1 *Payments of cash that are not expenses* - purchase of non-current assets; investing in other companies; repaying loans; payments to buy stocks of goods that are not sold until the next period; payments to creditors for expenses incurred in the previous period.
2 *Receipts of cash that are not revenues* - sale of non-current assets; borrowing money; proceeds from issuing shares; receipts from receivables this period in respect of sales for the previous period.
3 *Expenses that are not payments* - depreciation and amortization;[3] expenses incurred this period but which are not paid for until the next period; creating a provision; increase in a provision for bad debts; discount allowed to customers for settling their accounts promptly.
4 *Revenues that are not receipts* - sales that are made during this period, but the money is not received until the next period; discount allowed by suppliers for settling accounts promptly; reduction in a provision.

There are also examples where the cash receipt is very different from the revenue figure. When a non-current asset is sold, all the cash received is credited to the cash account. But in calculating profit, only the difference between book value and the sale proceeds is credited to profit, as shown in **Example 6.1**.

Example 6.1

The Floughin Company has a small assembly plant at Jurbeigh that originally cost £30,000; cumulative depreciation is £6,000. The government decided to develop an international airport nearby, and the company was able to sell its plant for £40,000. Calculate the profit for the year.

The receipt of cash is £40,000.

The net book value of the plant is (£30,000 − £6,000 =) £24,000.

Only the profit of £16,000 is credited towards profit for the year.

[2] Any profit on selling a non-current asset counts towards income for the year; the full amount of the sale proceeds does not.

[3] Amortization is really the same as depreciation, but the word is usually applied to leasehold property and to intangible non-current assets such as intellectual property or software licences. 'Impairment' of goodwill or other assets is comparable.

It is sometimes argued that cash flow would be a better basis for accounting than the accruals concept because it is more objective. But total cash flows (including receipts from borrowing and payments to acquire non-current assets) mean little unless there is some classification of the receipts and payments. The need for classification would remove the supposed objectivity. Almost all accountants agree that profit measurement[4] and the use of the accruals concept are essential.

6.3 Cash Flow Statements

A *cash flow statement* provides a reconciliation between the amount of profit generated during a period and the amount by which cash balances have increased or decreased during that period. The idea is that profits generate cash, but cash tends to flow away. The statement provides a clear indication of where this cash has gone.

It starts off by showing how much profit before tax was generated during the period; then, it shows what happened to the profits. Some of it may be tied up in additional inventory and receivables; some may have gone in paying interest and taxation; some may have gone in buying more non-current assets, or repaying loans. The final figure shows how much cash is left; that final figure at the end of a cash flow statement is the same as the cash balance shown on the statement of financial position at the year end.

It is useful to bear in mind that cash *in*flows are decreases in assets and increases in liabilities, while cash *de*creases are increases in assets and decreases in liabilities. Think that when buying a car, cash reduces, while when selling a car, cash increases. Most of the information required to prepare a cash flow statement can be found by comparing two statements of financial position. In **Illustration 6.1**, we can see that Ebbing plc made a profit in the year 2023.[5] But as the illustration shows, a company may be making and retaining decent profits, but because of the need to finance more non-current assets and higher levels of inventory and receivables, it ends the year with less cash than it started with. In **Illustration 6.2** Ebbing plc started year 2023 with £160,000 cash in the bank; it retained profits of £15,000 during the year (see note 5); but it ended the year with only £35,000 cash in the bank. By comparing the two statements of financial position in **Illustration 6.1**, at the beginning of the year and at the end of year, it is easy to see where the money went: £100,000 extra was tied up in non-current assets; there was an additional inventory of £40,000; and there was an additional £30,000 tied up in receivables. How were these additional assets financed? The money came partly from retained profits, partly by reducing cash balances, and partly by owing more to trade payables.

ILLUSTRATION 6.1

Statement of financial position of Ebbing plc as at 31 December

	Year 2022	Year 2023	Increase or decrease
Assets	£000	£000	£000
Non-current assets	200	300	100
Current assets			
Inventories	80	120	40
Trade receivables	60	90	30

[4] The reasons why profit is measured are explored in Chapter 5.

[5] Retained earnings increased from £120,000 to £135,000. Profits retained in year 2023 amounted to £15,000; that figure is after deducting dividends and taxation. Pre-tax profits would be much greater.

Statement of financial position of Ebbing plc as at 31 December			
	Year 2022	**Year 2023**	**Increase or decrease**
Cash	160	35	-65
	300	245	
Total assets	500	545	
Liabilities and equity			
Liabilities			
Current liabilities			
Trade payables	90	110	20
Non-current liabilities			
Long-term borrowings	50	60	10
Total liabilities	140	170	
Equity			
Share capital	240	240	0
Retained earnings	120	135	15
	360	375	
Total liabilities and equity	500	545	

Income statement of Ebbing plc for the year ending 31 December Year 2023	
	£000
Operating profit before interest and tax	48.5
Interest expense	4.0
Profit before taxation	44.5
Taxation	13.5
Profit for the year	35.0
Notes: Depreciation expense	£ 16,000
Dividends paid	£ 16,000

ILLUSTRATION 6.2

Cash flow statement of Ebbing plc for the year ended 31 December 2023		
Operating activities	£	£
Profit before taxation		44,500
Depreciation		16,000
		60,500
Increase in working capital		
Increase in Inventories	(40,000)	
Increase in Trade Receivables	(30,000)	
Increase in Trade Payables	20,000	(50,000)
Interest expense		4,000
Cash flow from operating activities		14,500

Cash flow statement of Ebbing plc for the year ended 31 December 2023			
Interest paid	(4,000)		
Taxation paid	(13,500)		
Dividends paid	(16,000)		
		(33,500)	
Net cash flow from operating activities		(19,000)	(A) Total outflow from operating activities
Investing activities			
Purchase of non-current assets[6]		(116,000)	(B) Investing outflow
Financing activities			
New loan issued		10,000	(C) Financing inflow
Decrease in cash		(125,000)	Net outflow A + B + C
Cash at start of the year 2023		160,000	
Cash at end of the year 2023		35,000	

The above reconciliation is rather simplified, and the cash flow statements published by companies are in a standardized format so that businesses can readily be compared with each other. They start by identifying cash flows from operations, which are as follows.

Operating activities

1 Profit before deducting taxation
2 Depreciation
3 (Increase) or decrease in working capital
4 Interest expense

= ***Cash flow from operating activities***

5 Interest paid
6 Taxation paid
7 Dividends paid

= ***Net cash flow from operating activities***

1 *Profit* is normally positive and is an inflow of cash. Where the business makes a loss, this outflow of cash is shown in brackets.

Any increase in retained profits can be established by comparing the statement of financial position at the end of the period with the statement of financial position at the beginning of the period. The figure required for a cash flow statement is profit before deducting taxation, which is found in the income statement.

2 *Depreciation* is shown as an inflow of cash. Profit is shown as if all expenses are outflows of cash. But depreciation is an expense that is not paid; there is no outflow of cash for depreciation. It is therefore necessary for depreciation to be added back to profit. It is an oversimplification to say that cash flow consists of profit plus depreciation, but it is useful to remember this as being the first part of a cash flow statement.

[6] Non-current assets at the end of year 2022 were £200,000. In the year 2023, the amount deducted for depreciation was £16,000. This would have reduced the amount to £184,000, i.e. the net book value. But at the end of the year 2023, the amount shown for fixed assets was £300,000; expenditure on additional non-current assets must therefore have been £116,000.

3 Any *increase in working capital* is an outflow of cash or a negative cash flow, and so it is shown in brackets. This usually means that profits have been used to finance higher levels of inventories and payables. Any reduction in working capital is shown as a cash inflow.

The main components of working capital are closing inventories, receivables and payables, and these can be shown individually instead of using a single figure for working capital.

Any increase in inventories and receivables is shown as an outflow of cash; any decrease in inventories and receivables is shown as an inflow of cash.

Any increase in payables is shown as an inflow of cash; any decrease in payables is shown as an outflow of cash. This is explained as follows:

a *Receivables* - Not all the revenue from sales (which is included in the profit figure) is immediately a cash inflow. Where the receivables have increased, this is treated as an outflow of cash (to reduce the inflow included in profit arising from sales). Where the receivables have gone down during a period, more money has been received from them, and the reduction is treated as an inflow of cash.

b *Payables* - Not all the expenses that have been recorded in arriving at the profit figure have in fact been paid. Where the amount of payables has increased, this is treated as an inflow of cash (to reduce the outflow included in profit in respect of purchases and expenses). Where the amount of payables has decreased during the period, this is treated as an outflow of cash (because more has been paid out than has been charged as an expense in calculating profit).

c *Inventories* - In calculating profit, only the cost of goods that have been sold is treated as an expense. The cost of goods that have not yet been sold (closing inventory) is not yet an expense, but those goods still have to be paid for. Any increase in inventory is therefore treated as an outflow of cash. Any reduction in inventory is treated as an inflow of cash.

4 *Interest expense* is added back since it might not have actually been paid but might be payable at a later date and have been, at least to a degree, accrued.

= Cash generated from operating activities. Items 1 to 4 are subtotalled to show the cash flow from trading activities

5 *Interest paid* is an outflow of cash and is shown in brackets. Any interest receivable is an inflow of cash. In some cases the interest receivable is greater than the interest payable, and so the net figure can be used, which in this situation, is an inflow of cash.

6 *Taxation paid* is an outflow of cash and is shown in brackets. Sometimes, there is a cash inflow where there has been a tax rebate, perhaps after the company has been making losses.

7 *Dividends paid* in the year[7]

= *Net cash outflow from operating activities*

The first part of a cash flow statement, dealing with cash flows from *operating activities*, is often the most complex. The second and third parts of the cash flow statement deal with *investing activities* (buying and selling non-current assets and investments) and *financing activities* (raising additional finance by issuing additional shares or debentures or perhaps reducing share capital and borrowings). The reconciliation of cash flow and profit for Ebbing plc is shown in the form of a cash flow statement in **Illustration 6.2**. Some additional information[8] has been included to make it more realistic.

[7] Interest and dividends received and paid may be classified as operating, investing or financing cash flows, provided that they are classified consistently from period to period (IAS 7.31).

[8] Additional information: depreciation £16,000; interest paid £4,000; taxation paid £13,500; dividends paid £16,000. The increase in retained profits for year 2023 is still £15,000, but profit before interest and taxation is (£15,000 + £13,500 taxation + £4,000 interest + £16,000 dividends) = £48,500.

International Accounting Standard 7 specifies that cash flow statements should report inflows and outflows of cash under three headings, as follows:

1 *Operating activities.* This should include all the receipts and payments resulting from sales and costs based on the profit figure. Not all the profit figure shows up as cash because of changes in current assets and current liabilities, as was illustrated with Ebbing plc in **Illustration 6.1** and **Illustration 6.2.**

   Depreciation has to be shown separately. It is treated as an expense in calculating profit as if cash has been paid out. But, unlike other expenses, no cash is paid out for depreciation. To arrive at a cash flow figure, it is therefore necessary to add depreciation (and amortization) to the net profit figure.

   Interest and taxation paid and dividends are also usually included as operating activities since they are likely to occur every year, although dividends can be shown as a financing activity.

   Ebbing plc made a decent enough profit, which, when added to depreciation, produced a cash inflow of £60,500. But after financing the increase in working capital, paying interest, taxation and dividends, there was a deficit of only £19,000, which was clearly not enough to pay for additional non-current assets.

2 *Investing activities.* This includes all payments for additional non-current assets and expenditure on buying investments in other businesses. Cash inflows include receipts from disposals of non-current assets. Ebbing plc spent £116,000 on additional non-current assets.

3 *Financing activities.* The main cash flows here are from issuing or redeeming shares and long-term loans. Cash outflows include redemption of loans, and a company may buy back some of its own shares.

   Ebbing plc raised a loan of £10,000 but did not raise any share capital during the period as it had enough cash to meet its needs this year since, fortunately, it had sufficient money to pay for them because it started the year with £160,000 in the bank.

The cash flows arising from operating activities is perhaps the most important figure, and it should be positive, even after paying interest, taxes and dividends. There is a cash deficit from operating activities in Ebbing plc (**Illustration 6.2**), but there is a cash surplus from operations in Reet Aylor plc (**Illustration 6.3**).

ILLUSTRATION 6.3

Cash flow statement of Reet Aylor plc for the year ended 31 December

	Year 2022	**Year 2023**
	£000	£000
Cash flows from operating activities		
Profit before tax	6,800	7,300
Depreciation	5,700	6,100
	12,500	13,400
Increase in trade receivables	(2,000)	(1,700)
Increase in inventories	(4,100)	(3,800)
Increase in trade payables	200	300
Interest expense	1,100	900
Cash flow from operations	7,700	9,100
Interest paid	(1,100)	(900)
Income taxes paid	(2,500)	(2,700)
Dividends paid	(1,300)	(1,400)
Net cash flow from operating activities	2,800	4,100

Cash flow statement of Reet Aylor plc for the year ended 31 December		
	Year 2022	**Year 2023**
Cash flows from investing activities		
Proceeds from disposal of equipment	400	300
Purchase of property and equipment	(9,300)	(6,600)
Net cash outflow from investing activities	(8,900)	(6,300)
Cash flows from financing activities		
Proceeds of issue of shares	200	3,300
Repayment of borrowings	(2,100)	–
Net cash used in financing activities	(1,900)	3,300
Net (decrease)/increase in cash	(8,000)	1,100
Opening cash	7,000	(1,000)
Closing cash	(1,000)	100

In the year 2022, Reet Aylor plc generated £2.8m from operating activities. But this was not enough to finance the £9.3m it spent on property and equipment. It raised some money from selling off equipment (£0.4m), but the net payment for investing activities was £8.9m. In most businesses, this would lead to the need to raise additional funds through long-term loans or issuing shares. But Reet Aylor plc started the year with £7m of cash in the bank, which was more than enough to finance the shortfall, and to pay the dividend for the year. The company decided to pay back some of its borrowings and ended the year with a £1m overdraft.

The financing activities in the year 2023 were rather different. The cash generated from operating activities was higher at £4.1m, but this was still not enough to finance the £6.3m of additional non-current assets in the year 2023. The shortfall was financed by a substantial share issue, which raised £3.3m. The additional funds raised were also used to pay off the £1m overdraft.

In a reasonably successful company the cash generated by operating activities should be enough to pay the regular annual payments of interest, tax and dividends, and some increase in non-current assets. Where there is a substantial increase in non-current assets, it is usually necessary for some financing activities to raise additional long-term funds.

In Reet Aylor plc the increase in dividend was very small considering the substantial increase in share capital. If the additional shares were issued towards the end of the year 2023, a substantial increase in the amount of dividends paid might be expected in the following year.

6.4 Interpreting Cash Flow Statements

Free cash flow

The term 'free cash flow' is widely used by financial journalists. The idea is that profit plus depreciation generates additional cash flows; some of this has to be used to finance increases in working capital and to pay interest and taxation. What then remains is free cash flow: companies are free to use it how they wish: to pay dividends, to invest in non-current assets or other businesses, and to repay borrowings or share capital.

It is perhaps easiest to regard free cash flow as being the net amount of cash arising from operating activities. For example, in Reet Aylor plc (**Illustration 6.3**), the amount was £4.1m in the year 2023.

Unfortunately, there is no clear definition of what is meant by free cash flow. Most companies do not identify such a figure. Some companies who show it use a variety of different definitions. Although companies are generally 'free' to decide whether or not to pay dividends, care is needed in interpreting cash flow statements: some companies show a free cash flow figure *before* deducting dividends, while others show free cash flow *after* dividends, as in Reet Aylor plc.

The treatment of non-current assets is also a problem. Businesses regularly need to replace some of their non-current assets as they come to the end of their lives; cash flow is not free if it has to be used for essential replacements. However, some non-current assets are purchased as part of an expansion plan, and companies are free to decide whether or not to go ahead with such expansions. It would be sensible to say that free cash flow is arrived at after payment for essential replacements of non-current assets, but before funding any expansion. Unfortunately, the distinction between essential replacements and non-current assets for expansion is hard to determine. Sometimes an arbitrary compromise is used, such as deciding that one-third of expenditure on non-current assets is for essential replacements; free cash flow is arrived at after deducting such a proportion of expenditure on non-current assets.

Cash flow ratios

Conventional ratio analysis can be adapted to use cash flow figures rather than profit figures. It is important that, in such analyses, a clear definition of cash flow is used consistently. The most straightforward figure to use is the net cash flow generated from operations in the first part of a published cash flow statement. It is seen as a key indicator of a business's ability to generate cash flows from its operations to pay dividends, repay debt and finance investments in fixed assets to maintain and increase its operating capability (without having to raise additional long-term shares or loan capital).

Unfortunately, IAS 7 does not have a firm definition of what is to be included in the net cash flow generated from operations with regard to interest and dividends. Interest paid is best included under operating activities, but the standard also allows it to be included under financing activities.

Interest and dividends received are best included under operating activities, but the standard also allows them to be included under investing activities (as they are the product of investments that have been made). Dividends paid are best included under financing activities, but the standard also allows them to be included under operating activities.

The following cash flow ratios are useful, provided the definition used for cash flow is clear and consistently applied. The term is sometimes used to mean simply profit plus depreciation. It would be better to use the total figure for operating activities taken from the cash flow statement.

Interest and dividend cover

These figures can be calculated to indicate the extent to which interest and dividend payments are covered by cash flows generated. The figures for Reet Aylor plc are as follows:

	Year 2022	Year 2023
	£m	£m
Net cash from operating activities plus dividends[9]	4.1	5.5
Dividends paid	1.3	1.4
Dividend times cover	3.15 times	3.93 times

The dividend cover has increased because, although the dividend payment has increased a little, the operating cash flow has increased by a bigger proportion.

	Year 2022	Year 2023
	£m	£m
Net cash from operating activities plus dividends[10]	4.1	5.5
Add back interest	1.1	0.9
Cash flow available to cover interest	5.2	6.4
Interest times cover	4.73 times	7.11 times

The interest cover has increased because the amount of interest payable has reduced (because some borrowings have been repaid), and the operating cash flow has increased.

Cash return on capital employed

This figure can be calculated to indicate the extent to which the business generates cash (as opposed to profit) for the shareholders.

$$\frac{\text{Net cash from operating activities}}{\text{Equity}} \times 100$$

Cash flow per share

This figure can be calculated in the same way as earnings per share (EPS), but using cash flow from operating activities instead of profit. The cash flow figure is divided by the number of shares in issue. Comparing cash flow per share with EPS is much the same as comparing total cash flow with total earnings.

Published cash flow statements

Published cash flow statements can be quite daunting and include many details and complexities that are hard to understand, even after wading through pages of complicated notes. Generally, figures shown in brackets are outflows of cash, and figures not shown in brackets are inflows of cash. But the proliferation of subtotals and negative figures (outflows) can be confusing, and sometimes the use of brackets is not consistent. It can be helpful to begin by summarizing the main figures and then asking a number of key questions. The following are likely to be helpful in respect of Reet Aylor plc.

	Year 2022	Year 2023
	£000	£000
Cash from operating activities	2,800	4,100
Cash (used in) investing activities	(8,900)	(6,300)
Cash (used in)/from financing activities	(1,900)	3,300
(Decrease)/increase in cash	(8,000)	1,100

[9] This figure is taken before deducting dividends; it is all available to cover dividends. Year 2022: 2,800 + 1,300 = 4,100; Year 2023: 4,100 + 1,400 = 5,500. Note the amounts are shown in thousands.

[10] This figure is provided *after* interest has been deducted; the interest is therefore added back to establish the amount available to cover interest.

Suggested questions in interpreting cash flow statements:

1 Was there a positive cash flow from operating activities? If so, how was it used? If not, why not?
2 Has working capital increased, and how was it financed? Has there been a reduction in working capital, and what is the significance of this reduction?
3 Have there been significant investing activities? Is there a substantial increase in non-current assets? Have there been substantial investments in other businesses? How were these financed?
4 Has there been a reduction in investments in non-current assets and other businesses? How much money was raised, and how was this used?
5 Has the business been raising substantial long-term financing? Why do these funds seem to be needed? Have they been invested in long-term assets? Were they needed to finance shortfalls in cash flows from operating activities? Were they needed to pay off overdrafts?
6 Are the cash flows from financing activities negative (i.e. has there been a reduction in long-term funding)? What do you think this would suggest? Is the business contracting? Or are cash flows from operating activities sufficient to finance expansion?
7 Has one form of long-term capital been used to redeem another (perhaps issuing shares to repay debentures)? Why might this have been done?
8 Did cash flows from operating activities cover the amount of dividends? Does the dividend appear to be justified by available cash flows?
9 Did the cash balance increase or decrease during the year? Why - what were the main contributors to this?

A cash flow statement provides useful information in relation to questions such as these, but it may not provide full answers. It is important (as always with an interpretation of financial statements) to compare this year's figures with the previous year's and to identify trends. It is also usually necessary to examine the statement of financial position and income statement for further explanation. All three statements should be considered together.

Interpretation

A quick overview of the 2023 cash flow statement for Thorn plc, in the retail sector (see **Illustration 6.4**) shows that it generated a small profit from operations, but its cash flow from operations, after paying interest, taxation and dividends, was substantial and not much lower than in 2022. Although there was a substantial increase in inventories, there was also a substantial increase in trade payables. The increase in trade payables might have a negative effect on Thorn's relationship with its suppliers. There were substantial purchases of non-current assets, repayments of loans and payments against assets acquired on long-term lease arrangements.

ILLUSTRATION 6.4

A published cash flow statement

Statement of group cash flows of Thorn plc, a cocoa retailer, for years ended June

	2023	2022
	£000	£000
Net cash outflow from operating activities[11]		
Profit before tax	852	7,582
Depreciation and amortization	12,197	11,244

[11] Taken from note 32, regrouped and simplified.

Loss/(profit) on disposal of non-current assets	148	(76)
Other items	(110)	379
Increase in inventories	(6,625)	(5,023)
Decrease/(increase) in trade receivables	264	(1,723)
Increase in trade payables	7,265	3,265
Increase in provisions	2,162	609
Increase in post-employment benefit obligations	(1,330)	(1,134)
Cash generated from operations	14,823	15,123
Interest received	12	177
Interest paid	(1,802)	(1,890)
Taxes paid	(1,392)	(2,255)
Dividends paid	(4,054)	(4,553)
Net cash outflow from operating activities	7,587	6,602
Cash flows from investing activities		
Purchase of property, plant, equipment	(4,208)	(4,605)
Proceeds of sale of property, plant, equipment	46	136
Net cash outflow from investing activities	(4,162)	(4,469)
Cash flows from financing activities		
Net proceeds from issue of shares	–	18
Capital element of finance leases rental payments	(2,499)	(3,613)
Borrowings (repaid)/advanced	(800)	2,500
Net cash outflow from financing activities	(3,299)	(1,095)
Net increase in cash and cash equivalents	126	1,038
Cash and equivalents at beginning of year	1,626	588
Cash and equivalents at end of year	1,752	1,626

In 2022, the pattern of cash flows is quite similar, although there was a significant improvement in the working capital since the receivables were lower compared to that in 2023. In both years, 2023 and 2022, there were substantial repayments of loans and no share issues. Perhaps, given the state of the economy and difficulties experienced in the retail sector, the company was happy to increase its cash balances and survive the period.

6.5 Format for Cash Flow Statements

A company's statement of financial position shows how much cash (bank) it has. Comparing this year's statement of financial position with last year's shows whether it has higher or lower cash now than a year ago or whether its overdraft has increased. It is worth comparing the profit that the company has made with what has happened to its cash balances.

The Stuaper Company (**Illustration 6.5**) made a profit during the year 2023, but it ended up with less cash at the end of the year than it had at the beginning. This is not unusual. If we compare the statements of financial position at the end of years 2022 and 2023, we can see what has happened to a lot of its cash. Where assets have increased (items 1, 2 and 3), we can assume that cash has flowed out of the business to pay for them. Where liabilities have been reduced (items 4 and 5), we can assume that cash has flowed out of the business to (re)pay them. In total, £140,000 has flowed out of the business to buy more assets or to pay liabilities.

ILLUSTRATION 6.5

Simplified statement of financial position of Stuaper Company as at 31 December

	Year 2022		Year 2023	
	£000	£000	£000	£000
Non-current assets		200		250
Current assets				
Inventories and	60		80	
Receivables	40		60	
Cash	160	260	40	180
		460		430
Current liabilities				
Trade payables		40		30
Non-current liabilities				
Borrowings		70		30
Equity				
Share capital	200		200	
Retained earnings	150	350	170	370
		460		430

Simplified income statement of Stuaper Company for the year ended 31 December

	Year 2023
	£000
Sales revenue	660
Cost of sales	440
Gross profit	220
Operating expenses	120
Operating profit	100
Finance expenses	(7)
Profit before tax	93
Corporation tax	(30)
Profit after tax	63

Cash balances have decreased from £160,000 to £40,000, an outflow of £120,000. But these outflows of cash have been partly offset by the fact that the company has made a profit. The statement of financial position shows that retained earnings have increased from £150,000 to £170,000: the company must have made (at least) £20,000[12] profit.

	£000
1 Non-current assets have increased, so it seems that it has bought more non-current assets during the year (250 - 200)	(50)
2 Inventories have increased, so it seems that more money is tied up in inventories (80 - 60)	(20)
3 Receivables have increased, so it seems that more money is tied up in receivables (60 - 40)	(20)
4 Current liabilities have gone down, so it seems that more money has been paid out (30 - 40)	(10)
5 Borrowings have gone down, so it seems that cash has been paid out to repay them (30 - 70)	(40)
6 Total outflows of cash	(140)
7 Reduction in cash balance	120
8 Increase in retained earnings	20

One way of preparing a cash flow statement is simply to compare each item on this year's statement of financial position with last year's. Every increase in assets or reduction in liabilities,[13] is an outflow of cash. Every decrease in assets or increase in liabilities,[14] is an inflow of cash. Arithmetically, this will reconcile this year's cash balance with last year's. But this is not satisfactory for a number of reasons:

1 A reconciliation is not an explanation, and it is better to present a cash flow statement in accordance with international accounting standards to make comparisons easier.
2 One simple figure for an increase (or decrease) in non-current assets is not satisfactory because (at least) two things have usually happened:
   a additional non-current assets have been bought (and some may have been revalued or disposed of);
   b non-current assets have been depreciated.

   Careful examination of the notes to the accounts might show the depreciation charge for the year and the amount spent buying additional non-current assets. The net figure of £50,000 does not tell us what we want to know.
3 The £20,000 increase in retained earnings is not a very useful figure. It is more useful to need to know how much the **profit before tax** was (before deducting taxation and dividends) as a first step to finding out how much cash was generated from operations. If we find that the company paid dividends of £43,000 during the year, the total profit after tax would be £63,000, leaving additional retained earnings of £20,000.

IAS 7 requires that cash flows should be classified under three headings:

1 Operating activities
2 Investing activities
3 Financing activities

Although international standards are not totally prescriptive about what should be included under each of the three headings, **Illustration 6.6** complies with generally accepted practice.

12 Some profits have been paid out as dividends. The statement of financial position shows only the *retained* earnings.
13 Or equity.
14 Or equity.

ILLUSTRATION 6.6

Summarized statement of financial position of Kione Halby as at 31 December

	Year 2022		Year 2023	
	£000	£000	£000	£000
Non-current assets				
Machinery at net book value	20		15	
Vehicles at cost	–	20	45	60
Current assets				
Inventories	30		50	
Receivables	30		35	
Cash	10	70		85
Total assets		90		145
Current liabilities				
Trade payables		20	18	
Overdraft			4	22
Non-current liabilities				
Debentures				50
Equity				
Share capital	40		40	
Retained earnings	30	70	33	73
		90		145

Summarized income statement for the year ended 31 December 2023

	£000
Sales revenue	200
Cost of sales	(170)
Gross profit	30
Profit on sale of non-current asset	1
Depreciation of machinery	(5)
Other operating expenses	(11)
Profit for the year	15

Additional information

1 During the year machinery, which had a net book value of £3,000, was sold for £4,000.

2 The motor vehicles were bought on the last day of year 2023, and no depreciation will be charged on them until year 2024.

3 Dividends paid were £12,000.

Ignore interest and taxation.

Summarized statement of financial position of Kione Halby as at 31 December				
	Year 2022		**Year 2023**	
	£000	£000	£000	£000

Kione Halby Cash flow statement for the year ended 31 December 2023			
	£000	£000	
Cash generated from operating activities			
Profit before tax		15	
Depreciation		5	
Other items			
Profit on sale of machinery		(1)	
		19	
Increase in working capital			
Increase in inventories (30–50)	(20)		
Increase in receivables (30–35)	(5)		
Decrease in payables (20–18)	(2)	(27)	
Interest paid	–		
Dividends paid	(12)	(12)	
Net cash outflow from operations		(20)	
Cash used in investing activities			
Purchase of machinery	(3)		See note 1
Purchase of vehicles	(45)		
Proceeds of disposal of non-current assets	4	(44)	
Cash used in financing activities			
Debentures issued	50	50	
Decrease in cash during year		(14)	
Opening cash balance		10	
Closing cash balance		(4)	

Note 1: The net book value of machinery at the beginning of the year was £20,000; machinery with a net book value of £3,000 was sold, and depreciation of £5,000 was charged; these would reduce the balance to £12,000. The balance at the end of the year was £15,000, indicating that additional machinery of £3,000 had been purchased.

In the above statement the convention has been adopted that outflows of cash are shown in brackets.

Cash generated from/used in operating activities

The above presentation shows cash generated from operating activities in three stages:

1 *Profit before tax plus depreciation and similar items and interest expense.* This is almost always an inflow of cash. Even when a business makes a loss, this is often more than offset by the depreciation charge for the year. The figure for Kione Halby is a cash flow of £19,000 (15,000 + 5,000 - 1,000).

2 *Changes in working capital.* This is typically an outflow of cash when a business is expanding. But careful management, reducing inventories and receivables, and delaying paying payables can produce an inflow of cash. Kione Halby had an outflow of £27,000 (20,000 + 5,000 + 2,000).

3 *Interest, taxation and dividends paid.* These are usually outflows of cash. However, sometimes a company receives more interest than it pays out; and negative tax charges do exist (for example, after losses, and/or substantial writing-down allowances for new non-current assets).

4 According to IAS s7.18, the direct method of presentation for operating cash flow is the preferred method. The direct method consists of gross cash receipts and gross cash payments and the operating cash flow would take the following format:

a

Direct method for calculating operating cash flow	**£**
Cash receipts from customers	xx
Cash paid to suppliers	xx
Cash paid for other operating expenses	xx
Interest paid	xx
Income taxes paid	xx
Net cash from operating activities	**xx**

The indirect method adjusts the accrual basis of net profit/loss for the effects of non-cash transactions. The operating cash flow using the indirect method would be shown as follows:

b

Indirect method for calculating operating cash flow	**£**
Profit before interest and income taxes	xx
Add back depreciation	xx
(Increase)/decrease in receivables	xx
(Increase)/decrease in inventories	xx
Increase/(decrease) in trade payables	xx
Interest paid	xx
Income tax paid	xx
Net cash from operating activities	**xx**

Illustration 6.6 is simplified, and Kione Halby made no payments for interest or taxation. Overall, in a successful business, there should be a cash inflow from operating activities. But with Kione Halby there was an overall outflow of cash of £8,000 (19,000 - 27,000) from operating activities because of the substantial increase in working capital.

Cash generated from/used in investing activities

The main items here are purchase of non-current assets, or other businesses, which are outflows of cash. There are usually some inflows as well, resulting from sales of non-current assets or parts of the business. Kione Halby paid £48,000 (45,000 + 3,000) for additional non-current assets, which was slightly offset by receipts of £4,000 for selling old non-current assets. The net cash outflow was £44,000.

Cash generated from/used in financing activities

Inflows and outflows are about equally likely under this heading. Dividends paid are classified as payments of operating activities, although they can also be classified as an outflow of cash under financing activities. The repayment or redemption of debentures and shares. Inflows result from additional borrowings or from raising more share capital. Kione Halby obviously needed a lot more cash (to finance the increases in working capital and the additional non-current assets), and it raised £50,000 by issuing debentures.

The total of the three categories of cash flow added together show a net outflow of £14,000, as follows:

	£
Cash used in operating activities	(20,000)
Cash used in investing activities	(44,000)
Cash generated from financing activities	50,000
Net cash outflow	(14,000)

The total of the cash flows in each of these categories must be equal to the difference between the cash that the business had at the beginning of the year and the amount at the end of the year. Kione Halby started the year with £10,000 in the bank; it ended the year with an overdraft of £4,000; this means that £14,000 had flowed out of the business. The cash flow statement shows the main items that made up that outflow.

6.6 How to Prepare a Cash Flow Statement

In order to prepare a cash flow statement, it is important to have a clear format in mind, such as the one shown in **Illustration 6.6**. Then, it is helpful to list each of the items that have to be found in the statement of financial position, income statement or notes to the accounts, as shown in **Illustration 6.7**. It is a good idea to leave a line or two between each item as there are likely to be additional figures or 'adjustments'[15] to be slotted in.

ILLUSTRATION 6.7

Cash generated from operating activities

1 Profit before tax

2 Depreciation

3 Other items such as profit or loss on the sale of non-current assets

4 Interest expense

(Increase)/decrease in working capital

5 (Increase)/decrease in inventories

6 (Increase)/decrease in receivables

7 Increase /(decrease) in payables

= *Cash inflow/(outflow) from operating activities*

8 Interest paid

9 Taxation paid

[15] It sounds better if you are 'making an adjustment' rather than just correcting a mistake!

10 Dividends paid*

= *Net cash inflow (outflow) from operating activities*

Cash used in investing activities

11 Purchase of non-current assets

12 Disposal of non-current assets

Cash used in financing activities

13 Issue/(repayment) of loan

14 Issue/(redemption of shares

Increase/(decrease) in cash during year

+ **Opening cash balance**

= **Closing cash balance**

* Can be shown as a financing activity

There is almost no limit to how complicated financial statements can be, and a competent and experienced accountant would be needed to produce a decent cash flow statement for any large, listed company. The following provides a guide to how the main figures can be found in a reasonably straightforward situation. The items are numbered in **Illustration 6.7** for convenience; this numbering has no official status. The format illustrated complies with international standards, but some variations are also acceptable.

1 Profit before tax should be easy to find on an income statement, even if it is not separately labelled as such.

It may be useful to see what cash flows have been generated before deducting interest, taxation and dividends, but these obviously have to be paid. They are usually shown as separate items (8, 9 and 10 in **Illustration 6.7**).

2 Depreciation is regarded as being a cash inflow because profit before tax is calculated after charging depreciation for the year as if depreciation was an outflow of cash. But it is not an outflow; it is charged as an expense and so has to be added back to profit as if it is a cash inflow.

Depreciation is not usually shown as a separate item on the face of an income statement. It is tucked away in the note; usually the note that applies to non-current assets on the statement of financial position. There is a schedule that shows the balance at the beginning of the year[16] for non-current assets: the balance at the end of the year, and the explanation of the differences; additional non-current assets acquired during the year; and disposals of non-current assets during the year. There is a similar schedule for depreciation showing the total cumulative depreciation at the beginning of the year, the depreciation charge for the year, the amount of depreciation for non-current assets disposed of, and the total cumulative depreciation remaining at the end of the year.

3 There are often other items, such as depreciation, which have been charged as expenses, but there has been no outflow of cash. These have to be added back to profit. They include: amortization; write-offs for impairment of goodwill and other assets; and increases in provisions.

Some of these items can be the other way around: profits have been boosted by items that produce no cash flows, and which therefore have to be deducted from operating profit. A reduction in a provision is an example of this.

There is also a problem with any profit or loss arising from the sale of non-current assets. If a non-current asset is sold during the year for more than its net book value, the profit arising is correctly treated as part of the profit in preparing the income statement. The total amount of cash received on

[16] The non-current assets are shown at cost (or revalued amount).

disposal of a non-current asset is shown under item 10, and this includes the amount of profit as part of the cash inflow. As the profit on disposal cannot be included twice on a cash flow statement (as part of the profit and as part of the proceeds of disposal), it has to be taken out of the profit figure; this is done by deducting it from profit - as if it is a cash outflow.

If a non-current asset is sold for less than its net book value, the loss is correctly charged against profit when the income statement is prepared (even if it is not separately identified). But as there is no cash outflow for that loss, the amount has to be added back to profit in preparing the cash flow statement. The proceeds of disposal are shown under item 10 in the cash flow statement.

4 The interest expense must be added back, too, because it might be an accrued expense and not paid at all or to an extent in the year.

5 The increase or decrease in inventories is easily calculated by comparing this year's statement of financial position with last year's. If the difference between the two inventory figures is an increase, the amount is shown on the cash flow statement as an outflow of cash. If inventories have decreased, the cash flow statement shows this as an inflow.

6 The increase or decrease in receivables is easily calculated by comparing this year's statement of financial position with last year's. If the difference between the two receivables figures is an increase, the amount is shown on the cash flow statement as an outflow of cash. If receivables have decreased, the cash flow statement shows this as an inflow.

7 The increase in payables is easily calculated by comparing this year's statement of financial position with last year's. If the difference between the two payables figures is an increase, the amount is shown on the cash flow statement as an inflow of cash. If payables have decreased, the cash flow statement shows this as an outflow.

8 It is easy to find the interest charge for the year on the income statement: it is labelled 'finance costs'. In some cases, there is also 'finance income' (interest receivable), and it is acceptable to show a single net figure for interest on a cash flow statement.

The amount shown on the cash flow statement should be the amount actually paid (or received) during the year, which is sometimes different from the amount shown on the income statement. The income statement should show the amount *due and chargeable as an expense* during the year; the cash flow statement should show the amount actually paid. Sometimes an amount due for the year ended on 31 December is not actually paid until January of the following year. The interest paid, to be shown in the cash flow statement, is the interest payable in the opening statement of financial position, plus the interest expense in the income statement less the interest payable in the closing statement of financial position.

9 It is easy to find the taxation charge for the year on the income statement. Sometimes this might not be the same as the amount actually paid during the year, which is required for the cash flow statement. The amount actually paid can be calculated if sufficient information is available, as shown in **Illustration 6.8**. It is much like the calculation of interest paid. The tax paid in the year, to be shown in the cash flow statement, is the tax liability at the beginning of the year, plus the tax charge in the income statement minus the tax liability at the year end.

10 The dividend paid in the year is usually disclosed in a note to the accounts, very often in the 'statement of changes to equity' note.

11 The amount paid for additional non-current assets can be found in the (statement of financial position) notes to the accounts, as explained in 2 above (additional non-current assets acquired during the year). There may be several different items included under the general heading of non-current assets.

Any increase in the amount of non-current assets that is due to a revaluation involves no cash flows and is not included on a cash flow statement.

12 The amount included on a cash flow statement for disposals of non-current assets must be the actual amount of cash received, not the book value. The book value of assets disposed of is easily established. As explained in 2 above, the statement of financial position notes to the accounts in respect of

non-current assets show both the cost[17] of the assets disposed of and the depreciation relating to them; the difference between the two is the net book value. The sale proceeds are the book value, plus any profit arising, or minus any loss arising. Profits or losses on disposals of non-current assets are included in the income statement, but it may be necessary to hunt around in the notes to find the amounts.

ILLUSTRATION 6.8

Statement of financial position extract from current liabilities

	At 31 December	At 31 December
	Year 2022	Year 2023
Corporation tax	£50,000	£60,000

The income statement showed a tax charge of £58,000 for the year ended 31 December 2023.

To calculate the amount actually paid during the year 2023, we can assume that the whole of the £50,000 shown as a current liability at the end of year 2022 was paid during that year.

During the year 2023, an additional £58,000 became payable, making a total of £108,000 due to be paid. By the end of the year 2023, only £60,000 was still due to be paid. We can therefore assume that the difference, £48,000, was actually paid, and this is the figure to be shown on the cash flow statement. A similar calculation is made to determine the interest actually paid in the year.

13 If any loans have been repaid, the amounts can be established by comparing this year's statement of financial position with last year's. There may be increases or reductions in non-current borrowings or both. Details are provided in the notes to the financial statements.

14 Other items include the cash inflows arising from the issue of any shares during the year, including the amount of any premium. The company may also have bought its own shares and cancelled them, which involves an outflow of cash. The overall picture is easily seen by comparing two years' statements of financial position, and more detail (such as the number of shares issued or redeemed) is provided in the notes to the accounts.

Summary

In many businesses, generating profits and generating cash flows go hand in hand. Good profits are likely to result in healthy cash flows. But the two are unlikely to be identical. In many circumstances, the profit (or loss) for the year can be very different from the increase (or decrease) in cash. The differences between the two show up well on a cash flow statement. Having cash available to meet liabilities as they fall due is essential for business survival, and healthy businesses should generate healthy cash flows. Businesses also need to generate profits if they are to survive and be healthy. If a business makes a profit, its wealth increases. That increase in wealth is used in many different ways (such as paying dividends and investing in more assets); it is unlikely to be matched by an exactly equal increase in cash.

It is vital that users of accounts can see where cash has been generated and how it has been spent in terms of operating activities, investment in non-current assets and elsewhere and in financing, in order to see the 'quality' of profits.

We could debate whether cash flow or profit is more important to the survival and success of businesses. That is like debating whether eating or drinking is more important to the survival and success of people. Both are essential.

17 Or revalued amount.

Review of key points

- Profit is not the same as cash flow. The accruals concept may be seen as being the theoretical justification and explanation of the difference.
- A cash flow statement provides a reconciliation between profit before tax for the year and the net increase or decrease in cash during the year.
- A company's operating profit may be used to finance higher levels of inventory and receivables; to pay interest, taxation and dividends, and to buy additional non-current assets.
- A detailed cash flow statement shows other differences between cash flow and profit in a standardized format.
- A cash flow statement should be interpreted alongside the related statements of financial position and income statements, and can reveal important aspects of a company's performance.
- Some differences between cash flow and profit are relatively minor, relating to the timing of receipts and payments compared with the timing of recognition of revenues and expenses.
- Depreciation is an important expense in calculating profit; there is no equivalent payment in cash terms.
- Cash *in*flows are decreases in assets and increases in liabilities, while cash *de*creases are increases in assets and decreases in liabilities.
- Some of the biggest receipts and payments (such as issue of shares; purchase of non-current assets; paying back loans) have no direct effect on profit.
- The availability of cash to meet liabilities as they fall due is essential to business survival. Making profits is essential if the business is to become 'better off'.

Self-testing questions

1 What is meant by the 'accruals concept'? Why is it important in financial accounting?

2 In what circumstances is a very profitable business likely to find that it has serious cash shortages?

3 Is it possible for a company to make losses year after year but still increase its cash balances? Explain.

4 What is meant by 'free cash flow'? Estimate the amounts of free cash flow for
   a Ebbing plc for the year 2023 (**Illustration 6.2**)
   b Reet Aylor for years 2022 and 2023 (**Illustration 6.3**)

5 You are given the cash flow statements for the last two years for Deek Lining plc, which are as follows:

Cash flow statement of Deek Lining plc for the year ended 31 December

	Year 3	Year 4
	£000	£000
Cash flows from operating activities		
Profit before tax	3,200	(1,350)
Depreciation	2,600	2,800
	5,800	1,450

Cash flow statement of Deek Lining plc for the year ended 31 December

	Year 3	Year 4
	£000	£000
Interest expense	200	150
(Increase) Decrease in trade receivables	(600)	300
(Increase) Decrease in inventories	(400)	200
(Decrease) Increase in trade payables	(100)	100
Cash inflow from operations	4,900	2,200
Interest paid	(200)	(150)
Income taxes paid	(1,300)	(100)
Dividend paid	(600)	(700)
Net cash flow from operating activities	2,800	1,250
Cash flows from investing activities		
Proceeds from disposal of equipment	100	1,100
Purchase of property and equipment	(3,700)	(150)
Net cash from investing activities	(3,600)	950
Cash flows from financing activities		
Proceeds of issue of shares	–	–
Increase (Decrease) in borrowings	200	(1,000)
Net raised cash from (used in)	–	–
financing activities	200	(1,000)
Net (decrease)/increase in cash	(600)	1,200
Opening cash	700	(100)
Closing cash	100	1,100

An extract from the chairperson's statement reads as follows:

> *Year 4 was another successful year, producing a positive cash flow which enabled us to pay off a substantial amount of borrowings, to invest in new fixed assets, and to increase the dividends for ordinary shareholders.*

Critically appraise this statement.

6 You are required to produce a cash flow statement for Daubyhaven Ltd for the year ended 31 December year 2.

Summarized statement of financial position of Daubyhaven Ltd as at 31 December

	Year 1		Year 2	
Non-current assets	£000	£000	£000	£000
Machinery at cost	120		130	
Provision for depreciation	(60)	60	(68)	62
Current assets				
Inventories	30		50	
Receivables	30		35	

Summarized statement of financial position of Daubyhaven Ltd as at 31 December

	Year 1		Year 2	
Cash	10	70	-	85
Total assets		130		147
Current liabilities				
Trade payables		20	18	
Overdraft			12	30
Non-current liabilities				
Debentures		30		20
Equity				
Share capital	50		60	
Retained earnings	30	80	37	97
		130		147

During the year ending 31 December year 2:

a A machine that had originally cost £15,000 and on which £12,000 depreciation had been charged was sold for £4,500.

b Operating profit, including the profit on the sale of the machine, was £35,000.

c Interest of £2,000, taxation of £8,000 and dividends of £18,000 were paid.

7 You are required to prepare a cash flow statement for Fistard Neash plc for the year ended 31 December Year 6.

Summarized statement of financial position of Fistard Neash plc as at 31 December

	Year 5		Year 6	
Non-current assets	£m	£m	£m	£m
Intangible assets		100		90
Property, plant and equipment	120		140	
Provision for depreciation	(50)	70	(66)	74
Current assets				
Inventories	40		65	
Receivables	60		55	
Cash	10	110	8	128
Total assets		280		292
Current liabilities				
Trade payables		45		40
Non-current liabilities				
Debentures		55		6

Summarized statement of financial position of Fistard Neash plc as at 31 December

	Year 5		Year 6	
Equity				
Share capital	150		170	
Share premium	-		40	
Retained earnings	30	180	36	246
		280		292

Income statement for year ended 31 December year 6

	£m
Sales revenue	440
Cost of sales	(330)
Gross profit	110
Profit on sale of Scottish factory	7
Distribution costs	(47)
Administrative expenses	(40)
Impairment of goodwill	(10)
Operating profit	20
Finance costs	(2)
Profit before taxation	18
Corporation tax	(4)
Profit for the year	14

During the year ending 31 December year 6:

a The Scottish factory had originally cost £24m, and depreciation of £8m had been charged on it. It was sold for £23m.

b Dividends paid were £8m.

c Interest of £2m and taxation of £4m were paid.

Assessment questions

1 Explain the effect of the accruals concept on the treatment of inventories, capital expenditure, receivables and payables.

2 Shareholders are mainly interested in a company's ability to pay dividends. If a company increases the amount of cash it has available during the year, it is able to pay more dividends. A company should therefore aim to maximize the amount of cash it has available. Explain the flaws in these statements.

3 You are given the following cash flow statements for Ink Reasing plc.

Cash flow statement of Ink Reasing plc for the year ended 31 December

	Year 1	Year 2
	£000	£000
Cash flows from operating activities		
Profit before financing costs	1,800	2,500
Depreciation	1,500	1,900
	3,300	4,400
Increase in trade receivables	(800)	(1,200)
Increase in inventories	(600)	(1,300)
Increase in trade payables	100	200
Cash from operations	2,000	2,100
Interest paid	(600)	(600)
Income taxes paid	(400)	(600)
Net cash from operating activities	1,000	900
Cash flows from investing activities		
Proceeds from disposal of equipment	-	100
Purchase of property and equipment	(2,100)	(4,000)
Net cash from investing activities	(2,100)	(3,900)
Cash flows from financing activities		
Proceeds of issue of shares	2,000	-
(Repayment of) increase in borrowings	(600)	2,200
Dividends paid	(400)	(500)
Net cash (used in) raised from financing activities	1,000	1,700
Net (decrease)/increase in cash	(100)	(1,300)
Opening cash	400	300
Closing cash	300	(1,000)

a Write a report explaining what the above cash flow statements reveal.

b The company's bankers stated that, in view of the £1m increase in the company's overdraft and the additional borrowings of £2.2m, the increase in the amount of dividends paid is not justified. Do you agree? Explain.

4 Ballamauda Ltd

Summarized statement of financial position as at 31 December

	Year 1		Year 2	
Non-current assets	£000	£000	£000	£000
Machinery at cost	80		70	
Provision for depreciation	(40)	40	(44)	26

Summarized statement of financial position as at 31 December

	Year 1		Year 2	
Current assets				
Inventories	50		35	
Receivables	38		28	
Cash	-	88	90	153
Total assets		128		179
Current liabilities				
Trade payables	30		39	
Overdraft	16	46	-	39
Non-current liabilities				
Debentures		-		40
Equity				
Share capital	40		40	
Retained earnings	42	82	60	100
		128		179

During the year ending 31 December year 2:

a A machine, which had originally cost £10,000 and on which £6,000 depreciation had been charged, was sold for £3,400.

b The profit before tax, after deducting the loss on the sale of the machine, was £35,200.

c Interest of £2,400, taxation of £6,400 and dividends of £6,000 were paid.

You are required to produce a cash flow statement for Ballamauda Ltd for the year ended 31 December year 2.

5 Soldriction plc

The summarized statement of financial position as at 31 December

	Year 3		Year 4	
Non-current assets	£m	£m	£m	£m
Intangible assets		50		55
Machinery at cost	90		104	
Provision for depreciation	(30)	60	(44)	60
		110		115
Current assets				
Inventories	30		36	
Receivables	44		48	
Cash	-	74	8	92
Total assets		184		207

The summarized statement of financial position as at 31 December

	Year 3		Year 4	
Current liabilities				
Trade payables	28		20	
Overdraft	13	41	-	20
Non-current liabilities				
Debentures		-		38
Equity				
Share capital	90		90	
Retained earnings	53	143	59	149
		184		207

Income statement for year ended 31 December year 4

	£m
Sales revenue	216
Cost of sales	(144)
Gross profit	72
Loss on sale of machinery	(4)
Distribution costs	(24)
Administrative expenses	(20)
Impairment of goodwill	(6)
Operating profit	18
Finance costs	(3)
Profit before taxation	15
Corporation tax	(4)
Profit for the year	11

During the year ending 31 December year 4:

a The company sold machinery, which had cost £12m, and on which £5m depreciation had been charged, for £3m.

b The company bought a number of manufacturing businesses in South Asia for £37m, of which £26m was for property, plant and equipment, and £11m for goodwill.

c Dividends paid were £5m.

d Interest of £3m and taxation of £4m were paid.

You are required to produce a cash flow statement for Soldriction plc for the year ended 31 December year 4.

6 You are given the following summarized statements of financial position and income statements for the Solverham Company for the past two years.

Statement of financial position as at 31 December

	Year 1		Year 2	
	£000	£000	£000	£000
Non-current assets at cost		200		220
Provision for depreciation		(60)		(82)
Net book value		140		138
Current assets				
Inventories	95		70	
Receivables	80		50	
Cash	-	175	25	145
Total assets		315		283
Liabilities and equity				
Current liabilities				
Payables	40		60	
Overdraft	80	120	-	60
Non-current liabilities				
12% debentures		110		135
Equity				
Share capital	50		50	
Retained earnings	35	85	338	88
		315		283

Income statement for the year ended 31 December

	Year 1	Year 2
Sales	520	500
Cost of sales	376	375
Gross profit	144	125
Administration expenses	(35)	(36)
Depreciation	(20)	(22)
Distribution costs	(22)	(24)
Operating profit	(67)	(43)
Interest paid	(14)	(17)
Net profit before tax	53	26
Taxation paid	16	8
Net profit after tax	37	18

Dividends paid in year 1 were £10,000, and in year 2 were £15,000.

a Prepare a cash flow statement for the year ended 31 December year 2.

b Explain how cash flow differs from profit.

c The company's managing director is pleased that the company has money in the bank, having paid off a significant overdraft. He is particularly pleased that he ignored his chief accountant, who said that the company could not afford to buy more fixed assets or to increase the dividend. Critically assess the chief accountant's advice.

7 Malcolm, the son of the founder of Solverham plc, is aware that the managing director of the company believes that the company is strong, and is doing well, but the chief accountant says that the company's position is rapidly deteriorating. You are required to produce a report on the company's financial position and performance based on the information given for question 6, Solverham Company. Your answer should include calculations of the ratios shown below for each year, and comments on them.

a Current ratio

b Liquidity ratio

c Capital gearing ratio

d Interest times cover

e Return on shareholders' funds

f Return on total long-term capital employed

g Operating profit as a percentage of sales

h Asset turnover

i Gross profit ratio

j Distribution costs as a percentage of sales

k Administrative expenses as a percentage of sales

l Sales/non-current assets

m Sales/current assets

n Inventory turnover ratio

o Trade receivables ratio

p Trade payables ratio

Group activities and discussion questions

1 A small business is more likely to prosper and to control its operations effectively by monitoring cash flows than by listening to its accountant. Discuss.

2 In what ways is a cash flow statement likely to be useful?

3 Why should small businesses produce accruals-based accounts (as opposed to relying on controlling cash and banking)?

4 The published accounts of companies have steadily become more complicated, with additional statements, notes and disclosures, as required by accounting standards. Conventional financial accounting is a waste of time and effort for small businesses. Discuss.

5 Analyse a number of companies' cash flow statements. Which figures seem to give the best indication of a company's performance? Can 'free cash flow' be assessed, and does it provide a useful indicator?

6 Analyse a number of companies' statements of financial position and calculate their current ratios, liquidity ratios and capital gearing ratios for the last two years. What do these ratios tell you about the companies' liquidity problems or strengths? What useful information does the companies' cash flow statements add to this?

7 The financial statements of a small business are likely to reveal any liquidity problems; the financial statements of a major listed company are more likely to disguise them. Discuss.

8 It is useful for companies to have detailed analysis and control of all cash flows. Why would they want additional, accruals-based information?

Accounting in context

Discuss and comment on the following report, based on an article from the press, with particular reference to the distinction between making profits and generating cash and an analysis of the sources and uses of cash.

BenevolentAI

BenevolentAI is one of the largest private AI companies globally and the leader in applying AI for scientific innovation. Founded in 2013 by Ken Mulvany, it analyses vast amounts of medical data to assist researchers in finding new disease treatment methods and creating personalized drugs for patients who would benefit the most.

In 2018, BenevolentAI raised £86m in capital, but its 2018 accounts showed only £63.6m from 'the issue of share capital net of costs'. The company's statement claims only 36,195 shares were issued for cash, amounting to £29.6m worth of equity. The remaining shares were issued as part of an acquisition of BenevolentAI Cambridge Ltd for £30.7m. The acquisition payment was £21.4m in stock and £9.3m in cash. In total, this amounts to only £51m of equity, which is £13m short of the £64m stated in the cash flow statement. Initially, the company did not respond to this discrepancy.

The company later clarified that the shares issued for the acquisition were separate from those issued for the capital raise. Also, the 36,195 shares issued for cash were net of redemptions of shares and were not the total shares issued to raise the £63.6m. BenevolentAI has also indicated that the £63.6m represented the cash drawn down to date from the raise. The remaining balance will be reflected in the 2019 financial statements, and the money raised totalled £84.1m.

Before the acquisition, BenevolentAI Cambridge was known as Proximagen Ltd. This company was owned by one of its key investors and was once part of BenevolentAI's CEO Ken Mulvany's old business. Despite the Cambridge facility losing £5m over 10 months in 2018, Mulvany was keen to be reunited with a part of his old business. A few months after the acquisition closed, the Evenstads injected at least £48m into BenevolentAI via the capital raise. BenevolentAI's press release on the acquisition did not mention that the Cambridge facility was owned by one of its key investors and was once part of Mulvany's old business. It instead focused on how the acquisition of a loss-making research lab meant that BenevolentAI was now 'an AI company ... across every stage of the drug discovery process'.

In a September 2018 blog post, the new CEO Joanna Shields stated that they acquired a drug development facility in Cambridge, making them the only AI company that can take their own drugs from discovery to the clinic. This vision is alluring, as it is a business that can aid quicker drug discovery and can now develop the drugs itself.

Sources: Jamie Powell (2019) Inside BenevolentAI: The $2bn Tech Company Backed by Neil Woodford. *Financial Times*, 18 June, https://www.ft.com/content/29f97812-d440-3ff2-a6e4-8b52d3d1b664

http://www.benevolent.ai

References and further reading

Black, G. (2009) *Introduction to Accounting and Finance* (2nd edn.). Harlow: FT Prentice Hall.

Elliott, B. and Elliott, J. (2022) *Financial Accounting and Reporting.* Upper Saddle River, NJ: Pearson Education.

Siegel, M.A. (2006) *Accounting Shenanigans on the Cash Flow Statement.* New York: New York State Society of Certified Public Accountants.

Tamimi, O. and Orbán, I. (2022) The Correlation Between Statement of Cash Flows, IAS 7, and Earnings per Share, IAS 33: A Case Study at Daimler Ag (Mercedes-Benz). *Intelektine Ekonomika,* 16(2). https://doi.org/10.13165/IE-22-16-2-01.

Wood, F. and Sangster, A. (2012) *Business Accounting* (vol. 1) (12th edn.). Harlow: FT Prentice Hall.

https://www.iasplus.com/en-gb/standards/ias/ias7

www.frc.org.uk (UK accounting standards)

www.ifrs.org (international accounting standards)

Chapter 7

Advanced Interpretation of Company and Group Accounts

Chapter contents

7.1 Introduction
7.2 Calculating Ratios from Published Accounts
7.3 Consolidated (Group) Financial Statements
7.4 Solvency and Predicting Financial Distress
7.5 Selective Performance
7.6 Other Information from Annual Reports

Learning objectives

After studying this chapter you will be able to:

- ✓ Identify key information in published financial statements required to assess companies' solvency and profitability
- ✓ Understand the terminology used in consolidated accounts and produce straightforward group statements of financial position
- ✓ Explain how financial accounting information can be used to calculate Z-scores and predict financial distress and understand the main elements included in Z-scores
- ✓ Analyse the performance of companies using most of the detailed information included in published financial statements
- ✓ Describe segmental reporting and make use of the information disclosed to assess the performance of different segments
- ✓ Make use of financial information disclosed by companies in addition to that included in statements of financial position, income statements and cash flow statements

7.1 Introduction

Chapter 4 showed how 20 widely used 'ratios' can be used to assess three key aspects of a company:

- Its solvency and ability to meet its liabilities as they fall due
- Its profitability and how this can be increased
- How its shares are rated on the stock market.

It is not too difficult to calculate these ratios when the information is provided by a textbook in a convenient format. It is more difficult to find and use appropriate information from a complex-looking annual report and accounts.

This chapter begins by providing extracts from the 2023 published annual report of Marks and Spencer plc. The 20 ratios are calculated for 2022, together with guidance on selecting the appropriate figures and some interpretation. Students are invited to calculate the equivalent 20 ratios for 2023 and to provide a more detailed interpretation.

The second part explains how group (or consolidated) statements of financial position are produced. The third and fourth parts of the chapter provide more detailed guidance on assessing solvency and profitability. A more detailed consideration of a company's performance on the stock market is provided in **Chapter 6**. The final part of this chapter examines other information available from annual reports and accounts.

7.2 Calculating Ratios from Published Accounts

The information provided in respect of Marks and Spencer plc is from pages 144 to 146 of their 2023 annual report and accounts and part of notes 2, 3, 17 and 19. The information in respect of ratios 17–19 assumes the share price to be 158p in 2022, and 167p in 2023. These figures show a 5.7 per cent increase in that one-year period. Share prices, as a whole, as indicated by the FTSE 100 index growth was less than 4 per cent in that period. Hence, Marks and Spencer shares performed very well in comparison with the market, as a whole (see **Illustration 7.1** and **Illustration 7.2**).

ILLUSTRATION 7.1

Marks and Spencer plc

Consolidated statement of financial position 1 April 2023

	Notes	2023 £m	2022 £m
Assets			
Non-current assets			
Intangible assets	14	**163.1**	192.5
Property, plant & equipment	15	**5,203.7**	4,902.3
Investment property		**11.8**	15.0
Investment in joint venture & associates	29	**767.9**	810.9
Retirement benefit asset	11	**482.0**	1,043.9
Other	16	**7.9**	4.5

Marks and Spencer plc			
Consolidated statement of financial position 1 April 2023			
	Notes	**2023 £m**	**2022 £m**
Trade and other receivables	17	**298.7**	270.6
Derivative financial instruments	21	**0.1**	21.4
Deferred tax assets	23	**7.6**	–
		6,942.8	7,261.1
Current assets			
Inventories		**764.4**	706.1
Other financial assets	16	**13.0**	17.6
Trade and other receivables	17	**280.6**	217.1
Derivative financial instruments	21	**22.6**	43.6
Cash and cash equivalents	18	**1,067.9**	1,197.9
Other		**6.5**	–
		2,155.0	2,182.3
Total assets		9,097.8	9,443.4
Liabilities			
Current liabilities			
Trade and other payables	19	**2,048.8**	1.960.9
Borrowings	20	**444.0**	247.2
Partnership liability to the pension scheme	12	**73.0**	71.9
Derivative financial instruments	21	**58.1**	3.2
Provisions	22	**44.0**	53.6
Current tax liabilities		**38.5**	34.0
		2,706.4	2,370.8
Non-current liabilities			
Retirement benefit deficit	11	**4.6**	5.7
Trade and other payables	19	**181.3**	188.2
Partnership liability to the pension scheme	12	**51.8**	120.4
Borrowings	22	**3,184.0**	3,561.0
Derivative financial instruments	21	**7.1**	0.4
Provisions	22	**75.4**	91.8
Deferred tax liabilities	23	**72,3**	187.2
		3,576.5	4,154.7
Total liabilities		**6,282.9**	6,525.5
Net assets		**2,814,9**	2,917.9
Equity			
Share capital	24	**19.8**	19.7

Marks and Spencer plc			
Consolidated statement of financial position 1 April 2023			
	Notes	**2023 £m**	**2022 £m**
Share premium		**910.7**	910.6
Capital redemption reserve		**2,680.4**	2,680.4
Hedging reserve	21	**(31.9)**	17.6
Cost of Hedging reserve	21	**4.2**	3.6
Other reserve		**(6,542.2)**	(6,542.2)
Foreign exchange reserve		**(69.6)**	(73.9)
Retained earnings		**5,839.1**	5,897.9
Total shareholders' equity		**2,810.5**	2,913.7
Non-controlling interests in equity		**4.4**	4.2
Total equity		**2,814.9**	2,917.9
Total liabilities and equity		**9,097.8**	9,443.4

The financial statements were approved by the Board on 23 May 2023.

Stuart Machin	Katie Bickerstaffe
Chief Executive Officer	Co-Chief Executive Officer

Marks and Spencer plc, Consolidated income statement for the year ended 1 April 2023

	Notes	**2023 £m**	2022 £m
Revenue	2,3	**11,931.3**	10,885.1
Cost of sales	2,3	**(7,786.7)**	(7,130.3)
Gross profit	3	**4,144.6**	3754.8
Selling and administrative expenses	3	**(3,609.2)**	(3,244.1)
Other operating income	3	**23.2**	80.1
Ocado results		**(43.5)**	(18.6)
Operating profit		**515.1**	572.2
Financed income	5, 6	**166.1**	33.9
Finance costs	5, 6	**(205.5)**	(214.4)
Profit before tax	4, 5	**475.7**	391.7
Tax	7	**(111.2)**	(82.7)
Profit for the year		**364.5**	309.0
Basic earnings per share	8	**18.5p**	15.7p
Dividends per share	9	**–**	–
Total dividend paid	9	**–**	–

Marks and Spencer plc, Notes to the financial statements

17 Trade and other receivables

Marks and Spencer plc

Consolidated statement of financial position 1 April 2023

	Notes	2023 £m	2022 £m
		2023 £m	**2022 £m**
Current assets			
Trade receivables (net)		**122.9**	98.2
Other receivables		**36.8**	27.2
Prepayments		**97.0**	76.8
others		**0.9**	0.8
Accrued income		**23.0**	14.1
		280.6	217.1
19 Trade and other payables			
Current liabilities			
Trade payables		**801.7**	732.8
Other payables		**560.0**	523.5
Social security and other taxes		**85.3**	59.1
Accruals		**554.5**	595.2
Deferred income		**47.3**	50.3
		2,048.8	1,960.9
24 Share capital			
	2023		2022
Allotted and issued ordinary shares of £0.01 each fully paid	**1,964,933,931**		1,958, 905, 344
Ordinary shares of £0.01 each, £m	**19.8**		19.7

ILLUSTRATION 7.2

Ratio	2022	2022	2023	2023
1 Current ratio	$\frac{2,182.3}{2,370.8}$	0.92 : 1		
2 Liquidity (quick) ratio	$\frac{(2,182.3 - 706.1)}{2,370.8}$	0.62 : 1		
3 Capital gearing ratio	$\frac{4,154.7}{2,917.9}$	142%		
or	$\frac{4,154.7}{4,154.7 + 2,917.9}$	59%		
4 Interest times cover	$\frac{572.2 + 33.9}{214.4}$	2.83 times		
5 Return on shareholders' funds	$\frac{309}{2,917.9}$	11%		

Ratio	2022	2022	2023	2023
6 Return on total long-term capital employed	$\frac{572.2 + 33.9}{2,913.7 + 4,154.7}$	9%		
7 Operating profit as a percentage of sales	$\frac{572.2}{10,885.1}$	5.3%		
8 Asset turnover	$\frac{10,885.1}{9,443.4 - 2,370.8}$	1.54 times		
9 Gross profit ratio	$\frac{3,754.8}{10,885.1}$	34%		
10 Selling and administrative expenses as a percentage of sales	$\frac{3,244.1}{10,885.1}$	30%		
11 Other operating expenses as a percentage of sales	**Not available**			
12 Sales/non-current assets	$\frac{10,885.1}{7,261.1}$	1.5 times		
13 Sales/current assets	$\frac{10,885.1}{2,182.3}$	4.99 times		
14 Inventory turnover ratio	$\frac{365 \times 706.1}{7,130.3}$	36 days		
15 Trade receivables ratio	$\frac{365 \times 98.2}{10,885.1}$	3.3 days		
16 Trade payables ratio	$\frac{365 \times 732.8}{7,130.3}$	37.5 days		
17 Price/earnings ratio	$\frac{158}{15.7}$	10.06		
18 Dividend yield	No dividend paid			
19 Dividend cover	No dividend paid			
20 Net assets per share or shareholders' equity per share	2,913.7 / 1,959.9	£1.487		

Comments on Marks and Spencer plc 2023 figures

Readers should complete the ratio table for 2023.

1 The **current ratio** is the ratio of current assets to current liabilities. It is lower than many companies but its inventory is readily saleable and goods are sold for immediate payment. The current ratio of this company is higher than that of a supermarket group, such as Tesco (0.76). Comparative figures for Tesco are found using the Fame database.

2 The **liquidity ratio** is the ratio of current assets excluding inventories to current liabilities. This is also low because the company has few trade receivables (customers pay for their purchases on sale yet the company buys its goods on credit). These two liquidity ratios are neither too high nor two low when judged against similar companies.

3 The **gearing ratio** relates debt (or borrowings) to equity. In this instance, for convenience, the total amount for non-current liabilities has been used. Non-current liabilities are shown as a percentage of total long-term capital (non-current liabilities plus equity). It is also acceptable to use borrowings as a

percentage of equity. Although gearing is on the high side, Marks and Spencer has the strength and reputation to maintain such a level of gearing.

If current liabilities are added to non-current liabilities (£2,370.8m + £4,154.7m = £6,525.5m), the total amount of short and long term 'debt' is seen to be higher than the amount of equity (£2,917.9m), which may be a cause for concern.

4 Interest cover is calculated by taking the profit available for paying interest and dividing it by the amount of interest paid (shown as finance costs). Although it depends on the type of business, interest cover of more than about 5 looks reasonably comfortable.

5 The profit for the period (after tax) is expressed as a percentage of the total amount for shareholders' equity. It is the return earned for ordinary shareholders. A return of more than 20 per cent is quite impressive, given the state of the retail sector.

6 Operating profit and finance income (before deducting interest paid and taxation) is expressed as a percentage of total capital employed, using the figure from number 3 above. It is the return earned by the company on the total of its long-term capital employed. It is important to use equivalent figures when comparing one year with another, and also when relating income statement figures to statement of financial position figures. As the assets generating finance income have been included on the statement of financial position[1] the 'return' must include all returns on those assets.

It is difficult to be completely consistent and correct. The figure used for capital employed includes all non-current liabilities. It excludes those 'loans and borrowings' that are part of current liabilities. The figure provided for finance costs includes interest on both non-current and current liabilities. It would be possible to estimate how much of the finance costs relate to short-term borrowings, and treat these as an operating expense. In ratio analysis there is inevitably some approximation, and it is necessary to be consistent. In this analysis all interest has been treated as if it is in respect of non-current liabilities.

The return, using both ratios 5 and 6, looks reasonable. It is more useful to compare two or more years and to note trends.

7 Operating profit is expressed as a percentage of sales revenue (turnover). This calculation, as with most profitability ratios, means little except when compared with other years, or with other companies in a similar line of business.

8 Sales revenue (turnover) is divided by operating assets; this includes all operating assets regardless of what long-term financing was used. It is usually taken as the total of all assets (current and non-current), *minus* current liabilities. It is equal to equity plus non-current liabilities.

9 Gross profit is expressed as a percentage of sales revenue (turnover).

10 Most companies disclose two categories of operating expenses - distribution costs and administrative expenses that can be expressed as a percentage of sales revenue (turnover). In this instance only selling and administrative expenses have been separately identified and disclosed.

11 In addition to distribution costs and/or administrative expenses one can also use operating profit as a percentage of sales revenue.

12 Sales revenue (turnover) is divided by the total for non-current assets to show the number of times that non-current assets were 'turned over' during the year.

13 Sales revenue (turnover) is divided by the total for current assets to show the number of times that current assets were 'turned over' during the year. This is then analysed in more detail in ratios 14 and 15 (and 16).

14 Cost of sales is used here, not sales, because the inventories figure is shown at cost price (not selling price). Inventories are divided by cost of sales (which is sales *minus* gross profit); this is then multiplied by 365 to show how many days inventories are held.

[1] It would be included in 'investments accounted for using the equity method'.

15 The sales figure is used here (not cost of sales) because receivables are shown at selling price. Trade receivables are divided by sales (turnover) and then multiplied by 365 to express the amount of receivables in days, which indicates how long receivables take to pay. Here, the figure for receivables is very low because people pay for their purchases as they buy them. When a company sells goods and is paid by credit card, the seller receives the money almost immediately.

16 Cost of sales is used here, not sales, because the amounts owing as trade payables are at cost price. Trade payables are divided by cost of sales, and then multiplied by 365 to indicate the number of days taken to pay trade payables.

17 This is calculated as the share price (current, perhaps taken from the *Financial Times*) divided by the amount of earnings per share, as shown in **Chapter 5**. The higher the price/earnings (PE) ratio, the more confident the stock market is in the company's growth prospects.

18 The dividend paid in the year usually comprises last year's final dividend, which is paid in the first half of this financial year, and this year's interim dividend, which is paid in the second half of this financial year. The dividend is expressed as a percentage of the current share price. However, Marks and Spencer did not pay any dividends in 2022 or 2023.

19 This can be computed as the profit after tax divided by the dividend paid, or the earnings per share is divided by the dividend per share.

20 The amount shown for total shareholders' equity is divided by the number of shares, which is taken from note 24. The share price on the stock market was higher than the statement of financial position value per share, reflecting that the expected benefits of owning these shares exceeds the carrying value of the net assets as reflected in the statement of financial position.

7.3 Consolidated (Group) Financial Statements

Most large listed public companies are really groups: a parent company with a number of subsidiary companies. When interpreting their financial statement, it is usually better to use the figures for the group rather than just for the (parent) company. In order to interpret these, it is necessary to know some of the principles and terminology of **consolidated accounts**.

Illustration 7.3 shows the simplified statements of the financial position of Quinnie plc and Krown Ltd on 31 December year 1, immediately after Quinnie bought all the shares of Krown. The group statement of financial position, which combines the two companies, looks like that of Quinnie, except that Quinnie's investment in Krown (£240,000) has been replaced by the net assets[2] of Krown (which also happens to be £240,000). Hence, in **Illustration 7.3**, the consolidated statement of financial position for Quinnie plc there is no goodwill.

ILLUSTRATION 7.3

Summarized statements of financial position of Quinnie plc and Krown Ltd at 31 December year 1

	Quinnie plc	Krown Ltd
	£000	£000
Non-current assets	260	200
Investment in Krown Ltd at cost	240	–
Current assets	80	100
Total assets	580	300

[2] Non-current assets, plus current assets, minus current liabilities.

Summarized statements of financial position of Quinnie plc and Krown Ltd at 31 December year 1

	Quinnie plc	Krown Ltd
	£000	£000
Current liabilities	100	60
Ordinary share capital	300	200
Retained earnings	180	40
	580	300

Quinnie bought 100 per cent of the shares of Krown Ltd on 31 December year 1. The group/consolidated statement of financial position as at 31 December year 1, using the acquisition method for consolidation, is prepared as follows:

Consolidated statement of financial position of Quinnie plc and its subsidiary at 31 December year 1

	Workings	£000
Non-current assets	(260 + 200)	460
Current assets	(80 + 100)	180
		640
Current liabilities	(100 + 60)	160
Ordinary share capital	Parent only	300
Retained earnings		180
		640

It is unlikely that when one company buys another company, the price that it pays will be exactly the fair value of the net assets acquired. If the company that is acquired is doing reasonably well,[3] the acquiring company will have to pay something extra for *goodwill*. In **Illustration 7.4**, the net assets of Fourthing are shown as £70,000,[4] but Pinnie paid £90,000 to acquire all the shares. On the consolidated statement of financial position, goodwill is therefore shown as £20,000, which is the difference between the cash paid by Pinnie and the net assets acquired of Fourthing.

Some of the main principles are shown in **Illustration 7.4**. There are two separate companies, Pinnie plc and Fourthing Ltd, and each produces its own statement of financial position. Pinnie is the parent company: it owns all of Fourthing's shares and controls its financial and operating activities. A group statement of financial position combines the statements of financial position of the two companies in a specific way: the first part of the group statements of financial position includes all the assets and liabilities of both companies; the second part shows who owns them all, and how it was financed. Goodwill appears on the group statement of financial position where the parent company has paid more for the subsidiary company than the fair value of the net assets that it acquires.

[3] In 2009 many companies were doing badly, and it was possible to buy companies for less than the statement of financial position value of their assets; the assets should be valued at 'fair value', but that may be difficult to determine in a depressed market.

[4] 50 + 60 − 40 = 70.

ILLUSTRATION 7.4

Summarized statements of the financial position of Pinnie plc and Fourthing Ltd at 31 December year 4

	Pinnie plc	Fourthing Ltd
	£000	£000
Non-current assets	100	50
Investment in Fourthing Ltd at cost	90	–
Current assets	80	60
Total assets	270	110
Current liabilities	30	40
Ordinary share capital	100	50
Retained earnings	140	20
	270	110

Pinnie bought 100 per cent of the shares of Fourthing Ltd on 31 December year 4. Pinnie plc's group/consolidated statement of financial position as at 31 December, year 4, using the acquisition method for consolidation, is prepared as follows:

Consolidated statement of financial position of Pinnie plc and its subsidiary as at 31 December year 4

	Workings	£000
Non-current assets	(100 + 50)	150
Goodwill	90 – (50 + 60 – 40)	20
Current assets	(80 + 60)	140
		310
Current liabilities	(30 + 40)	70
Ordinary share capital	Parent only	100
Retained earnings	Parent's retained earnings and any post-acquisition profits of the acquired company	140
		310

The rules for consolidated accounts may be summarized as follows:

1 Goodwill is the difference between the price paid for the subsidiary company (£90,000) and Pinnie's share of the net assets acquired. In this instance, Pinnie acquired 100 per cent of the net assets. Fourthing's net assets are non-current assets + current assets - current liabilities: £50,000 + £60,000 – £40,000 = £70,000. It is probably easier to think of this as the amount of equity (which is ordinary share capital + retained earnings: £50,000 + £20,000.

Goodwill must be calculated at the date of acquisition (in this case, it is easy: 31 December year 4). The goodwill arising from the acquisition of a subsidiary is subject to an annual impairment review. This requirement ensures that the asset of goodwill is not being overstated in the group's financial statements.

2 Share capital: the group statement of financial position shows only the parent company's share capital, not the subsidiary's.

3 Illustrations 7.3 and 7.4 - Retained earnings: the consolidated statement of financial position shows only the parent company's share of retained earnings at the statement of financial position date. In the case of Pinnie and Fourthing, the statements of financial position are prepared as at the date of acquisition; Fourthing has not yet made any 'post-acquisition' profits. In the future, the consolidated statement of financial position will show the parent company's share of any retained profits made by the subsidiary *after* the date of acquisition.

4 The figures shown on the consolidated statement of financial position for non-current assets, current assets and current liabilities are simply the amounts shown for each company, added together. This applies even if the subsidiary company is only partly owned.

A subsidiary company is controlled by a parent company, usually by owning a majority of its shares. In **Illustration 7.5**, Florrie plc owns 80 per cent of the shares of Tanner Ltd. This illustration has an additional complication: the subsidiary was acquired on 31 December year 4; a consolidated statement of financial position is now required for 31 December year 6.

The principles are much the same when a subsidiary is only partly owned. In **Illustration 7.5**, the holding company owns 80 per cent of the subsidiary, and so there is a 'non-controlling interest' of 20 per cent. The first part of the group statement of financial position still includes 100 per cent of the non-current assets, current assets and current liabilities. The second half includes an item 'non-controlling interest' that shows (as at the statement of financial position date) the amount of net assets owned by shareholders outside the group.

ILLUSTRATION 7.5

Summarized statements of financial position of Florrie plc and Tanner Ltd at 31 December year 6

	Florrie plc	Tanner Ltd
	£000	£000
Non-current assets	162	120
Investment in Tanner Ltd at cost	118	–
Current assets	20	80
Total assets	300	200
Current liabilities	15	50
Ordinary share capital	160	60
Retained earnings	125	90
	300	200

Florrie bought 80 per cent of the shares of Tanner Ltd on 31 December year 4. At that date, Tanner's retained earnings were £65,000. Florrie plc's group/consolidated statement of financial position as at 31 December, year 6, using the acquisition method for consolidation, is prepared as follows:

Consolidated statement of financial position of Florrie plc as at 31 December year 6

	Workings	£000
Non-current assets	162 + 120	282
Goodwill	118 – ((80% × (60 + 65))	18
Current assets	20 + 80	100
		400
Current liabilities	15 + 50	65
Non-controlling interest	20% × (90 + 60)	30
Ordinary share capital	Florrie i.e. Parent only	160
Retained earnings	125 + ((80% × (90 – 65))	145
		400

The main difficulty is with retained earnings. All of Florrie's retained earnings (£125,000) belong to the group and are included on the group statement of financial position. But only part of Tanner's belongs to the group: only 80 per cent of the retained earnings that Tanner has accumulated since it was acquired are included on the group statement of financial position. Retained earnings have increased from £65,000 to £90,000 since the acquisition, meaning that post-acquisition retained earnings are £25,000 (£90,000 - £65,000). The group's share of this (80 per cent) is £20,000.

The principles for calculating goodwill are the same. The price paid for Tanner was £118,000. Florrie's share of Tanner is 80 per cent, but it is necessary to calculate the net asset value of Tanner *at the date of acquisition*. This was share capital of £60,000, plus retained earnings that were £65,000. Equity at the date of acquisition was, therefore, £125,000; Florrie's share of that (80 per cent) was £100,000. Goodwill was, therefore, the difference between the £118,000 paid and the £100,000 that was the group's share of the net assets as of the date of acquisition.

Negative goodwill

Sometimes, a company buys another for less than the net book value of its assets. Perhaps it pays £2m for £3m worth of assets. Traditionally, this was regarded as 'negative goodwill'. But in the world of international accounting standards (IASs), this should not arise. Assets and liabilities should be revalued to 'fair value' at the date of acquisition. The assets shown at £3m were probably worth a lot less, and there may have been substantial unrecognized liabilities. Most of what was regarded as negative goodwill should disappear when assets and liabilities are restated at 'fair value'. If, on revaluation, there is still a 'profit' left,[5] then it should be taken to the income statement.

Group accounts in practice

The basic principles of group accounts, as outlined here, apply in what are frequently much more complex situations. Many companies have a number of subsidiaries, which, in turn, have their own subsidiaries, or 'sub-subsidiaries' of the parent company, all of which may be owned in different proportions, with part or all acquired or disposed of on different dates. The first part of a group statement of financial position shows 100 per cent of the assets and liabilities of parent and subsidiary companies; the second part shows who owns them: part belongs to the non-controlling interest - shareholders who own the minority part of the subsidiary.

The first part of a group income statement shows 100 per cent of the revenues, expenses and profit of the group. The second part shows that part of them are attributable to the non-controlling interest; the rest belong to the group.

In addition to subsidiaries, there may be *associates* and *joint ventures*. Here, the parent normally owns between 20 per cent and 50 per cent of the shares, and full consolidation does not take place. The group statement of financial position would show an amount for investment in such companies, which would reflect their share of net assets. The group income statement shows the group's share of the profits[6] of the associate or joint venture. When interpreting published financial statements, it is normally best to use the figures for the group as a whole, including the results for associates and joint ventures. These may be shown as 'investments accounted for using the equity method'.[7] More detailed analysis may exclude them. The important thing, as always with interpretation, is to ensure that comparisons are made on a consistent basis.

---

[5] If you have paid £2m for net assets that really are worth £2.1m, then you show the difference as £100,000 profit.

[6] Or losses.

[7] Joint ventures may be shown using either the equity method, or proportional consolidation.

7.4 Solvency and Predicting Financial Distress

The words 'financial distress' are widely used to cover a variety of different situations in which a company may find itself when it is unable to meet its liabilities as they fall due. Liquidation, receivership, bankruptcy and voluntary or compulsory winding up are all variations on a theme. Companies can negotiate arrangements with their bankers and other creditors. A few years ago, the debts of companies like Marconi and Eurotunnel were too great, and the companies gave their creditors substantial amounts of share capital in return for cancelling debt, so that previous shareholders soon held only a tiny proportion of the companies, the value of which was much reduced. By 2012, many well-known companies were in serious financial difficulties. Many professional football clubs have got into serious financial difficulties. In recent years, major banks collapsed and were taken over by the government - for example, Northern Rock in the UK - or by foreign banks.[8] The COVID-19 pandemic and the resulting quarantine measures have dealt a severe blow to brick-and-mortar stores that were previously enjoying a steady income for years. Many such establishments have seen their revenues plummet to almost nothing. The year 2023 saw two major shocks in the banking sector: the collapse of Silicon Valley Bank and the forced sale of Credit Suisse due to disaster. Swift action prevented a global economic crisis, but threats remain.

Sometimes companies may be the unwilling victim of a takeover bid; an agreed bid or merger may be sought, or parts of the business may be sold off to a variety of different companies, venture capitalists and other investors and institutions. When a company is in financial difficulties, the ordinary shareholders can lose most or all of their investment; creditors can suffer direct financial loss, and employees and suppliers suffer in different ways.

In the end, a company gets into financial difficulties for one reason only: they are unable to pay their debts. All sorts of factors can lead to this situation: bad management, poor products, a weak economy, problems with exchange rates, government policies, poor industrial relations, and changes in demand for products and services. There is usually no shortage of explanations for poor performance, and it can be difficult to identify these various factors - until it is too late. But the warning signs of impending financial difficulty are usually there for those who take the trouble to interpret financial information, and are brave enough to heed it.

Some of the warning signs are:

1. *Excessive debt.* This can be inferred from current ratios, liquidity ratios, gearing ratios and interest cover, especially if there is a deteriorating trend. It is also important to look at total debt, including both short and long term.

   Some aspects of published accounts can be hard to interpret - such as deferred taxation.[9] Obligations under finance leases can also be a problem. The important thing is to treat items consistently so that ratios are comparable. There are also companies, such as privatized utilities, which are not endangered by high levels of debt.[10]

   It may be useful to compare the amount of interest paid by a company with the amount of debt shown on its statement of financial position. An unusually high figure may suggest that, for most of the year, the level of debt was much higher than the amount shown at the year end. An unusually low figure may suggest that debt built up substantially before the end of the year and may still be increasing.

2. *Falling profits or losses.* A one-off loss, perhaps due to exceptional items, may not be a problem. But a profitable company is generally more safe and able to pay its liabilities than one that is making losses.

[8] Notably the bank of Santander. The government took a majority shareholding in the Royal Bank of Scotland that owned NatWest and the Isle of Man Bank. Halifax Bank of Scotland became part of the Lloyds Group.

[9] Deferred taxation is a 'liability' that may never have to be paid.

[10] Because of their near monopoly positions, and near certain revenues.

3 *Cash flows.* Sometimes companies generate profits that never seem to show up as cash - perhaps the company keeps pouring money into expansion. If there is 'creative accounting', the profits may be questioned. In the end, it is cash that pays the bills. Creditors such as bankers are usually interested in cash budgets to monitor the company's ability to repay what is due.

4 *Assets.* Assessments of solvency depend on the quality and valuation of the assets shown on the statements of financial position. Some assets are very specialized and may be of doubtful value in a forced liquidation.

5 *Share price.* When a company's share price goes down significantly more than the market generally, that is a warning sign. Companies do not suddenly get into financial difficulties, and the market price usually reflects problems well in advance.

6 *Other factors.* The financial press may draw attention to other warning signs, such as key executives leaving, difficulties in renegotiating loan agreements or significant loss of market share.

None of these warning signs alone necessarily indicates that a company will fail. A number of models exist that combine the various factors to give more or less reliable predictions of financial distress, including the 'Z-score'. The Altman Z-score is a numerical measurement that can be used to assess the state of financial distress, i.e. whether the company will go into bankruptcy or not.

Altman Z-scores

It is possible to find out which factors have been most closely associated with companies finding themselves in a situation of financial distress. A list of companies that have 'failed' in one way or another is produced. The financial data for those companies is compiled for a number of years, including amounts of profit, equity, working capital (WC), cash flows, and so on. The data is then manipulated until a way of selecting and arranging it is found that would best predict impending failure.

Altman (1968) found that the key data were:

- Working capital
- Total gross assets
- Retained profits
- Earnings before interest and tax
- Market value of equity
- Book value of debt
- Sales.

By arranging these as five ratios, and giving a weighting to each, Altman calculated a Z-score, which gave the best prediction of corporate failure.

Ratio	Weighting
1 Working capital ÷ total gross assets	× 1.2
2 Retained profits ÷ total gross assets	× 1.4
3 Earnings before interest and tax ÷ total gross assets	× 3.3
4 Market value of equity ÷ book value of debt	× 0.6
5 Sales ÷ total gross assets	× 1.0

Source: Adapted from Altman et al. (2019, p. 194).

Altman did not claim to state the causes of failure; it was a statistical calculation that, in his sample, gave the best results. Companies with a Z-score of more than 2.99, using the above calculation, did not fail; companies with a Z-score of less than 1.81 did fail. The outcome of companies with a score of between 1.81 and 2.99 was less predictable but, overall, the prediction was accurate in 96 per cent of cases.

Altman's model suggests that the following are important in predicting failure:

- The amount of working capital (in relation to total assets)
- The amount of retained profits (in relation to total assets)
- Some measure of return on capital employed (ROCE)
- Some measure of gearing and the market value of equity
- Some measure of utilization of assets (or turnover of assets).

Altman's model calculation suggests that Marks and Spencer is below the 'safe' level of 2.99 (see **Illustration 7.6**). A lower Z-score suggests that a company is more likely to face bankruptcy. If a company's Z-score is below 1.8, it implies that the business is in financial distress and has a high probability of going bankrupt. On the other hand, if the Z-score is 3 or above, the company is considered safe, and there is a low probability of bankruptcy. If the Z-score falls between 1.8 and 3, the company is in a grey area, and there is a moderate risk of bankruptcy. Typically, the lower the Z-score, the higher the chances of a company being in financial trouble.

ILLUSTRATION 7.6

Z-score for Marks and Spencer plc 2023

	£m			Weighting	
Current assets	2,155				
Less Current liabilities	(2,706)				
Working capital (WC)	(551)				
Non-current assets	6,943				
Current assets	2,155				
Total assets (TGA)	9,098				
Retained profits (RP)	5,839				
Profit before interest and tax (PBIT)	681				
Market capitalization (MV):					
1,965 million @ £1.67	3,283				
Current liabilities	2,706				
Non-current liabilities	3,577				
Total liabilities (BV)	6,283				
Sales	11,931				
1 WC/TGA	(551)	=	(0.061)	1.2	(0.073)
	9,098				
2 RP/TGA	5,839	=	0.642	1.4	0.899
	9,098				
3 PBIT/TGA	681	=	0.075	3.3	0.247
	9,098				

Z-score for Marks and Spencer plc 2023

	£m			Weighting	
4 MV of equity/BV of debt	3,283 / 6,283	=	0.523	0.6	0.314
5 Sales/TGA	11,931 / 9,098	=	1.311	1.0	1.3211
Z-score					2.698

Altman's sample was based on manufacturing companies in the USA in 1968. But similar work has been done by Taffler (1983) and Taffler and Tisshaw (1977) in the UK. Taffler found that the key ratios included:

	Weighting %
1 Profit before taxation ÷ current liabilities	53
2 Current assets ÷ total liabilities	13
3 Current liabilities ÷ total assets	18
4 (Immediate assets ÷ current liabilities) ÷ operating costs excluding depreciation	16

Taffler did not publish full details on the calculations, but it is clear that the key information, manipulated in different ways, could give very good indications of corporate failure in a different environment.

The message is clear: published financial statements, if interpreted with skill and care, can give very good indications of a company's solvency or how safe it is from financial collapse. Important information is available from financial statements, the most important being profits, assets, liabilities, cash flows and Z-scores. But other information is also important, including trends, quality of management, competition, and what is happening in the markets in which the company is operating.

7.5 Selective Performance

At an introductory level, most interpretation of accounts concentrates on the performance of a company as a whole. Profitability is measured using return on capital employed, and this is analysed into its various components showing (a) costs and profits in relation to turnover;[11] and (b) utilization of assets,[12] relating sales or cost of sales to different categories of assets in varying degrees of detail. Cash flows are also analysed for the company as a whole.

There are good reasons for wanting to analyse selectively the performance of different parts of the business. Suppose investors and analysts are interested in forecasting a company's future sales, profits and cash flows. In that case, they are likely to assume different growth rates, different rates of profitability and varying amounts of risk for different types of business - even if they are unable to do it exactly. At the end of the twentieth century, it was assumed that there were great growth prospects in areas such as telecommunications, pharmaceuticals and leisure. But investors were disappointed in the short run.

[11] Chapter 4, ratios 7, 9, 10 and 11.
[12] Chapter 4, ratios 8, 14 and 15.

Investors are also concerned with assessing the competence of management. Many companies are becoming increasingly diversified, making money in one area where they have expertise and success, then investing it in other areas that need careful monitoring.

In many cases, diversification is very successful: as one area declines, another expands. But some attempts at diversification are not successful, and it is useful to monitor the performance of different parts of the business. To facilitate this, there are official disclosure requirements that enable us to find out about different *segments* of a business, about *continuing and discontinued* operations, and about the results of investments in *associates* and *joint ventures*.

The idea that the financial performance of a company can be distilled into a single figure is appealing, and the *earnings per share* (EPS) figure is the most suitable for this purpose. If the EPS increases each year, that must be a good thing. If they fall, that must be a bad thing.

But a single measure of performance is likely to cover a multitude of sins. Investors who are trying to forecast future EPS figures need to consider whether or not this year's EPS figure has taken into account the following:

- The results of parts of the business that have since been discontinued
- The results of new acquisitions that have yet to come fully on stream
- Any exceptional items such as large, one-off profits on the sale of non-current assets or investments
- Exceptional write-offs of goodwill or other assets
- Exceptional provisions for future reorganizations and redundancies
- Impairment of goodwill
- Depreciation
- Interest
- Unrealized profits on revaluation of assets
- Exchange rate gains or losses on translating the financial statements of overseas subsidiaries.

Although IAS 33 clearly specifies how EPS should be calculated, companies are free to show additional versions of the figure, and it is important to be clear which version is being used and how the above items have been treated.

Segments

Most large companies have a number of different 'segments', which may be geographical (e.g. UK, Europe, Asia, USA) or 'business' segments (e.g. women's clothes, men's clothes, children's clothes). It is difficult to have a standard approach for defining segments for very different businesses, and the standard-setters have continuously revised their rules and guidelines on how segments should be defined and what information should be disclosed for each. IFRS 8 Operating Segments is intended to be a step towards a worldwide accounting standard.

A careful examination of the annual reports and accounts of most large companies reveals information about the different segments of the business that enables us to assess the performance of the different parts of the business using both business segments and geographical segments. Marks and Spencer discloses information for the following business segments: UK Clothing and home; UK Food; International; Ocado; and Others. It provides a great deal of segmental information, but care is needed in comparing one year with another. The information that it provided in 2023 is summarized in **Illustration 7.7** and **Illustration 7.8**.

ILLUSTRATION 7.7

	2023	2023	2023	2023	2023	2023
	UK Clothing and Home	UK Food	International	Ocado	Others, e.g. M&S Bank and M&S Energy	Group
	£m	£m	£m	£m	£m	£m
Revenue	3,658.3	7218.0	1055.0	–	–	11,931.3
Operating profit/ loss,	323.8	248.0	84.8	(29.5)	(0.5)	626.6
Finance income						58.1
Finance cost						(202.7)
Adjusting items						(6.3)
Profit/(loss) before tax	323.8	248.0	84.8	(29.5)	(0.5)	475.7

ILLUSTRATION 7.8

Other segmental information

	2023	2023	2023	2023	2023	2023
	UK Clothing and Home	UK Food	International	Ocado	Other segments	Group Total
	£m	£m	£m	£m	£m	£m
Additions to property, plant and equipment and intangible assets other than goodwill	170.4	221.1	29.9	–	–	421.4
Depreciation and amortization	(267.9)	(274.8)	(35.7)	–	–	(578.4)
Impairment charges, impairment reversals and asset write-offs	10.2	6.1	(1.9)			14.4
Assets						Not shown
Non-current assets						Not shown

These figures must be treated with care, but we can see the degree to which the sales and the profits arising from the different activities in which the company is engaged and where the assets are located. This information gives us an analysis of the degree to which the company depends on its various activities and the locations in which it operates. This can help in assessing risks and growth prospects.

The use of conventional accounting ratios provides more useful information to the extent the company provides information. For example, we can compute ratio 7 (operating profit as a percentage of sales) (from **Chapter 4**) for the UK and for international activities, and we can compute sales/total assets. These are shown in **Illustration 7.9** for the year 2023.

ILLUSTRATION 7.9

	2023 UK Clothing and Home	2023 UK Food	2023 International	2023 Ocado	2023 Other	2023 Group
Revenue, £m	3,658.3	7,218.0	1,055.0	nil		11,931.3
Revenue as a percentage of total group figure	0.3	0.6	0.1			1.0
Operating profit , £m	323.8	248.0	84.8	-29.5	-0.5	626.6
Operating profit as a percentage of total group	0.5	0.4	0.1	0.0	0.0	1.0

The international activities appear to be more profitable than the UK activities, but we must bear in mind that the international activities are a much smaller percentage of the total activity.

It is worth analysing the performance of the different segments of a company in this way and comparing this with the comments made by the chairperson or directors about the progress and prospects of different parts of the company. Producing detailed analyses for a number of years can give a better indication of trends, but the way in which the information is produced can change from year to year, making such comparisons difficult.

IASs require companies to publish more information and on a more comparable basis so that the published financial statements of major international companies are a mine of information, providing an ever-increasing resource for more detailed analysis.

Investments

It is possible to assess how successful management has been in making investments in other companies, although the information required for this may not be as full and clear as necessary. It is usually possible to establish a value for each category of investment and the return earned on that investment. There are three categories of investment:

1. Subsidiaries where control is usually achieved by owning 50 per cent or more of shares. Group accounts are prepared as shown in **Section 7.2**.
2. Associates where significant influence is exercised, usually by owning between 20 per cent and 50 per cent of the shares, and joint ventures where two or more jointly control a company in which they have invested. These are mostly[13] accounted for using the equity method, with the proportion owned (the investment) shown as an asset on the group statement of financial position and the share of the profit earned shown on the income statement.
3. Investments in companies where there is no significant influence, where only a small proportion of the shares is normally held. An amount for the investment is shown on the statement of financial position, and dividends receivable (not a share of profits) are shown on the income statement.

7.6 Other Information from Annual Reports

Users of financial statements may be concerned with other aspects of a company's activities, not just their solvency and profitability. They may be seeking a more detailed explanation of what is revealed by the statement of financial position, the income statement and the cash flow statement, and they may be looking for

[13] Proportional consolidation is also permitted for joint ventures.

information about future prospects and performance. Companies may choose to disclose all sorts of things in their annual reports, and there is often a chairperson's statement full of fine-sounding information in the style of advertising and public relations. But there is also quite a lot of useful additional information that is required by law and which is presented by companies in a fairly standard way.

Directors' report

The Companies Act 2006 (s415) states that the directors of a company must prepare a directors' report for each financial year.

The objectives of the directors' report are to communicate the company's performance, disclose significant risks and events, demonstrate good corporate governance and aid in decision-making. All companies, including those that qualify for the small companies' exemptions, must include a directors' report in their annual report.

The content of the directors' report varies depending on the size of the company, the number of employees and whether it is a quoted company. However, the report generally includes a lot of formal information that is fairly standardized, such as the following:

- *Names of the directors* of the company during the financial year
- *Principal activities* of the company and any changes
- *Business review* of the activities during the year and of the position at the year end
- *A fair view of the company's business*
- *Future developments*
- *Information about environmental matters, employees and social and community issues*
- *Research and development activities*
- *Statement of events after the reporting periods*: any important changes and events since the statement of financial position date
- *Value of land and buildings*: significant differences between the statement of financial position values and market value of land and buildings
- *Statement about employee involvement*: policies on providing information to employees, consulting them, any schemes for employees' shares, and increasing understanding of shared ideas about factors affecting the company's success (in companies with over 250 employees)
- *Number of disabled employees* and employment policies regarding disabled employees (in companies with over 250 employees)
- *Donations* to charities and political parties are each disclosed separately
- *Purchase of own shares*: number of shares purchased, amount paid and reasons for doing it
- *Information about directors*: their names and the number of shares held by each at the beginning and end of the year
- *Going concern*
- *Supplier payment*: the company's policy should be disclosed, and a calculation of the average number of days taken to pay trade payables
- *Disclosure of information to auditors*.

Substantial information is also provided about **directors' remuneration** and how it is determined, and about **corporate governance** and how the directors run the company. There is an independent **auditor's report** that usually looks fairly complicated but uses standard wording and says very little. The principal point of interest is if the auditors state whether or not it is their opinion that the financial statements show a 'true and fair view' (an unqualified or 'clean' audit report) or, alternatively, express some specific or general reservations (a 'qualified' opinion), and a statement of directors' responsibilities, which makes it clear that the financial statements are the responsibility of the directors, not the auditors.

Auditor's report

An auditor's report is a written account appearing in a company's annual report, providing a report on the audit of the financial statements, a report on the audit of the financial statements of the company, written and signed by the independent auditor and addressed to the shareholders expressing their opinion on whether the accounts show a 'true and fair view' and comply with the Companies Act and other specified regulations, such as IFRSs. The auditor aims to provide reasonable assurance that financial statements are free from material misstatement due to fraud or error and to issue an auditor's report containing the auditor's opinion.

Auditors have two options for providing opinions on financial statements - an unmodified/unqualified opinion, also known as a 'clean' opinion, or a modified/qualified opinion. An unmodified opinion is provided when the auditor believes that the financial statements accurately depict the company's financial position and performance for the given accounting period. However, due to increasing economic uncertainty both in the UK and globally, we may witness a rise in modified audit opinions.

There are several reasons why an auditor may issue a qualified opinion on a company's financial statements. These reasons include:

- The auditor was unable to obtain enough appropriate audit evidence for certain elements in the financial statements.
- The financial statements did not follow the generally accepted accounting principles (GAAP) or international accounting standards.
- There is a limitation on the scope of the auditor's work.
- The auditor has substantial doubt about the company's ability to continue as a going concern.

Forming an audit opinion

For the reasons above, the auditor must give a modified version of their opinion. Depending on the nature and severity of the matter being considered, there are three types of modifications: qualified opinion, disclaimer of opinion, and adverse opinion. Examples are provided for each opinion below:

1. Qualified opinion - limitation of scope

The audited company's turnover includes cash sales, but there was no reliable internal control system to ensure their accuracy. Hence, the auditors' opinion is that they are unable to adopt any other satisfactory audit procedures to check for significant misstatements in the recorded turnover.[14] Therefore, it will be determined that there is a limitation in the scope of work. However, the auditors can confirm that, in all other respects, the financial statements provide a true and fair view.

2. Qualified opinion - disagreement with management

A disagreement arises over the inclusion of a trade receivable shown on the statement of financial position due from the customer who has now ceased trading. Additionally, the company has no security for the collection of this debt. On the basis that this amount is not receivable, the auditor's opinion is to make a full provision for impairment for the amount and reduce profit before taxation for the year and the net assets for

[14] This example to illustrate limitation of scope has been adapted from https://www.hkicpa.org.hk/professionaltechnical/assurance/example_auditors/SME-FRS-Jul2009.pdf; https://www.iod.com/resources/governance/governance-explainer-qualified-audit-opinion/

the amount at that date. The auditor has determined that this misstatement could impact the decisions of users of the financial statements but that, in all other respects, the financial statements give a true and fair view.

3. Disclaimer of opinion

The auditor shall disclaim an opinion when the auditor is unable to obtain sufficient appropriate audit evidence on which to base the opinion, and the auditor concludes that the possible effects on the financial statements of undetected misstatements, if any, could be both material and pervasive. An auditor may make a statement indicating that a restriction on the extent of the audit report is significant enough to prevent them from attaining enough evidence to support an opinion on the financial statements, thus distancing themselves from providing any opinion at all related to the financial statements. In some cases, auditors may not be allowed to observe certain operational procedures or review specific procedures for groups that have a significant number of overseas subsidiaries. This can result in the auditor being unable to audit the results of these overseas subsidiaries and may lead to a disclaimer. As a result, the auditor cannot form an opinion on whether the financial statements provide a true and fair view.

4. Adverse opinion

The auditor judges, having obtained sufficient evidence, that there is a material and pervasive misstatement in the financial statements and that, because of the significance of the matter, the financial statements do not give a true and fair view. The opinion section will be headed up 'Adverse opinion'. When a company's financial statements deviate significantly from the accounting standards, auditors may issue adverse opinions. Such opinions can lead to the removal of the company's stock from the stock exchange. In 2017, Toshiba Corp. of Japan narrowly escaped this fate as their auditors gave a qualified opinion, rather than an adverse one, on the company's financial statements. Nevertheless, the auditing firm did issue an adverse opinion on the company's internal auditing controls, which is a less severe matter but still requires the company's attention.

The financial statements

The financial statements include an **income statement**, a **statement of financial position**, a statement of *changes in equity* and a **cash flow statement**. With large listed companies, there are usually parent company versions of these statements together with a consolidated version (which includes all the subsidiary companies). These are followed by substantial *notes to the financial statements* that include complex but vital information, which may sometimes lead to more obfuscation than clarification. There is usually also a *five-year summary* of results, although these vary considerably: it may not be for five years, and the companies may disclose very little or a great deal of information for previous years in a standardized format. Serious analysts may want to analyse previous years' financial statements for themselves or to follow up on particular items; most large listed companies now have good websites from which it is possible to download previous years' annual reports and financial statements.

Summary

It is not very difficult to learn to calculate a dozen or so standard accounting ratios based on the simplified versions of company accounts that are usually presented in textbooks and examinations. But when examining the complexities of real companies' financial statements it is easy to be overwhelmed. Relatively straightforward real company financial statements were introduced early in the book. More complicated financial statements, many of which are for groups of companies, should be seen as a challenge and as an opportunity: a challenge to answer the same basic questions about solvency and profitability that have already been introduced; and an opportunity to make use of more detailed information that is available to produce a fuller analysis.

Substantial and detailed information is available to assess the solvency of a company, its performance and how its profitability might be improved, and the performance of its shares on the stock market. The amount of information disclosed is generally increasing, partly in response to official requirements, and partly because companies want to enhance their social, environmental and political reputations and, not least in the market place, to support their share price.

Review of key points

- Interpreting published financial statements is more complex than most textbook examples, and the exact information required is not always available.
- Group or consolidated statements of financial position show goodwill and non-controlling interests. Retained earnings for the group include all those of the parent company, but only the appropriate proportion of retained profits made by subsidiaries since acquisition.
- More sophisticated assessments can be made of a company's solvency than the main ratios shown in **Chapter 1** and **Chapter 4**, particularly by using Z-scores.
- Companies disclose key information that enables us to analyse the performance of the different business and geographical segments in which the business operates.
- The published annual reports of most large companies include a wealth of useful information that companies are required to publish, including the notes to the accounts and the directors' report.
- Many annual reports include additional information that is not required by law, about such matters as the company's products and progress, directors, and environmental and social performance. Much of this is of a public relations nature and needs to be interpreted with care.

Self-testing questions

1 Calculate the 20 ratios for Marks and Spencer plc for 2023 to complete the table in **Illustration 7.2**, and write a report on the company's financial position and performance based on those ratios.

2 What accounting information is most useful in assessing a company's solvency?

3 The summarized statements of the financial position of Grand plc and Pony plc at 31 December year 6 were as follows:

	Grand plc	Pony plc
	£m	£m
Non-current assets	180	75
Investment in Pony plc at cost	90	-
Current assets	80	20
Total assets	350	95
Current liabilities	30	15
Ordinary share capital	150	45
Retained earnings	170	35
	350	95

Grand bought 60 per cent of the shares of Pony on 31 December year 3. At that date, Pony's retained earnings were £55m. Since that date, the fair value of goodwill has been impaired by £20m. Prepare a group statement of financial position as at 31 December year 6.

4 What key information is disclosed to assess the profitability of the various segments of a company?

5 You are given the following information about Gobbiediggan International plc:

Segment	**UK**		**Africa**		**South America**	
	Year 1	**Year 2**	**Year 1**	**Year 2**	**Year 1**	**Year 2**
	£000	**£000**	**£000**	**£000**	**£000**	**£000**
Sales	800	860	300	270	100	180
Operating profit	80	78	40	44	20	21
Operating assets	900	760	200	175	40	60

Making use of appropriate ratios, comment on the performance of each of the geographic segments.

One of the directors of the company considers that the UK market should be abandoned because profits are declining. A second director considers that the Africa market should be abandoned because sales are declining. A third director considers that the South America market should be abandoned because it keeps needing additional investment. Critically assess each of these views.

6 Calculate the Z-score for Marks and Spencer for 2023 and 2022. What are the main reasons for the change between 2023 and 2022?

Assessment questions

1 Select one or two companies' annual reports and accounts and assess the financial position and performance of its various segments and investments in as much detail as the information permits.

2 If a company analyses the ROCE of every division, branch, investment or segment that it operates, and closes down all those with a below average ROCE, then the average ROCE for the company as a whole is bound to increase. Assess this approach to managing a large business.

3 The summarized statements of the financial position of Yourow plc and Sentus Ltd at 31 December year 6 were as follows:

	Yourow plc	**Sentus Ltd**
	£000	**£000**
Non-current assets	700	400
Investment in Sentus Ltd at cost	450	-
Current assets	250	300
Total assets	1,400	700
Current liabilities	220	170
Ordinary share capital	1,000	430
Retained earnings	180	100
	1,400	700

Yourow bought 75 per cent of the shares of Sentus on 31 December year 2. At that date the retained earnings of Sentus were £70,000. At 31 December year 6 the original value of goodwill had been impaired by £32,000. Prepare the group statement of financial position as at 31 December year 6.

4 You are given the following segmental information about the Willaston Company:

Segment	**Men's things**		**Women's things**		**Children's things**	
	Year 1	**Year 2**	**Year 1**	**Year 2**	**Year 1**	**Year 2**
	£000	**£000**	**£000**	**£000**	**£000**	**£000**
Sales	400	405	800	820	60	130
Operating profit	80	95	90	92	(20)	(4)
Operating assets	200	180	250	260	10	11

Making use of appropriate ratios, comment on the performance of each of the segments.

5 You are given the following information about the Goodwynne Company:

	Year 2	**Year 3**
	£000	**£000**
Sales	1,000	1,100
Operating profit	100	115
Operating assets	700	800

Making use of appropriate ratios, assess the view that the company should concentrate on reducing its operating assets.

6 Interpretation of accounts tends to concentrate on statements of financial position, income statements and cash flow statements. Critically assess the value of other information included in annual reports *either* (a) for companies in general *or* (b) for one or two particular companies.

Group activities and discussion questions

1 What information would you like to see disclosed in company annual reports and accounts in addition to that which is at present required? Examine the annual report of a few companies that provide a lot more information than the minimum required. To what extent does that information provide you with what you want?

2 It is possible to calculate an almost infinite number of ratios from a company's annual report. What ratios other than the 20 emphasized in this chapter do you think would be useful? Why?

3 Think of a number of companies, or types of company, that have gone bankrupt or have found themselves in serious financial difficulties recently (perhaps airlines, banks or retailers). What do you think led to their financial difficulties? Try to identify some comparable companies, and examine their annual report and accounts. Is there evidence of impending financial difficulties?

4 It is unrealistic to assess the performance of a company on the basis of one figure, such as EPS. To what extent do the complexities in producing this figure undermine its usefulness?

5 Companies that generate cash surpluses can afford to diversify, but they should return the money to the shareholders, and it is for the shareholders to decide the extent to which they wish to diversify their investments. Companies that cannot afford to diversify often borrow money that they cannot afford and

make their shareholders' investments more risky; it is for the shareholders to decide whether or not they want more risk. Critically assess these statements.

6 Z-scores are only the beginning. Sophisticated statistical models that produce accurate predictions of share prices are becoming available. Discuss the practicability, limitations and implications of these statements.

Accounting in context

Discuss and comment on the following report based on articles in the press.

New CEO and profit pressure

In the past, a new CEO's first annual results, released just two months after arrival, would have been a prime prospect in setting their vision and achievements. However, António Simões, the new CEO of Legal & General, presented a lacklustre set of numbers, which he described as 'resilient'. The company's revenue decreased by 7 per cent to £902m, while operating profits remained almost unchanged at £1.66bn, and post-tax profits declined from £782m to £457m.

Legal & General has a unique business model, which includes life insurance, housebuilding, venture capital and investment operations. The Legal & General Capital division (LGC), which is responsible for these non-insurance activities, contributed to one-third of the group's operating profit in 2023, despite accounting for only 1.7 per cent of total assets. However, LGC's activities are highly volatile, and Simões, with his banking background, is expected to reassess these activities. He may decide to focus more on the company's core businesses of pensions and investment instead.

Legal & General's five reportable segments (Annual Report 2022, p. 220) are Retirement Institutional (LGRI), Retail Retirement (LGRR), L&G Capital (LGC), Investment Management (LGIM), and Insurance (LGI), LGRI focuses on defined-benefit pensions in the UK, Canada, America and the Netherlands, and has been the company's star performer. It has made significant profits from the booming pension risk transfer market and aims to enter similar deals worth £8bn to £10bn annually in the UK alone.

The key indicator of Legal & General's prospects is its capital position under the European Union's Solvency II Directive. This ratio measures the eligible capital of an insurance company to its regulatory capital requirement and is administered in the UK by the Prudential Regulation Authority. The company's ratio, which fell from 236 per cent to 224 per cent last year, is still healthy, with a £9.2bn surplus. This provides ample room for growth and dividend increases. The total dividend was increased by 5 per cent to 20p, as expected.

Legal & General's shares are a complex mix of interest rates, stock markets, economy, housing, and its core businesses of pensions and investment. The shares have remained between 200p and 300p since November 2020, despite the steady rise in dividends. A new CEO and improving interest rate environment could help the shares reach their pre-COVID peak of 313p, or shareholders could enjoy a rising dividend.

Sources: William Kay (2024) Plenty of Time for the Kitchen Sink. *The Times*, 6 March.

Patrick Hosking (2024) New L&G Boss Takes Time to Think Despite Profit Pressure. *The Times*, 7 March.

Legal & General Group plc, Annual Report 2022.

References and further reading

Altman, E.I. (1968) Financial Ratios, Discriminant Analysis and the Prediction of Corporate Bankruptcy. *Journal of Finance (New York)*, *23*(4), 589-609. https://doi.org/10.1111/j.1540-6261.1968.tb00843.x

Altman, E.I., Hotchkiss, E. and Wang, W. (2019) *Corporate Financial Distress, Restructuring, and Bankruptcy: Analyze Leveraged Finance, Distressed Debt, and Bankruptcy* (4th edn.). Hoboken, NJ: Wiley.

Boakes, K. (2010) *Reading and Understanding the Financial Times*. Harlow: FT Prentice Hall.

Financial Times (daily newspaper). Available online at www.ft.com.

Gray, R., Bebbington, J. and Gray, S. (2010) *Social and Environmental Accounting* (SAGE Library in Accounting and Finance).

McKenzie, W. (2010) *Financial Times Guide to Using and Interpreting Company Accounts* (4th edn.). Harlow: FT Prentice Hall.

O'Regan, P. (2006) *Financial Information Analysis* (2nd edn.). Chichester: Wiley.

Rees, B. (2011) *Financial Analysis* (4th edn.). Harlow: Pearson Education.

Sugden, A., Gee, P. and Holmes, G. (2008) *Interpreting Company Reports and Accounts* (10th edn.). Harlow: FT Prentice Hall.

Taffler, R.J. (1983) The Assessment of Company Solvency and Performance Using a Statistical Model: A Comparative UK-based Study. *Accounting and Business Research*, 15(52): 295–308.

Taffler, R.J. and Tisshaw, H. (1977) Going, Going, Gone: Four Factors which Predict. *Accountancy*, March, p. 6.

https://www.accountancyage.com/2017/08/11/toshiba-narrowly-escapes-delisting-as-pwc-finally-signs-off-on-accounts/

https://corporate.marksandspencer.com/investors/ (gives Marks and Spencer Group accounts in full)

https://www.frc.org.uk/library/standards-codes-policy/audit-assurance-and-ethics/auditors-responsibilities-for-the-audit/

https://www.ft.com/video/85b22857-9e8f-420a-9016-89bb3694c0ae (The Worst Year for Banks since 2008, *Financial Times* film)

https://www.icaew.com/technical/audit-and-assurance/audit/reporting-and-completion/understanding-audit-reports

https://www.investorschronicle.co.uk/signup/newsletters (a variety of information about companies, interpretation and performance)

www.cifc.co.uk (select: benchmarking and interfirm comparison; a standardized basis for using ratios to compare different firms)

www.experian.com (a credit rating agency)

www.legislation.gov.uk/ukpga/2006/46/part/15/chapter/5/crossheading/directors-report/enacted?view=plain

Chapter 8

Current Issues in Financial Reporting

Chapter contents

8.1 Introduction
8.2 What Is Creative Accounting?
8.3 Some Problem Areas
8.4 How to Curtail Creative Accounting
8.5 Social and Environmental Reporting

Learning objectives

After studying this chapter you will be able to:

- ✓ Explain what is meant by *creative accounting* and understand that the term is sometimes applied to very different practices
- ✓ Explain why creative accounting has developed
- ✓ Give examples of a number of creative accounting practices
- ✓ Describe and evaluate the various approaches to dealing with creative accounting
- ✓ Explain what is meant by *corporate social reporting,* and understand its relationship with corporate social responsibility
- ✓ Appreciate the application of corporate social reporting in particular areas, such as employees and the environment
- ✓ Discuss the role of accountants in corporate social reporting
- ✓ Describe and assess corporate social reporting in practice

8.1 Introduction

Financial accounting and reporting has gradually developed over the last two centuries to help to make the directors of companies accountable to their shareholders. In the mid-nineteenth century, when companies first became popular entities, it was relatively easy for directors to set up companies that did little more than defraud shareholders and creditors of their money. In return for the privilege of 'limited liability', governments steadily introduced stricter requirements for accounting, financial reporting and auditing. As new and more complex abuses developed, so stricter accounting regulations were introduced through a series of Companies Acts.

In the last few decades of the twentieth century 'creative accounting' became a fine art, and developed more quickly than governments were able to regulate through Companies Acts. The accounting profession took on the role of producing 'accounting standards' that specified definitions, measurement and disclosure in financial accounting. By the first decade of the twenty-first century these bodies had become more powerful, with the backing of governments, and more international.

It has long been recognized that companies are accountable to both shareholders and creditors who have an interest in the survival and prospects of companies. But other groups in society, and indeed society generally, also have an interest in the activities of companies, and it may be argued that companies are accountable to society generally for both their social and environmental activities and impacts.

The first part of this chapter deals with creative accounting, its continuing problems and attempts to control it. The second part deals with endeavours to develop social and environmental reporting. In conventional financial accounting 'the bottom line' refers to the profit for the year figure, or perhaps earnings per share (EPS). Many now advocate a 'triple bottom line' showing performance in three areas: (1) financial or economic; (2) ecological or environmental; and (3) social. This may be characterized as concerns with profit, the planet and people.

The section on creative accounting shows how difficult it is to establish and enforce rules that measure financial or economic performance. The second part of the chapter deals with the issue of social and environmental accounting.

8.2 What Is Creative Accounting?

The term 'creative accounting' is used in relation to a variety of different accounting practices. The *Oxford English Dictionary* explains creative accounting as 'the modification of accounts to achieve a desired end; falsification of accounts that is misleading but not necessarily illegal'. At one extreme it is used to describe fraudulent and criminal activities. At the other extreme it might be viewed more benignly: as being no more than producing an honest presentation that emphasizes the favourable aspects of a company's performance. There is a natural desire for companies to put a positive spin on their financial position and performance.

It is unlikely that a company's annual report will say:

> ***The company has three divisions. Division A is the largest and is a complete disaster; losses continue to mount. Division B is going downhill and is now running at a loss. Division C is small, but it did make a tiny profit.***

A more optimistic version, such as the following, is more likely to appear:

> ***Division C has expanded rapidly and sales and profits are at record levels. Division B is coping well with difficult world economic conditions. Division A has made good progress in meeting its targets and is expected to show further progress in the coming year.***

Investors and other users of annual reports and accounts can look at the published, audited figures to establish the relationship between management claims and the 'real' financial performance and position.

The development of creative accounting

In the late 1960s there were some serious and high-profile accounting scandals from which it seemed that companies could choose almost any accounting principles they liked. What was a profit to one accountant would be a loss to another, and confidence in the accountancy profession was at a low ebb.

The accountancy profession set up the Accounting Standards Committee (ASC) which, in the 1970s and 1980s, produced a series of Statements of Standard Accounting Practice (SSAPs) which were intended to raise standards of financial reporting, and to reduce the areas of difference and variety in accounting practice. They had some success in improving financial reporting, but it was in the 1980s that the term 'creative accounting' came to be widely used, even in the media.

Popular books on creative accounting by Griffiths (1986), followed by Jameson (1988), argued that companies had a wide choice of accounting principles, policies and practices, and could justify almost any profit figures that they wished. The reputation of the ASC suffered, and, following the recommendations of the Dearing Committee (1988), the accounting standards-setting arrangements were revamped, and the Accounting Standards Board (ASB) was established.

The situation improved in the 1990s, but the scandals did not go away. In a new version of his book, Griffiths (1995) argued that some order had been brought to the chaos of the regulatory framework of accounting, and that the ASB had made tremendous progress in restoring the integrity and credibility of accounting standards. The more flagrant abuses had been banned, but an extensive range of techniques was still available that could be used to massage the figures. The Financial Reporting and Review Panel (FRRP) was demonstrating that it could be effective in enforcing the application of accounting standards. But, he argued, 'creative accounting still flourishes ... there is still tremendous scope for manipulation'. He concluded that his basic 1986 premise still held: companies were still fiddling their profits.

Other books popularized the idea that creative accounting was (and probably still is) widespread and a global issue. Smith and Hannah (1991) highlighted a number of creative accounting practices. Some of the creative accounting policies identified in Smith and Hannah include: changes in provisions. extraordinary items, off-balance-sheet financing, interest capitalization, brand accounting, depreciation policies, pension fund surpluses, deferred consideration, low tax charge and currency mis-matching. They produced a list of major companies, and put a number of 'blobs' against them; one blob for each of the questionable practices that the company adopted. Some companies came out with a clean bill of health, but serious questions were raised about the credibility of the financial statements of others. Smith (1992, 1996) shows that the problems have not gone away. Smith, in addition to the above, included other creative accounting policies such as: pre- acquisition write-downs, disposal of fixed assets/businesses taken through the profit and loss account or deconsolidation of subsidiaries or classifying associates as trade investments prior to sale, contingent liabilities, and convertible stocks with put options (see Pierce-Brown and Steele, 1999). Other books in the 1990s (e.g. McBarnet and Whelan, 1999; Pijper, 1993) continued to highlight the problems of creative accounting in the UK.

But, in 2001/2, the limelight was taken by US companies with a number of major accounting scandals that overshadowed what came to be seen as relatively minor problems in the UK.

In November 2001, Enron, one of the world's largest energy groups, admitted that between 1997 and 2000 various 'special purpose entities' should have been included in the group's accounts, which would have substantially reduced profits. In December 2001, they filed for bankruptcy. Arthur Andersen, Enron's auditors, admitted shredding or deleting thousands of relevant documents and were found guilty of obstructing the course of justice. Arthur Andersen, one of the world's largest accountancy firms, collapsed, and its business was split up and taken over by rival firms. For the year 2001, Arthur Andersen had been paid $25m in audit fees and $27m for other non-audit services.

The demise of Arthur Andersen shook the accounting profession worldwide. Many of the accounting policies that were criticized at the peak of the controversy had previously hardly been a matter for comment. Suddenly the climate changed and they were presented as scandals or abuses. The main problems seemed to be in the USA, and action was taken by establishing stricter requirements under the Sarbanes-Oxley Act 2002. Former Enron chief executives, Kenneth Lay and Jeffrey Skilling, were found guilty of the biggest fraud in corporate history after their energy giant collapsed into bankruptcy. Others became more cautious as the effects of the Sarbanes-Oxley Act were felt, and the enhanced role of the International Accounting Standards Board (IASB) became effective, with more clear-cut accounting standards and moves towards international harmonization.

Other scandals have occurred since 2001, including Bernie Madoff, Anglo Irish Bank and Olympus Corporation. The most notorious scandal at the centre of the global economic crisis involved the financial services giant, Lehman Brothers. Lehman had borrowed huge sums to finance loans in sub-prime housing mortgages. At first, the company disclosed huge profits from this activity but did not recognize in their accounts the risks attaching to these loans, ignoring the accounting concept of 'prudence'. And when the housing market collapsed, massive losses arose on these loans. During 2008, as the horrible truth of the overvaluation of these assets became apparent, Lehman's share price collapsed and in September 2008, the company filed for bankruptcy protection. However, in spite of the collapse of Enron, Lehman Brothers, and other names that now trip off the tongue of newspaper readers, and the humiliation of their senior executives, creative accounting has not disappeared and a number of problem areas remain.

The effects

Creative accounting is sometimes used to:

1. *Boost reported profits (or reduce reported losses).* As long as the profits are credible, this is likely to lead to higher share prices. But share prices can collapse rapidly when credibility goes. Senior managers and directors often have remuneration packages, bonuses, shares and options, the value of which is increased by higher profits. The temptations of 'aggressive accounting' are obvious.
2. *Smooth profits.* In a year of very high profits, the creative accountant might understate them, and keep something back to supplement reported profits in leaner years. Investors are probably more impressed by a company that manages to increase its profits every year than by one that seems to swing from profits to losses. 'Income smoothing' may help to maximize shareholders' wealth. It is, of course, contrary to accounting rules, but it is likely that, at the margin, judgements in some companies are exercised in a more prudent way when the profits are very good and in a less prudent way when profits have fallen.
3. *Manipulating ratios.* Creative accounting can also be used to manipulate some key ratios that are used by analysts, and to produce more healthy-looking statements of financial position. If a company wants to demonstrate that it has a high return on capital employed it will want to maximize profits; but it will not want to see high figures for capital employed. Such companies may avoid increasing asset values, and find ways of reducing asset values that do not hit profits too hard, particularly in relatively lean years.
4. *Facilitate borrowing.* Creative accounting can show higher asset values to support borrowing and reduce gearing levels. Borrowings often come with covenants, to protect lenders, requiring specified gearing or current ratios. If land and buildings are revalued (upwards), that automatically increases the equity figure and shows lower gearing.

5 *Flattering management.* Directors and managers want to look good and to keep their jobs. After a takeover bid, the new management team are likely to be under pressure to prove that they are more successful than their predecessors. Poor performance can be blamed on the previous management, while strikingly better results appear to have been produced by the new management.

Judgement becoming creative

There is inevitably a need for judgement in many areas of accounting. With depreciation, we can rarely be sure how long a non-current asset will be used or what its residual value will be. If an airline changes its depreciation policy so that aircraft are depreciated over 25 years rather than 15 years, it will make a massive difference to profits. In a year when profits are a little low it would not be surprising if a company's manager decides that non-current assets will have longer lives so that depreciation is reduced and profits are increased.

We cannot be sure what the net realizable value of inventories of unsold goods are.[1] When a company is doing well, it may have time to check that all inventories really are written down to net realizable value. When profits are looking a little low, there may be other priorities than estimating the latest net realizable value figures and ensuring that everything has been written down accordingly.

Perhaps provisions for bad debts are more prudent in some years than others. Similarly, in a year of low profits, there may be no harm if a few repairs and renewals get classified as capital expenditure. And it is only natural to delay doing repairs when times are hard. Profits can be understated a little in the good years, so that when the bad years come, accounting policies can be reviewed to release something held back by previous caution.

Over time, there may be a growing expectation to boost profits, which can lead to accounting policies being manipulated in a way that benefits the company's bottom line. Initially, these actions might be lawful and compliant. However, they can eventually become questionable, unlawful and even criminal.

A company might operate a number of hotels and be reasonably successful for many years. Then occupancy levels drop. Keeping the hotels in a good state of repair, and maintaining their appearance is a major expense that hits profits. At first the company might decide to try to maintain profits by deferring all but essential repairs. Carpets are not replaced until they are threadbare and dangerous; rooms are not redecorated until the paper is peeling off the walls and the smart white paintwork has either turned to a gentle shade of puce or gone mouldy; and the furniture is starting to fall apart. After a few years it is not repairs that are needed, but a total refurbishment. Fortunately, refurbishment can be classified as capital expenditure, and does not damage profits. A new policy emerges: the expense for repairs virtually disappears; all hotels are refurbished every four or five years.

If there are still no profits from running the hotels, more extreme accounting policies are needed. Suppose that the company owns a hotel that originally cost £8m, but now needs £2m spending on it for refurbishment. It has a market value of £10m. The company sells the hotel to a friendly building company for £10m. The building company does the refurbishment, and sells the hotel back to the hotel company for £13m. The building company is happy with the contract: it has made £1m profit. The hotel company is happy with the arrangement: what might have been an expense for repairs, over the years, of £2m has become a profit (on sale of the hotel) of £2m. And its statement of financial position looks better. Instead of having a tatty old hotel shown at £8m, it has a newly refurbished one shown at £13m. And it had to borrow only £3m to achieve this.

It could get worse and more dubious, and illegal. Maybe the hotel is not really worth £10m. But there may be ways of finding a building company willing to enter into a contract to buy it for £10m, if there is a guaranteed profit of £1m. Perhaps there is more profit to be made from specialized arrangements to buy and sell hotels than there is from actually running hotels.

---

[1] Inventories should be shown at the lower of cost and net realizable value. It is, of course, necessary to know what the net realizable value is if it is to be compared with cost.

Other strange contracts can be created. A hotel might find that it expects spare room capacity worth £1m at quiet times of the year. It might be glad to sell that spare capacity to a package holiday company for £500,000 - giving the hotel company £500,000 of revenues that it would not otherwise have had. The package holiday company might then find that it has more capacity than it needs and sell on half of what it has bought to a conference company for £600,000 (making £100,000 profit for doing almost nothing). Then the conference company sells part of what it has bought - and the conference company buys some surplus capacity on an airline's routes from London to one of the places where it has hotel capacity; the airline has bought that spare capacity from another airline, and it had bought it from a hotel that had bought it from another airline - or perhaps it was the original airline, or hotel, or conference company. This had happened, similarly, in earlier years when telecommunication companies made profits by selling spare capacity to each other.

Creative accounting can start with cautious use of judgement that varies a little from year to year, depending on the circumstances. It can end with serious fraud and criminal activity; and with the company going into liquidation - with lots of people losing their livelihood, their pensions and their savings. But some people probably manage to get out in time, after making a lot of money. Creative accounting can be a mechanism for redistributing wealth from the poor, weak and vulnerable to those who are strong, clever and ruthless. Financial accounting has an important role to play in trying to prevent and disclose such activities.

How bad are the various techniques?

Where there are suggestions or accusations that creative accounting has been used, we could ask, on a scale of 1-10, how bad is it? Number 1 would be almost nothing wrong at all; number 10 would be the worst possible. The following is not intended to be authoritative or definitive. But it does give an idea of the range of different activities that some might classify as being 'creative accounting':

1. There is nothing questionable about the financial statements, but information has been presented to emphasize the more favourable aspects of financial position and performance, and to de-emphasize the least favourable.
2. The emphasis on the favourable aspects is so strong as to suggest more of a propaganda exercise than a balanced report.
3. All financial statements are properly drawn up, but somehow the rules seem to flatter the company's performance whereas a different selection of accounting policies and measurements would be less flattering.
4. All financial statements have been properly drawn up in accordance with the requirements of company law and accounting standards. Where the official accounting requirements allow choice or flexibility, the company selects those options that tend to flatter the financial statements.
5. There are departures from accounting standards, but these have been properly disclosed and explained, and the financial effects have been quantified.
6. There is a suspicion that there are departures from accounting standards that have not been disclosed. Some of the figures are questionable.
7. Rules and definitions have been pushed to the limit, and perhaps a little beyond. Judgements have been exercised to come up with treatments that the auditors have been persuaded to accept, but which, on the face of it, other accountants would find unacceptable.
8. Transactions and arrangements seem to have been deliberately designed to take advantage of, or to avoid, particular rules or accounting treatments.
9. *Clear* breaches of accounting standards without proper disclosure of departures or reasons for them.
10. Criminal activity, fraud and deception.

8.3 Some Problem Areas

One of the difficulties of describing the problem areas and neatest tricks of creative accounting is that by the time they come to be described in books such as this, they have become so well known that the accounting standard-setters have brought in measures to limit them.

Non-recurring items

Extraordinary Items

In the 1970s, we had a plethora of 'extraordinary items' that were 'below the line' and did not affect profit or EPS.

Under previous accounting guidelines, items were required to be classified as extraordinary only if they were both unusual and infrequent. If an event or transaction met the criteria for classification as extraordinary, it was to be separated from the results of ordinary operations and displayed separately in the income statement, net of tax, after income from continuing operations. Furthermore, disclosure of income taxes relating to extraordinary items was also required. Entities were required to present or disclose earnings-per-share data applicable to extraordinary items.

Examples of non-recurring items included losses on the sale of a manufacturing plant, exceptional write-offs of goodwill and other non-current assets, inventory write-offs, foreign currency losses, and costs of reorganizations and closures. The formal use of extraordinary items has been eliminated under Generally Accepted Accounting Principles (GAAP), so this discussion should be considered historical in nature. International Financial Reporting Standards (IFRS) do not use the concept of an extraordinary item at all.

Exceptional Items

Exceptional items can be defined as items in the profit and loss account (or the income statement) that have been incurred from the ordinary activities of the entity and are not expected to occur regularly.

IAS 1 requires the separate disclosure of certain items within an entity's ordinary activities. These items must be disclosed in the financial statements to ensure they present a fair view if they are of significant size, nature or incidence. Typically, this disclosure is made in a note to the financial statements rather than on the statement of profit or loss and other comprehensive income. However, if the items are sufficiently material, they may be disclosed on the face of the statement.

Examples of items that may require separate disclosure include asset write-downs, enterprise restructuring, discontinued operations, property disposals, long-term investments, and litigation settlements. The presentation of information is left to the entity's discretion, and they may choose to present exceptional items as a line item on the face of the accounts, in a disclosure note, or in columnar format.

Determining how to classify items as operating or exceptional requires judgement. IAS 1 warns against excluding operating costs from the results of operating activities to improve key performance indicators such as return on equity and earnings per share, as this would mislead users and impair comparability.

Accounting considerations for the COVID-19 pandemic

The Financial Reporting Council (FRC) has issued additional guidance on reporting exceptional items and Alternative Performance Measures (APMs) in the context of the COVID-19 pandemic. Increased disclosures and explanations are likely to be required to help users understand the impact of the pandemic in these areas.

According to IAS 1, Presentation of Financial Statements, companies must disclose material items either individually on the income statement or in the notes to their accounts. Companies should also evaluate whether additional income and expenditures resulting from the COVID-19 crisis should be separately disclosed according to their existing policies for 'exceptional' or similar items.

Each entity must assess the significance of items such as restructuring costs, impairment charges, incremental health and safety costs, and the costs of onerous contracts. The presentation of any such items should be useful to users of the accounts. Additionally, one can find further information about the effect of these or similar items on cash flows, their timing, and relevant tax implications.

Guidelines for disclosure include being transparent and fair in identifying gains and losses; avoiding describing amounts as 'non-recurring' or 'one-off' if they will also occur in the future; not labelling costs as exceptional solely because of a COVID-19-related reduction in or elimination of revenue streams; and not identifying incremental costs as exceptional if they result in incremental revenue that is not also considered exceptional - for example, additional staff costs related to managing unusually high levels of sales of in-demand items.

In cases where the effects of the COVID-19 pandemic are pervasive and difficult to quantify, it would be beneficial for companies to include narrative disclosures explaining the nature of the items and the uncertainties surrounding them. The FRC does not encourage companies to arbitrarily disclose and split discrete items in an attempt to quantify the portion relating to the pandemic in their accounts.

Alternative Performance Measures (APMs)

Many companies use APMs to enhance their financial reporting by offering additional information beyond what is provided under IFRS. This can include profit that has been adjusted for exceptional items. However, it is crucial that APMs are clearly labelled, explained, reconciled to the closest IFRS measure, and presented consistently year after year.

For example, there may be circumstances where the COVID-19 crisis results in changes to the APMs used to manage and monitor the business. In these circumstances, readers should be informed of any such changes and provided with an explanation of why they provide reliable and more relevant information.

While there may be changes to APMs that are due to the COVID-19 pandemic, APMs that attempt to provide a measure of normalized or pro-forma results by excluding the estimated effect of the pandemic are highly subjective and potentially unreliable. Therefore, the FRC does not expect companies to include such results in their income statement presentation.

Provisions

Provisions are liabilities with an uncertain timing or amount, either legal or constructive. Constructive obligations arise when an entity's actions indicate it will accept responsibilities, creating an expectation to discharge them. Examples include warranty obligations, restoring facilities and retailer refund policies.

Entities recognize a provision when it is probable that an outflow of cash or resources is required; otherwise, it is a contingent liability. Provisions are measured by the amount rationally paid to settle the obligation or transfer it to a third party at the end of the reporting period, accounting for risks and uncertainties, and discounted to present value.

IAS 37 specifies recognition and measurement requirements for three cases: (1) future operating losses cannot be recognized, (2) an onerous contract creates a provision, and (3) restructuring costs are recognized when the entity has a constructive obligation and announced the plan to those affected.

This is all rather more subjective than is desirable and still allows some scope for creative accounting.

Goodwill

Accounting for goodwill is a key part of business combinations. Goodwill arises when one entity (the parent company) gains control over another entity (the subsidiary company) and is recognised as an asset in the consolidated statement of financial position. Under IFRS 3, Business Combinations, goodwill is an asset representing the future economic benefits arising from other assets acquired in a business combination that are not individually identified and separately recognized. IAS 36, Impairment of Assets, requires an entity to assess, at the end of each reporting period, whether there is any impairment for an entity's non-financial assets. For goodwill and intangible assets with indefinite useful lives, the standard requires an annual impairment test. and when indicators of impairment exist.

If a company has a net asset value of, say, £10m, it is very unlikely that the owners of that company would be willing to sell it for £10m, especially if the company has had a good profit record for a number of years. At acquisition, the net assets of the acquired entity should be revalued to 'fair value'. A company might have net assets with a statement of financial position value of £10m and a 'fair value' of, say, £12m. But if the company is successful and profitable, anyone wanting to take it over should expect to pay more than £12m. Perhaps they pay £15m.

If a business has net assets of £12m, and £15m is paid for that business, there is no problem recording the payment of £15m, or the net assets of £12m. But £3m has been paid for goodwill. Is the £3m to be recorded as an expense or as an asset? Treating it as an expense would damage the profits for the year. Showing it as an asset might be open to question: does the business really own something worth £3m? Standard practice for accounting for goodwill has varied over the years. IFRS 3 does not permit systematic amortization but instead, there is an annual impairment review to assess each year whether there are any indications that the goodwill is not worth the amount paid for it.

Various factors can cause the impairment of goodwill, such as a decrease in the expected benefits from the subsidiary, loss of customers, significant changes in technology, or the departure of key staff. If the parent company concludes that the goodwill is impaired, it must be written down to its recoverable amount.

It is important to note that the impairment of goodwill cannot be reversed once it is done. So, it is essential to assess the value of goodwill every year to ensure that the company's financial statements are accurate.

In a recent takeover announcement, Nationwide Building Society has agreed to purchase Virgin Money UK for £2.9bn ($3.7bn). The all-cash deal is set to create the UK's second-largest savings and mortgage provider. Nationwide's offer of 220p per Virgin Money share represents a premium of 38 per cent as of 6 March 2024. The deal will be funded through the mutual's existing cash resources.[2]

Reducing choices

In a number of areas, several accounting choices exist under IFRS and can create hurdles for analysis while adding little valuable information. Standard-setters are attempting to reduce the choices available to management by establishing criteria for deciding between alternatives. In the past, there was often a free choice, but the criteria for making those choices have steadily become clearer, leaving less scope for creative accounting – or perhaps making the activities of the creative accountant more complex.

---

[2] Sinead Cruise and Yadarisa Shabong (2024) Nationwide Challenges UK's Big Banks with $3.7 bln Virgin Money Bid. *Reuters*, 7 March. https://www.reuters.com/markets/deals/nationwide-buy-virgin-money-uk-29-billion-pound-deal-2024-03-07/#:~:text=LONDON%2C%20March%207%20(Reuters),largest%20savings%20and%20mortgage%20provider.

Development expenditure

Research and development costs are accounted for differently under IFRS and US GAAP. In accordance with IAS 38, Intangible Assets, expenditure on research activities is recognized in the income statement, while development costs are capitalized as an intangible asset if they meet certain criteria, such as technical feasibility and the generation of future economic benefits. The asset is then amortized on a straight-line basis for up to 15 years from the date it is put into service. IFRS has broad-based guidance that requires companies to capitalize development expenses when certain criteria are met, but US GAAP expenses R&D costs as they are incurred.

The key challenge for companies under IFRS is to differentiate between costs related to research activities and those related to development activities Although the definition of research and development is almost the same in both IFRS and US GAAP, neither provides a clear distinction between the two. To make this distinction, companies need to establish processes and controls based on the nature of different activities.

Under US GAAP, there are specific requirements for cloud computing costs, motion picture films, software development costs and website development. In contrast, IFRS has more general guidance that applies to all development expenditures. Hence, differences in accounting treatment between the two standards can make it more complex for companies to apply IFRS.

Expenditures that are incurred during the development phase of a project can be capitalized when the company is able to demonstrate the following criteria. First, the technical feasibility of completing the intangible asset so that it can be used or sold. Second, the intention to complete the intangible asset and use or sell it. Third, the ability to use or sell the intangible asset. Fourth, how the intangible asset will generate probable future economic benefits. Fifth, the availability of adequate technical, financial and other resources to complete the development and to use or sell the intangible asset. And sixth, the ability to reliably measure the expenditure attributable to the intangible asset during its development. However, the primary factor in the above list is technical feasibility.

Capitalization of interest

Capitalization of interest is a way of calculating the cost of an asset that more accurately reflects the total investment made by a business. This method involves charging the cost of acquiring a resource that will benefit future periods against the revenues of the period it benefits. Its primary goal is to obtain a more accurate measure of cost that relates to the future benefits of the asset.

If an entity acquires, constructs or produces a qualifying asset, it must include the borrowing costs that are directly attributable to it as part of the cost of that asset. However, determining the exact amount of borrowing costs that can be attributed to a qualifying asset requires judgment. According to IAS 23, Borrowing Costs, specific borrowings must be taken into account first, followed by all general borrowings outstanding during the period. A qualifying asset is one that takes a substantial period of time to get ready for use or sale. It is important to note that investments accounted for under the equity method are not considered qualifying assets. Eligible borrowing costs may include exchange rate differences from foreign currency borrowings.

Financial instruments

IFRS 9 simplifies financial asset classification and measurement after initial recognition with fewer exceptions. It is based on fair value, where changes are recognized in profit and loss (FVPL) except in cases where restrictive criteria are met for classifying and measuring the asset at either amortized cost or fair value through other comprehensive income (FVOCI). The new model can result in profit and loss volatility, especially for entities holding non-loan/receivable instruments or portfolio investments in equity. Derivatives embedded in financial assets under IFRS 9 must be measured at FVPL in almost all cases.

Revenue recognition

It is not always clear exactly when a sale takes place and when the revenues from sales should be recognized. For bookkeeping convenience, a sale may be recognized in an accounting system when the invoice is sent to the customer. But, sometimes, companies who are not doing very well are tempted to bring forward the date on which sales are recognized; this will have the effect of increasing the sales in the current period.[3] They might, for example, choose to recognize the revenue when an order for goods or services is first received, and this is allowed.

Prior to the introduction of IFRS 15, Revenue from Contract with Customers, revenue recognition and measurement were governed by two accounting standards: IAS 18 Revenue and IAS 11 Construction Contracts. These former standards applied different rules and principles to the recognition of revenue from goods and services and provided little guidance for complex situations. In developing the new standards, both the IASB and FASB wanted to provide common principles for revenue recognition measurement for all types of revenue and all industries. The IFRS 15 is a standard that outlines the principles an entity needs to follow when reporting information about revenue and cash flows from a contract with a customer. IFRS 15 requires entities to recognize revenue in a way that accurately depicts the transfer of promised goods or services to the customer based on the amount of consideration that the entity expects to receive in exchange for those goods or services.

IFRS 15 introduced some changes, such as replacing the concept of transfer of 'risks and rewards' with 'control' and introducing 'performance obligations' alongside extensive disclosures. These changes are likely to put more pressure on accountants and auditors to scrutinize client contracts and challenge directors' judgements.

To recognize revenue under IFRS 15, an entity must follow these five steps:

1. Identify the contract(s) with the customer.
2. Identify the performance obligations in the contract. Performance obligations refer to promises in a contract to transfer goods or services that are distinct.
3. Determine the transaction price, which is the amount of consideration that an entity expects to receive in exchange for transferring promised goods or services to the customer. If the contract's consideration includes a variable amount, the entity must estimate the expected consideration.
4. Allocate the transaction price to each performance obligation based on the relative stand-alone selling prices of each distinct good or service promised in the contract.
5. Recognize revenue when a performance obligation is satisfied by transferring a promised good or service, which is when the customer obtains control of that good or service. A performance obligation may be satisfied at a point in time (typically for the transfer of goods to a customer) or over time (typically for the transfer of services to a customer). For a performance obligation satisfied over time, an entity would select an appropriate measure of progress to determine how much revenue should be recognized as the performance obligation is satisfied.

The problem of 'revenue recognition' is explored more fully in **Section 12.2** of **Chapter 12**.

Share options

If a company wants to minimize the salaries that count as expenses, employees can be paid with share options instead of money. This became fairly common practice at the height of the dotcom boom of the late 1990s (see **Example 8.1**).

[3] If sales are brought forward to be included in this year, the sales figure for the following year is reduced.

Example 8.1

Dorothy accepted a job with the e.vilwich company, selling potions on the Internet. The job carried no salary or commission, but she was given the option of buying 100,000 shares in the company for £1 each. When she joined the company the market price of the shares was only 50 pence. But before she left the company the market price had gone up to £11.

Dorothy bought her 100,000 shares for £100,000, and then immediately sold them for £1,100,000. She had received no salary; she had cost the company nothing; and she had become a millionaire.

Share options appear to cost the company nothing, and were not usually recorded as an expense. But existing shareholders do lose out: when someone exercises their options to buy, existing shareholders suddenly own a smaller portion of the company, and in a sense, the person who exercises the options has made a gain at their expense. Generally, such share option schemes are approved by shareholders at a general meeting and they will approve of such schemes if they believe the share option scheme will motivate directors and senior staff to focus upon increasing the company's share price. Such share options cannot be exercised within three years of the date they are granted and so senior management will benefit only if the share prices rise in that period. IFRS 2 now requires full reporting of share-based payments and detailed disclosure.

Suspicious treatments

Sometimes accountants are creative in producing profit figures that are not supported by the company's underlying performance. Perhaps people who work for the company know that it is going downhill, or perhaps there are terrible delays in paying creditors, but still, healthy-looking profit figures are produced.

One way of detecting questionable accounting is to compare the amount of tax a company is paying with its reported profit figures. If a company is paying virtually no corporation tax it must be telling HM Revenue and Customs that it is making virtually no profits. But if at the same time, it is declaring substantial profits in its annual reports, it is worth further investigation. It may be that the company has invested heavily in non- current assets and so has generous capital allowances for corporation tax purposes. Or it may be more suspicious. Companies might be engaging in questionable tax-saving schemes, which might, in due course, be overturned by the courts.

A cash flow statement can also give indications of what is 'really' going on if profit figures seem questionable. It is easier to generate fictitious profit figures than to produce fictitious cash. Sooner or later a company is going to need more cash to keep going. A genuinely profitable company generates cash, and a healthy company can usually raise cash without much difficulty, typically by borrowing. But if a company keeps needing to borrow more, it may raise questions, and its statement of financial position will start to look very weak if burdened by too much debt. The company may try to borrow in ways that do not appear on the statement of financial position.

When a company wants more non-current assets, it may:

1. Borrow the money and buy the non-current assets
2. Lease the non-current assets.

In the first instance, there is clearly an asset and a liability; both appear on the statement of financial position. In the second instance, the financial effects are very similar: the company has the use of the asset just as if it owns it and it has to make repayments, just as if it had borrowed the money. Leasing was seen as a way of, in effect, borrowing money, but keeping the borrowings off the statements of financial position. Creditors would not know the extent of the company's commitments to make payments under leasing agreements and might be misled into lending more money.

But accounting standards (currently IFRS 16 Leases) put a stop to this.

The objective of IFRS 16 is to report information that (a) faithfully represents lease transactions and (b) provides a basis for users of financial statements to assess the amount, timing and uncertainty of cash flows arising from leases. To meet that objective, a lessee should recognize assets and liabilities arising from a lease.

IFRS 16 introduces a single lessee accounting model and requires a lessee to recognize assets and liabilities for all leases with a term of more than 12 months, unless the underlying asset is of low value. A lessee is required to recognize a right-of-use asset representing its right to use the underlying leased asset and a lease liability representing its obligation to make lease payments.

Increasingly sophisticated, even devious, forms of off-statement of financial position finance were developed, and the need to report the 'economic substance' of an arrangement rather than its legal form became accepted. Now, the requirements of IAS 32 and IAS 39 are detailed and complex. Whatever the legal technicalities might be, if a company has incurred a financial commitment, it must be shown as such. In the USA, the rules appear to be stricter, but the more strict and clear the rules are, the easier it is to create financial arrangements that just fall within the letter of the rules but are a breach of the spirit of them. The UK approach errs on the side of principle rather than strict rules, and the idea of 'economic reality' takes priority over 'legal form'. It may be, however, that the international standards will be increasingly 'rules-based' in line with US standards.

Fuzzy rules

The accounting standard-setters have tried to move away from allowing companies a free choice between alternative treatments. They have done this by specifying the circumstances in which each should apply. Unfortunately, such specifications and rules tend to become fuzzy at the edges as some companies interpret them creatively.

The fuzzy rules, and the choice between the 'acquisition' (or 'purchase') and the 'merger' (or 'pooling of interests') methods of producing consolidated accounts, all but disappeared when strict criteria were specified for the use of the merger method. Now, with IFRS 3, there is no choice: the merger method is prohibited.

There are other areas where the standard-setters have tried to establish clear rules, including provisions, deferred tax, the definition of associates, recognition of profits on uncompleted long-term contracts, the basis on which production overheads are included in inventory valuations, and defining exactly which leases should be shown on the statement of financial position. The rules appear to be clear; there appears to be no choice. But there is always some fuzziness in rules in marginal cases. It is always possible that companies structure financial transactions in a particular way so as to be able to use the accounting treatment that shows their results in the best light.

Conclusion

Accounting standard-setters are steadily becoming more strict: they are reducing and eliminating choices, and more effective enforcement mechanisms are being implemented. But it seems unlikely that the problems of creative accounting will ever be completely solved. Perhaps it is unrealistic to expect (m)any problems to be completely solved. The present trend is for a steady increase in the length and complexity of accounting standards. But as the rules get fuller and more detailed, so some practitioners find increasingly complex ways around them. This, in turn, leads to the need for even more detailed standards to close loopholes that have been found. In spite of the efforts of the accountancy profession and the standard-setters, many would argue that creative accounting is still alive and well. A wide range of choices in the way that companies can measure and report their financial performance still remains.

8.4 How to Curtail Creative Accounting

Many different suggestions have been made for dealing with the problem of creative accounting, many of them building on what is already happening. The main ones are as follows.

Accounting standards

1. The production of clearer accounting standards that reduce or eliminate choices.
2. The 'benchmark' argument recognizes that there will never be 100 per cent agreement or standardization. There can be a single recommended treatment that is a 'benchmark'; where companies adopt a different treatment, the financial effects of doing this should be quantified and disclosed.
3. Stronger legal backing for accounting standards.
4. Enhancing the role of international accounting standards.
5. More effective monitoring and enforcement.
6. Principles rather than rules. The US approach seems to be more 'rules-based' - and it is always possible to find ways around the letter of the rule. The UK and international standards emphasize principles, and the importance of 'substance' (economic reality) rather than legal form.
7. Current cost accounting is favoured by some as a way of having clearer principles about asset valuation. But others see it as introducing more flexibility.
8. Cash flow accounting, if based simply on receipts and payments of cash, would reduce creativity. But there would be some subjectivity in classifying cash flows, and a serious loss of accruals-based information (like statement of financial positions).

The term 'cash flow accounting' is sometimes used to mean something quite different. Some people advocate the production of statements of financial position that use valuations based on the net present value of the future cash flows that an item is expected to generate. The amount of profit for a period would be based on the increase in the net asset value of the business between the two statement of financial position dates. This could lead to more creativity.

Auditing

There have been many criticisms of auditing arrangements, particularly relating to their perceived lack of independence from management. There is certainly a gap between what some people expect of auditors and what are more realistic expectations, as shown in **Illustration 8.1**.

ILLUSTRATION 8.1

Expectation	More realistic
1 The financial statements are prepared by the auditors; the auditors agree with everything in them and are responsible for them	The directors are responsible for preparing the financial statements. Auditors agree only that they represent one of perhaps several possible 'true and fair' views
2 The financial statements are correct and accurate; a different auditor would produce the same financial statements from the same basic information	The auditors do not prepare the financial statements, and as there are many areas requiring judgement, different accountants would probably come to different conclusions More skills and training is needed on complex and subjective issues, such as IFRSs 2, 3, 9, 16 and 17 and IAS 36.

Expectation	More realistic
3 The financial statements show what a company is worth; assets have been properly valued	Most assets are shown at some variation of historic cost. Even if they were shown at some sort of current value, the value of the business as a whole would almost certainly be very different from the value of the separable assets less liabilities
4 The auditors have checked and ascertained that no significant fraud or irregularities have taken place	The auditors are on the look-out for fraud, but they are not responsible for finding it all. And even if they find some, provided it is not too enormous, they will still say that the financial statements show a true and fair view
5 The business is a going concern and is not likely to collapse or fail in the foreseeable future	The auditors check to see if there are any doubts about the business being a going concern, and report accordingly. But there can be no guarantee that it will not collapse in the near future
6 The management of the company is reputable, competent, efficient and effective	Auditors are usually happy to take fees from even the most hopeless managers and are not likely to disclose any incompetence!
7 The audit report draws attention to any doubts about the company's finances	If there are doubts about the company's immediate financial survival, the auditors should comment
8 Auditors are independent and cannot be got rid of by directors	In theory auditors have great security and independence. But directors can easily put an audit out to tender, and replace existing auditors
9 Auditors are controlled and disciplined by a professional body that clearly specifies what is required of them	This is a reasonable expectation
10 Auditors are more concerned with their duty to the public and their reputation than with maximizing their own remuneration	This is more a matter of opinion!
11 Auditors are experts and are competent to determine if the financial statements show a 'true and fair view'	In some industries, such as banking, some transactions, some assets and some liabilities are so highly specialized and their complexity so constantly evolving, that it is unlikely that most people in the industry, let alone the auditors, really fully understand them

Improvements might be made in a number of ways, such as the following:

1 Rotating senior audit partners more often so that they do not work too closely with management.
2 Audit fees being set by an independent body rather than being negotiated by management.
3 Auditors being appointed by an independent body.
4 Prohibiting auditors from non-audit work for audit clients.
5 Restricting companies in recruiting their accounting staff from the firms that audit them.

Punishing offenders

Where it is clear that illegal creative accounting has taken place there is a case for more transparent and effective punishment of offenders. Various voluntary codes exist in the UK for improved corporate governance, relying particularly on non-executive directors. These have achieved some success. In the USA the Sarbanes-Oxley Act (2002) is much stricter in making it clear who is responsible, and what sanctions are likely.

Radical proposals

Various more radical proposals have been made, both right wing and left wing.

Right wing

We could argue that the whole regulatory approach to accounting is a waste of time and money; it serves only to build up the bureaucratic empires of the regulators; it will always be unsatisfactory, and will always lead to demands for more resources for the regulators. Accounting and auditing is a matter for agreement between the shareholders and the directors.

A right-wing perspective could take a laissez-faire approach, or it could rely on freedom of access to information.

1. *Laissez-faire.* The market-based argument is that there is no need for legislation or public involvement in the ways in which companies do their accounting, or in the existence, role or operations of auditing firms. Companies have a vested interest in supplying credible information to capital markets, and auditing firms have a financial interest in maintaining their reputations. Companies that supply duff information will be punished in the capital markets; share prices will collapse; the companies will be taken over at bargain basement prices; and the directors will lose their jobs when their more credible competitors take over. Similarly, auditing firms that give their names to incredible accounting treatments will soon lose credibility, and be of no use to their clients. Eventually they will end up like Arthur Andersen - the major international accounting firm that collapsed with the Enron scandal. The market takes care of everything. There is no need for public involvement.

   This argument is out of favour at present. As long as there are financial scandals, governments want to be seen to play a role in dealing with the problems. The UK approach tends to be gentle and consultative and the accountancy profession can usually talk governments around to their way of thinking. Following Enron, WorldCom and other scandals, the USA adopted very strong measures with the Sarbanes-Oxley Act.

2. *Freedom of access to information.* Financial statements provide summaries of transactions and of what can be a huge amount of financial data. In the early days of companies, when there were fewer shareholders and fewer financial transactions, it was practicable to open up the books of account to individuals[4] who could see all transactions for themselves. If someone chose to present 'creative' accounts of what had happened, it would be difficult to pull the wool over the eyes of shareholders who could inspect everything for themselves. Such an approach became impractical as the number of shareholders, and the number of financial transactions, increased enormously. Shareholders became dependent on the version of events that was created for them by accountants, directors and auditors. But computerization may have changed all of that. When we read that schoolboys with computers in their bedrooms can penetrate the secrets of Pentagon defence systems, and fraudsters or pranksters can penetrate the security of banking systems - perhaps just for fun - we can no longer pretend that company accounting systems are inviolate. The public need no longer be dependent on accountants as intermediaries to present company financial stories in ways that suit company directors.

   Such open access to information is potentially revolutionary, and could be associated with a dramatic shift of power in society. There could be no secrets in relation to creative accounting. But, unfortunately, very few people seem to be interested in the details of company transactions.

[4] Something similar happens with local authorities today.

Accounting and auditing arrangements are no longer a matter just for directors and shareholders. When companies are listed on stock markets, the listing agreement requires appropriate arrangements to be in place. A stock exchange does not want its reputation undermined by companies that have chosen to opt out of accounting regulations. The most substantial shareholders are institutional investors, such as pension funds. They are unlikely to invest in companies that lack normal accountability mechanisms.

Left wing

Many assume that there is a legitimate public interest in the numbers that purport to represent the profits, assets and liabilities of companies. This is because they are relevant in the allocation of resources in the economy, the amount of taxation paid by companies, or because of the importance attached to 'the system' and avoiding financial scandals. The left-wing view would be that it is better to rely on a public sector body to act in the public interest, rather than relying on the accounting profession, a variety of power groups and vested interests. When, as happens from time to time, there are accounting scandals, and financial reporting seems to be collapsing, there are increasing demands for more direct government/public control.

1. *HM Revenue and Customs Rules OK.* Many Europeans are surprised to find that, in this country, profits for financial reporting purposes do not simply follow the rules laid down by the government for taxation (and other) purposes, and that this is deemed to be quite legitimate. The idea that companies can choose to depreciate ships, or aircraft over 10 or 20 or 30 years - or almost any period they like - seems quite fantastic. Perhaps it is central to the Anglo-American notion of 'freedom', which includes freedom to be creative with accounting.

   If we want to argue for clearer, more effective and enforceable accounting rules to curb creative accounting, we can argue that this should come from the government, and it can build on what HM Revenue and Customs already does. To someone from Eastern Europe this would seem only natural. But the argument is rarely advanced in Anglo-American accounting cultures. It is argued that governments lack the necessary expertise in accounting, and that they would be too slow to respond to changing business and accounting circumstances and practices. Moreover, the tax regulations are not always designed with the intention of the accounts showing a 'true and fair view'. Accelerated capital allowances are arranged to encourage companies to acquire the latest technology, thereby improving productivity.

   And if governments lack accounting expertise, they can easily buy it, as companies do. And if governments are slow to respond to changing circumstances they may be no worse than the accounting profession. The Chancellor of the Exchequer is usually criticized for producing too many changes in the taxation system too quickly, not for slowness to respond.

2. *A State Auditing Board.* It may be too extreme to suggest nationalizing the whole of the auditing profession. However, if auditing is seen as not operating in the public interest, but is, instead, operating for the benefit of vested interest groups, this must remain the ultimate solution. A State Auditing Board could do much to shift the balance of power without full nationalization. If there is a public interest in auditors being independent from directors (which is supposed to be the case), it is hard to defend a system where, in effect, the directors:
   - Decide which firm of auditors should be appointed, and how long they should serve
   - Decide what level of remuneration to pay to auditors
   - Allocate substantial contracts to auditors for non-audit work.

A public or state auditing board could be responsible for appointing auditors to particular companies, determining the level of fees and the period of appointment, and deciding to whom non-audit work should be allocated.

Such a board would also have a vested interest in establishing and implementing clear-cut accounting rules that could be expected to minimize creative accounting.

Accountancy and power

Anyone who believes that there is such a thing as 'correct' accountancy is likely to favour existing accountancy arrangements whereby accounting standard-setters struggle with the problem of how particular items should be measured and reported. They then produce general reporting standards, and accountants and auditors have to ensure that these are properly applied.

But many accounting numbers and accounting standards are the result of negotiation, rather than being based on any underlying truth, principle or economic reality. Accounting standard-setters have changed their conclusions and recommendations on issues such as the amortization of goodwill, providing for deferred taxation, and capitalization of development expenditure. A negotiated settlement is reached, but it may be changed a few years later. No new 'truth' is discovered. In negotiations the strongest usually get their way, and the way in which accountancy is applied is as a result of bargaining among powerful interest groups. Any serious attempt to change the way in which accountancy is applied in practice would involve a change in the balance of power between the different vested interest groups in society that influence accounting.

8.5 Social and Environmental Reporting

This section provides an overview of the social and environmental reporting on a historical basis to understand the development of the new wave in this area, followed by the current development.

Definition and overview

There has been increasing recognition of the idea that companies and other organizations should be more widely accountable:

- To interest groups other than just shareholders and creditors
- For social and environmental issues, not just financial.

The Corporate Report, which was published by the Accounting Standards Steering Committee (ASSC) in 1975,[5] adopted a very wide view of accountability. It took a wide view that every significant entity had an implicit responsibility to report publicly and to a wide range of users. It defined the various user groups as:

1. Equity investors
2. Loan creditors
3. Employees
4. Analysts and advisers, including financial analysts, economists, statisticians, researchers, trade unions, stockbrokers and credit rating agencies
5. Business contacts, including customers, trade creditors and suppliers, competitors, and those interested in mergers and takeovers
6. The government, including tax authorities, central government departments and local authorities
7. The public, including taxpayers, ratepayers, consumers, and community and environmental and other special interest groups.

The Corporate Report assumed that organizations would publish a single, multi-purpose report. As this was intended to meet the needs of such a diverse range of users, it was difficult to define their information needs, but six additional statements were advocated:

[5] https://www.icaew.com/library/subject-gateways/corporate-reporting/the-corporate-report

1 A statement of value added
2 An employment report
3 A statement of money exchanges with the government
4 A statement of transactions in foreign currency
5 A statement of future prospects
6 A statement of corporate objectives.

The first two of these were fashionable for a few years; the second two did not catch on. The final two 'softer'[6] ones have been largely incorporated into directors' reports and operating and financial reviews. The *Corporate Report* had almost nothing to say about environmental issues: it was nearly 20 years before these concerns became fashionable.

In the decades following the publication of the *Corporate Report* there have been many attempts to define what is meant by 'social ' and to operationalize it.

Gray et al. (1987) define corporate social reporting as:

> ***the process of communicating the social and environmental effects of organisations' economic actions to particular interest groups within society and to society at large. As such, it involves extending the accountability of organisations (particularly companies), beyond the traditional role of providing a financial account to the owners of capital, in particular shareholders. Such an extension is predicated upon the assumption that companies do have wider responsibilities than simply to make money for their shareholders.***

They use the abbreviation CSR to mean corporate social *reporting*; unfortunately, the same abbreviation is widely used to mean corporate social *responsibility* (see the next section). Their definition is in no way limiting. Gray et al. (1996) say that CSR 'can take a potentially infinite range of forms ... to fulfil any one or more of a wide range of objectives. It can cover a myriad of different subjects ... It is not a systematic, regulated, or well-established activity.' It seems that CSR can be almost anything! It is necessary to distinguish between:

1 What some companies actually do. There are many companies that include some sort of social and/or environmental report with or in their normal annual reports. It may be a few paragraphs, or a supplementary booklet of a dozen or more pages
2 What is advocated by a wide range of groups and individuals.

The term 'corporate social reporting' is reasonably clear. It means reporting by companies and other organizations on matters of concern to society and groups in society; it involves disclosing information in addition to conventional financial accounting statements; and at present it usually means mainly voluntary disclosure, although there are some matters of social concern that Companies Acts require to be disclosed. Those who argue in favour of corporate social reporting either:

1 advocate that legislation should require additional disclosures;
2 favour continued experimentation with voluntary disclosures.

Some advocate both, with experimentation continuing until a consensus on clear disclosure requirements emerges. Most advocate continuing research and experimentation. Many use corporate social reporting to include environmental (or 'green') reporting.

---

6 'Soft' in the sense that they do not include much 'hard' data like conventional accounting statements.

Corporate social responsibility

The idea that companies should increasingly recognize their social responsibilities is widely accepted. The government even has a corporate social responsibility website[7] that publishes its views. In a recent update, Stephen Timms, who was Minister for Corporate Social Responsibility (CSR), stated that the government wanted to see UK businesses taking account of their economic, social and environmental impacts, which it saw as supporting its strategy on sustainable development. The government took 'compliance with legal requirements' as the base for corporate social responsibility, but encouraged companies to go beyond that. There are no radical proposals for compulsory additional social and environmental disclosures, but it favours building on the statutory Operating and Financial Review.

Although politicians can produce fine-sounding statements on the subject, there is little commitment to specific proposals for corporate social *reporting*. The 2004 government update recognized that corporate social responsibility continued to be highly topical and much debated; that it has increasingly provided the focus for exploration of broad philosophical questions about the roles and responsibilities of companies, and about a range of (almost random!) questions about employee volunteering, health concerns about mobile phones, poverty eradication and even AIDS. The paper asks, perhaps rhetorically, 'Does this mean that CSR risks being about everything and nothing?'

It is recognized by the government paper that we are a long way from consensus on what CSR means, and its value, and it lists some of the different ways in which it is seen:

1 As glossy reports and public relations
2 As a source of business opportunity and improved competitiveness
3 As sound business practice
4 As a distraction or a threat.

The government accepts the idea that many are concerned with the social and environmental impacts of companies, and refers to the idea of socially responsible investment (or ethical investment).[8] But it is cynical about the relationship between 'practice and communication'. In other words, there may be companies that are good at public relations, have a high public profile and appear to take their social responsibilities seriously, but they may not be socially responsible businesses. Similarly, there may be other companies that concentrate on 'doing' CSR rather than reporting on it. Increased disclosure means increased transparency and accountability; but it does not necessarily make companies more socially responsible.

Employees

There are two distinct approaches to social reporting in relation to employees:

1 Giving information to employees. This may involve special employee reports that might be simplified versions of the usual annual report and accounts. It can also involve providing more detailed information about employment, performance and prospects at particular locations. It does not necessarily involve published reports; detailed information may be provided where it is requested by employees and their representatives.
2 Giving information about employees, perhaps mainly to investors. This was the approach adopted by the *Corporate Report,* which advocated the publication of an employment report showing:
    a numbers employed;
    b broad reasons for changes in numbers during the year;

[7] www.csr.gov.uk

[8] Some investors want to buy shares only in companies that behave ethically, and want companies to publish information to show how ethical they are. For example, does the company produce weapons or warfare, or use child labour?

c age distribution and gender of employees;
d functions of employees;
e geographical locations of major employment centres;
f major plant and site closures, disposals and acquisitions during the year;
g hours worked and scheduled with detail for different groups;
h costs and benefits of pension schemes and ability of schemes to meet commitments;
i names of trade unions recognized for collective bargaining and membership figures (or a statement that the trade union did not make the information available);
j health and safety information, including frequency and severity of accidents and incidence of occupational diseases;
k selected ratios related to employment.

The 1970s saw many experiments in employment reports, and employee reporting. Today, most companies disclose little more than the legal minimum in their annual reports but there is usually a paragraph headed 'Employees' in which it is typically the chairperson who pays tribute to all their good work.

The environment

Since the 1990s, the popular concern has been with the environment and 'green' issues. Companies do a lot to damage the environment, perhaps permanently or irretrievably, and they should stop it at once! It is difficult to see how accountants could achieve this. Perhaps they can try to get others to measure the amounts of pollution, put a cost on it, and then ensure that 'the polluter pays' by imposing appropriate taxation. Or reporting requirements could be imposed in the expectation that public shaming might inhibit their polluting behaviour. An alternative view would be that unacceptable pollution would be illegal, and it is for governments, rather than accountants, to establish and enforce such laws.

There are also concerns about over-exploitation of the world's natural resources, such as oil and other minerals, and companies should be committed to sustainable development. Perhaps accounting-type monitoring and reporting mechanisms could be applied to encourage companies to use sustainable raw materials. Those who believe in markets argue that if oil is in short supply, its price will increase, and companies will continue to find ways of using less oil as its price increases. It may be that increases in oil prices have done more to encourage the development of the electric car than governments or accountants have done.

Most generation of electricity, however, also pollutes the environment. The amount of power that can be generated by wind, sun, water and tides seems to be inadequate, and environmentalists complain about the appearance of wind farms and fear for wildlife if an ambitious scheme like the River Severn Barrier is constructed. Nuclear power seems clean and almost infinite to many, but others consider it extremely dangerous to the environment because of the possibility of accidents, radiation leaks, terrorism, and the problem of what to do with radioactive waste, particularly at the end of the plant's life.

The potential problem of global warming was of major concern in the 1990s, and mathematical models[9] were constructed showing that, within a couple of generations, most of the planet would be uninhabitable. By the early years of the twenty-first century, the cry of global warming was superseded by the cry of 'climate change'. The conventional wisdom[10] today is that climate change is caused by human activities and that by reducing carbon emissions, we can slow down the rate of global warming. The pressure is on to reduce carbon

[9] In 1900 less sophisticated mathematical models showed that, if traffic continued to increase at the rate then prevailing, by 2000 London would be waist deep in horse manure. But the car replaced the horse! In the 1970s mathematical models showed that, if the accountancy profession continued to expand at the rate then prevailing, by the middle of the twenty-first century every man, woman and child in the UK would be an accountant. The main thing we learn from history is that we learn nothing from history!

[10] An alternative view is that, over the centuries, the world sometimes gets warmer, and sometimes colder, and that we do not really understand the reasons for this.

emissions by using less electricity and oil, increasing the use of recycled materials, reducing air travel, and buying food locally rather than shipping it for thousands of miles. Accountants may have a role in calculating whether the carbon footprint is more increased by shipping food from the other side of the world than by growing it in the UK and in assessing whether the benefits of recycling materials exceed the costs of so doing.

Environmentalists are concerned with a broad range of issues, many of which relate to sustainable procurement, production and development. They are also involved in developing measures of green accounting and environmental reporting. Issues include pollution, the survival of different species, biodiversity and dealing with climate change. Accountants have the most to offer in areas where objective measurement is required, especially if it is financial and in reporting to the public.

Environmental accounting

Regardless of what is publicly reported, many companies have internal accounting systems that keep track of environmental impacts. Environmental accounting is also called green accounting and can be defined as:

> *The collection, analysis and assessment of environmental and financial performance data obtained from business management systems, environmental management and financial accounting systems. The taking of corrective management action to reduce environmental impacts and costs plus, where appropriate, the external reporting of the environmental and financial benefits in verified corporate environmental reports or published annual reports and accounts.*

The government's Environment Agency produced this definition and stated the department's own commitment to develop an environmental accounting system to integrate environmental performance measures into core financial processes and to track internal environmentally significant expenditure. This is regarded as vital to assist in the management of environmental risks and operational costs. It is, of course, easier to collect and classify, and perhaps also to report, costs than it is to measure environmental impacts.

The definition is odd in that it assumes that separate corporate environmental reports would be 'verified' in some way, presumably in line with the way in which external financial reports are audited. Where environmental impacts and costs are included in the normal annual report and accounts, companies are free to report whatever information that they wish, in whatever way they wish, with no assumption that it should be included as part of the financial statements that are audited.

Who decides? Is it accountancy?

If companies are to produce corporate social reports someone has to decide what is to be included in them, and how it is to be defined, measured and reported. With financial disclosures, governments and the accounting standard-setters have determined what should be disclosed, and they are continually refining their standards. There are a few items, which are as much financial as social, that have to be disclosed by law, such as political and charitable donations, how long on average it takes a company to pay its trade creditors, and some information about employees. Otherwise, it is companies themselves that decide what kind of social and environmental disclosures they will make.

The danger of leaving it to companies to disclose what they wish is that many will use the idea of corporate social reporting mainly as a public relations opportunity. It is worth examining in detail the contents of companies' annual reports and analysing the extent to which they disclose information in a way that really holds them to account for their social responsibilities, and the extent to which these disclosures are designed mainly to enhance their image. Some companies have always used their annual reports as a public relations opportunity, and it may be of some benefit to society if they choose to boast about their social and environmental performance if that goes hand in hand with real improvements.

In general, the accountancy profession has built on statutory requirements, with more detailed guidance on implementing Companies Acts for financial accounting purposes. There are already some legal requirements regarding social responsibilities that are or could easily be, incorporated into annual reports. These relate to payment policies and timing in relation to trade payables, employment policies and the number and gender of employees, number of industrial injuries, number of disabled employees, and political and charitable donations. Governments are perhaps more likely to increase companies' legal social responsibilities rather than reduce them. Where governments impose reporting requirements on companies, at least in relation to financial matters, it has long been the role of the accountancy profession to develop reporting recommendations and standards on how these should be implemented.

Sustainability report

The importance of sustainability reports for companies is growing because investors and other stakeholders are calling on companies to provide more information about their sustainability activities and ESG strategies. Several new legislative documents on ESG requiring companies to disclose sustainability information have already become effective or are currently being prepared. These documents include the EU (1) Taxonomy Regulation (REGULATION (EU) 2020/852 of the European Parliament and of the Council of 18 June 2020 on the establishment of a framework to facilitate sustainable investment), (2) the Corporate Sustainability Reporting Directive (CSRD), (3) the Directive on Corporate Sustainability Due Diligence (CSDD), and the (4) Proposal for a Regulation of the European Parliament and of the Council establishing a framework for setting ecodesign requirements for sustainable products.

What is the UK doing?

Existing UK disclosure obligations

In the UK, companies are obligated to comply with environmental and climate-related disclosure requirements. This includes regulations such as the Companies Act 2006, the Listing Rules, the Disclosure Guidance and Transparency Rules (DTR), and the Taskforce on Climate-related Financial Disclosure (TCFD) recommendations. Companies that fall under this category must report annually on environmental and climate-related matters in their directors' reports, strategic reports, and other sections of their annual reports. Similarly, Limited Liability Partnerships (LLPs) are also required to disclose information on greenhouse gas emissions, energy efficiency measures, and total energy consumption in their annual reports.

UK Sustainability Disclosure Standards

The UK government is creating UK Sustainability Disclosure Standards (UK SDS) by assessing and endorsing the global corporate reporting baseline of IFRS Sustainability Disclosure Standards. UK SDS will require companies to disclose sustainability-related risks and opportunities, including those arising from climate change.

UK SDS will be based on the IFRS Sustainability Disclosure Standards issued by the International Sustainability Standards Board (ISSB). The Secretary of State for Business and Trade will consider endorsing the IFRS Sustainability Disclosure Standards by July 2024. UK-endorsed standards will divert from the global baseline only if necessary for UK-specific matters.

Once endorsed, UK SDS may be referenced in legal or regulatory requirements for UK entities. The UK government and the Financial Conduct Authority will make independent decisions to require disclosure for UK entities.

Using the IFRS Sustainability Disclosure Standards as a baseline, UK SDS aims to make company disclosures globally comparable and decision-useful for investors. These disclosures will help investors compare information between companies, facilitate decision-making, support the efficient allocation of capital, and ensure the smooth running of the UK's capital markets.

During the 2021 UN Climate Change Conference in Glasgow, the ISSB was unveiled with the mission of establishing a worldwide foundation for sustainability reporting. Thus providing legitimacy, as a board within the International Financial Reporting Standards (IFRS) Foundation, the ISSB is committed to promoting sustainability in business practices. Recently, the ISSB announced the release of two new standards on 26 June 2023: IFRS S1, which outlines general requirements for disclosing sustainability-related financial information, and IFRS S2, which focuses on climate-related disclosures.

In broad terms, IFRS S1 sets out overall requirements for an entity to disclose sustainability-related financial information about its sustainability-related risks and opportunities. It is designed to underpin all other IFRS SDS in terms of setting scope, objectives, core content and presentation requirements. The objective of IFRS S1 is to provide information that is material to meeting the information needs of existing and potential investors, lenders and other creditors.

IFRS S2 endorses the content requirements of IFRS S1 but supplements those core disclosure requirements with specific climate-related risk management disclosures and reporting metrics such as qualitative disclosures regarding the risks and opportunities of lower-carbon transition plans, scenario analysis, and quantitative data measuring the entity's greenhouse gas emissions.

It is important to note that the IFRS SDS diverge from the EU CSRD (and the European Sustainability Reporting Standards) in significant respects, for example, in relation to materiality. This, along with any country-specific adjustments to the incorporation of the IFRS SDS into national regimes, will pose a challenge to interoperability and the ability of businesses to adopt a wholly unified approach to disclosures.

The UK government has taken a proactive approach to assessing and recommending IFRS S1 and IFRS S2 and any resulting UK SDS implementation. To facilitate this process, the government has established two committees: the UK Sustainability Disclosure Technical Advisory Committee (TAC) and the UK Sustainability Disclosure Policy and Implementation Committee (PIC).

TAC, which comprises a chair and members from various professional backgrounds, will evaluate the IFRS Sustainability Disclosure Standards from a technical perspective and provide impartial recommendations on endorsement to the Business and Trade Secretary via DBT. The Financial Reporting Council (FRC) will support TAC's operations, including the provision of a secretariat.

On the other hand, PIC is responsible for advising on endorsement decisions based on TAC and PIC's analyses and recommendations. It will also analyse the IFRS Sustainability Disclosure Standards' interactions with current UK legislation and regulation. If the Business and Trade Secretary approves the standards, PIC will coordinate the UK government and FCA's implementation of UK SDS. PIC's membership includes various UK government departments and regulators, such as the Bank of England.

Overall, the UK government's establishment of these committees demonstrates its commitment to transparency, sustainability and good governance. The committees will ensure that the UK adopts and implements high-quality sustainability disclosure standards, which will benefit businesses, investors and the wider public.

Corporate social reporting in practice

Most large companies include something on their social and/or environmental responsibilities and activities in their annual reports and accounts, but the quantity and quality of the information disclosed varies enormously. Some produce substantial additional reports, while others include just a few paragraphs. In 2023, AstraZeneca plc produced 40 pages for their ninth annual 'Sustainability Report, which is aligned with the materiality assessment as of 2021. However, for 2024, this will be amended in accordance with the new requirements, including the EU Corporate Sustainability Reporting Directive and a new materiality assessment. AstraZeneca plc has nine material focus areas grouped under three priorities and provides comparative empirical data from 2021 to 2023:

1 *Access to healthcare*: equitable access, affordability and pricing, and health system resilience.
2 *Environmental protection*: ambition zero carbon, product sustainability and natural resources.
3 *Ethics and transparency*: ethical business culture, inclusion and diversity and workforce safety and health.

AstraZeneca plc provides in detail their work on sustainability and social responsibility as shown in **Illustration 8.2** and **Illustration 8.3**.

ILLUSTRATION 8.2

Extract from AstraZeneca plc Sustainability Report 2023

The Sustainability Report is prepared on a consolidated basis.

Access to healthcare

Scope of equitable access (p. 10)

To drive equitable access to healthcare by embedding practices across the product portfolio – including digital health, clinical trial diversity, patient centricity, investing in rare diseases, open innovation and intellectual property (IP) sharing arrangements.

Strategic approach equitable approach

Improving access to healthcare for patients worldwide, including our innovative product portfolio. Our approach involves incorporating programs into local systems and providing affordable medicines to patients. We aim to promote positive global health outcomes by addressing unmet medical requirements and access barriers, increasing the speed and range of patient access, driving excellence in product lifecycle management, and comprehending the long-term effects of scientific advancements.

Scope of affordability and pricing (p. 12)

To drive the accessibility of medicines for diverse, equitable, and inclusive patient groups through company policy and programming, including core pricing principles and access programmes.

Strategic approach to affordability and pricing

AstraZeneca has implemented four primary pricing principles that aim to promote our global affordability initiatives. These principles are as follows:

• Sustainability: ensure the sustainability of both the healthcare system and research-led business model.

• Value: pricing reflects medicines' clinical benefits to patients and their broader societal impact. Reducing the need for additional medical intervention has a positive economic impact on the healthcare system.

• Access: work collaboratively with payers and providers to develop solutions that enable sustainable access to our medicines.

• Flexibility: offer flexible pricing options that reflect variations in healthcare system needs and patient ability to pay.

Source: https://www.astrazeneca.com/sustainability/resources.html

As outlined in the sections above, the group has continued to make good progress on corporate responsibility throughout the year. In addition, it provides some information on ethics as shown in **Illustration 8.3**.

ILLUSTRATION 8.3

Extract from AstraZeneca plc Sustainability Report 2023

Ethical business culture

Scope of ethical business culture (p. 25)

Ensure high social standards by driving conduct and accountability beyond compliance, covering anti-bribery and anti-corruption, product safety, use of human tissue and animals for research, and human rights while building supplier capabilities.

Strategic approach to ethical business culture (p. 26)

Code of Ethics and Values that guides and ensures that we provide life-changing medicines in a responsible way. We make sure that all our employees and third parties receive annual Code of Ethics training to reinforce our commitment to ethical business conduct. We emphasize values-based decision-making and encourage a sustainability mindset that reflects our core values among our workforce and suppliers. We believe that being transparent about the business and making it visible supports the learning and development of the employees, suppliers, and partners. It is essential to meet the expectations of patients, investors, and broader society.

Scope of Inclusion and Diversity (p. 27)

Establish a workplace where every employee feels a sense of belonging. Appreciated for their contributions, regardless of their age, gender, disability, ethnicity, gender identity, nationality, pregnancy, race, religion, sexual orientation, country of origin, or any other form of diversity. This includes providing equal opportunities for development and growth, as well as fair rewards. In addition, we extend our Inclusion and Diversity priorities to our value chain by promoting supplier diversity efforts that benefit local communities and enhance our socio-economic impact.

Some companies have a preference for disclosing information that is easily quantified, such as the number of complaints received per customer, perhaps comparing the number with the average for the industry. Some confine themselves to bland statements about being nice to one or more of employees, customers, suppliers, the environment and local communities. Often there are general statements about increasing the use of recyclable paper and other consumables, many of which are supported by quantitative statements and comparisons.

There have been attempts to quantify and compare, in financial terms, the total social and environmental good and harm that a company has done. But these are fraught with difficulties in deciding what should be disclosed, and with definitions and measurement. These may be compared with the difficulties in financial accounting, but corporate social and environmental reporting is at a much earlier stage in its development, and it remains to be seen how far it will go.

Summary

Many accounting and financial scandals arise because of illegal (sometimes criminal) activity by company directors and others. It is often normal accounting and auditing routines and reports that uncover the problems.

Creative accounting also arises where the rules are not clear and so technically there is no wrongdoing. There will continue to be problems with creative accounting as long as directors have substantial control over the ways in which financial reports are presented. The problems of creative accounting can only be curbed, not cured; and the process may be slow, especially if reliance is placed on moderate, evolutionary changes. The UK is unlikely to implement radical right- or left-wing proposals, and will proceed by international consensus.

There may be potential for restricting creative accounting by requiring companies to use HM Revenue and Customs' taxation rules for measuring profit, as is (or was) the case in some European countries. But, somehow, the US-UK approach usually seems to win in any contest with European approaches. It may be unrealistic to expect a thorough, authoritative set of measurement rules to be developed and enforced that will close all the creative accounting loopholes. Substantial improvement can come from fuller and more clear-cut disclosure requirements. The most effective curbs would come from the most significant shifts of power over the presentation of accounting information.

The most likely outcome is that we will continue with gentle reforms, become increasingly international, and largely preserve the status quo. More effective changes come as statutory requirements for additional specific disclosures are increased; and from restricting the powers of directors over auditing and accounting. Those who have the power to do so create knowledge, accounting principles, and determine accounting practice. If creative accounting flourishes, it is because it is in the interest of those who have the power to allow it. Perhaps it can be effectively restricted only if there is a radical shift away from the existing power structures of the accountancy profession, standard-setters, directors and auditors.

Ever increasingly, however, either in response to regulation, recognition of pressure from interest groups or in recognition of the need for transparency and accountability, listed companies are increasing disclosure in the area of corporate social responsibility such as public safety, their impact upon the environment and their ethical stance on dealing with customers and the public.

Review of key points

- The term 'creative accounting' is applied to a wide range of accounting practices.
- The exercise of judgement is inevitable in some areas of accounting, and it may be tempting to exercise it in a creative way, and to extend this to other areas.
- Some companies use questionable accounting practices to boost profits, to improve key ratios, to boost equity on the statement of financial position and to smooth out profits and losses from year to year.
- Problem areas have included exceptional and extraordinary items, provisions, goodwill and off-statement of financial position finance.
- Accounting standard-setters have reduced the scope for creative accounting, but there are some 'fuzzy' rules, and some areas of choice remain.
- Moderate evolutionary changes are steadily reducing the scope for creative accounting.
- Creative accounting is still a problem and more radical solutions may be considered.
- Listed companies are disclosing information on corporate social responsibility in a sustainability report, on their impact on the environment and sustainability, public safety issues, and their ethical stance on such issues as how staff are expected to conduct themselves through their decisions, actions and communications.

Self-testing questions

1 In what areas of accountancy has there always been a need for subjective judgement, and scope for creative accounting?

2 Give examples of techniques that have been used in 'creative accounting'.

3 Is creative accounting illegal?

4 In what ways can accounting standards be improved to restrict creative accounting?

5 In what ways have auditors been criticized for lack of independence?

6 The Platto Company produced the following draft income statements in early January year 9, shortly before being taken over by the Uppit Company in February year 9.

	Draft income statement for year ended 31 December year 8	Budgeted income statement for year ended 31 December year 9
	£000	£000
Sales revenue	800	790
Opening inventory	80	90
Purchases	650	636
	730	726
Closing inventory	(90)	(88)
Cost of sales	640	638
Gross profit	160	152
Depreciation	(40)	(38)
Operating expenses	(90)	(92)
Profit	30	22

In February year 9, the Uppit Company revised the draft accounts of the Platto Company for year 8 as follows:

a Closing inventories were written down to net realizable value, estimated at £50,000.

b Non-current assets in Chipping Sodbury were written down to an estimated fair value that led to an impairment charge of £55,000. The net book value of the assets was reduced from £120,000 to £65,000.

During year 9, the actual results of the Platto Company were much the same as had been budgeted, except that:

c Sales were reduced by £32,000 because inventories left from year 8, which were originally expected to be sold for £112,000, were, in fact, sold for £80,000.

d The non-current assets in Chipping Sodbury were sold for £90,000; as a result, the total depreciation charge for year 9 was reduced from a budgeted level of £38,000 to an actual level of £26,000. The total of other operating expenses was unaffected.

Required:

i Show the summarized income statement for the Platto Company for year 8, as modified by the Uppit Company.

ii Show the summarized income statement for the Platto Company for year 9.

iii Explain and comment.

7 What information could annual reports include about the social performance of companies?

Assessment questions

1. In what ways are the problems of creative accounting being tackled at present?
2. What more radical solutions do you think should be considered?
3. In what areas is it particularly difficult to restrict creative accounting?
4. Examine the case for more government involvement in the setting and enforcing of accounting standards, and in the regulation of auditors.
5. What is likely to happen to a company that overstates its profits year after year?
6. Why should 'corporate social reporting' be considered as being part of the responsibility of accountants?
7. With regard to environmental issues, should accountants be more involved in:
   a. Management accounting-type measurement of costs and impacts; or
   b. External reporting?

Group activities and discussion questions

1. Obtain the annual reports of four companies, two being major, well-known companies, and two being much smaller. Compare the reports in terms of the public relations material and the 'spin' that they put on the results. Can the reports be ranked on a scale indicating the extent of 'spin'? Do some reports contain little or nothing more than the minimum required? Why do some companies provide a lot more information, comment and explanation than is strictly required?
2. A company has a duty to maximize reported profits. If it uses creative accounting techniques to do so, it does not matter as long as those profits have credibility. Discuss.
3. Examine a number of company accounts in detail. Express the taxation charge as a percentage of the profit before taxation and compare the companies. Examine the companies' cash flow statements. Do these comparisons reveal anything that causes you to question reported profit figures?
4. Produce a list of recent accounting standards, and select a few for detailed examination. Read the stated objectives in the standards, and try also to read between the lines. Can you suggest what 'creative accounting' techniques (if any) they are designed to address?
5. Should governments lay down the rules for profit measurement?
6. Select a few companies' annual reports and analyse their social and environmental reporting. Assess the value of the reported information.
7. To what extent, and in what ways, is a requirement to report particular information likely to affect the behaviour of companies?
8. Examine disclosures in the annual report of a listed company relating to the environment, sustainability and ethics and consider whether you believe businesses seeking to prosper in an economic slump and pay dividends to shareholders should be required to disclose such information.

Accounting in context

Discuss and comment on the following, based on an item taken from the *Financial Times*. What does it reveal about responsible investment and shareholder activism?

Responsible investment: winners and losers

At the annual meeting of Shell, a group of 26 investors, led by Amundi, Europe's largest asset manager, are forcing Shell to significantly improve its climate targets. This is the largest shareholder push on climate policy that the oil and gas group has faced so far. The resolution, coordinated by the activist group, 'Follow This', has urged Shell to align its 'medium-term' greenhouse gas emissions target with the Paris Agreement to limit global warming. To meet these targets, global emissions must fall by almost half by 2030. Shell claims that its targets are already in line with the Paris Agreement, but the activist group wants the company to do better. This would include accounting for all the emissions of its products sold to its customers, known as scope 3.

'We urge Shell to set a credible scope 3 absolute emissions target', said Diandra Soobiah, head of responsible investment at UK pension fund Nest.

The investors are urging Shell to set a credible scope 3 absolute emissions target, which would demonstrate leadership and show that Shell is serious about transitioning its business towards generating real-world change. Since 2016, the shareholder activists have organized similar motions at Shell meetings. However, support for the upcoming resolution has drawn the most investment managers, according to 'Follow This' founder Mark van Baal. Together, the investors oversee more than €3.8tn and own about 5 per cent of Shell. These investors include both UK and international: UK pension fund London CIV, Rathbones, Candriam and Edmond de Rothschild, Swedish pension fund AP4, and the Ethos Foundation, representing Swiss investors.

Last year, two shareholders co-filed the resolution at Shell and drew the backing of about 20 per cent of the total investors who voted. 'With 2023 being the warmest year on record, and COP28 signalling "the beginning of the end of the fossil fuel era", we are more aware than ever that climate change will create winners and losers,' said Matt Crossman, stewardship director at Rathbones, referring to the UN climate summit agreement in the previous month to shift away from fossil fuels.

Historically, traditional investment groups have avoided filing shareholder resolutions, preferring to rely on behind-the-scenes talks. But some have become frustrated by a lack of action. Shell's CEO, Wael Sawan, outlined plans after he took over the role last year to keep investing in fossil fuels. He argues that to meet global energy demand and maintain shareholder returns, Shell must continue to invest in oil production and expand its gas business, even as it also invests in different forms of energy with lower emissions such as biofuels, hydrogen and renewable sources.

Shell's aim is to cut absolute emissions from its own operations, also known as scope 1 and scope 2, by 50 per cent by 2030. By the end of 2022, Shell had reduced carbon emissions from operations by 30 per cent compared with 2016 on a net basis, more than halfway towards the target of a 50 per cent reduction by 2030. Shell has committed to reduce the 'net carbon intensity' of its products by 20 per cent by 2030 but not their absolute emissions. Carbon intensity is a contentious measure that represents emissions as a proportion of all the energy it sells. Using this accounting treatment allows Shell to offset the carbon produced by its oil and gas business against its lower-carbon products. Shell has said that the shareholder resolution is 'unrealistic and simplistic' and 'broadly unchanged' from the resolution filed by 'Follow This' last year.

Source: A. Mooney and T. Wilson (2024) Europe's Largest Investor Pushes Shell for Better Climate Policy: Amundi Joined by 26 Asset Managers Oil Group Urged to Exceed Paris Goals', *Financial Times,* 16 January.

A. Mooney and T. Wilson (2024) Shell under Fire from Europe's Largest Asset Manager over Climate Policy. *Financial Times*, 15 January, https://www.ft.com/content/8e530a5c-6f67-424a-a9d9-a14d395ee4c1

https://reports.shell.com/sustainability-report/2022/

References and further reading

Accounting Standards Board (1999) *Statement of Principles*. ASB.

Astolfi, P. (2021) Did the International Financial Reporting Standards Increase the Audit Expectation Gap? An Exploratory Study. *Accounting in Europe,* 18(2): 166–195. https://doi.org/10.1080/17449480.2020.1865549.

De la Torre, I. (2008) *Creative Accounting Exposed*. Basingstoke: Palgrave Macmillan.

Dearing Committee (1988) *The Making of Accounting Standards*. ICAEW.

Department for Business and Trade (August 2023) *UK Sustainability Disclosure Standards*. https://www.gov.uk/guidance/uk-sustainability-disclosure-standards.

Economica (monthly journal of the Institute of Chartered Accountants in England and Wales). www.icaew.com/economia.

Gilbert Welytok, J. (2006) *Sarbanes-Oxley for Dummies*. New York: Hungry Minds Inc.

Gray, R. (n.d.) *Discovering Social and Environmental Accounting*. Centre for Social and Environmental Accounting Research Website (St Andrews University).

Gray, R. (2001) Thirty Years of Social Accounting, Reporting and Auditing: What (if Anything) Have We Learnt? *Business Ethics: A European Review*, 10: 9–15. https://doi.org/10.1111/1467-8608.00207

Gray, R., Owen, D. and Adams, C. (1996) *Accounting and Accountability: Changes and Challenges in Corporate Social and Environmental Reporting*. Upper Saddle River, NJ: Prentice Hall.

Gray, R., Owen, D. and Maunders, K. (1987) *Corporate Social Reporting: Accounting and Accountability*. Upper Saddle River, NJ: Prentice Hall.

Griffiths, I. (1986) *Creative Accounting: How to Make Your Profits What You Want Them to Be*. London: Sidgwick and Jackson.

Griffiths, I. (1995) *New Creative Accounting*. Basingstoke: Macmillan.

Jameson, M. (1988) *A Practical Guide to Creative Accounting*. London: Kogan Page.

Jones, M. (2011) *Creative Accounting, Fraud and International Accounting Scandals*. New York: Wiley.

Jones, M. and Stanton, P. (2021) Negative Accounting Stereotype: Enron Cartoons. *Accounting History*, 26(1): 35–60. https://doi.org/10.1177/1032373220981424

McBarnet, D. and Whelan, C. (1999) *Creative Accounting and the Cross Eyed Javelin Thrower*. Chichester: Wiley.

Mulford, C.W. and Comiskey, E.E. (2005) *The Financial Numbers Game: Detecting Creative Accounting Practices*. New York: Wiley.

Napier, C. (1995) The History of Financial Reporting in the United Kingdom. In P. Walton (Ed.), *European Financial Reporting: A History*. London: Academic Press, pp. 259–283.

Oxford English Dictionary (2023) Oxford University Press, https://doi.org/10.1093/OED/4515462058.

Pierce-Brown, R. and Steele, T. (1999) The Economics of Accounting for Growth. *Accounting and Business Research*, 29(2): 157–173. https://doi-org.uow.idm.oclc.org/10.1080/00014788.1999.9729576

Pijper, T. (1993) *Creative Accounting: The Effectiveness of Financial Reporting in the UK*. London: Macmillan.

Schilit, H. (2002) *Financial Shenanigans: How to Detect Accounting Gimmicks and Fraud in Financial Reports*. New York: McGraw-Hill.

Smith, T. (1992, 1996) *Accounting for Growth: Stripping the Camouflage from Company Accounts*. London: Century Business.

Smith, T. and Hannah, R. (1991) *Accounting for Growth*. UBS Phillips and Drew.

Tilt, C., Rao, K. and Dissanayake, D. (2024) Social Reporting: Trends, Determinants, and Implications. In M. Magnan and G. Michelon (Eds.), *Handbook on Corporate Governance and Corporate Social Responsibility*. Cheltenham: Edward Elgar, pp. 324–343. https://doi.org/10.4337/9781802208771

https://finance.ec.europa.eu/capital-markets-union-and-financial-markets/company-reporting-and-auditing/company-reporting/corporate-sustainability-reporting_en

https://kpmg.com/us/en/articles/2023/ifrs-vs-us-gaap-rd-costs.html

https://www.astrazeneca.com/sustainability/resources.html

https://www.icas.com/professional-resources/coronavirus/latest-updates/the-frc-has-issued-additional-guidance-on-reporting-on-exceptional-items-and-apms-during-covid-19

https://www.ifrs.org/issued-standards/list-of-standards/ias-37-provisions-contingent-liabilities-and-contingent-assets/

https://www.ifrs.org/issued-standards/list-of-standards/ias-38-intangible-assets/

https://www.ifrs.org/issued-standards/list-of-standards/ifrs-15-revenue-from-contracts-with-customers/

https://www.ifrs.org/issued-standards/list-of-standards/ifrs-16-leases/

https://www.pwc.com/sk/en/environmental-social-and-corporate-governance-esg/esg-reporting.html

www.environment-agency.gov.uk/business/topics/performance

www.fasb.org

www.ifrs.org

Chapter 9

Bookkeeping to Trial Balance

Chapter contents

9.1 Introduction
9.2 Bookkeeping in Practice
9.3 Bookkeeping Systems

Learning objectives

After studying **Section 9.1** you will be able to:

- ✓ Record straightforward transactions using double-entry bookkeeping
- ✓ Prepare a trial balance summarizing those transactions
- ✓ Introduce closing inventory and convert the trial balance into a set of final accounts

After studying **Section 9.2** you will be able to:

- ✓ Produce ledger accounts in a good format
- ✓ Record a wide range of transactions using double-entry bookkeeping, including discounts and returns
- ✓ Use a cash book and separate petty cash from bank transactions

After studying **Section 9.3** you will be able to:

- ✓ Understand how accounting systems operate
- ✓ Appreciate the role of day books, ledgers and control accounts
- ✓ Prepare a simple bank reconciliation statement

9.1 Introduction

Consider the following example:

Keith opened a business, Keith Ltd, and opened a bank account in the name of the business. In the first week, the following transactions take place:

Day 1: Keith puts £1,000 of his own money into the bank account

Day 2: The business buys 100 shirts, each costing £10

Day 3: Sells 70 shirts for £30 each

Day 4: The business pays its shareholders a dividend of £100

When compiling business accounts, it is important to understand that every transaction affects two figures in the accounts.

In transaction 1, the bank balance increases by £1,000. This is because the shareholders have purchased share capital from the business.

In transaction 2, the bank balance decreases by £1,000. This is because the asset inventory has risen by £1,000.

In transaction 3, the bank balance goes up by £2,100 because the business has sales totalling £2,100 (70 × £30). Also, the inventory has been reduced by £700 (70 shirts at £10). Why? Because 70 of the shirts are no longer assets; instead, they have been sold, and the cost of the goods sold is £700.

In transaction 4, the bank balance falls by £100. Why? The business has paid a dividend of £100 to the shareholders. In reality, this would not be possible because we have ignored taxation and the legal restrictions on dividend payments.

The accounts are shown at the end of each day, and two figures are affected by each transaction (see **Illustration 9.1**).

ILLUSTRATION 9.1

Keith Ltd	£	£	£	£
	Day 1	**Day 2**	**Day 3**	**Day 4**
Statement of financial position at the end of day				
Assets:				
Inventory		1,000	300	300
Cash	1,000	0	2,100	**2,000**
Total assets	**1,000**	**1,000**	**2,400**	**2,300**
Share capital	1,000	1,000	1,000	1,000
Retained profits			1,400	1,300
Total equity	**1,000**	**1,000**	**2,400**	**2,300**
Income statement for the period ended	**Day 1**	**Day 2**	**Day 3**	**Day 4**
Sales			2,100	2,100
Cost of goods sold			700	700
Profit for the period			**1,400**	**1,400**
Dividends paid			–	100
Retained profits			**1,400**	**1,300**

You can see that:

1. Every transaction affects two figures.
2. The statement of financial position always balances.
3. The balance sheet (or statement of financial position) equation is assets = equity + liabilities (there are no liabilities in this example), but equity is a company's liability to its shareholders.
4. The profit increases the equity.
5. Opening equity + capital introduced + profit for the period − dividends = closing equity. Or to rearrange that equation:
6. Profit for the period = closing equity − opening equity + dividends − capital introduced.

In this simple example, we have been able to prepare a statement of financial position, with a list of the various assets, equity and liabilities and an income statement after each transaction. However, in a real business, where there are hundreds or thousands of transactions of different types taking place, a system must be devised to record these transactions from which the two main accounting statements (the statement of financial position and the income statement) can be prepared from time to time.

Businesses use double-entry bookkeeping to record all transactions. For a very simple operation, it might be possible to keep only a cash account that records all the money that the business receives and all the money that it pays out.

But most businesses operate using credit (buying goods and paying for them at a later date; selling goods and receiving payment for them at a later date); they own non-current assets that have to be depreciated; and many are financed by borrowing. It is, therefore, necessary to keep account not only of what has been received and paid but also of how much the business owes to various people, payables and other creditors and of how much is owed to the business by customers (receivables) and other assets. Double-entry bookkeeping has been developed to meet this need. It is also useful in producing a trial balance, which is a list of the various assets and liabilities and types of income, such as sales and the various expenses from which the two primary statements (the statement of financial position and income statement) will be prepared.

The rules for double-entry bookkeeping are straightforward: a few rules, consistently applied, are all that is needed. There are more detailed rules for anyone who wants to be a bookkeeper (introduced in **Section 9.2**), but the basic principles outlined below are simple.

Rule 1 – cash account

A cash account shows all receipts of cash on the left-hand side (known as the debit side, *Dr*) and all payments of cash on the right-hand side (known as the credit side, *Cr*), as shown below.

Cash account					
Receipts			Payments		
(Dr)			(Cr)		
Date	Description	Amount	Date	Description	Amount
2023		£	2023		£
1 Jan	Capital - Catherine Fox	100,000	4 Jan	Rent	2,000
3 Jan	Loan from HSBC	50,000	5 Jan	Vehicle	20,000
8 Jan	Sales	3,300	6 Jan	Purchases of books	4,000

From the above cash account, it can easily be inferred what has happened.

Catherine Fox started a business (as a bookseller) on 1 January 2023 with £100,000 of her own capital, which she paid into a business bank account. The money was 'received' into the business cash or bank account. She then borrowed £50,000 from HSBC. The next day, she paid rent of £2,000, then £20,000 to buy a vehicle, and then she paid £4,000 to buy some books. Two days later, she sold some books for £3,300.

Anyone with no training in accountancy would soon devise a system of record-keeping such as the above. Recording receipts and payments is essential to keep track of the business's money.

A professional bookkeeper would separate 'petty cash' (notes and coins) from money in the bank, but this need not trouble us here.[1] It is all money and will be called cash. But the above cash account is too simple, and it is not double-entry bookkeeping.

Rule 2 – each transaction is recorded twice

Every transaction must be recorded twice: on the left-hand side of one account and the right-hand side of another account. These accounts are like separate pages in a book, each ruled by the letter 'T'; hence, they are known as 't-accounts'.

The next steps should follow naturally. Payments must be on the right-hand (Cr) side of the cash account; payments are usually to pay for assets, expenses such as salaries, or purchases of goods for resale. Separate t-accounts are needed for each of these, and the amounts will be recorded on the left-hand (Dr) side of the assets, expenses, and purchases t-accounts.

Receipts must be on the left-hand (Dr) side of the cash account. They may be from the original capital provided or from borrowings, but they are mainly from sales. Separate accounts are needed for each, and the amounts will be recorded on the right-hand (Cr) side of the capital, loan, and sales accounts.

These are illustrated below.

Capital account					
Date	Description	Amount	Date	Description	Amount
Dr			Cr		
2023		£	2023		£
			1 Jan	Cash	100,000

HSBC loan account					
Date	Description	Amount	Date	Description	Amount
Dr			Cr		
2023		£	2023		£
			3 Jan	Cash	50,000

[1] It is explained in Section 9.2.

Sales account					
Date	Description	Amount	Date	Description	Amount
Dr			Cr		
2023		£	2023		£
			8 Jan	Cash	3,300

Rent account					
Date	Description	Amount	Date	Description	Amount
Dr			Cr		
2023		£	2023		£
4 Jan	Cash	2,000			

Vehicle (Non-current asset) account					
Date	Description	Amount	Date	Description	Amount
Dr			Cr		
2023		£	2023		£
5 Jan	Cash	20,000			

Purchases account					
Date	Description	Amount	Date	Description	Amount
Dr			Cr		
2023		£	2023		£
6 Jan	Cash	4,000			

There should be no difficulty in deciding what description to use for a transaction: it is simply the name of the account where the other half of the double entry is to be found. Payments for purchases are shown on the right-hand (Cr) side of the cash account and labelled as purchases; the transaction also appears on the left-hand (Dr) side of the purchases account, labelled as cash.

But many, or most, business transactions are not conducted on a cash basis. Purchases are typically made on credit, and the payment is made a month or so later. Sales to other businesses are normally made on credit, and the money is received a month or so later. Purchases and sales that take place on a credit basis must not be shown on the cash account when the transaction first takes place. Entries in the cash account will be made when the cash is received or paid. But there is a need to record the sales and purchases as soon as they are made - not least because there is a need to keep track of how much is owed to suppliers and how much is owed to the business by customers. Each t-account accumulates all the transactions of the same type, so all transactions relating to the bank account are recorded in the cash t-account, while all transactions relating to purchases are recorded in the purchases t-account.

Rules 3 and 4 follow naturally from what we have already seen.

Rule 3 – purchase account

The purchases account records all purchases made, whether they are cash or on credit.

Rule 4 – sales account

The sales account records all sales that have been made, whether they are on a cash basis or on credit; in other words, all transactions of the same type or for the same reason are 'posted' to the t-account with that name or heading. It is much like in a postal sorting office where all letters and parcels going to Edinburgh will be put in the same place. Here, all the rent payments will be recorded in a t-account called 'rent', and at the end of the year, we will know the total rent cost to the business.

Catherine Fox specializes in buying remaindered books on credit from UK publishers and selling them, on credit, to overseas colleges. Her purchases account, and sales account for January are shown below.

Purchases Account					
Date	**Description**	**Amount**	**Date**	**Description**	**Amount**
Dr			**Cr**		
2023		£	2023		£
6 Jan	Cash	4,000			
18 Jan	Pinwin Publishers	8,000			
22 Jan	Grohill Publishers	7,000			

Sales account					
Date	**Description**	**Amount**	**Date**	**Description**	**Amount**
Dr			**Cr**		
2023		£	2023		£
			8 Jan	Cash	3,300
			10 Jan	College Alpha	5,500
			27 Jan	College Beta	8,500

It is clear what has happened: she has bought books on credit from two suppliers, Pinwin Publishers and Grohill Publishers, and she has sold books on credit to College Alpha and College Beta. No cash has changed hands with respect to these transactions (yet), so the cash account has not been affected. However, she does need to keep track of her trade payables and trade receivables. She must also follow Rule 2 and complete the double entry, as shown below.

Purchases made on credit are shown on the left-hand (Dr) side of the purchases account and on the right-hand (Cr) side of the payables account.

Pinwin Publishers (Payables) account					
Date	**Description**	**Amount**	**Date**	**Description**	**Amount**
Dr			**Cr**		
2023		£	2023		£
			18 Jan	Purchases	8,000

Grohill Publishers (Payables) account					
Date	Description	Amount	Date	Description	Amount
Dr			Cr		
2023		£	2023		£
			22 Jan	Purchases	7,000

Sales made on credit are shown on the right-hand (Cr) side of the sales account and on the left-hand (Dr) side of the receivables account.

College Alpha Receivables account					
Date	Description	Amount	Date	Description	Amount
Dr			Cr		
2023		£	2023		£
10 Jan	Sales College Alpha	5,500			

College Beta Receivables account					
Date	Description	Amount	Date	Description	Amount
Dr			Cr		
2023		£	2023		£
27 Jan	Sales College Beta	8,500			

Catherine Fox will, in due course, pay some of what she owes to her suppliers, and these payments (like all payments) must be recorded on the cash account, as shown below.

Cash account					
Date	Description	Amount	Date	Description	Amount
Dr			Cr		
2023		£	2023		£
1 Jan	Capital - Catherine Fox	100,000	4 Jan	Rent	2,000
3 Jan	Loan from HSBS	50,000	5 Jan	Vehicle	20,000
8 Jan	Sales	3,300	6 Jan	Purchases of books	4,000
			24 Feb	Pinwin Publishers	6,000
			25 Feb	Grohill Publishers	6,500

She also needs to complete the double-entry bookkeeping by recording the transactions on the left-hand (Dr) side of her two suppliers' accounts, as shown below.

Pinwin Publishers (Payables) account					
Date	Description	Amount	Date	Description	Amount
Dr			Cr		
2023		£	2023		£
25 Feb	Cash	6,000	18 Jan	Purchases	8,000

Grohill Publishers (Payables) account					
Date	Description	Amount	Date	Description	Amount
Dr			Cr		
2023		£	2023		£
25 Feb	Cash	6,500	22 Jan	Purchases	7,000

The balance on Pinwin's account now shows that Catherine Fox owes it £2,000. The balance on Grohill's account now shows that Catherine Fox owes it £500.

The money owed to Catherine Fox by her credit customers should, in due course, be received. These receipts, like all receipts, must be recorded on the left-hand (Dr) side of the cash account, as shown below.

Cash account					
Date	Description	Amount	Date	Description	Amount
Dr			Cr		
2023		£	2023		£
1 Jan	Capital - Catherine Fox	100,000	4 Jan	Rent	2,000
3 Jan	Loan from HSBC	50,000	5 Jan	Vehicle	20,000
8 Jan	Sales	3,300	6 Jan	Purchases of books	4,000
26 Feb	College Alpha	3,000	24 Feb	Pinwin Publishers	6,000
28 Feb	College Beta	8,500	25 Feb	Grohill Publishers	6,500

Again, it is necessary to complete the double entry by recording the amount that has been received on the right-hand (Cr) side of the receivables (debtors) accounts, as shown below.

College Alpha (Receivables) account					
Date	Description	Amount	Date	Description	Amount
Dr			Cr		
2023		£	2023		£
10 Jan	Sales	5,500	26 Feb	Cash	3,000

College Beta (Receivables) account					
Date	Description	Amount	Date	Description	Amount
Dr			Cr		
2023		£	2023		£
27 Jan	Sales	8,500	28 Feb	Cash	8,500

The balance on the College Alpha account shows that it still owes £2,500. College Beta has paid in full, so there is no balance remaining in its account.

The above example shows most types of transactions. There may be dozens of different types of expenses (rent, rates, insurance, postage, stationery, telephone, wages, salaries and so on), but in principle, they are all the same. They are shown on the left-hand (Dr) side of an expense account, such as electricity, and the right-hand (Cr) side of the cash account when they are paid.

It is easy to understand the words left and right. However, the words 'debit' and 'credit' often seem to cause problems. They are just more professional-sounding words for the same simple idea.

Rule 5 – debiting and crediting

Recording a transaction on the left-hand side of an account is called debiting it. Recording a transaction on the right-hand side of an account is called crediting it. If an account has more debited to it than credited to it, it is said to have a debit balance. If an account has more credited to it than debited to it, it has a credit balance.

Enough transactions have been illustrated above to be able to make the following generalizations:

- A sales account has a credit balance.
- A purchase account has a debit balance.
- An expense account, such as rent, has a debit balance.
- An asset account, such as receivables, has a debit balance.
- A creditor's account, such as payables or a loan, has a credit balance (unless we have paid our suppliers too much by mistake!).
- A trade receivables account has a debit balance (unless our customers have paid us too much by mistake!).
- A cash or bank account has a debit balance, provided more has been received than paid out (an asset). If more has been paid out than received, it will have a credit balance, which is an overdraft (a liability).

If every transaction is recorded twice, on the debit side of one account and correctly on the credit side of another account, the totals of all the debits must equal the totals of all the credits. This can be checked and summarized in the form of a trial balance, which is simply a list of the balance on each t-account, as shown in **Illustration 9.2**.

It is called a 'trial' balance because we are trying to see if it balances or if there are errors and omissions. If it does not balance, there is definitely something wrong. If it does balance, there could still be some errors: items completely missing or 'compensating errors', such as where a debit item and a credit item for the same amount have been omitted or where an entry has been 'posted' correctly but to the wrong account.

ILLUSTRATION 9.2

Trial balance of Catherine Fox as at 28 February 2023

	Debit	Credit
	£	£
Capital		100,000
Loan		50,000
Vehicle	20,000	

Trial balance of Catherine Fox as at 28 February 2023		
	Debit	Credit
	£	£
Cash (£164,800 − £38,500)	126,300	
Pinwin (trade payable)		2,000
Grohill (trade payable)		500
College Alpha (trade receivable)	2,500	
Rent	2,000	
Purchases	19,000	
Sales		17,300
	169,800	169,800

The trial balance is also useful in summarizing all transactions. Even if there have been hundreds of sales, we just have one figure for the total. A cash account may have hundreds of debits and credits, but on the trial balance, we just show one figure. In the above trial balance, there are two trade payables; a normal business might have hundreds, but the trial balance would show just one figure for the total amount of the trade payables.

The trial balance provides the basis of the information that is needed to produce a statement of financial position and an income statement since it shows the sum total of the result of the transactions in the period. However, some additional information is usually needed, and this leads to the adjustment of the figures appearing in the 'after all-transactions trial balance'. Each 'adjustment' to the trial balance must involve a debit and a credit; otherwise, it would not balance. In any case, Rule 5 states every debit has a credit.

In Catherine Fox's case, the figure for closing inventory (the amount of unsold books at the end of the period) must be added to the trial balance. It will appear on the statement of financial position as a current asset, and it will be deducted from purchases to arrive at the cost of goods sold on the income statement. If her closing inventory is £6,000, her income statement and statement of financial position can be prepared as shown in **Illustration 9.3**.

ILLUSTRATION 9.3

Income statement of Catherine Fox for the two months ended 28 February 2023		
	£	£
Sales		17,300
Cost of goods sold		
Opening inventory	0	
Purchases	19,000	
	19,000	
Less Closing inventory	6,000	
		13,000
Gross profit		4,300
Expenses – rent		2,000
Net profit		2,300

Income statement of Catherine Fox for the two months ended 28 February 2023		
	£	£

Statement of financial position of Catherine Fox as at 28 February 2023		
	£	£
Assets		
Non-current assets – van		20,000
Current assets		
Inventories	6,000	
Trade receivables	2,500	
Cash	126,300	134,800
Total assets		154,800
Liabilities and equity		
Current liabilities		
Trade payables		2,500
Non-current liabilities		
Loan from HSBC		50,000
Total liabilities		52,500
Equity		
Capital	100,000	
Profit for the period	2,300	
Total equity		102,300
Total liabilities and equity		154,800

When looking at a statement of financial position and income statement like this for the first time, it is a good idea to check where each item has come from. It is important to note that the profit figure calculated at the end of the income statement account is added to the capital figure on the statement of financial position.[2]

Remember the following:

1 Every debit has a credit.
2 Debits are increases in assets or expenses or decreases in liabilities or revenues.
3 Credits are increases in liabilities or revenues or decreases in assets or expenses.

9.2 Bookkeeping in Practice

Section 9.1 provides enough information about bookkeeping to understand how a system works, record straightforward transactions, and produce a trial balance. However, bookkeeping systems are more sophisticated, and this section explains how bookkeeping operates in practice.

[2] In a company's income statement, any amount for dividends that shareholders receive is deducted to arrive at a 'retained' profit for the year. These items are shown on a separate 'statement of changes in equity' that links the income statement with the statement of financial position.

Balancing accounts

In **Section 9.1**, there were very few transactions, and it was easy to see the balance on an account. For example, in the account of a payable, Grohill Publishers, there was a debit item of £6,500 and a credit item of £7,000. As the credit item is greater than the debit item, we say that there is a credit balance on the account.

Where there are more transactions on the account (e.g. Catherine Fox's cash account), we have to add up all the debit items, which made a total of £164,800, then add up all the credit items, which made a total of (£38,500); then deduct the credit items from the debit items to arrive at the balance on the account, which is (£164,800 − £38,500 = £126,300); this is a debit balance because the total of debits is greater than the total of credits.

Calculating the balance on an account is done at the end of a period, typically monthly, and the balance is recorded twice on the account (as a debit and as a credit, keeping to the rules of double entry) and shown as a balance carried down (c/d), and then as a balance brought down (b/d), as shown in two of Catherine Fox's accounts below.

Grohill Publishers (Payables) account					
Date	Description	Amount	Date	Description	Amount
Dr		£	Cr		£
25 Feb	Cash	6,500	18 Jan	Purchases	7,000
28 Feb	Balance c/d	500			
		7,000			7,000
			1 Mar	Bal b/d	500

Cash account					
Date	Description	Amount	Date	Description	Amount
Dr		£	Cr		£
1 Jan	Capital	100,000	4 Jan	Rent	2,000
3 Jan	Loan from HSBC	50,000	5 Jan	Vehicle	20,000
8 Jan	Sales	3,300	6 Jan	Purchases of books	4,000
26 Feb	College A	3,000	24 Feb	Pinwin Publishers	6,000
28 Feb	College B	8,500	25 Feb	Grohill Publishers	6,500
			28 Feb	Balance c/d	126,300
		164,800			164,800
1 Mar	Balance b/d	126,300			

Remaining balances on accounts, including receivables, payables, cash and other assets and liabilities, are summarized in the form of a statement of financial position that is, in effect, a statement of remaining balances. Accounts that deal with expenses and revenues are dealt with differently: the balances are transferred to the income statement, which is part of the double-entry bookkeeping system. The income statement is summarized and presented in the form of an income statement.

Cash and bank

Accountants often use the word 'cash' to include both petty cash (coins and notes) and money in the bank. But in practice, it is necessary to record the two separately. Businesses are usually operated mainly through bank accounts recorded in the cash book, and it is necessary to keep a cash float to pay modest routine expenses (e.g. window cleaning, newspapers, coffee), such transactions being recorded in a petty cash book.

Discount allowed and discount received

Businesses often offer their customers a cash discount of perhaps 2.5 per cent or 5 per cent for prompt account settlement.

Discount allowed is an expense and reduces the amount owed by trade receivables and is accounted for as follows:

Debit: discount allowed account

Credit: the trade receivables (debtor's) personal account

The total on the discount allowed account is treated as an expense on the profit and loss account.

Discount received reduces the amount owed to creditors, and is treated as income to be added to gross profit, and is accounted for as follows:

Debit: the trade payables (creditor's) personal account

Credit: discount received

The amounts shown for sales and purchases are not affected by discounts allowed and received. The full amount (before deducting any cash discounts) is shown for sales and purchases. Discounts allowed and received are dealt with in the income statement after calculating gross profit and are included in the profit for the year shown on the income statement.

Discounts allowed and received should not be confused with 'trade discounts'. Suppliers often charge higher prices to the general public than they do to wholesalers and other businesses. These trade discounts are not entered into the accounting system. The transactions are recorded at the price actually charged.

Returns inwards and returns outwards

Customers often return goods that they have received to the supplier for various reasons, and in such circumstances, a credit note (to all intents and purposes, a 'minus' or 'negative' invoice) is issued. Generally speaking, such credit notes will be entered in the sales day book or the purchases day book as negative figures. Where the original sale was made on credit, the returns are accounted for as follows.

Returns inwards (or sales returns) are goods that a business has sold but have then been returned by the customer.

Debit: sales account

Credit: the trade receivables personal account

In this way, the inward returns are deducted from the total sales figure shown on the income statement.

Returns outwards (or purchases returns) are goods that a business has bought but then returned to the supplier. They are recorded as follows:

Debit: trade payables (creditor's) personal account

Credit: purchases

In that way, the returns outward are deducted from the total purchases figure shown on the income statement.

The recording of discounts and returns is shown in **Example 9.1**.

Example 9.1

Extracts from the ledger accounts of G. Maye

Sales account

			1 Mar	Bal	51,000

Purchases account

1 Mar	Bal	17,000			

S. Oldrick (Receivable)

1 Mar	Bal	23,000			

Cass Hawin (Payable)

			1 Mar	Bal	11,000

During March, the following transactions took place:

		£
3 Mar	Sales on credit to S. Oldrick	14,000
6 Mar	Purchases on credit from Cass Hawin	7,000
12 Mar	Purchases on credit from Cass Hawin	4,000
16 Mar	Returned goods to Cass Hawin	2,500
19 Mar	Sales on credit to S. Oldrick	21,000
21 Mar	S. Oldrick returned goods	4,600
26 Mar	Sales on credit to S. Oldrick	18,000
28 Mar	Paid the balance on Cass Hawin's account after taking a 4% discount	
30 Mar	Received a cheque from S. Oldrick for £50,730 who had taken discount of £2,670	

Required:

Show the above transactions in the form of T-accounts.

Solution

Purchases account

Date	Detail	Amount £	Date	Detail	Amount £
1 Mar	Bal	17,000			
6 Mar	C. Hawin	7,000			
12 Mar	C. Hawin	4,000	16 Mar	C. Hawin (return)	2,500

Sales account

Date	Detail	Amount £	Date	Detail	Amount £
			1 Mar	Bal	51,000
			3 Mar	S. Oldrick	14,000
21 Mar	S. Oldrick (return)	4,600	19 Mar	S. Oldrick	21,000
			26 Mar	S. Oldrick	18,000

S. Oldrick (Receivables)

Date	Detail	Amount £	Date	Detail	Amount £
1 Mar	Bal	23,000	21 Mar	Returns inwards	4,600
3 Mar	Sales	14,000	30 Mar	Discount allowed	2,670

Cass Hawin (Payables)

Date	Detail	Amount £	Date	Detail	Amount £
16 Mar	Returns Outwards	2,500	1 Mar	Balance	11,000
28 Mar	Discount received[3]	780	6 Mar	Purchases	7,000

[3] 4% × (£11,000 + £7,000 + £4,000 − £2,500) = 4% × £19,500 = £780

Date	Detail	Amount £	Date	Detail	Amount £
19 Mar	Sales	21,000	30 Mar	Cash	50,730
26 Mar	Sales	18,000	31 Mar	Bal c/d	18,000
		76,000			76,000
1 Apr	Bal b/d	18,000			

Date	Detail	Amount £	Date	Detail	Amount £
28 Mar	Cash	18,720	12 Mar	Purchases	4,000
		22,000			22,000

Discount allowed

Date	Detail	Amount £			
30 Mar	S. Oldrick	2,670			

Discount received

			Date	Detail	Amount £
			28 Mar	C. Hawin	780

Returns inwards are debited to sales, while returns outwards are credited to purchases and thereby affect the amount of gross profit. The figures to be included in the income statement from **Example 9.1** are as follows:

	£
Sales	99,400
Purchases	25,500

Discounts received and allowed do not affect gross profit. Discount received is added to gross profit. Discount allowed is a normal expense shown after calculating gross profit.

Accruals and prepayments

Accruals and prepayments are subject to the normal rules for double-entry bookkeeping. However, to prepare final accounts from a trial balance, particularly in an examination, adjustments can be made directly onto the statement of financial position and/or income statement. In practice, full double entry is required, as shown below.

Accrual

A company pays its electricity bill quarterly as follows:

3 April	£800
5 July	£600
4 October	£700

The company's year-end is 31 December, and the fourth electricity bill has not been received, recorded or paid by that date. It has to be accrued. An accrual is an expense incurred in one year but which is billed and paid for the following year. It may be estimated, or the actual bill, for example, £750, may be used for the accrual. It is likely to be received early in January before the financial statements have been finalized. The three payments will have been recorded early in the year: debit electricity[4] and credit cash. Since the business has used this electricity, even though it has not paid for it or been invoiced for it by 31 December, nevertheless the cost of this electricity must be accounted for. At the end of the year, it is necessary to add £750 to the amount of electricity expenses; it is also necessary to show £750 as a short-term creditor (an accrual) on the statement of financial position. The bookkeeping is done as follows:

[4] Alternatively, the account might be called 'lighting and heating'.

Electricity account					
Date Dr	Description	Amount £	Date Cr	Description	Amount £
3 Apr	Cash	800			
5 Jul	Cash	600			
4 Oct	Cash	700			
31 Dec	Accrual c/d	750	31 Dec	Income statement	2,850
		2,850			2,850
			1 Jan	Accrual b/d	750

This may seem a complicated way of proceeding, but it achieves three things:

1 The full amount of the electricity charge for the year (£2,850) is shown on the income statement (debit income statement; credit electricity account), although all of it has not yet been paid as at 31 December. This is because we are not accounting on a cash basis but in accordance with the accruals concept.

2 The balance brought down at 1 January (a credit balance) is the balance that will be shown on the statement of financial position as an accrual, part of short-term creditors.

3 When the final bill for the year, £750, is actually paid early in the following year, the bookkeeping will be debit electricity; credit cash. The electricity account already shows a credit balance brought down of £750; this will offset the payment made in respect of the previous year so that the new year, in effect, starts with a zero balance.

Prepayment

A company pays its rent bill quarterly, in advance, as follows:

3 January	£1,000	for January to March
25 March	£1,000	for April to June
24 June	£1,000	for July to September
29 September	£1,000	for October to December
24 December	£1,000	for January to March in the following year

The company's year end is 31 December, and at the end of the year, the company has paid not only the rent for the year but also the rent for the following three months. This final payment is considered to be a pre-payment, a payment in one year for which the benefits are going to arise in the following year. This sum of £1,000 is not considered to be an expense in this year but instead is regarded as a current asset, which will be 'consumed' in the following year. The accounting adjustment recording this prepayment is debit prepayments and credit rent. At the end of the year it is necessary to deduct £1,000 from the amount of the rent expense; it is also necessary to show £1,000 as a current asset (a prepayment) on the statement of financial position. The bookkeeping is done as follows:

Rent account					
Date Dr	Description	Amount £	Date Cr	Description	Amount £
3 Jan	Cash	1,000			
25 Mar	Cash	1,000			

Rent account					
Date	Description	Amount	Date	Description	Amount
Dr		£	Cr		£
24 Jun	Cash	1,000			
29 Sep	Cash	1,000	31 Dec	Prepayment c/d	1,000
29 Sep	Cash	1,000	31 Dec	Income statement	4,000
		5,000			5,000
1 Jan	Prepayment b/d	1,000			

This may seem a complicated way of proceeding, but it achieves three things:

1 The full amount of the rent charge for the year (£4,000) is shown on the income statement[5] (debit: income statement; credit: rent account), although £5,000 has been paid in the year to 31 December.
2 The balance brought down at 1 January (a debit balance) is the balance that will be shown on the statement of financial position as a prepayment, part of current assets.
3 In the following year's income statement, the rent for January to March will be shown as part of the rent expense, even though this was paid in the previous year. The rent account already shows a debit balance brought down of £1,000. As with electricity, we are not accounting on a cash basis but on an accrual basis.

Carriage inwards and carriage outwards

The cost of transporting goods, whether inwards or outwards, is an expense and is included on the trial balance as a debit. Often, there is no cost for carriage inwards because the seller pays delivery costs. Where the buyer pays the delivery costs (or carriage inwards), the expense is added to the cost of purchases and so affects the gross profit figure.

The cost of carriage outwards does not affect the gross profit. It is a normal expense and is included in the income statement, often as part of 'distribution costs'.

Depreciation of non-current assets

Companies usually have a number of categories of non-current (or fixed) assets (e.g. land and buildings; plant and machinery; fixtures and fittings; vehicles). They should maintain two t-accounts for each category:

1 *Non-current assets at cost (or valuation).* This shows all non-current assets that the company owns, usually at the original cost price; the account has a debit balance. Sometimes, a non-current asset is revalued, and then the amount on the non-current asset at cost is changed. If there is an increase in value, the non-current asset account is debited, and the increase is credited to the revaluation reserve, which is shown as part of equity on the statement of financial position.
2 *Provision for depreciation.* This shows the cumulative (or aggregate) depreciation that has been built up over a number of years; the account has a credit balance. Each year, the depreciation charge is debited to the income statement (to be included in expenses on the income statement) and credited to the provision for depreciation account. The credit balance on the provision for depreciation account increases each year until some non-current assets are sold.

[5] The term 'profit and loss account' is still sometimes used for recording transactions; the summary of it for final presentation is usually called an 'income statement'.

On the statement of financial position, the amount shown for non-current assets is the net book value. The cumulative depreciation figure is deducted from the cost (or revalued amount) to give the net book value.

When a non-current asset is sold, its cost must be removed from the cost t-account and its accumulated depreciation from the provision for depreciation t-account. Both amounts are transferred to a 'disposal (or sale) of non-current asset account', as shown in **Example 9.2**.

Example 9.2

The Salov Company bought a car for £20,000. The company's accounting policy is to depreciate cars over four years at 25 per cent per annum on a straight-line basis. The company estimates that the car will be sold for £2,000 at the end of its estimated economic life. The depreciation charge for each year will be (cost less estimated sale price, divided by four years, that is, £4,500 per annum. The company's non-current asset account and provision for depreciation account and depreciation expense account for the car in year 1 are shown below.

The effect of these transactions and the depreciation adjustment are also shown below.

Car at cost account

Cash	£20,000		

Provision for depreciation on car account

		Depreciation expense	£4,500

Depreciation of car expense account

Provision for depreciation (year 1)	£4,500	Income statement	£4,500

Sale of non-current assets

When a non-current asset is sold, its cost and accumulated depreciation must be removed from the cost and the provision from t-accounts and transferred to the disposal of non-current asset t-account in order to compute the profit or loss on its disposal.

As can be seen in **Example 9.3**, the machine that is disposed of has to be removed from the machinery at cost account and transferred to the disposal of the non-current asset account. This is done by crediting the machinery at the cost account and debiting the disposal of the non-current asset account.

Example 9.3

The Salov Company bought a machine some years ago for £20,000; cumulative depreciation in respect of the machine amounts to £16,000. The machine was sold last week for £5,500. The company's non-current asset account and its provision for depreciation account had balances brought forward immediately before the disposal, as shown below.

Machinery at cost account

Balance brought forward	£85,000		

Provision for depreciation on machinery account

		Balance brought forward	£55,000

The accumulated depreciation in respect of the machine that is sold has to be removed from the provision for depreciation on the machinery account and transferred to the disposal of the non-current asset account. This is done by debiting the provision for depreciation on the machinery account and crediting the disposal of the non-current asset account.

The effect of these two transactions is shown below.

Machinery at cost account

Balance brought forward	£85,000	Disposal of non-current asset	£20,000

Provision for depreciation on machinery account

Disposal of non-current account	£16,000	Balance brought forward	£55,000

Disposal of non-current asset account

Non-current asset at cost	£20,000	Provision for depreciation on machinery	£16,000

After these two transfers, the balance on the disposal of the non-current asset account is a debit of £4,000. This is the net book value of the machine. As the machine was sold for £5,500, a profit on sale of £1,500 was made. This profit is credited to the income statement and debited to the disposal of the non-current asset account. The cash received is debited to the cash account and credited to the disposal of the non-current asset account. The effect of these two transactions is shown below.

Disposal of non-current asset account

Non-current asset at cost	£20,000	Provision for depreciation on machinery	£16,000
Income statement	£ 1,500	Cash	£ 5,500
	£21,500		£21,500

The effects of a sale of non-current assets is included in **Self-testing question 6** (Ellie's Ltd) in **Chapter 10**.

9.3 Bookkeeping Systems

Bookkeeping systems are designed, or have evolved over the years, so that they achieve a number of objectives:

1. All transactions and adjustments are recorded using double entry.
2. They facilitate the preparation of trial balances and statement of financial position and income statement.
3. Transactions can be traced and verified by the organization's own staff, and by external auditors.

4 Errors can be identified, traced and corrected.
5 Several different people can work on different parts of the system at the same time; there are separate books and ledgers for different parts of a system, whether it is handwritten or computerized.
6 One part of the system, or set of records, is used to check on another part of the system.
7 Bookkeeping/accounting fraud occurs when somebody within a company dishonestly takes certain actions regarding accounting documents or records with a view to making a financial gain or causing a loss. Accountants must be aware of common warning signs that may include unusual transactions or accounting entries, missing or incomplete documentation, sudden changes in financial performance, lack of transparency, and unusual behaviour by company executives, which require further investigation.

Ledgers, day books and journals

All transactions end up being included in double-entry accounts in a 'ledger'. This is usually done on a computer using an accounting package. In a small business, with very few transactions, everything may be recorded in a single 'general ledger'. In a large organization there are likely to be several day books[6] and ledgers in which each individual transaction is recorded.

Where there are hundreds or thousands of items of sales, each item is usually recorded in a sales day book (or sales journal) and the total amount for a week's or a month's sales is shown in the ledger. Similarly, there is likely to be a purchases day book (or purchases journal). There might also be a purchases returns (or returns outwards) journal and a sales returns (or returns inwards) journal.

The main day books are:

1 Sales day book
2 Purchases day book
3 Cash book
4 Petty cash book
5 Journal.

A journal may be used to record one-off or special transactions such as adjustments to the trial balance at the end of the period, or corrections of errors.

There may be several cash books and a petty cash book or a combined one. They may be analysed to show the amounts for different sorts of transaction (e.g. expenses, payments to trade payables, receipts from trade debtors). The cash book is regarded as being both a day book (showing each individual transaction) and a ledger account in its own right.

It is essential to keep a separate personal account for each individual trade receivable and each individual trade payable to be clear what transactions have taken place, and the net amount owed to or by each individual. Where a business has a large number of different suppliers and credit customers, their personal accounts are kept in two different ledgers:

1 The sales ledger (or sometimes called 'trade receivables' ledger)
2 The purchase ledger (or sometimes called the 'trade payables' or 'bought' ledger).

The remaining t-accounts will be recorded in a nominal ledger.

[6] Or 'journals', or 'books of prime entry'.

Control accounts

Where a business has many trade receivables, it is likely that some errors are made in individual personal accounts, and it is important that the bookkeeping system checks for such errors so that they can be corrected.

It is possible to arrive at the total figure for receivables at the end of a period without examining the individual receivables accounts. The figure can be arrived at by starting with the total amount of receivables at the beginning of the period, then adding all credit sales made during the period (minus any sales returns); from that is deducted any discount allowed to receivables, and any amounts of money received from them. The remaining balance should be equal to the total on the individual personal accounts.

It is useful to have this total on the receivables control account that can be used in the trial balance and to prepare the final accounts, even before errors on individual personal accounts have been corrected.

The position is similar with a trade payables control account (see **Example 9.4**), but the opposite way around. For example, the amount owed to payables is a credit balance (whereas the amount owed by receivables is a debit balance); payments are made to payables (whereas money is received from receivables); discounts may be received from payables (whereas discounts are allowed to receivables); and returns are made outwards to payables (whereas they are received inwards from receivables).

Example 9.4

Trade receivables control account

Debit	*£000*	*Credit*	*£000*
Opening balances b/d	45	Cash received	197
Sales invoices total	210	Discounts allowed	2
Dishonoured cheques	2	Sales credit notes	6
		Bad debts	2
		Purchase ledger contra	3
		Closing balances c/d	47
	257		257
Opening balances b/d	47		

Trade payables control account

Debit	*£000*	*Credit*	*£000*
Cash paid	135	Opening balances b/d	26
Discounts received	2	Purchase invoices total	128
Purchase credit notes	4		
Sales ledger contra	3		
Closing balances c/d	10		
	154		154
		Opening balances b/d	10

Bank reconciliations

The cash book, or the bank column of a cash book, shows the amount of money that the business has in its bank account. When a statement is received from the bank, the amount on that statement will, in theory, agree with the cash book. In reality, the balance in the cash book and the balance in the bank statement are very unlikely to agree for two main types of reasons:[7]

1 First, the company might have made errors or omissions in recording its bank transactions. A business records all the transactions it is aware of, but it might only be aware of some transactions once it reads the bank statement. For instance, it might not know what bank charges have been charged until the statement has been received. Some customers might have paid money directly into the company's bank account through a direct banking system, which the company only learns about when reading the bank statement. Such 'missing' transactions must now be entered into the cash book.

2 Second, cheques and other payments made by the company at the end of the month and money banked at the end of the month might not have cleared the BACS system (Banking Automated Clearing System) by the date of the last day of the month when the bank statement is produced. Such 'timing differences' must be entered in a 'bank reconciliation statement' in order to verify the corrected cash book balance with the bank statement balance.

The above adjustments are shown in **Example 9.5**.

Example 9.5

Grenaugh Ltd's cash book showed a debit balance of £13,000 on 31 December year 9.

The bank sent it a statement showing the same date but that there was £16,400 in the bank.[8] Further investigation revealed the following:

1 Unpresented cheques, which had not cleared at 31 December, amounted to £5,000.

2 Grenaugh Ltd deposited £2,000 cash into the bank on 31 December, but this was not shown on the bank statement until 5 January.

3 The bank statement showed that the dividends received were £500 and had not yet been recorded in the cash book.

4 The bank charges for December amounted to £100.

Cash book

	£
Balance according to cash book	13,000
Add Dividends received not yet recorded (3)	500
Deduct Bank charges not yet recorded (4)	(100)
Updated cash book balance	13,400

[7] An additional factor is that, from the business's point of view, the money in the bank is an asset while from the bank's point of view, they owe the business money and, hence, the business is a liability. So, if the business pays £100 into a new bank account, this will be a debit balance in the books of the business while it will be a credit balance in the books of the bank. Transactions in the records of a business will be a mirror image of those same transactions in the records of the bank.

[8] A credit balance of £16,400 in the bank's books.

Bank reconciliation statement

	£
Balance according to bank statement at 31 Dec year 9	16,400
Add Cash deposited on 31 Dec, not yet cleared (2)	2,000
Deduct unpresented cheques, not yet cleared (1)	(5,000)
Updated bank statement balance	13,400

Suspense accounts

Suspense accounts are t-accounts, which are temporary holding accounts for a bookkeeping entry and generally arise for one or both of two different reasons. First, if extracting a trial balance after recording and posting transactions, the trial balance does not agree. Temporarily, and until the error is identified, a t-account is opened with the balance needed to make the trial balance agree. If the debit balances exceed the credit balances by, say, £500, then a suspense account with a credit balance of £500 is required, while if the credit balances exceed the debit balances by £500, then a debit balance will appear in the suspense account. The second cause of a suspense account is when one accounting entry is known, but the other entry is not. For example, if a customer pays £1,000 directly into a company's bank account but the identity of that customer is unknown, then the t-account 'bank' will be debited. Since the company does not know which customer's t-account in the receivables ledger should be credited, in order that the trial balance will agree and in order that 'every debit has a credit', the suspense account will be credited with £1,000. The suspense account is temporary and once the errors and unknowns' which gave rise to it have been remedied, as shown in **Example 9.6**, then the balance on the suspense account will be zero (or nil, whichever you prefer).

Example 9.6

The trial balance of Hue Limited, after all postings, at 31 December included a suspense account with a debit balance of £770. Further investigations reveal the following:

1. The company's payment of £1,500 to supplier Agro Limited had been correctly entered in the cash book but had not been posted to Agro's account in the purchase ledger.
2. The purchases account in the ledger had been undercast[9] by £200.
3. When a receipt paid directly into the company's bank account of £930 was entered in the cash book, the company was unaware which customer had made the payment. It has now been established that Customer Byro Limited had made this payment to Hue Limited.

The steps required to zero the suspense account balance are to complete the debit or credit to correct the t-account that is wrong, and the double entry will be posted to the suspense account.

Journal entries

		Debit	Credit
		£3	£
1.	Dr: Payables (Agro Ltd)	1,500	
	Cr: Suspense account		1,500

[9] 'Casting' is the accounting term for 'adding up'. Undercasting is a total which is too low while overcasting is a total which is too high.

2.	Dr: Purchases	200	
	Cr: Suspense account		200
3.	Cr: Receivables (Byro Ltd)		930
	Dr: Suspense account	930	

Suspense accounts

		Debit		Credit
		£		£
	Opening balance	770		
1			Payables	1,500
2			Purchases	200
3	Receivables	930		
		1,700		1,700
	Closing Balance	nil		

In each case, we have corrected the t-account with an existing error or an omission, and the double entry is for the suspense account.

Errors that are not shown in a suspense account

Errors in accounting can occur due to various reasons. These errors can be categorized into the following types:

1. *Omission error.* This is when a transaction is completely omitted from the accounting records. For example, a cash sale of £1m was not recorded.
2. *Commission error.* This occurs when a transaction is recorded in the wrong account. For instance, a council rates expense of £5,500 has been debited to the rent account in error.
3. *Error of principle.* This is when a transaction has been conceptually recorded incorrectly. For example, a non-current asset purchase of $1m has been debited to the repair expense account rather than an asset account.
4. *Compensating errors* in accounting are errors that offset other accounting errors. These errors can be difficult to identify, especially when they occur in the same account and reporting period, as the net effect is zero. Compensating errors may also appear in different accounts, leading to correct total debits and credits in the trial balance but incorrect account balances. For example, if a rent bill of £200 is debited to the rent account as £200 and a casting error on the sales account has resulted in sales being overstated by £200, these two errors cancel each other out, resulting in a net effect of zero. Other examples include if the wages expense is overstated by £2,000 due to one error and the cost of goods sold is understated by the same amount due to a compensating error, the trial balance would still balance.
5. *Original entry error.* This is when the correct double entry has been made but with the wrong amount. For example, a cash sale of £7,197 has been recorded as £7,179.
6. *Reversal of entries.* This is when the correct amount has been posted to the correct accounts but on the wrong side. An example of this would be a cash sale of £5,000 being debited to sales and credited to bank.

Summary

It is essential that all transactions are recorded accurately and that bookkeeping systems (manual and or computerized) are designed to ensure that every item can be traced and verified and that most errors are shown up. Every transaction is recorded in a book of prime entry, and then every transaction is recorded twice: once as a debit and once as a credit in the ledger t-accounts. The total of all credits must be equal to the total of all debits. Once the transactions have been recorded and summarized on a trial balance, adjustments will be made to record accruals, prepayments, depreciation, and the sale of non-current assets. Bookkeeping systems are necessary to keep track of all assets and liabilities and to ensure that there is an accurate record of all amounts owed to and by the business. They are also necessary to provide the basic information for producing statements of financial position and income statements. The first section of the chapter provided an outline of bookkeeping that is sufficient for most users of financial statements. More details were provided in the second and third sections, including bank reconciliations, control accounts and suspense accounts.

Review of key points

- Every transaction is recorded twice, on the left-hand (debit) side of one account, and on the right-hand (credit) side of another, that is:

  Every debit has a credit.
- Debits are assets and expenses while credits are revenues and liabilities.
- All receipts of cash are recorded on the debit side of the cash account; all payments are recorded on the credit side.
- Not all transactions are shown in the cash account. In many businesses most sales and purchases take place on credit.
- The trial balance provides a summary of all transactions, and is the basis for producing a statement of financial position and income statement.
- Bookkeeping systems in practice include more detail than is shown in most textbook examples.
- The term 'cash' is often used loosely to include both bank transactions and petty cash transactions; the two must be recorded separately in practice.
- Bookkeeping systems include mechanisms such as bank reconciliation statements and control accounts as a check on accuracy and the removal of a suspense account which has arisen to reflect errors in the double entry or incomplete double entry.

Self-testing questions

For the purpose of these questions, there is no need to separate 'petty cash' from 'bank' transactions. They can be combined in a single 'cash account'.

1 Complete the double entry for each of the following transactions:

a Sales made for cash are credited to the sales account and debited to the ________________.

b Sales made on credit to Smith are debited to the Smith account and credited to the ________________.

c Purchases made for cash are credited to the cash account and debited to the ________________.

d Purchases made on credit from Anirroc Company are debited to the purchases account and credited to the ________________.

e Smith, a trade receivable, pays us part of what they owe; the amount is credited to the Smith account and debited to the ________________.

f The provision for bad debts is increased by £30. This amount is debited to the income statement (perhaps via an income statement) as an expense and credited to the ________________.

2 Which of the following accounts normally have a credit balance (as shown on a trial balance): sales, purchases, trade receivables, trade payables, non-current assets, share capital, and share premium?

3 Which of the following accounts normally have a debit balance (as shown on a trial balance): expenses, non-current assets, receivables, cash at bank?

4 Which of the following statements is true?

a Accounts for assets and expenses have credit balances.

b Accounts for liabilities, share capital, retained earnings and overdrafts have credit balances.

5 Record the following transactions of Carlos using double-entry bookkeeping; summarize them in the form of a trial balance, and prepare an income statement for the three-month period, and a statement of financial position as at the end of the period.

1 Jul	Carlos started a business dealing in second-hand cars and opened a business bank account with £40,000
3 Jul	Carlos borrows £15,000 from the Spano Bank
5 Jul	Pays £5,000 to rent premises
8 Jul	Buys furniture and equipment for £11,000
13 Jul	Buys cars on credit from Motosales Ltd for £50,000
19 Jul	Pays general expenses of £2,500
27 Jul	Sells one car for £4,000 cash
3 Aug	Sells cars on credit to Minki Cabs for £18,000
10 Aug	Buys one car for £3,300 cash
16 Aug	Buys cars on credit from Motosales Ltd for £22,000
30 Aug	Pays £40,000 to Motosales Ltd
6 Sep	Pays general expenses of £3,300
14 Sep	Receives £15,000 from Minki Cabs
21 Sep	Sells cars for £24,000 cash

The inventory of unsold cars, the inventory remaining at the end of September, was £38,100 at cost. Ignore depreciation.

6 Record the following transactions of Killip using double-entry bookkeeping; summarize them in the form of a trial balance, and prepare an income statement for the one-month period and a statement of financial position at the end of that period.

1 Aug	Started business as a management consultant with £5,000 capital, which was paid into the bank
2 Aug	Paid £4,100 for a computer, printer, scanner and photocopier
4 Aug	Paid £500 rent for office for one month
6 Aug	Arranged advertising in the Journal of Man at a cost of £250, to be paid for a month later
7 Aug	Bought stationery on credit from Dubya Smith at a cost of £120
11 Aug	Received £650 for work done for two small clients
15 Aug	Paid travelling expenses of £135
20 Aug	Completed work for OneAlpha Ltd and invoiced them for £2,200
23 Aug	Paid £700 to a subcontractor
29 Aug	Paid £80 to Dubya Smith
31 Aug	Received £550 from OneAlpha Ltd

Depreciation should be ignored.

7 Cass Hawin's bookkeeper had not balanced the cash book on 31 March year 7. It received a bank statement dated 31 March year 7, which showed an overdraft of £2,000. Further investigation revealed the following:

a Unpresented cheques amounted to £1,500

b On 31 March, Cass Hawin had deposited £3,600 cash into the bank, but this was not shown on the bank statement

c The bank statement showed interest received of £200, which had not yet been recorded in the cash book

d The bank charges for December amounted to £150

Required:

i Show the necessary adjustments to the bank statement in a bank reconciliation statement; and

ii Show what the cash book balance should be before making any necessary adjustments.

Assessment questions

1 Complete the double entry for each of the following transactions:

a When a business owner pays additional capital to the company, the cash account is debited, and it is credited to the ____________________.

b A business repays a loan; the cash account is credited, and it is debited to the

____________________.

c The provision for bad debts is reduced by £50; the provision for bad debts account is debited, and it is credited to the ____________________.

d Drawings paid are credited to the cash account and debited to the ____________________.

e A loss arising on the sale of a non-current asset is debited to the income statement and credited to the ____________________.

f Closing inventory is shown as a debit item on the statement of financial position and is credited to the ________________.

g A supplier allows a cash discount of £24; this is credited to the income statement and debited to the ________________.

h Costs of delivering goods to customers of £123 are incurred with Rodo Transport Ltd. This amount is credited to the Rodo Transport Ltd account and debited to the ________________.

i A customer returns goods as being unsatisfactory; the amount is debited to the sales account on the income statement. It is credited to the ________________.

j The cost of buying a new non-current asset (a car costing £20,000) has inadvertently been debited to the account for 'travelling expenses'. To correct this error, the 'travelling expenses' account is credited, and it is debited to the ________________.

k How would the answer to (j) differ if the car had been bought on credit from BWM Garages Ltd?

2 Record the following transactions of A Florist using double-entry bookkeeping; summarize them in the form of a trial balance, and prepare an income statement for the month of January, and a statement of financial position as at the end of the period.

1 Jan	Started business with £10,000 capital, paid into the bank
2 Jan	Bought second-hand van; paid £4,000 by cheque
3 Jan	Bought flowers on credit from Miss Daisy, £700
4 Jan	Sold flowers for cash, £120
5 Jan	Bought flowers, paying by cheque, £456
6 Jan	Paid one month's rent, £408
7 Jan	Sold flowers on credit to the University of Eastminster, £999
14 Jan	Sold flowers in Berwick Street Market for cash, £236
20 Jan	Paid Miss Daisy £400
28 Jan	Received a cheque from University of Eastminster for £899

At the end of January, the closing inventory of flowers amounted to £210 at net realizable value. Depreciation should be ignored.

3 Record the following transactions of Moorey using double-entry bookkeeping; summarize them in the form of a trial balance, and prepare an income statement for the one-month period and a statement of financial position at the end of that period.

1 Apr	Started business selling electronic equipment with £800,000 capital that was paid into the bank
1 Apr	Paid £560,000 for a retail shop
2 Apr	Bought shop fittings on credit from Quirky Fitters for £101,000
3 Apr	Paid £460 for advertising
4 Apr	Purchased electronic goods from a car boot sale, paying cash, £800
5 Apr	Received £150 for first sales
7 Apr	Purchased goods on credit from Sinofacturers for £34,000

8 Apr	Sold goods on credit to Eccentainers amounting to £18,000
15 Apr	Cash sales, £230
24 Apr	Paid general expenses, £333
28 Apr	Paid £51,000 to Quirky Fitters and £25,000 to Sinofacturers
31 Apr	Received £12,500 from Eccentainers

At the end of the month the inventory of goods remaining was £22,600. Depreciation should be ignored.

4 Banner Ltd's cash book showed a debit balance of £8,000 on 30 June, year 4. The bank sent a statement to the company, showing the same date, but that there was £11,800 in the bank.[10] Further investigation revealed the following:

a Unpresented cheques amounted to £6,000

b On 30 June, Banner Ltd had deposited £3,000 cash into the bank, but this was not shown on the bank statement

c The bank statement showed dividends received of £1,000 that had not yet been recorded in the cash book

d The bank charges for December amounted to £200

Prepare a bank reconciliation statement showing the updated cash book and bank statement balances.

5 At 31 March year 9, included in the trial balance of BC Limited were the following balances:

Purchase ledger control	170,367 (Cr)
Sales ledger control	236,703 (Dr)

The following additional information is given in relation to the y/e 31 March year 9:

1.	Goods purchased in the year	633,570	
2.	Goods returned in the year	16,665	
3.	Sums paid to suppliers	599,997	
4.	Discounts deducted from sums owing to creditors		3,270
5.	Goods sold to customers		996,633
6.	Goods returned by customers		18,435
7.	Settled by receipt of		717,000
8.	Bad debts written off		10,032
9.	Discounts allowed to customers		7,200
10.	At 31 March year 9, in relation to J. Smith, who is both a customer and a supplier, balances on the two ledgers are as follows:		
	Sales ledger balance		5,340 Dr
	Purchase ledger balance		5,985 Cr

It has been decided to offset the sales ledger balance against the purchase ledger balance.

Required:

i Draw up sales and purchase ledger control accounts for the year ended 31 March year 9.

ii Why might the balances on the purchase ledger control differ from the list of underlying balances?

---

10 A credit balance of £11,800 in the bank's books.

6 In preparing the trial balance, you notice that the debit side exceeds the credit side by £970. Upon investigation, you identify the following mistakes:
   a Goods returned to suppliers amounting to £250 have been entered as a debit in the purchases account by mistake.
   b A cash payment for £560 has been entered in the cash book as £650.
   c A computer purchased for £2,000 as an office machine has been entered as a debit in the purchases account.
   d A credit note for £220 given to a customer has been credited twice in the customer's account.
   e A cheque for £780 received from a customer has been entered in the cash book and subsequently banked before the end of the year. However, no other entry has been made to the customer's account.

Required:

Explain how each of the above mistakes should be dealt with in a suspense account.

Group activities and discussion questions

1 a Accountants cannot do their job effectively if they do not have a detailed understanding of the business's bookkeeping systems.
   b Bookkeeping is done by technicians and computers; it is not a matter for managers and accountants.

   Discuss these two statements. With which do you most agree, and why?

2 The power of accountants and accountancy lies mainly in their control of the official financial recording system. Discuss.

3 A French balloonist landed in a field somewhere in the south of England. He hailed a passer-by and said, 'Can you tell me where I am, please?' The passerby said, 'You are in a wicker basket in a field.' The Frenchman said, 'You are an accountant, aren't you?' The Englishman said, 'Yes. How do you know?' The Frenchman said, 'Because your information is totally accurate and totally useless.' Explain and comment.

4 What is the point of learning the principles of double entry and its application since generally, even in very small companies, the process of completing the accounting records and the preparation of annual accounts are both computerized?

Accounting in context

Discuss and comment on the following. Do you think that blockchain can enhance the accounting profession? Explain the use of blockchain technology in each of the following cases: Bitcoin cryptocurrency, interbank reconciliation, land registry, and smart/automated contracts.

Blockchain and accounting

Blockchain technology has the potential to revolutionize accounting by improving transaction and asset management efficiency. It can serve as a universal entry bookkeeping system, providing clarity on rights, obligations and provenance. With this capability, the accountancy profession can expand its scope and record a wider range of activities than before. Moreover, it enables a more thorough analysis of the underlying economic reality of recorded transactions (ICAEW, 2018). Some of the case studies discussed by ICAEW for implementing blockchain include Bitcoin Cryptocurrency, interbank reconciliation, land registry, and smart/automated contracts.

According to Deloitte's 2019 survey, blockchain is gaining acceptance and maturing in various industrial sectors, such as telecommunications, life sciences and healthcare, and company executives are expressing confidence in its potential.

Blockchains are a game-changer in the world of accounting. They offer a secure and efficient way to address the many issues plaguing current systems in almost every industry. The potential benefits are enormous, and it is time to embrace the future with blockchain technology. While there are certainly challenges to be faced, such as capital requirements, security concerns and the need for regulatory standards, these issues can be overcome with careful planning and implementation.

Sources: Deloitte (2019) Deloitte's 2019 Global Blockchain Survey: Blockchain Gets Down to Business. https://www2.deloitte.com/content/dam/Deloitte/se/Documents/risk/DI_2019-global-blockchain-survey.pdf

ICAEW (2018) Blockchain and the Future of Accountancy, https://www.icaew.com/technical/technology/blockchain-and-cryptoassets/blockchain-articles/blockchain-and-the-accounting-perspective

D.D. Jayasuriya and A. Sims (2023) From the Abacus to Enterprise Resource Planning: Is Blockchain the Next Big Accounting Tool? *Accounting, Auditing & Accountability Journal*, 36(1): 24–62, https://doi.org/10.1108/AAAJ-08-2020-4718

References and further reading

Barrow, C. and Tracy, J. (2011) *Understanding Business Accounting for Dummies* (3rd edn.). Chichester: Wiley.

Black, G. (2009) *Introduction to Accounting and Finance* (2nd edn.). Upper Saddle River, NJ: FT Prentice Hall.

Monger, R. (2010) *Financial Accounting*. Chichester: Wiley.

Pavlova, V. (2020) Accounting Fraud in the UK: How Recent Scandals Are Impacting Practices. *Accounting Age*. https://www.accountancyage.com/2020/01/15/accounting-fraud-in-the-uk-how-recent-scandals-are-impacting-practices/

Wood, F. and Sangster, A. (2012) *Business Accounting* (vol. 1) (12th edn.). Upper Saddle River, NJ: FT Prentice Hall.

Chapter 10

Trial Balance to Final Accounts

Chapter contents

10.1 Introduction
10.2 Sole Traders
10.3 Companies
10.4 Partnerships

Learning objectives

After studying this chapter you will be able to:

- ✓ Understand how a trial balance summarizes all transactions that have been recorded
- ✓ Classify items on a trial balance as being income, expenses, assets, liabilities or equity
- ✓ Produce statements of financial position and income statements from trial balances for sole traders, companies and partnerships
- ✓ Incorporate a wide range of adjustments into final accounts
- ✓ Deal with a variety of different profit-sharing arrangements in partnerships

10.1 Introduction

This chapter deals with the conversion of a trial balance to a set of final accounts, incorporating a range of different adjustments. A trial balance summarizes all the transactions that have been recorded by an organization and provides the main information for producing a set of 'final accounts'; that is, a statement of financial position and an income statement. Additional information and 'adjustments' are required to complete the process.

A statement of financial position shows assets, liabilities and equity. The way in which these are presented has been changed several times in recent history, most recently following the widespread adoption of International Accounting Standards (IASs). When dealing with trial balances, it may be easiest to think of a statement of financial position as follows:

Assets = Liabilities + Equity	
Debit	**Credit**
Assets	Liabilities
	Equity (liability of the business to the owners)

An income statement shows revenues (or income) and expenses, the difference being profit. The format for presenting these statements has varied over the years, but when dealing with trial balances it may be seen as follows:

Income - Expenses = Profit	
Debit	**Credit**
Expenses	Income or revenues

If the above two simplified formats are combined, they begin to look a bit like a trial balance:

Trial Balance	
Debit	**Credit**
Assets	Liabilities
	Equity
Expenses	Revenue (or income)

The above format should help to avoid mistakes when dealing with items on a trial balance. Almost all debit items are either assets to be shown on the statement of financial position or expenses to be shown on the income statement. Almost all credit items on a trial balance are either revenues (or income) to be shown on the income statement or liabilities to be shown on the statement of financial position.

A long trial balance can be daunting but becomes more user-friendly if each item is labelled as being one of the above.

10.2 Sole Traders

A simplified trial balance can be converted into a statement of financial position and income statement, as shown in **Example 10.1**.

Example 10.1

A simplified trial balance might appear as follows:

Trial balance of Sim Pull as at 31 December year 8		
	Debit	Credit
	£	£
Land and buildings	200,000	
Payables (creditors)		10,000
Capital as at 1 January year 8		150,000
General expenses	80,000	
Sales revenue		120,000
Total	280,000	280,000

This would be easily converted into simplified final accounts as follows:

Statement of financial position of Sim Pull as at 31 December year 8			
	£		£
Land and buildings	200,000	Payables	10,000
		Capital	150,000

Income statement of Sim Pull for year ended 31 December year 8			
	£		£
General expenses	80,000	Sales revenue	120,000

Both of the above final accounts do not balance because a profit of £40,000 has been made, and this has to be shown on both the income statement and the statement of financial position, where it can be added to capital (if it is not a company), or shown as a separate item, as follows:

Statement of financial position of Sim Pull as at 31 December year 8			
	£		£
Land and buildings	200,000	Payables	10,000
		Capital	150,000
		Profit	40,000
	200,000		200,000

Income statement of Sim Pull for year ended 31 December year 8			
	£		£
General expenses	80,000	Sales revenue	120,000
Profit	40,000		
	120,000		120,000

Most trial balances look much more complex than Sim Pull's above because:

a. there are more items; and
b. there are adjustments to be made.

Additional items

Below are the items that most frequently appear on trial balances, categorized under the main headings, i.e. elements of financial statements, to indicate where they appear in final accounts.

Assets

Assets are usually classified as long term ('non-current assets') or short term ('current assets').

Non-current assets

- Premises, land, buildings
- Furniture, fixtures, fittings
- Plant, machinery
- Vehicles, ships, aeroplanes
- Goodwill
- Intangible assets

Current assets

- Inventories
- Receivables
- Prepayments or payments in advance
- Cash in hand and cash at bank

Liabilities

Short term

- Payables
- Accruals
- Overdraft
- Taxation

Long term

- Debentures, loans, mortgages

Equity

- Capital (called 'share capital' in a company)
- Retained profits
- Profit for the year
- Drawings (in a sole trader's accounts): this is a debit item to be deducted from capital

Revenue (or income)

- Sales or turnover
- Dividends, interest, rent, commissions received or receivable
- Discount received

Expenses

There are probably hundreds of different expenses, sometimes grouped together under general headings such as distribution costs or administrative expenses. Examples of expenses include: wages, salaries, rent, rates, insurance, postage, telephone, stationery, travelling expenses, carriage inwards, carriage outwards and lighting and heating.

Provisions are either negative assets or estimated liabilities. A provision for depreciation is shown as a deduction from non-current assets on the statement of financial position. A provision for bad debts is shown as a deduction from receivables (or debtors) on the statement of financial position. A car manufacturer is likely to have a provision for warranty claims, an estimated liability.

How to tackle a trial balance question

There are many different ways of tackling a trial balance question, perhaps using an extended trial balance. The following stages often prove to be the fastest way of scoring marks in an examination:

1. Make sure that you have the format of a statement of financial position and income statement memorized. Set the format out, using a whole page for each statement and writing on alternate lines, leaving space for adjustments. You should then be clear where most items from the trial balance should appear, and there should be space for any additions or alterations. In a company, you will also need a 'statement of changes in equity" showing the retained profits brought forward shown in the trial balance, plus the profit for the year (which will be the final total of the income statement) less the dividends paid in the year.
2. Remember to correctly categorize each item on a trial balance as an asset, liability, expense, or income. Then, copy the amount for each item from the trial balance onto the statement of financial position or income statement in the appropriate place (e.g. current assets or current liabilities).

   At this stage, do not bother with adding up (the totals may have to be changed later, and there are not usually many marks in an examination for adding up), and do not try to make adjustments until every item has been copied from the trial balance to the appropriate place. If you try to make adjustments before completing the copying out of trial balance items, you may get confused or omit items, such as the second part of an adjustment.
3. Do each adjustment in turn, making sure that each item is dealt with twice; usually this is once on the income statement, and once on the statement of financial position.
4. Add up to produce subtotals under each heading, profit figures, and balance. There is no point in attempting to calculate profit until all the adjustments have been made.

Stages 2, 3 and 4 are demonstrated in **Illustration 10.1** (Jimmy's Junk).

The 'extended trial balance' approach[1] is more time consuming, but it is also more systematic and thorough. Items are dealt with using several columns: debits and credits from the trial balance, adjustments, and columns to show the amounts for the statement of financial position and income statement.

[1] Illustrated on the website of this book.

Adjustments

The bookkeeping for dealing with these is shown in **Illustration 10.3** but there is no need to do the detailed bookkeeping in order to produce correct final accounts from a trial balance in an examination.

1 Closing inventory

Most businesses are likely to have unsold inventory at the end of the accounting period. A closing inventory is usually introduced in a question as an extra item after completing the trial balance. It has to appear twice in the final accounts as a:

- Debit on the statement of financial position, shown as a current asset
- Credit on the income statement, deducted from the opening inventory and purchases in calculating cost of sales (or cost of goods sold); this can be shown directly on the income statement to avoid bothering with double-entry bookkeeping in an examination.

Example 10.2 shows how to deal with the adjustment for closing inventory.

Example 10.2

Trial balance of Rikki Bloderick as at 30 June year 2		
	Debit	Credit
	£	£
Bank	56,000	
Capital		27,000
Lighting and heating	6,000	
Receivables	5,000	
Purchases	118,000	
Payables		13,000
Rent and rates	26,000	
Sales revenue		220,000
Inventories at 1 July year 1	12,000	
Wages and salaries	37,000	
	260,000	260,000

Adjustments:

1 Closing inventory as at 30 June year 2 amounted to £15,000

Prepare the income statement for the year ended 30 June year 2, and the statement of financial position as at that date.

Solution:

The first part of the income statement compares the year's sales revenue with the cost of goods sold to arrive at the gross profit.

The trial balance includes inventories available for sale at the beginning of the year (£12,000) and purchases made during the year (£118,000). The amount of goods available for sale was therefore (£118,000 + £12,000 =) £130,000, but not all those goods were sold during the year. We are told that the closing inventory of goods unsold at the end of the year amounted to £15,000. The cost of the goods that were sold during the year was therefore (£130,000 – £15,000 =) £115,000.

Income statement of Rikki Bloderick for the year ended 30 June Year 2		
	£	£
Sales revenue		220,000
Opening inventory	12,000	
Purchases	118,000	
	130,000	
Deduct Closing inventory	15,000	
Cost of goods sold		115,000
Gross profit		105,000
Lighting and heating	6,000	
Rent and rates	26,000	
Wages and salaries	37,000	69,000
Net profit		36,000

Statement of financial position as at 30 June year 2	
	£
Current assets	
Inventory	15,000
Receivables	5,000
Bank	56,000
Total assets	76,000
Current liabilities	
Payables	13,000
Equity	
Capital as at 1 July Year 1	27,000
Add Profit for year	36,000
Total liabilities and equity	76,000

2 Depreciation

Most businesses have some non-current assets that should be depreciated each year. A trial balance usually includes a number of non-current assets that are shown at cost (debit items). It is best to leave this figure unchanged and to deal with 'provision for depreciation' as a separate item. A statement of financial position usually shows the original cost of the asset, the provision for depreciation, and then the net book value, as follows:

Extract from statement of financial position as at 31 December year 6	
Plant and machinery at cost	£50,000
Deduct Provision for depreciation	£15,000
Net book value	£35,000

Trial balances include a provision for depreciation (a credit item), which is usually the figure left from the previous year. In the above example it could be that the £15,000 provision for depreciation figure on the trial balance was £10,000 (as at 31 December year 5); to that £5,000 is added (and charged as an expense, a debit, on the income statement) to give a new provision for depreciation as at 31 December year 6.

The bookkeeping for dealing with depreciation is shown in **Chapter 9**, **Section 9.2**; the idea of depreciation is explained in **Chapter 2**. **Example 10.3** shows how to deal with the adjustment to the trial balance.

You should now be able to tackle Self-testing questions 1–4 (Noddy; Mona Ramsey; Sally Glen; Mary Rushen), which are found at the end of this chapter. Answers are supplied at the end of the book.

Example 10.3

Extract from trial balance as at 31 December year 6		
	Debit	Credit
	£	£
Plant and machinery at cost	50,000	
Vehicles at cost	80,000	
Provision for depreciation on plant and machinery as at 31 December year 5		10,000
Provision for depreciation on vehicles as at 31 December year 5		35,000

Adjustments:

1 Provision for depreciation is to be made on plant and machinery at 10 per cent per annum on cost (straight-line basis).

2 Provision for depreciation is to be made on vehicles at 25 per cent per annum on a diminishing balance (or reducing balance) basis.

The calculations could be shown as a 'working' on the face of the statement of financial position or a note, as follows:

Non-current assets				
		Plant and machinery	Motor vehicles	Total non-current assets
		£	£	£
Cost	At 31 December Y5	50,000	80,000	130,000
	Additions/(Disposals)	0	0	0
	At 31 December Y6	50,000	80,000	130,000
Depreciation	At 31 December Y5	10,000	35,000	45,000
	Depreciation charge for the year (note 1)	5,000	11,250	16,250
	At 31 December Y6	15,000	46,250	61,250
Net book value	At 31 December Y6	35,000	33,750	68,750

Note 1: Depreciation charge for the plant and machinery: £50,000 x 10% = £5,000; Depreciation charge for the motor vehicles: (£80,000 – £35,000) x 25% = £11,250

3 Drawings

Most sole traders withdraw money from their businesses from time to time, especially if it is profitable. If drawings have already been recorded, the amount has been taken from the bank, and the amount withdrawn is shown as a debit item on the trial balance; that amount is then shown as a deduction from capital plus profit on the statement of financial position.

If drawings are shown as an adjustment because they have not yet been recorded, the amount should be taken from the bank and shown as a deduction from capital plus profit on the statement of financial position.

4 Accruals

There are usually some expenses (e.g. electricity) that still need to be recorded or paid at the end of the year. The amount of the required adjustment is:

- Shown as a debit on the income statement, increasing the amount of the expense that has already been recorded
- Shown as a credit on the statement of financial position, as a current liability.

Where an accrual already exists in the trial balance, this will be the accrual from the beginning of the year, and it is usually necessary to change the amount at the end of the year.

When there is an *increase* in the accrual, the *amount of the increase* is included as an expense (a debit) - for example, electricity expense - on the income statement. The increase is added to (credited to) the existing accrual in the statement of financial position.

When there is a *reduction* in the accrual, the *amount of the reduction* is credited to the expense, electricity, in the income statement. The reduction is deducted from the accrual that is shown on the statement of financial position.

5 Prepayments

There are usually some expenses (e.g. rent) that have been paid in advance at the end of the year, so part of the expense that has already been recorded (and included on the trial balance) is in respect of the following year. The amount of the prepayment is:

- Shown as a debit on the statement of financial position, as a current asset 'prepayments', underneath receivables
- Shown as a credit on the income statement, reducing the amount of the expense that has already been recorded.

Where a prepayment already exists in the trial balance, this will be the prepayment from the beginning of the year, and it is usually necessary to change the amount at the end of the year.

When there is an *increase* in the prepayment, the *amount of the increase* is deducted (credited to) from the expense, say rent, on the income statement. The increase is added to (i.e. debited to) the existing prepayment in the statement of financial position.

When there is a *reduction* in the prepayment, the *amount of the reduction* is debited to the expense, rent, in the income statement. The reduction is deducted (credited) from the prepayment that is shown on the statement of financial position.

6 Bad debts written off

Bad debts written off are specific, where it is known that a specific trade receivable will not be paying, perhaps because of liquidation or bankruptcy. It is easier to keep the writing-off of specific bad debts separate from any provision for bad debts. The amount to be written off is:

- Shown as a debit (an expense) on the income statement
- Treated as a credit on the statement of financial position by reducing the amount shown for receivables.

7 Provision for bad debts

Where a provision for bad debts already exists, it is usually necessary to change the amount at the end of the year.

When there is an *increase* in a provision for bad debts, the *amount of the increase* is included as an expense (a debit) on the income statement. The increase is added to (credited to) the existing provision for bad debts. This credit balance is shown as a deduction from receivables in the current assets on the statement of financial position.

ILLUSTRATION 10.1

Trial balance of Jimmy's Junk business as at 31 December year 9

	Debit	Credit
	£	£
Bank	18,010	
Capital as at 31 December year 8		90,950
Fixtures and fittings at cost	1,200	
General expenses	14,000	
Insurance	5,000	
Interest paid	7,000	
Inventory at 31 December year 8 (opening inventory)	3,000	
Lighting and heating	12,000	
Loan from Bank of Ruristan		100,000
Payables		32,000
Provision for bad debts		1,880
Provision for depreciation on delivery van as at 31 December year 8		9,760
Provision for depreciation on fixtures and fittings as at 31 December year 8		720
Provision for depreciation on premises as at 31 December year 8		24,000
Purchases	47,000	
Trade receivables	41,100	
Sales revenue		225,000
Shop premises at cost	300,000	
Delivery van at cost	20,000	
Wages	16,000	
	484,310	484,310

Adjustments

1 Closing inventory as at 31 December year 9 amounted to £4,000.

2 Depreciation is to be provided on shop premises on a straight-line basis at 2 per cent per annum.
3 Fixtures and fittings are to be depreciated straight-line at 10 per cent per annum.
4 Depreciation is to be provided on the delivery van at 20 per cent per annum on a diminishing balance basis.
5 The electricity bill for the three months ending on 28 February year 10 amounts to £2,700 and has not yet been recorded in the accounts.
6 The insurance amount shown includes £1,200 for the three months from 1 November year 9 to 31 January year 10.
7 A specific debt of £1,100 is to be written off as irrecoverable.
8 The provision for bad debts is to be adjusted to be 5 per cent of receivables.
9 On 31 December, Jimmy took drawings from the business of £18,000, which has not yet been recorded.

Prepare the income statement for the year ended 31 December year 9 and the statement of financial position as at that date.

The solution in three stages

The following solution is designed to show three stages of producing final accounts from a trial balance. In stage 1, the figures that are taken from the trial balance are shown in normal font. Stage 2 adjustments are shown in **bold**. The results of the final stage, adding up, are shown in *italics*.

Income statement of Jimmy's Junk for the year ended 31 December year 9

	£	£	£
Sales revenue			225,000
Opening inventory		3,000	
Purchases		*47,000*	
		50,000	
***Deduct* Closing stock**		**4,000**	
Cost of goods sold			*46,000*
Gross profit			*179,000*
General expenses		14,000	
Wages		16,000	
Interest		7,000	
Insurance	5,000		
	−400	**4,600**	
Light and heat	12,000		
	+900	12,900	
Bad debt written off		**1,100**	
Increase in provision for bad debts		**120**	
Depreciation: premises		**6,000**	
Depreciation: fixtures and fittings		**120**	
Depreciation: vehicle		2,048[2]	
			63,888
Net profit			*115,112*

[2] This shows the workings for depreciation using the reducing balance method: Van at cost £20,000, minus provision for depreciation as at 31 December year 8, £9,760, gives a net book value of £10,240 at the beginning of the year. The depreciation charge is 20 per cent of £10,240 = £2,048.

Statement of financial position of Jimmy's Junk as at 31 December year 9

Non-current assets		Cost	Provision for depreciation	Net book value
Shop premises		300,000	24,000	
			+6,000	
			30,000	*270,000*
Fixtures and fittings		1,200	720	
			+120	
			840	*360*
Delivery van		20,000	9,760	
			+2,048	
			11,808	*8,192*
				278,552
Current assets				
Inventory			4,000	
Receivables		41,100		
Bad debt written off		**−1,100**		
		40,000		
Provision for bad debts	1,880			
Increase	+120	**2,000**	**38,000**	
Prepayment			**400**	
Bank	18,010			
Drawings	**−18,000**		10	
				42,410
Total assets				320,962
Liabilities and equity				
Current liabilities				
Accrual			**900**	
Payables			**32,000**	**32,900**
Non-current liabilities				
Loan from Bank of Ruritan				100,000
Total liabilities				132,900
Equity				
Capital as at 31 December year 8		**90,950**		
Add profit for year		115,112		
		206,062		
Deduct drawings		18,000		***188,062***
				320,962

When there is a *reduction* in a provision for bad debts, the *amount of the reduction* is credited to the income statement (as if it is additional income or perhaps as a negative expense). The reduction is deducted from the provision for bad debts that is shown as a deduction from receivables in the current assets on the statement of financial position.

A provision for bad debts is general, estimated at perhaps 5 per cent of trade receivables. It is the trade receivables figure *after* writing off any bad debts referred to in adjustment 6 above.

These adjustments are illustrated in **Illustration 10.1** (Jimmy's Junk).

Additional adjustments

There may be other adjustments when trial balances are produced in practice; for example, to correct errors. When a trial balance is first produced it is only a 'trial': the accountant is trying to see if it will balance. If not, a 'suspense account' is sometimes put in to make up the difference; errors are then traced, and each correction is debited to the correct account, and credited to the suspense account (or credited to the correct account, and debited to the suspense account) until the trial balance balances and the suspense account balance is zero.

Normal bookkeeping principles apply to all adjustments to the trial balance, and these are shown in **Chapter 9**.

10.3 Companies

In most ways, the final accounts of companies are much the same as those of sole traders. The main differences are as follows:

1 There are prescribed formats for company final accounts, as explained in **Chapter 1** and **Chapter 2**. However, sole traders have more freedom to present financial statements in their own way.

2 The owners of companies receive payments *as dividends*; the equivalent payments to sole traders are called *drawings*.

3 In companies, *share capital* is shown in an account kept separate from retained earnings and dividends. For sole traders, profits are usually added to the capital figure, and drawings are deducted from capital.

4 In companies, there is a heading for *shareholders' funds,* which can include a number of items such as *ordinary share capital, preference share capital, share premium, revaluation reserve and retained profits*. In sole traders, a single capital account usually includes all that the owners have invested in the business, capital and profits.

5 Companies are liable to pay *corporation tax*. Therefore, in an income statement, a profit before tax figure, followed by income tax expense and then a profit after tax figure or profit for the year is shown. At the end of the year, it is usually necessary to estimate the amount of corporation tax payable, and this is included as a debit in the income statement, usually as the final deduction before showing profit for the year. In the statement of the financial position, the profit for the year is included as a credit. Sole traders are liable to pay income tax as individual people; there is no taxation on the profits of the business itself.

6 A trial balance often shows that a *dividend* has been paid (a debit item). Companies, particularly listed companies, pay an interim dividend in the second half of the financial year and, after the year-end, decide to pay a second dividend for the year, the final or proposed dividend. The shareholders usually approve this at the annual general meeting. These days, dividends are accounted for on a cash basis; that is, only when actually paid. Dividends are shown in the 'statement of changes in equity' and the notes to the accounts. The dividend paid is likely to comprise last year's proposed dividend, paid in the first half of this year, and this year's interim dividend, paid in the second half of this year.

7 Legislation requires that many expenses be disclosed in company accounts; these are often shown as notes to the accounts. The specified formats for income statement accounts require relatively little disclosure. Examples of expenses that must be disclosed, although they are included within more general headings on the income statement, are directors' fees, auditors' fees and expenses. The income statements of sole traders usually disclose expenses in some detail, according to the preferences of the individual concerned.

8 Most companies have to pay some *interest* (finance expense), whether on long-term loans, such as *debentures* or on overdrafts. It can be useful to show profit before charging interest ('operating profit') and profit after charging interest ('profit before taxation').

A simplified company trial balance question for Scarlett Ltd is shown in **Illustration 10.2**.

ILLUSTRATION 10.2

The trial balance of Scarlett Ltd as at 31 December year 4

	Debit	Credit
	£	£
Administrative expenses	24,000	
Cash	48,500	
Distribution costs	57,000	
Dividend paid	4,500	
Inventories at 31 December year 3	14,000	
Payables		53,000
Plant and equipment at cost	660,500	
Provision for depreciation on plant and equipment as at 31 December year 3		135,000
Purchases	730,500	
Retained earnings as at 31 December year 3		69,000
Receivables	68,000	
Sales		900,000
Share capital, ordinary £1 shares		450,000
	1,607,000	1,607,000

Adjustments

1 Inventories as at 31 December year 4 cost £18,000.

2 The depreciation charge on plant and equipment for the year ended 31 December year 4 is to be £48,000.

3 Corporation tax of £15,000 is to be provided.

Income statement of Scarlett Ltd for the year ended 31 December year 4

	£	£
Revenue (from sales)		900,000
Cost of sales		
Opening inventory	14,000	
Purchases	730,500	
	744,500	
Deduct Closing inventory (note 1)	(18,000)	726,500
Gross profit		173,500
Distribution costs	57,000	
Administrative expenses	24,000	
Depreciation	48,000	(129,000)
Profit before tax		44,500
Corporation tax		(15,000)
Profit for the year		29,500

Statement of changes in equity for the year ended 31 December year 4

	Share Capital	Retained Earnings	Total
	£	£	£
Balance as at 31 December year 3	450,000	69,000	519,000
Profit for the period		29,500	
Less: dividends paid		(4,500)	
Balance as at 31 December year 4	450,000	94,000	544,000

Statement of financial position as at 31 December year 4

	£	£
Assets		
Non-current assets		
Property, plant and equipment at cost		660,500
Deduct Provision for depreciation (135,000 + 48,000)		(183,000)
Net book value		477,500
Current assets		
Inventories	18,000	
Trade receivables	68,000	
Cash	48,500	
		134,500
Total assets		612,000
Liabilities and equity		
Current liabilities		
Payables (creditors)		53,000
Corporation tax		15,000
		68,000
Equity		
Ordinary share capital	450,000	
Retained earnings (69,000 + 29,500 − 4,500)	94,000	
		544,000
Total liabilities and equity		612,000

Additional adjustments

There may be other adjustments with company financial statements, for example, the issue or redemption of shares and debentures. There may be additional accruals for interest payable. Sometimes there might be revaluations of land or impairment of goodwill. Closing inventories, for example, should be shown at the lower of cost and net realizable value. Any reduction in the amount shown for assets is shown as a credit to the statement of financial position item (reducing the amount of the asset) and as a debit on the income statement (reducing profit). As always, normal bookkeeping principles apply to all adjustments. You should now be able to tackle **Self-testing question 6** (Ellie's Ltd) at the end of this chapter. A solution is provided at the end of the book.

Summary of adjustments

1 **Inventory**

Dr: Cost of sales

Cr: Inventory with the opening inventory

Dr: Inventory

Cr: Cost of sales with the closing inventory

2 **Depreciation charge for the year**

Dr: Depreciation expense

Cr: Accumulated depreciation with depreciation charge for the year

3 **Bad debt written off**

Dr: Bad debt expense

Cr: Trade receivables

4 **Provision for bad debts**

Dr: Bad debt expense

Cr: Provision for bad debts

with increase in provision required based on given percentage of closing net trade receivables (or the opposite, if the provision is to be reduced).

5 **Accrued charges**

Dr: Electricity expense

Cr: Accrued charges

with an increase in the accrual, over and above any accrual in the trial balance from the beginning of the year. A decrease in the accrual is the opposite entry.

6 **Prepayments**

Dr: Prepayments

Cr: Rent

with an increase in the prepayment, over and above any prepayment left in the trial balance from the beginning of the year. A decrease in the prepayment is the opposite entry.

7 **Disposal of a non-current asset**

Dr: Disposal of non-current asset account

Cr: Cost of non-current assets

Dr: Accumulated depreciation of non-current asset

Cr: Disposal of non-current asset account

with the cost and accumulated depreciation of the asset sold, respectively.

8 **Revaluation of land**

Dr: Valuation of land in non-current assets

Cr: Revaluation reserve (in equity)

with an increase in the carrying value of land

9 **Corporation tax**

Dr: Tax charge in income statement

Cr: Corporation tax creditor with corporation tax charge for the year

Extended trial balance

Another method of tackling the problem of producing accounts from a trial balance and adjustments is by extended trial balance (see **Illustration 10.3**).

ILLUSTRATION 10.3

Gadol Ltd is a distributor of imported clothes and accessories. The following is a list of balances extracted from its accounting records at 31 December year 9:

	Debit	Credit
	£000	£000
Land, at valuation	2,250	
Buildings: cost	3,200	
Buildings: accumulated depreciation at 1 January year 9		320
Inventory at 1 January year 9	700	
Motor vans: cost	1,625	
Motor van: accumulated depreciation at 1 January year 9		975
Trade receivables	980	
Provision for doubtful debts at 1 January year 9		80
Prepayment rent at 1 January year 9	75	
Accrued heat and lighting		20
Cash	1,075	
Trade payables		630
8% debentures: year 14		800
Share capital: ordinary 50p shares		2,000
Share premium		1,000
Revaluation reserve		850
Retained earnings		1,270
Sales		9,050
Purchases	4,415	
Wages and salaries	1,150	
Heat and lighting	525	
Distribution costs	350	
Rent	480	
Insurance	56	
Interest paid	64	
Disposal account		130
Dividend paid	180	
	17,125	**17,125**

You are given the following information:

1 Inventory at 31 December year 9 cost £450,000. Included in this is womenswear, which cost £120,000 and has become out of fashion. To sell these garments quickly, it has been decided to sell them at 70 per cent of their cost.

2 The land was purchased in year 2. Two years ago, ZTD, Commercial Property Agents, revalued it at £2,250,000. The directors decided to reflect the revalued amount in the statement of financial position. In December year 9, ZTD valued the land at £2,500,000, and the directors wish to include the revalued amount in the statement of financial position.

3 Rent for the shops is payable quarterly in advance. The last quarterly payment of £120,000 was made on 1 December year 9. There were no other types of prepayment, other than rent, at 31 December year 8 or 31 December year 9.

4 During the year, motor vans purchased on 30 June year 7 for £300,000 were sold for £130,000. The sales proceeds have been credited to the disposal account, but no other entries have yet been made in the company's records regarding this transaction. Details of the depreciation policy on the motor vans appear in note 5 below.

5 Land is not depreciated. Buildings are depreciated over 50 years to zero residual value. Motor vans are depreciated at a rate of 30 per cent on a reducing value basis. The company provides full depreciation in the year of acquisition and none in the year of disposal.

6 Accruals at 31 December year 8 relate to heat and lighting. The final heat and lighting payment in year 9 was paid up to 31 October year 9. The next heat and lighting invoice for the three months to 31 January year 10 was £150,000.

7 Included in trade receivables at 31 December year 9 is one of the company's customers that has recently gone into liquidation, owing £60,000. Additionally, the provision for bad debts of 5 per cent of trade receivables is required.

8 Corporation tax of £230,000 on the current year's profits is to be provided.

9 The company issued 300,000 additional shares at 50p each on 30 December year 9. The proceeds of £310,000 were paid into a separate bank account, and no entries have been made in the company's accounting records regarding this transaction.

Task: Prepare an extended trial balance for Gadol Ltd as at 31 December year 9 and then prepare the income statement for the year ended 31 December year 9 and the statement of financial position as at 31 December year 9.

The next section explains in detail how to complete an extended trial balance and then prepare the financial statements.

How to tackle an extended trial balance question

The following stages show how to produce the figures for an income statement and statement of financial position using an extended trial balance. The extended trial balance has four pairs of columns, each pair with a debit and a credit column. The first pair is the balance arising from the balances on each t-account arising from the transactions recorded in the ledgers at the year end. The second pair, headed *adjustments*, will record the accruals, prepayments, depreciation, and any other adjustments required at the year end arising from notes 1-9. Pairs 3 and 4 are headed *income statement* and *statement of financial position*.

1 List the balances from the question. You will notice that some of the balances are the sum total of transactions in the year: for example, sales, purchases and rent. Others are year-end balances: for example, cash, receivables and payables. Other balances are balances at the beginning of the year,

unchanged during the year: for example, inventory, prepayments, accruals and provision for bad debts. Remember that each row on the trial balance is the balance on t-accounts.

2 In the *adjustments* columns, complete the debits and credits arising from notes 1–9, bearing in mind our basic rules that 'every debit has a credit' and the nature of debits and credits. It might be that new rows will need to be added for assets, liabilities, revenues and expenses for which no balances appear in the 'after all transactions' columns. Check at the end of stage 2 that the total of debits column and the credit column agree. This will prove that you have done a debit for every credit.

3 Taking a ruler to each row on the trial balance, compute the arithmetic result of the row. If the result is a debit, if it is an asset, it will be 'extended' and be written as a debit in the statement of financial position columns; if it is an expense, it will be 'extended' and be written as a debit in the income statement columns. If the result is a credit, if it is a liability or equity, it will be 'extended' and be written as a credit in the statement of financial position columns; if it is a revenue, it will be 'extended' and be written as a credit in the income statement columns.

4 When adding the two income statement columns, if the credits exceed the debits, the difference indicates the profit before tax. In this case, in the statement of financial position columns, the debits should exceed the credits by the same figure, and this difference also signifies the profit before tax. You will recall that the profit increases the retained profits, in the equity section of the statement of financial position.

5 Finally, the figures in the income statement and the statement of financial position columns are simply copied onto the two statements in the standard formats.

	After all transactions		Adjustments		Income statement		Balance sheet	
	Dr	Cr	Dr	Cr	Dr	Cr	Dr	Cr
Land: valuation	2,250		250				2,500	
Buildings: valuation	3,200						3,200	
Buildings: accrued								
Depreciation		320		64				384
Motor vans: cost	1,625			300			1,325	
Motor vans: accrued								
Depreciation		975	153	150.9				972.9
Inventory	700		414	700			414	
Trade receivables	980			60			920	
Provision for bad debts		80	34					46
Prepaid rent	75		5				80	
Cash	1,075		310				1,385	
Trade payables		630						630
Accrued heat and lighting		20		80				100
8% debentures		800						800
Share capital 50p shares		2,000		150				2,150
Share premium		1,000		160				1,160
Revaluation reserve		850		250				1,100
Retained profits		1,270						1270
Sales		9,050				9,050		
Purchases/cost of sales	4,415		700	414	4,701			

	After all transactions		Adjustments		Income statement		Balance sheet	
Wages	1,150				1,150			
Heat and lighting	525		80		605			
Distribution expenses	350				350			
Rent	480			5	475			
Insurance	56				56			
Interest expense	64				64			
Disposal account		130	300	153	17			
Dividend paid	180						180	
Depreciation expenses			64 + 150.9		214.9			
Bad debt expense			60		60			
Provision for bad debts:								
Decrease				34		34		
Totals	17,125	17,125	2,520.9	2,520.9	7,692.9	9,084	10,004	8,612.9
Difference (i.e. profit before tax)					1,391.1			1,391.1

1 The closing inventory is valued at the lower of cost and net realizable value. The net realizable value of the items costing £120,000 is £84,000; that is, a loss of £36,000. Hence, the closing inventory is £414,000. So,

Dr: Cost of sales 700,000

Cr: Inventory 700,000

with the opening inventory

Dr: Inventory 414,000

Cr: Cost of sales 414,000

2 The land is to be revalued upwards by £250,000.

Dr: Land 250,000

Cr: Revaluation reserve 250,000

3 The rent paid in year 9 prepaid at the end of the year is two months out of the £120,000 paid in December. So the prepayment at the year end is £80,000. The prepayment already in the trial balance is £75,000, so the prepayment needs to be increased by £5,000.

Dr: Prepayments 5,000

Cr: Rent 5,000

4 The motor vans sold had a cost of £300,000. Depreciation in year 7 was 30 per cent of £300,000; that is, £90,000. The depreciation in year 8 was 30 per cent of £300,000 - 90,000); that is, £63,000. Hence, the accumulated depreciation on the vans sold is £153,000.

Dr:	Disposal account	300,000
Cr:	Motor vans: cost	300,000
Dr:	Motor vans: accumulated depreciation	153,000
Cr:	Disposal account	153,000

5 Depreciation on the buildings is £3.2m divided by 50; that is, £64,000. Depreciation on the remaining motor vans is 30 per cent of £1,325,000 less £822,000 (i.e. £975,000 - £153,000). The net book value is £503,000, so the depreciation is £150,900.

Dr:	Depreciation expense	60,000
Cr:	Buildings: accumulated depreciation	60,000
Dr:	Depreciation expense	150,900
Cr:	Motor vans: accumulated depreciation	150,900

6 Heat and lighting has been paid to October year 9. We need to accrue the two months of November and December. November to January cost £150,000, so the accrual will be two-thirds of £150,000; that is, £100,000. There is an accrual already in the trial balance of £20,000, so we need to increase the accrual by £80,000.

Dr:	Heat and lighting	80,000
Cr:	Accrued charges	80,000

7 A bad debt of £60,000 must be written off. The remaining receivables will be £920,000. The provision for bad debts is to be 5 per cent of £920,000, that is, £46,000. There is a provision in the trial balance of £80,000, so the provision must be *reduced* by £34,000.

Dr:	Bad debt expense	60,000
Cr:	Trade receivables	60,000
Dr:	Bad debt provision	34,000
Cr:	Reduction of provision expense	34,000

8 Corporation tax for the year is £230,000. Since the purpose of the extended trial balance is, among other things, to calculate the profit *before* tax, tax provisions are not adjusted on the trial balance but are put directly onto the income statement in the appropriate place in the standard format and shown in the statement of financial position as a current liability.

9 The cash increases by £310,000, the nominal value of the shares by 300,000 × 50p; that is, £150,000 increases the share capital while the excess sum raised over the par value increases the share premium, that is, £160,000.

Dr:	Cash	310,000
Cr:	Share capital	150,000
Cr:	Share premium	160,000

Income statement of Gadol Ltd for the year ended 31 December year 9

	£000	£000	£000
Sales revenue			9,050
Cost of goods sold			(4,701)
Gross profit			4,349
Wages		1,150	
Heat and lighting		605	
Distribution expenses		350	
Rent		475	
Insurance		56	
Interest		64	
Loss on disposal of van		17	
Depreciation		214.9	
Bad debts written off		60	
Decrease in bad debt provision		(34)	
			(2,957.9)
Profit before tax			1,391.1
Tax			(230)
Profit for the year			1,161.1

Statement of financial position of Gadol Ltd as at 31 December year 9

	£000	£000	£000
Non-current assets	Cost	Provision for depreciation	Netbook value
Land	2,500		2,500
Buildings	3,200	384	2,816
Motor vans	1,325	972.9	*352.1*
	7,025	1,356.9	5,668.1
Current assets			
Inventory		414	
Receivables	920		
Less: Bad debt provision	(46)	874	
Prepayment		80	
Bank		1,385	
			2,753
Total assets			8,421.1
Liabilities and equity			
Current liabilities			
Payables			630
Accrual			100
Corporation tax			230
			960
Non-current liabilities			800
Total liabilities			1,760

Equity		
Share capital	2,150	
Share premium	1,160	
Revaluation reserve	1,100	
Retained profits	2,251.1	
		6,661,1
Total equity and liabilities		8,421.1
Note: The retained profits is as follows:		
Balance at January year 9		1,270.0
Plus: profit for the year		1,161.1
Less: dividend paid		(180.0)
Balance at 31 December year 9		2,251.1

10.4 Partnerships

In most ways, partnerships' final accounts are similar to those of sole traders. The main differences arise because (a) the profit must be divided between the partners, and (b) separate accounts must be kept for each partner for capital, drawings and current transactions.

A partnership's income statement is prepared in the same way as that of a sole trader until the net profit is arrived at. After that, there is an 'appropriation account' on which the amount of profit due to each partner is calculated.

A partnership's statement of financial position is prepared in the same way as for a sole trader, except that (a) there is a separate capital account for each partner and (b) in addition to the capital accounts, there is a 'current account' for each partner to keep track of the amounts of profits credited to each, and the amount of drawings taken. A partner's total capital is the sum of the balances on their capital account and their current account.

In the simplified **Illustration 10.4**, it is assumed that there are no accruals or prepayments, and the only adjustments are for depreciation and closing inventory.

ILLUSTRATION 10.4

Trial balance of Orry, Mona and Michael as at 31 December year 7

	Debit	**Credit**
	£	£
Cash	95,200	
Expenses	44,400	
Premises	280,000	
Provision for depreciation on		
premises at 31 December year 6		33,600
Purchases	240,000	
Sales		400,000

Inventory at 31 December year 6	25,000	
Capital accounts at 1 January year 7		
Orry		160,000
Mona		100,000
Michael		30,000
Current accounts at 1 January year 7		
Orry		30,000
Mona	40,000	
Michael	29,000	
	753,600	753,600

Adjustments

1 Inventory at 31 December year 7 amounted to £35,000.
2 The provision for depreciation on premises is to be increased by £5,600.

Income statement of Orry, Mona and Michael for the year ended 31 December year 7

	£	£
Sales revenue		400,000
Opening inventory	25,000	
Purchases	240,000	
	265,000	
Deduct Closing inventory	35,000	
Cost of sales		230,000
Gross profit		170,000
Expenses	44,400	
Depreciation	5,600	50,000
Net profit		120,000

Explanations

The profit is calculated in the same way as that of a sole trader. In most cases, there would be more assets and expenses, more adjustments, and additional items such as receivables (debtors) and payables (creditors).

In a sole trader the net profit is added to the capital account on the statement of financial position, which should then balance.

In a partnership, it is necessary to know how the profit is to be divided between or amongst the partners. If there is £120,000 profit to be divided equally between three partners, it would be possible to credit £40,000 to each of the partner's capital accounts, and that would be the end of the matter. The statement of financial position (1) of Orry, Mona and Michael would balance if the £120,000 profit was added to the capital or current accounts.

More detail is usually required because:

1 The partners do not necessarily share the profits equally. In this example, Orry has much more money invested in the business (£160,000 + £30,000 = £190,000) than Michael, who seems to have drawn almost as much money out of the business as he has invested in it. But perhaps it is Michael who does

most of the work and deserves a regular salary. Orry may be more or less retired ('a sleeping partner'), but as he has a substantial sum invested in the business (and perhaps he set it up in the first place), he deserves some extra return to reflect that. It might be agreed that Michael should have a 'salary' from the profits of £40,000 a year, that Orry should have half of the remaining profits, and that Mona and Michael should have one-quarter each. Statement of financial position (2) shows the effect of appropriating the profits in this way.

2 There are usually separate accounts for partners:
   a Capital, with the amounts remaining much the same from year to year unless there is a major change
   b Current accounts, which change regularly each year as appropriations of profit are credited to them and drawings debited to them
   c Drawings, which may be shown in a separate account and debited to the current accounts at the end of the year

Statement of financial position (1) of Orry, Mona and Michael as at 31 December year 7 (before appropriation of profits)

	Orry	Mona	Michael			
Non-current assets					£	£
Premises						280,000
Deduct Provision for depreciation (33,600 + 5,600)						(39,200)
						240,800
Current assets						
Inventories					35,000	
Cash					95,200	
						130,200
Total assets						371,000
Capital accounts	**Orry**	**Mona**	**Michael**			
	£	£	£	£		
	160,000	100,000	30,000	290,000		
Current accounts	**Orry**	**Mona**	**Michael**			
	£	£	£			
	30,000	(40,000)	(29,000)	(39,000)		
				251,000		

Statement of financial position (2) of Orry, Mona and Michael as at 31 December Year 7 (after appropriation of profits)

	£	£
Non-current assets	£	£
Premises		280,000
Deduct Provision for depreciation (33,600 + 5,600)		(39,200)
		240,800
Current assets		
Inventories	35,000	
Cash	95,200	
		130,200
		371,000

Capital account					
Orry	**Mona**	**Michael**			
£	£	£			
160,000	100,000	30,000		290,000	
Current accounts					
	Orry	**Mona**	**Michael**		
	£	£	£		
Opening balance	30,000	(40,000)	(29,000)		
Salary	–	–	40,000		
Profit	40,000	20,000	20,000		
	70,000	(20,000)	31,000	81,000	
					371,000

Other issues in partnership accounts

Partners can agree among themselves to share the work and benefits of the partnership business in any way they like, and this is best done with a formal written agreement. In the absence of any agreement to the contrary, the provisions of the 1890 Partnership Act apply, the key parts of which are that partners share profits and losses equally; they share equally in the management of the business; there are no partners' salaries, interest on capital or drawings; if a partner loans money to the business, interest will be allowed at 5 per cent per annum; and no new partner can be admitted unless all agree. The partnership is dissolved if one partner resigns, dies or becomes bankrupt or insane.

A general example of partnership accounts is provided in **Illustration 10.5**, with additional questions at the end of this chapter.

ILLUSTRATION 10.5

Before preparing the appropriation account, the profit and loss account of Knobby and Bee-Gears showed a net profit of £150,000, and their summarized statement of financial position as at 31 December year 2 was as follows:

	£	£
Net assets		700,000
Profit for the year (before appropriation)		150,000
Capital accounts		
Knobby	500,000	
Bee-Gears	100,000	600,000
Current accounts		
Knobby	50,000	
Bee-Gears	(40,000)	10,000
Drawings accounts		
Knobby	(10,000)	
Bee-Gears	(50,000)	(60,000)
		700,000

The partnership agreement provides for charging interest on drawings at the rate of 10 per cent of the balances on the drawings accounts at the end of the year; interest on capital is to be 5 per cent per annum; Bee-Gears is to receive a salary of £30,000 a year; Knobby is to be credited with two-thirds of remaining profits and Bee-Gears with one-third.

ILLUSTRATION 10.6

Appropriation account of Knobby and Bee-Gears for the year ended 31 December year 2

	£	£
Net profit		150,000
Interest on drawings		
Knobby	1,000	
Bee-Gears	5,000	6,000
		156,000
Salary – Bee-Gears	30,000	
Interest on capital		
Knobby	25,000	
Bee-Gears	5,000	60,000
		96,000
Share of profit		
Knobby	64,000	
Bee-Gears	32,000	96,000

Summarized statement of financial position of Knobby and Bee-Gears as at 31 December year 2

	Knobby	Bee-Gears	
Net assets			700,000
Capital accounts	Knobby	Bee-Gears	
	500,000 Cr	100,000 Cr	
			600,000 Cr
Current accounts	Knobby	Bee-Gears	
	50,000 Cr	(40,000) Dr	
Interest on drawings	(1,000) Dr	(5,000) Dr	
	49,000 Cr	(45,000) Dr	
Salary	–	30,000 Cr	
Interest on capital	25,000 Cr	5,000 Cr	
Share of profit	64,000 Cr	32,000 Cr	
	138,000 Cr	22,000 Cr	
Drawings	(10,000) (Dr)	(50,000) (Dr)	
	128,000 (Cr)	(28,000) (Dr)	100,000 Cr
			700,000

Explanations

The income statement and statement of financial position have already been prepared in the usual way, taking into account depreciation, accruals and other adjustments. The net profit to be allocated between the partners is £150,000, which is a credit balance remaining on the income statement. For each appropriation of profit (salary, interest on capital and share of profit), the bookkeeping is to debit the profit and loss appropriation account and to credit the current account of each partner.

The idea of charging interest on drawings is rather different. The charge (the debit) is made to the partners' current accounts; the credit is to the profit and loss account, which has the effect of increasing the amount to be divided between the partners.

At the end of Year 2, the partners' drawings accounts can be netted off against their current accounts. The drawings accounts for Year 3 will then show only the drawings made in Year 3. Knobby may think that Bee-Gears ought to be charged more interest because he still has a debit balance on his current account in Year 3, even before making any drawings.

The partners' capital accounts usually remain unchanged from year to year unless it is agreed that additional capital is introduced (or withdrawn).

Summary

The basic recording of financial transactions, using double-entry bookkeeping, is the same with sole traders, companies and partnerships, and most of the adjustments to trial balances are much the same. Unincorporated businesses (sole traders and partnerships) are free to present their statements of financial position and income statements in traditional ways, often including expenses in some detail.

It is acceptable for profits to be added to capital and drawings to be deducted from capital with sole traders. In partnerships, there are usually separate accounts for each partner's capital, current transactions and drawings.

In company accounts, share capital must be clearly separated from other reserves and retained earnings. Companies Acts and accounting standards govern company financial statements and the formats shown in IAS 1 for statements of financial position and income statements are generally being adopted.

Review of key points

- The trial balance is a summary of all transactions that have been recorded in the double-entry bookkeeping system and is the basis for preparing statements of financial position and income statements.
- Adjustments and additional information are required to produce a statement of financial position and income statement. Each of these has to be dealt with twice: once as a debit and once as a credit.
- Adjustments for closing inventory, depreciation, the disposal of non-current assets, revaluation of land, accruals, prepayments, bad debts written off, and provisions for bad debts are the same in all types of organizations.
- Drawings are deducted from capital in sole traders' accounts. In partnerships, drawings are shown separately from capital and separately for each partner.
- A company's income statement concludes by showing profit for the period. Dividends are shown on a separate statement, 'changes in equity for the period'.
- Statements of financial position and income statements for all types of organization are increasingly following the formats illustrated in IAS 1.

Self-testing questions

1 The trial balance of Noddy's Business as at 31 December year 6 is as follows:

	Debit	Credit
	£	£
Shop premises	400,000	
Capital as at 1 December year 6		370,000
General expenses	120,000	
Payables (creditors)		20,000
Sales		130,000
	520,000	520,000

Prepare an income statement for the year ended 31 December year 6, and a statement of financial position as at that date.

2 The trial balance of Mona Ramsey as at 30 September year 3 was as follows.

	£	£
Bank	24,321	
Capital		27,000
General expenses	8,000	
Inventory at 1 October year 2	20,000	
Payables		13,000
Purchases	188,000	
Receivables	11,000	
Rent, rates and insurance	17,000	
Sales revenue		267,321
Wages	39,000	
	307,321	307,321

Adjustment

a Closing inventory as at 30 September year 3 amounted to £15,000.

Prepare an income statement for the year ended 30 September year 3, and a statement of financial position as at that date.

3 The trial balance of Sally Glen's business as at 31 December year 8 is as follows:

	£	£
Bank	23,000	
Capital as at 31 December year 7		370,000
General expenses	8,000	

	£	£
Inventory at 31 December year 7	18,000	
Provision for depreciation on premises as at 31 December year 7		21,000
Provision for depreciation on delivery van as at 31 December year 7		14,000
Payables		20,000
Purchases	242,000	
Receivables	60,000	
Rent, rates and insurance	23,000	
Sales revenue		365,000
Shop premises at cost	350,000	
Delivery van at cost	32,000	
Wages	34,000	
	790,000	790,000

Adjustments

a Closing inventory as at 31 December year 8 amounted to £19,000.

b Depreciation is to be provided on shop premises on a straight-line basis at 2 per cent per annum.

c Depreciation is to be provided on the delivery van at 25 per cent per annum on a diminishing balance basis.

Prepare an income statement for the year ended 31 December year 8, and a statement of financial position as at that date.

4 The trial balance of Mary Rushen's business as at 30 June year 5 was as follows.

	£	£
Capital as at 30 June year 4		238,200
Cash and bank	7,400	
Fixtures and fittings at cost	44,000	
Freehold buildings at cost	400,000	
General expenses	13,000	
Inventory at 30 June year 4	12,000	
Payables		18,000
Provision for depreciation on freehold buildings as at 30 June year 4		80,000
Provision for depreciation on fixtures and fittings as at 30 June year 4		30,800
Purchases	155,000	
Receivables	8,000	
Repairs and maintenance	10,600	

	£	£
Sales revenue		320,000
Wages	37,000	
	687,000	687,000

Adjustments

a Closing inventory as at 30 June year 5 amounted to £7,000.

b Depreciation is to be provided on freehold buildings on a straight-line basis at 2.5 per cent per annum.

c Depreciation is to be provided on the fixtures and fittings on a straight-line basis at 10 per cent per annum.

Prepare an income statement for the year ended 30 June year 5, and a statement of financial position as at that date.

5 The trial balance of Brad Head as at 31 December year 3 was as follows:

	£	£
Bank	6,400	
Capital as at 31 December year 2		35,000
Fixtures and fittings at cost	22,000	
General expenses	9,000	
Interest paid	3,500	
Inventory at 31 December year 2	28,000	
Heat and lighting	19,000	
Loan from SHC Bank		50,000
Payables		31,000
Plant and machinery at cost	220,000	
Provision for bad debts		1,800
Provision for depreciation on vehicles as at 31 December year 2		15,000
Provision for depreciation on fixtures and fittings at 31 December year 2		13,200
Provision for depreciation on plant and machinery as at 31 December year 2		24,000
Purchases	255,000	
Receivables	98,100	
Rent, rates, and insurance	65,000	
Sales revenue		660,000
Vehicles at cost	60,000	
Wages	44,000	
	830,000	830,000

Adjustments

a Closing inventory as at 31 December year 3 amounted to £13,000.

b Depreciation is to be provided on plant and machinery on a straight-line basis at 10 per cent per annum.

c Depreciation is to be provided on fixtures and fittings on a straight-line basis at 10 per cent per annum.

d Depreciation is to be provided on the delivery van at 20 per cent per annum on a diminishing balance basis.

e An electricity bill for the three months ending on 31 January year 4 amounts to £3,000 and has not yet been recorded in the accounts.

f Rent for the three months ending on 28 February year 4, amounting to £6,600, was paid at the beginning of December year 3.

g A specific debt of £2,100 is to be written off as irrecoverable.

h The provision for bad debts is to be adjusted to be 2.5 per cent of debtors.

i On 31 December year 3 Brad Head took drawings from the business of £6,000, which have not yet been recorded.

Prepare an income statement for the year ended 31 December year 3, and a statement of financial position as at that date.

6 The trial balance of Ellie's Ltd as at 31 December year 1 was as follows:

	Debit	Credit
	£	£
Inventory at 1 January year 1	19,500	
Trade receivables	61,000	
Trade payables		13,400
Share capital: 100 £1 shares		100
Share premium		11,600
Retained profits at 1 January year 1		17,100
Printing and stationery	2,400	
Provision for bad debts		600
Wages and salaries	12,300	
Purchases	167,000	
Sales revenue		248,300
Cash at bank	450	
Rent	1,500	
Electricity	1,100	
Fixtures and fittings at cost	12,000	
Fixtures and fittings: provision		
for depreciation at 31 December year 0		2,000
Van at cost	8,400	

	Debit	Credit
	£	£
Van: provision for depreciation at		
31 December year 0		4,200
Van: disposal proceeds		4,750
Car at cost	20,000	
Car: provision for depreciation at		
31 December year 0		5,000
General expenses	1,400	
	307,050	307,050

Additional information

a Inventories as at 31 December year 1 was £21,000.
b Rent prepaid as at 31 December year 1 was £400.
c Accrued electricity as at 31 December year 1 was £200.
d A receivable of £500 is to be written off.
e The provision for bad debts is to be increased to £650.
f Depreciation is to be provided for the year as follows: fixtures and fittings – 25 per cent per annum on a reducing balance basis; and vehicles – 25 per cent per annum on a straight-line basis.
g The company's accounting policy is to charge no depreciation in the year that a non-current asset is sold.
h Corporation tax of £15,000 is to be provided.

Prepare an income statement for the year ended 31 December year 1 and a statement of financial position as at that date.

7 The trial balance of Bulgham, Dhoon and Barony as at 31 December year 9 is as follows:

	£	£
Cash	47,000	
Furniture at cost	90,000	
General expenses	45,000	
Inventories as at 31 December year 8	37,000	
Provision for depreciation on		
furniture as at 31 December year 8		27,000
Purchases	320,000	
Rent	28,000	
Sales revenue		490,000
Capital accounts as at 1 January year 9		
Bulgham		40,000
Dhoon		30,000

	£	£
Barony		20,000
Current accounts as at 1 January year 9		
Bulgham		10,000
Dhoon	22,000	
Barony	28,000	
	617,000	617,000

Adjustments

a Inventory as at 31 December year 9 amounted to £31,000.

b Furniture is to be depreciated on a straight-line basis at 10 per cent per annum.

c Rent of £6,000 was paid on 30 November year 9 for the three-month period ending on 28 February year 10.

d Profits are to be appropriated as follows:

i 5 per cent interest on capital to each partner;

ii salaries of £18,250 each to Dhoon and Barony;

iii the remaining profits to be divided equally among the three partners.

There were no drawings during the year. Prepare an income statement for the year ended 31 December year 9, and a statement of financial position as at that date.

Assessment questions

1 The trial balance of E. Zee's Business as at 31 December year 7 was as follows:

	Debit	Credit
	£	£
Workshop	170,000	
Payables		15,000
Capital as at 1 January year 7		145,000
General expenses	50,000	
Sales revenue		60,000
	220,000	220,000

Prepare an income statement for the year ended 31 December year 7, and a statement of financial position as at that date.

2 The trial balance of Isabella Stanley as at 31 March year 9 was as follows:

	£	£
Administration expenses	43,000	
Bank	61,000	
Capital		30,000

	£	£
Inventory as at 1 April year 8	18,000	
Payables		33,000
Purchases	234,000	
Receivables	17,000	
Sales revenue		370,000
Selling expenses	26,000	
Distribution costs	34,000	
	433,000	433,000

Adjustment

a Closing inventory as at 31 March year 9 amounted to £22,000.

Prepare an income statement for the year ended 31 March year 9, and a statement of financial position as at that date.

3 The trial balance of Michael Orry's business as at 31 March year 2 is as follows:

	£	£
Administrative expenses	43,000	
Capital as at 31 March year 1		250,000
Cash and bank	170,000	
Drawings	36,900	
Distribution costs	11,000	
Inventories as at 31 March year 1	18,000	
Payables		18,000
Plant and machinery at cost	180,000	
Provision for depreciation on plant and machinery as at 31 March year 1		108,000
Provision for depreciation on vehicles as at 31 March year 1		21,000
Purchases	120,000	
Receivables	16,000	
Repairs and maintenance	27,900	
Rent and rates	36,200	
Sales		390,000
Vehicles at cost	48,000	
Wages	80,000	
	787,000	787,000

Adjustments

a Closing inventory as at 31 March year 2 amounted to £21,000.

b Depreciation is to be provided on plant and machinery on a straight-line basis at 10 per cent per annum.

c Depreciation is to be provided on vehicles on a reducing balance basis at 25 per cent per annum.

Prepare an income statement for the year ended 31 March year 2, and a statement of financial position as at that date.

4 Andreas, Jude and Sandy are in business together, sharing profits in the proportion 3 : 2 : 1. Their partnership agreement provides for interest on their fixed capital balances of 8 per cent per annum, and that Sandy should receive a salary of £13,400 per annum. Their trial balance as at 30 June year 3 was as follows:

	£	£
Bank	42,800	
Business expenses	38,150	
Capital accounts as at 30 June year 2		
Andreas		120,000
Jude		150,000
Sandy		100,000
Payables		8,000
Current accounts as at 30 June year 2		
Andreas		15,000
Jude		13,000
Sandy	4,600	
Receivables	11,150	
Drawings accounts as at 30 June year 3		
Andreas	51,000	
Jude	72,000	
Sandy	38,400	
Plant and equipment at cost	290,000	
Goodwill	100,000	
Inventories as at 30 June year 2	12,000	
Provision for depreciation		
as at 30 June year 2		50,000
Purchases	78,900	
Sales		283,000
	739,000	739,000

Adjustments

a Non-current assets are to be depreciated at 20 per cent per annum on a reducing balance basis.
b Closing inventory amounted to £18,900.
c Business expenses of £2,735 have been incurred but not yet recorded.
d A provision for bad debts amounting to 10 per cent of receivables is to be created.

Prepare an income statement and an appropriation account for the year ending 30 June year 3, and a statement of financial position as at that date.

5 The trial balance of Faraway Retailers Ltd as at 31 December year 1 is shown below.

	Debit	Credit
	£000	£000
Inventories as at 1 January year 1	545	
Trade receivables	705	
Trade payables		600
Share capital: £1 shares		1,500
Share premium		750
8% debentures		1,200
Retained profits at 1 January year 1		190
Printing and stationery	750	
Provision for bad debts		40
Wages and salaries	890	
Distribution costs	100	
Bad debt written off	20	
Purchases	3,350	
Sales		7,900
Cash at bank	51	
Rent and rates	320	
Electricity	55	
Debenture interest	48	
Land and buildings at cost	3,000	
Land and buildings provision for depreciation as at 31 December year 0		90
Fixtures and fittings at cost	1,500	
Fixtures and fittings provision for depreciation as at 31 December year 0		600
Plant and machinery at cost	2,800	
Plant and machinery provision for depreciation at 31 December year 0		1,264
	14,134	14,134

Additional information

a The inventory check on 31 December year 1 revealed the following:

	Cost	Net realizable value
	£000	£000
Home furnishing	500	1,000
Clothing	440	410

b Rent and rates include a rent payment of £144,000 for the period 1 April year 1 to 31 March year 2.

c Electricity for the three months ended 31 January year 2 of £18,000 was paid in February year 2.

d A trade receivable of £5,000 is to be written off.

e The provision for bad debts is to be adjusted to be 5 per cent of trade receivables.
f Depreciation is to be provided for the year as follows: land and buildings, 2 per cent per annum on a straight-line basis; fixtures and fittings, 20 per cent per annum on a straight-line basis; and plant and machinery is 25 per cent per annum on reducing balance.
g A full year's debenture interest is payable.
h Corporation tax of £615,000 is to be provided.

Prepare an income statement for the year ended 31 December year 1, and a statement of financial position as at that date.

Group activities and discussion questions

1 Would you rather be in business as a sole trader, in a partnership, or a company? Why?
2 What are the various ways of sharing profits between partners, and why are they used?
3 Is there, or should there be, a standard format for the financial statements of unincorporated businesses? Why or why not?
4 Why is there a need for 'adjustments' to a trial balance at the year end?
5 Bookkeeping records transactions; trial balances, statement of financial positions and income statements summarize and present the results of those transactions. It is unrealistic to expect such summaries to be 'useful', except in a very narrow sense. Discuss. How useful would you like financial statements to be? How realistic is it to expect financial statements to meet the needs of various users of accounts, given the way in which they are derived?

Accounting in context

In relation to the following reports based on information from the website of a well-known accounting software package developer and articles referring to software packages, what advantages arise from using such a package instead of a manual system of accounting demonstrated in **Chapters 9** and **10**? Do you think there are any differences in principle between accounting using a traditional approach and a computerized accounting system?

Background information on VT Software from the company website

VT Final Accounts, our final accounts software, runs in Microsoft Excel and produces professionally formatted company accounts (including tax computation), sole trader accounts and partnership accounts from trial balance stage upwards. A trial balance can be entered directly into VT Final Accounts, or imported from the VT Transaction+ bookkeeping software package at the touch of a button. VT Final Accounts can also be used to generate an iXBRL account or tax computation file from any Excel workbook (the VT workbooks are pre-tagged).

• iXBRL • Extended trial balance • Automatic hiding of lines and notes with nil balances • Automatic note numbering • Automatic cash flow statement • Abbreviated accounts • Choice of audit or accountants report • Automatic export to tax software packages • Unlimited number of clients/companies

VT Transaction+ is an easy to use bookkeeping software package which runs directly in Windows. It can be used to process incomplete records or to record day-to-day transactions.

• Rapid data entry screen for posting a mixture of payments and receipts directly from bank statements • Transactions can be easily edited or deleted • Fully integrated cash book, sales, purchase and nominal ledgers • Profit and loss account and balance sheet in self-assessment tax return format can be printed out or exported to tax software packages. Includes column for disallowable expenses • Unlimited number of clients/companies

VT Software is dedicated to producing easy to use and inexpensive bookkeeping and accounts production software.

Source: http://www.vtsoftware.co.uk

VT launches iXBRL final accounts program

By John Stokdyk

Like Sage and several other accounts production software developers, VT faced a big challenge to adapt its product for the new electronic filing format. The program is now ready, giving users two months to implement it and test their processes before online filing of Corporation Tax returns becomes mandatory.

VT managing director Philip Hodgson has been keeping members of **AccountingWEB.co.uk** updated on the program's progress and confirmed the planned 31 January launch date last month in the VT Software discussion group after rumours a rival developer had reportedly been circulating negative rumours about the product.

Costing £199 per user in the first year (and £150/year after that), VT Final Accounts includes a Generate iXBRL File command that can be used with any Excel workbook, not just the pre-tagged VT templates. UK GAAP, UK IFRS and UK Corporation Tax taxonomies are supported and the software will also be able to 'tag up' customisations to the standard templates, or other accounts spreadsheets.

This extra facility took a little time to get exactly right, Hodgson said: 'We needed to build in the self tagging features so that users could customise the VT workbooks and it was only a little more work to make the self tagging features apply to any workbook.'

'If you have already done your own thing in Excel, especially if you have a single template from which you derive all your accounts, then self tagging may well be the most efficient way forward.'

The VT Final Accounts package will also include two tools that may help those determined to pursue the DIY tagging route:

- VT Fact Viewer – a tool that displays the tags in any iXBRL file.
- VT Taxonomy Viewer, which lists the tags available in any taxonomy.

Source: http://www.accountingweb.co.uk/topic/tax/vt-launches-ixbrl-final-accounts-program/476766

TaxCalc expands FRS 102 capabilities to include limited liability partnerships

Tom Herbert states that Compliance suite TaxCalc has extended its FRS 102 Revenue under UK GAAP accounts production offering to include limited liability partnerships (LLPs), as the UK prepares for what could be the biggest shake-up to the accounts production scene since the XBRL transformation of the 2010s.

TaxCalc has added the ability to prepare accounts under the full FRS 102 standard for LLPs following the addition of FRS 102 formats for individual limited companies in spring 2023.

The upgraded version of TaxCalc's accounts production feature has been specifically designed to cater to the complex requirements of accounting firms that serve LLPs accounts. It offers the same level of functionality as the original feature for other formats, including the ability to analyse individual figures in detail, generate personalized reports, and automatically tag iXBRL. With this upgrade, TaxCalc confidently meets the growing needs of accounting firms for more advanced and tailored services.

The company, based in Wokingham, plans to expand into additional areas including group accounts and charities by 2024, with other specialist formats potentially being developed in the future based on customer demand.

'We've had great feedback from customers on our FRS 102 for individual limited companies formats,' TaxCalc chief product officer, Pauline Smith told AccountingWEB. 'We made a promise to deliver products for practices of all sizes, and we're delivering features that our customers are getting genuine value from and solving their problems. The more formats our customers have available, the better results they can achieve for their clients.'

TaxCalc simplifies and streamlines financial processes, ensuring compliance in a complex landscape. It allows sole traders, partnerships, LLPs and micro, small, medium and large limited companies to accurately prepare financial statements, therefore freeing up their time to spend on higher-value services.

Source: https://www.accountingweb.co.uk/tech/accounting-software/taxcalc-expands-frs-102-capabilities-to-llps

References and further reading

Barrow, C. and Tracy, J. (2011) *Understanding Business Accounting for Dummies* (3rd edn.). Chichester: Wiley.

Black, G. (2009) *Introduction to Accounting and Finance* (2nd edn.). Upper Saddle River, NJ: FT Prentice Hall.

Monger, R. (2010) *Financial Accounting.* Chichester: Wiley.

Wood, F. and Sangster, A. (2012) *Business Accounting* (vol. 1) (12th edn.). Upper Saddle River, NJ: FT Prentice Hall.

Part 2

Financial Management

Chapter 11

Financing a Business

Chapter contents

11.1 Introduction
11.2 Share Capital
11.3 Borrowing
11.4 Retained Profits
11.5 Other Sources of Finance

Learning objectives

After studying this chapter you will be able to:

- ✓ Describe the main sources of finance used by companies
- ✓ Appreciate the differences between the various sources, and evaluate the appropriateness of each in different circumstances
- ✓ Understand the advantages and disadvantages of high gearing
- ✓ Evaluate different dividend policies
- ✓ Understand how published accounts indicate companies' financing needs and policies
- ✓ Take an overall view of the financing of businesses, combining a number of different approaches

11.1 Introduction

Businesses own a variety of different assets, and statements of financial position show how these have been financed. These assets are non-current assets (such as land and buildings, plant and machinery, furniture and fittings) and current assets (such as inventories, trade receivables and cash at the bank). These have been financed from three main sources:

1 *The money or capital that was put into the business by its owners* - in a company, this is the share capital, which is part of 'equity' or shareholders' funds.

2 *Borrowing* - a company may borrow money on a long-term basis (e.g. by issuing debentures) and on a short-term basis (e.g. as a bank overdraft).

3 *Retained profits* - a successful company makes profits, some of which are paid out to shareholders as dividends; what is left is retained in the business, financing an increase in net assets.

When starting a business, the owners usually put in a large amount of their own money ('equity') and/or borrow substantial sums. If the business is to expand, the business will need to make profits, retaining some within the business. There are, however, other ways of financing the setting up of a business and its subsequent growth. Although businesses tend to own the premises that they occupy and the vehicles and equipment that they use, they may choose to lease them instead. Although many businesses finance inventories of goods, many find that, by buying on credit, they do not need to provide the finance themselves. Similarly, many businesses finance 'receivables' themselves, whereas others manage to get their customers to pay cash (so that there are few, if any, trade receivables) or even to require them to pay in advance. It can be very expensive to finance a manufacturing facility (factory premises, plant and machinery; inventories of raw materials, components, work in progress and finished goods); an alternative is to subcontract (or 'outsource') the manufacturing, perhaps to a country where these things cost less, leaving the subcontractor to provide the finance.

The three main sources of finance for a business (share capital, borrowing and retained profits, as shown in **Illustration 11.1**) are examined in the first three parts of this chapter. However, it is always worth considering other ways of financing. Careful control of working capital can substantially reduce financing requirements, and ways of doing this are examined in the fourth part of the chapter. Finally, 'other sources of finance' are considered, including other ways of doing business that reduce the need for external finance. In most situations, a combination of different ways of financing the business is used.

ILLUSTRATION 11.1

The three main sources of finance (share capital, borrowing and retained profits) are shown in the following simplified company statement of financial position:

	£
Non-current assets	
Property, plant and equipment	2,600
Current assets	
Inventories, trade receivables and cash	1,200
Total assets	3,800
Liabilities and equity	
Current liabilities	
Trade payables	800
Non-current liabilities	
Debentures	1,000
Total liabilities	1,800
Equity	
Share capital	1,000
Retained earnings	1,000
	2,000
Total liabilities and equity	3,800

In this instance, the three long-term sources of finance (share capital, borrowing and retained profits) are each £1,000, making a total of £3,000. There is also short-term funding (current liabilities or trade payables) of £800. The £800 has financed most of the current assets; perhaps the company's trade payables have financed their inventory of goods. The £3,000 has financed all the long-term assets of £2,600, leaving £400 for working capital.

11.2 Share Capital

Share capital is perhaps the most important source of finance for companies, and it is mostly 'ordinary' share capital. There are other types of shares, including a variety of preference shares.

Ordinary shares

When a company is established it issues a number of ordinary shares. With a small, new company, they may be issued only to a few family members. The shareholders are the owners of the company. They also bear most of the risk. If the company gets into financial difficulties, all the creditors have to be repaid before anything is returned to the shareholders. Shareholders can lose everything that they put into a company, but their liability is limited to that amount. There can be no call on the shareholders' personal assets to pay any amounts due to creditors; that is the nature of limited liability.

A company may start as a small, private limited company with a restricted number of shares. If it grows and wants more shareholders, it will become a public limited company. Very large successful companies may become listed on a stock market (such as the London Stock Exchange) to raise additional finance from many more shareholders with an Initial Public Offering (IPO) of shares. There are many very large private companies in the UK, such as Virgin Atlantic, John Lewis Partnership and Anglian Water, that are not listed on a stock exchange.

The initial nominal (or par) value of the shares may be £1 each (or 50 pence, or 10 pence, or any amount). In a successful expanding company, the market value of shares is likely to increase. If the company needs new funding, it may issue a rights issue to the existing shareholders. New shareholders will not be invited to buy shares at an old, low price. New shares are normally issued at a premium, as shown in **Example 11.1**, where additional £1 shares are issued for £2.50; the premium is £1.50 per share.

There is no requirement for a company to pay dividends on ordinary shares. In a very small company, where there are only two or three shareholders, they may easily agree on the amount of dividends, if any, are to be paid. In large, listed companies, the directors normally propose a dividend for shareholders to approve at the annual general meeting. There is usually an interim dividend paid part-way through the year and a final dividend after the year end. Companies sometimes decide not to pay a dividend, perhaps because they have been making losses or have some other financial problem. Many companies pay regular and increasing dividends. In the first quarter of 2024, companies such as Lloyds, GSK, Beazley, Schroders, and Reckitts raised their dividends, whereas WPP and Unilever dividends did not change. However, companies like Shell are increasingly using share buybacks, i.e. buying back their own shares.[1]

The fact that ordinary shares are not required to pay a dividend may make them seem like an attractive, cost-free source of finance. But many shareholders, especially institutional shareholders (such as pension funds), expect and rely on a steady (and increasing) stream of income from dividends. The shareholders are the company's owners, and directors who regularly disappoint shareholders are likely to find themselves out of a job.

[1] James Gard (2024) Top FTSE 100 UK Dividend Paying Stocks. *Morningstar*, 31 May, https://www.morningstar.co.uk/uk/news/111721/top-ftse-100-uk-dividend-paying-stocks–isa-season-special.aspx

Growing companies might not seek a full listing on the stock exchange to begin with. They may first invite a financial institution or venture capitalist to buy some shares. Companies such as venture capitalist 3i Group plc invest in growing companies that are not yet large enough for a stock market listing. The formalities, administrative burden and costs of a full stock market listing may be too much for companies of modest size and they are likely to seek a listing on the Alternative Investment Market (AIM). AIM is regulated by the London Stock Exchange (LSE) but has less demanding rules, and a listing is less costly than being on the LSE's Official List.

Example 11.1

Share premium

Big Company agrees to pay £2,500,000 to take over Little Company. Big Company's shares are highly regarded by investors. Their market value is £2.50 per share, and the nominal value is £1.00 per share. The £2,500,000 is paid not in cash but by the issue of one million £1 shares.

The effect of this transaction is that Big Company's statement of financial position will show £1,000,000 of additional share capital and £1,500,000 of share premium. The total, £2,500,000, was issued in exchange for assets (the Little Company).

Shares may be issued in exchange for cash or any assets.

Companies often increase their share capital a little each year, especially when there is some sort of incentive scheme for directors and other staff that provides them with shares. But any significant increase in funding through the issue of shares is a major event for a company, and does not happen very often. Similarly, a company may, from time to time, buy back some of its own shares and so reduce share capital. Companies do not keep a supply of shares for investors to buy and sell: investors buy and sell shares from each other, usually via a stock exchange. Investors cannot go to Marks & Spencer and buy a few shares along with their new underwear and microwave dinner! They have to go via some sort of stockbroker, and there are lots of easy and flexible ways of buying and selling shares via a range of banks and other financial institutions, and on the internet.

Rights issue

When a company wants to raise substantial additional funds by issuing shares, it often makes a *rights issue* to existing shareholders. This usually means that it offers new shares at a price lower than the current market price (see **Example 11.2**).

Example 11.2

The Right Company has one million ordinary shares with a nominal value of 50 pence each and a market value of £2 each. The company decides to make a rights issue, offering existing shareholders one share for every five that they already hold, at a rights price of £1.50 per share.

Shareholders might choose to exercise their rights (by buying the additional shares) or to sell them.

After the rights issue the theoretical value of the company will be:

Existing one million shares at £2 each	£2,000,000
Cash raised from rights issue 200,000 at £1.50	300,000
	£2,300,000
Number of shares after issue	1,200,000

$$\textit{Theoretical ex-rights price}\left(TERP\right) = \frac{£2,300,000}{1,200,000} = £1.92$$

An alternative solution:

$$TERP = ((5\ \textit{existing shares} \times £2.00) + (1\ \textit{right} \times £1.50)) / 6 = £1.92$$

A *rights issue* is the normal way in which established companies raise additional funds and it is intended to be attractive to existing shareholders. If the current market price of a company's shares is £2, the right to buy more shares at £1.50 each sounds attractive. After the rights issue, the total value of the company will, in theory, be worth the amount it was worth before the rights issue, plus the amount of money raised from the rights issue. In practice, if investors believe that the additional funds will be invested sufficiently profitably, the total value of the company will increase by more than the amount of cash raised.

If shareholders exercise all their rights, they will continue to own the same proportion of the company. The right to buy shares cheaply may look attractive, but the record of rights issues is mixed. Sometimes, it seems that companies issue rights issues because they are in financial difficulties. Sometimes, it is a sign of success, and additional funds are needed for expansion.

Bonus issue

A bonus issue (or a scrip issue) is quite different: it raises no additional funds, and so should not really be included in a chapter on sources of finance!

Many shareholders like receiving a bonus issue, although they really receive nothing. Most people would probably rather have two pieces of cake than one. But if the second piece of cake is created just by cutting the original piece of cake in half, there is no gain. In effect, that is what a bonus issue does. A one-for-one bonus issue means that everyone has twice as many shares, but nothing has changed; each still owns the same proportion of the same total. In **Example 11.3** there was a 'two-for-one' bonus issue. For example, anyone who held 200 shares would be given an additional 400 shares, giving them a total of 600 shares. The total number of shares the company had, therefore, increased from 2m to 6m; share capital was increased by £4m; retained earnings were reduced by £4m. However, the assets (and liabilities) of the company are unchanged.

Example 11.3

Scriptease plc	Before bonus issue	After bonus issue
	£000	£000
Non-current assets	5,300	5,300

Scriptease plc	Before bonus issue	After bonus issue
Current assets		
Inventories and receivables	3,000	3,000
Cash	500	500
Total assets	8,800	8,800
Trade payables	300	300
Equity		
Share capital (nominal value: £1 per share)	2,000	6,000
Retained earnings	6,500	2,500
	8,800	8,800

In practice, a bonus issue is more likely to be one new share for every three, four, or five shares already held. Shareholders may think that they will still receive the same amount of dividend per share, and so they will be better off. Bonus issues are often associated with good performance and optimism, which could lead to an increase in demand for the shares and, therefore, an increase in share price and the total value of the company.

One of the justifications for bonus issues is that it is often said that share prices higher than about £8 or £10 become less 'marketable': shareholders would rather buy five shares at £2 each than one share for £10. But there are plenty of successful companies where the share price is much higher; for example, on 16 April 2024 AstraZeneca plc closed at £108.78 with a P/E of 35.98 times.

Preference shares

The classification of preference shares depends on their respective terms and conditions. For example, preference shares that provide for redemption at the holder's option give rise to a contractual obligation and are, therefore, classified as financial liabilities.

Preference shareholders take less risk and can expect less reward than ordinary shareholders. Preference shares have a fixed dividend rate, for example, 7 per cent. This means that for each £1 preference share, investors receive a 7 pence dividend each year. Sometimes a company might decide not to pay the preference dividend (perhaps when profits are low). But if no preference dividend is paid, then no ordinary dividend can be paid either. The preference shareholders have a preference over ordinary shareholders with dividend payments.

Preference shares are usually *cumulative*, which means that if the preference dividend is not paid in some years, all arrears of preference dividends must be paid before any ordinary dividends can be paid. However, preference shares are not very popular for a number of reasons. Ordinary shareholders always have the prospect that the company might do really well, and there could be a substantial increase in profits, dividends and share price: they might make loads of money! Preference shareholders are more secure, but their level of dividend is fixed, whether the company does well or badly.

Preference shares can be made more attractive if they are *participating* and/or if they are *convertible*. Participating preference shares can participate in higher levels of dividends when the company does well and ordinary dividends rise above some predetermined level. Convertible preference shares can be more attractive: they can be converted to ordinary shares at a predetermined rate (see **Example 11.4**). Since preference shares are generally redeemable at some future date, they are viewed more like liabilities than like equity and, as a result, IAS 32 requires that preference shares be classified as liabilities, and since there is an obligation to pay the preference share dividend, such dividends are classified much like interest payments. The classification is not quite as simple as it seems. For example, preference shares required to be converted into a fixed number of ordinary shares on a fixed date or on the occurrence of an event that is certain to occur should be classified as equity.

Example 11.4

The Fastgro company issues £1 ordinary shares at a premium of 50 pence per share. On the same date, it issues 6 per cent convertible £1 preference shares, giving the shareholders the right to convert three preference shares into one ordinary share at any date they choose.

In the early years, preference shareholders are unlikely to give up three preference shares worth about £3, while one ordinary share is worth £1.50. But if the company is successful, the market price of the ordinary shares might increase steadily to, say, £10 per share. An investor with 900,000 preference shares, worth about £900,000, could then convert them to 300,000 ordinary shares worth £3m; this would give a profit of over £2m!

The prospect of a substantial capital gain, if the company is successful, can make convertible preference shares seem very attractive to investors; they get a decent dividend in the short term, with reasonable security. But the dividend is likely to be very expensive to the company, mainly because dividends (unlike interest) are not allowable as an expense to be charged against taxation. If we assume a corporation tax rate of 30 per cent, then a company needs to earn £10 profit to pay a £7 dividend. However, it is cheaper for the company to borrow money: a company earning £10 profit could pay £7 in interest and still have £3 (pre-tax) profit left for shareholders.

Interpretation of statements of financial position

When interpreting statements of financial position, for most purposes the total figure for 'equity' is used. **Equity (or ordinary shareholders' funds) includes all ordinary shareholders' funds (share capital, share premium and all reserves/retained profits) except preference share capital.** This figure is used in calculating gearing, and in calculating the net assets per share. It is also used in calculating the profitability of ordinary shareholders' funds: net profit after tax (and after deducting any preference share dividends) is expressed as a percentage of equity. It is usually a mistake (often made by students) to use the share capital figure instead of including all shareholders' funds.

The nominal value of shares is of little or no importance except perhaps in calculating the number of shares that make up share capital. Calculations of earnings per share (EPS), dividend per share and net assets per share are based on the number of ordinary shares.

11.3 Borrowing

Some very prudent individuals and businesses may think that borrowing is dangerous since the business may not be able to meet the interest and repayments, and there is always the risk of insolvency if the business gets into difficulties. Those who want to minimize risk probably want to minimize borrowing. But if they are so risk averse, they should probably not go into business and will probably never make much money.

It is safest and easiest to put your money in a bank and earn a steady, low rate of interest with little or no risk. But people invest in businesses because they think that it is worth the risk in order to earn more money. If banks are paying, say, 5 per cent interest, investors hope to earn more than that by investing in companies. Perhaps they expect a return on capital employed (ROCE) of 10 per cent or more. A business could argue that if the cost of borrowing is less than the ROCE that they can earn, then the more they borrow, the more profit they will make. If you can borrow money at 7 per cent per annum, and invest it to earn 10 per cent per annum, then the more money you borrow, the more profit you will make, as shown in **Example 11.5**.

Example 11.5

Two companies in the same industry each have a return on capital employed of 10 per cent, and they are each able to borrow money at the same interest rate of 7 per cent.

Prudent plc borrows an extra £1m	
Cost of additional borrowings: £1m at 7%	£70,000 per annum
Additional earnings: £1m at 10%	£100,000 per annum
Net additional earnings	£30,000 per annum
Profitable plc borrows an extra £100m	
Cost of additional borrowings £100m at 7%	£7,000,000 per annum
Additional earnings: £100bn at 10%	£10,000,000 per annum
Net additional earnings	£3,000,000 per annum

Borrowing can increase the return to shareholders, as is demonstrated in **Example 11.6**. Borrowing can also be relatively cheap and is a cheaper source of finance than issuing ordinary shares because the interest is allowable as an expense for tax purposes. Shareholders expect a higher return as they are taking more risk than lenders. But what they expect and what they get can be very different.

Example 11.6

Low-geared company Capital structure			Equity	£100m
			10% debentures	£10m
				£110m
	Year 1	**Year 2**		
	£m	£m		
EBIT	10	12	+20%	
Interest	1	1		
Pre-tax profit	9	11		
Tax (say) 30%	2.7	3.3		
Profit after-tax	6.3	7.7	+22.2%	
High-geared company Capital structure			Equity	£50m
			10% debentures	£60m

EBIT	10	12	+20%	£110m
Interest	6	6		
Pre-tax profit	4	6		
Tax (say) 30%	1.2	1.8		
Profit after-tax	2.8	4.2	+50%	

In both cases, EBIT (earnings before interest and taxation) increased by 20 per cent between years 1 and 2. However, the effect of gearing was a larger increase in the profit after tax earned by the ordinary shareholders. In the low-geared company, the return earned by ordinary shareholders increased by 22.2 per cent, whereas in the high-geared company, it increased by 50 per cent.

There are other good reasons for borrowing rather than issuing more shares. In a family-controlled company, the existing shareholders and directors might not want to risk issuing more shares if it results in new and different people becoming shareholders and perhaps controlling the company. In spite of what some textbooks say, directors do not always make rational economic decisions: many like to keep their positions of power and influence, even if (by not issuing more shares) they restrict the growth and profitability of the company. The costs involved in issuing shares also tend to be higher than the costs of obtaining loans.

Another advantage of borrowing is that it comes in many forms and can be very flexible. It may be short or long term. The most flexible way of borrowing is through an overdraft. Interest rates are negotiable and are usually a number of percentage points above the base rate. Individuals with unauthorized overdrafts may find that they are charged ridiculously high interest rates, perhaps even 10 or 15 points above the base rate. A company ought to be able to negotiate an overdraft interest rate just a little above the base rate. The base rate is what the Bank of England charges other banks and other lenders when they borrow money. The Bank of England's Monetary Policy Committee on 19 June 2024 maintained the Bank Rate at 5.25 per cent per annum. Some businesses are seasonal and need to borrow at particular times of the year.

A business such as a seaside hotel is likely to be flush with cash in October, after the holiday season, but by March, they need short-term borrowings until the money starts coming in for the next holiday season. Many businesses have plenty of money in the middle of the month but need to borrow at the end of the month when wages and salaries are paid. Overdrafts are most appropriate for such short-term financing because interest is payable only for the actual days that the overdraft facility is used. There is no point in having a fixed loan throughout the year (as it will require paying interest throughout the year) if the money is needed only for a few days each month or for a few months each year.

Although overdrafts are supposed to be a short-term source of finance, many individuals and companies have significant (and increasing!) overdrafts that go on for years. Banks are interested in converting overdrafts into fixed loans for a few years if they can earn more interest. Businesses need to work out carefully how much it is appropriate to borrow with fixed-term loans and fixed interest rates and how much it is appropriate to use overdraft facilities.

Debentures are a form of long-term borrowing (typically 5–10 years), usually with a fixed rate of interest, which can be listed on a stock market. Investors can, therefore, sell them when they wish, and the company can choose to buy them back on the market if they have nothing better to do with their money. Debentures are usually 'secured' on some non-current assets of the company, perhaps on land and buildings. Perhaps a floating charge can be used as security for borrowings or other indebtedness. A floating charge security will be placed on a certain class of assets, which could be current assets. This means that the disposal of some of these assets is allowed. However, if there is a default, such as non-payment of interest, the floating charge will become a fixed charge on the specified class of assets. A famous court case is National Westminster Bank plc v Spectrum Plus Ltd and others [2005] UKHL 41.[2]

[2] Judgments – National Westminster Bank plc (Respondents) v. Spectrum Plus Limited and others and others (Appellants), https://publications.parliament.uk/pa/ld200506/ldjudgmt/jd050630/nat-1.htm (accessed 11 July 2024)

Debentures are sometimes 'convertible' into ordinary shares, which can make them very attractive to investors if it is expected that the company's shares will do very well in the future. Investors in a new or expanding business may be attracted by the security of a debenture with a reasonable interest rate to begin with, together with the possibility of conversion to ordinary shares (and increases in the share price, and increasing dividends) once the venture has proved to be successful.

The main attraction of borrowing is the idea that the more you borrow, the more profit you can make. It may be an attractive idea, but there are a number of problems with ever-increasing borrowings:

1 Borrowing may be no problem as long as the company can be sure of always having earnings above the required level of interest payments. But businesses tend to have good years and bad years; the economy tends to run in cycles; some industries are particularly cyclical; some industries run into bad patches, with bad luck and/or bad management. If, in some years, the company does not earn enough to make the necessary interest payments, lenders may repossess vital assets and force the business to curtail its activities or close down.
2 The more you get into debt, the more difficult it is to borrow more money. There is probably always someone or some bank that will lend to you, but as you get more into debt, the interest rates become higher to compensate the lender for additional risk.
3 Lenders usually look for some security. It is easy to borrow money secured on land and buildings. Lenders may be happy to take some 'floating charge' on whatever other assets the company has. But when all assets have already been used as security, it is increasingly difficult to borrow more money.
4 Those who have already lent money to the company often lay down conditions to restrict the company's ability to borrow more. These 'restrictive covenants' could include conditions like maintaining certain financial ratios, annual audits, or no dividend payments and may specify that a company's total borrowing must not exceed some multiple of the amount of equity. The following are some common ratios used: Debt/EBITDA; Debt/Equity, EBIT/Interest.
5 Companies that are heavily in debt may get a reputation as being 'high risk', and other businesses may be reluctant to do business with them. Sometimes investors steer clear because the risk is too great.

A good old-fashioned view might be that a company should keep increasing its borrowing as long as it can get away with it. Theory suggests that, eventually, lenders will see that the company has borrowed too much (gearing is too high), and they will start to charge higher interest rates. As borrowing increases, interest rates increase until, eventually, the cost of borrowing is higher than the return that the company can generate from the borrowings. High levels of borrowing are also associated with high risk, and this can affect the share price, especially if it starts to look as if the company is so heavily in debt that it might be forced into liquidation. There is, thus, an optimal level of borrowing (although it is difficult to establish what this level is) in this traditional view.

Modigliani and Miller (1958) offered a different perspective, suggesting that the level of gearing does not affect the share price. Even if the amount of borrowing changes, it is still the same business, with the same earnings stream and the same business risk. Modigliani and Miller's presentation is sophisticated, but it depends on a number of unrealistic assumptions, and it is often misinterpreted. Their emphasis is on the value of the company, which depends on the investments that they have and the cash flows that they will generate; how the company is financed is a secondary issue. More recent work, recognizing the impact of taxation (interest is an allowable expense for taxation, and so the cost of borrowing is likely to be lower than the cost of equity), together with lower interest rates and the actual behaviour of companies, suggest that there may be some optimal level of gearing; but this is hard to find, and views about acceptable levels of gearing change from time to time.

In practice, many companies borrow as much as they can get away with. Some companies constantly need additional funds because of expansion and development. But some companies (like some individuals!) do not seem to be able to live within their means and borrow until they go bust.

In **Illustration 11.1** the company had total long-term funds of £3,000, of which £1,000 was borrowed. In other words, one-third of its long-term funding was borrowed, or its gearing ratio was 33⅓ per cent. There is, of course, no 'correct' or 'best' level of borrowing, nor is there a single correct way of measuring gearing.[3] Companies that are able to borrow extensively are likely to have a steady, secure income stream so that they can be confident about being able to pay the necessary interest every year. They are also likely to have lots of good quality assets (particularly land and buildings) to offer as security to lenders. Companies in very cyclical industries should avoid high gearing, but many do not, and they get into financial difficulties. The airline industry is noticeably susceptible to epidemics of war, terrorism, and disease, sudden and rapid rises in the price of oil, and the recent economic downturn. Many airlines are highly geared, and many have found themselves in serious financial difficulties in recent years.

When the telecommunications industry was expanding and share prices were booming at the end of the twentieth century, many companies got away with very high levels of borrowing for a while. Then, the business climate turned against them, and many share prices collapsed. BT had a debt mountain of £30bn, which did not look too bad in relation to the market value of its equity when share prices were high. But in comparison with the statement of financial position value of equity it looked terrible. And when telecommunications share prices took a nosedive, the amount of debt looked unsustainable in relation to the market value of equity. BT has taken decisive action, and has substantially reduced the debt.

The mandate of the Monetary Policy Committee unequivocally states that the inflation target remains in force at all times, underscoring the paramount importance of maintaining price stability within the framework of UK monetary policy. The central banks, such as the Bank of England, have had to increase interest rates in order to curb inflation. In times of lower interest rates, higher levels of gearing had become acceptable. Sometimes one company buys another company and finances the purchase almost entirely by borrowing; this is called a 'leveraged buyout'.[4] Since, the buyouts rely on leverage to finance their transactions, the increase in interest rates affects them significantly.

This suggests that with rising interest rates buyout funds can no longer rely on obtaining cheap debt and increasing their valuation.

11.4 Retained Profits

A successful company makes profits that materialize in the form of additional cash or other net assets. The company may choose to pay out all its profits as dividends, in which case profits will not be a source of funds. Most companies choose to pay out a proportion (perhaps around 40 per cent) of their profits as dividends; the rest are retained and used to finance the business. Obviously, the more profit a company makes, the greater is the potential for using retained profits as a source of finance. Raising finance through retained profits depends on how profitable the business is. It also depends on the company's dividend policy.

Dividend policy

In deciding how much dividend to pay, or what proportion of profits are to be paid out as dividends, companies need to consider some important matters. Dividend policy usually requires striking a balance between (a) paying out *all* profits as dividends, and (b) paying *no* dividends at all.

Pay out all profits as dividends

There is a case for paying out all profits as dividends: profits belong to the shareholders, not the directors. The directors might see retained profits as being too easy a source of finance, and not bother to ensure that they

[3] If borrowing is represented as D, and equity is represented as E, gearing can be measured by taking D as a percentage of D + E; or as a percentage of E. D is sometimes taken to include overdrafts; sometimes it refers only to long-term borrowing.

[4] The purchase of another business can, instead, be financed by issuing additional ordinary shares.

are reinvested in the company properly and profitably. As profits are earned, they may simply disappear into higher levels of inventories and receivables, or even cars and 'conference centres' for the comfort of directors.

Many companies find themselves with surplus funds that they invest in disastrous diversification (ad)ventures or waste on more or less (un)successful takeover bids and mergers. Northern Rock lost millions of pounds attempting to move from its secure base in retail banking into areas of wholesale banking where it had no experience.[5] The British retailer Marks & Spencer ceased its franchise agreement with FiBA, its Turkish franchise partner in Russia, taking a charge of £31m.[6] Some companies have a history of merging with others and then demerging or selling off the bits they no longer want. For example, the history of the BT Group goes as far back as 1846, when it started as The Electric Telegraph Company.[7] BT Group was created in 2001 following the demerger of BT Wireless - BT's mobile business, re-branded as mmO2 - from British Telecommunications plc on a one-for-one share basis. This is an interesting case study as it provides examples of debt crisis, sale and demergers. The evidence so far suggests that a takeover is more likely to destroy shareholder value than to create it.

There are, of course, plenty of exceptions: well-managed companies that succeed in reinvesting retained profits year after year and which have a good record in increasing profits and dividends - some even succeed in increasing their return on capital employed, and, with a bit of luck, the company's share price. There are also many companies where the directors know that they are unable to do this. GEC sat on mountains of cash rather than risk wasting it on ill-advised investments. Other companies, knowing that there are limited opportunities for successful investment of surplus funds, simply return them to shareholders as special dividends, or they use the money to buy their own shares on the market and cancel them.[8]

Many companies or their directors cannot be trusted to invest retained profits successfully. But there are good reasons for not expecting companies to pay out all their profits as dividends:

1. Rising prices, or inflation, usually mean that companies need to retain some of their profits, not for expansion, but merely to maintain the existing level of operations. More funds are required to finance receivables (as selling prices increase), to finance inventories (as replacement costs increase), and to replace non-current assets as the cost of these increases. Inflation in the UK in recent years has been very low, and the cost of replacing many items (e.g. computers and electronic equipment) has actually fallen. However, few businesses can afford to finance even their existing level of operations without retaining some profits.
2. Investors, particularly financial institutions, generally want to see dividends increasing steadily each year, preferably by rather more than the rate of inflation. **Illustration 11.2** shows how company profits can fluctuate, but attempts are made to keep dividends steady.

ILLUSTRATION 11.2

The EPS and the dividend per share of the Cycle Company for the last few years are shown below (in pence).

Year	**1**	**2**	**3**	**4**	**5**	**6**	**7**
EPS	100	134	60	116	180	10	191
Div	50	53	56	59	63	64	70
Cover: EPS/Div	2	2.5	1.1	2.0	2.9	0.2	2.7

[5] HM Treasury (2009) *The Nationalisation of Northern Rock*. National Audit Office, https://www.nao.org.uk/wp-content/uploads/2009/03/0809298.pdf

[6] J. Davey (2022) Britain's M&S Pulls Out of Russia and Warns on Outlook. *Reuters*, 25 May. https://www.reuters.com/business/retail-consumer/britains-ms-warns-outlook-profit-jumps-2022-05-25/

[7] BT Group, Our History. https://www.bt.com/about/bt/our-history

[8] This is a way of increasing EPS; even if total earnings do not increase, the number of shares decreases and so the EPS increases.

3 Many companies boast that they have succeeded in increasing dividends every year since anyone can remember. Compared with dividend expectations, profits are less predictable, less controllable, more cyclical, and more affected by one-off 'exceptional' items. Companies usually prefer to increase dividends only modestly in the very good years so that there is more scope for maintaining or increasing dividends in the lean years.

Pay out no dividends

There is a case for paying no dividends at all, even in successful companies. When a company is making serious losses or when it has massive borrowings, scrapping the dividend for a year or two makes good sense. Companies at an early stage of their development need all the money that they can get hold of, and so are not inclined to pay dividends. In the great dotcom and TMT[9] bubble of the late 1990s, many companies did not pay dividends. A quick look at the *Financial Times* will show which companies are not paying dividends; usually, there are plenty of mining companies and pharmaceuticals and biotechnology companies that have not yet found their pot of gold or wonder drug and are burning up cash in their efforts; there is unlikely to be a dividend until a worthwhile discovery has been developed.

If a company can invest the shareholders' money and earn a better rate of return than the shareholders can themselves, then there is a case for the company to keep the money and not pay dividends. If the money stays within the company, the value of its shares should increase. If shareholders need some income, they can sell a few shares; and (they hope!) the value of their shares will increase because of all the retained profits being reinvested. If they sell a few shares, they may have to pay capital gains tax, but for many shareholders, the taxation of capital gains is lower than the taxation on income from dividends. Paying no dividends at all may suit some companies and some shareholders - sometimes.

Dividend policy in practice

When making a dividend decision, companies need to take into consideration a variety of often conflicting factors. First, from a legal perspective, a company can only distribute its retained profits. Second, it needs to have the cash in the bank in order to pay a dividend, or an overdraft which will enable it to pay a dividend. Then, as will be seen in **Chapter 14**, if a company needs money to invest in attractive investment opportunities, that would usually reduce its dividend payment since it needs that money for profitable investment. By the same token, if it has available cash but no significant investment opportunities, that would be an argument in favour of paying a larger dividend. Furthermore, some companies tend to pay out a small dividend and that will attract shareholders who do not want a dividend but are attracted to companies which focus on growth, while other companies favour a high dividend policy which would tend to attract shareholders who are investing for high annual dividend income, perhaps the elderly.

Companies generally follow a consistent dividend payout policy, and so shareholders will be attracted to invest in companies with the dividend policy they prefer. Most companies do not opt for the extremes of no dividends or 100 per cent distribution. Usually, a proportion of profits is distributed. Listed companies typically pay out less than half of their profits as dividends. Recent constituents of the FTSE 100 index are shown in **Illustration 11.3** for the fiscal year 2023.

Company profits tend to fluctuate from year to year, not least because of 'exceptional' items such as profits or losses arising from the sale of non-current assets, or closing down part of the business. As shown in **Illustration 11.2**, it makes more sense to try to maintain a record of steady and increasing dividends rather than to pay out the same proportion of profits each year. Some companies pay an extra 'special' dividend in a particularly good year. But most try to keep an upward trend, even when profits fall. In general, there is no magic number that defines an ideal payout ratio as it largely depends on the sector in which a company operates.

[9] Technology, media and telecommunications.

ILLUSTRATION 11.3

	3i Group plc	Barclays Bank	Burberry	BAE systems plc	Lloyds Banking Group	BT Group
Dividend per share, pence	0.53	0.08	0.61	0.03	0.03	0.08
Dividend yield (5-year average), %	3.56	3.07	2.09	3.88	4.41	4.07
Dividend growth rate (5 year), %	12.05	–	8.11	6.21	−2.98	−12.94
Payout ratio (TTM), %	12.04	28.62	38.39	46.15	23.70	28.77

Source: Financial Times, 17 April 2024

In making dividend decisions, companies need to consider what 'signal' any change in dividends gives to investors. A sudden reduction in dividends suggests that directors are not confident about future years. Companies also need to consider what cash is available to pay dividends and their plans for expansion, investment and borrowing.

11.5 Other Sources of Finance

Companies are assumed to need funds to finance the purchase of fixed assets and inventories, and to pay expenses until the profits come rolling in, in the form of cash. In addition there is a need to finance working capital, but careful management of working capital can also be seen as a source of finance. If receivables or inventories are reduced, or if the time taken to pay trade payables is increased, funds are freed up to use for other purposes. The management of working capital is dealt with in **Chapter 12**.

There are various ways of avoiding, or minimizing, the need to raise finance:

1. Non-current assets can be leased instead of buying them. Obviously this applies to premises, but most machinery, equipment and vehicles can be leased if necessary. It is sometimes possible to arrange for an initial rent-free period to minimize initial funding requirements. But most lessors will not rent out equipment to any individual: the lessee usually needs to produce evidence that they are creditworthy.
2. Sale and leaseback. A business can raise finance by selling assets that it owns and wants to continue using through a finance company (such as a bank or insurance company), and then leasing the asset back from that company. This is often done with premises, and many chains of retail shops no longer own the freehold of their premises: they made a sale and leaseback arrangement. This can make sense both for the finance company and for the retailer. The finance company gets a guaranteed return in rental income at the going rate (say 5–7 per cent per annum); the retailer continues to use the premises and raises additional funds at a reasonable cost. The transaction will look good if the premises are sold for more than their book value: the profit contributes to an increase in earnings per share (EPS). This may be further boosted if the funds raised are used to increase profits or to reduce the number of shares.

   A cautious proprietor may prefer to retain the freehold of business premises; it can be used to provide security for loans where additional finance is needed.

3 Businesses often find that they have more non-current assets than they need, especially when they are in financial difficulties. Warehouses can be 'rationalized': the company may find that it can manage with two instead of six and raise substantial sums by selling off uneconomic premises.
4 Outsourcing or subcontracting some activities (e.g. computing, accounting, catering, manufacturing, cleaning, transport - indeed, almost anything) may free up surplus assets that can be sold to raise funds. It can also minimize the finance required for expansion.
5 Careful management of working capital can effectively reduce the financing needs of a business; reductions in working capital can produce additional cash.
6 Factoring or invoice discounting the company's trade receivables. These involve borrowing funds from a 'factor', usually a department of a bank, equivalent to an agreed percentage of trade receivables. Usually, the factor will manage the collection of those debts from customers, while in invoice discounting, the company itself will manage credit control.
7 Increasing profits also generates additional funds. This can be done either by reducing costs (e.g. eliminating a layer of management or transferring production to developing countries, such as China) or by increasing sales (the volume of sales and/or selling prices).
8 Reducing dividends, or even not paying dividends for a year or two, is another way of making more funds available.
9 Careful cash budgeting can also make more funds available when needed by delaying major payments at times when there is a particular shortage of cash. Sometimes the easiest way to deal with a cash shortage is to delay capital expenditure programmes.

Businesses rely mostly on funds contributed by their owners (sole proprietors, partners or shareholders), on borrowing money, and on generating profits that are ploughed back into the business. But there are more creative ways of financing businesses.

Summary

The published financial statements of companies show how they have been financed, and indicate the balance between safety and solvency, on the one hand, and risk and profitability, on the other. The safest way of financing a company is to issue more shares, but this can be an expensive business, and shareholders expect a high return. Borrowing is in many ways easier and cheaper, but excessive gearing can lead to excessive risk, which can adversely affect share prices, and increase the cost of borrowing. Retained profits are also an attractive source of funds, and companies need to have dividend policies that strike a balance between keeping shareholders happy, and retaining profits to finance expansion, where such reinvestment is justified. High gearing can enhance profitability, particularly during a period of low interest rates; but it also increases risk. Similar issues arise with the management of working capital. Minimizing levels of inventories and receivables can minimize the need for external finance, and enhance return on capital employed. But lowering levels of working capital make companies look less solvent. There are various more creative ways of financing a business, and there are no 'correct' solutions. Policies on gearing, dividends and working capital change as circumstances change, and a combination of several different approaches to financing a company is usually appropriate.

Review of key points

- The three main sources of funds for companies are share capital, borrowing and retained profits.
- There is no requirement to pay dividends to ordinary shareholders; they bear most of the risk of the business, and, if the business does well, will get substantial rewards.
- Borrowing can 'gear up' the return to the owners of the business, but excessive gearing is risky.
- Profits may be paid out to shareholders as dividends, or reinvested in the business as they are earned.
- Dividend policy strikes a balance between retaining funds within the business that are needed, and maintaining a payment record to satisfy shareholders.
- Much of business activity can be financed without using share capital, borrowing or retained profits.
- Published financials statements indicate the way in which a business has been financed, its dividend, gearing policies, and the effectiveness of its working capital management.

Self-testing questions

1 What are the three main sources of finance for businesses?
2 What are the main differences between preference shares and ordinary shares?
3 Explain the advantages and disadvantages of a company increasing its gearing.
4 You are given the following information about two companies:

Summarized statements of financial position as at 31 December

	TimeBall Company		DownsPier Company	
	Year 6	Year 7	Year 6	Year 7
	£000	£000	£000	£000
Total assets	350	402.2	400	354.1
Liabilities and equity				
Liabilities				
Current liabilities	50	60	100	70
9% debentures	100	140	100	50
	150	200	200	120
Equity				
Share capital	100	100	100	115
Share premium	-	-	-	15
Retained profits	100	102.2	100	104.1

Summarized statements of financial position as at 31 December

	TimeBall Company		DownsPier Company	
	Year 6	**Year 7**	**Year 6**	**Year 7**
	£000	**£000**	**£000**	**£000**
Total equity	200	202.2	200	234.1
Total liabilities and equity	350	402.2	400	354.1
Summarized income statements for year ended 31 December				
Sales	100	110	100	95
Gross profit	40	44	40	41
Operating profit	20	21.6	20	17.5
Interest	9	12.6	9	4.5
Pre-tax profit	11	9	11	13
Taxation	3.3	2.7	3.3	3.9
Profit after-tax	7.7	6.3	7.7	9.1
Dividends	4	4.1	4	5
Retained profit for the year	3.7	2.2	3.7	4.1

a You are required to calculate for each company for each year:
   - i capital gearing ratio;
   - ii interest cover;
   - iii dividend cover;
   - iv proportion of profits paid out as dividends.

b Explain what each shows.

c Comment on the financial performance and position of the two companies making use of appropriate ratios.

5 Explain what factors affect a company's dividend distribution in a year.

Assessment questions

1 Why might a company issue convertible preference shares rather than debentures?

2 The capital structure of two companies is as follows:

	Loborough plc	**Hiborough plc**
	£m	£m
Equity	180	50
11% debentures	20	150
	200	200

The EBIT of both companies was as follows:

Year 1	£19m
Year 2	£22.8m
Year 3	£15.2m

The rate of corporation tax on profits is 25 per cent.

a Calculate the net profit after-tax earned for ordinary shareholders for each year and for each company.

b Comment on the effect that gearing has had on the results.

3 The directors of the Palazine Company are seeking funding of £50m to finance an expansion programme. The summarized financial statements for the most recent year are set out below:

Income statement for the year ended 31 December year 6		**£000**
Sales		120,000
Cost of sales		90,000
Gross profit		30,000
Distribution costs	8,000	
Administration expenses	12,000	(20,000)
Operating profit		10,000
Debenture interest		(5,000)
Net profit before taxation		5,000
Taxation		(3,000)
Net profit after taxation		2,000
Dividends		(1,000)
Retained profit for year		1,000

Statement of financial position as at 31 December year 6		£000
Non-current assets		
Land and buildings (market value £55m)		45,000
Plant and machinery		18,000
Investments at cost (market value £30m)		45,000
		108,000
Current assets		
Inventories	8,000	
Receivables	5,000	
Cash	1,000	14,000
Total assets		**122,000**
Current liabilities		
Payables		24,000

Income statement for the year ended 31 December year 6		£000
Non-current liabilities		
10% debentures (secured)		50,000
Equity		
Share capital	30,000	
Retained earnings	18,000	48,000
		122,000

The following suggestions have been made for raising the additional finance. You are required to explain the effects of each suggestion and comment on their practicability.

The company could:

i issue more debentures;

ii make a sale and leaseback arrangement on its premises;

iii sell its investments (although some directors object to this as it would involve a loss of £15m);

iv reduce inventories by one-half;

v halve the period that trade receivables are allowed to pay (assume all sales are on credit);

vi extend the period for paying trade payables by 50 per cent;

vii use the reserves;

viii issue more ordinary shares;

ix obtain a bank overdraft.

4 The earnings per share, the dividend per share and the share price of Uppen Down plc for the last few years are shown below (in pence):

	Year 1	Year 2	Year 3	Year 4	Year 5	Year 6	Year 7
EPS	20	25	18	30	10	13	24
Div	10	10.4	10.8	11.2	11.7	12.2	12.7
Share price	300	400	200	270	250	270	300

a You are required to calculate the dividend cover for each year, the payout ratio as the proportion of profits that were distributed as dividends, and the dividend yield based on the share price at the year end given above.

b Comment on the company's dividend policy.

c Since the end of year 7 the dividend yield, as shown in the *Financial Times*, has increased to 10 per cent. What is this likely to indicate?

5 An extract of Sky High plc's statement of financial position as at 1 October year 6 is given below:

	£000
Ordinary share capital @ £1 each	1,000
Revaluation reserve	2,500
Retained profits	3,200
	6,700

On 1 January year 7, the company issued 1 right share for every 5 in issue for £4 each when the market price was £5.

a Show how the rights issue should be accounted for in the statement of financial position.

b Calculate the theoretical share price of Sky High plc after the rights issue. Explain why, in reality, the share price may differ from the theoretical price.

Group activities and discussion questions

1 What is the minimum amount of funding with which it is possible to start a business? Could a business be started with zero funds? What sort of business could each member of the group start, with little or no funding? Prepare a (very brief) business plan. Would it be necessary to raise substantial funding to develop the business so that it becomes large scale? How would you define 'large scale' (big enough to provide you with a suitable lifestyle; big enough for a stock market listing)?

2 Prepare a list of companies that are not currently paying dividends. (Look for shares with a zero yield in the *Financial Times*'s listing.) Why are these companies not paying dividends? Each member of the group could research a number of companies. Can the companies be classified into groups each with similar reasons for not paying dividends (e.g. developing new products/services; recent losses)?

3 Why are some companies high-geared, and others low-geared? Each member of the group should examine the statements of financial position of a number of companies, probably in different sectors. It may be easiest to do this using the companies' websites. The group should agree the way in which gearing should be measured (e.g. is short-term borrowing to be included with long-term borrowing?). Are utility companies more highly geared than retailers? Are breweries more highly geared than oil companies? Can you identify what factors seem to be associated with high gearing and low gearing?

4 Prepare a list of companies which have arranged bonus (scrip) issues in the last three months. (You can look at the *Financial Times* website for this information.) Note down the share price before and after the bonus issue and the market capitalization (shown in Monday's *Financial Times*) before and after the scrip issue. How much has the total value of the company (market capitalization) changed as a result of the bonus issue?

Accounting in context

Discuss and comment on the following report taken from the press with reference to the evolution in the sources of capital available to companies.

KKR – $6.4bn raised for second Asian infrastructure fund

KKR, the renowned investment firm listed on the New York Stock Exchange, has raised a record $6.4bn for its latest Asian infrastructure fund, topping a month of strong investment movement in the sector despite some slake in fundraising by the broader private equity firms. At $6.4bn, KKR's Asia Pacific Infrastructure Partners II fund is the largest pan-regional infrastructure-dedicated fund.

The private equity group has added a second fund to its Asian infrastructure business, bringing its assets under management to $13bn. The company has been focusing its investments on markets such as India and Southeast Asia and has avoided investing in China despite it being the region's largest economy.

Infrastructure has become a popular investment for private equity firms due to its stable long-term returns, especially in the energy transition and digitalization sectors amid global volatility.

David Luboff, who is the co-head of Asia-Pacific and also the regional head of infrastructure at KKR, stated that he anticipates increased dealmaking activity in the current year, following a lull in 2020. He expects this trend to continue due to the emergence of new sources of capital, including direct investors, along with private equity players. Luboff said the new fund would apply 'modest leverage' in its deals and focus on 'geographies where we felt the track record, as well as the supply of opportunities, the regulatory backdrop, was supportive'. That included India, South Korea, the Philippines, Japan, Singapore, Australia and New Zealand, he added.

BlackRock purchased Global Infrastructure Partners for $12.5bn to create the world's largest infrastructure firm, while the Australian Macquarie Group raised over €8bn for its new European infrastructure fund.

Blackstone, Stonepeak and I Squared Capital have expressed increasing interest in infrastructure investments as governments face funding pressures.

Source: R. Mercedes and K. Wiggins (2024) KKR Raises $6.4bn for Infrastructure Fund in Asia. *Financial Times*, 2 February.

References and further reading

Adrian, T. (2023) Higher-for-Longer Interest Rate Environment is Squeezing More Borrowers. *IMF Blog*, 10 October. https://www.imf.org/en/Blogs/Articles/2023/10/10/higher-for-longer-interest-rate-environment-is-squeezing-more-borrowers (accessed 13 May 2024).

Boakes, K. (2010) *Reading and Understanding the Financial Times*. Upper Saddle River, NJ: FT Prentice Hall.

Financial Times (daily newspaper) www.ft.com.

Hillier, D., Ross, S., Westerfield, R., Jaffe, J. and Jordan, B. (2010) *Corporate Finance* (1st European edn.). Maidenhead: McGraw-Hill Education.

Investors Chronicle (weekly magazine).

Kershaw, D. (2016) The Market for Corporate Control: Value, Stakeholders, and Governance, in *Principles of Takeover Regulation* (online edn.). New York: Oxford Academic. https://doi.org/10.1093/oso/9780199659555.003.0001 (accessed 17 April 2024).

McKenzie, W. (2010) *Financial Times Guide to Using and Interpreting Company Accounts* (4th edn.). Upper Saddle River, NJ: FT Prentice Hall.

Modigliani, F. and Miller, M. (1958) The Cost of Capital, Corporation Finance and the Theory of Investment *American Economic Review*, June: 261–97.

Rees, B. (2011) *Financial Analysis* (3rd edn.). Upper Saddle River, NJ: FT Prentice Hall.

Vernimmen, P., Quiry, P., Dallocchio, M., Le Fur, Y. and Salvi, A. (2009) *Corporate Finance: Theory and Practice*. Chichester: Wiley.

Watson, D., Head, A., Chan, D., and Watson, D. (2023) *Corporate Finance: Principles and Practice* (9th edn.). London: Pearson.

https://markets.ft.com/data/equities/tearsheet/summary?s=AZN:LSE

https://www.accaglobal.com/uk/en/student/exam-support-resources/professional-exams-study-resources/strategic-business-reporting/technical-articles/debt-equity.html

https://www.iasplus.com/en-gb/standards/ias/ias32

www.londonstockexchange.com

Chapter 12

Management of Working Capital

Chapter contents

12.1 Introduction
12.2 Definition and Importance of Working Capital
12.3 Economic order quantity (EOQ)

Learning objectives

After studying this chapter you will be able to:

- ✓ Define working capital and explain its importance in relation to solvency, overtrading and profitability
- ✓ Explain how to manage receivables and calculate the financial implications of different policies for managing receivables
- ✓ Discuss the control of inventories and apply the economic order quantity (EOQ) model
- ✓ Explain how to plan, control and manage cash, and how to manage and avoid cash crises
- ✓ Understand the role of control and management of payables

12.1 Introduction

The planning and management of working capital is an important part of the financing of a business. High levels of inventories and receivables tie up large amounts of finance; reductions in inventories and receivables, and increases in payables, provide extra finance for the business.

12.2 Definition and Importance of Working Capital

A large part of a company's capital is usually tied up in non-current assets such as buildings and machinery for a period of years. But companies also need some capital to finance short-term assets such as inventories and receivables, and there is a need for some cash for day-to-day operations. The amount of long-term capital available after financing non-current assets is known as 'working capital', which may be defined as:

Long-term funds − non-current assets = working capital

Alternatively, working capital represents the net current assets available for maintaining the day-to-day operational activities. Working capital can easily be calculated as the difference between the current assets and the current liabilities.

From the statement of financial position in **Illustration 12.1** we can see that working capital in years 1 and 2 was:

Long-term funds = equity + non-current liabilities

Year 1 85,000 + 110,000 − 140,000 = £55,000
Year 2 88,000 + 135,000 − 138,000 = £85,000

ILLUSTRATION 12.1

Statements of financial position of Solverham Company Ltd as at 31 December

	Year 1	**Year 2**
	£000	**£000**
Non-current assets (at cost)	200	220
Provision for depreciation	(60)	(82)
Net book value	140	138
Current assets		
Inventories	95	70
Receivables	80	50
Cash	–	25
	175	145
Total assets	315	283
Current liabilities		
Payables	40	60
Overdraft	80	–
	120	60
Non-current liabilities		
12% debentures	110	135
Equity		
Share capital	50	50

Statements of financial position of Solverham Company Ltd as at 31 December		
	Year 1	Year 2
	£000	£000
Retained earnings	35	38
	85	88
Total liabilities plus equity	315	283

The more usual definition of working capital is:

Current assets − current liabilities = working capital

From the statement of financial position above we can see that working capital is:

Year 1 175,000 − 120,000 = £55,000
Year 2 145,000 − 60,000 = £85,000

The two definitions appear to be different, but provided all items on the statement of financial position are classified under the same five headings, the two approaches will produce the same figure.

Although most businesses finance their inventories and receivables partly from their long-term funds, current assets are also partly financed by payables and other current liabilities. In year 2, Solverham (**Illustration 12.1**) had inventories of £70,000; £60,000 of this was financed by current liabilities. In some companies, particularly retailers, inventories are wholly financed by short-term creditors.

How much working capital should a business have?

There is usually a relationship between a company's turnover and the amount of working capital it has. In **Chapter 4**, ratios 14, 15 and 16 express inventories, receivables, and payables in relation to the cost of sales or turnover. As turnover increases, we can expect working capital to increase in proportion. If turnover goes up by 25 per cent, it does not mean that the amount of cash coming into the business immediately goes up by 25 per cent: there is likely to be an increase in inventories and receivables (partly financed by an increase in creditors).

However, companies should do more than watch working capital drift upwards; there is a need for proper planning and control. There is, however, no ideal level for working capital. It is a question of balancing (a) *solvency* against (b) *profitability*, that is, risk against reward.

Objectives of working capital management

A critical aspect of managing working capital is ensuring that a business has enough liquidity available to meet its obligations in a timely manner. If a company has inadequate working capital, it may struggle to pay its employees, suppliers and other creditors on time, leading to negative consequences such as loss of trust, supplier discounts and harm to the credit score. In the worst-case scenario, a business may be forced to sell its assets if it cannot repay its creditors.

The other primary goal of working capital management is to optimize profitability. Funds tied up in working capital typically provide minimal or no returns. Consequently, a business with excessive working capital may not generate the anticipated return on investment expected by its investors, which is calculated as operating profit divided by total equity and long-term liabilities.

As a result, it is essential to find the right balance between liquidity and profitability when determining the optimal level of working capital.

A company that is very safe in terms of solvency will have lots more current assets than current liabilities. There will always be more than enough current assets, either in the form of cash or receivables (and even inventories), that will soon become cash to meet short-term liabilities as they fall due. This short-term financial strength can be expressed in the form of *current ratios* and *liquidity ratios*. In **Illustration 12.2**, the first of the four companies (Alice Ltd) has the most working capital, the strongest current ratio (3:1), and the strongest liquidity ratio (2:1). The fourth company (Dora Ltd) has the least working capital: a negative amount! Dora also has a very low current ratio (0.17:1) and a very low liquidity ratio (0.1:1).

ILLUSTRATION 12.2

	Alice Ltd	Bertha Ltd	Colin Ltd	Dora Ltd
	£000	£000	£000	£000
Non-current assets	150	150	150	150
Current assets				
Inventories	100	50	100	4
Receivables	150	80	150	2
Bank/cash	50	10	–	4
	300	140	250	10
Current liabilities				
Payables	100	80	200	60
Overdraft	–	–	50	–
	100	80	250	60
Working capital	200	60	–	(50)
Net assets = capital employed	350	210	150	100
Profit	35	35	35	35
Return on capital employed	10%	16.7%	23.3%	35%

A company that is more concerned with profitability than with appearing to be solvent will concentrate on keeping down the amount of working capital. In order to maximize return on capital employed companies need not only to maximize profits or returns, but also to minimize capital employed (ROCE) in relation to profits. Other things being equal, companies that manage with the least working capital are likely to be the most profitable ones.

Each of the four companies in **Illustration 12.2** has the same amount of non-current assets and the same amount of profit. The only difference between the companies is the amount of working capital they have. As working capital decreases, so the ROCE increases. The company with the lowest amount of working capital (Dora Ltd has £50,000 *negative* working capital) has the highest ROCE (35 per cent).

In terms of solvency or liquidity, however, Dora looks very weak. There are payables of £60,000, but current assets amount to only £10,000. Few businesses would have such a pattern of working capital (perhaps a florist's shop; inventories would be low because fresh flowers do not keep for long). Retailers tend to sell mostly on a cash basis, and so a low receivables figure is to be expected. Retailers buy mostly on credit and so a significant creditors' figure is normal.

Although there is no 'normal' level of working capital, we can see that higher levels of working capital are associated with higher levels of solvency; and lowering levels of working capital can increase profitability.

Overtrading

Having too little working capital is associated with 'overtrading'. This occurs when a company is trying to do too much business with too little long-term capital. If a company generates lots of cash and manages its working capital carefully, it may survive and prosper even if it appears to be overtrading. But having insufficient liquid resources (or access to them) to meet liabilities as they fall due is fatal for businesses.

The problem can start with a major outflow of cash, perhaps to buy additional non-current assets or another business, to repay a loan, or to pay too much out as dividends. It is sometimes the result of success: rapid expansion can lead to a rapid outflow of cash (inventories, receivables and non-current assets all increase) before the cash comes in from customers. High levels of inflation make the problem worse: the amount of cash required to replace assets increases in line with inflation.

Overtrading can also be the result of failure. A company that makes substantial losses is likely to find that cash is haemorrhaging out of the business. A mild case of overtrading is easily treated with various tactics to bring in cash more quickly. Accounts receivables can be pressed to pay more quickly; inventories can be reduced by control of new purchases and by extra efforts to sell inventory; and payments to creditors may be delayed.

A cash shortage, the effects of reducing inventories and receivables, and the increase in payables soon reduce a company's current ratio. A trend of falling current ratios is a matter of concern.

In a serious case of overtrading, the symptoms get worse, and attempts to deal with it can lead to further deterioration. The overdraft limit can often be increased, but if an increased limit is breached, the bank may demand the closure and repayment of the overdraft immediately. If a company reduces its inventories too much, it will soon find that it is losing business because it is unable to supply what its customers want. Customers will go elsewhere if they are pushed too hard to pay their bills too quickly. Trade payables will usually put up with a little delay, but most will not tolerate repeated or increased delays. If a company cannot pay its bills without excessive delay, it will soon find that it is unable to obtain supplies on credit. If it is to continue in business, it has to find cash to buy supplies, which makes the original problem worse.

Many of us have been in shops where the signs of overtrading are obvious. There is very little on the shelves because suppliers are no longer willing to sell to them on credit. Each day, the shopkeeper hopes to bring in a few hundred pounds from customers so that they can go to their local cash and carry to replace what they have sold; they cannot buy very much because they have to use some of the cash to pay off some of the amounts due to whichever creditors are pressing hardest.

Often, it is a wage bill that precipitates the crisis, especially at the stage when the bank is no longer willing to honour cheques because the business has (again!) exceeded its overdraft limit. At this stage, desperate measures are needed. When difficulties first arise, surplus assets are sold off to raise cash. Towards the end, it even has to sell essential assets and sell off stocks at ridiculously low prices to bring in some cash to survive another day. At this stage, the business has little chance of survival.

It is not difficult to spot the early symptoms of overtrading, and good financial planning and management can avoid a crisis. The usual problem is trying to do too much with too little money, especially where there is too little long-term finance. Solutions include raising more long-term capital and careful management of working capital and profitability, with a particular emphasis on cash budgeting so that crises can be identified and averted before they become critical to survival (see **Example 12.1**).

Example 12.1

Basic working capital cycle

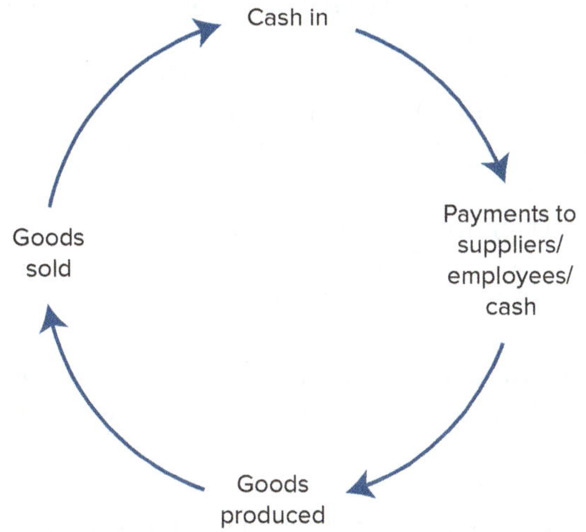

A manufacturer buys goods on credit, uses those goods in production, and then sells those finished goods. At each stage in this process, there is a time gap. It takes time between buying goods and production, between production and selling the goods, and the objective is to minimize the gap between each stage. Additionally, there is a time delay from each stage in its effect on cash. A business will try to minimize the time between paying for goods it has purchased to manufacture and sell and receipts of cash from its customers. In order to optimize its management of working capital and the effect of these time delays on its bank balance, it must control its stockholding and production process, its credit control by managing its receivables and the positive effect on its bank balance in paying its suppliers.

Managing receivables

Financial managers may prefer to minimize the amounts tied up in accounts receivables (debtors). This minimizes the requirements for external funding. If accounts receivables are reduced, cash is brought into the business more quickly, the amount of capital employed is reduced, and profitability is increased.

Some businesses sell on a cash-only basis: there are no receivables. Some (such as mail-order companies) require customers to pay in advance, and their account receivables can be negative. Others (particularly service providers such as airlines) require part of full payment in advance; this reduces the amount tied up in account receivables.

Offering credit facilities to customers may be an important part of marketing strategy, and it is usually essential when supplying governments and other major organizations. But it has its costs: bad debts, administration of customers' accounts, credit control (chasing customers to pay on time), and the cost of capital (money tied up in receivables may be used more effectively elsewhere). If a company is partly financed by an overdraft that costs 10 per cent per annum, and the level of their receivables is £100,000, then the cost of financing those debtors is £10,000 per annum. It is worth calculating whether the costs of offering credit facilities are justified by the contribution earned by the additional business generated.

If a business decides that it will sell on credit, the following steps should be taken to encourage customers to pay on time, and to minimize losses through bad debts.

Accepting credit customers

It would be foolish to sell on credit to every individual; there are always a few dodgy customers who will not pay up. There are various ways of deciding who is likely to be creditworthy:

1. *Personal judgement and the impression someone creates.* This is still important and no amount of investigation or calculation can eliminate the need for personal judgement. Even the most reputable companies and individuals (and even countries' governments) get into financial difficulties and are unable to pay their bills. But we should not rely on a smart suit and a flashy car being the guarantee of financial strength; they can be financed by excessive borrowing. A visit to a customer's premises can be revealing: many businesses with impressive internet sites and publicity are operated from a backroom above a shop or a teenager's bedroom.
2. *Bankers' references.* Although they may say very little that is useful, with current money-laundering regulations, the mere fact that someone has a bank account is some indication that they exist and have an address (or they did when they opened the account).
3. *Business annual reports and accounts.* These can be checked before accepting a credit customer. They show what liabilities a business already has and indicate its financial strength and ability to pay liabilities as they fall due. It is also worth calculating its payables ratio: how long it seems to take to pay existing creditors.
4. *Ask other creditors how reliable a company is in paying its bills.* This can be done formally by obtaining trade references. It may be more revealing if done informally through business contacts. Often it becomes widely known when a particular company becomes a slow payer.
5. *Credit-rating agencies.* Agencies such as Experian, Moody's, and S&P Global provide information on the creditworthiness of individuals and firms; this can be done immediately by telephone or the Internet.

How much credit to allow

The amount of credit allowed to customers should be limited in four ways:

1. *Time.* It is important to be clear about how long customers are allowed to pay, perhaps within 30 days. It is wise to have a contract with the agreed terms for payment, with penalties for delay.
2. *Amount of money.* Each customer should have a credit limit based on their size and creditworthiness. It could be millions of pounds for a government body, but perhaps only £100 for a student!
3. *Maximum for an individual receivable.* Many businesses rely too heavily on one or two major customers. If one such customer does not pay up, the business may go bankrupt. It is important for a business to know that there is not an individual receivable owing an amount large enough to bring the business down if they do not pay.
4. *Maximum total receivables figure.* It may be prudent to estimate the maximum total receivables figure that the business can afford to finance. Profitable expansion usually looks attractive, but if it involves additional working capital that the business cannot afford, it could be very risky.

Collecting the money

The first step in collecting the money from trade receivables is to send out the paperwork promptly and correctly and for it to be clear when payment is due. Small businesses are often lax about this: proprietors are often more keen on their product or service than they are on paperwork. Larger businesses usually have fairly tight - sometimes aggressive - credit control systems.

When payments come in, it is necessary to check the amounts received carefully; some customers are skilled at disputing invoices, delaying payments and taking discounts to which they are not entitled.

Offering cash discounts for prompt payment can be an effective way of encouraging customers to pay within, say, 14 days. But the cost of offering such discounts needs to be carefully calculated. A 10 per cent discount may encourage customers to pay up, say, one month early. But a 10 per cent discount for one month is very expensive - equivalent to 120 per cent per annum! Even a discount of 4 per cent may prove too expensive, as shown in **Example 12.2**. More modest discounts of, say, 1 per cent, may not be enough incentive for early payment. It might be more cost-effective to employ a competent credit controller to chase debtors to pay up promptly. Another approach is to charge interest on late payments.

Example 12.2

Last year, the Vinelia Building Company's turnover was £12m. All sales were made on credit. Their account receivables figure was £3m at the statement of financial position date, and that figure was typical throughout the year.

The company usually has a large overdraft and their cost of capital is 15 per cent per annum. The sales director recommends offering customers a 4 per cent discount for prompt payment and estimates that this would halve the receivables figure.

The costs and benefits of this proposal would be as follows:

		£000s
Current account receivables		3,000
Revised account receivables		1,500
Reduction in account receivables		1,500
Saving on interest cost	1,500*15%	225
Cost of discount	12,000*4%	480
Net cost of using early settlement discount		(225)

The cost of offering the discount is more than the saving in interest. Therefore providing a discount for early settlement of the accounts receivable is not financially acceptable.

It is important to have a credit control system that carefully monitors the payment record of customers, and what has been done about late payers. It is usual to produce an 'age analysis' of receivables, showing minimal detail if the sale took place only a month or two previously but where amounts have been outstanding for more than two or three months, the amounts and dates should be carefully detailed for each customer, together with what action had been taken, and what promises and payments have been received. As a basic part of the credit control system, the analysis should be regularly examined so that any appropriate follow-up action may be taken. The financial costs and benefits of a credit control system can be seen in **Example 12.3**.

Example 12.3

The Vinelia Building Company (as in **Example 12.2**) is considering employing a credit controller and instituting more effective procedures for collecting money from receivables. The annual cost of doing this is expected to be £40,000. If the average period taken by receivables to pay their bills is reduced from three months to two and a half months, would this expense be justified?

		£000s
Current account receivables	£12m × 3/12	3,000
Revised account receivables	£12m × 2.5/12	2,500
Reduction in account receivables		500
Annual savings in interest	£500,000 × 15%	75
Additional costs		40
Net benefit		35

An additional expenditure of £40,000 a year is justified if it reduces the average level of receivables by £500,000 and interest costs by £75,000 a year.

When payments do not come in on time the next step is a prompt and polite reminder. Problems arise when customers have still not paid a few weeks after the due date. There are three main approaches to get customers to pay up:

1 *Phoning them, following up promises to pay and visiting them.* Sales staff are not usually keen on the sordid business of asking their customers for money. But continuing to supply customers who do not pay can be fatal to a business.
2 *Withdrawing supplies to customers.* Sometimes, it may be best to negotiate a compromise: supplies will continue if the customer pays for them on delivery and begins to pay off some of the amounts due for previous supplies.
3 *Threatening legal action.* The threat should be enough to frighten most customers into paying promptly. Legal action can be very expensive, but threats are cheap: a routine letter (that appears to come) from solicitors may be cost effective.

The costs and benefits of different approaches

The costs of having receivables include:

1 Cost of capital
2 Administration
3 Bad debts
4 Discount allowed.

Companies need to evaluate the costs and benefits involved in different strategies. Sometimes they may want to increase sales by offering more attractive payment terms. If we know the contribution/sales ratio of a company[1] we can estimate the additional profits that will be brought in by an increase in sales. We can also estimate the amount by which receivables will be increased by offering more attractive credit terms. If we also know the company's cost of capital, we can estimate the annual cost of an increase in debtors. We can then calculate if it appears to be worthwhile to offer more generous credit terms to customers, as shown in **Example 12.4**.

[1] Contribution as a percentage of sales, as explained in Section 17.2.

Example 12.4

The Tightar Company specializes in surfacing driveways and minor roads. It has a strict credit control policy because it is short of funds, and depends on an overdraft that has an interest rate of 18 per cent per annum.

It does not undertake work for public institutions or building contractors because such customers are slow to pay, taking on average 10 weeks.

The company's annual turnover is £520,000, and its average receivables figure at any one time is £30,000.

The direct costs of surfacing a driveway amount to 40 per cent of the selling price.

Would it be worth extending its average credit period to 10 weeks if it could double turnover?

Direct costs as a proportion of turnover	40%		
Contribution as a proportion of turnover	60%		
Proposed additional sales	£520,000		
Additional contribution (60%)	£520,000 × 60%	=	£312,000
Existing receivables figure			£ 30,000
New turnover	£520,000 × 2	=	£1,040,000
New receivables figure	$\frac{10 \text{ weeks}}{52 \text{ weeks}}$ × £1,040,000	=	£200,000
Increase in receivables	£200,000 - £30,000	=	£ 170,000
Annual interest cost of the increase in receivables	18% × £170,000	=	£ 30,600
Therefore, a net benefit	£312,000 - £30,600	=	£281,400

It is worthwhile to pay interest on the necessary additional borrowings because the cost of the interest is substantially lower than the additional contribution generated.

Factoring and invoice discounting

A business can outsource or subcontract almost any activity, including the management of receivables. With factoring, most of the money tied up in receivables (typically 75–80 per cent) can be turned into cash immediately rather than waiting for the duration of the credit term.

When it comes to factoring, there are two options, as explained below:

1. *Recourse factoring.* If a company chooses this option, the factor can ask for money back from the company if it is unable to collect payment from trade receivables.
2. *Non-recourse factoring.* With this option, the factor takes on all the risk of uncollectible receivables, and the company is not liable for them.

Factoring companies usually charge a lower rate for recourse factoring because they are not taking on all the risk. With non-recourse factoring, the factor is taking on all the risk, so they charge a higher rate to compensate for that risk.

The factoring company provides the money and charges interest for so doing; it can also provide the administration of the client's sales accounting, invoicing and credit control, for which they also charge a fee, typically between 0.75 per cent and 2 per cent turnover. These costs may be more than offset by savings in the business's own administration and advantages in getting the money in more quickly so that it can be used for other, more profitable purposes. Factoring is likely to be particularly appropriate in small, rapidly growing businesses where the business has relatively little expertise in credit control. The factor is likely to be more efficient and effective, with economies of scale in carrying out its specialist activity. Using a factor can mean that cash from debtors becomes readily available as the business expands; otherwise, the need to finance working capital can be a significant constraint on growth: increased sales usually require increases in inventory and receivables that are only partly financed by payables. Factoring can be a way of financing growth.

Factoring can be done confidentially so that customers do not know that a third party is collecting a company's receivables. A business should be careful when calculating the costs and benefits of using a factor: it may seem to be more expensive, but if it is more effective in the long run, it may prove to be more economical. It usually has to be a long-term arrangement: once a business becomes reliant on getting the cash in quickly by using a factor, it is difficult to go back and establish a replacement source of finance and set up a credit control function again. Another disadvantage of factoring is that, sometimes, the factor may be unwilling to take on particular types of customers where it anticipates problems.

Invoice discounting is usually a short-term way of using receivables to quickly make cash available. In effect, the receivables are 'sold' to a financial institution that provides around 75 per cent of the amount immediately. The client (not the financial institution) continues with the administration of receivables and continues to bear any risks of bad debts. This usually applies only to selected receivables and can be a useful source of short-term finance.

Managing inventories

Inventories of raw materials, work in progress, and finished goods can be reduced by careful budgeting and planning and the use of techniques such as the economic order quantity (EOQ).

It is always handy to have lots of materials in stock just in case it might be needed. But holding stock is a very expensive business. There are all the costs involved in providing storage space, including rent, rates, lighting, heating, insurance, security and administration. But the most substantial costs of holding stocks are:

1. *The cost of capital.* A company's cost of capital might typically be 10-15 per cent per annum. This means that, just in terms of the cost of capital, it costs between £10,000 and £15,000 a year to have an average inventory of £100,000.
2. *Obsolescence.* Clothes go out of fashion, publications go out of date, and technological items are soon superseded. Stocks of computers, software or mobile phones that are only a year or two old are worth very little. Inventories of goods for sale, and even raw materials and components, rapidly become out of date.
3. *Physical deterioration.* Inventories physically deteriorate - or even disappear - in various ways. Some things are eaten by rats and other creatures; some things evaporate, go mouldy, or become unusable in a variety of ways.

Holding inventories is expensive, typically costing perhaps 25 per cent per annum. A company that, on average, holds an inventory of £100,000 is likely to incur costs of about £25,000 a year. In order to maximize profitability, there is pressure to reduce inventory levels. Various approaches are used to achieve this.

Where finished goods inventory appears to be excessive, there has presumably been a mismatch between the sales budget and the production budget - too much has been produced. This can be tackled by using appropriate control information more quickly and considering special offers to clear existing inventories.

It is also worth concentrating only on the most valuable items in stock. Sometimes as much as 90 per cent of the value of inventory may be in only 10 per cent of the items. It may not be worth bothering too much about lots of small items of little value.

12.3 Economic Order Quantity (EOQ)

Various quantitative techniques are available for effective management of inventories. If the aim is to keep inventories at as low a level as practicable, there is a need to order small quantities at frequent intervals. But every time an order is placed, there are significant administrative costs: placing the order, checking what has been received, and checking and paying invoices. The administrative costs of ordering suggest that it would be better to order larger quantities less frequently. It is possible to balance these two factors, as shown in **Example 12.5**.

Example 12.5

The Chemvee company uses 10,000 special-purpose disks each year and pays 50 pence each. The ordering cost associated with each order is £200, and annual stockholding costs are estimated at 25 per cent per annum. Calculate the economic order quantity (EOQ).

$$\text{EOQ} = \sqrt{\frac{2 \times \text{annual demand} \times \text{ordering cost}}{\text{Price per unit} \times \text{stockholding cost}}}$$

$$= \sqrt{(2 \times 10{,}000 \times £\,200) \div (£\,0.50 \times 0.25)}$$

$$= \sqrt{4{,}000{,}000 \div 0.125} = 5{,}657$$

The EOQ is 5,657 units.

If the company orders 5,657 units at a time, it will have to order (10,000 ÷ 5,657 = 1.77) just less than twice a year: about once in 29 weeks. The average annual ordering cost will be 1.77 × £200 = £354 per annum.

When it receives each new order, it will have 5,657 units in inventory that will be gradually whittled down to zero units. On average, it will have half of the 5,657 units in inventory (2,828½ each costing 50 pence), amounting to £1,414. Annual stockholding costs amount to 25 per cent of the inventory (0.25 × £1,414 = £354).

We can see that the EOQ is the quantity at which the annual inventory holding cost is equal to the annual ordering cost. If the company ordered more often, the annual cost of ordering would increase, as would the annual inventory holding cost.

A formula such as this is useful in drawing attention to two key variables in determining inventory levels and providing rough guidelines. In practice, it might be difficult to determine ordering costs and stockholding costs with the accuracy inherent in the formula's use. Even annual demand may not be so predictable. A more serious weakness of the EOQ formula is that it ignores quantity discounts. It is often possible to negotiate price reductions in return for more substantial order quantities.

Just in time

The just-in-time approach to inventory planning and control is that goods are purchased or produced only when they are needed. A fine line is drawn so that inventories are neither too high, with the associated stockholding costs, or too low, so that customers cannot be supplied. A just-in-time policy is only suitable when there is reliable sales forecasting and when the supply of materials and production is fast and reliable. Supermarkets have fresh bread delivered every day, just in time to meet customers' demands. Similarly, manufacturers can have components delivered just in time to meet production schedules; this minimizes the amount of inventories held. It is highly dependent on managing good quality relationships with suppliers. Traditional managers may be tempted to keep large inventories 'just in case' they are needed. But the pressures of financial management lead to the use of a variety of approaches to minimizing inventory levels.

Managing cash

Planning and control of cash (and bank) is an essential part of financing a business. New and rapidly expanding businesses are often short of cash; unplanned overdrafts can incur very high rates of interest. In serious cases, the bank may withdraw support, and the business is then unable to meet its liabilities. In some businesses, excessive amounts of cash can be a problem and lead to underperformance. The business may earn interest on its deposits at modest rates (currently 4 or 5 per cent per annum), but shareholders expect their funds to be used more profitably. Sometimes companies have large hoards of cash that they keep to be ready to buy another business; sometimes companies have surplus funds, and they do not seem to know what to do with them; and sometimes these surplus funds are returned to shareholders as extra dividends, or the company buys up its own shares on the market and cancels them.

Careful planning and control of cash should ensure that sufficient long-term funds are available to finance all long-term assets; that additional funds are retained or raised to meet planned high levels of investment whether in non-current assets or acquiring other businesses; and that working capital is properly planned and financed, partly from current liabilities. Overdrafts are an appropriate source of finance to meet temporary or seasonal requirements. Cash budgeting is an essential tool of financial management, and businesses should plan their financing requirements over a three- to five-year period. Cash budgeting is dealt with in **Chapter 7** and the main approaches to raising finance are outlined in this chapter. Liquidity problems become apparent in interpreting financial statements, as shown in **Chapter 4**, and cash flow statements can be used to review a company's performance, as shown in **Chapter 7**.

Where a company has liquidity problems, the ideal solution may be to raise more equity finance (by issuing shares); but a number of approaches suggested below may minimize the problem in the short term.

Liquidity problems can be minimized by good housekeeping. Prompt banking of all receipts will minimize cash shortages and interest charges. Centralized banking should ensure that any cash shortages in one part of the business are offset by surpluses elsewhere. Payments should not be made ahead of schedule and sending a cheque rather than using a bank transfer helps to retain funds within the business for a few more days. But customers should be encouraged to pay by the fastest means. Creditors should be paid at the time of the month when the business normally has most money in the bank, not at the same time as it pays wages and salaries. It is also important to maintain good relationships with bankers, letting them see budgets, and keeping within agreed limits; the role of bankers can be vital when times are tough. Careful planning and monitoring can avoid liquidity problems.

Where there are more serious liquidity problems, the business may need to take emergency measures that could include a desperate trip to the bank. Banks are always willing to help if they are sure that the customer will repay (and has assets as security), but can make high charges in situations that look risky, and may refuse to help if they have no confidence in the management of the business. Delaying payments to payables may be necessary. Receivables can be encouraged to pay more quickly. Selling off stocks at low prices will bring in cash, at the expense of profits. Capital expenditure can be postponed or cancelled. Surplus assets can be sold off: many businesses have some assets that are underutilized. Sometimes large companies, in times of crisis, suddenly appear to discover that they have expensive head office buildings in the centre of London, or country houses, or sports grounds (or even executive jets) that they do not really need. Smaller businesses can consider transferring their main administrative office to the spare bedroom at home! And businesses can free up cash by selling off company cars and using taxis or bicycles instead, especially when the only realistic alternative is bankruptcy. It may be possible or necessary to defer the payment of taxes; this can usually be negotiated with HM Revenue & Customs, although, of course, interest will be payable. The payment of dividends can also be delayed, reduced or cancelled, although it looks better if this is planned.

Some short-term crisis measures can do more harm than good, especially if there is an underlying problem, such as overtrading. But tackling a problem promptly and harshly is better than undue optimism - a key cause of business failure.

Managing payables

To some extent, inventories and receivables are financed by payables, and such trade credit is an attractive source of finance. It is cost-free, and the amount of payables tends to increase in line with increases in sales, inventories and receivables. When a company has short-term liquidity problems, the easiest thing to do is to delay paying trade payables. This does not cause much of a problem if it is only for a week or two, especially if, after a short-term blip, the company goes back to paying its payables on time. But there is a danger that a company may be unable to resume normal payment periods, and that further delays will occur if it becomes too heavily dependent on creditors as a source of short-term funding.

Excessive delay in paying creditors is not cost-free. Payables soon lose patience with slow payers and are likely to cut off supplies, take legal action or add interest to the amount due. If supplies are cut off because of slow (or non-) payment, it may be difficult to get supplies on credit elsewhere, especially if a company gets a reputation as being a poor payer.

There is much to be said about cultivating good relationships with suppliers, keeping to the terms of the contract, and concentrating on the quality of the relationship, including payment. A company that delays making payments is in a weak position when it comes to negotiating improvements in the quality of goods or services received from suppliers.

In some businesses, such as retailers, the amount of payables is greater than the total of current assets; in this case, short-term creditors are, in effect, financing some of the company's long-term assets. But a 'normal' working capital cycle would show that inventories represent a number of days' sales; receivables represent a number of days' sales, and this is only partly offset by the number of days' sales represented by payables (see **Example 12.6**).

Example 12.6

Ground Limited is a frozen food manufacturer. Figures from the annual accounts are as follows:

	Year 2	Year 1
	£000	£000
Sales	3,427	2,981
Cost of goods sold	2,124	1,789
Inventory	500	374
Trade receivables	492	324
Trade payables	218	347

Chapter 4, ratios 14, 15, and 16 express inventories, receivables and payables in relation to the amount of (cost of) sales. These three ratios for the two years are as follows:

		Year 2 days		Year 1 days
Inventory period	500 x 365/2124	86	500 x 365/2124	76
Trade receivables period	492 x 365/3427	52	324 x 365/2981	40
Trade payables period	218 x 365/2124	(37)	347 x 365/2124	(71)
Working capital period		101		45

So, although the sales have increased, the working capital period has more than doubled, and this is likely to put a strain on the ability of the business to survive with its existing level of capital.

Summary

Working capital is the inventory, receivables, cash and payables tied up in the day-to-day operations of the business. It is vital for the optimal effectiveness of the business that there is neither too much money tied up in working capital nor too little. If there is too much in working capital that will be a drain on cash; it will affect the possibility of investing in new projects and buying new non-current assets or other businesses. On the other hand, if there is too little working capital, this is likely to affect relationships with suppliers, result in the inability to supply customers and could result in overtrading and the collapse of the business. In this chapter, we have examined these issues, looked at the working capital cycle, how to optimize the quantity and reordering of inventory, the management of cash, credit control of receivables and issues relating to paying suppliers. These procedures and considerations will increase the company's efficiency.

Review of key points

- Working capital is usually measured as current assets minus current liabilities.
- Insufficient working capital is likely to be associated with liquidity problems; excessive working capital restricts profitability.
- Receivables should be managed to minimize bad debts and to encourage receivables to pay up quickly.
- The cost-effectiveness of different ways of managing receivables should be assessed.
- Carrying excessive inventories is expensive for companies.
- Careful planning and control of cash is essential.
- Trade payables should be paid in accordance with agreed terms; some companies prefer the short-term financial advantage of delaying paying their creditors.
- Calculations and estimates can be made of the costs and benefits of different policies for managing each element of working capital.

Self-testing questions

1 Why might a company want high levels of working capital?

2 Can a company operate with zero or negative levels of working capital?

3 How would you detect overtrading, and why does it matter?

4 What steps can be taken to speed up the collection of receivables? Why might a company deliberately allow an increase in the time taken for receivables to pay?

5 What factors are taken into consideration in the conventional model for calculating economic order quantities (EOQs)?

6 How can a company avoid having liquidity crises?

7 The Congle Company uses 40,000 wongles a year. Each wongle costs £1.25 to buy; stockholding costs are estimated to be 32 per cent per annum of the cost of the inventory held; each order costs £20 to place. What ordering quantity will minimize costs? How many orders will be placed each year? How often will goods be delivered, and what is the average inventory level? What is the annual stockholding cost?

8 Fleshwick Traders has a large overdraft on which interest of 17 per cent per annum is being charged. The directors are considering offering cash discounts to customers to encourage prompt payment. Annual sales, all on credit, amount to £365,000, and the receivables figure at present is £90,000. The sales director considers that a discount of 2.5 per cent for settlement in 10 days would be taken up by about one-third of their customers. The finance director thinks that a larger discount would be required to achieve this result. Assuming that the sales level remained constant:

  a Would it be worth offering the discount if the sales director is right?

  b What is the largest discount the company could offer without a reduction in profits?

  c Assume that each £1 of sales contributes 20 pence to non-current costs and profits. If the company decided to offer a 5 per cent cash discount for payment in 10 days, and it is taken up by one-third of its customers, how large an increase in sales would be required to maintain profits?

9 Stokeypokey Wholesalers Ltd is proposing to set up a branch in Northern Ireland. Experience elsewhere suggests that sales will start off at £100,000 a month in January, and then increase by £100,000 a month until reaching £400,000 in April. Then sales will increase by £80,000 a month until they reach £640,000 in July. In August sales are expected to reach £700,000 a month and remain at that level until the end of the year. Customers are expected to pay two months after the sales are made.

The cost of purchases is 80 per cent of the sales figure, and they are paid for in the month following the purchase. In January purchases will amount to £240,000; then, each month they purchase the amount of goods required for the following month.

Rent of £100,000 per quarter is payable at the beginning of January, and then in March, June, September and December. Other expenses, payable in the month that they are incurred, are expected to amount to £10,000 per month for the first four months; they will increase to £15,000 a month in May, and then to £16,000 a month in August-December.

The only capital expenditure is for purchase of fittings, with £50,000 payable in January and £50,000 in September. Depreciation is at 10 per cent per annum, with a full year's depreciation being charged in the first year.

The Northern Ireland branch starts business with an interest-free loan of £1 million from Stokeypokey Wholesalers, which is put into a separate bank account.

  a Prepare a summarized income statement for the first year of business.

  b Prepare a statement of financial position as at the end of the first year.

c Prepare a cash budget showing receipts and payments for each month for the year.
d Comment on the results, highlighting key learning points.

Assessment questions

1 How can a company operate with minimum levels of working capital?
2 Working capital should be managed to maximize profitability. Explain and comment.
3 What steps can be taken to minimize bad debts?
4 What are the main limitations of the EOQ model?
5 The Scottish Cake Company has annual sales of £1,200,000. Annual non-current costs are £150,000 and last year's profit was £50,000. At the year end the receivables figure was £100,000.

The company has been offered a contract for supplying cakes to the Swaysco Supermarket Group in England. Sales would be £300,000 in a year, and Swaysco would require three months' credit. The Scottish Cake Company's cost of capital is estimated at 15 per cent per annum. Is the proposed expansion worthwhile if all customers are given three months' credit? Is the proposed expansion worthwhile if only Swaysco is given three months' credit?

6 The summarized statement of financial position of the Warmel Trading Company as at 31 December last year was as follows:

	£	£
Non-current assets		3,000,000
Current assets		
Inventories	500,000	
Trade receivables	600,000	
Cash	10,000	1,110,000
Total assets		4,110,000
Current liabilities		
Trade payables		110,000
Equity		4,000,000
Total liabilities and equity		4,110,000

Last year sales amounted to £3,600,000 and net profit before tax was £600,000. The company's target ROCE is 15 per cent. It is estimated that variable costs amount to 50 per cent of sales, and that non-current costs amount to £1,200,000 per annum.

The purchasing manager is concerned about the very small amount of cash available and that the company may be unable to meet its current liabilities as they fall due.

The financial accountant says that the level of receivables is too high, and proposes to appoint a credit controller at an annual cost of £25,000. He reckons that by doing this the amount of receivables could be halved.

The sales manager believes that many customers are put off by the strict credit control policies, and would like to allow three months' credit to customers. If this policy was adopted he reckons that sales would increase by at least 10 per cent. The finance director estimates that such a policy would result in receivables taking, on average, four months to pay, that inventory and payables would each increase by 10 per cent, and that bad debts would increase by £18,000 per annum.

Required:

a Evaluate the comments made by:

 i the purchasing manager

 ii the financial accountant

 iii the sales manager and finance director.

b What would you recommend and why?

7 The following information has been extracted from the most recent annual report and accounts of Greyhound Leather Manufacturers Ltd:

Income statement	**Year 1**	**Year 2**
	£000	£000
Sales	20,000	22,000
Cost of sales	16,000	17,800
Gross profit	4,000	4,200
Operating profit	2,000	2,050
Net profit after tax	1,500	1,300
Statement of financial position		
Non-current assets	6,200	12,680
Inventories		
Raw materials	1,600	2,000
Work in progress	400	420
Finished goods	2,000	2,500
Receivables	5,000	3,200
Bank	2,000	-
Total assets	17,200	20,800
Current liabilities		
Payables	2,200	2,800
Overdraft	-	2,000
	2,200	4,800
Equity	15,000	16,000
Total liabilities and equity	17,200	20,800

a The finance director is pleased with the management of working capital, but the chairperson is more concerned about profitability. Using appropriate calculations, you are required to look at the financial management of the company and comment on the two points of view expressed.

b What is meant by the working capital cycle? Illustrate your answer with appropriate calculations for Greyhound Leather Manufacturers Ltd.

c What steps can a company take to improve inventory turnover?

d The company uses one million hides of leather a year, which it buys for £16 each. Stockholding costs are estimated to be 25 per cent per annum of the cost of the items in inventory. Administration costs for placing and receiving an order are estimated to be £50. How many hides should the company order at a time (i.e. calculate the EOQ)?

e Illustrate the financial effects of implementing the EOQ in practice and suggest its limitations.

8 The directors of Woebun Standard Components plc have been very successful in persuading their customers to pay, on average, in one month. However, they believe that this policy restricts sales and that sales would increase by 15 per cent if the average collection period for receivables was allowed to increase from one month to two months.

The selling price of the component is £40 per unit, and variable costs per unit are £30. Annual sales revenue is £6m. A sales increase of 15 per cent would lead to an increase in inventory of £400,000 and an increase in trade payables of £100,000.

Woebun expects a ROCE of 27 per cent per annum.

a Should the company allow its customers to enjoy the two-month extended credit period on purely financial grounds?

b Assess the practicability and financial viability of restricting the two months' credit to new customers only.

c What are the main causes and symptoms of *overtrading*? To what extent and in what ways can effective management of debtors avoid the problems of overtrading?

9 The Bonjarron Decorating Company uses 14,400 large-size cans of white gloss paint in a year. It uses different suppliers and, on average, pays £20 per can. It has limited storage space and reckons that the annual stockholding costs amount to 20 per cent of the cost of the stocks held. Administration costs amount to £50 per order placed.

a Calculate the EOQ.

b For what reasons might the company use (i) a much higher or (ii) a much lower ordering quantity?

Group activities and discussion questions

1 Many small businesses may be seen as 'overtrading'. Accountants are too conservative about such things. To be successful, a rapidly expanding small business needs to sail close to the wind. Discuss these views.

2 Large businesses should not have working capital problems. It is easy for them to borrow large sums on a long-term basis. The problem for large businesses is not working capital; it is excessive gearing. Discuss.

3 Discuss the effects on 'just in time' of increasing proportions of manufacturing (for the UK) taking place in Eastern Europe, Africa and Asia.

4 Can working capital, like manufacturing, be 'outsourced'? Could a company operate with zero or negative capital employed, make some profits, and therefore have a ROCE of infinity?

5 Large companies can bully small customers to pay up promptly, while they need not bother paying their own bills on time. Small companies have to pay up promptly if they are to continue to receive supplies, but they cannot force large customers to pay them promptly if they are to continue to make sales. Discuss these views.

6 How does cash budgeting for a business differ from the way in which you do your own, personal cash budgeting. Should it differ? (Other than the amounts of money being very different!)

7 Distinguish between factoring and invoice discounting. Explain the circumstances in which a company considering these two forms of finance would be likely to prefer factoring rather than invoice discounting.

Accounting in context

Discuss and comment on different ways as to how the company can finance its working capital. One such way is to use asset finance.

Indebted New York fitness group needed to refinance $1.2bn in debt after pandemic closures led to a liquidity crunch.

Equinox, the high-end gym chain, has secured $1.8bn in funding from a consortium of private capital investors to refinance $1.2bn in debt that is soon to mature. This move has given the company greater financial flexibility. Sixth Street and Silver Lake, two of the world's biggest private lenders, are leading the group of investors. They will provide $1.8bn in debt to refinance maturing loans, as well as to fund working capital and the expansion of new clubs. The refinancing will be carried out in two loan arrangements and will not include any preferred equity or other debts that could dilute the ownership of Equinox's existing equity holders.

Equinox experienced financial challenges due to the COVID-19 pandemic. The gym chains were closed for several months, resulting in a liquidity crisis and a decrease in memberships. Although Equinox's financial situation improved later on, the high debt level and rising interest rates restricting its refinancing options, raising concerns about the company's viability. Both S&P Global and Moody's placed Equinox on watch for downgrades in the junk territory, fearing that the company may face restructuring if it failed to refinance its loans. S&P Global noted that Equinox only had $44m in cash, and it may not generate enough cash flow to cover fixed charges if it refinanced its debts at current rates. Luckily, a group of private capital organizations and some of Equinox's existing investors arranged the refinancing, preventing the crunch.

Equinox is confident - revenues have increased 27 per cent in the previous year, and the group is building 25 new clubs, expanding its footprint by about 20 per cent.

Source: A. Gara and E. Platt (2024) Luxury Gym Chain Equinox Raises $1.8bn to Avert Cash Crunch. *Financial Times*, 8 March, https://www.ft.com/content/be39a2d6-4757-402f-aa66-2d04761cabde

References and further reading

Atkinson, A., Kaplan, R., Matsumura, E. and Young, M. (2012) *Management Accounting (*6th edn.). Harlow: Pearson.

Dyson, J.R. (2010) *Accounting for Non-accounting Students* (8th edn.). Upper Saddle River, NJ: FT Prentice Hall.

Proctor, R. (2009) *Managerial Accounting for Business Decisions* (3rd edn.). Harlow: Pearson.

Seal, W., Garrison, R.H. and Nooreen, E.W. (2011) *Management Accounting* (4th edn.). Maidenhead: McGraw-Hill.

Watson, D., Head, A., Chan, D., and Watson, D. (2023) *Corporate Finance: Principles and Practice* (9th edn.). Harlow: Pearson.

Part 3

Introduction to Management Accounting

Chapter 13

Introduction to Management Accounting

Chapter contents

13.1 Introduction
13.2 The Origins of Management Accounting
13.3 Management Accounting and Financial Accounting
13.4 Budgetary Control
13.5 Manufacturing Accounts
13.6 Absorption and Marginal Costing
13.7 Standard Costing and Variance Analysis
13.8 Developments in Management Accounting

Learning objectives

After studying this chapter you will be able to:

- ✓ Distinguish between management accounting and financial accounting
- ✓ Outline the development of management accounting
- ✓ Appreciate the roles of budgets and budgetary control
- ✓ Understand manufacturing accounts and basic costing terminology
- ✓ Distinguish between absorption and marginal costing
- ✓ Outline the main areas of management accounting

13.1 Introduction

This chapter introduces the main areas of management accounting that are developed in subsequent chapters. Management accounting techniques have been developed to help managers make decisions affecting the performance of the company. These will include short-, medium- and long-term decisions. Short-term decisions are often those which must be made in a short period of time, and while they will affect the company's performance, they are unlikely to make or break the company. Such decisions include break-even analysis, which is dealt with in **Chapter 17**. Perhaps I am asked to run a graduation ball and need to decide how many tickets need to be sold in order to break even. Medium-term management accounting techniques include budgetary control and are examined in **Chapter 15**. Here, the company is creating a financial plan for its activities for each of the next few years. This will enable the company to determine its objectives and plan what resources it needs in terms of materials, labour and other 'inputs' such as indirect costs like rent, non-current assets and capital. And, as we will see, having established its budget, after the event, management will compare the 'actual' results with the 'budget' to establish what went right and what went wrong in order to improve the company's performance. Long-term management accounting techniques include capital investment appraisal when massive future projects are assessed. On an inner-city piece of land, should we build a shopping centre or an office block or sell the land to a property developer? Such decisions very often involve enormous sums of money and are likely to have a major impact on the company's future performance and survival. Capital investment appraisal is introduced in **Chapter 14**.

In this chapter, we examine the origins of management accounting and then distinguish management accounting from financial accounting. We briefly look at budgetary control, manufacturing accounts, some important costing terminology, two different ways of defining the cost of a unit of production - absorption costing and marginal costing - and then introduce standard costing and variance analysis. These techniques are introduced in this chapter but will be dealt with in subsequent chapters.

13.2 The Origins of Management Accounting

Management accounting[1] evolved during the twentieth century because managers needed systematic and reliable financial information to help them to *manage* their businesses. They needed financial information to make plans, to monitor the effectiveness of those plans[2] and to help them decide between alternative courses of action.

A small or new business can cope without management accounting, or perhaps without any accounting at all. As long as it keeps an eye on its bank statements, and makes sure that the money it receives is more than it pays out, it will survive. But, sooner or later, it will need to calculate profit figures. HM Revenue & Customs will expect tax to be paid on any profits. Bankers or anyone lending to the business will expect to see conventional financial statements. If the business is large enough to have partners, or to become a company owned by a number of shareholders, the owners will want to know how much profit has been made, and how it is to be shared out between them.

Companies are required to produce annual reports, including income statements (showing profit for the year), statements of financial position and cash flow statements. But managers need to monitor and control the financial performance of their organizations more often than once a year. Even a very basic accounting system would include monthly financial statements. Managers would examine these monthly financial statements, and perhaps be pleased that they are better than expected. Or perhaps they would be disappointed if the results are poorer than expected. They presumably have *some* expectations - if only that they make a profit, or do better than the previous year.

Financial plans, or budgets, detail the results that an organization is expected to achieve: its planned results. If the actual monthly results shown in the financial statements are then compared with the results that were intended, we have a rudimentary system of *budgetary control*. Budgetary planning and control is examined in **Chapter 15**.

[1] Management accounting is also referred as 'managerial accounting', if you think that sounds more impressive.

[2] Or to 'control' the business - by comparing actual results with planned results.

13.3 Management Accounting and Financial Accounting

Financial accounting has been developed within a framework of company law, mainly to provide information for shareholders and creditors rather than to provide information for the managers of a business. Managers can have whatever information they want as a basis for planning and controlling the business and making decisions. They do not need to rely on financial accounting, and systems of management accounting have been developed that differ from financial accounting in a number of ways, as shown in **Illustration 13.1**. Management accounting has developed from costing systems.

ILLUSTRATION 13.1

Comparison of financial accounting and management accounting

Financial accounting	Management accounting
Companies are required by law to produce financial accounting information	No formal requirements
The ways of producing and presenting the information are determined by company law and international financial reporting standards	No formal requirements. Statements are prepared in different formats for different purposes
Information is mainly a record of what has already happened	Information is a basis for decisions about the future and includes forecasts, plans and budgets
Emphasis on precise accuracy (statements of financial position must balance), although this leads to delays in producing information	Emphasis on relevance and immediacy; approximations are acceptable
Information is intended mainly for users outside the organization, especially shareholders and creditors	Information is intended for directors and managers within the organization for decision making
Information is public	Information may be private
Published information is for the company as a whole (with some additional information for main segments)	More emphasis on detailed analysis
Annual reporting is a requirement	Emphasis on frequent production of control information

For many organizations, particularly those involved in manufacturing or producing a number of different products, financial accounting information does not provide sufficient information. In particular, they need to know the *costs* of the different products - or services - that they provide. Detailed costing systems were developed, particularly during the First World War, as a basis for determining how much companies should charge to the government for supplying armaments, clothing and other supplies necessary for war. Knowing how much it costs to produce each different product helps to determine the price to be paid for it. Early costing systems were based on 'cost plus' pricing: the government agreed to pay for the costs of direct materials and direct labour[3] plus a percentage to cover the manufacturer's overheads and to allow a profit. These costing systems were based on *absorption costing*, which is explained and illustrated in **Chapter 16**.

Absorption costing is also necessary for financial accounting purposes. As explained in **Chapter 15**, gross profit is the difference between the sales figure for the year and the cost of the goods that have been sold, as

[3] The terms 'direct materials' and 'direct labour' refer to the materials and labour in the production process and are explained further in Chapter 16.

shown in **Illustration 13.2**. The *cost of sales* figure is calculated by adding opening inventory to purchases, then deducting closing inventory. The point is that costs have been incurred to buy some goods (in this instance, £50,000) that are not part of the cost of goods sold during year 10. They are to be carried forward as an expense for the following year: they will be opening inventory in year 11, and part of the cost of sales for that year.

ILLUSTRATION 13.2

Income statement for 'a retailer' for year ended 31 December year 10

		£000
Sales revenue		300
Cost of sales		
Opening inventory	40	
Purchases	260	
	300	
Closing inventory	(50)	
		250
Gross profit		50
Operating expenses		(35)
Operating profit		15

In a retail business this is straightforward: it buys goods, it sells goods, and an adjustment for unsold inventories has to be made, as shown in **Illustration 13.2**.

In a manufacturing organization the principle is the same: we need to calculate the cost of the goods that have been sold. During a year all sorts of costs will be incurred, some of which are part of the cost of goods sold, and some of which have to be carried forward to the following period. In addition, there will be a range of other costs - overheads or operating expenses - which have to be written off as they are incurred. These are included in a manufacturing account, as shown in **Illustration 13.3**. Exam questions often ask to calculate or explain prime cost. Prime cost is the sum of the direct costs, which are the direct materials, direct wages and direct expenses in **Illustration 13.3**.

ILLUSTRATION 13.3

Manufacturing account for 'a manufacturer' for year ended 31 December year 10

Direct materials	£000	£000
Inventory at 1 January year 10	12	
Purchases during year 10	148	
	160	
Inventory at 31 December year 10	17	
Cost of direct materials consumed		143
Direct wages		86
Direct expenses		11
Prime cost		240
Production overheads		
Various		345

Manufacturing account for 'a manufacturer' for year ended 31 December year 10		
Direct materials	£000	£000
Total production costs incurred		585
Add work in progress 1 January year 10		35
		620
Deduct work in progress 31 December year 10		(50)
Production cost of goods completed		570
Transferred to income statement		
Income statement for 'a manufacturer' year ended 31st December year 10		
		£000
Sales revenue		900
Cost of sales of finished goods		
Opening inventory	60	
Production cost	570	
	630	
Closing inventory	(80)	
		550
Gross profit		350
Operating expenses		(35)
Operating profit		315

13.4 Budgetary Control

Many businesses use financial accounting as a basis for planning future activities, making decisions between different courses of action, and controlling their financial position and performance. They do not wait until the end of the year to see how things have turned out, after the statement of financial position and income statement have been produced. Instead, they plan ahead. They decide what they want next year's financial results to look like. They set themselves a target,[4] perhaps to increase the return on shareholders' funds to 16 per cent, or to increase earnings per share to 13 pence. These objectives may be set out in the form of a planned or budgeted set of final accounts for next year - perhaps with a budgeted income statement, statement of financial position and cash flow statement for each month. Then, as the year progresses, each month's actual results can be compared with what was planned. In this way, some financial control is established, and where the results that are actually achieved are not good enough, the need for some sort of corrective action becomes clear. This comparison and control takes place monthly or more often.

Budgetary control is dealt with more fully in **Chapter 15**.

[4] They may have several targets, such as increasing market share, reducing short-term borrowings and increasing profitability.

13.5 Manufacturing Accounts

Manufacturing accounts illustrate the link between financial accounting and management accounting. There is always a need to produce an income statement, but more detailed statements are required to arrive at the figure for cost of sales.

At first sight a manufacturing account looks complicated. We need to see that there are three inventory adjustments for:

1 *Direct materials.* Calculate the cost of direct materials consumed during the period (as opposed to the direct materials *purchased* during the period).
2 *Work in progress.* Calculate the costs incurred in making finished goods (and to exclude the costs incurred in manufacturing items that are not completed during the period and so are not available for sale).
3 *Finished goods.* Calculate the cost of the goods that were actually sold (and to exclude closing inventories of finished goods that were available for sale, but not sold).

As with a retailer, there are unsold inventories at the end of a period, and these are not included in the cost of sales (they are shown as a deduction). A retailer's cost of sales is: opening inventories, *plus* purchases, *minus* closing inventories. The income statement of a manufacturer is the same, except that we are dealing with finished goods that they have made. It shows opening inventories of finished goods, *plus* the manufacturing cost of finished goods, *minus* closing inventories of finished goods.

Terminology

Prime cost is the sum of all the direct production costs: direct materials, direct labour and direct expenses or direct overheads.

All *prime costs* are part of *production cost* (may also be called *manufacturing cost* or *factory cost*). Where a company makes a number of different products (e.g. tables, desks, chairs), prime costs are allocated directly to each different product so that it is possible to calculate the prime cost of manufacturing a table or a chair or a desk.

Production cost also includes both direct and indirect costs such as *production overheads*,[5] which become part of the cost of finished goods. The costs are charged as an expense in the income statement (as part of the cost of sales) when the items are sold. Costs incurred in making goods that are not sold are carried forward in closing inventory to be treated as an expense in the following period. It is not possible to allocate manufacturing overheads directly to individual items produced: they are usually apportioned in some way, perhaps in relation to direct labour costs.

Operating expenses include distribution costs and administrative expenses. These are not part of manufacturing costs and are not carried forward as part of closing inventories; they are *period costs*, which means that they must be charged as an expense during the period in which they are incurred. Finance expenses (or interest payable) are also a period cost and are not carried forward in closing inventories.

Cost behaviour

Costs can be classified based on their behaviour. This means that costs behave differently depending on the level of activity. Costs can be classified as either fixed, variable, stepped fixed or mixed cost. They are illustrated graphically in **Example 13.1**.

[5] Which may be called manufacturing overheads or factory overheads.

In **Example 13.1**, the first graph shows that total *variable costs* change directly in line with the volume of production. If the company stopped making desks, it would save all the costs of direct materials and direct labour. There would also be some reduction in production overheads - less power would be used, maintenance costs would probably be lower (if the machinery is used less), and there might be a reduction in 'indirect labour' costs (supervisors and others in the factory who are not direct labour). It should be noted that variable cost per unit remains constant. Variable costs are directly proportionate to activity or output within a stated range but can change beyond that range. In materials, there can be economies of scale whereby additional material can be purchased at a lower price per unit. On the other hand, with labour, there can be diseconomies of scale whereby workers work beyond their normal weekly hours and overtime is paid at a higher rate per hour.

Fixed costs are costs which, within a stated range of output, do not vary, that is, they remain constant. This is illustrated in **Example 13.1**. Fixed costs continue at much the same level, regardless of the volume of production. The fixed cost per unit will decline with increases in output or level of activity. Such costs would include the rent, rates, lighting and heating of the factory, most of the costs of supervisory staff, and most machinery and maintenance costs. However, beyond that range, these fixed costs can increase. So, it might be possible for a supervisor to manage the production of 10,000 cars, but if production increases beyond that level, the company will need to employ another supervisor. Hence, supervisors' salaries will be *stepped fixed costs*. The stepped fixed costs are shown graphically in **Example 13.1**.

Semi-variable costs are those with a fixed annual cost and a variable cost per unit consumed. The semi-variable costs are shown graphically in **Example 13.1**. Utility costs such as electricity, water and telephone are sometimes priced in this way.

Example 13.1

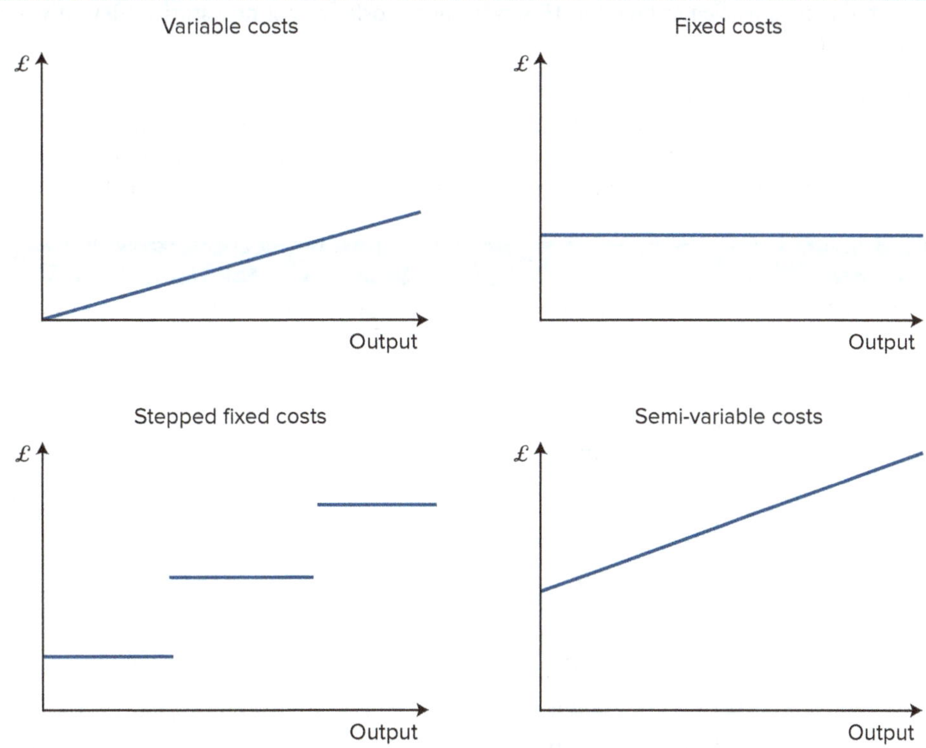

Direct costs are costs that can be identified with an individual cost unit. A cost unit could refer to a unit of production, such as a car or a cost unit could be a department of a business. In the case of a car, for example, direct costs would include materials and labour, while in the case of a department of a business, direct costs would also include the rent of the building.

Indirect costs, however, are costs that cannot be identified with the individual cost unit. The rent of the factory would be an indirect cost in determining the cost of a car.

Terminology, and issues arising, are examined more thoroughly in **Chapter 16**.

13.6 Absorption and Marginal Costing

Traditional costing systems are based on *absorption costing*, where the costs shown for inventories of manufactured goods include their full share of manufacturing overheads.[6] This is necessary for financial accounting and the calculation of profit. Detailed costing systems enable companies to show the costs incurred in making particular products, providing different services, and engaging in a variety of different activities. **Chapter 16** explains how this is done.

Marginal costing provides a different approach. It requires *fixed costs* to be separated from *variable costs* and provides a more useful basis than absorption costing for making decisions. This is explained in **Chapter 17**.

Although accountants try to produce accurate and reliable costing figures, costing systems do not necessarily produce a 'correct' cost for any particular purpose. A system can ensure that all costs are recorded and that they are coded and allocated in particular ways to calculate what costs have been incurred by a particular activity or in producing a particular product. However, those costs are not necessarily relevant when making a particular decision.

In **Illustration 13.4**, if the total of *all* costs is divided by the number of items sold, the average cost per item sold was £5, but Jeremy Paul sold them for £2 each; based on this, the business may not be viable. However, we should not assume that £5 will be the average cost per item sold in subsequent months; as shown in the illustration, the greater the volume of sales is, the lower the cost per unit is. This is normal in business.

ILLUSTRATION 13.4

Jeremy Paul started a business selling hamburgers and hot dogs. In April, he hired a van and incurred total costs of £5,000. He sold 1,000 hamburgers and hot dogs for £2,000.

Sales and costs in the first six months were as follows:

	Number sold	**Total costs**
		£
April	1,000	5,000
May	2,000	5,500
June	3,000	6,000
July	5,000	7,000
August	5,500	7,250
September	5,200	7,100

[6] Manufacturing or production overheads include factory rent and electricity, and depreciation on the equipment used in production, and are explained further in Chapter 16.

	Total costs incurred, £	Number sold	Cost per item, £	Selling price per item, £	Profit/(loss) per item, £
April	5,000	1,000	5	2	(3.00)
May	5,500	2,000	2.75	2	(0.75)
June	6,000	3,000	2.00	2	0.00
July	7,000	5,000	1.40	2	0.60
August	7,250	5,500	1.32	2	0.68
September	7,100	5,200	1.37	2	0.63

The answer to the question 'How much does it cost to produce a hamburger?' depends on how many you produce.[7] It is easier to say how much it actually cost in (say) June, but the answer would be different for July. A costing system shows what something *did* cost, but projections of those costs into the future are fraught with danger.

Some costs are more relevant than others in decision-making; it is usually better to separate fixed from variable costs (and use 'marginal costing'). Costs should be calculated in whatever ways are most useful to management and most 'relevant' to a particular decision.

13.7 Standard Costing and Variance Analysis

Some businesses use standard (or planned) costs rather than actual costs as a basis for making decisions, partly because actual costs can fluctuate a lot, and standard costs may provide a better guide. Where standard costs are used, together with budgets, it is important to compare actual costs with what was planned. Variances can then be calculated to show where and why actual results were not what was expected so that action can be taken to control the business.

13.8 Developments in Management Accounting

Management accounting is constantly changing and developing to meet the needs of particular businesses and circumstances. More accurate ways of identifying overhead costs with particular products and activities are required and more accurate activity-based costing has developed, which is outlined in **Chapter 16**.

As international businesses have become more competitive, and the life cycles of products have become shorter as new products are developed, a range of techniques has emerged. Some of these are outlined in **Chapter 9**.

[7] Perhaps the answer to most questions is, 'It depends on what assumptions you are making.'

Summary

Management accounting is concerned with providing information that is useful to managers in planning and controlling their businesses. The following chapters develop the main areas of management accounting: **Chapter 15** deals with budgetary control; **Chapter 16** with absorption costing; **Chapter 17** with marginal costing and decision-making; **Chapter 18** with standard costing and variance analysis; and the **Appendix** introduces a range of other management accounting techniques.

Review of key points

- Financial accounting is concerned with meeting the needs of shareholders, creditors and others who are outside the business. Management accounting is concerned with meeting the needs of managers within the business.
- Financial accounting follows laws and accounting standards. Managers are free to develop management accounting and information systems that meet their particular needs.
- Management accounting is particularly concerned with providing information for planning, decision-making and control.
- Budgets are the usual tool for annual financial planning; budgetary control subsequently provides actual financial results for comparison with budget.
- Absorption costing ensures that all production overheads (variable and fixed) are 'absorbed' (charged to) products and included in closing inventories.
- Absorption costing is required to show the cost of closing inventories, but it is not usually the best basis for decision-making.
- Marginal costing separates fixed costs from variable costs and identifies 'contribution' as the difference between sales and variable costs.
- Marginal costing is a much better basis for decision-making but is based on rather simplistic assumptions.
- Standard costing provides a systematic way of analysing 'variances', which are the difference between planned financial results and actual financial results.
- Many different management accounting techniques have been developed to meet the needs of particular circumstances.

Self-testing questions

1 Which of the following is true?

Management accounting, when compared with financial accounting, is:

a More subject to regulation

b More accurate and verifiable

c Focused more on the future
d Distributed more widely to shareholders

2 What is the difference between a direct and an indirect cost? Give an example of each.
3 In what circumstances is labour (a) a variable cost and (b) a fixed cost.
4 Which of the following is included in closing inventories of finished goods?
a Cost of direct materials consumed
b Finance costs
c Administrative expenses
d Selling and distribution costs

5 The trial balance of JackDannie, a manufacturer, as at 30 June year 7 was as follows:

	Debit	Credit
	£000	£000
Administrative expenses	420	
Bank	300	
Capital		370
Direct wages	270	
Direct materials: inventory as at 1 July year 6	64	
Distribution costs	320	
Factory electricity	11	
Factory rent	76	
Indirect manufacturing wages	90	
Finished goods: inventory as at 1 July year 6	70	
General factory expenses	12	
Machinery	140	
Payables		66
Provision for depreciation on machinery as at 1 July year 6		40
Purchases of direct materials	390	
Receivables	420	
Repairs to machinery	8	
Sales		2,200
Work in progress: inventory as at 1 July year 6	85	
	2,676	2,676

Additional information:

i Inventories at 30 June year 7 were:

	£000
Direct materials	67
Work in progress	78
Finished goods	92

ii Machinery is to be depreciated at 10 per cent per annum on a straight-line basis.
iii Ignore taxation.

You are required to prepare the manufacturing account and income statement for JackDannie for the year ended 30 June year 7, and a statement of financial position as at that date.

Assessment questions

1 Which of the following is *not* true?

Financial accounting, when compared with management accounting, is:

- a intended mainly for shareholders, creditors and others outside the business
- b more accurate and verifiable
- c mainly concerned with providing information to managers
- d a legal requirement.

2 Which of the following are included in the *prime cost*?

- a manufacturing overheads
- b direct materials
- c direct labour
- d distribution costs.

3 The trial balance of Stujerpa, a manufacturer, as at 31 March year 10 was as follows:

	Debit	**Credit**
	£000	£000
Administrative expenses	17,320	
Bank	15,068	
Capital		44,200
Direct wages	87,100	
Direct materials: inventory at 1 April year 9	2,500	
Distribution costs	9,100	
Factory power	850	
Factory rent, rates, insurance	8,400	
Factory supervisor's salary	35,600	

	Debit	Credit
	£000	£000
Finished goods: inventory as at 1 April year 9	380	
General factory expenses	1,340	
Machinery	29,000	
Maintenance of machinery	8,550	
Payables		26,760
Provision for depreciation on machinery as at 1 April year 9		5,800
Purchases of direct materials	92,510	
Receivables	44,231	
Sales		275,400
Work in progress: inventory as at 1 April year 9	211	
	352,160	352,160

Additional information:

1 Inventories as at 31 March Year 10 were:

	£000
Direct materials	2,200
Work in progress	189
Finished goods	444

2 Machinery is to be depreciated at 10 per cent per annum on a straight-line basis.

3 Ignore taxation.

You are required to prepare the manufacturing account and income statement for Stujerpa for the year ended 31 March year 10, and statement of financial position as at that date.

4 Explain the differences between financial accounting and management accounting.

5 Draw the following cost behaviour charts:

i A supervisor's salary.

ii The cost of raw materials is £15 per unit for the first 100 units, £10 per unit for the next 100 units and £5 per unit for the next 100 units.

iii Direct hourly labour with a 50 per cent surcharge for overtime.

iv The cost of water comprises an annual fixed charge and an amount for each cubic metre used.

Group activities and discussion questions

1 Would you rather be a management accountant or a financial accountant? Why?

2 Examine the idea that financial accountants act in the public interest but management accountants act only in the interest of managers.

3 Businesses have financial accounts, and bank statements. Why do they need additional information?

4 Discuss which of the costs of running a car are 'fixed' and which are 'variable' in relation to the number of miles run.

Accounting in context

Discuss and comment on the following report based on an article from the press, with reference to fixed costs and whether the company, Superdry, should de-list from the stock exchange.

Superdry to de-list from the London Stock Exchange, subject to shareholder approval

Superdry is a British clothing company known for its jackets and clothing inspired by American vintage styles and Japanese graphics. In 2003, Julian Dunkerton, chief executive and co-founder of Superdry, began trading initially by selling T-shirts from a market stall in Cheltenham. The business was publicly listed in March 2010. Although Dunkerton resigned as CEO in 2015, he resumed his position in 2019 following a boardroom conflict where he censured the previous management for the company's decline. Experts have noted that the brand has experienced difficulty in attracting younger consumers.

The brand has been struggling amid difficult consumer retail market conditions and weak wholesale orders. As part of a profound three-year restructuring plan, Superdry will quit the London Stock Exchange and pursue rent savings for its stores. If the management did not push ahead with the turnaround, it would be forced into an insolvency procedure.

Superdry expects the restructuring to result in rent reductions in 39 of its 94 UK locations as part of a plan to resume a 'more stable footing'. Superdry is also hoping to raise up to £10m in fresh funds and Dunkerton said that he will not be making an offer for any further shares that he did not own.

The restructuring is conditional on the business receiving the proceeds of the equity fundraising, which is supported by Dunkerton.

Unfortunately, Dunkerton's efforts did not yield the desired results. The company continues to face profit warnings and is currently operating at a loss. As a result, there are concerns about its viability as a going concern, such that trading in the company's shares was briefly halted after a sharp fall. Tom Waite wrote in *Morningstar* on 4 September 2023 that Superdry's stock had dropped more than 20 per cent. This happened after the company released its delayed annual results. Trading in the shares on the London main market had been momentarily suspended after Superdry missed a deadline for publishing results for the financial year that ended on 29 April. The company blamed the delay on having a new auditor.

In 2023, there were serious concerns over the financial stability of the company, which were made public. The auditors in the 2023 annual report emphasize 'that a material uncertainty exists that may cast significant doubt on the Group and Parent Company's ability to continue as a going concern. The Group made a post-tax loss of £148.1m for the period.'

Dunkerton comments: 'The reality is we're losing money ... [and] so we have to make sure that we're right-sizing this business, cutting our **fixed costs**, making sure that we are here for the next ten or twenty years, [that] we save jobs and we have a positive outlook on the future.' He added that de-listing from the stock market would allow him to 'focus on the business and also seriously cut costs'. He said audit fees had risen significantly from £1m five years ago to an 'unsustainable' £5m.

Dunkerton considers that the costs of being a listed company are too high and that if you remove them the company will be in a much better place. Eighty per cent of his time is spent doing things that may be categorized as non-productive from a brand perspective. Hence, de-listing from London's main market will mean that it is going to be a lot easier taking the company private.

Dunkerton has expressed his hope that most of the stores would remain open if landlords agreed to rental deals that are in line with the market rates. However, in cases where such agreements cannot be reached, a few closures may be inevitable.

Dunkerton has stated that Superdry, the fashion brand, has been facing several challenges such as Brexit, the discontinuation of VAT-free shopping for tourists, and business rates. The company has found it difficult to conduct international business efficiently due to Brexit. Superdry is planning to be de-listed by July, but it is subject to approval from shareholders.

Update from the London Stock Exchange:

Superdry provides a further update regarding the cancellation of the listing of its ordinary shares on the Official List maintained by the Financial Conduct Authority and their trading on the London Stock Exchange's main market for listed securities (the 'de-listing'), as originally announced on 16 April 2024 and as approved by shareholders at the general meeting held on 14 June 2024.

Shareholders are reminded that the last day of trading in Superdry's ordinary shares on the main market is 12 July 2024. The de-listing will become effective at 8:00 a.m. on 15 July 2024.

Source: J. Hurley and I. Fish (2024) Superdry Decides to Turn its Back on London Market. *The Times*, 17 April.

References and further reading

Atkinson, A., Kaplan, R., Matsumura, E. and Young, M. (2012) *Management Accounting* (6th edn.). Harlow: Pearson.

Bhimani, A.C.T., Datar, S.M., Horngren, C.T. and Foster, G. (2012) *Management and Cost Accounting* (5th edn.). Upper Saddle River, NJ: FT Prentice Hall.

Drury, C. (2008) *Management and Cost Accounting* (7th edn.). Andover: Cengage Learning.

Dyson, J.R. (2010) *Accounting for Non-accounting Students* (8th edn.). Upper Saddle River, NJ: FT Prentice Hall.

Proctor, R. (2009) *Managerial Accounting for Business Decisions* (3rd edn.). Harlow: Pearson.

Seal, W., Garrison, R.H. and Nooreen, E.W. (2011) *Management Accounting* (4th edn.). Maidenhead: McGraw-Hill.

Watson, D., Head, A., Chan, D., and Watson, D. (2023) *Corporate Finance: Principles and Practice* (9th edn.). Harlow: Pearson.

Weetman, P. (2006) *Management Accounting: An Intro.* Upper Saddle River, NJ: FT Prentice Hall.

Chapter 14

Investment Appraisal

Chapter contents

14.1 Introduction
14.2 Investment
14.3 Methods of Investment Appraisal
14.4 Cost of Capital
14.5 Uncertainty and Risk

Learning objectives

After studying this chapter you will be able to:

- ✓ Understand the difference between using cash flow and profit in making investment appraisals
- ✓ Calculate and interpret the return on investment (ROI), or return on capital employed of a project and appreciate its uses and limitations
- ✓ Calculate and interpret the payback period of a project and appreciate its uses and limitations
- ✓ Understand the principles of discounting and calculate a project's net present value (NPV) and internal rate of return
- ✓ Evaluate the strengths and weaknesses of discounted cash flow (DCF) approaches to investment appraisal
- ✓ Understand which cash flows are relevant and should be included in a DCF calculation, and which are not
- ✓ Appreciate the importance of cost of capital in investment appraisal, and evaluate the relevance of cost of capital calculations
- ✓ Understand that there is always uncertainty and risk in investment appraisal and appreciate various ways of dealing with this

14.1 Introduction

Financial accounting is concerned with reporting to shareholders on the success of management in achieving what shareholders want. It may be assumed that the objective is to maximize shareholders' wealth. To achieve this, they should use proper investment appraisal techniques to ensure that shareholders' funds are used only to finance activities that will produce an adequate return. They must strike a balance between high-risk projects that seem to promise a high return and safer projects producing a lower return. They should also be aware of a company's cost of capital. A company with a cost of capital of 10 per cent per annum will find that projects yielding 12 per cent per annum are attractive and can increase the value of the company. Those with a higher cost of capital (e.g. 15 per cent) will find that fewer projects are attractive.

14.2 Investment

Individuals and companies invest money in the short term with the idea of getting back more, in the longer term, than the initial cost of the investment. This is a straightforward enough idea, but there are a number of issues that have to be addressed if we are to 'appraise' our investments properly.

1. How much do you need to get back to justify the amount invested?
2. How quickly does the money need to come back? If you can invest £100 today, and get back £300 after 50 years, the return might look brilliant, but the timing is not!
3. Risk. How sure are you that you will get back the amount suggested? There are various ways of allowing for risk and uncertainty in investment appraisal, but there is still a need for judgement and recognition that some uncertainty is inevitable in most businesses and projects.

Before considering the various approaches that are used in investment appraisal, it is necessary to be clear whether the returns that we expect an investment to make will be measured as:

a. profit, or
b. cash flow.

Profit and cash flow

Profits are measured in accordance with all the usual rules that apply to income statements. Profit, by definition, should always mean after depreciation has been charged as an expense. But as depreciation is not 'paid' (no cash goes out of the business), the annual *cash flows* from a project are usually much higher than the annual *profits*. This is clearly shown in Elizabeth's project in **Example 14.1**.

Example 14.1

Elizabeth was made redundant recently and was given a severance payment of £55,000 which she uses to buy a special purpose delivery vehicle. She employs a driver. Each year she receives money from customers for delivering goods; each year she pays all her expenses in cash (wages, petrol, repairs, insurance, etc.); and each year she pockets what is left: this amounts to £15,500 a year, which she reckons is a pretty good return on her initial capital of £55,000.

Unfortunately, Elizabeth forgot to allow for depreciation. After five years the vehicle is worn out, and she manages to sell it for £5,000. She should have allowed £10,000 a year for depreciation.

In terms of cash flow, Elizabeth made £15,500 a year. In terms of profit she made only £5,500 a year.

In this simple business we can see that:

Profit	+	Depreciation	=	Cash flow
£5,500	+	£10,000	=	£15,500

The first of our four methods of investment appraisal, return on investment (ROI), uses profit. The other three methods use cash flow.

14.3 Methods of Investment Appraisal

Return on investment (ROI)

Return on investment (ROI), also known as return on capital employed (ROCE)[1] and accounting rate of return (ARR), is a key performance indicator that measures the profitability of an investment project relative to the amount of capital invested. While there are different approaches to defining ROI, they all focus on quantifying the amount of accounting profit generated in proportion to the capital deployed in a given investment initiative. It uses accounting profits that are calculated after charging depreciation.

It can be expressed as follows:

$$\frac{\text{Average annual profits}}{\text{Amount initially invested}} \times 100$$

Elizabeth's return may be calculated as follows:

$$\frac{5{,}500}{55{,}000} \times 100 = 10\%$$

Using ROI is an appealing approach to investment appraisal in a number of ways. It is, in many ways, consistent with conventional financial accounting. If the performance of a company as a whole is judged on the basis of profitability, using return on capital employed, then it makes sense to judge the performance of each part of the business using ROCE. If a company wants to achieve ROCE of, say, 15 per cent per annum, it can be sure of achieving this if every part of the business and every project achieves this return.

But calculating the return on the *initial* amount invested is likely to understate the returns that a company subsequently achieves. If a project has no scrap value, that is, the capital employed at the end of its life is zero, then the average capital employed is exactly half of the initial capital employed. The return on average capital employed will be double the return on initial capital employed.

Effect of depreciation with Elizabeth's project, where the initial amount invested is £55,000

After one year's depreciation, the investment amount will be reduced to £45,000. After two years, it will be £35,000. After three years, it will be £25,000. After four years, it will be £15,000. At the end of five years, it will be down to £5,000. We can say that the *average* amount invested in the project is the amount halfway

[1] ROCE is usually applied to the business as a whole, but it can be applied to parts of the business or individual projects.

through its life, that is, after two and a half years. The average amount invested is £30,000, calculated as follows:

$$\text{Average investment (or capital employed)} = \frac{\text{Initial investment} + \text{Value at end}}{2}$$

$$£30{,}000 = \frac{£55{,}000 + £5{,}000}{2}$$

$$\text{Return on investment} = \frac{5{,}500}{30{,}000} \times 100 = 18.3\%$$

Elizabeth

Return on initial capital employed	£5,500/£55,000	10%
Return on average capital employed	£5,500/£30,000	18.3%

It may be better to use the *average* amount invested, rather than the *initial* amount invested. This is less prudent: using the *average* amount invested shows a higher return (see **Example 14.2**). Elizabeth should not reject what might be a perfectly good project on the basis that it achieves a return on initial investment of 'only' 10 per cent.

Example 14.2

The Trudo machine will cost £50,000 and will have a four-year life with zero scrap value at the end of five years. It will generate cash flows as follows:

Year 1	£10,000
Year 2	£16,000
Year 3	£20,000
Year 4	£20,000
Total	£66,000

To calculate average annual profit, it is necessary to calculate average annual depreciation charges.

There is no need to know what method or rate of depreciation will be used. The total amount to be written off, whatever method is used, is £50,000. The total cash flows are £66,000. The total profits must therefore be £16,000. Averaged over four years, the profits are £4,000 a year.

We could work out average annual profits as follows:

Average annual cash flows	£66,000 ÷ 4 = £16,500
Average annual depreciation	£50,000 ÷ 4 = £12,500
Average annual profit	£4,000

The return on the initial amount of capital employed is:

$$\frac{£4{,}000}{£50{,}000} \times 100 = 8\%$$

The return on average capital employed is:

$$\frac{£4{,}000}{£25{,}000} \times 100 = 16\%$$

It is difficult to relate the ROI of a project to the company's cost of capital. It would be appealing to say that if a company's cost of capital is, say, 12 per cent, any project with an ROI of greater than 12 per cent should be accepted because it would increase the company's average return on capital employed and so increase the value of the company. There are several important reasons why such a neat rule of thumb could lead to poor decisions:

1 There are different ways of calculating ROI, and care is needed to ensure that like is compared with like.

2 ROI ignores the timing of future cash flows and profits. It simply averages profits over the life of the project. It assumes that making £10,000 profit next year is the same as making £10,000 profit after three years. But shareholders want to see results within a relatively short time. The problem is shown in **Illustration 14.1** with two projects: one generates cash flows and profits more quickly, and the other generates more profit and cash flow but over a longer period.

   In **Illustration 14.1**, the Jaggie project makes only £40 profit, but the Lardie project makes £45 profit. The ROI is, therefore, higher for the Lardie project than it is for the Jaggie project. But the Jaggie project makes money much more quickly, and it might be a better project.

3 The use of ROI is also criticized because it depends on all of the usual assumptions in financial accounting. The usefulness of ROI is limited by variations in accounting policies, the use of 'creative accounting', and any questionable assumptions in measuring profits or capital employed.

ILLUSTRATION 14.1

	Jaggie project			Lardie project		
Year	**Cash flow**	**Depreciation**	**Profit**	**Cash flow**	**Depreciation**	**Profit**
	£	£	£	£	£	£
0	(100)			(100)		
1	45	20	25	10	20	(10)
2	40	20	20	20	20	–
3	35	20	15	30	20	10
4	10	20	(10)	40	20	20
5	10	20	(10)	45	20	25
Total	140	100	40	145	100	45

	Jaggie	Lardie
Average annual profits	£40 ÷ 5 years = £8	£45 ÷ 5 years = £9
Average capital employed	(£100 + £100)/2 = £50	(£100 + £100)/2 = £50
Return on average investment	£8 x 100/£50 = 16%	£9 x 100/£50 = 18%

In deciding between Jaggie and Lardie, we need a method of investment appraisal that takes into account not just the amounts of cash flows or profits that a project generates but also their timing. It is better to get our money back sooner rather than later.

In both of these projects, there are years when no profit is being made. However, as long as a project generates positive net cash flows, it is usually worth continuing.

ROI, or ROCE, is the only method of investment appraisal that uses profit figures rather than cash flow figures. The 'return' means profit, and in calculating profit, depreciation has to be deducted from the cash flow.

Other methods of investment appraisal are based on cash flows, not profit. Depreciation is not deducted from cash flows when calculating the payback period or discounted cash flow.

Payback period

The easiest way to deal with the timing of future returns is to ask the simple question: how quickly do we get our money back? A project that gives you your money back in three years is likely to be better than one that takes five years.

A quick look at Jaggie and Lardie shows that both require an initial investment of £100, but Jaggie claws it back much more quickly. After only two years, Jaggie has already produced cash flows of £95 and will have paid back the full £100 a couple of months into the third year. But Lardie is much slower: it has not repaid the full £100 until the end of the fourth year.

As a method of investment appraisal, the payback period has a number of clear advantages:

1. It is easy to calculate, easy to understand and easy to present.
2. It is based on cash flow, not profit, and so is seen as being more objective, with less dependence on questionable accounting assumptions.
3. It emphasizes the need for projects to repay quickly, which is important, especially considering the cost of the funds invested in a project.
4. Projects with shorter payback periods are likely to be less risky than projects that take longer to pay back the initial investment.
5. In forecasting the results of a project, we can be much more certain about costs and revenues in the first few years than we can be about what might happen 5 or 10 years into the future.

If we combine ROI with a payback period, we might make reasonable investment decisions. ROI takes into account all the profits that a project makes throughout its life; it ignores timing. The payback period considers only the length of time it takes for cash flows to amount to the original investment; it ignores cash flows after the payback period.

Using only the payback period as a method of investment appraisal could lead to unrealistic decisions and may not increase the company's value. The payback period is illustrated in **Example 14.3**.

Example 14.3

Rudi pays £100,000 for a three-year lease on an office building that will generate cash inflows of £50,000 a year for three years and has no residual value at the end of the three years.

Duri pays £100,000 for the freehold of some shop premises, which will bring him cash inflows of £12,500 a year for many years into the future.

Payback computation for Rudi and Duri:

Rudi			Duri		
Year	Cash flow, £	Cumulative cash flow, £	Year	Cash flow, £	Cumulative cash flow, £
0	(100,000)	(100,000)	0	(100,000)	(100,000)
1	50,000	(50,000)	1	12,500	(87,500)
2	50,000	0	2	12,500	(75,000)
3	50,000		3	12,500	(62,500)
			4	12,500	(50,000)
			5	12,500	(37,500)

Rudi			Duri		
Year	Cash flow, £	Cumulative cash flow, £	Year	Cash flow, £	Cumulative cash flow, £
			6	12,500	(25,000)
			7	12,500	(12,500)
			8	12,500	0

Rudi's payback period is two years.

Duri's payback period is eight years.

If the two investments were compared solely on the basis of the payback period, Rudi's would clearly be the better investment. But in this case, it is worth waiting longer to get a lot more money back. Duri's project is the better one (unless the cost of capital is very high).

The disadvantages of using the payback period are:

1 It ignores cash flows after the initial amount has been paid back.
2 It does not consider the timing of cash flows in a systematic way.

Looking at the payback period may be a convenient way of initially screening out projects that take far too long to pay back, but it does not indicate whether or not a project is worthwhile. A project must produce enough total cash flows and to do so within a reasonable period. It is important to consider the *timing* of cash flows more precisely; this is best done using discounted cash flow.

Discounted cash flow method: net present value

It is obviously better to receive £100 today than to receive £100 in one year's time, even if we ignore risk and inflation. £100 received today can be invested, and after a year, it might be worth £104 or more, depending on how successful the investment is. If we have to wait for the money, we lose the opportunity to use it to generate a return, even if the return is only 4 per cent interest. But shareholders expect a higher return than they could get from putting their money in a bank and might expect the company to 'make', say, 10 per cent per annum for them. Companies should have better investment opportunities than individuals.

If we have the choice of receiving £100 today, or £120 in a year's time, the decision is a little more difficult, but it is always worth waiting to receive money *if* we are going to receive extra money to compensate for the delay. Indeed, that is the whole nature of investment: we pay out money in the short term in order to receive more back in the future. If a company's cost of capital[2] is 10 per cent, it is well worth waiting a year to receive £120 rather than having only £100 today. Where a company's cost of capital is 10 per cent per annum, then the cost of waiting to receive money is 10 per cent per annum, and DCF should be used to calculate if it is worth waiting for the expected returns.

If we know the cost of a project and the future cash flows it will generate, then it is a matter of arithmetic to determine whether or not an investment is worthwhile. If the company's cost of capital is 10 per cent, we apply a 10 per cent discount rate to future cash flows. If we have to wait one year to receive £100, that is the equivalent of receiving £90.91 today. This is because if we received £90.91 today, we could invest it at 10 per cent for a year, and then it would give us exactly £100 in a year's time.

If we have to wait two years for it, then the 'present value' is £82.64. If we have to wait three years for it, then the NPV is £75.13. If we have to wait four years for it, then the NPV is £68.30, and so on.

2 Cost of capital is the discount rate applied to the cash flows in calculating the net present value of a project.

It is easy to check this. If we had £68.30 today, and it earned 10 per cent a year interest, at the end of four years, it would amount to £68.30 × 1.1 × 1.1 × 1.1 × 1.1, which comes to £100.

If a company's cost of capital is 10 per cent per annum, we assume that it has investment opportunities that would enable £100 today to become £110 after one year. If this is the case, we can make the following statements:

1. Receiving £100 today is equivalent to receiving £110 after one year.
2. Waiting one year to receive £110 is equivalent to receiving £100 today.
3. Waiting one year to receive £100 is equivalent to receiving £90.91 today. This is because if we have £90.91 today, and we invest it at 10 per cent, we will make £9.09 interest in one year, which will give us (£90.91 + £9.09 =) £100 after one year.
4. Waiting two years to receive £100 is equivalent to receiving £82.64 today. This is because if we have £82.64 today, and we invest it at 10 per cent, we will make £8.26 interest in the first year, giving us (£82.64 + £8.26 =) about £90.90,[3] which, after another year at 10 per cent, will give us £100.
5. We can look at any future cash flows and discount them in this way.

This is all very important in investment appraisal. The nature of investment is that we pay out money now and expect to get returns in the future. To start with, we need to work out what those future returns are likely to be and to assess the timing of them. Then we need to 'discount' the future cash flows to take into account the cost of having to wait for them. We will continue to assume that the cost is 10 per cent per annum, but equivalent calculations can be made for any 'discount rate'.

We have already established that receiving £100 after

1 year	is equivalent to receiving	£90.91 today
2 years	is equivalent to receiving	£82.64 today

We can continue as follows:

3 years	£75.13
4 years	£68.30, and so on

Another way to explain this is if the future value of £90.91 invested at 10 per cent = $90.91 \times (1 + i)^n$

$$= 90.91 \times (1 + 0.1)^n$$
$$= 90.91 \times (1.1)^1$$
$$= £100$$

So, to establish the 'present value' of £100 to be received at the end of year 1,

$$\text{the 'present value'} = 100 \times \frac{1}{(1+i)^n}$$
$$= 100 \times \frac{1}{(1.1)^1}$$
$$= 100 \times 0.909$$
$$= £90.91$$

$$\text{If the 'future value' of £82.64 invested at 10\%} = 82.64 \times (1+i)^n$$
$$= 82.64 \times (1 + 0.1)^2$$
$$= £100$$

[3] There are usually slight rounding differences with DCF.

So, to establish the 'present value' of £100 to be received at the end of year 2,

$$
\begin{aligned}
\text{the 'present value'} &= 100 \times \frac{1}{(1+i)^n} \\
&= 100 \times \frac{1}{(1+1)^2} \\
&= 100 \times 0.826 \\
&= £82.64
\end{aligned}
$$

The easiest way of finding these 'discount factors' is to look them up in a present value table, as shown in **Illustration 14.2.** Part 1 shows the present values of £1, which equals $1/(1 + i)^n$, where i is the interest or discount rate on the investment and n is the number of periods into the future where the £1 is to be received or paid. Part 2 is the present value of an annuity of £1 - an annuity is a regular sum of money to be received or paid at the end of period 1 and at the end of each succeeding year until year n. You will see from Part 1 that the present value of £1 received at the end of year 1 is £0.909, at the end of year 2 is £0.826, and at the end of year 3 is £0.751. The total present value of an annuity of £1 to be received at the end of years 1-3 is, therefore, £2.486. A quicker way to compute the present value of £1 to be received at the end of years 1-3 is to look at Part 2, where the PV of an annuity of £1 for all years 1 to 3 is £2.487. The difference is a small rounding difference.

ILLUSTRATION 14.2

Part 1: Present value of £1

%	1	2	3	4	5	6	7	8	9	10
Period										
N										
1	0.990	0.980	0.971	0.962	0.952	0.943	0.935	0.926	0.917	0.909
2	0.980	0.961	0.943	0.925	0.907	0.890	0.873	0.857	0.842	0.826
3	0.971	0.942	0.915	0.889	0.864	0.840	0.816	0.794	0.772	0.751
4	0.961	0.924	0.888	0.855	0.823	0.792	0.763	0.735	0.708	0.683
5	0.951	0.906	0.863	0.822	0.784	0.747	0.713	0.681	0.650	0.621
%	11	12	13	14	15	16	17	18	19	20
Period										
1	0.901	0.893	0.885	0.877	0.870	0.862	0.855	0.847	0.840	0.833
2	0.812	0.797	0.783	0.769	0.756	0.743	0.731	0.718	0.706	0.694
3	0.731	0.712	0.693	0.675	0.658	0.641	0.624	0.609	0.593	0.579
4	0.659	0.636	0.613	0.592	0.572	0.552	0.534	0.516	0.499	0.482
5	0.593	0.567	0.543	0.519	0.497	0.476	0.456	0.437	0.419	0.402

Part 2: Present value of an annuity of £1

%	1	2	3	4	5	6	7	8	9	10
Period										
1	0.990	0.980	0.971	0.962	0.952	0.943	0.935	0.926	0.917	0.909
2	1.970	1.942	1.913	1.886	1.859	1.833	1.808	1.783	1.759	1.736
3	2.941	2.884	2.829	2.775	2.723	2.673	2.624	2.577	2.531	2.487

4	3.902	3.808	3.717	3.630	3.546	3.465	3.387	3.312	3.240	3.170
5	4.853	4.713	4.580	4.452	4.329	4.212	4.100	3.993	3.890	3.791
%	11	12	13	14	15	16	17	18	19	20
Period										
1	0.901	0.893	0.885	0.877	0.870	0.862	0.855	0.847	0.840	0.833
2	1.713	1.690	1.668	1.647	1.626	1.605	1.585	1.566	1.547	1.528
3	2.444	2.402	2.361	2.322	2.283	2.246	2.210	2.174	2.140	2.106
4	3.102	3.037	2.974	2.914	2.855	2.798	2.743	2.690	2.639	2.589
5	3.696	3.605	3.517	3.433	3.352	3.274	3.199	3.127	3.058	2.991

We can then apply these discount factors to the cash flows of a particular project to find the 'present value' of the future cash flows, assuming a cost of capital of 10 per cent. This is applied to Jaggie and Lardie, as shown in **Illustration 14.3**. Clearly, the present value of £1 being paid out now (period 0) is £1. The present value of £1 received at the end of year 1 (period 1) is £0.909, at the end of year 2 (period 2) is £0.826, and so on.

ILLUSTRATION 14.3

	Jaggie project			Lardie project		
Year	Cash flow	Discount factor	Net present value	Cash flow	Discount factor	Net present value
0	(100)	1	(100)	(100)	1	(100)
1	45	0.909	40.91	10	0.909	9.09
2	40	0.826	33.06	20	0.826	16.53
3	35	0.751	26.30	30	0.751	22.54
4	10	0.683	6.83	40	0.683	27.32
5	10	0.621	6.21	45	0.621	27.94
Total	140		+ 13.31	145		+3.42

Hence, adding the present value of all future cash inflows and deducting the present value of all outflows, using a 10 per cent discount factor, we can see that the total NPV for each of the projects is as follows:

Jaggie (£113.31 − £100) = £13.31
Lardie (£103.42 − £100) = £3.42

Although Lardie brings in more money than Jaggie, it is not worth waiting for. Jaggie earns enough to cover the cost of capital and an extra £13.31. Lardie also covers its cost of capital and has a positive NPV. But Jaggie has a greater NPV, and so is the better investment.

Discount rates can be applied in this way to most projects. Once the discount rate or cost of capital has been decided, the best project is the one that produces the highest NPV.

If discount tables are not available, the figures for Jaggie can be calculated, as shown in **Example 14.4**.

Example 14.4

The cash flows in this illustration are from **Illustration 14.3** in respect of Jaggie.

Year 1 Divide the cash flow by 1 + the discount rate. Divide the cash flow by 1.1 for a 10 per cent discount rate

$$\text{Cash flow} = £40.91 = \frac{45}{(1 + 10\%)^1}$$

Year 2 Divide the cash flow by 1.1 × 1.1 to allow for two years (i.e. 1.1 squared)

$$\text{Cash flow} = £33.06 = \frac{40}{(1 + 10\%)^2}$$

$$\text{or } \frac{40}{(1.1)^2}$$

Year 3 Divide the cash flow by 1.1 × 1.1 × 1.1 to allow for three years (i.e. 1.1 cubed, or 1.1^3)

$$\text{Cash flow} = £26.30 = \frac{35}{(1 + 10\%)^3}$$

Year 4 Divide the cash flow by 1.1 × 1.1 × 1.1 × 1.1 to allow for four years (i.e. 1.1^4)

$$\text{Cash flow} = £6.83 = \frac{10}{(1 + 10\%)^4}$$

Year 5 Divide the cash flow by 1.1 multiplied by itself five times to allow for five years (i.e. 1.1^5)

$$\text{Cash flow} = £\ 6.21 = \frac{10}{(1 + 10)^5}$$

For those who are not particularly good at mathematics, it is easier to use discount tables. But if you want to do it without tables, here are the three easy steps:

1 Decide on the discount rate, and add it to 1, as follows:

5%	becomes	1.05
10%	becomes	1.1
15%	becomes	1.15

2 Multiply the figure given in (1) by itself once for year 1; twice for year 2; three times for year 3; four times for year 4, and so on.

3 Divide the cash flow for each year by the figure given in (2) above to 'discount' it to give the 'present value'.

When we have identified all the future cash flows and then allowed for the delay in receiving them by 'discounting' them, we know the NPV of the future cash inflows. This can be compared with the amount of the initial outflow to see if the project has earned us the 10 per cent that we specified as the cost of capital. Investment decisions should be based on choosing those projects that give the maximum cash flows after applying the appropriate discount rate. This is called the NPV.

The NPV decision rule is:

1 Accept a project if the NPV is > 0
2 Reject a project if the NPV is < 0.

If choosing between mutually exclusive projects, accept the project with the highest NPV.

Part 2 of **Illustration 14.2** shows the discount factors for the receipt of payment of the same sum of money for several years. For example, calculating the present value of £150 received at the end of year 1, year 2 and year 3, using the present value table, is:

(150 × 0.909) + 150 × 0.826) + 150 × 0.753) = £373.20

A quicker way of doing this calculation is using the present value of an annuity table.

Illustration 14.2, Part 2, shows that the present value of £1 received or paid in each of years 1, 2 and 3 is £2.487. The present value of £150 is:

£150 × 2.487 = £373.05

The result is the same, of course, with a small rounding difference, but using the present value of an annuity table is a quicker route to the answer (see **Example 14.5**).

Example 14.5 Using the annuity factor to calculate net present value

Assume Nairobi, in year 0, has invested £95,000 for a machine making ice cream. The project will last five years, and there is no scrap value at the end of the project in year 5. She expects to generate a net cash flow of £30,000 per year. Using the annuity factor at a discount rate of 10 per cent, calculate the net present value. The annuity factor for year 5 at 10 per cent is 3.791, as given in **Illustration 14.2**. The net present value is positive £18,730. Therefore. Nairobi should accept the purchase of the machine.

Present value = £30,000 × 3.791) = £113,730
Less initial investment = (£95,000)
Net present value = £18,730

Discounted cash flow: internal rate of return (IRR)

With the NPV approach to investment appraisal, we need to select a discount rate; then, the NPV of the project is calculated. With Jaggie, the NPV was £13.31. With Lardie, the NPV was £3.42. The answer will always be a sum of money (it could happen to be zero).[4]

If we do not know what discount rate to use, we could put the question the other way around: what discount rate would make future cash flows exactly equal to the amount of the initial investment? In other words, we need to find the discount rate when the project breaks even or gives a zero NPV - see **Illustration 14.4**, where the project will break even at an IRR of 17.09 per cent and the NPV is zero. The internal rate of return (IRR) is the 'yield' of the project. If the IRR equals or exceeds the company's required rate of return, that project is acceptable to the company.

4 The sum of money could be positive, negative or zero.

ILLUSTRATION 14.4 What an IRR graph looks like

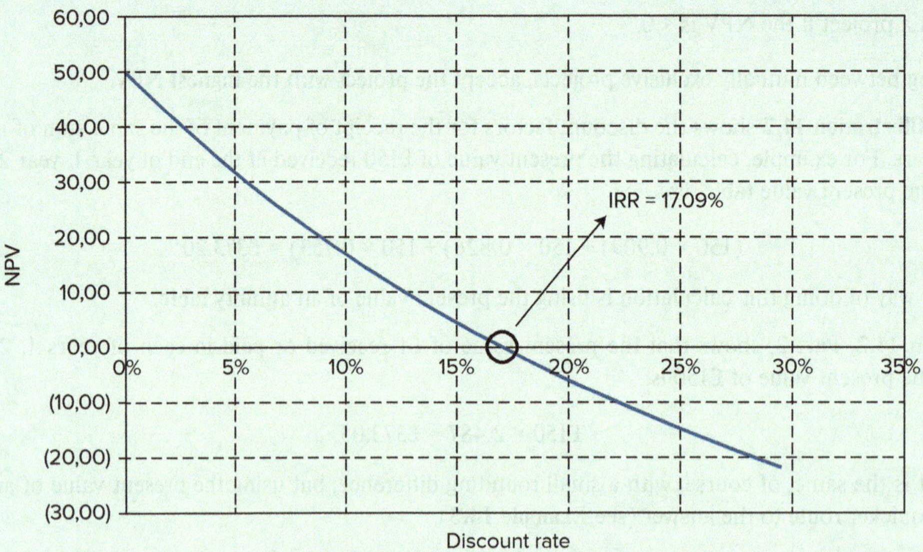

With the IRR, we do not assume a discount rate. Instead, we try to find a discount rate at which the NPV of the project is zero. The answer will always be a percentage. A quick glance at Jaggie and Lardie suggests that the IRR of Jaggie is well above 10 per cent. As Lardie has a much smaller NPV, its IRR is likely to be not much above 10 per cent. In the calculations in **Illustration 14.5**, 20 per cent is chosen as a guess for Jaggie and 15 per cent for Lardie to find the second NPV at this discount rates.

ILLUSTRATION 14.5

	Jaggie project			Lardie project		
Year	Cash flow	Discount factor 20%	Net present value	Cash flow	Discount factor 15%	Net present value
0	(100)	1	(100)	(100)	1	(100)
1	45	0.833	37.50	10	0.867	8.70
2	40	0.694	27.78	20	0.756	15.12
3	35	0.579	20.25	30	0.658	19.72
4	10	0.482	4.82	40	0.572	22.87
50	10	0.402	4.02	45	0.497	22.37
Total	+40		(5.63)	+45		(11.22)

When the cash flows of Jaggie and Lardie are discounted using higher discount rates, we can see that the totals amount to less than the £100 originally invested. Comparing these results with those shown using a 10 per cent discount rate, we can say that:

Jaggie earns more than 10 per cent: it has a positive NPV of £13.31 when discounted at 10 per cent.

Jaggie earns less than 20 per cent: it has a negative NPV of (£5.63) when discounted at 20 per cent.

Jaggie's IRR is between 10 per cent and 20 per cent; but it is closer to 20 per cent.

Lardie earns more than 10 per cent: it has a positive NPV of £3.62 when discounted at 10 per cent.

Lardie earns less than 15 per cent: it has a negative NPV of £11.22 when discounted at 15 per cent. *Lardie's* IRR is between 10 and 15 per cent, but it is closer to 10 per cent.

A better estimate of IRR can be made using interpolation.

The formula is shown below:

$$\text{IRR} = ra + \frac{NPVa}{NPVa - NPVb} \times (rb - ra)$$

ra = lower discount rate

rb = higher discount rate

NPVa = NPV at lower discount rate

NPVb = NPV at higher discount rate

We know that Jaggie's IRR is between 10 and 20 per cent. It is 10 per cent plus a part of 10 per cent.

$$\begin{aligned}\text{IRR} &= 10\% + \frac{13.31}{(13.31 - (5.63))} \times (20\% - 10\%)\\ &= 10\% + (0.7 \times 10\%)\\ &= 17\%\end{aligned}$$

We know that Lardie's IRR is between 10 and 15 per cent. It is 10 per cent plus a part of 5 per cent.

$$\begin{aligned}\text{IRR} &= 10\% + \frac{3.62}{(3.62 - (11.22))} \times (15\% - 10\%)\\ &= 10\% + (0.24 \times 5\%)\\ &= 11.2\%\end{aligned}$$

We can now compare the two investments, Jaggie and Lardie, using different approaches to investment appraisal.

	Jaggie	Lardie
Return on average investment	16%	18%
Payback period	2.14 years	4 years
Net present value at 10%	£13.31	£3.62
Internal rate of return	17%	11.2%

Jaggie is clearly the better project. Lardie showed a better return on investment because it produces slightly more profits. However, because Jaggie produces cash flows more quickly, it shows a shorter payback period, and it is better to use discounted cash flows.

Advantages of using an internal rate of return are:

1 It deals properly with the timing of all cash flows, that is, the time value of money.

2 Seeing an answer as a percentage appears to be easy to understand and can be compared with a company's cost of capital.

The main disadvantages of using an internal rate of return are:

1 It involves more calculations than other methods.

2 It is technically flawed and can lead to incorrect decisions. This is particularly true where there are irregular patterns of cash flows (perhaps with inflows coming before outflows) and high discount rates, and multiple IRRs can exist in those circumstances.

3 It cannot distinguish projects requiring large investments from those with small investments.
4 It cannot distinguish between projects involving investment from those requiring borrowing.
5 It cannot distinguish between mutually exclusive projects. We cannot assume that a project with a higher IRR is better than one with a lower IRR since the project with the higher IRR might have a lower NPV, as can be seen in **Illustration 14.6**.

ILLUSTRATION 14.6 NPV versus rate of interest (i)

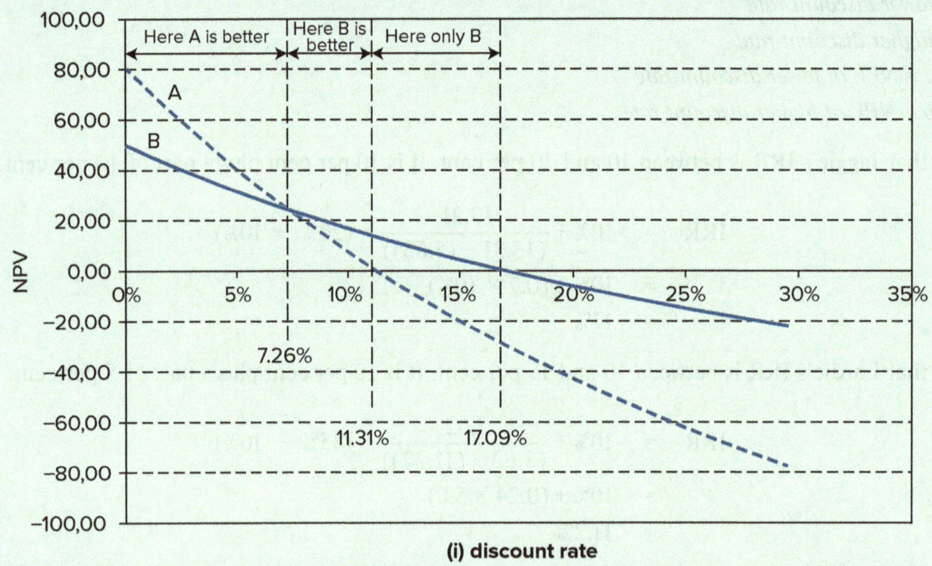

A variety of different techniques for investment appraisal may be used. Sometimes the use of one technique rather than another can lead to a different, and perhaps a poor, investment decision. The best approach is to use DCF to calculate the NPV. In order to do this it is necessary to know what discount rate to use, or the 'cost of capital'.

Calculation of NPV and IRR using Excel

Illustration 14.7 provides information for the Buttler Group, which wants to invest £100,000 in a machine for manufacturing cricket bats. The machine will last five years and has a scrap value of £5,000 at the end of year 5. The cash flows are shown below:

ILLUSTRATION 14.7

Cell number on Excel	Description	Discount rate/Cash flows, £
A2	Discount rate 8%	0.08
A3	Initial investment	(100,000)
A4	Net cash flow in year 1	23,200
A5	Net cash flow in year 2	25,200
A6	Net cash flow in year 3	35,280
A7	Net cash flow in year 4	35,222
A8	Net cash flow in year 5 + scrap value	30,000

NPV calculation using Excel

$NPV formula: = NPV(A2, A4 : A8) + A3$

$NPV = £17,399.54$

IRR calculation using Excel

$IRR\ after\ 5\ years: = IRR(A3 : A8)$

$IRR\ after\ 5\ years: = 14\%$

Which cash flows to include: relevant costs

It is easy to get lost in the technicalities and complications of DCF and overlook the fact that the calculations can be no better than the basic data on which they are based. Estimates have to be made of the cost of the project, the timing and amount of future cash inflows and outflows that it will generate, and the cost of capital. There is always an element of risk and uncertainty.

The appraisal should take into account all cash flows that would result from the project being undertaken, and exclude all cash flows that would arise whether or not the project is undertaken. There are a number of problem areas, including those shown below. It is important not only to have the best estimates of the amounts of the cash flows, but also to be clear about the timing of them (see **Example 14.6**).

Example 14.6

A company owns a machine that it originally bought for £100,000 and on which depreciation of £80,000 has been charged. The company could sell it for scrap for £10,000; alternatively, it could hire it out to another manufacturer, and the net present value rentals receivable for doing this would be £15,000.

The net book value of £20,000 (£100,000 – £80,000) is irrelevant. The opportunity cost of using the machine for another purpose is £15,000.

1 *Working capital.* Where a project involves expansion, there is usually a requirement for additional working capital (e.g. inventory and trade receivables) at the beginning, which is treated as a cash outflow. It is usually assumed that at the end of the project's life the additional working capital will no longer be required,[5] and so becomes a cash inflow.

2 *Installation.* Where a new piece of equipment is being bought, the cash outflow for it should include any payments for installation and setting it up.

3 *Scrap values.* If a new machine is being bought there is often a cash inflow from the sale of the old machine. If this scrapping is a direct result of buying the new machine, then the cash inflow from the scrap value should be included in the appraisal. When the new machine comes to the end of its life, we usually assume that there will be a cash inflow from selling it.

4 *Taxation.* The amount of corporation tax to be paid should be included in the appraisal. This can be rather complicated[6] and there are three aspects to it:

   a If the project makes additional profits (which is usually the intention), additional corporation tax is payable.

[5] Inventories are sold; receivables pay up; there is an inflow of cash.

[6] Sometimes profit is made in one year, and the tax is paid in the following year. The actual timing of payments has to be taken into account in DCF computations.

b HM Revenue & Customs allows profits to be reduced for tax purposes by substantial 'capital allowances' for depreciation[7] (usually more generous than the amounts that the company charges in its financial accounts).

c The timing for tax liability and the capital allowances for depreciation must be the same.

Example 14.7 shows two methods of dealing with these amounts. Method 1 shows a single tax payment each year, with capital allowances deducted from each year's profits. Method 2 deals with writing down allowances separately from the tax on additional annual profits by calculating the amount for each year, discounting them, and then deducting them from the initial cost of the asset. Method 2 is useful in 'sensitivity analysis' where the effects of differing assumptions are calculated.

Example 14.7

DCF and taxation

Question:

A company is proposing to invest in a new machine that will cost £100,000. It will generate additional profits of £19,000 a year for five years. At the end of year 5, it is expected to have a scrap value of £10,000. Assume depreciation is calculated on a straight-line basis.

Corporation tax is 30 per cent of taxable profits; the capital allowance is a 'writing down allowance' of 25 per cent per annum using a reducing balancing method.

Answer:

1 Calculate annual cash flows (before considering taxation)
Annual profits will be £19,000
Depreciation will be £90,000 ÷ 5 = £18,000 per annum
Cash flows (before considering taxation) will be £18,000 + 19,000 = £37,000 a year for the first four years, with an additional £10,000 in year 5

2 Assuming that capital allowances is the writing down allowance of 25 per cent calculated on the reducing balance basis, as follows:

Cost of asset	£100,000
Year 1 WDA 25%	25,000
	75,000
Year 2 WDA 25%	18,750
	56,250
Year 3 WDA 25%	14,062
	42,188
Year 4 WDA 25%	10,547
	31,641
Year 5 WDA 25%	7,910
	23,731
Proceeds of scrap	10,000
Balancing allowance	13,731

[7] And 'balancing allowances': any 'loss' when the asset is sold at the end of its life. If it is sold at a 'profit', tax is payable on the excess of the sale proceeds over the amount to which it is written down for tax purposes.

3 *Method 1* – Calculate amount of tax payable based on profits after deducting writing-down allowances. The DCF is then done on a single, all-embracing cash flow figure.

Year	0	1	2	3	4	5
		£	£	£	£	£
Profit before deducting depreciation		37,000	37,000	37,000	37,000	37,000
Less WDA		(25,000)	(18,750)	(14,062)	(10,547)	(7,910)
Balancing allowance		–	–	–	–	(13,731)
Taxable profit		12,000	18,250	22,938	26,453	15,359
Cash flows						
Tax payable (30%)		(3,600)	(5,475)	(6,881)	(7,936)	(4,608)
Net cash flows		33,400	31,525	30,119	29,064	32,392
Scrap value						10,000
						42,392
10% discount factor	1.0	0.909	0.826	0.751	0.683	0.621
Present values		30,361	26,040	22,619	19,851	26,325
Sum of the present values						125,196
Initial investment						(100,000)
NPV						25,196

4 *Method 2* – Two separate discounting calculations: (i) the cost of the asset together with the value of the taxation allowances and the final scrap value; (ii) other cash flows, including profits and the taxation on them.

Present value of writing-down allowances

Year	0	1	2	3	4	5	Total
WDA		25,000	18,750	14,062	10,547	7,910	
Balancing allowance (BA)					13,731		
30% of WDA/BA		7,500	5,625	4,218	3,164	6,492	
10% discount factor	1.0	0.909	0.826	0.751	0.683	0.621	
NPV		6,817	4,646	3,168	2,161	4,032	20,824

Cost of machine	£100,000
NPV of WDAs and balancing allowance	(£20,824)
Net cost of machine (after deducting taxation allowances)	£79,176
Deduct NPV of final scrap value £10,000 × 0.621	£6,210
NPV of the net cost of the machine	£72,966

Annual pre-depreciation profits	£37,000	
Deduct tax at 30%	£11,100	
Annual cash flows after tax	£25,900	
Annuity 10% for 5 years	× 3.791 =	£ 98,187
NPV		£25,221

The two different methods produce the same positive net present value of £25,200. There are slight rounding differences. The second method facilitates 'sensitivity analysis': the results of lower sales or higher costs can be calculated without changing the cost of the machine.

5 *Incremental costs.* Some costs will be incurred, and the payments made, whether or not the project is undertaken. A project may be charged its share of fixed overheads (such as the costs of providing a factory and its administration), but as those costs will be incurred whether or not the project is undertaken, the cash flows for fixed overheads are usually excluded. Only incremental fixed costs, those which would arise as a result of this project, are relevant costs.

6 *Sunk costs.* There are often significant payments for market research and feasibility studies that are undertaken before a decision is made on whether or not to go ahead. As those costs have already been incurred or paid (they are 'sunk'), or if the company is committed to paying these costs in the near future ('committed'), such costs are irrelevant in deciding whether or not to go ahead with the project and should be ignored in the project appraisal.

7 *Opportunity costs.* The cost of using an asset (or materials or labour) for a particular project is often the 'opportunity cost' of the best alternative use. If the asset or other input could be sold, if not used in the project under consideration, the selling price would be the relevant cost. Or if the resource is presently producing a contribution from its existing use, using it for the project under consideration, the contribution forgone would be the relevant cost.

8 *Costs of disposal.* If the cost of using a required material which is in stock but has no alternative use but would otherwise need to be safely disposed of, perhaps by health and safety regulations, a *cost saving* would arise in using it for the project equal to the cost of its safe disposal.

14.4 Cost of Capital

The preferred method of investment appraisal is discounted cash flow: net present value (see **Section 14.3**), using a 'given' discount rate, perhaps 10 per cent. The best projects are those that show the highest NPV when discounted at 10 per cent. (In **Illustration 14.5**, Jaggie is better than Lardie.)

The choice of 10 per cent might almost be arbitrary and there is something to be said for having a clear policy: any project giving a positive NPV when discounted at 10 per cent is acceptable. This would work well if unlimited funds are available at a cost of no more than 10 per cent per annum. It is important to establish what the company's cost of capital is, to be used as a 'hurdle' rate, and there are various ways of approaching this.

1 *Opportunity cost.* If there are plenty of projects available that show a positive NPV when discounted at 14 per cent, and only limited funds are available, then the hurdle rate should be 14 per cent, not 10 per cent. There is no point in tying up limited funds on projects that achieve only, say, 11 per cent if there is the opportunity to invest in projects that achieve 14 per cent or more. In **Illustration 14.5** the company should not invest in Lardie if they would then not have sufficient funds to invest in Jaggie.

It is important that a company has a sensible hurdle discount rate for investment appraisal. If it is set too low, perhaps at 7 per cent, then the company is likely to invest in projects that barely earn their keep, that disappoint the owners of the business, and that result in the value of the business falling. If it is set too high, perhaps at 22 per cent, then the company is likely to reject projects that more than earn their keep. If projects that earn a good return are rejected, then the business loses opportunities to increase its value.

2 *Weighted average cost of capital.* Companies are usually financed partly by borrowing and partly by shareholders' funds. At first sight, it is not difficult to establish the cost of borrowing: the interest rate on borrowings is usually specified. The cost of shareholders' funds is more difficult. As there is no requirement for companies to pay dividends on ordinary shares, we might be tempted to think that shareholders' funds have no real cost. They are 'free', and provided the company makes *some* profit, that is OK. But directors who do not meet shareholders' expectations in terms of profit will probably soon find themselves out of a job. Low profits lead to low share prices; low share prices invite takeover bids; and when another company acquires a company that is seen to be failing, it will soon get rid of the previous managers.

The cost of ordinary shareholders' funds depends on market expectations. The company should aim to invest in ways that increase the value of the company, not in ways that reduce it. Attempts to identify a company's cost of capital are attempts to identify the discount rate that projects must achieve in order to maintain the value of the company at least.

A company might be half-financed by borrowing, which costs 8 per cent per annum, and half-financed by shareholders' funds, which cost 14 per cent per annum. In this case the company's average cost of capital is 11 per cent.

Another company might be 25 per cent financed by borrowing, which costs 8 per cent per annum, and 75 per cent financed by shareholders' funds, which cost 14 per cent per annum. In this case the company's weighted average cost of capital is 12.5 per cent.

25% × 8%	=	2%
75% × 14%	=	10.5%
		12.5%

In calculating the weighting of the different types of capital (e.g. shareholders' funds 75 per cent; loan capital 25 per cent), it may be better to use the *market* value of shareholders' funds and the *market* value of borrowings rather than the amounts shown on the statement of financial position.

a *Cost of borrowing.* A company might have issued £1m of 10 per cent debentures, but that does not necessarily mean that the cost of those debentures is 10 per cent per annum. If the market value of debentures falls below the statement of financial position value, the amount of interest payable remains the same, but the *effective* rate (interest payable as a percentage of market value) will be higher. Similarly, if the market value of debentures increases, the effective interest rate declines. A number of other factors have to be taken into consideration:

i Interest is an allowable expense for corporation tax purposes. If the company's effective rate of corporation tax is 25 per cent, then the effective cost of 10 per cent interest to the company is only 7.5 per cent.

ii Most debentures are redeemable at some future date, perhaps 5 or 10 years into the future. They may be redeemable at par (which is book value or face value), at a discount (e.g. £100 debentures redeemable at £95), or a premium (e.g. £100 debentures redeemable at £110).

The calculation of the cost of debentures can look like doing a DCF calculation to arrive at the internal rate of return, as shown in **Example 14.8**.

Example 14.8

The market value today of Air UK's 6 per cent debentures is £80 for £100 par value. The debentures are redeemable at £105 four years from today. The company is profitable and its effective rate of taxation is 30 per cent.

The cost of interest each year is 70 per cent of £6, which is £4.20. At first sight, the cost of the loan capital looks like 70 per cent of £6 per annum, that is, 4.2 per cent. But the effective cost is increased by the premium payable on redemption and by the fact that the current market value of the debentures is well below the £100 par value.

The cash flows associated with it are shown in the second column below. As the cost of the debentures is likely to be more than 6 per cent, as a first guess, we try discounting the cash flows at 10 per cent.

Year	Cash flow	Discount factor 10%	Net present value	Discount factor 15%	Net present value
0	(80)	1	(80)	1	(80)
1	4.2	0.909	3.81	0.870	3.65
2	4.2	0.826	3.47	0.756	3.18
3	4.2	0.751	3.15	0.658	2.76
4	109.2	0.683	74.59	0.572	62.44
			+ 5.02		(7.97)

When discounted at 10 per cent, the future cash flows associated with the debenture are more than the price of the debenture now. The cost of the debentures to the company (in relation to the current market value) is, therefore, more than 10 per cent per annum.

When discounted at 15 per cent, the future cash flows associated with the debenture are less than the price of the debenture now. The cost of the debentures to the company (in relation to the current market value) is, therefore, less than 15 per cent per annum.

$$\text{Interpolation suggests a cost of } 10\% + \frac{5.02}{(5.02 + 7.97)} \times (15 - 10)$$
$$= 11.9\%$$

If the company has nothing better to do with its money, it should consider buying up the debentures on the stock market. But if the company's opportunity cost of capital is 12 per cent or more, it should be able to find a more profitable use of funds.

b *Cost of equity (cost of ordinary shareholders' funds).* Establishing the cost of equity is more difficult: there is no requirement to pay dividends, and it might be tempting to think that there is no cost attached to shareholders' funds. Shareholders have money invested in the business, and if they are lucky, they will receive dividends, and the value of their shareholdings will increase. If they are unlucky, there will be no dividends, and the value of their shareholdings will decline.

In a small company, where one or two directors own all the equity, the company can do what it likes. If it chooses to regard shareholders' funds as having zero cost and invest in duff projects, that is its own business.

If a listed company decided that shareholders' funds were cost-free, it might not produce enough profits or dividends, the market value of the shares would decline, and the directors would soon find their position threatened.

In order to determine the cost of a company's equity, we need to know what rate of return is needed to maintain or increase the value of the company. This really depends on shareholders' expectations. If they are expecting a return of 10 per cent, and the company generates 15 per cent, then the value of the company should increase. If they are expecting 15 per cent, and the company generates only 10 per cent, then we can expect the value of the company to decrease.

It is not clear how investors' expectations can be quantified. Even if we could find out what it is that determines future share prices, by the time we have found out, the picture would have changed; any model that predicts share prices based on historical data needs to be constantly updated to maintain credibility.[8] Sometimes companies seem to promise a lot, and their share price goes up and up. But if they then disappoint, the share price will collapse. It seems sensible to manage expectations: to plan and promise only what can be delivered with reasonable certainty.

In assessing shareholders' expectations, as in so many areas of accounting, we need to consider whether they should be expressed in terms of profit or cash flow. ROCE and price/earnings (P/E) ratio are two indications of shareholders' expectations based on profits. The dividend growth model is based on dividends. The capital asset pricing model (CAPM) can also be used to assess a company's cost of capital. Companies should not undertake projects that are likely to lower the company's returns and share price. When they cannot find sufficiently profitable opportunities for investing available funds, they should return those funds to shareholders as dividends or use them to buy up the company's shares. There are plenty of examples of companies that have invested surplus funds unwisely and so have reduced the value of the company.

3 *ROCE.* If a company has a ROCE of, say, 15 per cent, shareholders may expect this rate to continue in the future. If the company fails to achieve this, the share price is likely to fall. This does not, however, mean that the company's cost of capital for DCF purposes is 15 per cent. ROCE provides only a rough indication of shareholders' expectations, and there is no clear relationship between a company's ROCE and its cost of capital to be used for DCF.

4 *P/E.* A company's P/E ratio is also an indication of investors' expectations about the future profits of a company. Where substantial growth is expected, the share price is likely to be high in relation to the current level of profits, so the P/E ratio is high. Where growth in earnings is expected to be low, then the company's share price is likely to be low in relation to the current level of profits, so the P/E ratio is relatively low. There is, however, no easy way to convert the P/E ratio into a cost of capital figure.

5 *Dividend growth model.* A company's share price in relation to the last known level of dividends is also a good indicator of shareholders' expectations. If a company has a low dividend yield, this means that the share price is high in relation to the last known level of dividends; shareholders' expectations are high, and future dividends are expected to grow at a relatively high rate. The growth rate in dividends over recent years can be calculated and incorporated into a 'model', or formula, that indicates the cost of a company's equity capital.

The cost of share capital is assumed to be the dividend yield on the shares (dividend expressed as a percentage of share price), adjusted for an assumed rate of growth (see **Example 14.9**).

[8] There is more chance of maintaining credibility than of revealing truth!

Example 14.9

Last year's dividend per share: 20p

Current share price: £5 or 500p

Assumed rate of dividend growth: 15 per cent per annum

1 Calculate next year's dividend: 20p * (1 + 15%) = 23p

2 Express next year's dividend as a percentage of the current share price: $\frac{23}{500} \times 100 = 4.6\%$

3 Add assumed rate of growth: 15% + 4.6% = 19.6%

Cost of capital is assumed to be 19.6 per cent.

The model obviously has limitations and, in this example, a very high growth rate is assumed for dividends, which results in an unusually high cost of equity capital.

6 *CAPM.* The CAPM assumes that the cost of capital is based on:

a a 'risk-free' interest rate; to this is added

b an extra return to allow for the risk of investing in shares generally; this second element is adjusted to allow for

c the specific risk of a given company.

It is easy to find the 'risk-free' interest rate: it is the interest yield on government bonds, currently about 4 per cent.

The second element is more difficult to estimate, but we might say that in recent decades investors in ordinary shares have had returns of about, say, 8 per cent over and above the rate on government bonds.

The specific risk of a given company is measured as a 'beta', which might be average (1.0), above average (say, 1.2), or below average (say, 0.8).

The cost of capital of a company with high risk might be:

$$4\% + (8\% \times 1.2) = 4\% + 9.6\% = 13.6\%$$

The cost of capital of a company with low risk might be:

$$4\% + (8\% \times 0.8) = 4\% + 6.4\% = 10.4\%$$

Calculations are complex, but the answers produced seem to be reasonable: typically the cost of equity may be between 10 and 15 per cent per annum.

Evaluation of different approaches to the cost of capital

It is difficult to establish the cost of ordinary shareholders' funds with any certainty and without making some assumptions. Average returns on ordinary shares for the twentieth century can be calculated, and shareholders might expect this level of returns to continue. But in the first three years of the twenty-first century, they were disappointed: returns on ordinary shares were negative, and share prices fell. In the following three years, there was a return of growth. Although we do not know how long this will continue, it is reasonable to assume that there is little change in long-term expectations.

Estimates of the cost of borrowing are likely to be more accurate. The cost of borrowing is likely to be lower than the cost of ordinary shareholders' funds because it is seen as lower risk and because interest is an allowable expense for corporation tax purposes.

Given that the cost of borrowing is likely to be lower than the cost of equity, it is worth calculating a weighted average cost of capital figure. This approach assumes that the more a company relies on borrowing, the lower its cost of capital is likely to be. However, if a company relies too much on borrowing, the amount of risk increases, and this is likely to increase the cost of capital.

In practice, many companies do not bother with the more sophisticated approaches to determining the 'correct' cost of capital figures. It is acceptable to choose a reasonable rate, and stick to it. For low-risk projects 10 per cent is acceptable. For higher-risk projects it could be increased up to about 15 per cent.

14.5 Uncertainty and Risk

All investments are based on assumptions about the future, and there is usually some uncertainty about our forecasts and a degree of risk. There are some 'risk-free' investments, such as lending money to the government by buying 'gilts'. But managers are more likely to be involved in evaluating projects where there is some uncertainty and risk in estimating:

1 The initial cost of the project: with major projects the initial capital expenditure often turns out to be much higher than was originally planned.
2 The cash inflows that the project will generate: forecasts may prove to be much too high or much too low.
3 The cash outflows, including costs, that will be involved.
4 The timing: A project may take longer to complete and generate cash flows than anticipated. And it is difficult to be sure how long a project will last. It is easy to 'assume' a five-year life, but it is difficult to know how long it will really continue.

There are various ways of dealing with risk and uncertainty, all of which involve some subjectivity but help to credibly establish forecasts and appraisals.

One approach is to use a higher discount rate for projects that are seen as involving more risk than others. This is appealing, but it is difficult to know how much extra risk there is and by how much the discount rate should be increased.

A second approach, where there are several possible outcomes, is to apply probability theory to arrive at an 'expected value'. For example, if there is a 20 per cent chance that a cash flow will be £10,000, a 45 per cent chance that it will be £20,000, and a 35 per cent chance that it will be £30,000, the 'expected' cash flow can be calculated as follows:

20% × £10,000	=	£2,000
45% × £20,000	=	£9,000
35% × £30,000	=	£10,500
Expected cash flow		£21,500

The actual cash flow for a particular project is unlikely to be the 'expected' figure calculated in this way. But if probabilities can be applied in this way to a number of different projects, on average, the actual results are likely to be in line with what is expected. The problem is, of course, knowing what the probability is for any particular outcome.

A third approach is to recognize that a range of different outcomes is possible and to produce one appraisal based on rather pessimistic assumptions, one based on rather optimistic assumptions, and one 'realistic' appraisal between these two extremes. This may be attractive in terms of saying (a) this is the worst that is likely to happen - this is the downside risk; (b) this is the best that is likely to happen; and (c) this is what is most likely to happen. If (a) looks pretty dreadful, then a pretty good (b) might be needed to make the risk look worthwhile. This may give a useful 'feel' for a project and provide a basis for considering other likely outcomes. It may not be too difficult to agree on a range of likely outcomes, which can help to make decisions. But it is very subjective. There is no way of determining how dreadful the pessimistic assumptions should be or how brilliant the optimistic assumptions should be.

A fourth approach is to use 'sensitivity analysis' to consider a wider range of different possible outcomes. The appraisal can be done again and again, using different assumptions, to see how sensitive the decision is to particular changes in each variable. It may be uncertain whether a project will last for 5 years, 10 years, or somewhere in between. Sensitivity analysis might show that it is brilliant if it lasts for 10 years, but it is still viable if it lasts for only 5 years. It may be uncertain whether the initial project cost will be £1m, or £2m, or somewhere in between. Sensitivity analysis might show that it is a brilliant project if it costs only £1m, a waste of money if it costs £2m, and that, provided it does not cost more than £1.6m, it is viable. Wherever there is uncertainty, the proposal can be recalculated to see how sensitive it is to a change in assumptions. This approach does not remove subjectivity, but it does enable the financial effects of particular uncertainties relating to each variable in the calculation to be quantified and provides a basis for judgement and decision-making.

Summary

In theory managers use investment appraisal techniques to ensure that a company's funds are used in ways which maximize shareholders' wealth. In practice managers may have their own agendas, favouring particular projects, seeking to impress their superiors, enhancing their reputation, increasing their personal remuneration packages, and getting promotion by claiming credit for all that goes well, and blaming others for all that goes badly. It is easy to gain approval for a pet project by producing forecasts and appraisals that meet the company's criteria and show it as being viable. It is important that companies have 'post-investment appraisal' procedures in place that check if actual results are in line with the figures that were included in the appraisal that the company approved. Successful managers will have done some, or all, of the following:

- Made sure that actual results are in line with the original appraisals.
- Been promoted and transferred so that they are no longer around to take the blame.
- Kept a careful record of all the forecasts that made up the appraisal, and made sure that someone else is responsible for each element that made up the total appraisal. If the project does not come up to expectations, it is Bill's fault because the sales forecasts were wrong; or Jane's fault because she underestimated the original cost; or Jo's fault because production costs were way out of line.

Successful investment projects are the key to the financial success of a company, and to maximizing shareholder value. Management cannot avoid the results of their investment activities being assessed by the outside world through their published financial statements. For individual managers, taking credit for successful investment projects is important to success. All managers need to understand investment appraisals if they are to be the ones who take the credit, and not the ones who end up taking the blame. Good managers ensure that decisions are taken on the basis of information that is as honest as possible, with risks and uncertainties specified and taken into account. Good decisions are taken by responsible groups of managers who understand the limitations of the data, and the techniques used for appraising the data.

Review of key points

- The ROI of a project is calculated using profits, not cash flow, and is comparable with the return on capital employed for the company as a whole.
- The payback period is calculated using cash flows, not profits, and tells us how quickly a project is likely to pay for itself.
- DCF properly allows for the timing of cash flows.
- The NPV method of DCF is the preferred method of investment appraisal.
- It is necessary to know the company's cost of capital to use NPV.
- DCF calculations can be no better than the underlying data that are based on estimates, and there is always some risk and uncertainty.

Self-testing questions

1 How is ROI calculated?

2 The Row Sea Company's most recent annual report and accounts show a profit after tax of £1m last year, and the statement of financial position shows total shareholders' funds of £10m. It is considering buying a ship that will cost £2m and generate operating profits (after charging depreciation) of £180,000 a year.

Would the investment increase the company's return on capital employed?

3 The PBP company has £1m to invest and is considering the following two projects:

a Project A will generate annual net cash flows of £200,000 for eight years.

b Project B will generate cash flows of £400,000 in year 1, £350,000 in year 2, £300,000 in year 3, £100,000 in year 4, £50,000 in year 5, and then about £5,000 a year for another few years.

On the basis of this information, and without considering DCF, which of the two projects is better?

4 What are the main advantages and disadvantages of using the following methods of investment appraisal?

a ROI

b Payback period

5 Is there a case for investing in the following project?

A new machine costs £200,000 and will have a five-year life with no residual value at the end. It is expected to generate profits of £35,000 a year for five years.

What is the highest cost of capital at which the project would be acceptable?

6 The Peel Company is considering two alternative investment opportunities: a Kippering Project and a Queenies Project. Each would involve an initial outlay of £50,000 and is expected to have a five-year life with no scrap value at the end. The additional cash flows (before deducting depreciation) that each project is expected to generate are as follows:

Year	Kippering	Queenies
	£	£
1	25,000	5,000
2	20,000	15,000
3	15,000	25,000
4	10,000	25,000
5	5,000	20,000

You are required to calculate the following for each project and suggest how a decision should be made between the two projects:

a average annual profits;

b return on initial capital employed;

c return on average capital employed;

d payback period;

e NPV using a 10 per cent discount factor;

f NPV using a 25 per cent discount factor;

g an approximate internal rate of return.

7 The Maroc Production Company is considering manufacturing and selling an economy video camera for use by small retailers for security purposes. A firm of management consultants has carried out a feasibility study for them at a cost of £25,000, which has not yet been paid. There would be two requirements for machinery:

a Some existing machinery could be modified at a cost of £100,000 to undertake the first stage of production.

b For the second stage of production, the company already has suitable machinery that is not in use; it has a book value of £80,000, which would be difficult to dismantle and dispose of, and its net realizable value at present is zero.

If the project goes ahead, maintenance costs of the machinery would be £10,000 per annum; there would be additional working capital requirements of £50,000 at the beginning of the project, which would be recovered at the end of four years; initial marketing costs, to be paid for as soon as the project is approved would be £60,000; and annual marketing costs would be £20,000 per annum for the full four years.

The cost and selling price per unit is expected to be:

	£	£
Selling price		60
Materials	11	
Direct labour	6	
Variable overheads	13	
General fixed overheads	12	
Interest	2	44
Profit		16

The management consultants have suggested that the product would have a four-year life before being superseded by better cameras and that the pattern of sales would be:

	Sales in units
Year 1	3,000
Year 2	7,000
Year 3	4,000
Year 4	1,000

The company's cost of capital is assumed to be 20 per cent per annum.

Making careful use of the above information, calculate the NPV of the project. Ignore taxation.

Make and state appropriate assumptions where necessary.

8 Soderby plc has £10m of 10 per cent debentures that are due to be redeemed at par in five years' time. Their current market value is £98, and corporation tax is 30 per cent. What is the cost of the debt capital?

9 The market value of Chipperby's ordinary shares yesterday, immediately after paying a dividend of 40 pence, was £12. Dividends are expected to grow at the rate of 5 per cent per annum.

   a Calculate the cost of Chipperby's equity capital using the dividend growth model.

   b The return on ordinary shares in recent years has averaged 11 per cent; the risk-free interest rate at present is 3 per cent; and Chipperby's beta is 0.75. Calculate the cost of Chipperby's equity capital using the CAPM.

Assessment questions

1 How is the payback period calculated? Why is it widely used, although it can suggest wrong decisions?

2 The Leongwei Company decided that there would be no additional purchases of fixed assets unless they had been subject to investment appraisal and showed a positive NPV when discounted at 10 per cent. The policy was implemented five years ago, but the company's return on capital employed is still only 7 per cent per annum.

   Explain the apparent inconsistency.

3 A project with an initial cost of £200,000 is expected to make profits of £44,000 per annum for five years, at the end of which it will have a scrap value of £20,000. Calculate:

   a average annual depreciation charge
   b average annual cash flows
   c payback period
   d total profits made during the five years
   e return on initial investment
   f return on average investment
   g NPV assuming a cost of capital of 20 per cent
   h internal rate of return.

4 Respirer Ltd is a small company that specializes in the manufacture of electronic devices for surveillance purposes. Recently, it has been involved in producing devices to detect drugs and the presence of live animals or humans in import and export consignments. It has designed and produced a prototype of a device that it calls the 'Kensington', and that can be worn by lorry drivers.

A report from a large firm of management consultants suggests that in order to produce the device, the company will need to set up a new production line at a cost of £600,000 and that an old assembly shop could be used. The assembly shop originally cost £500,000 and depreciation on it of £350,000 has been charged, but it has not been used for a number of years. The company was planning to sell it for £120,000, but the consultants' report recommends that it is used to produce the new device; modifications to the workshop for this purpose will cost £80,000.

The expected costs and selling price per unit of the Kensington are as follows:

	£	£
Selling price		110
Materials	18	
Labour	12	
Variable overheads	15	
General fixed overheads	8	
Interest	4	57
Profit		53

The anticipated sales in units are 5,000 in year 1, 10,000 in year 2, 16,000 in year 3, 12,000 in year 4, and 7,000 in year 5.

Additional working capital requirements will be £250,000, which will be recovered at the end of the project. An initial advertising campaign costing £400,000 will be required at the beginning of the project; continuing marketing costs will be £130,000 per annum.

The prototype cost £80,000, and those costs have been paid; the consultants' report cost £120,000, but those costs have not yet been paid.

The company's cost of capital is 15 per cent.

Making careful use of the above information, calculate the NPV of the project. Ignore taxation. Make and state appropriate assumptions where necessary.

5 The Bitchwood Company is considering two alternative investment proposals, details of which are as follows:

		Proposal 1	Proposal 2
		£	£
Initial investment		100,000	120,000
Cash inflow	Year 1	35,000	30,000
	Year 2	30,000	30,000
	Year 3	30,000	35,000
	Year 4	25,000	50,000
	Year 5	15,000	40,000

Assume that the amount of the initial investment will be depreciated on a straight-line basis over five years and that there will be no residual value.

a Calculate for each proposal:

  i payback period

  ii average annual profits

  iii return on initial investment

  iv NPV using discounted cash flow and assuming a cost of capital of 10 per cent

  v internal rate of return.

b Which of the two projects would you recommend, and why?

6 Redderby plc has £12m of 11.43 per cent debentures that are due to be redeemed at a premium of 5 per cent in four years' time. Their current market value is £104, and corporation tax is 30 per cent. What is the cost of the debt capital?

7 The market value of Presterby's ordinary shares yesterday, immediately after paying a dividend of 15 pence, was £6. Dividends are expected to grow at the rate of 8 per cent per annum.

  a Calculate the cost of Chipperby's equity capital using the dividend growth model.

  b The return on ordinary shares in recent years has averaged 13 per cent; the risk-free interest rate at present is 3.5 per cent; and Chipperby's beta is 1.2. Calculate the cost of Chipperby's equity capital using the CAPM.

Group activities and discussion questions

1 'The acceptability of an investment proposal depends on the company's cost of capital; a project that is acceptable to one company may not be acceptable to another.'

'Accurate assessments of cost of capital are not possible; choosing a figure of between 10 per cent and 15 per cent is a reasonable approximation.'

Explain, contrast and attempt to reconcile these statements.

2 With many well-publicized projects, it seems that proper investment appraisal techniques were not applied, were not possible or appropriate, or were ignored. Discuss this statement with reference to projects such as:

  a the Millennium Dome

  b fees paid by telecommunications companies for third-generation licences

  c the building for the Scottish Assembly in Edinburgh

  d the building of Wembley Stadium or the 2012 Olympic sites.

3 To what extent is the proper use of investment appraisal techniques likely to stop the development of projects that are for the benefit of society?

4 A post-investment appraisal is essential to ensure that a company's investment appraisal techniques have been properly applied. However, it is likely to reveal some uncomfortable facts. Discuss.

5 Sophisticated investment appraisal techniques are no substitute for sound judgement (or good luck). Discuss.

6 Effective managers usually succeed in getting approval for the projects that they want. A knowledge of the company's investment appraisal procedures enables them to produce figures that ensure that projects will be approved. The existence of sound investment appraisal procedures does not ensure that projected results are actually delivered. Discuss.

Accounting in context

Discuss what the UK water industry can learn from the banking industry failures.

UK water vs banking sector failures

'Ballooning leverage and excessive financial engineering are among the unnerving parallels with the 2008 financial crisis' (Jenkins 2024).

At first sight, the UK water industry has little in common with the banking sector – put aside liquidity problems caused by leaky pipes and the toxic assets otherwise known as sewage spills. Yet there are significant challenges confronting Thames Water, the UK's biggest water group, and many others among the UK's 17 suppliers of water and sewerage services that strongly align with the issues that banks faced in the period running up to the 2008 global financial crisis.

In October 2008, the UK Chancellor of the Exchequer commissioned the chairman of the UK's Financial Services Authority (FSA) to review the causes of the financial crisis and to make recommendations on the changes in regulation and supervision required to ensure a more robust banking system. Lord Turner's review (The Turner Review: a regulatory response to the global banking crisis) was published on 18 March 2009.

The commonly cited reasons for the Royal Bank of Scotland (RBS) failure:

1. RBS's capital position had significant weaknesses as a result of management decisions, which were permitted by an inadequate global regulatory capital framework.
2. The bank was overly reliant on risky short-term wholesale funding, which was also permitted by an inadequate approach to the regulation of liquidity.
3. The FSA conducted little fundamental analysis of RBS's underlying asset quality, which caused concerns and uncertainties.
4. Additionally, the bank suffered substantial losses in credit trading activities, eroding market confidence.
5. Both the bank and the regulator underestimated the extent of the losses.
6. The ABN Amro acquisition took place with inadequate due diligence. Furthermore, there was an overall systemic crisis, and banks in worse relative positions were extremely vulnerable to failure.

Parallels with the banking industry

There is the huge amount of debt that exists within the system. For instance, Thames Water has been permitted to operate with a gearing of 80–90 per cent, which is reminiscent of the banking system that allowed RBS to function with an insufficient core capital ratio. As a result, in 2008, RBS became the world's biggest bank failure and had to be bailed out by the UK government, which cost £45.5bn.

The parent company of Thames Water has defaulted on a £400m bond, which is part of the group's total debt of £18.3bn. Other water companies also have high levels of debt, which have been accumulated since they were privatized in 1989. However, as debt costs have risen over the years, and cash flows have decreased due to weak performance and larger regulatory fines, the leverage multiples, which compare debt with operating profit, have increased significantly. For example, in Thames Water's case, the multiple has doubled to around 15 times. Adding to the challenge of the stretched financing, the assets that these companies are backing have been artificially overvalued.

Just as illiquid securities were overvalued on bank balance sheets, excessive financial engineering also poses a problem. Back in 2008, bad mortgage lending to subprime US borrowers became a systemic issue due to investments in collateralized debt obligations. Similarly, the UK water sector has relied on complex corporate structures such as Thames's interlocking system of holding, operating and financing entities, which can be quite confusing. Investors' bond holdings are also insured in a similar way. Monoline insurance, which suffered greatly in 2008 due to its exposure to toxic bank securities, has underwritten a significant portion of the bonds issued by the most indebted UK water utilities.

Inadequate regulation

It is important to note the similarities between the regulation of banks before the financial crisis of 2008 and the regulation of water companies before the year 2024. Investors in the water industry argue that the rules imposed by regulator Ofwat have been too restrictive, with regard to investment levels and consumer charges. Similar to the banking industry, the focus on consumer pricing rather than the overall health of the sector has been short-sighted and has resulted in a lack of investment and opportunities for arbitrage. It remains to be seen if the water industry will face bank-style bailouts in the event of a crisis, but hopefully, this can be avoided.

Economist Dieter Helm suggests that an important reform would be to separate sewerage responsibilities from water operators. The investment horizons should include 10 to 20 years, which is crucial if they are to undertake the necessary climate-related infrastructure overhaul to prevent untreated sewage from polluting our rivers and seas. In considering positively the prospects of resetting the UK's privatized water sector, it is worth noting that private sector provision of water services is unusual around the world - 90 per cent of countries, says Professor David Hall at the University of Greenwich, have state-owned water operations. And here's an interesting scenario: in the Netherlands, public-sector water operators are funded by Nederlandse Waterschapsbank, a AAA-rated public-sector water bank. In other words, the common ground between water companies and banks is harnessed for the common good. And guess what: the Dutch water business is by some measure the best performing in Europe.

Water management faces a public relations issue similar to UK banking. Customers expect free services, believing water is essential and readily available. However, upgrading infrastructure requires significant spending. Water policymakers could learn valuable lessons from banking parallels, as they prepare to release a draft financial and regulatory regime for the next five years.

The similarities between banks before 2008 and water companies before 2024 are quite striking, especially in terms of ineffective regulation. Water company investors argue that the regulations have been overly strict, with the regulatory agency Ofwat controlling investment levels and consumer charges. This narrow focus on consumer pricing rather than the overall health of the sector has led to arbitrage opportunities and hindered investment, similar to what happened with banks before their collapse. If the current challenges facing water companies result in failure, should they receive bailouts similar to those given to banks?

Sources: P. Jenkins (2024) What UK Water Can Learn from Global Banking. *Financial Times* 15 April. https://www.ft.com/content/5de3b208-279a-4f7a-91b3-cb77c4908646

Clifford Chance (2009) The Turner Review and its Impact on the Future of Banking. https://www.cliffordchance.com/content/dam/cliffordchance/briefings/2009/04/Briefing___The_Turner_Review_and_its_impact_on_the_future_of_banking.pdf

J. Treanor and S. Bowers (2011) RBS Failure Caused by Multiple Poor Decisions. *Guardian*, 12 December. https://www.theguardian.com/global/2011/dec/12/royal-bank-of-scotland-fsa-report

J. Treanor (2017) The RBS Crisis: A Timeline of Events. *Guardian*, 21 May. https://www.theguardian.com/business/2017/may/21/royal-bank-of-scotland-a-timeline-of-events

House of Commons, Treasury Committee (2012) The FSA's Report into the Failure of RBS. https://publications.parliament.uk/pa/cm201213/cmselect/cmtreasy/640/640.pdf

References and further reading

Arnold, G. (2008) *Corporate Financial Management* (4th edn.). Upper Saddle River, NJ: FT Prentice Hall.

Brealey, R., Myers, S. and Allen, F. (2010) *Principles of Corporate Finance-Global Edition*. New York: McGraw-Hill.

Brealey, R.A., Myers, S.C. and Marcus, A.J. (2011) *Fundamentals of Corporate Finance* (7th edn.). New York: McGraw-Hill.

Das, S. (2012) *Extreme Money: The Masters of the Universe and the Cult of Risk*. Harlow: Pearson.

Drury, C. (2008) *Management and Cost Accounting* (7th edn.). Andover: Cengage Learning.

Rosenthal, J., Rouwenhorst, G., Thomas, J., and Xu, A. (2021) Hertz Global Holdings: Uses of Debt and Equity. *Yale School of Management*, Case 20-030, 11 January.

Vernimmen, P., Quiry, P., Dallocchio, M., Le Fur, Y. and Salvi, A. (2009) *Corporate Finance: Theory and Practice* (2nd edn.). Chichester: Wiley.

Watson, D., Head, A., Chan, D. and Watson, D. (2023) *Corporate Finance: Principles and Practice* (9th edn.). Harlow: Pearson.

Chapter 15

Budgetary Planning and Control

Chapter contents

15.1 Introduction
15.2 Budgets and Budgetary Control
15.3 Implementing Budgetary Control
15.4 Cash Budgets
15.5 Advantages of Operating Budgetary Control Systems
15.6 Problems of Budgetary Control in Practice
15.7 Zero-based and Rolling Budgets (ZBB)
15.8 Planning and Programming Budgeting System (PPBS)

Learning objectives

After studying this chapter you will be able to:

- ✓ Define budgets and budgetary control and explain how they operate
- ✓ Explain and illustrate the use of budgets and control information
- ✓ Understand and demonstrate the use of flexible budgets
- ✓ Explain the role of cash budgets and produce and interpret practical examples
- ✓ Describe the main advantages of operating budgetary control
- ✓ Critically assess the operation of budgetary control in practice
- ✓ Understand the role and limitations of ZBB and of PPBS

15.1 Introduction

We all start off with some sort of plans in mind, however vague, and hope that they will come to fruition and that we fulfil our dreams (or some of them). Then, on a regular basis, we will compare what is actually happening in our lives with what we hoped for. Perhaps we find that all is as we had hoped; or we change our plans;

or we decide what we need to do in order to fulfil our dreams, or attain our objectives. Some small businesses may operate in this way. But a well-managed business defines and quantifies its objectives, prepares detailed plans, and systematically compares the results that are actually achieved with those that were planned. Budgetary control does this in a systematic way and this chapter outlines how this is done in practice. Some of the difficulties in practice are discussed and two alternative approaches (ZBB and PPBS) are introduced.

15.2 Budgets and Budgetary Control

A starting point for preparing plans or budgets for next year is to look at this year's actual financial statements and estimate what will happen next year, adding a bit for inflation and a bit for growth.

In **Example 15.1**, the directors of Daniel Dhoon are forecasting a 12 per cent increase in sales and an increase in profits. This is to be achieved by instituting a delivery service. Unfortunately, this will lead to a substantial increase in distribution costs; it will also require the purchase of additional non-current assets (such as vans), and current assets (inventories and receivables) are likely to increase. Although a modest increase in net profit is expected, the increase in assets and equity is much greater. The end result is that the return on equity will fall from 3 per cent to 2.5 per cent. This may be a reasonable estimate of what could happen, but it needs to be a satisfactory plan or budget.

Example 15.1

Preparing a budgeted income statement and statement of financial position

The directors of the Daniel Dhoon Company were not satisfied with recent results: growth had been sluggish, and return on equity needed improvement. To increase the return on equity, they planned to expand sales by starting a delivery service in year 8. The draft budget for year 8, together with the actual results for year 7, are shown below.

Income statement for the year	Actual results Year 7	Forecast results Year 8	
	£	£	
1 Sales	400,000	448,000	12% increase
2 Cost of sales	300,000	318,000	
3 Gross profit	100,000	130,000	25% gross profit ratio, increasing to 29%
4 Distribution costs	(30,000)	(58,300)	
5 Administrative expenses	(53,000)	(54,000)	
6 Operating profit	17,000	17,700	
7 Finance expense	(8,000)	(8,000)	
8 Profit before taxation	9,000	9,700	

9 Taxation	(3,000)	(3,100)
10 Profit for year	6,000	6,600
Statement of financial position as at year end		
11 Non-current assets, net book value	270,000	315,000
12 Current assets	60,000	85,000
Total assets	330,000	400,000
13 Current liabilities	30,000	36,000
14 8% debentures	100,000	100,000
15 Equity	200,000	264,000
Total liabilities and equity	330,000	400,000
Return on equity:	6,000/200,000	6,600/264,000
profit for year/equity	= 3.0%	= 2.5%

Example 15.1 does not really show a budget. It looks as if someone has been asked to prepare financial statements on the basis that sales will increase by 12 per cent as a result of buying a vehicle for around £50,000 and spending £40,000 or so on employing a driver, petrol and other delivery costs. As a plan, it is not satisfactory because it does not attain a particular objective: return on equity will fall from 3 per cent to 2.5 per cent. It may be seen as a *draft* budget, providing a basis for revision. It can be changed again and again until it is more like a plan that can be implemented and which will succeed in increasing the return on equity.

Keywords in the definition of a budget are that it is prepared and *approved* before the period to which it relates and that it is a plan intended to achieve *a given objective.*[1] There could even be several objectives, such as achieving a particular amount of earnings per share, reduction in borrowings or increase in sales. The point is that management must approve and commit to the plan to ensure that it is implemented.

In revising the draft, consideration could[2] be given to the following:

1. Could the vehicle be hired instead of buying it? That would reduce the amount of capital employed and, in turn, the return achieved.
2. Could the delivery function be outsourced?
3. Is an appropriate charge being made for delivery?
4. Could the increase in current assets be held down[3] by restricting the amount customers are allowed to owe or by reducing inventory levels?
5. Are there other ways of increasing sales that would require less (capital and revenue) expenditure?

A budget may be defined as:

> ***A plan, quantified in monetary terms, prepared and approved prior to a defined period of time, which usually shows planned income to be generated and/or expenditures to be incurred during that period and the capital to be employed to attain a given objective.***

---

[1] If a budget is to be prepared and approved prior to (e.g.) year 8 (probably in November or December year 7), there is a problem in that the actual results for the whole of year 7 will not be available until after the end of the year. This is usually overcome by using actual results for January to October, and estimated results for November and December of year 7.

[2] It might be useful to start by applying and interpreting most of the set of ratios given in Chapter 4.

[3] Management of working capital is dealt with in Chapter 12.

There is also a need to check if the draft budget is realistic, particularly in relation to sales and cash. Starting a delivery service will likely increase sales, but it needs to be clarified why the gross profit ratio is expected to increase, and this would need to be explained. Perhaps they expect lower buying prices because of bulk buying, but their estimates suggest a very optimistic increase in the gross profit ratio for a modest 5 per cent increase in sales. Perhaps they expect to be able to charge higher prices (but they need to be careful in view of their sluggish growth). Or their delivery service will concentrate on products with a higher margin. A detailed sales budget - showing planned sales for all the different product lines - would help to produce more realistic plans.

It is also necessary to know when and how the cash will become available, particularly for the purchase of the van. A detailed cash budget is required, showing the receipts and payments expected for each month and the balances available or the overdraft (or other additional funding) that would be required.

After doing all the detailed work, it is possible that management would adopt the 'forecast' shown in **Example 15.1** on the basis that it is worth accepting a short-term reduction in return on equity as a step towards improving sales and profitability in future years once the delivery service has been fully established. It is more likely, however, that management would require some modifications to the estimates before accepting it as the plan designed to achieve their objectives for the following year.

A full budgetary control system requires a whole set of different budgets, as shown in **Section 15.3**.

After the budget has been adopted as the plan that the organization intends to implement, it is necessary to monitor the actual results achieved each month.[4] This is the idea of 'control'. Usually, the actual results achieved will be different from what was planned - that's life! Perhaps some sales and costs will be higher than planned, others will be lower, and overall, the changes do not matter very much. But some results may be seriously out of line. In **Example 15.1** the new delivery service may be a huge success - more than one van can cope with - and they will have to reconsider their options.[5] Or the service may be a failure with nowhere near enough additional sales to justify the costs. They may consider additional marketing initiatives that will help them to achieve their plans; or they could abandon their delivery service, or find other ways of doing it.[6] Control information provides information about *actual* results; these are compared with the plan, and where there are significant differences, action must be taken: either the budgets are changed, or additional effort has to be put in to achieve them.

Budgetary control may be defined as:

> ***The establishment of budgets relating the responsibilities of executives to the requirements of a policy, and the continuous comparison of actual with budgeted results, either to secure by individual action the objective of that policy, or to provide a basis for its revision.***

A key part of the definition is that specified managers should be responsible for implementing particular parts of the budget. There is not much point in establishing plans and just hoping they will come to fruition. Someone must be responsible. In **Example 15.1**, someone would be responsible for implementing the delivery service - and would be 'given a budget' - an allocation of what they were authorized to spend. There would also be someone responsible for monitoring the sales and costs of the delivery service.[7]

It is important to compare the actual results with the original plan or budget to see if the business is on course. Where actual results are different from what was planned, some corrective action is required.

In addition to a budgeted income statement and statement of financial position, it is usually important to produce a cash budget; often, this is required by the business's bankers who want to see when and how their loans and overdrafts can be repaid. Cash budgets are dealt with in **Section 15.4**.

---

[4] Or more frequently.

[5] Perhaps a second van; or making a delivery charge to reduce demand.

[6] Such as outsourcing.

[7] The delivery service could be a cost centre, profit centre or investment centre in its own right.

A full and formal system of budgetary control involves the production of a set of detailed budgets to include all the business's activities, which all culminate in a budgeted income statement, a budgeted statement of financial position, and a cash budget. Managers in each area of the business are involved in setting the budgets. The system is supposed to express the intentions of top management, detailed as a financial plan, with a commitment from all managers to achieve the results expected.

15.3 Implementing Budgetary Control

When budgets are used for planning and controlling a large and complex organization, different budgets have to be produced for each part of the organization, and for each major activity. Many people are involved in the process of setting budgets, and subsequently in dealing with the control information. Often it is necessary to produce a *budget manual*, specifying and standardizing how the budgets are to be produced. This will specify the various budgets that are used to compile the *master budget.*

The starting point in producing the master budget is the sales budget. It is necessary to know the likely level of sales in order to know what direct materials need to be purchased, how much labour to employ, the amount of machinery, overheads, and so on. A typical set of budgets is shown below. In a large organization, there may need to be budgets for each of a number of different product groups and/or for a number of different geographic areas. Different managers will be responsible for producing (and later for monitoring the implementation of) each budget; managers are generally dependent on information from other budgets to plan their activities.

1. Sales budget: showing budgeted sales for each month.
2. Finished goods inventories and production budget: once the level of sales has been planned, it is necessary to plan how much should be produced, making allowance for any inventories or finished goods.
3. Direct materials usage budget: once the level of production has been planned, it is necessary to plan what materials should be purchased (again making allowance for any inventories of direct materials).
4. Direct labour budget: obviously, this is dependent on the planned level of production.
5. Production overhead budget: this is partly dependent on the planned level of production but is also influenced by other factors, such as the purchase of better production facilities (capital expenditure budget).
6. Distribution cost budget.
7. Administration expense budget.
8. Budgeted income statement: all the above listed budgets are needed before a budgeted income statement can be produced.
9. Budgeted statement of financial position: Even when all the above have been produced, there is still not enough information to produce a budgeted statement of financial position. First, the budgets listed below must be produced.
10. Capital expenditure budget: additional capital expenditure may be planned if there is to be an increase in production or to reduce costs or improve quality. The capital expenditure budget will also include capital expenditure in relation to costs that are not directly linked to production, such as distribution costs and administrative expenses.
11. Cash budget: showing cash receipts and payments of cash and the resulting balances for each month (or more often).

This may seem like a lot, but in a manufacturing organization, it is necessary. There may be additional budgets, such as a budgeted cash flow statement and a research and development budget. Many of the above budgets will be made up of a number of departmental budgets, such as those for advertising or the human resources departments. The definition of budgetary control, provided by the Chartered Institute of Management Accountants (CIMA) notes that budgets are 'relating the responsibilities of executives to the requirements of a policy and the continuous comparison of actual with budgeted results'. In many organizations, there is a separate departmental budget for each departmental manager. Ideally, this should detail what each manager is expected to achieve; in practice, it often does little more than show how much money they are authorized to spend.

A *master budget*, or *summary budget*, is prepared from and summarizes all the other budgets. This is usually taken to mean the budgeted income statement and budgeted statement of financial position. It might be tempting to include the cash budget as part of the master budget, but the single figure for cash/bank on the statement of financial position cannot be properly produced without first producing a cash budget.

Budgeted figures are typically shown for each month. Sometimes the whole set of budgets is produced once a year, perhaps in November of the year, beginning two months later in January. With *annual* budgeting, new budgets are not produced until the following November. But many organizations produce *rolling budgets*. This means that the budget is produced for the following 12 months; then, each month, another month is added (and the old month is taken out). Typically, in November, year 7, the budget is produced for the year January to December, year 8. In December year 7, the budget is produced for the 12 months from February year 8 to January year 9. In January year 8, the budget is produced for the 12 months from March year 8 to February year 9. In this way, there are always budgets for the following 12 months.

The different budgeting approaches are discussed below:

A ***fixed budget*** assumes a given level of production and sales. The level may be different for each period during the year (many businesses are seasonal, and there may be plans for growth). A fixed budget is a budget that does not consider any circumstances that may result in actual activity levels being different from those on which the budget was initially based. In this type of budget, the cost allowances for each cost item remain the same for variable items without any changes being made. A flexible budget, on the other hand, takes into account changes in activity levels and adjusts the cost allowances accordingly.

One of the problems with fixed budgets is that actual cost figures are likely to be very different from the budget, especially if output increases significantly. In **Illustration 15.1**, actual sales are 20 per cent higher than the budget, and, as we would expect, costs have increased. But not all costs should increase by 20 per cent: there may be some increases or decreases in efficiency, but some overheads (such as managers' salaries or rents payable for premises) are 'fixed' - they do not increase as production increases. It is useful to separate 'fixed' costs from 'variable' costs, such as direct materials and direct wages, which are expected to increase in line with the volume of production. In this way, we can produce a ***flexed budget***, as shown in **Illustration 15.2**, using the principles of *flexible budgeting*.

A ***flexible budget*** is a financial plan that summarizes the expected revenues and expenses over a range of different activity levels. This is different from a fixed budget, which only considers one activity level. The flexible budget takes into account varying levels of activity and is an important tool for analysing business performance. To create a flexible budget, it is necessary to differentiate between fixed and variable costs.

ILLUSTRATION 15.1 A fixed budget

January Year 9	Budget	Actual
	£000	£000
Sales	100	120
Direct materials	30	35
Direct labour	20	25
Production overheads	30	32

January Year 9	Budget	Actual
	£000	£000
Administration and distribution overheads	12	13
Total costs	92	105
Profit	8	15

ILLUSTRATION 15.2 A flexible budget

January Year 9	Budget	Flexed budget	Actual
	£000	£000	£000
Sales	100	120	120
Direct materials	30	36	35
Direct labour	20	24	25
Production overheads	30	33	32
Administration and distribution overheads	12	13.2	13
Total costs	92	106.2	105
Profit	8	13.8	15

A ***flexible budget*** may be most practicable when the levels of production and sales fluctuate a lot and are hard to predict. The fixed budget shown in **Illustration 15.1** shows that profit has increased to £15,000 compared with £8,000 shown in the budget. But this is not due to efficiency. Sales have increased by 20 per cent, and direct material and labour costs can be expected to increase by about 20 per cent. However, overhead costs should increase by a smaller proportion because some overheads are 'fixed'; they do not increase as production increases.

In this instance, it has been assumed that half of the overhead costs are fixed and half are variable. In other words, when sales and production increase by 20 per cent, it is expected that overheads will increase by 10 per cent, and the 'flexed budget' column in **Illustration 15.2** has been prepared on that basis. When sales increase by 20 per cent, total costs are expected to increase from £92,000 to £106,200. In this instance, efficiency has increased: most costs have increased by less than the flexible budget would suggest (although direct labour costs have gone up by more than 20 per cent, indicating some decrease in efficiency).

A simple examination of the fixed budget in **Illustration 15.2** shows that all costs have increased, sales have increased, and profit has increased. It appears that everything is alright. But such control information is not very useful. There is no indication of any increases or decreases in efficiency, which are revealed by using a flexible budget.

Another disadvantage of using a fixed budget is that overheads are charged out to different jobs and products on the basis of the original fixed budget. In this instance, direct labour was originally budgeted at £20,000, and production overheads were £30,000. If absorption costing is used, production overheads could be charged to products at the rate of 150 per cent of direct labour. This means that the amount *charged* for overheads increases in line with the increase in output,[8] but the amount of overheads *incurred* would increase by a smaller proportion. In **Illustration 15.1**, the amount of production overhead incurred was £32,000, but the amount charged to particular jobs would be £37,500 (150 per cent of £25,000).[9] Production overheads of £5,500 would be 'over-recovered'. Most of this problem is eliminated if marginal costing is used.

[8] Or, more accurately in this instance, in line with the increase in direct labour costs.

[9] The direct labour cost incurred.

15.4 Cash Budgets

Most of us have some sort of cash budget in mind for our own personal receipts and payments. A personal cash budget is unique to each individual and is influenced by factors such as age, lifestyle, personal preferences and standard of living. We would like to know that each month there is enough coming in to meet the payments that we plan to make. Or we may plan it the other way around: we will spend no more than the cash that will be available to us. Failure to plan properly can lead to unexpected overdrafts and credit card borrowing with high charges.

It is a similar story for companies. They need to plan their monthly[10] receipts and payments for at least the next year. It may be that a company is very profitable and expanding rapidly, but it may need to generate more cash to meet its monthly commitments. Some companies make substantial profits, but at the end of the year, they have less cash than they had at the beginning of the year. Other companies may be less profitable, but they generate lots of cash. Comparing a company's budgeted income statement with its cash budget for the coming year shows how its monthly cash flows differ from its monthly profits or losses and why. The budgeted income statement gives a good indication of the viability of the business. The cash budget shows whether it is likely to have cash surpluses (which it may wish to invest) or whether there is going to be insufficient cash to get by. If a cash shortage problem is identified in advance, ways around the problem can be planned before it becomes a crisis. This can be seen by examining **Example 15.2**, the Holly Day Company.

Example 15.2

Cash Budget

The Holly Day Company manufactures seasonal goods for holiday-makers and supplies them to retailers in many seaside resorts. Its seasonal sales patterns have remained the same in recent years. Sales start at £15,000 a month in January and increase by £15,000 a month until they peak at £120,000 a month in August; they fall to £90,000 a month in September, £30,000 a month in October, and then to £15,000 a month in November and December. Customers pay for the goods, on average, two months after the sales are made.

The materials are bought and used in the month before sales take place; they are treated as an expense in the month that the finished goods to which they relate are sold, and they are paid for one month after purchase (i.e. in the month that the sale takes place). The cost of materials for making the goods amounts to one-third of the selling price.

The basic labour force costs £4,000 a month from October to January each year. This increases to £6,000 a month in February and £8,000 a month in March. The labour costs in the busy time of the year are £16,000 a month, from April to September inclusive.

The only other expense is depreciation, which amounts to £3,000 a month. One of the machines is approaching the end of its life and will be replaced by a new one, costing £60,000, which will be paid for in June. Depreciation on the new machine will be charged at 20 per cent per annum on a straight-line basis. The old machine will be sold for £15,000 (which is its net book value) at the end of the year (in December).

Taxation of £50,000 is payable in March, and dividends of £55,000 will be paid in May.

Required:

a Prepare the income statement for the coming year, showing sales, expenses, and profit for each month, as well as the total.

[10] Or weekly or even daily.

b Prepare the cash budget for the coming year, showing receipts and payments for each month, the net cash surplus or deficit for the month, and the bank balance at the end of each month. Assume that the business starts the year with £50,000 in the bank.

Answer:

a Budgeted income statement

Sales	15	30	45	60	75	90	105	120	90	30	15	15	690
Expenses													
Materials	5	10	15	20	25	30	35	40	30	10	5	5	230
Wages	4	6	8	16	16	16	16	16	16	4	4	4	126
Depreciation	3	3	3	3	3	4	4	4	4	4	4	4	43
	12	19	26	39	44	50	55	60	50	18	13	13	399
Profit	3	11	19	21	31	40	50	60	40	12	2	2	291

b Cash budget of the Holly Day Company

	£000	£000	£000	£000	£000	£000	£000	£000	£000	£000	£000	£000	£000
	Jan	Feb	Mar	Apr	May	Jun	Jul	Aug	Sep	Oct	Nov	Dec	Total
Receipts													
From debtors	15	15	15	30	45	60	75	90	105	120	90	30	690
Sale of machine												15	15
	15	15	15	30	45	60	75	90	105	120	90	45	705
Payments													
Materials	5	5	10	15	20	25	30	35	40	30	10	5	230
Wages	4	6	8	16	16	16	16	16	16	4	4	4	126
New machine						60							60
Taxation			50										50
Dividends					55								55
	9	11	68	31	91	101	46	51	56	34	14	9	521
Net receipts or (Deficit)	6	4	(53)	(1)	(46)	(41)	29	39	49	86	76	36	184
Opening balance	50	56	60	7	6	(40)	(81)	(52)	(13)	36	122	198	—
Closing balance	56	60	7	6	(40)	(81)	(52)	(13)	36	122	198	234	234

A cash budget shows all the (planned or expected future) receipts and payments of an organization, typically on a monthly basis for the next year.

The receipts figure includes all cash that comes in directly from cash sales. It also includes receipts from customers (trade receivables); they usually come in a month or two after the sales are made, so the figure is different from that shown on an income statement. In **Example 15.2**, it was assumed that all sales were on credit. There may be other receipts, such as money that comes in from dividends, interest, rent, commission and royalties. The cash budget will show the money as a receipt in the month when the money is expected. An income statement shows it in the month in which it is earned (or it 'accrues'), regardless of when the cash is received.

Some receipts do not appear on an income statement. These include receipts from issuing shares or debentures, borrowing money, and sales of non-current assets.[11]

[11] The profit arising on the sale of a non-current asset is included in the income statement. That is the difference between the net book value of the asset and its sale proceeds.

The payment figure includes all the money that is expected to be paid out. Payments for purchases are usually made a month or so after the purchases are made (and recorded for income statement purposes). The cash budget also shows payments for expenses that will also appear on the income statement. With most expenses, the payment is made after the expense is incurred. Some expenses (such as rent and perhaps advertising) are paid in advance. Again, in the cash budget, it is the period in which the payment is actually made that matters. In the income statement, it is when the expense is incurred that matters.

The cash budget also shows when the taxation liability and dividends are to be paid. These items also appear on the income statement, but, again, the timing might be different. A company typically shows its taxation charge on the income statement of one year, but the cash is actually paid in the following year. Similarly, a company typically decides on their final[12] dividend in one year and the cash is paid out in the following year.

Some payments do not appear at all on an income statement. Cash has to be paid out to acquire non-current assets (fixed assets), and there may be payments to buy investments, such as shares in other businesses, and to repay loans.

A cash budget shows the change in the cash balance each month. There is an opening balance at the beginning of the month. Total receipts and total payments are calculated to give a figure for net receipts (or payments) for the month. Net receipts are added to the balance at the beginning of the month to show the closing balance for the month. That then becomes the opening balance for the next month.

Figures can, of course, be the other way around. If the budget shows an overdraft at the beginning of the month, net receipts for the month will reduce the overdraft.

The budget should also show the total increase or decrease in cash expected during the year. This will be different from the budgeted profit figure, and it is useful to compare the two to see how and why the profit figure for the year differs from the cash flow figure. This is illustrated in this chapter with the Holly Day Company (**Example 15.2**), Rachel's business (**Self-testing question 6**), and Judas (**Assessment question 5**).

15.5 Advantages of Operating Budgetary Control Systems

Budgetary control (like many management techniques) is sometimes presented as if it is a panacea, a solution to all the problems of management. If it is operated well, it has a number of functions and can certainly improve the management of an organization in a number of ways:

1 *Objectives.* It ensures that the objectives of an organization are defined, quantified and set down in plans in such a way that managers (and perhaps all staff) know what they are supposed to be achieving and the contribution that they are expected to make towards the attainment of the company's objectives.

2 *Limiting factors.* The budgeting process should ensure that any limiting factors are identified. The amount that the company is able to sell is often the limiting factor, and production volumes and expenses have to be planned on the basis of likely sales. But there could be different limiting factors, such as production capacity; where this is identified, ways may be planned to overcome it, such as increasing capacity through shift working, additional capital expenditure, or outsourcing. Alternatively, it may be possible to increase selling prices to reduce demand and redirect the advertising budget to emphasize the quality of the higher-priced product. Availability of funding may also be a limiting factor: when the cash budget and the master budget have been prepared it may be that the company cannot afford to do what all the other

[12] Companies typically pay an interim dividend part way through the year, and a final divided after the end of the year.

budgets have suggested, and additional funding may be planned. The point is that if limiting factors are identified a month or two before the year begins, there is a good chance of overcoming them in advance, which is better than waiting for a crisis to hit.

3 *Authorizing.* Departmental managers are typically given budgets *authorizing* the amounts they can spend. This enables them to plan their expenditure in a systematic way and avoids the need to seek permission for each item.
4 *Responsibility.* Budgetary control systems can help define what each manager or budget holder is responsible for. Advertising managers are not just allowed to spend a given sum of money; they are expected to achieve a given level of sales. Human resources managers are not just allowed to spend money on recruitment; they are expected to ensure that the staff specified in the budget are actually recruited and in the jobs that were planned.
5 *Delegation.* Budgetary control facilitates the delegation of a great deal of responsibility to managers at different levels. The board of directors is usually seen as being responsible for the company achieving its objectives, but the overall objectives need to be broken down into individual chunks of responsibility, tasks and objectives that individual managers are expected to achieve. The board should know that managers are doing what their budgets specify and leave them to get on with it.
6 *Management by exception.* Senior management should concentrate on the exceptions. They do not need to scrutinize piles of detailed reports for every part of the business and try to judge whether or not things are going well. Control information should highlight where actual results are significantly different from plan - the 'exceptions' - and where management needs to take action. Where everything is going more or less according to plan, senior management can leave well alone. They can concentrate on managing the exceptions.
7 *Control.* It is possible to 'control' an organization only if there are plans or expectations of results to be achieved. Budgetary control systematically provides 'control' information comparing actual results with planned results.
8 *Motivation.* In some organizations, employees do not have much motivation, especially when they do not know what is expected of them. Budgetary control should clearly establish the objectives and plans for each part of the organization. This can help to motivate managers and others to do their best to ensure that plans are implemented successfully. Budgetary control establishes targets, and if they are realistic, they can improve motivation. Evidence shows that budgets should be 'tight but attainable'. If a car salesman who sold 100 cars last year is given a budget of 170 this year, he is likely to be utterly demotivated. But if he has a budget to sell 110 cars this year, he might consider this difficult but achievable and is likely to 'give it a go'.
9 *Performance evaluation.* Incentive schemes and bonuses are designed to motivate employees to improve their performance. Budgets provide a useful basis for measuring performance so that good performance can be rewarded.
10 *Communication and co-ordination.* These should be improved. It is necessary, for all parts of the organization to know what the plans are. It would cause problems if the sales team was busy securing orders that the company could not fulfil, or if the volume of production was being increased while the labour force was being reduced and purchases of direct materials cut back. It is necessary for managers in every part of the organization to know what the plans are for the organization as a whole.

Much of the above could be summarized in a single word: planning. Preparing budgets and operating a system providing regular feedback that compares actual results with budgeted results is essential for managing and controlling an organization. It can also help to achieve the benefits listed above.

15.6 Problems of Budgetary Control in Practice

In practice budgetary control may not be as successful as intended and there are many problems in implementing and operating successful budgetary control systems.

1 *Level of performance.* Realistic financial plans are needed to ensure that sufficient cash and other resources are available to meet the expected level of sales; and the budgeted level of sales should not be exaggerated, otherwise the organization would be in danger of arranging for too much labour and materials to be available, and resources will be wasted if the capacity that has been planned is not used. But if the budget is also intended to motivate staff, it may be necessary to set targets based on ambitious levels of performance, even if they are not likely to be achieved. Budgets that work in motivating staff are probably not a suitable basis for planning resources.

2 *Participation.* It is usually claimed that a budgetary control system works better if staff who are responsible for implementing particular parts of the plan are involved in establishing the plan. Where managers think that plans are realistic and have been involved in establishing them, they are more likely to identify with them. But it may be difficult to get some managers to participate, especially those with little understanding of finance.

   When a set of budgets has been produced, with effective participation, they are then put together as a master budget, which, it is hoped, will achieve the objectives that are established by the board of directors. Unfortunately, a set of budgets that results from extensive participation often does not show the results required; the board may decide that the profits shown are inadequate and decide that all the budgets need to be revised. In particular, it might seek to reduce expenditure. All those managers who had conscientiously participated in determining what levels of expenditure are necessary may suddenly find that their proposed budgets are arbitrarily cut by a fixed percentage. This undermines the effectiveness of their participation and may alienate some managers from the budgeting process.

3 *Reward schemes.* Where budgets are used as a basis for determining staff bonuses, promotions or other rewards, there are particular problems with participation and setting an appropriate level of performance. When sales managers are invited to participate in setting their budgets, if they think they can achieve sales of £5m a year, they may keep that opinion quiet and advocate a budget of only £4.5m a year because they know that they can easily achieve that level, and be rewarded accordingly. Similarly, advertising managers who reckon they need an annual budget of £100,000 to achieve the budgeted sales level are likely to press for budgets of perhaps £120,000 to make their lives easier. In this way, where participation is encouraged, managers are inclined to build in *budgetary slack* so that it is fairly easy for them to achieve what the budgets require.

4 *Competition for resources.* Although the budgeting process is intended to improve co-operation and co-ordination within an organization, managers often find themselves competing for resources. It is only to be expected that heads of departments such as advertising, human resources and research and development want to maximize the resources available to them. Sometimes, it could happen that all managers sit down and discuss idealistically how much the organization really needs to spend on each activity, and the resulting budget will be what is 'best' for the organization. More often, there is likely to be some overall limit on what can be spent on these different activities, and managers will find themselves competing with each other to maximize their share with a generous budget that authorizes how much they can spend in the coming year. Those managers who are most confident in dealing with finance may be the winners - perhaps at the expense of the organization as a whole.

5 *Incremental budgeting.* The easiest way to produce a budget is simply to base it on the previous year's actual results and add a bit for inflation and a bit more for growth. But this is *estimating* what is likely to happen; it is not *planning* to achieve the desired results. It is likely to produce budgets that are easily

achievable but this 'easy' approach is not best designed to help the organization to achieve its objectives. Sometimes managers are mainly motivated by empire-building and ensuring that the budget allocated to them increases each year.

6 *A paperwork exercise.* Unless senior management enthusiastically endorses the budgets and is determined to check that actual results are in line with plans, budgetary control can sometimes be little more than a paperwork exercise, something that the accounts department produces once a year and of which no one takes much notice. This is particularly true where managers have little understanding of or training in finance. Each month, vast quantities of control information are produced that most managers do not understand or use or care about. It is too much information and may be too late to be of much use. Managers often produce their own 'control' information and argue that the 'official' information is neither accurate nor relevant. A management accountant has to be very able and determined to operate a budgetary control system effectively.

7 *Tendency to spend up to budget.* Where managers have a budget for some expenditure, they sometimes treat it as if it were a bag of money that they have been given to spend within the year. Often, if they underspend their budget, that money is 'lost' to them, and they are likely to be given a smaller budget for the following year. When managers are more interested in empire-building than in doing what is best for the organization, they will tend to spend all that they can and seek a bigger budget allocation for the following year. In organizations where the year end is 31 March, there is often a rush to spend money during February to ensure that the budget is used up by the end of the year and that the budget will not be cut for the following year. Many suppliers expect such a rush from public sector organizations before their year end. Some find important conferences to go to in sunny climates, order large amounts of stationery or spend money on repairs (like repainting the inside of cupboards) just before the end of the financial year. The problem can be reduced if managers are allowed to 'carry forward' unspent balances to the following year. It is, however, more difficult to eliminate an empire-building attitude.

8 *An end in itself.* There is a danger that managers are expected 'only' to achieve what the budget shows and that opportunities for more profitable activities are ignored because they are not in the budget. An unexpected but potentially profitable sales enquiry from China may be ignored because there is no money in the budget for the necessary travelling expenses. Similarly, an opportunity to take over a competitor at a knock-down price may be missed because it was not in the budget. Budgetary control can play a valuable role in helping an organization achieve its objectives, but once budgets are approved, they should not be set in stone: there must always be some flexibility when opportunities arise.

9 *Defining objectives.* For simplicity in setting budgets, a single objective may be assumed, such as achieving a given level of earnings or return on capital employed. However, organizations often have multiple and even conflicting objectives, such as achieving sales growth (which might imply low selling prices) and improving the quality of their products (which might imply higher selling prices). Sometimes different managers within an organization may seem to be pursuing different objectives. The problem of defining objectives and measuring the extent to which they are achieved is more difficult in a public sector or not-for-profit organization. In theory, the budgeting process ensures that objectives are defined and quantified, but in practice, it may not be easy to secure agreement on objectives.

Most management techniques are more difficult in practice than their proponents would suggest. There are all the usual difficulties, such as the costs of implementation and the need to train staff to operate the systems effectively. But budgetary control is well established in most medium and large organizations and is operated with varying degrees of success.

Budgetary control is sometimes seen as a game in which the players (managers) are involved in setting their own budgets. Then, the accountants put all the individual budgets together in a master budget: the budgeted income statement, statement of financial position and the cash budget. It may be that all the budgets fit neatly together, revealing no cash shortages and achieving all the intended targets. But this is not possible to happen. It is more likely that once the first draft of the master budget is prepared, the finance director or senior management will insist on revisions: expenditure to be cut back, sales to be increased, capital expenditure to be reduced and deferred. All the careful planning put in by individual managers is overturned. However, experienced managers know that this will happen, so they put some 'slack' into the first version of the budget because experience tells them that the final version will be tougher. And the finance director knows that they know and that they have included slack, so tougher cut-backs are demanded. But very experienced managers know this, and have included even more slack than the finance director would expect. But very experienced finance directors know this ... and so all is set for another round of the game of budgetary control.

One approach to making budgetary control more effective - and to avoid the tendency for expenditure to drift upwards every year ('incremental drift') - is to use *zero-based budgeting* (ZBB). This means that, instead of taking the previous year's figures as a basis for planning future expenditure, the basis is taken as zero. The starting point is that each activity will spend nothing in the coming year unless it can be justified. This may be valuable in some areas: perhaps there is no need for company cars if it is cheaper to use taxis; perhaps there is no need for a mail room if most communication is done by email. But it is usually too much hassle, expense and bureaucracy to review every activity every year, and incremental budgeting still predominates.

If budgets are seen as the official expressions of the plans and intentions of top management, they are likely to be taken seriously and provide an effective means of controlling the business. They are likely to be less effective if they are seen as being a paperwork exercise produced by the finance department, a pointless extra burden for management, a sterile figure-producing exercise that provides information that managers do not understand, is irrelevant to their needs and arrives in too much detail, and too late for them to act on. If they are to be successful, management accountants must produce financial information that is relevant and effective in planning, decision-making and control in the business.

15.7 Zero-based and Rolling Budgets

Zero-based budgeting (ZBB)

ZBB is one way of tackling the inefficiencies and budgetary slack of traditional incremental budgeting. Budget slack, also known as budget padding, is the intentional overestimation of expenses and underestimation of revenue during budget setting. Instead of basing each budget on the equivalent budget for the previous year, with adjustments for known changes, each year and each budget begin with an assumption of zero expenditure. Instead of arguing for an increase of 5 per cent or 10 per cent, departmental managers have to argue for any budget at all. If the head of advertising cannot defend expenditure on advertising as being cost-effective, there will be no advertising budget. If the head of distribution cannot demonstrate that it is worthwhile for the company to operate its own fleet of vehicles, Royal Mail and others will be invited to put in tenders for taking over the distribution function. The finance director may be astute at self-defence (or may be fed up with running the finance department!) and be able to fight off proposals to outsource the finance function to a large firm of chartered accountants. But it is quite likely that the payroll function will be outsourced. Even production departments may be given a zero budget (and be closed down) if it would be cheaper to cease manufacturing and buy in components, sub-assemblies or even finished goods - probably from some part of the world where production costs are lower.

The idea is to prepare a budget for each cost centre from a zero base, and every item has to be justified in its entirety if it is to be included in next year's budget. A questioning attitude is required to examine every item of expenditure and to clear out any 'dead wood'. The company's activities should be divided into separate 'decision packages'. These are evaluated according to the costs incurred and benefits generated by each activity and ranked in order of priority. Some activities will be closed down if they are hardly needed, generate little benefit, are outdated, or can be done more cost-effectively in another way, perhaps by outsourcing. Examples of cost-effectiveness include: embedding digital systems, cultivating a culture of continuous change to drive sustainable change, utilizing data to inform decisions, optimizing resources, and automating processes for greater efficiency.

ZBB has a number of advantages. For example, it helps to identify and remove obsolete, wasteful and inefficient operations and expenditures. It is a systematic way of responding to a changing business environment and can increase staff motivation towards greater efficiency. The systematic process and documentation challenge the status quo, appraise all operations, and ensure that alternatives such as outsourcing are considered. It should lead to a more efficient allocation of resources. ZBB is particularly useful in public sector and not-for-profit organizations where profitability is not an appropriate measure of efficiency and effectiveness.

ZBB is, however, expensive to apply. It involves a substantial volume of work and paper, and it seems excessive to do this every year. It can lead to rational economic decisions, but these decisions should perhaps be made on a long-term basis, within an overall framework, rather than on a short-term basis as part of an annual budgeting cycle. Systematic ZBB requires special training for staff, probably involving the use of consultants, and there is likely to be resistance if it seems likely to lead to redundancies. Existing information systems are likely to be inadequate, and it is difficult to evaluate the costs and benefits of all decision packages and functions.

Some of the questioning attitudes of ZBB can undoubtedly lead to the reduction and elimination of some activities and functions, improved resource allocation and greater profitability. But most organizations would only operate some of their budgets from a zero base every year.

Rolling budgets

Rolling budgets differ from traditional annual budgeting in that they are typically updated on a monthly or quarterly basis and projected for a much longer period. A rolling forecast uses historical data to predict a business's future performance over a continuous period, unlike static budgets that forecast the future for a fixed time frame, such as January to December. A rolling forecast is regularly updated throughout the year to reflect any changes, making it more adaptable to a business's evolving needs.

Advantages of rolling budgets

Using a rolling budget has several advantages over a static budget. Managers no longer need to wait until the next budgeting period to make any adjustments. By using a rolling forecast, a company can quickly respond to market changes and make necessary adjustments in a timely manner.

Businesses face constant changes in their environment, which can lead to increased risks. To mitigate these risks, a rolling forecast can be utilized, allowing the business to adjust to changing economic and industry conditions. This approach also allows the company to identify areas that require more attention. The rolling forecast is an improvement over traditional budgeting, as it involves recalibration of forecasts and resource allocation every month or quarter based on actual business performance. This involves re-examining a plan and correcting it in accordance with a new understanding or purpose,

Using rolling budgets enables the optimization of resource allocation by making decisions in real time. This allows for a more efficient funnelling of resources to where they are most needed. It also provides managers with a timely view of the next 12 months at any point during the year.

Disadvantages of rolling budgets

There are some clear issues when using rolling budgets. First, they demand more staff, resources and time. Since rolling budgets are frequently updated, they typically require more time and dedication from the responsible managers and leaders. Managers may also require training, which can be expensive and time-consuming.

Second, conflict may emerge regarding performance targets, as managers may complain about shifting goal-posts. Additionally, managers may spend too much time preparing the budget and not enough time controlling it. Third, the company may need to acquire new software that allows for regular updating of the budget. If the rolling budget is done on a stand-alone spreadsheet not linked to the company's internal systems, data integrity issues can arise.

Example 15.3

Marcus Group is a family business that produces cider for both online and supermarket sales. This is a competitive industry, with supermarkets' pricing pressure and the need to continually innovate. Marcus Group uses annual, incremental budgeting, created on a standalone spreadsheet, as its primary control tool and uses this budget as the basis for performance evaluation.

Required:

Prepare the rolling budget for the next four quarters.

The accountant has suggested the following assumptions to be included in the new rolling budget:

1. Sales volume would grow at the same fixed compound rate every quarter. Assume that sales, labour and material costs will go up by 3.5 per cent and should be applied from quarter 2.
2. Variable costs include direct material and direct labour costs.
3. Fixed production overheads would now be £10,000 higher beginning quarter 3 onwards.
4. Based on the previous quarter's costs, administration costs would increase by 8 per cent from quarter 3 to account for an increase in the lease of a new harvesting machine.
5. A new manager will be appointed and receive a salary of £60,000 per annum starting at the beginning of quarter 2.

The following budget has been prepared on a quarterly basis for the current year ending 31 December year 8:

Budget Marcus Group

	Quarter 1, year 8	Quarter 2, year 8	Quarter 3, year 8	Quarter 4, year 8	Actual Quarter 1, year 8
	£000s	£000s	£000s	£000s	£000s
Sales revenue	580	593	611	630	565
Direct material	-29	-30	-31	-32	-30
Direct labour	-58	-60	-62	-63	-58
Contribution	**493**	**503**	**518**	**535**	**477**
Fixed overheads	-144	-144	-154	-154	-144
Administration costs	-252	-252	-265	-278	-252
Profit	97	107	99	103	81

Answer:

Rolling Budget Marcus Group

		Quarter 2, year 8 £000s	Quarter 3, year 8 £000s	Quarter 4, year 8 £000s	Quarter 1, year 9 £000s
Sales revenue	Increase by 3.5% based on actual Q1	579	594	608	624
Direct material	Increase by 3.5% based on actual Q1	-31	-32	-33	-34
Direct labour	Increase by 3.5% based on actual Q1	-60	-62	-64	-67
Contribution		**494**	**511**	**529**	**547**
Fixed overheads		-144	-154	-154	-154
Administration costs		-252	-272	-294	-317
Manager salary	£80,000/4	-20	-20	-20	-20
Profit		75	65	61	56

15.8 Planning and Programming Budgeting System (PPBS)

PPBS is designed to improve programme evaluation and was developed particularly for public-sector organizations such as defence. Some would argue that there is obviously a need for more defence, perhaps listing particular problem areas, and so it is necessary to spend more on defence. But it is difficult to assess the efficiency and effectiveness of that expenditure unless it is clearly targeted to particular 'programmes' where expenditure can be measured and success assessed.

The PPBS framework comprises two crucial components. The first is the foundational principle of departmental accountability, which underpins the system's philosophy. The second is the distinct language of PPBS, which encompasses specialized terms such as objectives, programmes, programme options, outputs, progress measurement, inputs, alternative ways to do a given job, and system analysis. These terms create a unique vocabulary that distinguishes PPBS from other management structures.

If applied to a police force a number of programmes might be identified, such as (i) reducing drug crime in the Orriton area, (ii) reducing speeding and road accidents in the Searam area, (iii) reducing muggings in the Trandton area; (iv) reducing shop-lifting in the Brandwich area; and (v) reducing burglaries in the Julby area.

An important part of the planning process would be to define a number of programmes such as these rather than describe everything as 'policing'. Then, budgets allocate resources to each programme, and expenditure is classified so that it is identified with particular programmes (rather than seeming to disappear down a black hole). We can budget to spend £200,000 a year for reducing muggings in the Trandton area. Subsequent control information might show that only £170,000 was actually spent. More importantly, the effectiveness of the programme in Trandton can be measured. By how much were muggings reduced? What percentage reduction can be aimed for next year, or in a comparable programme?

The overall management of the public sector organization can control how much was spent on each programme, and see how effective that expenditure was. This can provide a basis for reallocations in subsequent years in the light of actual experience of how effective different expenditures on different programmes has been in practice.

The phrase 'PPBS' is not particularly widely used, but within the public sector, there is increasing emphasis on identifying 'programmes' and assessing the effectiveness of expenditures on different programme areas.

Summary

Budgetary control is a well-established management accounting technique that is widely used in all but the smallest organizations. It defines objectives, establishes plans for achieving those objectives, and makes each area in the organization responsible for its part of the plan. Control information compares the results actually achieved with those that were planned on a regular basis. Although it is impossible to predict the future, budgeting helps reduce uncertainty and anticipate problems. There are many 'behavioural' problems in practice with budgetary control that militate against the advantages that can be gained from an effective system.

Review of key points

- Budgets are financial plans showing how the objectives of an organization can be achieved.
- Budgetary control provides regular feedback information.
- A budget manual details how budgetary control is to be applied in a particular organization and shows all the different budgets to be produced.
- A master budget, also known as the budgeted statement of financial position and income statement, shows the results of all the detailed budgets.
- A cash budget shows planned receipts and payments of cash, typically on a monthly basis for the next year.
- The budgeted net receipts of cash are likely to be very different from the budgeted profit figure.
- The availability of cash to meet liabilities as they fall due is essential to business survival.

Self-testing questions

1 Define the term 'budget' and draw attention to the most important parts of the definition.
2 Distinguish between fixed budgets and flexible budgets.

3 The owner of a car servicing and repair business, with five employees, produces an annual statement of financial position and income statement, and monitors his bank statement on a monthly basis. Examine the case for and against introducing a system of budgetary control.

4 Produce a flexible budget for the Dhoon Glen Manufacturing Company and comment on the company's results for August. Assume that:

   a fixed production overheads are £100,000 per month
   b fixed distribution costs are £20,000 per month
   c fixed administration overheads are £50,000 per month.

	Budget August	**Flexed budget**	**Actual results**
	Year 6	August, Year 6	August, Year 6
	£000	£000	£000
Sales	600		690
Direct materials	120		140
Direct labour	100		117
Production overheads	200		223
Distribution costs	80		95
Administrative overheads	60		70
Total costs	560		645
Profit	40		45

5 In what circumstances is a very profitable business likely to find that it has serious cash shortages?

6 Rachel owns a specialist boring-digging machine that she hires out, together with an operator/driver, to builders and farmers. A few years ago her accountant worked out that she should charge £500 a day and that should give her a comfortable living. In the last year demand has fallen, particularly in the winter months when the weather restricts the use of the machine, and in the summer months when many people are on holiday. In the coming year (year 3) she estimates that she will have 10 days' work a month in January and February; 20 days' work a month in March, April, May and June. Then it will fall to 12 days a month in July and August. In September, October and November she expects 20 days' work a month, and only 5 days in December. At the end of year 2 her debtors figure was £5,000, of which she expects to receive half in January and half in February.

On average customers pay two months after the work is done.

Operating expenses, including fuel and labour, amount to £100 per day.

Expenses are paid in the month that they are incurred.

Her fixed overheads, including depreciation, are £3,000 per month. The machine originally cost £140,000 and is expected to have a five-year life, with a residual value of £20,000. She uses straight-line depreciation.

At the end of last year she had only £1,000 in her business bank account.

Rachel would like to take £45,000 a year out of the business to cover her personal living expenses. But she does not want to have an overdraft; and she does not want to be living off capital.

Required:

   a Prepare the income statement for the coming year, showing sales, expenses and profit for each month, and in total.

b Prepare the cash budget for the coming year, showing receipts and payments for each month; the net cash surplus or deficit for the month; and the bank balance at the end of each month. Assume that the business starts the year with £50,000 in the bank.

c Explain why the company has generated more cash than profit during the year.

d How much do you think that she can afford to take out of the business as drawings (or dividends if it is a company) during the year? Give your reasons.

Assessment questions

1 Define the term 'budgetary control' and critically discuss the most important parts of the definition.

2 Distinguish between annual budgets and rolling (or continuous) budgets.

3 What behavioural problems are likely to arise in operating a system of budgetary control?

4 Produce a flexible budget for the Gorrie Production Company and comment on the company's results for May. Assume that:

a fixed production overheads are £100,000 per month

b fixed distribution costs are £20,000 per month

c fixed administration overheads are £50,000 per month.

	Budget May	Flexed budget	Actual results
	Year 3	August, Year 3	May, Year 3
	£000	£000	£000
Sales	900		810
Direct materials	200		178
Direct labour	250		227
Production overheads	240	210	
Distribution costs	100	103	
Administrative overheads	109	90	
Total costs	899	808	
Profit	1	2	

5 Judas has developed a plan for a rapidly expanding business selling and installing software for individuals using computers at home. He will operate on a 100 per cent mark-up (50 per cent gross profit ratio) on the software that he sells, and will employ a team of highly paid technician/sales staff. He has piloted his business model on a number of customers and he knows that they are particularly afraid of computer viruses; he will provide a guarantee of 12 months free of viruses. But, somehow, after a year or so he knows that there will always be a return of viruses and most of his customers will request his services again. During the next 12 months he aims to build up his customer base, and make a small profit.

He has discussed his business plan with his accountant, and the following seems to be soundly based:

a Sales in January will be £220,000 and will then increase by £20,000 per month. Customers pay two months after the sale is made.

b Suppliers are paid one month after purchases are made. Stocks amounting to £100,000 will be bought in the first month and maintained at that level. Purchases will be made each month that are sufficient to supply sales for that month.

c Wages and expenses will be £100,000 a month for the first four months of the year; then they will increase to £150,000 a month for the following three months; then they will be £200,000 a month for the next five months. They are paid during the month that they are incurred.

d At the beginning of the year he will spend £840,000 on non-current assets. All non-current assets are depreciated over 10 years. Depreciation is charged on a monthly basis. In June additional fixed assets of £360,000 will be bought.

His accountant advises him that, although the business should make a modest profit, there will be substantial cash outflows to begin with. She prepared a monthly budgeted income statement, and a monthly cash budget. But Judas had £1m available to finance the business and reckoned that there would be no problem. He refused to pay her fees and so she did not show him the monthly budgets.

Required:

i Prepare a monthly income statement for the first year of the business, showing the profit or loss each month, and for the year in total.

ii Prepare a cash budget for the year, showing the receipts and payments for each month, and the cash surplus or deficit each month.

iii Explain and comment on the results.

Group activities and discussion questions

1 What plans do you have for this year? Would it be helpful to define and quantify them? What do you do when what actually happens is very different from what you had planned?

2 If you have work experience, did you see evidence that your employer operated a system of budgetary control? What were the attitudes of your colleagues towards budgets and budgetary control?

3 Do you prepare a cash budget for yourself for the coming year? What is the case for and against bothering to do this? Is it *essential* for a company to prepare a cash budget? Is it *essential* for you?

4 Should large companies publish their budgets for the coming year? Do companies publish any forecasts?

5 Is budgetary control too idealistic? Is it inevitable that powerful employees will feather their own nests and empire-build rather than working to achieve the objectives of the company?

Accounting in context

Discuss and comment on the following case study with reference to the pros and cons of zero-based budgeting.

Zero-based budgeting transferable to zero-based management

Launching an anonymous public attack on one's own employees is never a wise decision, especially during the later stages of a pandemic. Despite this, UK government officials and ministers have complained about the productivity of their remote-working civil servants. One cabinet minister was quoted by *The Times* as saying, 'There must be the suspicion that some people have spent the last 15 months working from home but haven't actually been doing very much.' Another source added, 'It's hard to know who is deserving of a promotion when people are working remotely.' These comments seem to be an attempt to force employees to return to their offices, but they reveal much more about the bosses than the workers. If after 15 months, you only have a 'suspicion' about what your people are up to and find it 'hard to know' who are your top performers, then you are guilty of neglect at best and mismanagement at worst.

The concern is that if managers continue to oversee their employees in the same way as before the pandemic, regardless of whether they are working in the office or remotely, it will likely result in the same problems. Carly Moulton, a representative of Zapier, a company with a completely remote workforce, stated during a panel discussion at the Academy of Management annual meeting that the issue with remote work is not the work itself but rather the lack of proper management and culture. Managers now have the opportunity to review their management strategies. Just as finance directors may conduct zero-based budgeting to assess each division's funding, leaders should practice zero-based management. They should question whether they would organize their team or company in the same way if they had to start from scratch. Phil Libin, a former CEO of Evernote who currently runs All Turtles, a product studio that has adopted distributed working, believes that large companies attempting to bring knowledge workers back to the office are being unrealistic. It is not sensible to assume that forcing employees to commute will inspire loyalty and creativity.

Sources: A. Hill (2021) Leaders Must Stop Blaming Their Bad Management on Remote Workers. *Financial Times*, 15 August. https://www.ft.com/content/2ce5ee7f-e94a-4cf0-b9a3-83a35e1530a8

References and further reading

Allen, R., and Clifton, R. (2023) From Zero-base Budgeting to Spending Review: Achievements and Challenges. *Development Southern Africa*, 1–17. https://doi.org/10.1080/0376835X.2023.2226164

Atkinson, A., Kaplan, R., Matsumura, E. and Young, M. (2012) *Management Accounting* (6th edn.). Harlow: Pearson.

Bhimani, A.C.T., Datar, S.M., Horngren, C.T. and Foster, G. (2012) *Management and Cost Accounting* (5th edn.). Upper Saddle River, NJ: FT Prentice Hall.

Chartered Institute of Management Accountants (2000) *Management Accounting Official Terminologies*, CIMA.

Chartered Institute of Management Accountants (2005) *Management Accounting Official Terminologies*, CIMA.

Drury, C. (2008) *Management and Cost Accounting* (7th edn.). Andover: Cengage Learning.

Dyson, J.R. (2010) *Accounting for Non-accounting Students* (8th edn.). Upper Saddle River, NJ: FT Prentice Hall.

Proctor, R. (2009) *Managerial Accounting for Business Decisions* (3rd edn.). Harlow: Pearson.

Seal, W., Garrison, R.H. and Nooreen, E.W. (2011) *Management Accounting* (4th edn.). Maidenhead: McGraw-Hill.

https://online.hbs.edu/blog/post/importance-of-budgeting-in-business

Chapter 16

Absorption Costing

Chapter contents

16.1 Introduction
16.2 Role and Origins of Costing Systems
16.3 Classification of Costs
16.4 Direct Materials and Pricing
16.5 Direct Labour
16.6 Direct Expenses
16.7 Production Overheads
16.8 Allocation, Apportionment and Absorption
16.9 Evaluation of Absorption Costing
16.10 Activity-based Costing

Learning objectives

After studying this chapter you will be able to:

- ✓ Explain how absorption costing developed
- ✓ Understand how product costs are accumulated using absorption costing
- ✓ Apply the main classifications of costs
- ✓ Understand and apply the main pricing systems for materials issued
- ✓ Calculate production overheads using different methods
- ✓ Evaluate absorption costing
- ✓ Understand and apply ABC

16.1 Introduction

Costing systems are used to determine the cost of producing something, usually a 'cost unit'. It might be a car, a piece of furniture, a thousand bricks, a house, or the product of a service organization such as a hair-cut, a successful student, or a task undertaken by a firm of solicitors. The two main systems of costing are *absorption costing*, sometimes known as *full costing*, which is examined in this chapter; and *marginal costing*, which is dealt with in **Chapter 17**.

16.2 Role and Origins of Costing Systems

Most costing systems have developed gradually during the last 100 years in response to the needs of management who need to establish a cost for closing inventories, to price goods for sale, to make a variety of different decisions about which products to make, and to plan and control costs.

In financial accounting, it is necessary to establish the cost of closing inventories. This is needed for calculating profit. Gross profit is the difference between the revenue earned from sales and the cost of the goods that have been sold. The cost of goods that have not been sold ('closing inventory') is carried forward to be shown as an expense in the following period; it is not charged as an expense until the goods are sold. Costs that have been incurred, therefore, have to be allocated between (a) cost of sales, which is treated as an expense on the income statement, and (b) closing inventory,[1] which is carried forward on the statement of financial position as a current asset. For this purpose costs include all production (or manufacturing costs), which include not only direct materials and direct labour, but all production overheads. All these costs have to be attributed to what has been produced in a fair and reasonable manner so that the cost of sales and the cost of closing inventory include the total of all manufacturing costs.[2]

It is important to establish the costs of producing different products or services or orders or contract, if only to give some indication of what price should be charged for each product. During the First World War, 'cost plus' pricing systems were developed for businesses that supplied goods for the war effort (such as weapons, uniforms and vehicles), direct material and direct labour costs were carefully recorded, and a percentage was agreed upon (the 'plus') to cover overheads and profit. Companies wanted to ensure that all their costs and a margin for profit were covered in the price agreed.

In some ways, this 'cost plus' approach lives on. Costing systems typically record and classify direct material and direct labour costs in detail, then a percentage is added to cover production overheads, and then perhaps another percentage to cover other overheads and profit. This approach is now usually too crude. As manufacturing processes have become more automated, direct labour has become a smaller proportion of production costs, and production overheads have become a much larger proportion. Moreover, competition means that it is not usually possible simply to calculate the costs and then add some percentages, and then determine a price that covers everything; somehow costs have to be planned and managed with a price in mind that the market will bear.

It is, of course, important to know what it costs to produce something so that relevant decisions can be made: whether to produce more or less of a particular product, or to abandon some, or outsource, or increase prices. But absorption costing is not a good basis for making such decisions; marginal costing is usually more appropriate. Care should be taken in deciding to eliminate a 'loss-making' product (such as desks in **Illustration 16.1**). This is explained more fully in **Chapter 17**. Absorption costing is a necessary basis for some decisions, such as quoting a price for major construction projects (such as the Channel Tunnel, Crossrail, or the facilities for the Olympic Games). Sometimes it might make good business sense to agree to selling prices that do not cover full production costs, but the scope for this is limited. Somehow, a business must have selling prices that cover not only all production costs but also all administration, distribution and finance costs, and also make a profit. Where selling prices do not cover all such costs, businesses soon fail, as selling price pressures remain elevated due to inflationary pressures and worsening economic conditions.

[1] Closing inventory should be shown at the lower of cost and net realizable value. It is therefore necessary to know both the cost, and the net realizable value, in order to establish which is the lower.

[2] But manufacturing costs exclude administration costs, selling and distribution overheads, and finance costs.

Absorption costing

ILLUSTRATION 16.1 Absorption costing

	Total	Tables	Desks	Chairs
	£000	£000	£000	£000
Sales	757	254	276	227
Direct materials	300	100	120	80
Direct labour	160	50	60	50
Prime cost	460	150	180	130
Production overheads	160	50	60	50
Production cost	620	200	240	180
Distribution and administrative overheads	124	40	48	36
Total costs	744	240	288	216
Profit	13	14	(12)	11

Absorption costing is also important in planning and controlling costs. A budgetary control system includes budgets for all costs and involves regular comparisons of actual costs with those that were planned. Ideally, control systems are designed so that managers who are responsible for particular costs can actually control those costs. It is too easy to say that an individual production manager cannot control some production overheads because they are predetermined and relatively fixed. But someone has to be responsible for all costs, and all costs should be planned and controlled. Absorption costing can help to ensure that someone is responsible for all costs.

16.3 Classification of Costs

Accounting systems are designed to classify and record costs in various ways that are useful. Typically, as costs are incurred, they are given code numbers; these code numbers may indicate a number of things, such as:

1 the nature of the cost (e.g. rent, insurance, wages, materials, utilities, maintenance);
2 whether it is a production cost (which may be included in closing inventories), or a period cost, which must be charged as an expense during the period in which it is incurred;
3 who is responsible for authorizing the cost. This can be related to cost centres, budget centres and the whole business of budgetary control.

In a manufacturing organization, production costs are classified as direct costs (direct material, direct labour and direct expenses) and as production overheads, as shown in the manufacturing account in **Chapter 17**.

Costs can be defined and classified in many different ways. It is useful to identify **sunk costs** and **relevant costs** when making future decisions (see **Glossary**).

16.4 Direct Materials and Pricing

Direct materials are materials and components that become part of the finished product and which are charged to individual jobs. In a garage repair business, a new fan belt for Mrs Shah's car is a direct material cost of the repairs for Mrs Shah. In a building business, for any particular job, the direct materials would include bricks, timber and partly made items such as staircases and window frames. In a manufacturing business, the direct materials could include the metal, timber, glass and chemicals that are incorporated into a particular product.

It is necessary to record which materials are used for which particular job or product so that the total cost of that job or product can be calculated. Where 'just-in-time' purchasing is used, purchases can be charged directly to a particular job as soon as they are ordered. Where purchases go into stores before being issued to production, some sort of 'requisition' note must be used each time materials are issued from stores; this will specify which job the materials are required for, to ensure that they are charged to that job.

There may also be 'indirect materials' where it is not worth the time and trouble of charging them for individual jobs. These include lubricants, cleaning materials and items of low value (perhaps adhesives or nails) that are included in general production overheads.

In a modern manufacturing environment, direct materials and components are ideally delivered to the factory 'just in time' to be used for a particular job, batch, product, or contract. From the moment the materials are ordered, they are known for which product they are intended, and there is no need for complicated costing procedures: all materials are allocated directly to jobs.

In some traditional manufacturing environments, large inventories of many different materials and components are kept 'just in case' they are needed. This is particularly true in many 'jobbing' industries where there is a regular demand for materials such as particular lengths of wood, metal, various screws, rivets, and so on. A problem can arise when identical materials are bought at different dates and different prices. In **Illustration 16.2** different quantities of an item are bought during March, with the price paid varying between £11 per unit and £14 per unit.

ILLUSTRATION 16.2

Date	Units purchased	Cost price per unit	Amount	Total
1 March	1,000	£12	£12,000	£12,000
13 March	2,000	£11	£22,000	£34,000
26 March	500	£14	£7,000	£41,000

A problem with all these methods is that the cost shown for a particular item varies from one date to another. It could happen that a job completed on one date is shown as being profitable, but an identical job completed on a different date is shown as being unprofitable. The difference between the two is due only to the issue of prices changing, and that, in turn, is due only to the pricing system used.

If some of the materials are then issued from the stores on 28 March, there are different ways of pricing those issues, as follows:

1 It could be assumed that the earliest prices (£12) are charged first until all 1,000 items have been issued; then subsequent issues are charged at £11 until 2,000 have been used up. This method is called first in first out, or FIFO. It is probably a sensible method of physically handling the goods (use up the oldest first), but where items are identical, this may not be possible. In any case, the way in which issues are priced can be different from the way in which they are physically handled.

2. It could be assumed that the most recent prices (£14) are charged first until all 500 items have been issued; then subsequent issues are charged at £11 until 2,000 have been used up. This method is last in first out, or LIFO.
3. An *averaging system* could be used. There are 3,500 items in stock that have cost £41,000; that is an average price of (about) £11.71. That average price could be used for all issues. The average could be recalculated on a regular basis (e.g. monthly or quarterly), or each time a new delivery is received.
4. *Standard cost*: a 'fairer' system of charging direct materials to jobs might be to use a standard price for all components, with that price being revised annually. This is normal when a standard costing system is used. In **Illustration 16.2**, it could be decided that the standard cost is £12 per item (or perhaps £12.50 to allow for a bit of inflation), regardless of the cost of different purchases during the year.
5. *Replacement cost* is sometimes used based on the current cost of purchasing more items at the date the item is to be used. This is likely to give more realistic decisions, especially where major long-term production is being considered, rather than relying on the chance of what happens to have been bought in the past.

During a period of rising prices, FIFO has the advantage that closing inventories tend to be at recent prices, which are likely to be relatively high and fairly realistic. But the items that are issued to production are likely to be at the oldest, and so probably the lowest, prices; costs of production are likely to be understated, and any further orders for the same product could not be produced at the same cost.

With LIFO, it is the other way around. During a period of rising prices, LIFO has the advantage since the most recent prices are charged to production, and these are likely to be fairly realistic.[3] But what is left as inventory will be shown at old, low and unrealistic prices - a prudent version of 'cost' when applied to valuing inventory.

An averaging system is likely to be 'fairer', but costs are still subject to the chance of what happens to have been purchased in the past. Standard cost is not only 'fair'; it is also as realistic as the standard price selected, but standards can rapidly become out of date. Replacement cost is likely to provide the best basis for decision-making, but it would often be too much trouble to establish and record replacement costs for every little item issued from stores. In general, accountancy is based on costs actually incurred and recorded; there is continuing debate about the extent to which it is worth moving to more 'relevant' figures.

16.5 Direct Labour

Direct labour costs are wages and employment costs that are charged directly to particular jobs. It may be that some employees work exclusively on one product (perhaps making standard tables), and so their wages are charged to that product. Other direct labour employees may have their time allocated to different products using some sort of time sheet. Such a system is used in many professional offices where lawyers or accountants have to complete time sheets showing how many hours were spent on each job so that their time can be charged accordingly.

'Indirect labour' costs are those costs of employing people that cannot be charged to particular individual jobs or products. Some indirect labour costs are part of production overheads; others are part of administrative expenses or distribution costs.

[3] But if ever the whole inventory of an item is used up, the oldest, lowest costs would be charged to production; this could result in costs being seriously understated.

16.6 Direct Expenses

Most 'expenses', such as hiring and maintaining machinery or using patents and trademarks, may be included in production overheads rather than charged to individual products or customers. A builder is likely to have a lot of machinery and equipment that is used on all jobs. But when it is necessary to hire a crane to build a high office block, the cost of hiring the crane would be a 'direct expense' that is charged directly to a particular job rather than being included in production overheads.

With materials, labour and expenses, the test is the same: they are 'direct' if they can properly be charged to individual jobs rather than being included in production overheads.

16.7 Production Overheads

Production overheads include all the costs of operating a factory or other production facility that cannot be charged to individual products or customers. They are the costs of the facilities that most or all products use to some extent. It is necessary to charge them indirectly to different products. They include the costs of providing and operating the factory, such as rent, rates, insurance, maintenance, lighting and heating; the costs of providing and operating the machinery and equipment, including depreciation, maintenance, lubrication and power; and the costs of employing all those who work in the factory who cannot be charged as direct labour, including supervisors, maintenance staff, storekeepers, cleaners and operators of fork-lift trucks and other lifting equipment.

The total cost of production overheads is easy to establish, but it is difficult to decide how much should be charged to each different product or job, and what basis would be 'fair'. In **Illustration 16.1** total production overheads for the period amount to £160,000, and it so happens that the total direct labour costs for the period are also £160,000. An easy way to charge production overheads to the three different products is to say that for each £1 of labour cost that they incur, they will be charged £1 for production overheads. Production overheads are charged on the basis of direct labour cost; in this instance it is 100 per cent of direct labour cost.

Percentage on direct labour cost

The percentage to be charged has to be recalculated each year, based on budgets for the forthcoming year. If the budget shows production overheads for the forthcoming year as £250,000, and labour costs as being £100,000, the percentage on direct labour will be 250 per cent, as shown in **Example 16.1**.

The rate calculated before the year begins will be charged on all jobs throughout the year. When the end of the year comes, there are two main possibilities:

1. Overheads will have been under-recovered. Perhaps 'actual' labour costs were only £90,000; production overheads charged would be 250 per cent of that, which is £225,000. But 'actual' overheads incurred might have been £265,000. *Under-recovered overheads* would be £40,000 (£265,000 = £225,000), that is, an extra charge when profits are calculated.
2. Overheads will have been over-recovered. Perhaps actual labour costs were £112,000; production overhead charges would be 250 per cent of that, which is £280,000. Even if actual overheads incurred had increased to £260,000, there would still be *over-recovered overheads* of £20,000 (£260,000 = £280,000), that is, an extra credit when profits are calculated.

Example 16.1

Budget for next year			
	Total	Machining workers	Assembly workers
Hours to be worked	10,000	2,000	8,000
Total direct labour cost	£100,000	£36,000	£64,000
Total production overheads	£250,000		
Production overheads as a percentage of direct labour	250%		
Direct labour hour rate	£25		

Direct labour hour rate

Charging production overheads on the basis of a direct labour hour rate seems much the same as charging them as a percentage of direct labour cost. In **Example 16.1**, if only the total column is used (and so assuming that direct labour is paid at £10 per hour) the two methods will give the same answer (see **Example 16.2**).

Example 16.2

Question:

Job 123A requires 20 hours of direct labour (5 hours machining, 15 hours assembly). Calculate the amount of production overheads to be charged to that job using the following methods:

1 Percentage on direct labour cost

2 Direct labour hour rate

Answer:

1 20 hours of labour at £10 = £200. 250% of £200 = £500

2 20 hours @ £25 per hour = £500

If a direct labour hour rate is calculated for production overheads that rate (£25 in this instance) is charged for all hours worked.

If a percentage of direct labour cost is used, and different workers are paid at different hourly rates, the amount of overheads charged will be different. For example, in **Example 16.2**, machining workers are paid at £18 per hour, and assembly workers are paid at £9 per hour. The production overhead cost of Job 123A would have to be calculated based on the labour cost.

Labour cost	Machining	5 hours @ £18 =	£ 90
		15 hours @ £9 =	£135
			£225
Production overheads 250% of £225			£562.50

The *average* labour cost in the factory was £10 per hour; this particular product required 20 hours of labour, which cost £225. If overheads are charged in accordance with the specific labour cost, then a higher overhead charge results.

In order to have more accurate charging of production overheads, factories are often divided into different cost centres, with different overhead rates for each. In **Example 16.2** it would probably be sensible to divide the factory into a Machining Department and an Assembly Department. Each would have different rates of overhead recovery and perhaps even different methods.

Machine hour rate

Where there is machinery that is particularly expensive to operate, there may be a separate cost centre for a particular machine or group of machines.

A factory has an electronic testing machine in a separate cost centre. The production overheads for that cost centre are £80,000 a year. The machine is expected to operate for 2,000 hours per annum.

The machine hour rate is £80,000 ÷ 2,000 = £40 per hour.

Each product is charged (in this instance) £40 for production overheads for each hour that the machine is used.

Other methods

Various other methods of charging production overheads to different products are possible. Overheads could be charged per unit produced, but usually only where all units produced are identical. They could be charged as a percentage of direct material costs or prime costs. Vehicles could be charged per mile.

The management (or accountants on their behalf) should determine which methods are most appropriate in their particular circumstances, and the first three methods described above are the most usual. Obviously, the use of different methods is going to produce different product costs. One method might show a particular product as being profitable, while a different method shows it as being unprofitable. It is inevitable that, whatever method is used, some products will sometimes be treated unfairly. Accountants are constantly seeking more accurate methods (such as activity based costing, as described later in this chapter); but every method is based on assumptions that may sometimes be of questionable validity. There is no such thing as a single 'correct' overhead cost. Those who use costing information should always be aware of the assumptions on which it is based and be prepared to question them.

16.8 Allocation, Apportionment and Absorption

Where a factory operates a number of separate cost centres (perhaps different workshops), the production overheads for each cost centre can be separately calculated.

Some costs can be directly *allocated* to different cost centres very accurately. Some members of staff ('indirect labour') may work exclusively in one cost centre, or their time can be specifically allocated between cost centres. Each cost centre can be separately metered to give accurate figures for lighting, heating and power. Machinery may be located exclusively in specific cost centres and so the cost of depreciation and maintenance of that machinery can be specifically allocated to that cost centre.

Other costs are more difficult to identify with particular cost centres and need to be *apportioned* to them in some equitable way. The cost of rent, rates, depreciation and repairs for the factory building may be apportioned to different cost centres on the basis of the square metres occupied. (This may also be done for lighting and heating where separate metering is not possible.) Some costs may be apportioned to cost centres on the basis of the number of employees in that cost centre; this might include some costs of supervision and indirect labour, and the costs of operating a canteen. Other costs may be apportioned on the basis of usage, perhaps the number of times a facility is used or the number of hours that a facility is used.

The costs of individual products are accumulated by adding together direct materials, direct labour (and perhaps some direct expense), and then the amount of production overheads (based on calculations such as those shown in **Section 16.7**) is *absorbed* by the product to give its total production costs.

It is sometimes useful to estimate the amount of administration, selling and distribution overheads that are incurred by a particular product, but these are period costs,[4] and do not become part of product costs.[5]

16.9 Evaluation of Absorption Costing

The traditional approach to managing fixed overhead production costs involves combining different cost types and deriving a single overhead absorption rate. This absorption rate is typically expressed as overhead cost per labour hour, overhead cost per machine hour, or a number of units. While this approach may oversimplify things, it is quick and convenient.

Absorption costing is the required method for valuing closing inventory. It is also useful in ensuring that all costs are 'recovered': that means charging every cost to a job or customer. If a business allocates only some of its costs to jobs, it could end up showing that all its jobs contribute some sort of overhead contribution, but overall, it makes a loss.

The process of charging out all costs inevitably involves approximations and arbitrary elements. The basis for charging is usually established at the beginning of the year, based on budgeted figures. As the year goes by, actual figures are likely to be different from budgeted figures, and the amount of overheads charged to jobs during the year is likely to be different from the amount of overheads actually incurred. At the end of the year, there are usually 'under-recovered' or 'over-recovered' overheads.

In the long run, a business must ensure that its sales revenue covers all of its production costs. Absorption costing is a method of attributing all production costs to individual products in the expectation that sales revenue will cover them. It is a method of recording and classifying costs that do not necessarily provide a suitable basis for short-term decisions.

Example 16.3

Rriskei Company manufactures luxury tents. In January, it produces 1,000 tents, of which 800 are sold by the end of the month, leaving 200 still in inventory.

Each tent uses £100 of labour and £400 of materials directly attributable to it. In addition, the production facility has £20,000 of total fixed overhead costs each month. Rriskei Company will assign £200 to each tent for fixed overhead costs (£20,000 total ÷ 1,000 tents produced in the month). Rriskei

[4] To be written off during the period in which they are incurred, whether or not the product is sold.

[5] Which are carried forward in the cost of closing inventory if the product is not sold in the current period.

Company uses the absorption costing method for all pricing decisions, which includes the total cost of the product.

Required:

Calculate the absorption cost per unit, the total cost of goods sold and the value of goods still remaining in the inventory.

Answer:

The absorption cost per unit:

£700 = (£500 labour and materials + £200 fixed overhead costs).

Total cost of goods sold:

Since 800 tents were sold,

£560,000 = (£700 total cost per unit × 800 tents sold).

The closing inventory will include:

£140,000 = (£700 total cost per unit × 200 tents still in the closing inventory).

16.10 Activity-based Costing

Partly because of the inadequacies and inaccuracies of absorption costing, developments such as activity-based costing (ABC) are intended to make overhead charges more accurate. In **Example 16.4,** central overhead costs are allocated to three different cost centres on a single, simple basis (as a percentage of sales revenue), which ignores the factors that really 'drive' costs. ABC attempts to identify the 'drivers' for each cost so that, for example, delivery costs are allocated to the different depots on the basis of miles covered (rather than being lumped in with other costs and allocated on the basis of sales revenue).

Example 16.4

The Brigstow Autoparts Company operates from a main warehouse in Brigstow and imports spare parts for specialist sports cars and sells them via three distribution depots: one in England, one in Wales and one in Scotland. The company's budget for the coming year is summarized as follows:

	England	Wales	Scotland
	£000	£000	£000
Sales	10,000	8,000	6,000
Cost of sales	5,600	4,600	3,800
Gross profit	4,400	3,400	2,200
Local operating costs	2,720	2,660	1,620
Operating profit	1,680	740	580
Brigstow: Central costs			

	England	Wales	Scotland
	£000	£000	£000
Warehouse			
Depreciation	200		
Storage	160		
Operating and despatch	240		
Delivery	600		
Head office			
Salaries	400		
Advertising	160		
Establishment	240		
	2,000		

Central costs are allocated to the three distribution depots as a percentage of the sales revenue of each depot, as follows:

	£000
Total sales	24,000
Total central costs	2,000
Central costs as a percentage of sales	8.33% (one-twelfth)

	England	Wales	Scotland
	£	£	£
Central costs	833	667	500
Operating profit	1,680	740	580
Net profit (loss)	847	73	80
Total £1,000,000			

Following the popularity of activity-based costing, management has decided their usual approach to allocating central overheads to the different distribution depots is too crude and simplistic and that each category of central costs should be allocated in accordance with cost drivers (what it is that really incurs the costs at each depot). These have been defined as follows:

1. Depreciation: in proportion to the amount of space occupied
2. Storage: in proportion to the amount of space occupied
3. Operations and despatch: in proportion to the number of despatches
4. Delivery: in proportion to the number of delivery miles
5. Salaries: 10 per cent of their time is spent on warehouse issues; the remainder is divided equally between the three depots
6. Advertising: to be allocated in proportion to sales
7. Establishment: to be allocated on the same basis as salaries

The necessary information for the three depots is as follows:

	England	Wales	Scotland
Number of dispatches	550	450	520
Total delivery distances (000 miles)	70	50	90
Storage space occupied (%)	40	30	30

Required:

Prepare a schedule showing the costs and profit of each depot using activity-based costing as specified above.

Answer:

Brigstow Autoparts Company

		England	Wales	Scotland
		£000	£000	£000
Sales		10,000	8,000	6,000
Cost of sales		5,600	4,600	3,800
Gross profit		4,400	3,400	2,200
Local operating costs		2,720	2,660	1,620
Operating profit		1,680	740	580
Central costs				
Depreciation (40:30:30): note 1		80	60	60
Storage (40:30:30): note 2		64	48	48
Operating and despatch (550:450:520): note 3		86.8	71.1	82.1
Delivery (70:50:90): note 4		200	142.9	257.1
	Warehouse			
Salaries (10:30:30:30): note 5	40	120	120	120
Advertising (10,000:8,000:6,000): note 6		66.7	53.3	40
Establishment (10:30:30:30): notes 7 & 5	24	72	72	72
Reallocation of warehouse (550:450:520; total is 1,520)	64	23.2	18.9	21.9
		712.7	586.2	701.1
Net profit		967.3	153.8	(121.1)
Total £1,000,000				

So, the overheads are allocated to the three locations according to what 'drives' or causes those costs. In that way, the overheads are more accurately allocated than in the 'traditional' methods of overhead absorption. However, whatever methods of allocating overheads are used, and however complex they are, there is inevitably an arbitrary element, and in making any particular decision, it is best to ensure that only the most appropriate or relevant specific costing information is used for that particular purpose. It is not possible to develop a costing system that produces costs that are accurate for all purposes. And, of course, ABC is more costly and complex to implement, so when comparing ABC to the traditional methods of overhead absorption, the costs and benefits need to be considered.

Summary

Absorption costing developed as a method of applying all production costs to individual products or jobs. This is needed partly to separate the costs of sales from closing inventories and for profit calculation. Absorption costing is not usually appropriate for short-term decision-making. In the long term it can help to ensure that all costs are 'absorbed' by products and to avoid selling at a loss. ABC is a more accurate but by no means perfect system for allocating overheads on the basis of cost drivers.

Review of key points

- Absorption costing is needed for valuing closing inventories rather than for short-term decision-making.
- Direct materials and direct labour can be allocated directly to the costs of individual products or jobs.
- Production overheads have to be absorbed by individual products or jobs on the basis of an hourly rate or a percentage addition that is 'fair'.
- The production cost shown for a particular product will be different if a different method of recovering overheads or pricing materials is used.
- Production overheads are allocated directly to cost centres where this is possible. Otherwise, they are apportioned to cost centres on an equitable basis.
- The production overheads for a cost centre are absorbed by products using different overhead recovery rates (and perhaps methods) for each cost centre.
- ABC is an absorption costing method in which fixed costs are allocated to products on the basis of what drives those costs.

Self-testing questions

1 Give examples of direct materials and indirect materials, and explain why and how they are treated differently.

2 The budget for the Mooarport Manufacturing Company for the coming year shows total production overheads as £23m. They plan to work 1.4 million hours.

   a Calculate the production overhead rate per hour.

   Total labour costs for the year are budgeted at £23m.

   b Calculate the average wage rate per hour.

   c Calculate the production overhead recovery rate as a percentage of direct labour cost.

The factory is divided into three departments; the budgets for each show:

	Department A	Department B	Department C
Production overheads	£1m	£2m	£20m
Hours worked	500,000	500,000	400,000
Direct wages	£5m	£8m	£10m

d Calculate the production overhead rate per hour for each department.

e Calculate the average wage rate per hour for each department.

f Calculate the overhead recovery rate as a percentage of direct labour cost for each department.

The company makes a product called PQ that requires 13 hours of direct labour.

g Calculate the production overheads for product PQ using the production overhead rate per hour for the factory as a whole, as in (a) above.

3 The Baldrine Company made the following purchases of Component WX:

Date	Units purchased	Cost price per unit	Amount	Total
1 March	1,000	£12	£12,000	£12,000
13 March	2,000	£11	£22,000	£34,000
26 March	500	£14	£7,000	£41,000

The company then undertook two contracts; one on 28 March, and the second on 31 March. Each used 1,500 units of component WX. Show the price that would be charged to each job using each of the following methods:

a FIFO;

b LIFO;

c weighted average.

4 Distinguish between allocation, apportionment and absorption of production overheads.

5 In what ways are administrative overheads and selling and distribution costs absorbed by different products?

6 The Canters Riding Centre is based in Cheshire. It offers three types of course. These are Pony Trekking, General Lessons and Advanced Riding Skills. The following budgeted figures relate to year 4.

	No. of courses per year	Staff hours per course	Brochures per course	Admin events per course	Insurance clauses per course
Pony trekking	40	25	30	10	14.15
General lessons	3000	2	1	4	1.5
Advanced riding skills	100	2	5	6	5

The centre currently uses the total number of participant days per year to absorb fixed overheads. Budgeted fixed overheads for year 4 are expected to be as follows (£):

Staff salaries	108,000
Administration	33,800
Brochures	7,050
Insurance	139,150

Required:

a Calculate the overhead absorption rate used by the centre.

b Calculate the cost of each course using traditional absorption costing.

c Reallocate the overheads using the most appropriate cost driver available, and calculate the cost of each course using ABC.

d Briefly discuss the advantages and disadvantages of ABC over traditional absorption costing.

7 The Breakaway Holiday Company has overheads totalling £800,000. Until recently it had applied its overheads on a traditional volume basis, based on the number of holidays sold. It sells two major products, package tours and adventure holidays.

Type of holidays	Number of holidays sold	Number of enquiries	Total number of brochures printed per holiday	Number of couriers on a holiday
Package tour	2,000	7	34	2
Adventure	1,200	5	10	1

Overheads have been split into the following activities:

	£
Enquiries	180,000
Publicity brochures	320,000
Courier trips	300,000
Total	800,000

Required:

a Calculate to the nearest £, the overhead cost of a holiday based on the traditional volume-based method.

b Recalculate the overhead costs of *both types of holiday* using an activity-based costing approach, showing how the costs differ from (a) above.

c Indicate what advantages and possible disadvantages an activity-based costing approach can bring to an organization.

Assessment questions

1 Give examples of direct labour and indirect labour, and explain why and how they are treated differently.

2 The Rumsea Production Company has annual production overheads of £1,000,000 and 50,000 direct labour hours per annum are worked, made up as follows:

Machining operatives	10,000 hours at £20 per hour
Assembly operatives	25,000 hours at £10 per hour
Finishing operatives	15,000 hours at £15 per hour

a Calculate, for the factory as a whole, the overhead recovery rates as a percentage of direct labour.

b The production overheads for each department are as follows:

Machining	£500,000
Assembly	£200,000
Finishing	£300,000

Calculate the overhead recovery rate as a percentage of direct labour for each department.

c A new product, the Rumbo, will require 10 hours of machining, 4 hours of assembly and 4 hours of finishing. How much production overhead should be charged? Explain and justify your calculations.

3 The Ballorna Company made the following purchases of component LMS:

Date	Units purchased	Cost price per unit	Amount	Total
11 Feb	500	£20	£10,000	£10,000
17 Feb	200	£22	£4,400	£14,400
21 Feb	300	£24	£7,200	£21,600
25 Feb	400	£23	£9,200	£30,800

The company completed two contracts, one on 28 February and the second on 11 March. Each used 600 units of component LMS. Show the price that would be charged to each job using each of the following methods:

a FIFO;

b LIFO;

c weighted average.

4 What are 'cost centres' and why are they used?

a GamesRus plc manufactures three types of electronic game. These are 'Dungeons and Druids', 'Alien Invader Force' and 'Sorcerers' Revenge'. The factory is set up to produce the games in batches of 1,000, and it plans to manufacture 1 million of each type of game during year 4 (i.e. 1,000 batches of 1,000 games each). In each case, the cost unit is a batch of 1,000 games.

The budgeted direct costs of manufacture are as follows:

Product	Direct labour hours per batch	Raw material costs per batch
Dungeons and Druids	3	£250
Alien Invader Force	5	£360
Sorcerers' Revenge	4	£270

Direct labour is paid at £8 per hour.

Total production overheads for year 4 are budgeted as follows:

	£
Machine set-up costs	405,000
Maintenance costs	155,000
Quality control costs	200,000
Packaging costs	140,000
	900,000

At present the company uses direct labour hours as a base to absorb these production overheads.

The company has started to investigate the possibility of using ABC and has identified some data that could be used to calculate cost driver rates. The following cost driver information is expected for *each batch of 1,000 games*:

	No. of setups per batch	**No. of quality inspections per batch**	**No. of packaging steps per batch**	**No. of maintenance events per year**
Dungeons and Druids	2	2	1	10
Alien Invader Force	3	1	2	10
Sorcerers' Revenge	4	2	4	20

Required:

b For each product, calculate *the total production cost* for each batch of 1,000 games of each product using the traditional absorption costing method for year 4.

c Calculate *the total production cost* for each batch of 1,000 games for each product using ABC for year 4.

d Briefly discuss ABC's advantages and disadvantages over traditional absorption costing. Your discussion should include a reference to ways in which managers could use ABC's cost information more meaningfully.

Activities and discussion questions

1 Costs based on absorption costing are not wholly accurate, and do not provide an appropriate basis for decision-making. Discuss.

2 Why is absorption costing widely used?

3 Cost accounting is a system of recording, classifying and accumulating costs; there is no reason why this should be useful in management accounting. Discuss.

4 Absorption costing is often used in the pricing of long-term government contracts, as in the case of the building of submarines for the Royal Navy. Discuss and identify the reasons for this.

Accounting in context

Discuss and comment on the following report based on articles from the press with reference to reducing costs, including overheads, in improving a company's performance.

UK drug shortages aggravated due to Brexit

'The Nuffield Trust report blames Brexit that has "exacerbated" the "underlying fragilities at a global and UK level" in drug supply chains.' Drug shortages in the UK have more than doubled between 2020 and 2023, and the main reason is that Brexit has impacted the medical supplies of drugs. The UK has found it challenging to ensure an adequate volume of its medicine supplies, according to research by the Nuffield Trust. These shortages include key areas such as antibiotics and epileptic drugs. These shortages have required the government to mitigate the problem by reimbursing the pharmacies for buying drugs above their standard cost, and these price concessions have significantly increased and peaked in late 2022. These problems are related to several factors: disruption of the supply chains of imports from Asian countries, COVID-19 lockdowns, inflation and global uncertainty. Additionally, the UK has seen a reduction in the number of alternatives available for its medical drugs. Generic pharmaceutical products make up the majority of drugs prescribed globally compared to the brand/innovator drugs. During the pandemic, the severe lockdown in China, the second-largest pharmaceutical market controlling 10 per cent of the world's market, also contributed to manufacturing delays.

Increased demand for popular medications, such as hormone replacement therapies, and UK pricing policies have undoubtedly exerted pressure on the country's supplies, as highlighted by the Nuffield Trust. The UK Medicines and Healthcare Regulatory Agency (MHRA) has been slower in approving new drugs compared to the EU. For example, the MHRA in 2021 (its first year of independence) approved 35 new drugs in the UK, compared to 40 in Europe and 52 in the US.

Sources: I. Johnston (2024) Brexit Has 'Exacerbated' UK Drug Shortages, Research Finds. *Financial Times*, 18 April. https://www.ft.com/content/e1c60543-f5fa-44ac-b180-4b4c60d86342

L. Alfaro and S. Jeong (2020) COVID-19: The Global Shutdown. Harvard Business School Case 320-108, May (revised July 2020). https://www.indiaassignmenthelp.com/uploads/1652205823COVID%2019%20The%20Global%20Shutdown.pdf

M. Hofer (2023) Post-Brexit Medicine Approvals: What We Know. Imperial College Business School. https://www.imperial.ac.uk/business-school/ib-knowledge/health/post-brexit-medicine-approvals-what-we-know/

Nuffield Trust (2024) Patients Face 'New Normal' of Medicines Shortages as UK Hampered by Supply Issues and Impact of EU Exit. Press release, 18 April. https://www.nuffieldtrust.org.uk/news-item/patients-face-new-normal-of-medicines-shortages-as-uk-hampered-by-supply-issues-and-impact-of-eu-exit#:~:text=Global%20supply%20problems%20have%20caused,trying%20to%20mitigate%20the%20problem.

References and further reading

Atkinson, A., Kaplan, R., Matsumura, E. and Young, M. (2012) *Management Accounting* (6th edn.). Harlow: Pearson.

Bhimani, A.C.T., Datar, S.M., Horngren, C.T. and Foster, G. (2012) *Management and Cost Accounting* (5th edn.). Upper Saddle River: FT Prentice Hall.

Drury, C. (2008) *Management and Cost Accounting* (7th edn.). Andover: Cengage Learning.

Dyson, J.R. (2010) *Accounting for Non-accounting Students* (8th edn.). Upper Saddle River, NJ: FT Prentice Hall.

Proctor, R. (2009) *Managerial Accounting for Business Decisions* (3rd edn.). Harlow: Pearson.

Seal, W., Garrison, R.H. and Nooreen, E.W. (2011) *Management Accounting* (4th edn.). Maidenhead: McGraw-Hill.

Chapter 17

Marginal Costing and Decision-making

Chapter contents

17.1 Introduction
17.2 Marginal Costing Presentation and Contribution
17.3 Separating Fixed and Variable Costs
17.4 Break-even Analysis
17.5 Break-even Charts and Profit/Volume Graphs
17.6 Marginal Costing and Decision-making
17.7 Advantages of Marginal Costing
17.8 Limitations of Marginal Costing

Learning objectives

After studying this chapter you will be able to:

- ✓ Distinguish between fixed and variable costs
- ✓ Calculate contribution and understand its meaning
- ✓ Understand the relevance, uses and assumptions of marginal costing
- ✓ Use marginal costing for a range of short-term decisions including break-even analysis, make and buy decisions and optimal use of scarce resource (limiting factor) decisions
- ✓ Be able to identify the advantages and limitations of marginal costing

17.1 Introduction

Absorption costing provides a means of ensuring that all products and services bear their fair share of costs, but it is not useful in decision-making. The full cost of producing desks may be £240,000 a year, but that does not mean that £240,000 a year would be saved if the production of desks was stopped. Nor does it mean that the costs would go up or down by 10 per cent if the volume of production was increased or decreased by 10 per cent. In decision-making, it is important to have knowledge of the *behaviour* of costs so that questions such as the following can be answered.

We need to ask questions as to what will happen to costs, for example, under the following circumstances:

1 the volume of output is increased or decreased
2 a production line is terminated
3 a new product is introduced (and what volume of production and sales will be required to cover costs)
4 new and better machinery is installed.

The key to establishing the behaviour of costs is to separate fixed costs from variable costs.

Fixed costs continue at much the same level, regardless of the volume of production. Such costs would include the rent, rates, lighting and heating of the factory, most of the costs of supervisory staff, and most machinery and maintenance costs.

Variable costs change directly in line with the volume of production. If the company stopped making desks, it would save all the costs of direct materials and direct labour. There would also be some reduction in production overheads - less power would be used, maintenance costs would probably be lower (if the machinery is used less), and there might be a reduction in 'indirect labour' costs (supervisors and others in the factory who are not direct labour).

17.2 Marginal Costing Presentation and Contribution

It is important to remember that absorption costing principles must be used when preparing financial statements for external purposes. One key principle of absorption costing is that inventory and units produced must include a share of all production costs, both fixed and variable, that were incurred to bring them to their present condition.

However, marginal costing principles are used for internal decision-making purposes, usually short term. As fixed costs are incurred regardless of the level of activity, the purpose of marginal costing is to consider the amount of contribution generated.

Marginal costing information can be presented for a business as a whole, or separately for each product, or combined, as shown in **Illustration 17.1**. Sales figures are shown first, and then all variable costs are deducted to show the 'contribution' that each product makes towards fixed costs and profits.

ILLUSTRATION 17.1 Marginal costing

	Total	**Tables**	**Desks**	**Chairs**
	£000	£000	£000	£000
Sales	**757**	254	276	227
Variable costs:				
Direct materials	**300**	100	120	80
Direct labour	**160**	50	60	50
Production overheads	**80**	25	30	25
Production costs	**540**	175	210	155

	Total	Tables	Desks	Chairs
	£000	£000	£000	£000
Distribution and administrative overheads[1]	**46**	15	18	13
Total variable costs	**586**	190	228	168
Contribution	**171**	64	48	59
Fixed costs:				
Production overheads	80			
Distribution and administrative overheads	78			
Total fixed costs	158			
Profit	13			

When using costing information to make decisions, it is useful to be able to separate fixed costs from variable costs. Ways of doing this are outlined in the section on marginal costing below. The figures from **Illustration 17.3** are presented in a marginal costing format in **Illustration 17.4**. Here, it is assumed that production overheads are half-fixed and half-variable and that distribution and administrative overheads are mainly fixed (£78,000 fixed; £46,000 variable).

The following points emerge from the marginal costing presentation:

1 Each of the three products makes a 'contribution' towards fixed costs. These fixed costs will be incurred whether or not desks are made.

2 Desks make a contribution of £48,000. It might be 'fairer' if desks made a larger contribution. But if the company stops making desks, the company will be £48,000 worse off;[2] and its (modest) overall profit of £13,000 would turn into a loss.

3 Using marginal costing, variable costs are charged to each product, but fixed costs are dealt with only in total (not charged to individual products).

4 *Contribution* may be defined as sales minus variable costs, and it is important to calculate the contribution for each product.

5 *Contribution* can also be calculated as fixed costs plus profit; but fixed costs and profit are not shown for each product.

6 The above may be summarized as sales minus variable costs equals contribution, which equals fixed costs plus profit. This may be expressed as:

$$S - V = C = F + P$$

$$\text{or} \quad S - V = F + P = C$$

S = Selling price or sales revenue

V = Variable cost

C = Contribution

F = Fixed cost

P = Profit

[1] Distribution and administrative overheads have been allocated to each product in proportion to total variable production costs. £46,000 is 8.52 per cent of £540,000; that percentage has been applied to the total variable production cost for each item: 8.52 per cent of 175,000 is £14,900, rounded to £15,000; 8.52 per cent of £210,000 is £17,900; 8.52 per cent of £155,000 is £13,200. Businesses are free to allocate overheads on whatever basis seems most appropriate to them.

[2] Unless it replaces desks with a more profitable product, or increases the selling price of desks.

Absorption costing and marginal costing systems each provide information that is useful for different purposes. However, if absorption costing is used, the value of the inventory will be based on the full production cost of a unit of product, whereas with marginal costing, the value of the inventory will be based on the total variable production cost of a unit of product. The result of this is that inventory values will be different based on which of the two costing methods are used, thereby affecting the profit.

17.3 Separating Fixed and Variable Costs

There are a number of ways of separating fixed from variable costs:

1 *Inspection, line by line.* Each item of expenditure can be examined and assessed as fixed or variable. Many items such as direct materials, direct labour, and some production overheads such as the power used to drive machinery are mainly variable. Other items such as rent, rates, insurance and most salaries are mainly fixed. The main problem with this approach is that some items are semi-fixed - for example, salaries where there is a bonus for higher levels of output or sales - and some items are semi-variable - for example, repairs to machinery and inspection of manufactured goods, which are likely to increase somewhat, but not by as much as the increase in production.

2 *Comparing two periods.* Where the level of profit and sales is known for two periods, a lot of information can be deduced by comparing the two periods.

   Illustration 17.2 does not seem to contain much information: sales have increased by 20 per cent in the month of April; profits have increased by 50 per cent in April; the higher increase in profits is due to the incidence of fixed costs. In **Illustration 17.3** a line for total costs (the difference between sales and profit) has been inserted, and the amount of change between March and April is shown. When sales increased by £20,000, variable costs increased by £15,000. We assume that fixed costs did not increase (because they are fixed), and so the whole of the increase in costs is an increase in variable costs. The relationship between variable costs and sales is therefore established: variable costs are 75 per cent of sales; this is shown in the fourth line of figures in **Illustration 17.3**. As total costs are made up of the two items (fixed costs; variable costs), the amount of fixed costs is simply the difference between line (iii) and line (iv); and it must be the same amount (in this case it is £15,000) for each month.

ILLUSTRATION 17.2 Separating fixed and variable costs

	March	April
	£	£
Sales	100,000	120,000
Profit	10,000	15,000

ILLUSTRATION 17.3 Separating fixed and variable costs

		March	April	Change
		£	£	£
i	Sales	100,000	120,000	20,000
ii	Plus profit	10,000	15,000	
iii	Total costs	90,000	105,000	15,000
iv	Less variable costs	(75,000)	(90,000)	
v	Fixed costs	15,000	15,000	

3 *Comparing several periods.* To see if the pattern suggested by just two periods is representative, it is more realistic to compare the level of costs with the level of output over a number of periods. This can be done in several ways:

a The measurements can be plotted on a graph, with a visual attempt at plotting a line that best fits the measurements. Cost levels at various levels of output can be read from the graph. Continuing that line down to a zero level of output suggests the amount of fixed costs (which is presumed to be the amount of costs the line shows at a zero level of output).

b Every measurement. Only two are considered - the highest level of output and the lowest. The calculation is then done using the highest and the lowest levels of production, using the method shown above for comparing two periods.

c Regression analysis, using the 'least squares' method, can be used to obtain a line of best fit, which takes all the available measurements into account. It assumes a straight-line relationship.

Greater mathematical precision in calculating the relationship in previous periods does not mean that the figures that are produced will provide a better basis for decision-making. The usefulness of all costing information, when used for decision-making, depends on what assumptions are made (particularly about future cost levels). Realistic assumptions are more important than more refined and detailed mathematical accuracy in measuring previous relationships between costs.

17.4 Break-even Analysis

Once we have separated total costs into fixed costs and variable costs, in a given situation we can easily calculate *contribution*, *break-even point* and *margin of safety*.

We know that profit is the difference between sales and costs; if we identify the two types of cost we can say that:

SALES minus VARIABLE COSTS minus FIXED COSTS equals PROFIT

This can be rearranged as:

SALES minus VARIABLE COSTS equals FIXED COSTS plus PROFIT

$$S - V = F + P = \text{Contribution}$$

That gives us two definitions of contribution:

(1) Contribution	=	Sales minus variable costs
(2) Contribution	=	Fixed costs plus profit

Each definition of 'contribution' should give the same answer. This can be illustrated using the figures for March from **Illustration 17.3**:

(1) Sales minus variable costs	= contribution
£100,000 − £75,000	= £25,000
(2) Fixed costs plus profit	= contribution
£15,000 + £10,000	= £25,000

The contribution/sales ratio can also be calculated. Expressed as a percentage it is contribution as a percentage of sales. It can also be expressed as contribution ÷ sales. Using the figures for March from **Illustration 17.3**, the contribution/sales ratio is:

$$\frac{£25,000}{£100,000} \text{ which is 25\%, of 0.25}$$

The *break-even point* is the level of sales at which neither profit nor loss is made. The sales revenue is equal to the costs incurred. Where a business makes many units that are identical, it can be expressed in terms of the number of units sold. Where a business makes a number of different products, it is expressed as the amount of sales in £'s rather than units. The calculation is as follows:

Break-even formula:

Break-even point in units = Fixed costs per annum ÷ contribution per unit

Break-even point in £'s sales = Fixed costs per annum ÷ contribution/sales ratio

The high-low method is linked to cost behaviour analysis and is a method used for separating semi-variable costs into their fixed and variable elements. Therefore, this method includes comparing the total costs at the highest and lowest levels of activity. When the variable cost is a fixed charge per unit and the fixed costs remain constant, it is feasible to determine the fixed and variable costs by solving the corresponding equations. It is easily calculated using a two-step process: The first step involves selecting the highest and lowest activity levels and their respective costs and calculating the variable cost per unit as shown in **Example 17.1**. The second step involves calculating the fixed cost using either of the two levels selected in Step 1. The fixed cost is now the difference between the total cost less total variable cost, as shown in **Example 17.1**.

Example 17.1

The volume of production in units and total production costs of the Soldrick Manufacturing Company in recent weeks were as follows:

Week	Number of units produced	Total production costs, £
1	80,000	176,000
2	76,000	170,000
3	82,000	177,000
4	84,000	180,000
5	77,000	170,750
6	82,000	176,500
7	79,000	106,200

The highest level of production was 84,000 units in week 4 at a cost of £180,000.

The lowest level of production was 76,000 units in week 2 at a cost of £170,000.

	Week 4	Week 2	Change
Production in units	84,000	76,000	8,000
Production costs	£180,000	£170,000	£10,000

It costs £10,000 to produce an extra 8,000 units. The variable cost per unit is therefore:

$$\frac{£10{,}000}{8{,}000} = £1.25 \text{ per unit}$$

Production costs can now be split between fixed costs and variable costs, as follows:

	Working	Week 4	Working	Week 2
Variable costs	£1.25 × 84,000	£105,000	£1.25 × 76,000	£95,000
Fixed costs	£180,000 - £105,000	£75,000	£170,000 - £95,000	£75,000

The *margin of safety* is the amount by which sales can fall before reaching the break-even point. If sales fall by more than the margin of safety, losses will be incurred. In **Example 17.2**, the expected level of sales is 50,000 units a year, and the margin of safety is 16,667 units because sales can fall to the break-even point, 33,333, before losses are made.

Example 17.2

Break-even point

Dulby Company produces and sells 50,000 dulbies a year for £25 each. Variable costs amount to £16 per unit. Annual fixed costs are £300,000. You are required to calculate the break-even point in units and sales revenue in £s.

The contribution per unit is £25 − £16 = £9 per unit.

(1) The break-even point in units is:

$$\frac{\text{Fixed costs}}{\text{Contribution per unit}} = \frac{£300{,}000}{£9} = 33{,}333 \text{ units}$$

The contribution/sales ratio is £9 ÷ £25 = 36% or 0.36

(2)The break-even point in sales revenue is:

$$\frac{\text{Fixed costs}}{\text{Contribution/sales ratio}} = \frac{£300{,}000}{0.36} = £833{,}33$$

The sale of 33,333 units at £25 each would yield sales revenue of £833,333.

The margin of safety can also be expressed in £s of sales revenue. In **Example 17.2,** the level of sales is (50,000 × £25 =) £1,250,000; this can fall to £833,333, giving a margin of safety of £416,667 (which is 16,667 units).

17.5 Break-even Charts and Profit/Volume Graphs

ILLUSTRATION 17.4 Break-even chart of Dulby Company

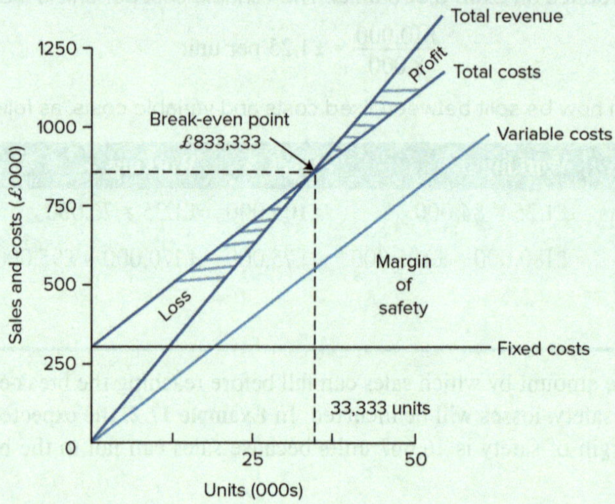

Note:

Break-even point is where total cost = total revenue

333,33 units and sales revenue of £833,325 : Margin of safety

= expected output − break-even point

= 50,000 − 33,333 units = 16,667 units

= £1,250,000 − 833,333 = £416,667 sales revenue

= 33%

ILLUSTRATION 17.5 Profit/volume chart of Dulby Company

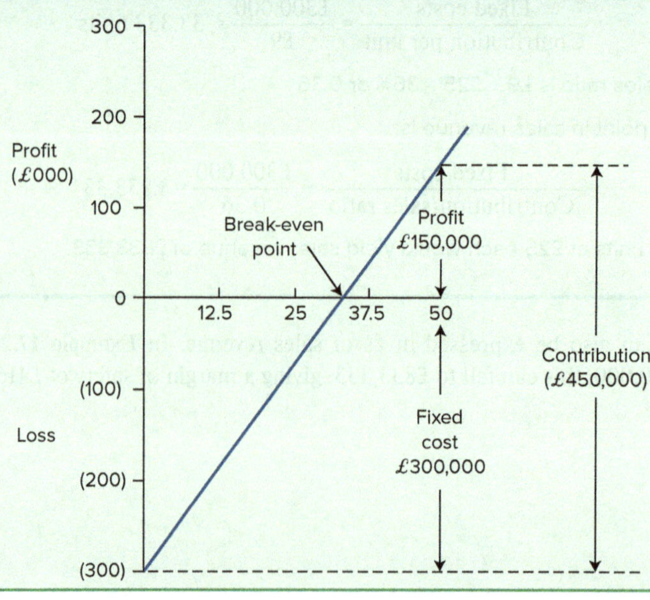

17.6 Marginal Costing and Decision-making

Once fixed costs have been separated from variable costs, it is possible to answer questions such as the following:

1 When launching a new product, what sales level is needed to ensure that all costs are covered?
2 When planning a price reduction, how many additional sales are required to make up for lost revenue?
3 By how much can the existing level of sales fall before the business starts to make losses?
4 What sales level is required to achieve a profit of, say, £50,000?
5 How can we maximize profitability when production is restricted by a limiting factor (such as limited machine capacity)?
6 Should we manufacture components in-house or buy them from outside ('make or buy' decisions)?

Examples of answers to the above six questions are shown in **Examples 17.3, 17.4, 17.5, 17.6, 17.7,** and **17.8.** A break-even chart (**Illustration 17.4**) or a profit/volume chart (**Illustration 17.5**) can show answers to the first four questions.

17.7 Advantages of Marginal Costing

The main advantage of marginal costing is in decision-making: it focuses on how costs will behave as a result of changes in the volume of production. It takes no account of the effect of fixed costs which, within a specified range of output, are assumed not to change, and the existence of economies of scale (e.g. materials), where the unit purchase price might fall, as quantities increase or diseconomies of scale (e.g. labour), where the production increases, overtime rates might increase the unit cost. The greater the volume of production, the more units there are, while the unit costs will not change, the total contribution will increase in direct proportion to the level of output. The focus is not on the 'profit' each product makes. It is on the 'contribution' that each product makes towards fixed costs that will be incurred regardless of the volume of production, and towards profit. A product may appear to be running at a loss (when absorption costing is used), but it is making a positive contribution to the fixed costs and profit of a business. In **Illustration 16.1** absorption costing showed desks losing £12,000 a year. But if the business stopped making them, it would be £48,000 worse off because desks make a contribution of £48,000 a year (**Illustration 17.1**).

Example 17.3

Question:

The Burjy Company is planning to launch a new type of burjy that will sell for £100 each. Fixed costs are £80,000 per annum; variable costs are £60 per unit. How many do they need to sell to break even?

Answer:

Contribution is (£100 − £60) = £40 per unit; need enough contribution to cover fixed costs of £80,000. £80,000 ÷ £40 = 2,000 units to break even.

Example 17.4

Question:

Mulby Company is planning to reduce the selling price of mulbies from £60 per unit to £50 per unit. Fixed costs are £900,000 per annum; variable costs are £30 per unit; 50,000 units per annum are made and sold. How many additional units must be sold to make up for the price reduction?

Answer:

Existing sales revenue	50,000 @ £60	£3,000,000
Existing costs 50,000 @ £30 = 1,500,000 + 900,000		£2,400,000
Existing profit		£600,000
Proposed contribution per unit (£50 − £30)		£20

Contribution required:

Fixed costs	£900,000
Profit	£600,000
	£1,500,000

Sales units required to make that contribution

£1,500,000 ÷ £20 = 75,000

An increase of 25,000 units is required

Example 17.5

Question:

The Gurby Company make and sells 1 million gurbies a year that sell for £20 each. Fixed costs are £600,000 a year and variable costs are £18 per unit. By how much can the existing level of sales fall before the company starts to make losses?

Answer using sales revenue:

Existing sales revenue 1 million @ £20	= £20,000,000
Contribution/sales ratio	£2 ÷ £20 = 10% or 0.1
Break-even point:	Fixed costs ÷ contribution sales ratio
	£600,000 ÷ 0.1 = £6,000,000

Sales can fall by £14m.

Answer using units:

Existing sales units	1,000,000
Contribution per unit	£2

Break-even point = fixed costs ÷ £2

£600,000 ÷ £2 = 300,000 units

Sales can fall by 700,000 units.

Comparing two answers: 700,000 units @ £20 = £14m sales revenue

Example 17.6

Question:

The summarized results of Pulby Company are as follows:

	£
Sales 10,000 units at £30 each	300,000
Variable costs at £25 each	250,000
Fixed costs	45,000
Profit	5,000

How many more units does it need to sell to make a profit of £50,000?

Answer:

It needs £45,000 additional contribution. Contribution is £5 per unit. It needs to sell an extra 9,000 units.

Example 17.7

Limiting factors

The Wink Company produces three types of wink: Fenwinks, Garwinks and Hoodwinks, details of which are as follows:

	Fenwinks	Garwinks	Hoodwinks
Demand in units per annum	100,000	140,000	200,000
	£	£	£
Selling price per unit	50	80	100
Variable costs per unit	20	40	55
Contribution per unit	30	40	45

If the company had unlimited production facilities, it would produce all it could sell. If demand were limited to 350,000 units per annum, it would produce all the Hoodwinks and Garwinks it could (340,000 units) because they each make the greatest contribution. It would produce only 10,000 Fenwinks.

Its problem is that, because of health and safety regulations, all products have to be treated by their safety-wink machine, which has a capacity of only 400,000 hours per annum. The time taken to treat each product is as follows:

Fenwinks	1 hour
Garwinks	1½ hours
Hoodwinks	2 hours

If it concentrated on producing only Hoodwinks (because they have the highest contribution per unit) its total production would be 200,000 units, using all the capacity of the safety-wink machine, which would give a contribution of 200,000 × £45 = £9,000,000.

Instead, it should concentrate on producing the items that give the greatest contribution per unit of limiting factor; that is, the greatest contribution per hour of the safety-wink machine.

	Fenwinks	Garwinks	Hoodwinks
Demand in units per annum	100,000	140,000	200,000
Contribution per unit	£30	£40	£45
Time on safety-wink machine	1 hour	1½ hours	2 hours
Contribution per hour of safety-wink machine	£30	£26.67	£22.50

The production plan should be as follows:

	Number produced	Contribution generated	Safety-wink hours used	Safety-wink hours remaining
Fenwinks	100,000	£3,000,000	100,000	300,000
Garwinks	140,000	£5,600,000	210,000	90,000
Hoodwinks	45,000	£2,430,000	90,000	0
Total contribution		£11,030,000		

By concentrating on making items that maximize the contribution per unit[3] of the limiting factor it has made a total contribution of just over £11m. If it had simply concentrated on producing items that maximized the contribution *per item of production,* the total contribution would have been only £9m.

However, this analysis assumed that there is no interrelated demand among these three products. If, for example, Nike were selling three products – trainers, t-shirts and caps – and the trainers had the lowest contribution per unit of scarce resource, it will still be necessary to make and sell this product because it is the trainers that create the demand for the other two products. Additionally, of course, it might be possible to remove or mitigate the constraint by acquiring another machine, finding another source for a scarce material or finding additional labour from abroad.

Ranking products in order of their contribution per unit of the limiting factor is the strategy when there is only *one* scarce resource; if there is more than one scarce resource, we then have to resort to *linear programming,* an operational research technique.

[3] In this case the unit of limiting factor is hours. It could be, for example, litres or kilos, if only a limited amount of a raw material was available.

Sometimes a business wants to quote low prices, perhaps in order to penetrate a new export market, or as a 'loss leader' to encourage customers to buy other products. By identifying the marginal cost of a product, it is possible to see the minimum selling price that would not produce a loss. Where pricing decisions consider only full absorption costs, there is little flexibility, and it is difficult to see the effects of different pricing decisions.

Example 17.8

Question:

The Baldwynne Company manufactures almost all of the components it uses in-house. An important component, the wynngie, costs £50 to produce. An outside supplier can provide wynngies at a price of £43 each. The production cost of a wynngie is as follows:

	£
Direct materials	14
Direct labour	12
Production overheads	24
	50

Production overheads, one-third of which are variable, are charged at 200 per cent of direct labour costs.

Should the company continue to produce, or buy in wynngies?

Answer:

The variable costs of production are £14 + £12 + £8 = £34 per unit. It is cheaper to make them than buy them (unless production capacity is limited, and an alternative product can make a greater contribution).

Break-even analysis clearly identifies the effects of changes in volume, the break-even point and the margin of safety.

Where marginal costing is used for valuing closing inventories, the resulting profit figures will be different from absorption costing and, arguably, more realistic. In **Illustration 17.6(a)**, closing inventories are shown at full absorption cost of £80 per unit, and gross profit is £18,000. In **Illustration 17.6(b)**, closing inventories are shown at marginal cost, which is £30, and gross profit is only £13,000. The difference arises because, in absorption costing, closing inventories include their share of fixed production overheads; these are carried forward to be treated as an expense in the following year. In marginal costing, closing inventories include only variable production costs; the whole of the fixed production overheads is written off as an expense in the current year. In **Illustrations 17.6(a)** and **17.6(b)** closing inventory is 100 units, and fixed production overheads are £50 per unit: this amounts to £5,000, which is the difference in gross profit between the two methods.

ILLUSTRATION 17.6(a) Absorption costing

		£
Sales	900 @ £100 each	90,000
	Opening inventory	0
	Absorption cost of production 1,000 @ £80 each	80,000

		£
	Closing inventory 100 @ £80 each	(8,000)
Production cost of goods sold		(72,000)
Gross profit		18,000

ILLUSTRATION 17.6(b) Marginal costing

		£
Sales	900 @ £100 each	90,000
	Opening inventory	0
	Variable cost of production 1,000 @ £30 each	30,000
	Closing inventory 100 @ £30 each	(3,000)
Marginal cost of goods sold		(27,000)
Contribution		63,000
Fixed production overheads		(50,000)
Gross profit		13,000

Which method is 'better' is debatable. Normal financial accounting standards require the use of absorption costing, so that closing inventories include their fair share of fixed production overheads. But if the net realizable value of closing inventories is less than the cost figure shown (in this case £8,000), they should be written down to realizable value.

17.8 Limitations of Marginal Costing

1 Marginal costing is not acceptable for the valuation of closing inventories in financial accounting.

2 The use of marginal costing might encourage selling at prices that are too low to cover fixed costs and to make a profit. The view is that all orders are worthwhile, provided the price covers variable costs and makes a positive contribution. But if there are too many orders that make only a small contribution, fixed costs will not be covered, and the business will make a loss. There are often occasions when it is worth taking some orders that make only a small contribution, but there will be serious problems if a company does not make a sufficient contribution overall.

3 The main danger of marginal costing and break-even analysis is that they are based on simplifying assumptions, which can lead to oversimplistic interpretations and to bad decisions. The following assumptions may be reasonable where only modest changes are expected, but would not be true in respect of major changes in levels of production.

   a Cost behaviour is linear; that is, total costs vary in line with the level of output, as shown on profit/volume graphs and break-even charts. In practice, the line of total costs would often be curved or go up in steps (e.g. when new production facilities come on stream).

   b Variable costs per unit remain constant. In practice, direct material costs per unit might decrease as output increases because of economies from bulk buying. Labour costs per unit might also decrease as employees become more efficient (the 'learning curve' effect). But in some circumstances, increased production may lead to material and labour shortages, and increased costs. Break-even analysis usually assumes that there are no changes in efficiency or productivity.

c All costs can be classified as fixed or variable. Although the behaviour of costs can be plotted over a period of time, and relationships assumed, those relationships can easily change as circumstances change.

d Fixed costs remain constant. This is unlikely to be true in the long run. If production is to increase beyond the capacity of current capacity, there will have to be a step up to increase production facilities. If production declines sufficiently, factories will close, and 'fixed' costs will be reduced. In the long run, most 'fixed' costs are variable.

e Variable costs vary in line with production. This may be true when there is time to adjust. But direct labour cannot usually be switched on and off instantly because of people's contracts of employment. In the short term, direct labour costs may be more like fixed costs.

If these limitations are borne in mind, marginal costing should provide a better basis for decision-making than absorption costing.

Summary

Fixed costs do not change with the level of output within a given range, while marginal costs vary with the level of output. In marginal costing, fixed costs are not associated with a unit of output and absorbed into the cost of a unit but are treated as period costs. Contribution per unit is the selling price less the variable costs and the contribution per unit is a contribution towards covering the company's fixed costs and after having covered the fixed costs (i.e. having broken even), each additional unit sold makes a profit equivalent to the unit contribution. Marginal or variable costs and contribution can be used to establish the number of units required to make a given profit, to calculate the number of units required to break even, and to help in making such decisions as whether to make or buy goods and what to make in the event that there are insufficient resources, materials or labour, for instance, to satisfy the demand for the company's output.

Like all management accounting models, marginal costing makes various assumptions and has some limitations but it is a very useful way of making several types of short-term decision.

Review of key points

- Total fixed costs are costs that do not vary with the level of production within a specified range of output and/or time.
- Total variable costs are costs that vary with production.
- Variable costs per unit are constant.
- Contribution per unit = selling price minus variable cost.
- PV ratio = contribution per unit/selling price per unit × 100.
- Break-even point = fixed costs/selling price per unit.
- Margin of safety = budgeted or expected output minus break-even point.
- Break-even point and margin of safety can be determined graphically as well as in a computation.

- With limiting factors, products should be 'ranked' in order of their contribution per unit of scarce resource.
- Marginal costing is based on classifying costs by behaviour: it assumes that costs can be classified according to whether they are fixed or variable.
- It is assumed that there are no economies or diseconomies of scale and that fixed costs, variable costs and revenues are all linear, varying in proportion to output.

Self-testing questions

1 Define 'contribution', 'break-even point' and 'margin of safety'.

2 How can fixed costs be estimated or measured separately from variable costs?

3 The Dannidhoon Company is planning to launch a new type of dhoon that will sell for £60 each. Fixed costs are £700,000 per annum; variable costs are £35 per unit. How many does it need to sell to break even?

	September	October
	£000	£000
Sales	600	650
Profit	100	120

From the above information calculate total costs for each month, variable costs as a percentage of sales, fixed costs, contribution/sales ratio and break-even point.

4 The Paradise Island Building Company builds three types of residence, details of which are shown below. It has always concentrated on the luxury end of the market where prices and profits are highest. Recently the government has required work permits for all building workers, and the company is allowed to use only (a) 30,000 hours a year or (b) 51,000 hours. What other factors might be taken into consideration in the decision?

	Holiday chalets	Terraced houses	Luxury villas
Annual demand	20	30	10
Labour hours to build a home	300	600	3,000
	£000	£000	£000
Selling price per home	100	200	800
Variable costs per home	70	120	420

You are required to calculate:

a the contribution for each type of home;

b the amount of contribution per unit of limiting factor, assuming first there are 30,000 labour hours available and, second, there are 51,000 labour hours available;

c its optimum building plan, and the total contribution it would generate;

d any other factors you think should be taken into consideration in making this decision.

5 Eagle Sandwiches makes and sells sandwiches in a local light industrial zone. The average variable cost of a sandwich is £1, while the average selling price is £3. Weekly fixed costs are £4,000, while budgeted sales are 2,400 units. Calculate the profit at the forecast level of sales, the break-even point in terms of both units and sales revenue, the margin of safety in terms of both units and sales revenue and as a percentage of sales revenue, and draw a break-even chart reflecting this decision.

Assessment questions

1 Define 'fixed costs' and 'variable costs'.

2 How does marginal costing differ from absorption costing?

3 The Cornay Company is planning to reduce the selling price of cornays from £110 per unit to £99 per unit. Fixed costs are £3,600,000 per annum; variable costs are £40 per unit; 80,000 units per annum are made and sold. How many additional units must be sold to make up for the price reduction?

4 The summarized results of the Poterin Company are as follows:

	£
Sales 6,000 units at £150 each	900,000
Variable costs at £130 each	780,000
Fixed costs	100,000
Profit	20,000

How many more units does it need to sell to make a profit of £90,000?

	February	**March**
	£	£
Sales	120,000	150,000
Profit	24,000	34,000

From the above information calculate total costs for each month, variable costs as a percentage of sales, fixed costs, contribution/sales ratio and break-even point.

5 Persie Limited is dedicated to the production and sale of highly fashionable sunglasses. The company's budgeted monthly production is 3,000 units. Variable manufacturing costs are £16 per unit, while variable selling costs are £4 per unit. Fixed selling costs are £24,000 per month, while monthly fixed manufacturing costs are £30,000. Each pair of sunglasses sells for £40. The company values stock on a first-in-first-out basis.

Other data relating to July and August were as follows:

Number of units	**July**	**August**
Opening inventory	400	100
Production	3,400	3,300
Sales	3,700	2,800
Closing inventory	100	600

Required:

a Prepare an income statement for Persie Limited for both July and August using:

  i marginal costing;

  ii absorption costing.

b Present a calculation explaining the differences between the profits arising from the two methods.

Group activities and discussion questions

1 'Break-even analysis is pointless, given the model's unrealistic and simplistic assumptions.' Identify these assumptions and discuss this statement.

2 Increasingly, companies are outsourcing activities that were previously handled in-house by employees. What activities do you believe are subject to such a policy? What are the advantages and disadvantages of such a policy?

3 In the circumstances that a manufacturer is operating with scarce resources, what are the dangers of determining production on the basis of the ranking of the products according to their contribution per unit of that scarce resource?

4 Absorption costing overstates a manufacturer's profit compared to marginal costing. Discuss why this might be argued.

Accounting in context

Discuss and comment on the following article from the press with reference to effect on fixed costs and profit margin.

BlackRock rolls out first generative AI tools

The world's largest money manager is working to gain a competitive edge in the emerging technology race and using generative AI to create a 'co-pilot' for its Aladdin and eFront risk management systems. Clients will be able to use BlackRock's advanced language model technology to assist them in extracting information from Aladdin. BlackRock, which already generates more than 8 per cent of revenue from technology services, is striving to surpass its asset management peers. Companies worldwide are competing to leverage generative AI to develop new products and extract proprietary data for financial advantage.

'GenAI will revolutionize how people interact with technology' to enhance productivity. It will effectively change users' expectations around GenAI advantages for frequency, timeliness, and simplicity. BlackRock is further developing tools to help investment professionals assemble financial and other data for research reports and investment proposals, as well as a language translator. Additionally, it will begin to integrate Microsoft's AI add-on into Office 365 productivity software. In all cases, the AI will be generating 'first drafts' that will undergo normal quality control, and all data will remain inside BlackRock's 'walled garden' rather than being shared with users of open-access generative

AI programs. The firm also aims to use the technology to democratize coding more broadly. BlackRock executives believe that using AI this way will help the money manager reduce fixed costs and increase margins.

Other financial services companies are also experimenting with AI tools both internally and for clients. Several banks, including Bank of America and Wells Fargo, offer AI-powered chatbots to help retail customers manage their finances. Citigroup is using advanced language models to improve developer productivity and test for software vulnerabilities – but not for credit scoring or other applications that affect customer access to financial products.

Source: Brooke Masters (2023) BlackRock to Roll Out First Generative AI Tools to Clients Next Month. *Financial Times*, 6 December. https://www.ft.com/content/3f3431f1-d6dc-4310-9edc-3bc8cdc46caa

References and further reading

Atkinson, A., Kaplan, R., Matsumura, E. and Young, M. (2012) *Management Accounting* (6th edn.). Harlow: Pearson.

Bhimani, A.C.T., Datar, S.M., Horngren, C.T. and Foster, G. (2012) *Management and Cost Accounting* (5th edn.). Upper Saddle River, NJ: FT Prentice Hall.

Drury, C. (2008) *Management and Cost Accounting* (7th edn.). Andover: Cengage Learning.

Dyson, J.R. (2010) *Accounting for Non-accounting Students* (8th edn.). Upper Saddle River, NJ: FT Prentice Hall.

Harris, E. (1995) *Marginal Costing*. London: CIMA Publishing.

Proctor, R. (2009) *Managerial Accounting for Business Decisions* (3rd edn.). Harlow: Pearson.

Seal, W., Garrison, R.H. and Nooreen, E.W. (2011) *Management Accounting* (4th edn.). Maidenhead: McGraw-Hill.

Chapter 18

Standard Costing and Variance Analysis

Chapter contents

18.1 Introduction
18.2 Direct Material Variances
18.3 Direct Labour Variances
18.4 Variable Overhead Variances
18.5 Fixed Overhead Variances
18.6 Sales Margin Variances
18.7 Summary of Variances
18.8 Another Approach
18.9 Evaluation

Learning objectives

After studying this chapter you will be able to:

- ✓ Understand the role of standard costing and variance analysis
- ✓ Calculate, analyse and interpret direct material, direct labour and overhead variances
- ✓ Calculate, analyse and interpret sales margin variances
- ✓ Use variances to analyse and explain differences between budgeted profit and actual profit
- ✓ Evaluate the role, strengths and weaknesses of standard costing and variance analysis

18.1 Introduction

Chapter 15 showed how budgeting can be used to 'control' a business. Plans or budgets that show how the company's objectives can be achieved are set down and approved. They provide the basis for controlling the business. Actual results are then compared with planned results to see how they differ and what changes need to be made.

Where actual profits turn out to be very different from those that were planned, the problems are to do with costs, and with sales revenues. If costs and sales are not at the levels that they *should be*, the reasons must be identified, and, if possible, corrective action taken. Standard costing shows what costs *should be*. Where actual costs are different from standard costs there are one or more 'variances'. Variance analysis can also be identified for sales.

It is possible to calculate a set of cost variances and sales margin variances that explain the difference between budgeted profits and actual profits achieved. The variances are intended to point management in the direction of improved performance. In **Examples 18.1** and **18.2** it is not surprising that profits are higher than budget because the volume of sales and the selling price are both higher than budget. But the increase in profit compared with budget is modest (only £1,000). Variance analysis can identify where their performance is unsatisfactory or inefficient, and where they have done well.

Example 18.1

Busy Airports plc plans to produce 100,000 meals per month and to sell them at £3.50 each.

The standard cost of production per meal is:

	£	
Direct materials	1.00	1/2 kg @ £2 per kg
Direct labour	0.50	3 minutes @ £10 per hour
Variable overheads	0.75	£15 per hour
Total variable costs	2.25	
Fixed overheads	0.80	£80,000 per month
	3.05	

Budgeted profit is 100,000 meals @ 45 pence = £45,000

Its actual costs and revenues last month were:

	£	£
Sales 110,000 meals @ £3.60		396,000
Direct materials 54 kg	118,000	
Direct labour 5,200 hours	53,000	
Variable overheads	87,000	
Fixed overheads	82,000	
Total costs		340,000
Profit		56,000

Example 18.2

		Standard costs	Flexed budget		Actual results	
	Per unit	Total for 100,000 meals	Total for 110,000 meals		Total for 110,000 meals	Per unit
	£	£	£		£	£
Sales	3.50	350,000	385,000	54 kg	396,000	3.60
Direct materials	1.00	100,000	110,000	5,200 hrs	118,000	1.073
Direct labour	0.50	50,000	55,000		53,000	0.482
Variable overheads	0.75	75,000	82,500		87,000	0.791
Fixed overheads	0.80	80,000	80,000		82,000	0.745
Total costs	3.05	305,000	327,500		340,000	3.091
Profit	0.45	45,000	57,500		56,000	0.509

Direct material and direct labour variances are very similar. If actual costs are higher than standard costs it is due to one or both of the following:

1 More materials or labour have been used than standard (direct material usage variance; direct labour efficiency variance), and/or

2 The price of materials or labour is higher than standard (direct material price variance; direct labour rate variance).

Variable overhead variances are typically in proportion to direct labour variances (variable overheads are typically charged as a proportion of direct labour hours).

When calculating cost variances it is important to compare actual costs with standard costs and to remember that the standard cost of production is what it should have cost to produce the amount that was *actually produced*; that is, using the flexed budget. Of course it costs more to produce more. The important question is: have costs gone up more, or less, than would be expected for *that volume* of production.

18.2 Direct Material Variances

As direct material costs should be £1 per meal, and 110,000 meals were produced, the cost should have been £110,000; but the actual cost was £118,000. This was not due to food being wasted; indeed, they used only 54 kg of food whereas the standard amount (for that volume of output) was 55 kg. The reduction in the amount of food saved was £2,000; that is the direct material usage variance. But the cost of buying food increased. It bought 54 kg of food, which should have cost £108,000 but actually cost £118,000. This extra £10,000 is the direct material price variance and is due to price increases (see **Illustration 18.1**).

ILLUSTRATION 18.1 Direct material variances

Actual cost		Actual quantities @ planned price		Standard cost
		54 kg @ £2 per kg		110,000 meals @ £1 each
£118,000		£108,000		£110,000
	Direct material price variance		Direct material usage variance	
	£10,000 adverse		£2,000 favourable	
	Direct material cost variance £8,000 adverse			
In sum:				
Total direct material variances	Price:	Actual quantity × (Actual price − Standard price)		
	Usage:	Standard price × (Actual quantity − Standard quantity)		

Managers need to consider why the variances have arisen. Perhaps the favourable usage variance was because less food was wasted (and maybe the quality of the meals suffered). Perhaps the adverse price variance was due to the demand suddenly increasing, and having to buy extra food at short notice from more expensive suppliers. Or perhaps market prices had increased generally.

In other circumstances where there is an increase in production, it might be expected that the variances would be the other way around. Purchasing greater quantities can mean obtaining bulk discounts, and favourable direct material price variances. And a sudden need to work more quickly can lead to more materials being wasted, and an adverse direct material usage variance. Perhaps the price and usage variances are interrelated; if there is a favourable price variance and an adverse usage variance, perhaps lower quality materials were purchased and that led to greater wastage.

The important thing for management is to identify what has gone wrong, why and what can be done about it.

Direct material cost variances can be analysed in more detail, identifying price and usage variances for each category of direct material. Where different direct materials are mixed together, it is possible to subdivide the usage variance into a mix variance (due to a change in the proportions used in the mixing), and yield variance (due to a higher or lower amount of end products emerging from the process). It is also possible to subdivide the price variance to see which materials have increased most in price, and perhaps which have gone down.

18.3 Direct Labour Variances

As direct labour costs should be 50 pence per meal, and 110,000 meals were produced, the cost should have been £55,000; but the actual cost was only £53,000. Clearly the workers were not lazy or inefficient; indeed, they needed to work for only 5,200 hours to produce 110,000 meals. The standard amount of time specified for producing that number of meals is 5,500 hours.

In this example production can be measured in units: number of meals. In a business that produces many different products, 'units' may not be comparable. Another way of measuring output is the 'standard hour'.

This is the amount of production that should be achieved in one hour. As each meal is expected to take three minutes to produce, in one hour 20 meals should be produced. Therefore 110,000 meals should take 110,000 ÷ 20 = 55,000 hours. The actual amount produced was 5,500 standard hours (or 110,000 meals).

Illustration 18.2 shows the calculation of variances using units, which is probably easier. **Illustration 18.3** shows the calculation of variances using standard hours as the measure of output, which is probably harder, but it is often the only method possible.

ILLUSTRATION 18.2 Direct labour variances

Actual cost	**Actual hours @ planned rate**	**Standard cost**
	5,200 hours @ £10 per hour	110,000 meals @ 50p each
£53,000	£52,000	£55,000

Direct labour rate variance £1,000 adverse

Direct labour efficiency variance £3,000 favourable

Direct labour cost variance £2,000 favourable

ILLUSTRATION 18.3 Direct labour variances

Actual cost	**Actual hours @ planned rate**	**Standard cost**
	5,200 hours @ £10 per hour	Standard hours for actual production 5,500 hours @ £10 per hour
£53,000	£52,000	£55,000

Direct labour rate variance £1,000 adverse

Direct labour efficiency variance £3,000 favourable

Direct labour cost variance £2,000 favourable

In sum:

Direct labour variances	Rate:	Actual hours × (Actual rate − Standard rate)
	Efficiency:	Standard rate × (Actual hours − Standard hours)

The rate variance (like a direct material price variance) is not too difficult. It is based on the actual number of hours worked (regardless of what was produced), and compares the planned rate of pay with what was actually paid. In this instance 5,200 hours were worked; that should have cost £10 per hour; the cost should have been £52,000. The actual cost was £53,000. There is an adverse direct labour rate variance of £1,000. There is no need to calculate the actual hourly rate of pay; the calculation can be done simply using the total amount paid.

The efficiency variance is based on the amount actually produced. It compares what that output should have cost with the hours actually taken to produce that. The amount actually produced can be calculated using *units*, as shown in **Illustration 18.2**, or *standard hours*, as shown in **Illustration 18.3**.

Using units, production was 110,000 meals, which, at £0.50 each, should have cost £55,000.

Using 'standard hours' as the measure, the production amounted to 5,500 hours, which should have cost £55,000.

The standard cost of production (£55,000 worth of production) is then compared with the actual number of hours it took to achieve that level of production (charged at the standard hourly rate): 5,200 hours were worked, which at £10 per hour, should have cost £52,000. The difference between the £53,000 and the £55,000 is the direct labour efficiency variance, which in this instance is favourable.

Any changes in the actual rate of pay are ignored in calculating the direct labour efficiency variance; they are separately calculated in the direct labour rate variance.

There is no need for the more complicated calculations used by those who like formulae.[1] The main variances can be calculated by using the three columns shown. On the left is the actual cost - easy enough. On the right is the standard cost: the only difficulty is to remember that it is the *actual* volume of production shown at what it should have cost. The middle column is more difficult: it is the actual number of hours, multiplied by the standard rate per hour.

The left-hand column and the middle column both include the actual hours worked: the only difference is that the left has been calculated using the actual rate of pay per hour; the middle column shows the standard rate of pay. The difference between the two columns is the rate variance.

It is worth investigating the causes of the variances. It is possible that workers were more efficient because they were paid more. Or perhaps there are some greater efficiencies with an increased volume of production. The adverse rate variance may have been because of the need to work overtime with higher rates of pay. Perhaps the rate and efficiency variances are interrelated; if there is a favourable rate variance and an adverse efficiency variance, perhaps lower grade workers were used and that led to inefficiencies.

It is also possible that the original standards specified were unrealistic.

18.4 Variable Overhead Variances

Variable overheads are in proportion to labour costs. In this illustration, labour costs are £10 per hour; variable overheads are £15 per hour. Although they worked only 5,200 hours, the amount of production achieved was 5,500 standard hours. The standard cost of the amount actually produced was 5,500 at £15 (the variable overhead recovery rate), which is £82,500. They were efficient, as with labour, in producing more 'hours worth' (or standard hours) of production than the number of hours they worked: 300 hours at £15 per hour is £4,500; that is the variable overhead efficiency variance.

Although variable overheads should have been £78,000 for the number of hours worked, they were, in fact, £9,000 more. Possible explanations for this would include an increase in the price of items within variable overheads, and perhaps the need for more supervision, inspection, transport, administration, and so on as a result of the increased output. It is possible to analyse the variable overhead expenditure variance to see the extent to which it is due to price increases, and the extent to which it is due to a greater volume of expenditure (see **Illustration 18.4**).

[1] For example, we could calculate that the actual rate of pay was £53,000 ÷ 52,000 hours = £10.192307 per hour. The standard rate of pay was £10 per hour. The variance in the rate per hour was £0.192307. As 52,000 hours were worked, the total adverse labour rate variance is 52,000 × £0.192307 = £999.99.

ILLUSTRATION 18.4 Variable overhead variances

Actual cost		Actual hours @ planned rate	Standard cost
£87,000		5,200 hours @ £15 per hour	110,000 meals @ 75p each
		£78,000	£82,500
	Variable overhead expenditure variance	Variable overhead efficiency variance	
	£9,000 adverse	£4,500 favourable	
	Variable overhead cost variance £4,500 favourable		
In sum:			
Variable overhead variances	Price:	Actual quantity × (Actual price − Standard price)	
	Efficiency:	Standard price × (Actual quantity − Standard quantity)	

18.5 Fixed Overhead Variances

Fixed overheads are not expected to vary with the amount of production. The company planned to spend £80,000 during the month, but actually spent £82,000. This adverse expenditure variance could be due to particularly large expenses having to be paid that month (rent, rates, maintenance) or to inflationary pressures (e.g. salary increases); or it could be that fixed overheads were not as fixed as had been thought, and some expenditure increased as production increased.

The standard cost of production (£88,000) is expected to be more than the amount budgeted because more was produced. Even if fixed overheads are totally fixed, using absorption costing, fixed overheads are still charged out at £16 per hour. If 10 per cent more is produced, the costing records will show that it cost 10 per cent more because of the way that costs are charged out. (The budget was £80,000; the standard cost was £88,000.)

In **Illustration 18.5** the difference between the Budget column and the Standard column arises because the volume of production was greater than had been budgeted. This is the fixed overhead volume variance. The company budgeted to work for 5,000 hours; it produced 5,500 hours worth of production. The favourable volume variance is 500 hours at £16, which is £8,000.

The volume variance is partly due to working more hours than specified in the budget (5,200 hours instead of 5,500 hours); and partly because the staff worked more efficiently.

The efficiency variance arises because they worked only 5,200 hours to produce 5,500 standard hours worth of production. This mirrors the direct labour and variable overhead efficiency variances; each is at a different rate per hour. Fixed overheads are charged at £16 per hour, and so the fixed overhead efficiency variance is 300 hrs × £16 = £4,800 favourable. The capacity utilization variance arises because they used more of their capacity than they planned. They worked for 5,200 hours instead of the 5,000 hours budgeted. This meant that more overheads were charged out, which is 'favourable'.

One advantage of calculating the variances using the columns shown in **Illustration 18.5** is that it is easy to see which variances are favourable, and which are adverse. If actual costs (on the left) are lower than standard costs (on the right), that is favourable. Indeed, if any item to the left is lower, that is favourable.

ILLUSTRATION 18.5 Fixed overhead variances

Actual cost	**Budgeted hours @ planned rate**	**Capacity used (hours worked)**	**Standard cost**
	5,000 hours @ £16 per hour	5,200 hours @ £16 per hour	110,000 meals[2] @ 80p each
£82,000	£80,000	83,200	£88,000

Fixed overhead expenditure variance

£82,000 – £80,000 = £2,000 adverse

Fixed overhead capacity utilization variance

£83,200 – £80,000 = £3,200 favourable

Fixed overhead efficiency variance

£88,000 – £83,200 = £4,800 favourable

Fixed overhead volume variance £8,000 favourable

Fixed overhead cost variance £6,000 favourable

Fixed overhead variances can be further analysed by showing, for example, separate variances for fixed production, administration and selling and distribution overheads.

In simple terms:

Fixed overheads variances	Expenditure:	Actual fixed overheads – Budgeted fixed overheads
	Volume:	Budgeted fixed overheads – (Actual quantity × Selling price per unit)

18.6 Sales Margin Variances

The amount of sales revenue earned during a period may be different from the amount budgeted because (a) the volume of sales is different from budget; and/or (b) the price of sales is different from budget. But in calculating the variances it is not the sales revenue that matters. What matters is the effect of changes in sales volume and sales price on profit; it is the margin between costs and selling price that is used in calculating sales variances. All cost variances should already have been identified; sales margin variances base the margin on standard costs; and on the margin between standard cost and actual selling price.

It is legitimate to refer to sales volume variance and sales price variance. But adding the word 'margin' to the names of the variances is a useful reminder that they are not based on sales revenues, but on the margins, or amounts of profit, that would be generated.

The sales margin price variance measures the effect of a change in price. The first and third columns in **Illustration 18.6** both show the actual volume of sales. The difference between them is that the first is based on the actual selling price; and the third is based on the budgeted selling price.

2 As with direct labour and variable overhead variances, the standard cost of production can be measured in standard hours. The standard hours of production is 5,500 hours, which, at the hourly rate of £16, is £88,000.

The sales margin volume variance measures the effect of a change in volume. The third and fifth columns in the table both show the budgeted profit margin. The difference between them is that the third column shows the actual volume of sales, and the fifth column shows the budgeted volume of sales.

In **Illustration 18.6** all the sales margin variances are based on the assumption that the cost of production was £3.05 per meal. The planned profit margin for each meal was 45 pence; but the actual selling price was 10 pence higher and so the actual profit margin was 10 pence higher.

ILLUSTRATION 18.6 Margin approach

Actual sales @ actual margin	**Actual sales @ planned margin**	**Budgeted sales @ budgeted margin**
110,000	110,000 hours	100,000 meals
@ 55 p	@ 45 p	@ 45 p each
£60,500	£49,500	£45,000
Sales price variance		Sales margin volume variance
£60,500 – £49,500 = £11,000 favourable		£49,500 – £45,000 = £4,500 favourable
Total sales variance £15,500 favourable		

Using the table, if the figures to the left are higher, that is favourable. With costs it is obviously the other way around: if actual costs to the left are higher, that is adverse.

As with most variances it is possible to subdivide them. This illustration assumes that there is only one product. Where there are a number of different products, price variances can be calculated for each. It is also likely that the actual mix of products sold will be different from what was budgeted; it is then possible to divide the volume variance into a mix variance and a quantity variance.

18.7 Summary of Variances

Where both cost and sales margin variances are calculated, the sum of all the variances should equal the difference between the budgeted profit for the period and the actual profit achieved and can be summarized in a 'performance report'. See **Illustration 18.7**.

ILLUSTRATION 18.7 Performance report: margin approach

	£	£	£
Budgeted profit for period			45,000
Sales price variance	11,000 favourable		
Sales margin volume variance	4,500 favourable		
Total sales margin variance		15,500 favourable	
Direct material price variance	10,000 adverse		
Direct material usage variance	2,000 favourable		
Direct material cost variance		8,000 adverse	
Direct labour rate variance	1,000 adverse		
Direct labour efficiency variance	3,000 favourable		
Direct labour cost variance		2,000 favourable	
Variable overhead expenditure variance	9,000 adverse		
Variable overhead efficiency variance	4,500 favourable		
Variable overhead cost variance		4,500 adverse	

	£	£	£
Fixed overhead expenditure variance	2,000 adverse		
Fixed capacity utilization variance	3,200 favourable		
Fixed efficiency variance	4,800 favourable		
Fixed overhead volume variance	8,000 favourable		
Fixed overhead cost variance		6,000 favourable	
Total variances			11,000 favourable
Actual profit for the period			56,000

Interpretation of these variances

The firm made £11,000 more profit than it had planned. This was overwhelmingly due to a favourable sales performance. It increased both the volume of sales, and the selling price, which would have increased profits by £15,500. There were, however, some adverse cost variances.

There were adverse expenditure variances on both fixed and variable overheads amounting to £11,000. This may have been due partly to cost increases with respect to various overhead items (e.g. increases in rents, rates, electricity); it may be that they spent a lot more on marketing to achieve the higher sales levels; and it could be that the distinction between fixed and variable overheads had not accurately been determined.

In other areas there were efficiency gains with savings on material usage, and due to the efficiency of labour.

18.8 Another Approach

Sales contribution variance

An alternative approach to the sales margin variance is the sales contribution variance, where the focus is upon the contribution variance rather than the change in margin. With the sales volume contribution variance, we are trying to isolate the change in the contribution of the business arising from a change in sales units. With this approach, the fixed overhead variance is simply the variance on fixed overhead expenditure; there is no need to calculate the fixed overhead volume variances.

The sales price variance measures the effect of a change in price. The first and third columns in **Illustration 18.8** both show the actual volume of sales. The difference between them is that the first is based on the actual selling price; and the third is based on the budgeted selling price.

ILLUSTRATION 18.8 Contribution approach

Actual sales @ actual contribution	**Actual sales @ planned contribution**	**Budgeted sales @ budgeted contribution**
110,000	110,000 meals	100,000 meals
@ £1.35	@ £1.25	@ £1.25 each
£148,500	£137,500	£125,000
	Sales price variance	Sales contribution volume variance
	£11,000 favourable	£12,500 favourable
	Total sales variance £23,500 favourable	

The sales contribution volume variance measures the effect of a change in volume. The third and fifth columns in the table both show the budgeted contribution. The difference between them is that the third column shows the actual volume of sales, and the fifth column shows the budgeted volume of sales.

In **Illustration 18.8** all the sales contribution variances are based on the assumption that the variable cost of production was £2.25 per meal. The planned contribution for each meal was £1.25; but the actual selling price was 10 pence higher and so the actual contribution was 10 pence higher.

Summary of variances

Where both cost and sales contribution variances are calculated, the sum of all the variances should equal the difference between the budgeted profit for the period and the actual profit achieved and can be summarized in a performance report (see **Illustration 18.9**).

ILLUSTRATION 18.9 Performance report: contribution approach

	£	£	£
Budgeted profit for period			45,000
Sales price variance	11,000 favourable		
Sales contribution volume variance	12,500 favourable		
Total sales margin variance		23,500 favourable	
Direct material price variance	10,000 adverse		
Direct material usage variance	2,000 favourable		
Direct material cost variance		8,000 adverse	
Direct labour rate variance	1,000 adverse		
Direct labour efficiency variance	3,000 favourable		
Direct labour cost variance		2,000 favourable	
Variable overhead expenditure variance	9,000 adverse		
Variable overhead efficiency variance	4,500 favourable		
Variable overhead cost variance		4,500 adverse	
Fixed overhead expenditure variance		2,000 adverse	
Total variances			11,000 favourable
Actual profit for the period			56,000

Interpretation of these variances

The firm made £11,000 more profit than it had planned. This was overwhelmingly due to a favourable sales performance. The firm increased both the volume of sales, and the selling price, which would have increased profits by £23,500. There were, however, some adverse cost variances.

There were adverse expenditure variances on both fixed and variable overheads amounting to £6,500. This may have been due partly to cost increases with respect to various overhead items (e.g. increases in rents, rates, electricity); it may be that it spent a lot more on marketing to achieve the higher sales levels; and it could be that the distinction between fixed and variable overheads had not accurately been determined.

In other areas there were efficiency gains with savings on material usage, and due to the efficiency of labour.

In sum there are two approaches to the sales variances:

Sales	Price	AQ × (AP − SP)
	Contribution volume	SC × (AQ − SQ)
	or margin volume	SM × (AQ − SQ)

18.9 Evaluation

Role and functions

The main appeal of standard costing and variance analysis is that it is a control mechanism that provides a systematic analysis of differences between planned performance and actual performance. It is intended to do so in such a way that, for each variance, it is possible to establish:

1. which managers are responsible for performance not being according to plan
2. which variances are unavoidable, and which are due to inefficiency
3. where it is possible to take actions to improve performance
4. which variances are significant or important, and which are small and of little consequence
5. which variances are favourable, and whether they are at the expense of adverse performance elsewhere
6. which variances are adverse, and whether they are offset by favourable variances elsewhere
7. a systematic basis for further investigation into the causes of poor performance.

Standard costing establishes a range of expected costs that can be used for a variety of purposes, in planning and making decisions. When planning new products it is straightforward to obtain the costs of the various direct materials and components. It may be possible to use synthetic standards in planning labour costs. Traditionally standard costing developed from the era of 'scientific management', and time and motion study (work study) techniques were used to develop standards, and assess the speed at which people should work. In recent years the development of 'target costing' has required renewed emphasis on minimizing labour costs. Standards can provide target costs that help to motivate staff towards greater efficiency.

Standard costing, particularly with labour costs, can also be used as a basis for remuneration, with bonuses, piece-work, and a range of schemes for performance-related pay. In traditional work study, people were expected to perform at a rate equivalent to walking at four miles an hour. Those who could walk (or work) faster would be paid more.

Overall, it is intended that standard costing and variance analysis should enhance efficiency. It can help in developing budgets, facilitate 'management by exception', and perhaps even improve staff motivation because expected levels of performance are defined.

In some organizations, standard costs are used as the basis for valuing inventories of work in progress and finished goods for financial accounting purposes.

Problems and limitations

Unfortunately, it is not always possible to establish 'standards' in a scientific or objective way. How long it should take to do a particular piece of work is often disputed. Moreover, it is not clear on what basis standards should be established, and the following are sometimes suggested:

1 Ideal standards, which are a very high target to aim for. It assumes working under ideal conditions with no wastage or hold-ups. In theory this may be what is aimed for, but it can be very demotivating if standards are set that are more like targets that cannot realistically be attained.
2 Attainable standards, which are stretching, but make some allowance for inevitable inefficiencies.
3 Current standards are based on what is currently happening with no expectation of significant improvement. These provide a realistic basis for planning, decision-making and valuing inventories.
4 Basic standards remain the same for long periods of time and can be useful for comparing efficiency from year to year.

Standard costs are sometimes discredited, especially when they are used as a basis for remuneration, and some people find ways around them. It is necessary to keep standards current, alive and real otherwise they can become discredited and unrealistic. When there are significant changes in the costs of raw materials and components, it is always a problem to know how often to change standards. Standard costing has tended to concentrate on direct materials and direct labour, but in modern manufacturing production, overheads are often much greater than direct costs, and are more difficult to control. The need for just-in-time manufacturing has also tended to de-emphasize standard costing. There is a need for continuous improvement across the board, rather than aiming for standards that are sometimes out of date and not very soundly based.

Summary

Standard costing is still widely used in manufacturing organizations, although it is seen as being a traditional technique, and has been much criticized. It can also be used in a range of professional and service organizations. The idea of establishing a standard, what something *should* cost, is inherently appealing, and provides a basis for control information. Once standards and budgets are established, it is possible to calculate 'variances' showing how actual performance differs from what it should be. Variance analysis provides a systematic approach to explaining differences. It does not provide all the answers; it points to where further investigation is likely to prove fruitful.

Summary of variance formulae

Sales	Price	AQ × (AP − SP)
	Contribution volume	SC × (AQ − SQ)
	or margin volume	SM × (AQ − SQ)
Direct materials	Price	AQ × (AP − SP)
	Usage	SP × (AQ − SQ)
Direct labour	Rate	AH × (AR − SR)
	Efficiency	SR × (AH − SH)
Variable overhead	Price	AQ × (AP − SP)
	Efficiency	SP × (AQ − SQ)
Fixed overheads	Expenditure	Actual FO − Budgeted FO
	Volume (when using the margin approach)	Budgeted FO − (AQ × SP per unit)

Review of key points

- Standard costing establishes standard costs for materials, labour and overheads and is the basis of a systematic control system.
- Variance analysis compares actual costs with standard costs to help establish where, how and why actual performance differs from standard performance.
- Analysis shows in many areas where differences are due to changes in efficiency or in price.
- Variances can also be calculated for sales.
- A comprehensive set of variances should explain the difference between planned performance and actual performance.
- Standard costing has a number of useful functions, but is only as good as the standards on which it is based.

Self-testing questions

1 Corrina planned to spend £10 to buy 10 kg of dough to make 10 loaves of bread.[3] Actually she spent £10.50 and bought 10.4 kg of dough and made 11 loaves of bread.

  a Calculate and explain the direct materials cost variance.
  b Calculate and explain the direct materials price and usage variances.

2 Anomelg solicitors employed Maggie to do their conveyancing work; she is treated as 'direct labour'. They planned to pay her £30 per hour for 100 hours a month and expect her to complete 10 conveyances.

  During April they paid her £2,400 for 84 hours work and she completed seven conveyances.

  a Calculate and explain the direct labour cost variance.
  b Calculate and explain the direct labour rate and efficiency variances.

3 The Wee Lee Cycle Company planned to produce 120,000 bicycles a year (10,000 a month) at a total cost of £80 each, and to sell them for £100 each.

  Last month it produced 11,000 bicycles at a total cost of £902,000, and sold them for £979,000.

  a Calculate the budgeted profit for the month.
  b Calculate the actual profit for the month.
  c Calculate sales margin and cost variances in as much detail as the information permits.
  d Evaluate the information disclosed.

4 The Wool Witch Company manufactures woollen dolls that sell for £28 each and the company plans to manufacture and sell 5,000 a month. The standard production costs per doll are:

Direct materials	1 kg at £3 per kg
Direct labour	1 hour at £10 per hour
Fixed overheads	£10,000 per month

[3] The standard cost (of materials) was therefore £1 per loaf.

Last month the company made and sold 4,000 dolls for £108,000. Its costs were:

Direct materials	3,900 kg costing £12,200
Direct labour	3,850 hours costing £39,500
Fixed overheads	£9,500

a Calculate the budgeted profit for the month.
b Calculate the actual profit for the month.
c Calculate cost and sales contribution variances in as much detail as the information permits.
d Evaluate the information disclosed.

5 Poleg Limited manufactures kitchen cupboards. The standard cost of each unit is £120, comprising:

		£
Direct materials	15 sq metres at £4.50 per sq metre	67.50
Direct labour	5 hours at £6 per hour	30.00
Variable overheads	5 hours at £3 per labour hour	15.00
Fixed overheads		7.50
		£120.00

The company had budgeted to make and sell 1,000 cupboards at a selling price of £150 in June. However, in June, the actual figures were as follows:

		£
Production and sales:	1,400 units	212,800
Direct materials	22,000 sq metres	121,000
Direct labour	6,800 hours	34,000
Variable overheads		15,000
Fixed overheads		6,000

Prepare a performance report reconciling the budgeted profit to the actual profit showing all the variances arising. Write a brief report advising management on your finding and possible reasons why each variance arose.

Assessment questions

1 Mary planned to pay Tom £50 for 5 hours to wash 20 cars.[4]

Last week Tom and a number of customers were on holiday. She actually paid Fred £45 for 4 hours to wash 15 cars.

a Calculate and explain the direct labour cost variance.
b Calculate and explain the direct labour rate and usage variances.

[4] The standard labour cost of washing one car was therefore £50 ÷ 20 = £2.50.

2 The Aanroc Manufacturing Company budget for May shows the following:

Fixed overheads	£256,000
Number of labour hours to be worked	16,000
Number of aanrocs to be produced	10,000

Actual results for May were as follows:

Fixed overhead costs	£266,000
Number of labour hours worked	17,000
Number of aanrocs actually produced	11,000

Required:

a Calculate and explain the fixed overhead cost variance.

b Explain and illustrate how the standard cost of production can be measured (i) in units, and (ii) in standard hours.

c Calculate and explain the fixed overhead expenditure, volume, capacity utilization and efficiency variances.

3 The standard cost of producing one kiredo is as follows:

Direct materials	5 kg at £12 per kg	£60
Direct labour	2 hours at £16 per hour	£32
Variable overheads	2 hours at £8 per hour	£16

Fixed overheads are expected to be £180,000 per annum, and the plan is to produce 12,000 kiredos per annum.

Last month 1,200 kiredos were produced and the costs incurred were:

Direct materials 5,900 kg costing	£70,000
Direct labour 2,000 hours costing	£44,000
Variable overheads	£18,600
Fixed overheads	£15,500

Calculate the cost variances in as much detail as the information permits and comment on the results.

4 The Nire Company plans to sell 2,000 nires a month, the standard marginal cost of which is £60 each, at a selling price of £80 each. Last month it sold 2,100 nires for £161,700.

Calculate the sales contribution price variance and the sales contribution volume variance.

5 The following is extracted from the standard unit cost card of RNM Ltd for the quarter ended 31 December year 9:

Selling price per unit	£25
Direct materials (2 kg @ £1 per kg)	2
Skilled labour 1 hour @ £8 per hour	8
Variable overheads	3
Fixed overheads	2
Net profit per unit	10
Budgeted sales	10,000 units

Variable overheads are determined by using the skilled labour hours, while fixed overheads are absorbed on the budgeted sale units. For the quarter ended 31 December year 9, the following results were reviewed:

	£
Sales (9,000 units)	234,000
Direct materials (16,000 kg)	20,000
Skilled labour (9,500 hours)	71,250
Variable overheads	30,875
Fixed overheads	22,000

Required:

Calculate the actual and budgeted profit for the quarter ended 31 December year 9. Reconcile these profit figures by providing the appropriate variances in a performance report.

What explanations would you give regarding the discrepancies between the actual and the budgeted results?

Group activities and discussion questions

1 How widely do you think standard costing could be applied? Discuss possible examples from non-manufacturing organizations.

2 Do you have any 'standard costs' in mind in your own life (e.g. the standard cost of buying lunch, or cooking dinner)? Is it useful to have such costs in mind?

3 If you were expected to produce something (e.g. a picnic, or a student newspaper) under a 'standard costing' system, would you find ways round the system? How?

4 What do you think of the idea that everyone should work at the same speed (or produce the same amount in a given time)?

Accounting in context

Discuss and comment on the following report with reference to the need for a company to regularly review 'standard price' in the light of changes in costs, selling price and demand caused by factors outside its control. For each of the costing methods listed below, explain the advantages and disadvantages of the costing method.

COVID-19: Hospitals need to change their costings methods

The healthcare industry has been profoundly affected by the COVID-19 pandemic, stretching its capacity to the limit. Both developed and developing nations have felt the impact on the healthcare system. Operational expenses have increased, leading to higher treatment costs. But most of the expense controversies were very much because COVID-19 is not unprecedented nor unpredictable. Similar cost escalations have occurred in the past due to shifts in policies and insurance packages.

While hospitals have established strategies to manage expenses without compromising the quality of care, it is crucial to review and adjust costs during each surge.

It is important to recognize that COVID-19 is likely to remain a long-term challenge, necessitating immediate action. A top priority is to evaluate the impact and develop cost-effective, sustainable strategies that prioritize patient welfare. Scientific cost management plays a crucial role in this effort.

Hospitals must thoroughly assess all cost components, such as inventory management, supply chain, and labour costs, which make up a large proportion of operational expenses. The remaining expenses, including marketing, operations, and financial costs, must be adapted to the management framework.

Healthcare reform has led to hospitals facing pressure to improve their practices as budgets shrink and demands increase. To effectively manage finances, it is crucial to clearly define, evaluate, analyse, and then redefine costs and processes. This requires a combination of analytical skills and costing techniques within hospital management. The absence of industry standards has led some to believe that all cost accounting methods are equally valid.

A few costing methodologies that hospitals can implement are:

RVU costing

The relative value unit (RVU) cost accounting is an objective method used to identify costs. RVU utilizes the Resource-Based Relative Value Scale (RBRVS), a methodology employed by the Centers for Medicare & Medicaid Services and private payers to determine physician payment. It takes into account fee schedules, a floor capitation rate, capitation payments, and the profitability of third-party payer reimbursement. By assessing this information, hospital administrations can determine the feasible cost of providing services and a more realistic fee, as well as negotiate better profitable contracts.

Kaizen costing

Deriving from a Japanese word, Kaizen means constant improvement in all aspects of the performance at every level. Healthcare Kaizen is a lean tool that focuses on small, continuous improvements throughout the workplace. Each small change results in a minor improvement. As time passes, these minor improvements add up to significant steps forward in efficiency, quality, safety, and workplace culture.

Kaizen's potential stems from its inclusive approach. Unlike other improvement programs, Kaizen's success depends on the participation of all employees. This means that directors, nurses, doctors, nursing assistants, technicians, accountants, purchasers, and administrators need to examine their daily routines and make suggestions for improvements. A key aspect of the Kaizen philosophy is its continual nature. Kaizen becomes part of the culture and improvements should focus on eliminating waste and simplifying work processes.

Essentially, hospitals do not rely on past cost data but assess each cost activity, such as the cost of the supply chain, administration, procurement, inventory, and transportation, as a new process. Furthermore, to offer operations managers a fresh perspective on reallocating resources and setting cost targets, it continuously adjusts all the costs incurred.

Standard costing

In this setting, hospitals establish a standardized cost for different procedures based on industry norms. They then compare the actual expenses to the fixed costs to determine any variances. Hospitals may utilize both a standard cost profile and a standard treatment protocol in this evaluation process.

Activity-based costing

Activity-based costing (ABC) is a widely used method in cost accounting. It determines the true cost of patient treatment by taking into account all relevant parameters and calculating the cost at each stage of the procedure. This method also enables hospitals to allocate resources more efficiently. With this approach, hospital management can analyse and identify cost discrepancies, taking into consideration factors such as the type of procedure, the attending physician, the patient's location, and the relevant department.

Along with these, hospitals can also use artificial intelligence (AI) as a critical tool for analytics, insights and the decision-making process. This will help them understand treatment variability and cost modelling while eliminating system waste and substantially reducing costs.

Hospitals may opt to combine the aforementioned methods to achieve a more effective outcome. However, regardless of the chosen technique, it is crucial that cost-cutting strategies are data-driven and consistent. Most importantly, these measures should never compromise the quality of healthcare provided by the institution.

Sources: Latesh Sen (2021) After COVID-19, Hospitals Need to Change How They Do Their Costings. *Gulf News*, 23 September. https://gulfnews.com/business/analysis/after-covid-19-hospitals-need-to-change-how-they-do-their-costings-1.82459378 (accessed 1 July 2024).

P. Selivanoff (2018) Selecting the Right Cost Model. Healthcare Financial Management Association, 29 October. https://www.hfma.org/accounting-and-financial-reporting/costing-and-managerialaccounting/62272/ (accessed 1 July 2024).

References and further reading

Atkinson, A., Kaplan, R., Matsumura, E. and Young, M. (2012) *Management Accounting* (6th edn.). Harlow: Pearson.

Bhimani, A.C.T., Datar, S.M., Horngren, C.T. and Foster, G. (2012) *Management and Cost Accounting* (5th edn.). Upper Saddle River, NJ: FT Prentice Hall.

Drury, C. (2008) *Management and Cost Accounting* (7th edn.). Andover: Cengage Learning.

Dyson, J.R. (2010) *Accounting for Non-accounting Students* (8th edn.). Upper Saddle River, NJ: FT Prentice Hall.

Proctor, R. (2009) *Managerial Accounting for Business Decisions* (3rd edn.). Harlow: Pearson.

Seal, W., Garrison, R.H. and Nooreen, E.W. (2011) *Management Accounting* (4th edn.). Maidenhead: McGraw-Hill.

Chapter 19

Sustainability and Accounting

Chapter contents

19.1 Introduction
19.2 Why Is Sustainability Important?
19.3 Integrated Reporting (IR) Framework
19.4 International Sustainability Standards Board Issues - IFRS S1 and IFRS S2
19.5 Value Chain for Sustainable Businesses
19.6 Climate Change Risks and the Associated Financial Implications
19.7 Recommendations of the Task Force on Climate-related Financial Disclosures (TCFD)
19.8 UN SDGs and their Significance for Organizations

Learning objectives

After studying this chapter you will be able to:

- ✓ Understand sustainability and the reasons why it is important
- ✓ Describe the use of an Integrated Reporting framework
- ✓ Explain climate change risks and the associated financial implications
- ✓ Explain the UN SDGs, their significance for organizations in terms of risks and opportunities and the definitions of impact

19.1 Introduction

The concept of sustainability is a multifaceted one, with a widely embraced definition that emerged from the United Nations Brundtland Commission in 1987. It characterizes sustainability as the capacity to fulfil the needs of the present without jeopardizing the ability of future generations to meet their own needs. In essence, this principle aims to guarantee the flourishing of all life forms for the long term. Additionally this definition assumes that resources are limited and should be used carefully to ensure there is enough for future generations without reducing the current quality of life. A sustainable society must be socially responsible, prioritize environmental protection and sustain equilibrium in human and natural systems.

The quantity and scope of social and environmental information provided by companies has significantly increased, often presented in separate reports alongside the annual report. These individual reports have become more detailed, covering a wider range of issues to meet the needs of different stakeholders. Recently, companies have begun integrating social and environmental information with financial information in single reports, marking a departure from earlier practices where social and environmental information was not combined with financial details. The new approach aims to integrate social, environmental, financial and governance information.

19.2 Why Is Sustainability Important?

Sustainability has numerous benefits, both in the short term and in the long term. Without embracing more sustainable choices, we risk compromising Earth's ecosystems and our way of life. Failure to address harmful processes could lead to the depletion of fossil fuels, the extinction of numerous animal species (biodiversity, and irreversible damage to the atmosphere. Clean air, non-toxic atmospheric conditions, reliable resource growth, and water quality are among the advantages of sustainability.

The concept of sustainability encompasses three pillars: environmental, social and economic, often referred to as profits, planet and people. These pillars are particularly relevant to corporate sustainability efforts.

1. Environmental protection is the most frequently discussed element, focusing on reducing carbon footprints, water usage, non-decomposable packaging, and wasteful processes in the supply chain. These practices are not only cost-effective and financially beneficial but also crucial for environmental sustainability.
2. Social development involves ensuring that employees, stakeholders and the community are treated fairly, ethically and sustainably by businesses. This includes offering benefits such as improved maternity and paternity leave, flexible scheduling, and learning and development opportunities. Additionally, it means operating with sustainable labour practices, by employing adult workers in safe environments and ensuring fair pay.
3. Economic development stands as one of the fundamental pillars of sustainability. For a business to thrive in the long term, it must be profitable and able to generate sufficient revenue. The challenge in achieving this sustainability lies in striking a balance. Instead of single-mindedly pursuing profit, companies should strive to generate profit while taking into account other elements of sustainability.

The Triple Bottom Line, often referred to as TBL, emphasizes the significance of considering social and environmental sustainability alongside economic performance. Coined by sustainability advocate John Elkington, the concept suggests that businesses should aim to create not only economic value but also environmental and social value. Elkington's perspective on the TBL highlights the need for a broader business goal beyond just financial gain.

As per the American Institute of Certified Public Accountants (AICPA), sustainability accounting involves aligning sustainability initiatives with company strategy, assessing risks and opportunities, and providing measurement, accounting and performance management expertise to ensure the integration of sustainability into the company's daily operations. The key responsibility of sustainability accounting encompasses sustainable reporting and sustainability assurance.

The Sustainability Accounting Standards Board (SASB), a part of the Value Reporting Foundation, emphasizes that companies are confronted with distinct challenges due to issues such as climate change, resource constraints, urbanization and technological innovation. While financial statements offer valuable information about a company's financial position, this information is seen as historic. Investors are ever more interested in how companies manage sustainability issues that impact long-term value.

The traditional business reporting model was designed for a time when the world looked significantly different. However, with globalization, resource scarcity, a growing global population, and heightened scrutiny from customers, investors, employees, and other users, there is a pressing need for sustainability reporting. Companies are now expected to demonstrate not only financial profitability but also social responsibility. Sustainability accounting ensures that this responsibility is based on credible, verifiable information.

Clearly, in response to stakeholder demands for greater transparency, sustainability reporting has emerged as a method to report on the social and environmental impacts alongside the traditional economic results. As the trend of publishing sustainability reports continues to increase, it is anticipated that accounting professionals will provide assurance similar to that of financial statements and reports. However, reporting and assurance are not the only way since companies may involve themselves by using dialogue in communicating with different stakeholder groups.

19.3 Integrated Reporting (IR) Framework

In 2009, the then HRH the Prince of Wales convened a meeting at St James's Palace to kickstart the journey of the International Integrated Reporting Council (IIRC). The meeting brought together a diverse group of representatives to promote integrated reporting.

In response to the global financial crisis of 2007-2008, the IIRC was established to undertake the need for solutions that could help prevent a future collapse of the financial system. Integrated reporting, initially a conceptual idea, was recognized as a potential method to alleviate the misallocation of resources and capital that had contributed to the crisis. Integrated reporting has achieved significant success, with over 2,500 companies across more than 70 countries embracing it and major stock exchanges incorporating it into their guidelines, thus lending it legitimacy. The principles of integrated reporting have now become an integral part of corporate governance reform globally. The IIRC has collaborated with leading framework providers and standard setters to develop a comprehensive, globally accepted reporting system that integrates both financial accounting and sustainability disclosure through partnerships with the Carbon Disclosure Project (CDP), the Climate Disclosure Standards Board (CDSB), Global Reporting Initiative (GRI), and the Sustainability Accounting Standards Board (SASB).

The IIRC's success can be attributed to the market-driven development of the principles-based International Integrated Reporting Framework. This framework has demonstrated its efficacy across businesses of varying scopes and industries worldwide, laying the groundwork for the integrated reporting movement. It articulates fundamental ideas such as value creation for the organization and others.

The Integrated Reporting (IR) Framework, which was introduced in December 2013, was a significant step towards bringing technical rigour and cohesion to a process that had nevertheless grown organically due to market pressure. This framework is aimed at furthering genuine and effective behavioural changes in the way businesses see, plan and develop a dialogue with their stakeholders. The benefits of integrated reporting are readily apparent in the form of improved stakeholder relationships and a deeper understanding of the actual drivers of value within a business. This enables businesses to proactively focus on the risks and opportunities of their business models beyond the balance sheet.

Integrated reporting aims to:

- Improve the quality of information available to providers of financial capital to facilitate the efficient allocation of capital. This involves promoting a more cohesive approach to corporate reporting, drawing on various reporting strands to communicate the full range of factors that materially affect an organization's ability to create value over time.
- Enhance accountability and stewardship for the broad base of capital by fostering an understanding of their interdependencies.
- Encourage integrated thinking, decision-making and actions that focus on value creation over time. The IR Framework highlights the importance of integrating thinking across an organization's operations, including its functional units. It emphasizes the critical role of the finance function in generating and delivering value for the organization. Integrated thinking involves aligning the organization's strategy, governance and performance with its wider economic, social and environmental context, enabling value creation. This approach fosters a deeper understanding of the interconnections among various organizational activities and their impact on long-term sustainability and performance. If one were to open a large listed company's sustainability report, it is easily observed that the report suggests interconnectedness and forward-looking information that encompasses diverse perspectives, all aimed at sustainable value creation.

In 2017, the IIRC established the Integrated Thinking and Strategy Group as part of the IR Business Network. This global group, composed of over 50 participants, embarked on developing a new framework for integrated thinking. In January 2020, the group released a report introducing the 'spring model' for implementing integrated thinking. This model centres on the interdependence of various resources and impacts associated with a business, with the primary focus on creating and safeguarding value for key stakeholders, thus fostering resilient and forward-looking businesses. Various networks have emerged globally as businesses convene locally to explore avenues for implementing integrated reporting within the framework of local regulations. Major networks exist in Australia, Brazil, India, Japan, Turkey, the US, as well as across Europe, Africa and the ASEAN region.

South Africa is recognized as a pioneer in integrated reporting, being the first country to embrace it as a fundamental aspect of corporate governance. It has made integrated reporting a mandatory requirement for all primary listings on the Johannesburg Stock Exchange, enhancing the trust and confidence of its stakeholders and the legitimacy of its operations. The Integrated Reporting Committee of South Africa aligns with the intentions of the King III report by adopting a stakeholder-inclusive perspective to promote sustainability and meet the legitimate expectations of stakeholders. This emphasis is not limited to listed companies but extends to all organizations. The latest guidance from the Integrated Reporting Committee of South Africa offers details on how organizations can adapt and enhance their reporting in response to the COVID-19 pandemic.

Japan is also leading the way in promoting integrated reporting, seeing it as a way to build strong, long-term relationships between businesses and their investors.

Leading adopters, such as the UK, Australia, Malaysia, and the Netherlands, have adopted a corporate governance approach to integrated reporting.

Corporate reporting is a crucial aspect of corporate governance as it reflects the purpose, values and activities of the business, and the behaviours of the board and management team. Integrated reporting is increasingly emphasized in corporate governance codes worldwide.

The purpose of the IR Framework is to facilitate the widespread adoption of integrated reporting globally. Its objectives are to:

- Enhance the quality of information to enable more efficient allocation of capital
- Encourage a comprehensive and efficient approach to corporate reporting that draws on diverse knowledge and data, and communicates all factors that are likely to impact value creation over time

- Strengthen accountability and stewardship for all the different types of capital a company uses or affects, and promote understanding of their interdependencies
- Facilitate integrated thinking, decision-making, and actions focused on creating value over the short, medium and long term.

19.4 International Sustainability Standards Board Issues – IFRS S1 and IFRS S2

The International Sustainability Standards Board (ISSB) issued its inaugural standards in June 2023 - IFRS S1 and IFRS S2 - steering in a new era of sustainability-related disclosures in capital markets worldwide. The standards aim to enhance trust and confidence in company disclosures about sustainability to better inform investment decisions. Importantly, these standards establish a common language for disclosing the impact of climate-related risks and opportunities on a company's outlook for the first time.

About the standards

IFRS S1 provides disclosure requirements for companies to communicate sustainability-related risks and opportunities to investors over the short, medium and long term. IFRS S2 sets out specific climate-related disclosures and is designed to be used with IFRS S1. Both standards fully incorporate the recommendations of the Task Force on Climate-related Financial Disclosures (TCFD). The ISSB developed IFRS S1 and IFRS S2 with extensive market feedback and in response to calls from the G20, the Financial Stability Board, and the International Organization of Securities Commissions (IOSCO), as well as leaders in the business and investor community. This broad support for a comprehensive global baseline of sustainability-related disclosures demonstrates the widespread demand for a consistent understanding of how sustainability factors affect companies' prospects. The ISSB standards ensure that companies provide sustainability-related information alongside financial statements, in the same reporting package. The standards have been developed to be used in conjunction with any accounting requirements. They are also built on the concepts that underpin the IFRS Accounting Standards, which are required by over 140 jurisdictions.

Adoption of the ISSB standards

Mary Schapiro, Head of the TCFD Secretariat, stressed the need for common reporting standards to enhance comparability in climate-related financial data globally. The ISSB standards, built upon the TCFD framework, provide a universal baseline for companies to disclose essential climate-related financial information, crucial for transparent markets and a smooth transition to a low-carbon economy.

Jean-François van Boxmeer, Chair of the European Round Table for Industry (ERT) and Vodafone Group, emphasized the importance of global alignment in providing a comprehensive view of a company's sustainability performance. He urged jurisdictions, including the EU, to adopt the ISSB standards to avoid double reporting and ensure greater comparability for users.

19.5 Value Chain for Sustainable Businesses

Value chain is a term developed by Michael Porter in 1985 in his book *Competitive Advantage: Creating and Sustaining Superior Performance*. Supply chain sustainability focuses on aligning environmental, social and community impact throughout the lifecycle of products and services. This involves implementing better policies and procedures to ensure a positive environmental, social and economic impact while adding value to stakeholders. Creating a sustainable supply chain is essential as it significantly impacts the environment and provides opportunities for organizations to make beneficial adjustments to reduce their environmental footprint. Implementing sustainable practices not only benefits the environment but also enhances a company's credibility and lowers costs. A clean and green supply chain involves businesses taking a holistic and ethical approach to reduce unnecessary resource use and emissions, emphasizing transparency and long-term impact. Integrating sustainability into the value chain can lead to improved resource consumption, reduced unnecessary spending, and enhanced profitability and performance for businesses.

The declining costs open up opportunities for long-term growth. By establishing a clear value chain, businesses can mitigate risks and build credibility. Creating a sustainable value chain requires strategic initiative, a structured approach and clear targets. It is important to build a team that understands sustainable change and prioritizes critical issues. Collaboration with suppliers is key for building awareness and capacity with a shared vision.

Competition, companies and the value chain

Companies are competing with one another in today's globalized economy, not just for a sizeable customer base but also for supplies. The dynamics of the market and how companies conduct business are changing in the current global environment as a result of the constantly expanding focus on organizational responsiveness to the social and ecological impact of their products and services.

Effective communication and collaboration with partners, suppliers and relevant parties is essential for companies to manage resources efficiently and mitigate risks in order to compete successfully. Overcoming these challenges presents opportunities for firms to innovate, drive effective action, achieve efficiency and increase market share when managed properly. Competent value chain management is crucial in today's business landscape and can complement other types of business management efficiency analysis. Starbucks is an intriguing company to analyse from a value chain perspective due to the significant value it adds from coffee bean procurement and distribution, as well as from store supply to customers.

19.6 Climate Change Risks and the Associated Financial Implications

At the COP 21 United Nations climate change conference in Paris, it was agreed that there is an urgent need for stronger and more ambitious climate action to achieve the goals of the Paris Agreement. This action should involve governments, cities, regions, businesses and investors, as everyone has a role to play in effectively implementing the Paris Agreement.

Climate change and biodiversity depletion are some of the most critical challenges we face today. They are prompting significant economic transformation, driving fundamental changes in business models, and necessitating a re-evaluation of what we consider to be business as usual.

Businesses are increasingly committing to achieving net-zero emissions and minimizing their impact on the planet. As the global shift towards decarbonization gains momentum and the far-reaching impacts of climate change unfold, businesses are gearing up for a low-carbon future. They are meeting the demands of stakeholders for accountability by preparing for this transition.

It is now expected that businesses not only set strong decarbonization targets and develop robust plans to decarbonize their operations and supply chains but also establish goals and take actions to reduce their impact on nature. Boards of directors are under significant pressure to address environmental issues, and it is imperative for businesses to fully grasp the implications of climate and nature-related risks and opportunities.

19.7 Recommendations of the Task Force on Climate-related Financial Disclosures (TCFD)

The Financial Stability Board (FSB) created the TCFD to develop recommendations on the types of information that companies should disclose to support investors enabling financial markets to price risk.

The main climate-related risks and opportunities that organizations should consider are described below.

Climate-related risks

The Task Force divided climate-related risks into two major categories: (1) risks related to the *transition* to a lower-carbon economy and (2) risks related to the *physical* impacts of climate change.

Transition risks

The transition to a lower-carbon economy necessitates significant policy, legal, technological and market adjustments to address the mitigation and adaptation requirements associated with climate change. These changes could pose varying degrees of financial and reputational risk to organizations based on their nature, speed and focus.

Policy and legal risks

Policy actions related to climate change continue to evolve, primarily falling into two categories: those that aim to limit actions contributing to the adverse effects of climate change and those that seek to promote adaptation. Examples include the implementation of carbon-pricing mechanisms, the shift toward lower emission energy sources, the adoption of energy-efficiency solutions, and the promotion of sustainable land-use practices. The risks associated with and the financial impact of policy changes depend on their nature and timing.

Another significant risk is litigation or legal risk, with a rise in climate-related litigation claims over recent years. Such claims have been brought before the courts by various entities, including property owners, municipalities, states, insurers, shareholders and public interest organizations, citing failures to mitigate impacts of climate change, to adapt to climate change and to disclose material financial risks adequately. With the growing value of loss and damage from climate change, litigation risk is anticipated to increase.

Technology risk

Technological advancements or innovations supporting the transition to a lower-carbon, energy-efficient economic system can significantly impact organizations. The development and application of emerging technologies such as renewable energy, battery storage, energy efficiency, and carbon capture and storage can influence the competitiveness of specific organizations, their production and distribution costs, and ultimately the demand for their products and services. The timing of technology development and deployment is a critical uncertainty in assessing technology risk.

Market risk

Climate change's impact on markets is complex, with one major effect being shifts in the supply and demand for specific commodities, products and services as climate-related risks and opportunities are increasingly considered.

Reputation risk

Climate change presents a potential reputational risk linked to changing consumer or community perceptions of an organization's contribution to or detraction from the transition to a lower-carbon economy.

Other risks

Physical risks stemming from climate change can be event-driven (acute) or result from longer-term shifts (chronic) in climate patterns. These risks can have financial implications for organizations, including direct damage to assets, supply chain disruptions, changes in water availability and quality, food security and extreme temperature changes impacting operations and employee safety. Acute risks are those driven by events like severe weather events, while chronic risks are associated with longer-term shifts in climate patterns, such as sustained higher temperatures leading to sea level rise or chronic heat waves.

Efforts to address climate change offer organizations various opportunities, such as resource efficiency, cost savings, adoption of low-emission energy sources, development of new products and services, access to new markets, and building resilience in the supply chain. These opportunities may vary depending on an organization's operational region, market and industry.

Potential financial impacts

Below are some of the financial impacts of the above risks. Note that this is not an exhaustive list.

- Higher operating expenses, such as increased compliance costs and higher insurance premiums
- Write-offs, asset impairment and premature retirement of existing assets due to policy modifications
- Increased costs or decreased demand for products and services as a result of fines and judgments because of not adhering to sustainability goals
- Diminished demand for goods and services due to changes in consumer preferences
- Increased production costs due to fluctuating input prices (e.g. energy, water) and output requirements (e.g. waste treatment)
- Sudden and unforeseen shifts in energy costs
- Changes in revenue mix and sources resulting in reduced revenues
- Re-pricing of assets (e.g. fossil fuel reserves, land valuations, securities valuations)

19.8 UN SDGs and their Significance for Organizations

Between 2000 and 2015, the Millennium Development Goals (MDGs) were a pivotal development framework that achieved success in various areas, including the reduction of poverty and the improvement of health and education in developing countries. Following the MDGs, the Sustainable Development Goals (SDGs) expanded the scope of challenges to be addressed in order to eradicate poverty, encompassing a wide range of interconnected topics across the economic, social and environmental dimensions of sustainable development.

The current economic situation, along with consumption patterns and increasing urbanization, is leading to resource depletion, climate change and other social and economic problems that impact people and the planet. This has prompted a portion of the population, non-governmental organizations (NGOs), governments and the United Nations (UN) to call for the development of strategies to mitigate or minimize the impacts of these issues. This resulted in a global action plan composed of 17 Sustainable Development Goals (SDGs), 169 targets and 232 indicators to advance sustainable development by 2030 (**Illustration 19.1**).

ILLUSTRATION 19.1 The United Nations Sustainable Development Goals

Goal 1	No poverty
Goal 2	Zero hunger
Goal 3	Health and well-being
Goal 4	Quality education
Goal 5	Gender equality
Goal 6	Clean water and sanitation
Goal 7	Affordable and clean energy
Goal 8	Decent work and economic growth
Goal 9	Industry, innovation and infrastructure
Goal 10	Reduced inequalities
Goal 11	Sustainable cities and communities
Goal 12	Responsible consumption and production
Goal 13	Action to combat climate change and its impacts
Goal 14	Conserve and sustainably use the oceans, seas and marine resources for sustainable development
Goal 15	Life on land
Goal 16	Peaceful and inclusive societies with access to justice for all and effective, accountable and inclusive institutions
Goal 17	Partnerships for the goals – strengthen the means of implementation and revitalize the global partnership for sustainable development

The SDGs offer a comprehensive framework for achieving a more sustainable and equitable future for all. These goals tackle global challenges such as poverty, inequality, climate change, environmental degradation, peace and justice. With 17 interconnected objectives, it is critical to accomplish all of them by 2030 to ensure inclusion for everyone. Despite some progress, notably in the adoption of zero-carbon technologies for climate mitigation, overall progress has been impeded by a combination of crises, including the COVID-19 pandemic, rising inflation, economic and environmental distress, regional and national unrest, conflicts and natural disasters. This disruption has significantly impacted progress towards the 2030 Agenda, underscoring the importance of valuing every incremental step forward.

Various mechanisms can aid in this endeavour, including technology transfer, financial support, scientific cooperation, education on sustainability-oriented policies and strategies, and the Clean Development Mechanism (CDM). Given that the CDM serves as a common link between technology transfer and sustainable development, this approach will be given special attention.

Example 19.1

The following are some examples of company sustainability goals:

Unilever has set a goal to achieve 'carbon-positivity' by 2030 by phasing out the use of fossil fuels in its operations and generating more renewable energy than it consumes.

Danone is committed to removing deforestation from its supply chain.

Beyond Meat's plant-based products require 99 per cent less water, 93 per cent less land, and emit 90 per cent less greenhouse gases compared to traditional meat-based products. The company has demonstrated significant market value through its IPO and is currently experiencing a surge in product sales. Given the impact of the COVID-19 pandemic, many companies are re-evaluating their product offerings, with certain consumer goods companies simplifying their supply chains. For these companies, now is an ideal time to also assess their environmental impact.

Advantages of SDGs

SDGs offer several advantages for corporations. Firstly, they provide a comprehensive framework for focusing on sustainability, encompassing social, environmental and economic goals with specific targets and indicators. Unlike the MDGs, the SDGs acknowledge the potential contribution of firms towards their achievement. This allows corporations' managers to align their activities with sustainable development and strengthen their relationships with stakeholders in various communities.

Secondly, the SDGs serve as a global classification system for the key challenges facing humanity, offering a common language for sustainable development. This system helps organizations prioritize and align their sustainability efforts with the 2030 Agenda, facilitating collaboration and identifying areas where they can have the most impact. Many large companies already claim to contribute to the SDGs, and tools like the SDG Compass and the SDG Action Manager have been developed to help firms benchmark their progress and ensure alignment with the goals.

Finally, the SDGs provide clear and urgent goals for achieving sustainability, with tangible targets and indicators that align with both firm-level metrics and country-level objectives. The 2030 deadline emphasizes the need for immediate action rather than long-term planning. Additionally, the goals were designed with input from businesses and civil society organizations, and tools have been developed to assist firms in implementing the SDGs. This shows that the SDGs are both relevant and actionable for large global corporations.

Drawbacks of SDGs

The UN SDGs are becoming a crucial mechanism for coordinating governments' efforts to address global challenges. However, their implementation by managers is challenging. The argument that reducing poverty is a complex issue deeply rooted in inequality and injustice is indeed compelling. The criticism of the SDGs being unfeasibly expensive, lacking prioritization, and not accounting for local contexts is noteworthy. The concern that the broad array of targets in the SDGs could lead to cookie-cutter development policies and act as a distraction from the urgent need to eliminate extreme poverty is valid.

The suggestion to reduce the SDGs to focus on ten goals squarely aimed at reducing poverty, boosting education, and improving health seems practical and could lead to more effective outcomes. Prioritizing poverty eradication and essential areas such as education and health could facilitate more targeted and impactful efforts.

It may be beneficial to explore ways to refine and streamline the SDGs to address these concerns and maximize their effectiveness in driving progress towards sustainable development goals. This could involve re-evaluating the current set of goals and modifying them to ensure a more practical, focused and impactful approach to addressing global development challenges.

Summary

This chapter has explored the historical development and significance of sustainability and accounting, showing how it has led companies to recognize a broader responsibility to stakeholders through sustainability reporting. The increasing global focus on integrated reporting underscores the fact that organizations cannot afford to overlook issues such as climate change. The global goals have resulted from a highly inclusive process that involved governments, businesses, civil society and citizens right from the start. There is a widespread consensus on the direction that the world needs to pursue. Achieving these goals will require an exceptional effort from all sectors of society, with businesses playing a crucial role in these endeavours.

It is no longer acceptable to ignore sustainability, environmental, health and safety, and climate change risks and stakeholder concerns regarding these issues. Although chief financial officers have traditionally not been at the forefront, there is now a growing expectation for them to take on a more active role.

Review of key points

- Sustainability includes the three pillars: environmental, social and economic.
- Integrated reporting (IR) adopts a stakeholder-inclusive perspective to promote sustainability and meet stakeholders' expectations and should be used by all companies
- The International Sustainability Standards Board (ISSB) issued IFRS S1 and S2.
- IFRS S1 provides disclosure requirements for companies to communicate sustainability-related risks and opportunities. IFRS S2 sets out specific climate-related disclosures.
- Supply chain sustainability aims to integrate environmental, social and community considerations across the life cycle of products and services. This aims to establish and enforce policies and procedures to achieve a positive environmental, social and economic impact while delivering value to stakeholders.
- Climate-related risks are classified into two groups: (1) risks related to the transition to a lower carbon economy and (2) risk related to the physical impacts of climate change.
- The UN's Sustainable Development Goals have both advantages and drawbacks.

Self-testing questions

1 Define sustainability.
2 What is integrated reporting?
3 For each climate-related risk, consider the potential financial impacts.

Group activities and discussion questions

Select a company from oil and mining, pharmaceutical, food or fashion. Download the integrated reports or sustainability report from the company's website and answer the following questions:

1 How big are the integrated reports?
2 Who is responsible for the integrated report?
3 List the stakeholders to whom the report is directed.
4 How has the company adopted the International Integrated Reporting Framework (IIRC Framework)?
5 What issues are discussed in the integrated report?
6 How does the company address climate change and biodiversity?

Accounting in context

Discuss and comment on the following report based on an article from the press. Are brands a means to drive social or environmental change, or should the primary focus in the twenty-first century be on prioritizing profits and meeting clients' needs?

Sustainable fashion

ESG concerns may undermine support for potential blockbuster flotation

Media reports on the adverse impact of ESG controversies on investment are certainly now more frequent

Online retailers are in dire problems, with ASOS resorting to strong discounting of their products and Boohoo struggling to retain customers. Concerns are rising as the Chinese-founded fast fashion online retailer, Shein, has registered with the Financial Services Authority to list on the London Stock Exchange (LSE). Environmental, social and governance (ESG) concerns about Shein may encounter obstacles in its London initial public offering (IPO) on the LSE. Despite being founded in China and primarily sourcing its suppliers there, the company is headquartered in Singapore. Many Chinese companies have quietly redomiciled or registered in Singapore to hedge against rising geopolitical risk as tensions between Beijing and Washington escalate.

Shein reported a profit of $2.0bn in 2023 and revenue of $30bn, whereas ASOS reported group revenue of £3.5bn and an operating loss of £248.5m in 2023. Shein is valued at $66bn (£52bn), compared to ASOS and Boohoo, who both have a market capitalization below £500m. Shein's listing on the LSE could enhance the City following a lack of substantial IPOs in recent years. Nevertheless, major UK institutional investors are cautious about investing in Shein due to concerns about the company's alleged use of forced labour. Human rights groups have accused Shein of employing forced labour in its cotton supply chain from Xinjiang, an allegation that Shein has refuted. Considering the ESG criteria, it appears improbable that responsible investors would consider purchasing Shein's shares. This suggests that there may be a potential risk of 'collateral brand damage', for the LSE.

The LSE might struggle to entice UK asset managers to back Shein's IPO due to the uncertainties surrounding ESG, corporate governance and other important factors with poor human rights practices and sustainability, despite the attraction of a large listing like Shein, with its global reach, substantial growth and strong profitability. However, investors argue that listings like Shein are vital for the exchange's future, especially as it has been losing companies to US counterparts offering higher valuations. Furthermore, relatively low-cost UK-listed companies are desirable as takeover targets for foreign investors. Wood Group, a British oilfield services and engineering firm, is in takeover discussions with Dubai-based Sidara. This could lead to the loss of its London listing as the company focuses on decarbonizing and as energy demand changes. Although ESG concerns persist for the fashion industry, not all investors are solely focused on them, as evidenced by the interest in fast fashion companies like Boohoo and luxury brands. Many asset managers rely on their own ESG standards to guide their stock selections.

Other problems of fashion observed in developing countries

The Atacama Desert in northern Chile, famous for its breathtaking landscapes, has unfortunately become one of the fastest-growing dumping grounds for discarded clothes in the world. This troubling trend is a result of the rapid rise of fast fashion, which has led to an overwhelming amount of waste declared as an environmental and social emergency by the UN. The impact is particularly felt in South Asia and Africa, where local facilities are struggling to cope with the massive influx of discarded clothing. For instance, in Ghana, a landfill near the capital city of Accra is 60 per cent clothes and 65 feet high, gaining international attention as a symbol of this crisis.

Unfortunately, the fashion industry has a significant environmental impact. Textile waste is often transported directly from the factory to global dumping grounds. The industry's manufacturing processes heavily rely on chemicals, water and non-renewable energy sources, making them major contributors to environmental damage. According to the European Environment Agency, the fashion industry is estimated to be responsible for up to 10 per cent of the world's total carbon emissions.

Resale markets, once helpful, are now overwhelmed by the growing volume of discarded clothing. New initiatives, both large and small, are underway to tackle clothing waste. The attention to the Atacama desert's issues may also motivate additional projects.

What can the fast/luxury fashion industry do to push for sustainability?

The fashion industry has made slow progress in sustainability. Some brands have 'take-back' schemes, but these have been criticized for encouraging more consumption. Around 369 companies have committed to science-based targets, but only 170 have been approved. Greenwashing, whereby brands market themselves as more climate-friendly and sustainable than they really are, is a common problem, and the EU has introduced a law to regulate environmental claims. The aim of the new law is to regulate how businesses verify their environmental claims. Statements that do not meet the minimum criteria set will be banned.

A fashion brand's main carbon footprint is generated indirectly through its value chain. Opting for renewable, sustainable fashion materials like organic cotton and bamboo can reduce the carbon footprint of the final product, and consumers are willing to pay more for these options. Additionally, recycled polyester, derived from open-loop recycling of 'PET bottles', can significantly diminish the environmental impact and realize a more sustainable future for packaging. The fibre market has also seen the emergence of new sustainable fashion innovations, such as The LYCRA Company's fibre, made from annually renewable field corn instead of fossil fuels, which can be seamlessly integrated into the manufacturing process.

Fashion brands can further consider their products' post-consumer life cycle by embracing sustainable and circular practices that prioritize reuse, recycling and repurposing. When designing, sustainable fashion brands may opt for biodegradable materials and provide clear disposal instructions to consumers. Moreover, they can establish in-house recycling programmes, like Madewell's denim recycling initiative, which allows customers to return pre-loved pairs of jeans for store credit, with the products repurposed for residential insulation by Habitat for Humanity.

Source: J. Bartlett (2024) Fast Fashion Goes to Die in the World's Largest Fog Desert: The Scale is Breathtaking. *National Geographic*, 5 March. https://www.nationalgeographic.com/environment/article/chile-fashion-pollution

S. Butler and L. O'Carroll (2024) EU Plan to Impose Import Duty on Cheap Goods Could Dent Shein and Temu. https://www.theguardian.com/business/article/2024/jul/03/eu-plan-to-impose-import-duty-on-cheap-goods-could-dent-shein-and-temu

E. Dunkley, M. Novik and I. Levingston (2024) Fund Managers Give Cool Reception to Prospect of Shein London IPO. *Financial Times*, 6 June.

F. Ferraro and A.S. de Tejada Cuenca (2024) Sustainability Business School Teaching Case Study: Can the Fashion Industry Be More Sustainable? *Financial Times*, 25 June. https://www.ft.com/content/bb1c4c8c-142a-478e-8b60-04e7178e9c4d

L. Indvik and A. Hancock (2023) Can Fast Fashion Kick its Dirty Habits? *Financial Times*, 27 August. https://www.ft.com/content/d9d93d98-eba5-4d4a-9a4d-21b7f824987b

J. Johnson (2024) A Shein Listing Could Further Rattle ASOS and Boohoo. *Investors' Chronicle*, 24–30 May, p. 10.

https://asos-12954-s3.s3.eu-west-2.amazonaws.com/files/7217/0065/7934/ASOS_Annual_Report_2023.pdf

https://www.madewell.com/do-well/recycling.html#tradein

https://www.shein.co.uk/SHEIN-Modern-Slavery-Statement-a-1067.html

References and further reading

BCG (2020) Your Supply Chain Needs a Sustainability Strategy. https://www.bcg.com/publications/2020/supply-chain-needs-sustainability-strategy

Cuervo-Cazurra, A., Doh, J.P., Giuliani, E., Montiel I. and Park, J. (2022) The United Nations' Sustainable Development Goals: Pros and Cons for Managers of Multinationals. *AIB Insights*, 22(1). https://doi.org/10.46697/001c.32530

Crane, A., Matten, D., Glozer, S. and Spence, L.J. (2019) *Business Ethics: Managing Corporate Citizenship and Sustainability in the Age of Globalization* (5th edn.). Oxford: Oxford University Press.

Economist, The (2015) The 169 Commandments. *The Economist*, 26 March. https://www-economist-com.uow.idm.oclc.org/leaders/2015/03/26/the-169-commandments

Gray, R. (2010) Is Accounting for Sustainability Actually Accounting for Sustainability ... and How Would We Know? An Exploration of Narratives of Organisations and the Planet. *Accounting, Organizations and Society*, 35(1): 47–62.

HM Treasury (2024) TCFD-aligned Disclosure Guidance for Public Sector Annual Reports. Updated 21 March 2024. https://www.gov.uk/government/publications/tcfd-aligned-disclosure-application-guidance/task-force-on-climate-related-financial-disclosure-tcfd-aligned-disclosure-application-guidance

Hoy, C. and Sumner, A. (2021) The End of Global Poverty: Is the UN Sustainable Development Goal 1 (Still) Achievable? *Global Policy*, 12(4): 419–429.

IFRS (2023) ISSB Issues Inaugural Global Sustainability Disclosure Standards. 26 June. https://www.ifrs.org/news-and-events/news/2023/06/issb-issues-ifrs-s1-ifrs-s2/

IIRC (2013) *The IIRC Pilot Programme Yearbook 2013: Business and Investors Explore the Sustainability Perspective of Integrated Reporting.*

Rinaldi, L. (2020) Integrated Thinking for Stakeholder Engagement: A Processing Model for Judgments and Choice in Situations of Cognitive Complexity. In C. de Villiers, P.-C. Hsiao and W. Maroun (eds.), *The Routledge Handbook of Integrated Reporting* (pp. 280–292). Abingdon: Routledge.

Rinaldi, L. (2023) Accounting and the COVID-19 Pandemic Two Years On: Insights, Gaps, and an Agenda for Future Research. *Accounting Forum*, 47(3): 333–364.

Solomon, J. (2021) *Corporate Governance and Accountability* (5th edn.). Wiley.

Solomon, J. and Maroun, W. (2012). Reporting Pre- and Post-King III: What's the Difference? Association of Chartered Certified Accountants Discussion Paper.

United Nations (2023a) *Framework for Reporting Climate Change Risks & Opportunities in Corporate Reports.* https://unfccc.int/climate-action/momentum-for-change/activity-database/momentum-for-change-framework-for-reporting-climate-change-risks–opportunities-in-corporate-reports

United Nations (2023b) *Times of Crisis, Times of Change: Science for Accelerating Transformations to Sustainable Development.* United Nations publication issued by the Department of Economic and Social Affairs.

https://am.jpmorgan.com/gb/en/asset-management/adv/investment-themes/sustainable-investing/child-labour-in-cobalt-mining/?_gl=1*1kyptmg*_up*MQ..&gclid=CjwKCAjwyo60BhBiEiwAHmVLJYP8DmaKEhkbW90vEMSak78lIzYfp0tRHQggtybx0MG6eLv7xOKuZhoC2NEQAvD_BwE&gclsrc=aw.ds

https://integratedreporting.ifrs.org/10-years/10-years-summary/

https://integratedreporting.ifrs.org/resource/integrated-thinking-strategy-state-of-play-report/

https://integratedreporting.ifrs.org/resource/international-ir-framework/

https://kpmg.com/xx/en/home/insights/2020/06/climate-change-and-decarbonization.html

https://news.un.org/en/story/2024/06/1151271

https://unglobalcompact.org/sdgs/about

https://www.ifrs.org/news-and-events/news/2023/06/issb-issues-ifrs-s1-ifrs-s2/

http://www.sdgcompass.org/

https://www.theguardian.com/business/2012/aug/07/credit-crunch-boom-bust-timeline

https://www.un.org/sustainabledevelopment/sustainable-development-goals/

Answers to Self-testing Questions

Chapter 1

1 A statement of financial position shows assets, liabilities and share capital. Expenses, sales and profit for the year are shown on the income statement.

2 Non-current assets (fixed assets) are intended to be retained and used by the business for more than a year.

Current assets are cash and things that are intended for conversion into cash within a year.

3 Land and buildings; plant and machinery; furniture, fixtures and fittings; vehicles, ships and aircraft.

Furniture owned by a furniture shop and intended for sale is a current asset. Vehicles owned by a garage and intended for sale are a current asset.

4 Assets minus liabilities equals equity.

5 Individual assets may be worth more or less than the statement of financial position value.

A successful business as a whole (including unrecorded goodwill) should be worth more than the statement of financial position shows because of the profits that it now produces, and expectations for the future.

6 a Current ratio = current assets : current liabilities

45,000 : 22,000 = 2.05 : 1

b Liquidity ratio = current assets excluding inventories : current liabilities

21,000 : 22,000 = 0.95 : 1

c

	Existing		Revised	
	£	£	£	£
Non-current assets		50,000		50,000
Current assets				
Inventories (at cost)	24,000		20,000	
Trade receivables	12,000		12,000	
Cash	9,000	45,000	17,000	49,000
Total assets		95,000		99,000
Current liabilities				
Trade payables		22,000		22,000
Equity				
Share capital	50,000		50,000	
Retained earnings	23,000	73,000	27,000	77,000
		95,000		99,000

d Current ratio = 49,000 : 22,000 = 2.2 : 1

Liquidity ratio = 29,000 : 22,000 = 1.3 : 1

As the business now has £4,000 less inventory, and £8,000 more cash, both the current ratio and the liquidity ratio have improved, or become stronger.

7 a £83,000, being the increase in shareholders' funds

b £83,000 + £10,000 − £20,000 − £30,000 = £43,000

8

	Domer Castle	Warmer Castle
Current ratio	34 : 17 = 2 : 1	34 : 17 = 2 : 1
Liquidity ratio	26 : 17 = 1.5 : 1	15 : 17 = 0.88 : 1
$\frac{\text{Debentures}}{\text{Debentures+Equity}}$	100 ÷ 331 = 30.2%	200 ÷ 331 = 60.4%
EBIT ÷ Interest payable	31,000 ÷ 10,000 = 3.1 times	32,000 ÷ 20,000 = 1.6 times

Warmer appears to be weaker. The two companies have the same current ratio, but a large part of Warmer's current assets is stocks and so it has a much lower liquidity ratio. Warmer also has much higher capital gearing and its interest cover is low.

9 a i Non-current assets − £ 80,000

Cash + £ 100,000

Retained earnings + £ 20,000

ii Inventories − £ 30,000

Receivables + £ 80,000

Retained earnings + £ 50,000

iii Cash − £ 40,000

Payables − £ 40,000

b

	Existing		Revised	
	£	£	£	£
Non-current assets		158,000		78,000
Current assets				
Inventories (at cost)	110,000		80,000	
Trade receivables	120,000		200,000	
Cash	20,000	250,000	80,000	360,000
Total assets		408,000		438,000
Current liabilities				
Trade payables		120,000		80,000
Equity				
Share capital	250,000		250,000	
Retained earnings	38,000	288,000	108,000	358,000
		408,000		438,000

Chapter 2

1 The statement of financial position is as at a particular date. An income statement is for a particular *period*, such as for a year.

   a A statement of financial position shows assets, liabilities and equity (which includes all retained profits).

   b An income statement shows revenues, expenses and the current year's profit.

2 An expense is the cost incurred in earning the revenues of a particular period. Some assets become expenses. Assets such as unsold inventories and non-current (fixed) assets may be seen as stores of value that have not yet been used up in generating revenues. Fixed assets become recognized as expenses as they are depreciated. Inventories become expenses when they are sold. Receivables become expenses if they are written off as bad debts.

3 Closing inventories are shown at the lower of cost and net realizable value. The valuation of closing stock has a direct effect on profits. If closing stock is overstated by £1m, then profits are overstated by £1m.

If closing inventories were shown at selling price, the company would be taking credit for profits before sales are made; it is not a good idea to claim profits that have not yet been earned.

4 Depreciation is charged to write off the cost of the fixed asset over a number of years, depending on its economic life. If an asset is shown at a revalued amount rather than at cost, then the revalued amount is written off in the same way.

5 Capital expenditure adds to fixed assets that are then written off (depreciated; an expense) over a number of years. Examples would include a retail shop buying a new delivery vehicle, having an extension to the shop built and buying new tills. Revenue expenditure is written off during the period in which it is incurred. Examples include lighting, heating and cleaning. (Some revenue expenditure is included in closing inventories that are carried forward and written off in the period in which they are sold.)

6 Profit after tax for the year, £12,000. This is because:

   a it is the amount that has been earned for them after charging all expenses and taxation; and

   b it is the basis for dividend decisions; dividends are the amounts actually paid to shareholders.

7 Kingsdun Company

	Delivery van	Boring machine
	£	£
Cost	25,000	25,000
Year 1 depreciation	6,250	2,500
Net book value at end of year 1	18,750	22,500
Year 2 depreciation	4,688	2,500
Net book value at end of year 2	14,062	20,000
Year 3 depreciation	3,516	2,500
Net book value at end of year 3	10,546	17,500
Year 4 depreciation	2,636	2,500
Net book value at end of year 4	7,910	15,000

8 Dargate Retailing Company

Product	Cost price	Mark-up	Selling price	Gross profit
	£	%	£	%
Fargs	100	25	125	20
Gargs	100	10	110	9.09
Hargs	50	100	100	50
Jargs	40	100	80	50
Kargs	80	50	120	33⅓
Largs	50	20	60	16⅔
Margs	30.77	30	40	23.1
Nargs	45	11.11	50	10
Pargs	75	33⅓	100	25

9 Banterbury Company Ltd

	Year 3		Year 4	
	£000	%	£000	%
Turnover	100	100	120	100
Cost of sales	60	60	73	60.83
Gross profit	40	40	47	39.17
Distribution costs	(12)	12	(14)	11.67
Administration expenses	(9)	9	(12)	10
Operating profit	19	19	21	17.5
Interest payable	(3)	3	(3)	2.5
Profit before taxation	16	16	18	15
Tax on profit for year	(4)	4	(3)	2.5
Profit after tax for the year	12	12	15	12.5

Turnover has increased by 20 per cent, but most costs have increased by a larger percentage than sales. Expressing all items as a percentage of sales, we can see that cost of sales has increased slightly, and so gross profit has gone down. There has been an increase in operating costs as a percentage of sales, and so operating profit as a percentage of sales has gone down. There has been no change in interest costs, and the company is fortunate that the amount of tax payable has gone down: the effect of these two is that there has been an increase in profit after tax as a proportion of sales.

The small improvement in profit as a percentage of sales is mainly due to the lower tax charge. Cost of sales and operating costs have both increased by a bigger proportion than sales. These results suggest that management have not been very successful in getting more profits out of the increase in sales.

Shareholders' funds are £109,000, and the profit after tax earned for them is £15,000, a return on shareholders' capital employed of 13.8 per cent, which is satisfactory.

Chapter 3

1 The main users of financial accounting information are: shareholders, potential shareholders and investors generally; creditors, and suppliers; lenders (such as banks and debenture holders); employees, and potential employees; customers; government and public sector bodies; HM Revenue & Customs; the company's managers and directors; financial analysts and advisers; competitors; and the public.

Different users may have a wide variety of different information needs, but financial accounting tends to concentrate on what investors want to know about the security of their company and its future prospects, as well as receiving an account of the directors' stewardship. Creditors also want to know about the security or solvency, and its future prospects as an indicator of how likely it is to be able to repay the amounts it owes.

2 An asset is a resource controlled by the enterprise as a result of past events and from which future economic benefits are expected to flow to the enterprise.

A liability is a present obligation of the enterprise arising from past events, the settlement of which is expected to result in an outflow from the enterprise of resources embodying economic benefits.

3 Provisions are a problem because the Companies Act, and conventional practice, are more liberal than the definition and treatment established by accounting standards. The Companies Act 1985 defined provisions as 'amounts retained as reasonably necessary to cover any liability or loss which is either likely or certain to be incurred'. Provisions were often created for future reorganizations, redundancies, legal liabilities, decommissioning costs, and future costs and losses of various sorts. This would exclude current *proposals* to incur liabilities or losses in future periods. IAS 37 defined a provision as 'a liability of uncertain timing or amount' and indicates that it must be a liability, a present obligation. This means that many traditional provisions are not allowed. But there is some flexibility because the provision can include an obligation that is 'constructive', where there are no legal commitments, but where the company has by its actions and announcements committed itself to a course of action.

4 IFRS 3 defines goodwill as 'future economic benefits arising from assets that are not capable of being individually identified and separately recognized'. It arises where one business has paid more for that business than the fair value of its assets.

5 'Pure' historic cost accounting would show all assets on the statement of financial position at cost price. Non-current assets need to be depreciated. Inventories have to be shown at net realizable value where this is below cost price. A provision for bad debts may have to be deducted from receivables. Some assets such as property and investments may be revalued.

6 Revenues are the amounts credited to the income statement in respect of the main activities of the business (sales, fees earned). Income includes any other amounts generated, for example from rentals or investments. Gains can be of any type, including revenues and income; they also include gains arising on revaluation of assets, which may be realized or unrealized.

7 Profit is seen as being important because: (a) it provides a guide to dividend decisions; (b) it indicates how much cash a company has generated; (c) it indicates how successful, or otherwise, a company and its management are; (d) it provides a basis for levying corporation tax; (e) it provides a guide to investors in choosing what shares to buy and sell; (f) it gives an indication to creditors about the company's ability to pay its liabilities; it indicates economic efficiency; and (g) it is of interest to different groups, including employees, politicians, customers and others who may be concerned about companies making excessive profits.

Chapter 4

1 a Current assets: current liabilities (e.g. 1.8 : 1)

b Current assets minus stocks : current liabilities (e.g. 0.9 : 1) c Capital requiring a fixed return (e.g. debentures) as a percentage of total long-term capital (equity plus debentures). This is often expressed as: $\frac{D}{D+E}$ e.g. 35%

It may also be expressed as $\frac{D}{E}$

It is usually calculated using statement of financial position values. It may be calculated using market values. Preference shares and all borrowings may be included with D.

d Earnings before interest and taxation ÷ interest payable (e.g. five times)

2 It might take a long time to convert stocks into cash; they are not a very 'liquid' asset.

3 Net profit for the year, after taxation, as a percentage of equity (including all reserves and retained earnings) as shown on the statement of financial position.

4 The 'return' is earnings before interest and taxation. If debentures are included as part of capital employed, the interest payable on them should be included as part of the return on capital employed (ROCE). It is important that the numerator and the denominator are consistent: where borrowings are included in the denominator, the interest on those borrowings should be included in the numerator. Return on ordinary shareholders' capital employed is usually measured after charging taxation for the year. If borrowings are included in capital employed, an earnings before interest and taxes (EBIT) is used as the numerator, it is taken before charging taxation; this is a matter of convenience, not a matter of principle.

5 An increase in the gross profit ratio does not tell us anything for sure about sales. They may have increased; selling prices may have increased. But an increase in the gross profit ratio may be entirely attributable to a reduction in cost of sales as a percentage of sales, which could be due to more effective buying, or reductions in purchase prices.

6 The company's financial position looks reasonably strong with some improvement in year 2. The current ratio is lower, but the liquidity ratio has increased. The gearing looks rather high, but has reduced; the company has reduced its long-term borrowing slightly; shareholders' funds have increased slightly; and interest cover has increased.

The company's current assets look rather high, and this can have an effect on profitability. It has generated substantial amounts of cash, and the cash balance is now excessive and should be used profitably. It may be the company's intention to further reduce its long-term borrowing.

The company has managed to increase its profitability slightly: both measures of ROCE have improved. But it appears to be struggling with sales and costs. Sales have increased slightly (5 per cent), but the gross profit margin has gone down a little. Operating costs have been kept under control (a slight decrease); and because of reduced borrowings, there has been a significant reduction in interest payable. After taxation, there has been an improvement in net profit as a percentage of sales.

Overall utilization of capital employed has hardly changed, but there have been improvements in the management of stocks and debtors. Stock turnover looks very slow, but has been improved substantially. The length of time that debtors take to pay has also been reduced substantially.

More detailed analysis of each item of expense as a percentage of sales could be undertaken; more detailed analysis of each item of assets and liabilities in relation to sales could be made. But the analysis shown below brings out the main points outlined above. The overall impression might be of reasonably successful financial management struggling to improve financial performance in difficult market conditions.

Solvency	Year 1	Year 2
Current ratio	1,868 : 434	2,100 : 600
	4.3 : 1	3.5 : 1
Liquidity ratio	688 : 434	1,100 : 600
	1.6 : 1	1.8 : 1
Gearing ratio	1,000 ÷ 2,434	900 ÷ 2,400
	41%	37.5%
Interest cover	295 ÷ 100	305 ÷ 90
	2.95 times	3.39 times
Profitability		
Return on ordinary shareholders' capital employed	135 ÷ 1,434	150 ÷ 1,500
	9.4%	10%
EBIT as a percentage of long-term capital employed	295 ÷ 2,434	305 ÷ 2,400
	12.1%	12.7%
Gross profit ratio	375 ÷ 3,600	384 ÷ 3,780
	10.42%	10.16%
Operating profit/sales	295 ÷ 3,600	305 ÷ 3,780
	8.19%	8.07%
Net profit after-tax sales	135 ÷ 3,600	150 ÷ 3,780
	3.75%	3.97%
Sales net assets	3,600 ÷ 1,434	3,780 ÷ 1,500
	2.51 times	2.52 times
Inventory turnover (days)	$\frac{1,200}{3,225} \times 365$	$\frac{1,000}{3,396} \times 365$
	136 days	107 days
Receivables ratio (days)	$\frac{600}{3,600} \times 365$	$\frac{500}{3,780} \times 365$
	61 days	48 days

Chapter 5

1 The three ratios may be calculated on a 'per share' basis, or for the company as a whole. The results should be the same.

a The price/earnings (P/E) ratio indicates whether the share price is expensive or cheap in relation to the most recent profits. It is calculated by dividing the share price by the earnings per share (EPS). A high P/E ratio (e.g. 30+) suggests that investors are optimistic about future increases in earnings. A low P/E ratio (e.g. 10 or less) suggests that investors are not very optimistic about future growth.

b The dividend yield indicates whether the share price is expensive or cheap in relation to the most recent dividends. It is calculated by dividing the most recent year's dividend per share by the share price. A high dividend yield (e.g. 5 per cent or more) suggests that shares are cheap in relation to the most recent dividend. A very high dividend yield (e.g. 8 per cent or more) suggests that there are serious concerns about the company: perhaps the share price has collapsed, and/or the level of dividends is not expected to be maintained at last year's level. A low dividend yield (e.g. 2 per cent or less) suggests that investors are optimistic about future growth.

c The dividend times cover relates the most recent year's dividends to the amount of profits earned in that period. It helps to indicate how 'safe' the dividends are. It is calculated by dividing the amount of earnings by the amount of dividends. A high cover (e.g. 2.5 or more) suggests that dividends are relatively safe. A low cover (e.g. 1.2, or even less than 1) suggests that the company would have difficulty maintaining the dividend, especially if there was a fall in earnings.

2 The market value of a successful company is likely to be higher than its statement of financial position value.

This is partly because statement of financial position values may be understated. It is mainly because the market value of a business is largely influenced by its profitability, and expectations that it will be at least maintained, and will probably increase. The value of a successful business as a whole, as a going concern, with internally generated goodwill that is unrecorded, is normally higher than the value of a collection of dead assets.

Sometimes the market value of a company falls below the net asset value, especially when the company is doing badly. In these circumstances the company may unwittingly attract an asset-stripping takeover bid. Another company may be attracted to buy up the assets of the company at a low price, and then split up the various parts of the company and sell them at a profit.

In some companies (e.g. property companies) assets may be fully valued, and prospects for growth in earnings are limited; the market value may then be lower than the net asset value.

3 The dividend yield refers to the last known dividend. The next dividend may be lower, or it may be zero. High dividend yields are associated with low share prices, and question marks about how likely the dividend is to be maintained.

4 The figures are shown in full below.

	Alemouth plc	Beermouth plc
Share capital (20p shares)	£1,600,000	£2,000,000
Retained earnings	£3,200,000	£18,000,000
	£4,800,000	£20,000,000
Net profit after tax for year	£3,520,000	£1,200,000
Dividends for year	£3,200,000	£800,000
Number of shares	8,000,000	10,000,000
Market price of shares	£4.40	£1.80
Market capitalization	£35,200,000	£18,000,000
EPS	£0.44	£0.12
Dividend per share	£0.40	£0.08
P/E ratio	10	15
Dividend times cover	1.1 times	1.5 times
Dividend yield	9.09%	4.44%
Net assets per share	£0.60	£2.00

5 The dividend yield of Alemouth plc is very high, which is associated with a low share price (the P/E ratio is only 10), a low dividend cover (1.1 times) and pessimism about future prospects.

6 The market capitalization of Beermouth is only £18m, although its net asset value is £20m. In most companies the market value is higher than the net asset value. There could be something seriously wrong with Beermouth's statement of financial position: perhaps the assets are overvalued, or there is a significant unrecorded liability; perhaps the company is about to be used for something. It is more likely that the market value of the company is very low because the company is expected to be making losses. The company's return on capital employed (ROCE) (£1,200,000/£20,000,000) was only 6 per cent last year. If the company makes losses of more than £2m in the current year, the net asset value would soon fall below the current market capitalization (which might then rise or fall, depending on investors' expectations).

Chapter 6

1 The accruals concept means that profit is not based on cash flows; it is not the difference between cash received during a period, and cash paid out during that period. The accruals basis of accounting means that profit is the difference between revenues earned during a period, and the costs incurred in earning those revenues. Revenues (sales and other income) are recognized when they are earned, not when the cash is received. Similarly, expenses are not recognized when payments are made; instead, they are 'matched' against the revenues earned during the period.

The accruals concept is important in financial accounting because profits are different from cash flows; a business can be profitable and expanding, but be short of cash. A business can generate cash (e.g. by selling off assets), but be running at a loss.

If business accounts were based entirely on 'receipts and payments', there would be no statement of financial position, and no measurement of profit. The accruals concept is essential for the preparation of statements of financial position and income statements.

2 A very successful business will have serious cash shortages if its profits are poured into additional assets. This may be a healthy expansion of inventories and receivables in line with sales; and investment in additional non-current assets, and buying shares in other companies. It may be unhealthy if poor control results in too many assets being bought, excessive inventory levels, and fixed assets that are not profitably utilized.

The situation could also arise if substantial loans are repaid, and if the company pays out more as dividends than it earns as profits.

3 If a company's depreciation charge is greater than its losses, it can still produce a positive cash flow. If a business is declining, additional cash could come in from reducing asset levels (inventories are sold off, receivables pay up and excess non-current assets are sold). But this could not continue indefinitely. Eventually non-current assets will be fully depreciated and/or sold off, leaving little more than a cash shell.

4 Free cash flow is the amount of cash flow that a company has generated during a period, which it is free to spend as it wishes. It is based on cash flow from operations after deducting non-discretionary payments such as interest and taxation (and including any dividends received). The company is free to spend as much of this free cash flow as it wishes on additional investments in fixed assets, paying dividends and repaying loans. The figure should be reduced to allow for the fact that there is usually some *essential* replacement of non-current assets.

a £7,000 minus essential asset replacement = approximately zero

b £4,100 minus, say, £3,100 = £1,000; £5,500 minus, say, £2,200 = £3,300

5 It is true that Deek Lining plc produced positive cash flows in year 4, but this was mainly as a result of reducing assets. Reducing stocks and debtors produced £500,000, and sales of fixed assets produced £1,100,000. The increase in the amount owed to creditors produced another £100,000.

It is also true that additional non-current assets were bought, but this amounted to only £150,000, while the proceeds of selling non-current assets were £1,100,000.

Borrowings were substantially reduced, as the chairman stated, and, as a result, there was a reduction in the amount of interest paid.

The most serious feature of year 4 was the substantial loss (£1.2m), compared with a profit of £3.4m in year 3. This demonstrates clearly the difference between cash flow and profit: although it made a loss in year 4, it produced a positive cash flow.

Year 3 generally looked more healthy, with a substantial profit, although it ended the year with less cash than it had at the beginning. It may be that it overexpanded in year 3 (with too much cash going into additional assets) and that some rationalization and careful housekeeping (including control of working capital) was required in year 4.

The increase in dividend is not justified by earnings: the company made a loss in year 4.

Although the chairman's statements are correct, it is difficult to justify the overall view that the company had a successful year in year 4. It made a substantial loss, and seemed to be selling off assets in order to raise additional cash.

6

Daubyhaven Ltd. Cash flow statement for year ended 31 December year 2		
Cash generated from operating activities	**£**	**£**
1 Operating profit	35,000	
2 Depreciation*	20,000	
3 Other items: profit on sale of machine	(1,500)	
		53,500
Increase in working capital		
4 Increase in inventories	(20,000)	
5 Increase in receivables	(5,000)	
6 Decrease in payables	(2,000)	
		(27,000)
7 Interest paid	(2,000)	
8 Taxation paid	(8,000)	
		(10,000)
		16,500
Cash used in investing activities		
9 Purchase of non-current assets**	(15,000)	
10 Disposal of non-current assets	4,500	
		(10,500)
Cash used in financing activities		
11 Repayment of loan	(10,000)	
12 Dividends paid	(18,000)	

Daubyhaven Ltd. Cash flow statement for year ended 31 December year 2	
	(28,000)
	(22,000)
Decrease in cash during year	
Opening balance	10,000
Closing balance	(12,000)

*At the beginning of the year the provision for depreciation was £60,000 During the year it was reduced by £12,000 in respect of a machine that was sold, to £48,000. It ended the year as £68,000, which means that it must have increased by £20,000, being the depreciation charge.

**At the beginning of the year machinery at cost was £130,000. During the year it was reduced by £15,000 in respect of a machine that was sold, to £115,000. It ended the year as £130,000, which means that it must have increased by £15,000, being the additional purchases of machinery.

7

Fistard Neash plc	£	£
Cash generated from operating activities		
1 Operating profit	20	
2 Depreciation*	24	
3 Impairment of goodwill	10	
Profit on sale of Scottish factory	(7)	
		47
Increase in working capital		
4 Increase in inventories	(25)	
5 Decrease in receivables	5	
6 Decrease in payables	(5)	(25)
7 Interest paid	(2)	
8 Taxation paid	(4)	(6)
		16
Cash used in investing activities		
9 Purchase of fixed assets**	(44)	
10 Disposal of fixed assets	23	
Cash used in financing activities		(21)
11 Redemption of debentures	(49)	
Issue of shares***	60	
12 Dividends paid	(8)	3
		(2)
Decrease in cash during year		
Opening balance	10	
Closing balance	8	

*At the beginning of the year the provision for depreciation was £50m. During the year it was reduced by £8m in respect of the Scottish factory that was sold, to £42m. It ended the year as £66m, which means that it must have increased by £24m, being the year's depreciation charge.

**At the beginning of the year plant, property and equipment at cost was £120m. During the year it was reduced by £24m, in respect of the Scottish factory that was sold, to £96m. It ended the year as £140,000, which means that it must have increased by £44m, being the additional purchases of property, plant and equipment.

***Share capital increased by £20m, and share premium increased by £40m. This indicates that shares with a nominal value of £20m were issued for £60m.

Chapter 7

1 Marks and Spencer plc

Ratio	2023	2023	2022	2022
1 Current ratio	2155.0 / 2706.4	0.8	2182.3 / 2370.8	0.92
2 Liquidity (quick) ratio	(2155.0 – 764.4) / 2706.4	0.51	(2182.3 – 706.1) / 2370.8	0.62
3 Capital gearing ratio: Debt/Equity	3576.5 / 2810.5	127%	4154.7 / 2913.7	142%
Debt/(Debt+Equity)	3576.5 / (3576.5 + 2810.5)	56%	4154.7 / (4154.7 + 2913.7)	59%
4 Interest times cover	(515.1 + 166.1) / 205.5	3.3 times	(572.2 + 33.9) / 214.4	2.83 times
5 Return on shareholders' funds	364 / 2814.9	13%	(572.2 + 33.9) / 214.4	11%
6 Return on total long-term capital	(515.1 + 166.1) / (3576.5 + 2810.5)	11%	(572.2 + 33.9) / (4154.7 + 2913.7)	9%
7 Operating profit as a % of sales	515.1 / 11931.3	4.3%	572.2/ 10885.1	5,3%
8 Asset turnover	11931.3 / (9077.8 – 2706.4)	1.87 times	10885.1 / (9044.3 – 2370.8)	1,54 times
9 Gross profit ratio	4144.6 / 11931.3	35%	3754.8 / 10885.1	34%
10 Selling and administrative expenses as % of sales	3609.2 / 11931.3	30%	3244.1 / 10885.1	30%
11 Other operating expenses as a % of sales	Not shown		not shown	
12 Sales/non-current assets	11931.3 / 6942.8	1.72 times	10885.1 / 7261.1	1.5 times
13 Sales/current assets	11931.3 / 2155.0	5.54 times	10885.1 / 2182.3	4.99 times
14 Inventory turnover ratio	764.4 × 365 / 7786.7	36 days	706.1 × 365 / 7130.3	36 days
15 Trade receivables ratio	122.9 × 365 / 11931.3	3.8 days	98.2 × 365 / 10885.1	3.3 days
16 Trade payables ratio	801.7 × 365 / 7786.7	37.6 days	732.8 × 365 / 7130.3	37.5 days
17 Price/earnings ratio	167 / 18.5	9.03	158 / 15.7	10.06
18 Dividend yield	*No dividend paid*		*No dividend paid*	
19 Dividend cover	*No dividend paid*		*No dividend paid*	
20 Net assets per share	2810.5 / 1964.9	£1.43	2913.7 / 1959.9	£1.49

When asked to 'write a report on the financial position and performance' of a company, it is not sufficient just to comment on each ratio. An attempt should be made to analyse and comment of key themes - perhaps more fully than that provided below.

Report on the financial position and performance of Marks and Spencer plc for the year 2023, which should be read in conjunction with the analysis of the 2022 figures appearing after **Illustration 7.2.**

- *Introduction.* This report is based on 20 ratios calculated from the published annual report of Marks and Spencer plc for 2023.
- *Financial position.* The current and quick ratios of the company have fallen, but the current ratio is still higher than Tesco's (0.72 in 2023). However, the quick ratio is lower than Tesco's (0.58) in 2023). The company has hardly had any change in the efficiency ratios between the two years, and the working capital cycle is very low at 2 days (36 + 3.8 - 37.6). There has been a small increase in share capital, the details of which appear in Note 24 of the Annual Report but further details show that this increase arises from the issue of shares in respect of employee share options. It is becoming increasingly common for large companies to delay in paying their suppliers and, while there is a cash flow benefit, ethical questions arise. There has been a substantial reduction in borrowing and the gearing ratio has fallen accordingly. Although gearing was on the high side, Marks and Spencer does, however, have the strength and reputation to maintain such a level of

gearing; clearly, a decision has been taken to reduce gearing. Associated with this reduction in gearing, the interest cover has risen. Overall, this indicates that shareholders' risk has fallen.

- *Overall profitability.* There was a 10 per cent increase in sales revenue and a 10 per cent fall in operating profit. Although the return on capital employed has increased to 11 per cent from the previous year's 9 per cent, the profitability of the company, including the gross margin at 34 per cent, has otherwise remained steady. The asset turnover has also improved.
- *Stock market.* The share price rose to 167p in 2023 while the FTSE 100 rose by 4 per cent in this year. The P/E ratio fell substantially, indicating the market's fall in confidence about the future prospects of the shares. The dividend yield has risen largely as a result of the fall in the share price. The dividend cover indicates that the company has maintained its policy of maintaining the proportion of profits distributed to shareholders. Even though the net assets per share have dropped by 4 per cent, the market seems to be confident in Marks and Spencer shares as an investment during this year.

2 Current ratio; liquidity ratio; capital gearing; interest cover. Profits, quality of assets and cash flows are also important. Z-scores take into account various combinations of similar information including working capital, total gross assets, retained earnings, earnings before interest and tax, market value of equity and book value of debt.

3 Group statement of financial position of Grand plc and its subsidiary at 31 December year 6

	£m	Workings
Non-current assets	255	180 + 75
Goodwill	10	90 − 60% (45 + 55) = 30
		30 − 20 impairment
Current assets	100	80 + 20
Total assets	365	
Current liabilities	45	30 + 15
Minority interest	32	40% (45 + 35)
Ordinary share capital	150	Grand only
Retained earnings		Grand 170. Deduct share of post-acquisitions loss 60% (55 − 35) = 12 Impairment 20
	138	170 − 12 − 20
Liabilities and equity	365	

4 Turnover, operating profit and net assets for each class of business and for each geographic sector.

5 The key ratios for Gobbiediggan International plc are calculated as follows:

Segment	UK		Africa		South America	
	Year 1	Year 2	Year 1	Year 2	Year 1	Year 2
Operating profit	80 900	78 760	40 200	44 175	20 40	21 60
Operating assets	8.9%	10.26%	20%	25.1%	50%	35%
Operating profit	80 800	78 860	40 300	44 270	20 100	21 180

Segment	UK		Africa		South America	
	Year 1	Year 2	Year 1	Year 2	Year 1	Year 2
Sales	10%	9.1%	13.3%	16.3%	20%	11.7%
Sales	800 900	860 760	300 200	270 175	100 40	180 60
Operating assets	0.89	1.13	1.5	1.54	2.5	3.0

It is true that profits in the UK are declining, in spite of a modest increase in sales. However, the UK produces the bulk of the company's profits; the amount of capital employed has declined, and the profitability of the UK (in terms of return on capital employed, ROCE) has increased. The UK may be a mature market, with limited long-term prospects, but for the foreseeable future it is still very important and profitable to the company.

It is true that sales are declining in the Africa market; but profits are increasing; profitability (in terms of ROCE) is higher than the UK and is increasing. The decline in sales may be a one-off blip, and the company should investigate its causes, and try to increase sales before abandoning the market.

It is true that the South America market has had additional investment of £20,000; but this sum is small compared with the substantial increase in sales, and the high level of profitability. The ROCE declined, but this may be because it will take a little while for the additional investment to generate substantial additional profits.

The ratios may suggest that the company has a reasonable balance of different markets. It may also suggest priorities for developing each of the markets.

6

	£m	Weighting	
Current assets	1,520		
Current liabilities	(1,891)		
Working capital (WC)	(371)		
Non-current assets	5,633		
Current assets	1,520		
Total assets (TGA)	7,153		
Retained profits (RP)	5,282		
Profit before interest and tax (PBIT)	852		
Market capitalization (MV)			
1,582 million @ £3.70	5,853		
Current liabilities	1,891		
Non-current liabilities	3,079		
Total liabilities (BV)	4,970		
Sales	9,537		
1 WC/TGA	$\frac{(371)}{7,153} = (0.052)$	1.2	(0.062)
2 RP/TGA	$\frac{5,282}{7,153} = 0.738$	1.4	1.034
3 PBIT/TGA	$\frac{852}{7,153} = 0.119$	3.3	0.393
4 MV of equity/BV of debt	$\frac{5,853}{4,970} = 1.178$	0.6	0.707

	£m	Weighting	
5 Sales/TGV	$\frac{9,537}{7,153} = 1.333$	1.0	1.333
Z-score			3.405

As with 2011 when the Z-score was 3.416, this is well above the 'safe level' of 2.99.

Chapter 8

1 Depreciation, valuation of inventories, the distinction between capital expenditure and revenue expenditure, provisions for bad debts, other provisions, impairment of goodwill.

2 Low depreciation figures; profits/losses on sales of non-current assets; other exceptional items; provisions; asset (re)valuations; capitalizing items in the grey area between capital and revenue expenditure; showing alternative earnings per share figures.

3 There is no agreed definition of creative accounting. At the moderate end of the spectrum of creative accounting practices, some exercise of judgement is perfectly legal. At the other extreme, deception is illegal.

4 Accounting standards could reduce or eliminate choices of accounting policy, and require additional disclosures. More effective systems for monitoring and enforcement could also be developed.

5 There may be a conflict of interest between the auditors' wish to earn additional fees from consultancy and their need to remain independent from directors. In practice it is the directors who determine the appointment and remuneration of auditors, although this is subject to approval by the shareholders. Many of the problems are criticisms of the arrangements for auditing rather than of the auditors themselves.

6 The Platto Company

	Draft income statement for year ended 31 December Year 8	Budgeted income statement for year ended 31 December Year 9	Answer (i) Revised income statement for year ended 31 December Year 8	Answer (ii) Actual income statement for year ended 31 December Year 9
	£000	£000	£000	£000
Sales revenue	800	790	800	758
Opening inventory	80	90	80	50
Purchases	650	636	650	636
	730	726	730	686
Closing inventory	(90)	(88)	(50)	(88)
Cost of sales	640	638	680	598
Gross profit	160	152	120	160
Profit on sale of asset				25
				185
Impairment			(55)	

	Draft income statement for year ended 31 December Year 8	Budgeted income statement for year ended 31 December Year 9	Answer (i) Revised income statement for year ended 31 December Year 8	Answer (ii) Actual income statement for year ended 31 December Year 9
Depreciation	(40)	(38)	(40)	(26)
Operating expenses	(90)	(92)	(90)	(92)
Profit	30	22	(65)	67

iii When the Uppit Company took over the Platto company it looked as if Platto's profits were steadily declining (from £30,000 in year 8 to £22,000 in year 9). Uppit produced a rapid improvement: it showed that Platto was not making a profit at all - it made a loss of £65,000 in year 8. By year 9, Uppit had turned this around: a profit of £67,000 was produced. But this was all done by 'creative accounting': there was no real improvement in the company's performance. Two extra charges were made against profits in year 8 (writing-down inventories, impairment of non-current assets); this led to extra profits in year 9 (a lower opening inventory figure; a profit on sale of non-current assets). Both of the additional charges in year 8 proved to be too high: the inventories sold for more than their supposed net realizable value; and the assets in Chipping Sodbury sold for more than their supposed fair value. There was no real improvement in performance (and it no longer has Chipping Sodbury!).

7 Information to appear in published accounts should help the various users to make informed decisions and since a company has a relationship with society in general, these days, that will include so-called 'corporate social reporting'. Thus, it is a relatively recent concern for accountants. An alternate view is that a business's primary responsibility is to maximize profit and while it will have to follow the law, there is no reason or requirement to go any further in terms of social responsibility and disclosure.

- The company might produce additional data since it might foresee imminent government regulations.
- The company might wish to build a reputation with the public (e.g. The Body Shop).
- The company might wish to demonstrate it is considering the needs of various user groups.
- The company might feel under pressure from various pressure groups (e.g. Shell).

Among the information that might be disclosed:

- About employees: numbers, salaries, benefits, conditions in developing countries, industrial accidents, policies on employing workers with disabilities, involvement with and secondment of staff to local charities.

Chapter 9

1 a Sales made for cash are credited to the sales account and debited to the *cash account.*

b Sales made on credit to Smith are debited to the Smith account, and credited to the *sales account.*

c Purchases made for cash are credited to the cash account, and debited to the *purchases account.*

d Purchases made on credit from Anirroc Company are debited to the purchases account and credited to the *Anirroc Company* (Anirroc is a creditor).

e Smith, a debtor, pays us part of what he owes; the amount is credited to the Smith account and debited to the *cash account.*

f The provision for bad debts is increased by £30. This amount is debited to the income statement as an expense, and credited to the *provision for bad debts account.*

2 Sales, creditors, share capital, share premium.

3 All of them.

4 Statement (b) is true.

5

Carlos cash account

Date	Description	Amount	Date	Description	Amount
		£			£
1 Jul	Capital	40,000	5 Jul	Expenses (rent)	5,000
3 Jul	Spano Bank	15,000	8 Jul	Furniture and equipment	11,000
27 Jul	Sales	4,000	19 Jul	Expenses	2,500
14 Sep	Minki Cabs	15,000	10 Aug	Purchases	3,300
21 Sep	Sales	24,000	30 Aug	Motosales	40,000
			6 Sep	General expenses	3,300

Carlos capital account

Date	Description	Amount	Date	Description	Amount
		£			£
			1 Jul	Cash	40,000

General expenses account

Date	Description	Amount	Date	Description	Amount
		£			£
5 Jul	Cash (rent)	5,000			
19 Jul	Cash	2,500			
6 Sep	Cash	3,300			

Furniture and equipment account

Date	Description	Amount	Date	Description	Amount
2004		£			£
8 Jul	Cash	11,000			

Purchases account

Date	Description	Amount	Date	Description	Amount
		£			£
13 Jul	Motosales Ltd	50,000			
10 Aug	Cash	3,300			
16 Aug	Motosales	22,000			

Motosales Ltd (payables) account

Date	Description	Amount	Date	Description	Amount
		£			£
30 Aug	Cash	40,000	13 Jul	Purchases	50,000
			16 Aug	Purchases	22,000

Sales account

Date	Description	Amount	Date	Description	Amount
		£			£
			27 Jul	Cash	4,000
			3 Aug	Minki Cabs	18,000
			21 Sep	Cash	24,000

Minki Cabs (receivables) account

Date	Description	Amount	Date	Description	Amount
		£			£
3 Aug	Sales	18,000	14 Sep	Cash	15,000

Trial balance as at 30 September

	Debit	Credit
	£	£
Capital		40,000
Spano Bank loan		15,000
Cash	32,900	
General expenses	10,800	
Furniture and equipment	11,000	
Purchases	75,300	
Payable (Motosales)	32,000	
Sales		46,000
Receivables (Minki Cabs)	3,000	
	133,000	133,000

Income statement of Carlos for the three months ending 30 September		
	£	£
Sales		46,000
Cost of sales		
Opening inventory	0	
Purchases	75,300	
Deduct Closing inventory	38,100	
Cost of goods sold		37,200
Gross profit		8,800
General expenses		10,800
Loss		2,000
Statement of financial position of Carlos as at 30 September		
Fixed assets		
Furniture and equipment		11,000
Current assets		
Inventory	38,100	
Receivables	3,000	
Cash	32,900	
		74,000
Total assets		85,000
Capital	40,000	
Loss	(2,000)	
		38,000
Loan		15,000
Payables (creditors)		32,000
		85,000

6 Killip's ledger accounts

Cash account

Date	Description	Amount	Date	Description	Amount
		£			£
1 Aug	Capital	5,000	2 Aug	Office equipment	4,100
11 Aug	Sales	650	4 Aug	Office expenses (rent)	500
31 Aug	OneAlpha Ltd	550	15 Aug	Travelling expenses	135
			23 Aug	Salaries and subcontracting	700
			29 Aug	Dubya Smith	80

Capital account

Date	Description	Amount	Date	Description	Amount
		£			£
			1 Aug	Cash	5,000

Office equipment account

Date	Description	Amount	Date	Description	Amount
		£			£
2 Aug	Cash	4,100			

Office expenses account

Date	Description	Amount	Date	Description	Amount
		£			£
4 Aug	Cash (rent)	500			
7 Aug	Dubya Smith (stationery)	120			

Advertising account

Date	Description	Amount	Date	Description	Amount
		£			£
6 Aug	Journal of Man	250			

Journal of Man (payable) account

Date	Description	Amount	Date	Description	Amount
		£			£
			6 Aug	Advertising	250

Dubya Smith (receivable) account

Date	Description	Amount	Date	Description	Amount
		£			£
29 Aug	Cash	80	7 Aug	Office expenses	120

Sales account

Date	Description	Amount	Date	Description	Amount
		£			£
			11 Aug	Cash	650
			20 Aug	OneAlphaLtd	2,200

Travelling expenses account

Date	Description	Amount	Date	Description	Amount
		£			£
15 Aug	Cash	135			

OneAlpha Ltd (receivable) account

Date	Description	Amount	Date	Description	Amount
		£			£
20 Aug	Sales	2,200	31 Aug	Cash	550

Salaries and subcontracting account

Date	Description	Amount	Date	Description	Amount
		£			£
23 Aug	Cash	700			

Trial balance as at 31 August

	Debit	Credit	Calculation of balances
Cash	685		6,200 − 5,515
Capital		5,000	
Office equipment	4,100		
Office expenses	620		500 + 120
Advertising	250		
Journal of Man		250	
Dubya Smith		40	120 − 80
Sales		2,850	650 + 2,200
Travelling expenses	135		
OneAlpha Ltd	1,650		2,200 − 550
Salaries and subcontracting	700		
	8,140	8,140	

Income statement for month ending 31 August

Sales		2,850
Office expenses	620	
Advertising	250	
Travelling expenses	135	

Statement of financial position as at 31 August

Non-current assets		
Office equipment		4,100
Current assets		
Debtors	1,650	

Sales and subcontracting	700	1,705	Cash	685	2,335
Profit		1,145	**Total assets**		6,435
			Current liabilities		
			Journal of Man	250	
			Dubya Smith	40	290
			Equity		6,145
			Capital	5,000	
			Profit	1,145	
					6,145
					6,435

7 Cass Hawin

Cass Hawin: bank reconciliation **Balance according to cash book**	**£***	
Add Interest received	200	
Deduct Bank charges	(150)	
Updated cash book balance	£100	
Balance according to bank statement	£(2,000)	
Unpresented cheques	(1,500)	increasing the overdraft
Add Cash deposited on 31 March	3,600	reducing the overdraft
Updated bank statement balance	£100	

*The balance in the cash book would be £50 (debit) before recording the interest received (debit) and the bank charges (credit).

Chapter 10

1 Noddy

Income statement of Noddy's business for the year ended 31 December year 6		**Statement of financial position as at 31 December year 6**		
	£			**£**
Sales	130,000	Shop premises		400,000
General expenses	(120,000)	**Total assets**		400,000
Profit	10,000	Payables		20,000
		Capital	370,000	
		Profit	10,000	
		Equity		380,000
		Total liabilities and equity		400,000

2 Mona Ramsey

Income statement of Mona Ramsey for the year ended 30 September year 3			Statement of financial position as at 30 September year 3		
		£			£
Sales revenue		267,321	**Current assets**		
Opening inventory	20,000		Inventory	15,000	
Purchases	188,000		Receivables	11,000	
	208,000		Bank	24,321	50,321
			Total assets		50,321
Deduct Closing inventory	15,000		**Current liabilities**		
Cost of goods sold		193,000	Payables		13,000
Gross profit		74,321	**Equity**		
General expenses	8,000		Capital at 1 October year 2	27,000	
Rent, rates, insurance	17,000		Profit for year	10,321	37,321
Wages	39,000	64,000			50,321
Net profit		10,321			

3 Sally Glen

Income statement of Sally Glen for the year ended 31 December year 8		
	£	£
Sales revenue		365,000
Opening inventory	18,000	
Purchases	242,000	
	260,000	
Deduct Closing inventory	19,000	
Cost of goods sold		241,000
Gross profit		124,000
General expenses	8,000	
Rent, rates, insurance	23,000	
Wages	34,000	
Depreciation: premises	7,000	
Depreciation: vehicle	4,500[1]	
		76,500
Net profit		47,500

[1] Van at cost £32,000 minus provision for depreciation at 31 December year 7, £14,000, gives a net book value of £18,000 at the beginning of the year. The depreciation charge is 25 per cent of 18,000 = £4,500.

Statement of financial position of Sally Glen as at 31 December year 8			
Non-current assets	Cost	Provision for depreciation	Net book value
	£	£	£
Shop premises	350,000	21,000	
		+ 7,000	
		28,000	322,000
Delivery van	32,000	14,000	
		+ 4,500	
		18,500	13,500
			335,500
Current assets			
Inventory	19,000		
Receivables	60,000		
Bank	23,000		102,000
Total assets			437,500
Current liabilities			
Payables			20,000
Equity			
Capital as at 31 Dec year 7		370,000	
Add Profit for year		47,500	
			417,500
Total liabilities and equity			437,500

4 Mary Rushen

Income statement of Mary Rushen for the year ended 30 June year 5		
	£	£
Sales		320,000
Opening inventory	12,000	
Purchases	155,000	
	167,000	
Deduct Closing inventory	7,000	
Cost of goods sold		160,000
Gross profit		160,000
General expenses	13,000	
Repairs and maintenance	10,600	

Income statement of Mary Rushen for the year ended 30 June year 5		
	£	£
Wages	37,000	
Depreciation: freehold buildings	10,000	
Depreciation: fixtures and fittings	4,400	
		75,000
Net profit		85,000

Statement of financial position of Mary Rushen as at 30 June year 5			
Fixed assets	**Cost**	**Provision for depreciation**	**Net book value**
	£	£	£
Freehold buildings	400,000	80,000	
		+ 10,000	310,000
Fixtures and fittings	44,000	90,000	
		30,800	
		+ 4,400	8,800
		35,200	318,800
Current assets			
Inventory	7,000		
Receivables	8,000		
Cash and bank	7,400		22,400
Total assets			341,200
Current liabilities			
Payables			18,000
Equity			
Capital as at 30 June year 4	238,200		
Add Profit for year	85,000		323,200
			341,200

5 Brad Head

Income statement of Brad Head for year ended 31 December year 3		
	£	£
Sales revenue		660,000
Opening inventory	28,000	
Purchases	255,000	
	283,000	

Income statement of Brad Head for year ended 31 December year 3		
	£	£
Closing inventory	13,000	
Cost of sales		270,000
Gross profit		390,000
General expenses		9,000
Light and heating 19,000 + 2,000		21,000
Rent, rates, insurance 65,000 − 4,400		60,600
Wages		44,000
Depreciation: fixtures and fittings		2,200
Depreciation: MV		9,000
Depreciation: plant and machinery		22,000
Increase in provision for bad debts		600
Bad debt written off		2,100
Total expenses		170,500
Operating profit		219,500
Interest paid		3,500
Profit for the year		216,000

Statement of financial position as at 31 December year 3			
Non-current assets	**Cost**	**Depn**	**NBV**
	£	**£**	**£**
Fixtures and fittings	22,000	13,200	
		2,200	6,600
Plant and machinery	220,000	24,000	
		22,000	174,000
Vehicles	60,000	15,000	
		9,000	36,000
			216,600
Current assets			
Inventories			13,000
Receivables (98,100 − 2,100)	96,000		
Provision for bad debts (1,800 + 600)	(2,400)		93,600
Prepayment			4,400
Cash (6,400 − 6,000)			400
Total assets			328,000

Equity		
Capital as at 31 December year 2	35,000	
Profit for year	216,000	
Drawings	(6,000)	245,000
Current liabilities		
Payables	31,000	
Accruals	2,000	33,000
Non-current liabilities		
Bank loan		50,000
		328,000

6 Ellie's Ltd

Income statement of Ellie's Ltd as at 31 December year 1	£	£
Sales		248,300
Cost of goods sold		
Opening inventory	19,500	
Purchases	167,000	
	186,500	
Less Closing inventory	21,000	165,500
Gross profit		82,800
Printing and stationery	2,400	
Wages	12,300	
Bad debt written off	500	
Increase in provision for bad debts (650 − 600)	50	
Rent (1,500 − 400)	1,100	
Electricity (1,100 + 200)	1,300	
Depreciation on furniture and fittings (25% × 10,000)	2,500	
Depreciation on cars (25% × 20,000)	5,000	
Profit on disposal of van (8,400 − 4,200 − 4,750)	(550)	
General expenses	1,400	26,000
Operating profit		56,800
Corporation tax		15,000
Profit after tax		41,800

Statement of financial position of Ellie's as at 31 December year 1			
Fixed assets	**Cost**	**Accumulated depreciation**	**Net book value**
	£	£	£
Fixtures and fittings	12,000	4,500	7,500
Vehicles	20,000	10,000	10,000
			17,500
Current assets			
Inventories		21,000	
Receivables (61,000 − 500)	60,500		
Less Provision for bad debts	(650)	59,850	
Prepaid rent		400	
Cash		450	
Total assets			81,700
Current liabilities			99,200
Payables		13,400	
Accruals		200	
Taxation		15,000	
			28,600
Equity			
Share capital		100	
Share premium		11,600	
Retained profits as at 31 December year 0	17,100		
For year to 31 December year 1	41,800	58,900	
			70,600
			99,200

Note
Dividends payable are now not normally recognized until after they have been approved by shareholders.
It may be assumed that the above financial statements were finalized after the annual general meeting.

7 Bulgham, Dhoon and Barony

Income statement of Bulgham, Dhoon and Barony for the year ended 31 December year 9		
	£	£
Sales revenue		490,000
Opening inventory	37,000	
Purchases	320,000	
	357,000	
Deduct Closing stock	31,000	

Income statement of Bulgham, Dhoon and Barony for the year ended 31 December year 9				
		£	£	
Cost of sales			326,000	
Gross profit			164,000	
General expenses		45,000		
Rent (28,000 − 4,000)		24,000		
Depreciation		9,000	78,000	
Net profit			86,000	
Profit and loss appropriation account				
Interest on capital				
Bulgham		2,000		
Dhoon		1,500		
Barony		1,000	4,500	
Salaries				
Dhoon		18,250		
Barony		18,250	36,500	
Profit share				
Bulgham		15,000		
Dhoon		15,000		
Barony		15,000	45,000	
			86,000	
Statement of financial position as at 31 December year 9				
Non-current assets				
Furniture at cost				90,000
Deduct Provision for depreciation (27,000 + 9,000)				36,000
				54,000
Current assets				
Inventories			31,000	
Prepayment			4,000	
Cash			47,000	82,000
Total assets				136,000
Capital accounts:	Bulgham	Dhoon	Barony	
	40,000	30,000	20,000	90,000
Current accounts:	Bulgham	Dhoon	Barony	
	10,000	22,000 Dr	28,000 Dr	
Interest	2,000	1,500	1,000	
Salaries	-	18,250	18,250	
Share of profit	15,000	15,000	15,000	
	27,000	12,750	6,250	46,000
				136,000

Chapter 11

1 - Owners' capital, which is share capital in the case of a company
- Borrowing, which may be short term (e.g. overdraft) or long term (e.g. debentures)
- Retained profits

In addition, expansion can be funded in a variety of ways such as factoring debtors, sale and leaseback of premises.

2 Preference shareholders receive a fixed rate of dividend. No dividend can be paid to ordinary shareholders unless the preference dividend has been paid. There is no fixed rate of dividend for ordinary shareholders: they may receive very substantial dividends, or none at all.

Preference shares are usually *cumulative*, which means that if their dividend is not paid for one or more years, all arrears of preference dividends must be paid before any ordinary dividends are paid.

3 The main advantages of gearing (or borrowing) are that, if the company is successful, it can 'gear up' the return to ordinary shareholders. If a company can borrow money at, say, 7 per cent, and invest it to earn, say, 10 per cent, the whole of the extra profits belongs to the ordinary shareholders. The more the company borrows, the more profit it will make. Such borrowing also has the advantage that it enables companies to finance expansion relatively quickly, and at a relatively modest cost. Interest is an allowable expense for corporation tax purposes. If the alternative to borrowing is to issue ordinary shares, the issue costs of shares are likely to be higher, and shareholders are likely to expect a higher return in due course.

The main disadvantage of gearing is the risk of borrowing too much, and the company getting into difficulty. If a company has excessive borrowing, suppliers and lenders may be reluctant to do business with it. As long as a company has to pay only, say, 7 per cent for its borrowing, and is able to earn, say, 10 per cent, it should be alright. But if interest rates rise very much, or (more likely) if earnings are significantly reduced - or the company has no earnings - in particular years, it is likely to get into serious financial difficulties. Substantial borrowing is usually secured on some of the company's assets, and if the company is unable to meet the repayments, the lenders may require the assets to be sold, and the company could be forced into liquidation.

High gearing exaggerates the effects of changes in earnings before interest and taxes (EBIT) on earnings for ordinary shareholders. When EBIT is good, it is very, very good for the ordinary shareholders. But when EBIT is bad, it can be horrid for the ordinary shareholders - there may be no dividends and the share price may collapse. High gearing is associated with high risk.

4 a

	TimeBall Co		DownsPier Co	
	Year 6	Year 7	Year 6	Year 7
Debentures	100	140	100	50
Debentures + equity	300	342.2	300	284.1
i Capital gearing ratio	33⅓%	40.9%	33⅓%	17.6%
Operating profit	20	21.6	20	17.5
÷ interest	9	12.6	9	4.5
ii Interest cover	2.2 times	1.7 times	2.2 times	3.9 times
Profit after tax	7.7	6.3	7.7	9.1
Dividend	4	4.1	4	5
iii Dividend cover	1.9 times	1.5 times	1.9 times	1.8 times
iv Proportion of profit paid as dividend	36%	46%	36%	38%

b i The capital gearing ratio shows the proportion of net assets financed by borrowing. The TimeBall Company increased its fixed assets plus current assets less current liabilities; a small part of this was financed by retained profits; it was mainly financed by additional borrowing. It became a higher risk company. The DownsPier Company reduced its fixed assets plus current assets less current liabilities; this was needed, plus an issue of additional shares, and a small amount of profit retained during the year, to provide enough to pay off half of the borrowing. The company's risk was reduced.

ii The interest times cover shows how much the company is earning in relation to the amount of interest payable. In year 6 the interest cover of both companies was very low (2.2 times), which means that nearly half of their EBIT was committed to interest payments. A serious dip in EBIT could make it very difficult for the company to pay the necessary interest. In year 7 the TimeBall Company's interest cover was lower, meaning that the situation became more risky. The DownsPier Company's interest cover increased significantly (though it is still on the low side), and risk was reduced.

iii The dividend cover shows how much profit after tax was available to pay the dividend that the company chose to pay. The TimeBall Company's profit after tax was lower in year 7 than in year 6, and there was a very small increase in dividend, both of which reduced the cover. The DownsPier Company's profit after tax increased significantly (by 18 per cent), but the increase in dividend was more substantial (25 per cent) and so the dividend cover was reduced.

iv The proportion of profits paid out as the dividend is the same information as in (iii) above, but expressed the other way around (the reciprocal expressed as a percentage).

c

	TimeBall Co		DownsPier Co	
	Year 6	Year 7	Year 6	Year 7
Return on shareholders' capital employed (ROSCE)				
Profit after tax	7.7	6.3	7.7	9.1
Shareholders' capital employed	200	202.2	200	234.1
ROSCE	3.85%	3.1%	3.85%	3.9%
Return on total long-term capital employed				
Operating profit	20	21.6	20	17.5
Debentures + equity	300	342.2	300	284.1
Return	6.7%	6.3%	6.7%	6.2%

In year 7 the TimeBall Company increased its operating profit, but because of extra debenture interest, its profitability was reduced.

In year 7 the DownsPier Company managed a small increase in the return on ordinary shareholders' capital employed; although its operating profit was lower than in the previous year, its debenture interest was halved. The ordinary shareholders had put more money into the company, and they earned just enough to make it worthwhile.

Gross profit/sales (%)	40	40	40	43
Operating profit/sales (%)	20	19.6	20	18.4

The TimeBall Company maintained the same gross profit ratio from year 6 to year 7, but its operating profit as a percentage of sales declined; this must have been due to operating expenses increasing more than sales.

The DownsPier Company's gross profit ratio increased from year 6 to year 7; perhaps it concentrated on its most profitable lines, and the total amount of sales declined. Its operating profit as a percentage of sales declined, although the gross profit had increased. This was because operating expenses had increased, both as a percentage of sales, and in total.

The TimeBall Company expanded sales and borrowing in year 6, and its financial position was weaker, as shown by the gearing ratio and interest times cover. But the expansion was not (yet?) worthwhile, and profitability declined. It managed a small increase in dividends, but this was not justified by profits.

The DownsPier Company seems a little safer. Sales declined, and borrowing was reduced, and the gross profit ratio increased, and the amount of net profit increased. The return on ordinary shareholders' capital increased very slightly and there was a substantial increase in dividend - more than was justified by the increase in profits.

5
- Legal position: balance of retained profits is the maximum sum payable.
- Cash flow position: there must be money available to pay a dividend.
- Investment opportunities: if cash is required for profitable investment, that would tend to reduce sums available to pay a dividend. And vice versa.
- Consistency of dividend policy: companies tend to follow a consistent payout policy and investors who approve of that policy would be attracted to become shareholders.
- Signal to the stock market: a company with poor performance this year might maintain its dividend in order to convey its confidence in its future performance.

Chapter 12

1 High levels of working capital make life easier for managers. Sales can be made to anyone without worrying about collecting the money in. Having large amounts of stock is convenient to satisfy all demands. Having substantial sums of money in the bank is also very convenient - there is no need to plan it properly, and there is always money available. High levels of working capital also lead to high current ratios, which make the company look financially stronger in terms of its ability to pay its creditors as they fall due.

2 Receivables can be reduced to little or nothing (or even negative) if customers are required to pay in advance. Some businesses have no inventories, or ensure that deliveries are 'just in time'. If there is a significant trade payables figure, then working capital can be negative. This is not unusual with retailers.

3 At first it arises with attempts to expand with insufficient long-term capital. There might be significant increases in non-current assets, inventory and receivables; but then the business finds that it is unable to finance these. Payables increase; current and liquidity ratios fall; and the company runs out of money. It may then have to operate on a cash only basis, and start to sell off assets.

4 Prompt paperwork, with invoices and reminders; follow-up letters and telephone calls; personal visits. Threatening to cut off supplies and/or legal action. Implementing threats. Offering cash discounts for early payment. Charging interest on late payment.

A company might deliberately increase the length of time that customers are allowed to pay if this is likely to lead to increases in sales, and to generate additional profits greater than the cost of financing the additional debtors.

5 Inventory holding costs; and the costs of ordering (which may include placing the order, monitoring receipt and payment of invoice). It also considers the volume of usage during the year, and the price per unit.

6 By careful planning and monitoring of cash receipts and payments; ensuring that there are sufficient funds to meet all planned requirements; and not authorizing unplanned payments.

7 Congle.

Applying the EOQ formula the ordering quantity will be the square root of the placed orders:

$$\sqrt{\frac{2 \times 40{,}000 \times £20}{1.25 \times 0.32}} = \sqrt{\frac{1{,}600{,}000}{0.4}} = \sqrt{4{,}000{,}000} = 2{,}000$$

The number of orders each year will be 40,000 ÷ 2,000 = 20.

The annual ordering cost = £20 × 20 times per annum = £400. Goods will be delivered (365 ÷ 20 =) every 18 days.

The average inventory level will be half of the amount delivered, i.e.

$$\frac{1}{2} \times 2{,}000 \times £1.25 = £1{,}250$$

The annual inventory holding cost is £1,250 × 32% = £400.

8 Fleshwick Traders

Annual cost of receivables now: £90,000 × 17% = £15,300.

Annual sales are £365,000, i.e. £1,000 per day.

Existing receivables figure is £90,000, i.e. 90 days.

Expected reduction in receivables applies to one-third of receivables, i.e. £30,000.

Reduction is from 90 days to 10 days, i.e. a reduction of (eight-ninths).

Eight-ninths of £30,000 is £26,667.

Annual interest saved is 17 per cent of £26,667 = £4,533.

Annual cost of discount on one-third of annual sales is £121,667 × 2.5% = £3,042.

a It is worth offering the discount because the amount of interest saved is greater than the cost of the discount offered.

b The annual interest saved is £4,533; discount costing up to £4,533 could be offered without reducing profits. £4,533 as a percentage of eight-ninths (one-third of annual sales) of £121,667 is 3.726%.

c Five per cent discount to one-third of existing customers would cost £6,085.

The annual interest saved would be £4,533.

The additional cost would be £6,085.

The additional contribution required would be £1,552.

Additional annual sales to achieve this contribution (contribution is one-fifth of sales) is 5 × £1,552 = £7,760.

This is near enough for most purposes, but for the mathematically inclined it is rather simplistic.

A more accurate calculation would be as follows:

Let I = the increase in sales required to finance the discount.

The cost of the discount is one-third (365,000 + I) × 0.05, less the interest saving, which is 17 per cent of eight-ninths of one-third of (365,000 + I). This will be equal to the amount of the additional contribution required, which is 20 per cent of the additional sales. We can say, therefore, that

$$\left[\frac{1}{3}(365{,}000 + I) \times 0.05\right] - \left[0.17 \times \frac{8}{9} \times \frac{1}{3} \times \frac{90}{365}(365{,}000 + I)\right] = 0.2 \times I$$

The amount of the additional contribution required (solving the above equation) is £7,913.

9 Stokeypokey

a Income statement

		£000
Sales		6,180
Cost of sales		4,944
Gross profit		1,236
Rent	400	
Other expenses	165	
Depreciation	10	575
Net profit		661

b Statement of financial position as at end of year

Non-current assets at cost		100
Less provision for depreciation		10
		90
Current assets		
Inventories	560	
Receivables	1,400	
Prepayment	100	
Cash	71	2,131
Total assets		2,221
Liabilities and equity		
Payables		560
Loan		1,000
Branch profit		661
		2,221

c

	Jan	Feb	Mar	Apr	May	Jun	Jul	Aug	Sep	Oct	Nov	Dec
	£000	£000	£000	£000	£000	£000	£000	£000	£000	£000	£000	£000
Receipts												
from receivables	-	-	100	200	300	400	480	560	640	700	700	700
Payments for												
purchases		240	240	320	384	448	512	560	560	560	560	560

	Jan	Feb	Mar	Apr	May	Jun	Jul	Aug	Sep	Oct	Nov	Dec
	£000	£000	£000	£000	£000	£000	£000	£000	£000	£000	£000	£000
Rent	100		100			100			100			100
Fittings	50								50			
Expenses	10	10	10	10	15	15	15	16	16	16	16	16
Opening												
balance	1,000	840	590	340	210	111	(52)	(99)	(115)	(201)	(77)	47
Net receipts	(160)	(250)	(250)	(130)	(99)	(163)	(47)	(16)	(86)	124	124	24
	840	590	340	210	111	(52)	(99)	(115)	(201)	(77)	47	71

Workings												
	Jan	Feb	Mar	Apr	May	Jun	Jul	Aug	Sep	Oct	Nov	Dec
Sales	100	200	300	400	480	560	640	700	700	700	700	700
Purchases	240	240	320	384	448	512	560	560	560	560	560	560

d The business looks highly profitable. Stokeypokey plans to put £1m into the Northern Ireland branch and expects to earn £661,000 profit: a return on capital of just over 66 per cent per annum.

The gross profit ratio is expected to be 20 per cent. The net profit/sales ratio is expected to be 10.7 per cent. The main reason for the high ROCE that capital employed is fairly low, partly because the premises are rented.

Although profits look very good, it will take a little longer to generate cash flows to match. Rapid expansion in sales means that cash receipts from receivables tend to lag behind payments. A rapidly expanding and profitable business is often 'cash hungry' in the early stages. In this venture the branch pays out more cash than it receives in each of the first nine months, and the initial £1m will not be sufficient to avoid an overdraft by September.

By careful planning it might be possible to avoid an overdraft. Perhaps it could arrange to delay some payments in September, such as for the additional fittings, or make an extra effort to get debtors to pay more quickly in August.

Depreciation is an expense in calculating profit, but it is not a cash payment.

Chapter 13

1 Only (c) is true.

2 Direct costs are directly attributable to a particular job, product or service. Indirect costs are costs that cannot be identified with the individual cost unit.

3 Hourly paid staff are a variable cost, while employees on a monthly salary are fixed costs.

4 Only (a) is true.

5 Manufacturing account for JackDannie for year ended 30 June year 7

Direct materials	£000	£000
Inventory as at 1 July year 6	64	
Purchases during years 6 and 7	390	
	454	

Inventory as at 30 June year 7	(67)		
Cost of direct materials consumed			387
Direct wages			270
Prime cost			657
Manufacturing overheads			
Factory electricity		11	
Factory rent		76	
Indirect manufacturing wages		90	
General factory expenses		12	
Depreciation on machinery		14	
Repairs to machinery		8	211
			868
Total manufacturing costs incurred			
Add Work in progress 1 July year 6			85
			953
Deduct Work in progress 30 June year 7			(78)
Manufacturing cost of goods completed			875
Transferred to income statement			

Income statement for JackDannie year ended 30 June year 7

			£000
Sales revenue			2,200
Cost of sales of finished goods			
Opening inventory		70	
Manufacturing cost		875	
		945	
Closing inventory		(92)	
			853
Gross profit			1,347
Administrative expenses			(420)
Distribution costs			(320)
Profit			607

Statement of financial position of JackDannie as at 30 June year 7

Non-current assets			
Machinery at cost			140
Provision for depreciation	40		
	14		(54)
			86
Current assets			
Inventories direct materials		67	
Work-in-progress		78	

Finished goods		92	
		237	
Receivables		420	
Bank		300	957
Total assets			1,043
Current liabilities			
Payables			66
Capital as at 1 July year 6	370		
Profit for year	607		977
			1,043

Chapter 14

1 The return on investment (ROI) takes the average annual profits during the life of a project and expresses them as a percentage of the capital employed in the project. It is sometimes based on the initial capital employed, and sometimes on the average capital employed over the life of the project.

2 The company's return on capital employed (ROCE) is 10 per cent (£1m as a percentage of £10m).

The ROI of the proposed project is 9 per cent (£180,000 as a percentage of £2m). But these figures are not strictly comparable: the £1m is after tax; and the £180,000 is operating profit (before tax).

If the company had surplus funds, the new ship would increase the company's ROCE because there would be no increase in capital employed, and profits would increase. If the £2m needed was in the bank, the increase in profits would depend on the amount of interest receivable that was lost as a result of buying the ship.

If the company had to raise additional equity, the total return on equity would be lowered because (a) the 9 per cent return is lower than the existing 10 per cent return; and (b) the additional £180,000 is operating profit: it would be less after tax.

If the ship was financed by borrowing, the company's return on equity would increase, assuming that the cost of borrowing was less than 9 per cent per annum.

3 Cash flows

Year	Project A £000	Project B £000
0	(1,000)	(1,000)
1	200	400
2	200	350
3	200	300
4	200	100
5	200	50
6	200	5
7	200	5
8	200	5
Total	1,600	1,215

The payback period of Project A is five years. The payback period of Project B is just less than three years.

Project A produces substantially more cash flows than Project B. If the time value of money is not considered, Project A is much better.

If the discounted cash flow (DCF) was used, whether or not it is worth waiting for the extra money would depend on the discount rate used.

4 a ROI is based on profits and so is compatible with financial accounts. The answer is expressed as a percentage which appears to be easy to understand. It is relatively easily calculated and understood.

However, the approach ignores the timing of the cash flows. A project may have a good ROI but not be worthwhile if the delay in receiving it is too long.

b Payback period is easy to understand and easy to calculate. It uses cash flows rather than profits, and the emphasis is on getting back the money quickly.

But payback period ignores cash flows received after the end of the payback period. Use of payback period could lead to a project being accepted that makes very little money, but pays back quickly; and a very profitable project could be rejected because it takes a little longer to pay back.

5 The project will generate £35,000 profits a year for five years, giving total profits of £175,000. This looks poor.

But, profits are measured after charging depreciation, which amounts to £40,000 a year. Annual cash flows are therefore £75,000 a year.

Using a discount rate of 10 per cent, the project gives a net present value (NPV) of about £84,300, as follows:

Year 1	0.909	×	75,000	=	68,175
Year 2	0.826	×	75,000	=	61,950
Year 3	0.751	×	75,000	=	56,325
Year 4	0.683	×	75,000	=	51,225
Year 5	0.621	×	75,000	=	46,575
	3.790	×	75,000	=	284,300

After deducting the initial cost of the investment (£284,300 − £200,000) the NPV of the project is £84,300, which makes it acceptable if the company's cost of capital is 10 per cent.

The project would still be just about acceptable with a cost of capital of 25 per cent (£75,000 × 2.689 = £201,675) because the net present values of the future cash flows would still be slightly above the initial cost.

6

		Kippering	Queenies
a	Average annual profits	£	£
	Total cash flows	75,000	90,000
	Total depreciation	50,000	50,000
	Total profits	25,000	40,000
	Average annual profits	5,000	8,000
b	Return on initial capital employed	10%	16%
c	Return on average capital employed	20%	32%

					Kippering		Queenies
d	Payback period				2⅓ years		3.2 years
				£000		£000	
e	NPV using 10%	1	0.909	25	22,727	5	4,545
		2	0.826	20	16,528	15	12,396
		3	0.751	15	11,269	25	18,782
		4	0.683	10	6,830	25	17,075
		5	0.621	5	3,105	20	12,418
					60,459		65,216
					(50,000)		(50,000)
	NPV				10,459		15,216
f	NPV using 25%	1	0.800	25	20,000	5	4,000
		2	0.640	20	12,800	15	9,600
		3	0.512	15	7,680	25	12,800
		4	0.410	10	4,100	25	10,250
		5	0.328	5	1,640	20	6,560
					46,220		43,210
					(50,000)		(50,000)
	NPV				(3,780)		(6,790)
g	Approximate internal rate of return						
	10% plus a proportion of 15%				$\frac{10,459}{(10,459 + 3,780)}$	$\frac{15,216}{(15,216 + 6,790)}$	
					0.735 × 15		0.691 × 15
					11.02		10.36
	+ 10				21.02%		20.36%

7 If it is decided to go ahead with the proposal the additional cash outflows at the beginning of the project would be:

Modifications to existing machinery	£100,000
Additional working capital	£50,000
Initial marketing costs	£60,000
	£210,000

The book value of the other machine is irrelevant; it has no alternative use or disposal value and so there is no 'opportunity cost'.

The cost of the consultants' report has already been incurred whether the project goes ahead or not, and so is irrelevant.

The cash flows generated by each unit of sales are:

Selling price		£60
Variable costs		
Materials	11	
Labour	6	
Variable overheads	13	£30
		£30

The costs of general fixed overheads and of interest will be incurred whether or not the project goes ahead and so they are not relevant.

	Year 0	Year 1	Year 2	Year 3	Year 4
Sales (units)	-	3,000	7,000	4,000	1,000
'Contribution' at £30 per unit		90,000	210,000	120,000	30,000
Machinery	(100,000)				
Working capital	(50,000)				50,000
Marketing	(60,000)	(20,000)	(20,000)	(20,000)	(20,000)
Maintenance		(10,000)	(10,000)	(10,000)	(10,000)
Net cash flow	(210,000)	60,000	180,000	90,000	50,000
20% discount factor	1.0	0.833	0.694	0.579	0.482
Present value	(210,000)	50,000	124,920	52,110	24,100

The NPV of the project discounted at 20 per cent is (£251,130 − £210,000 =) £41,130

8 Soderby plc cost of debt capital

Year	Cash flow	Discount factor 10%	NPV	Discount factor 5%	NPV
0	(98)	1	(98)	1	(98)
1	7	0.909	6.36	0.952	6.664
2	7	0.826	5.78	0.907	6.349
3	7	0.751	5.26	0.864	6.048
4	7	0.683	4.78	0.823	5.761
5	107	0.621	66.45	0.784	83.888
			(9.4)		10.71

Interpolation suggests the IRR is $5\% + \frac{10.7}{(9.4 + 10.7)} \times 5$

7.66%

9 a i Next year's dividend: 40 pence × 1.05 = 42 pence

ii Next year's dividend as a % of current share price: $\frac{£0.42}{12} = 3.5\%$

iii Add assumed rate of growth: 5% + 3.5% = 8.5%

b i Risk free 3%

ii Return on shares generally 11%; deduct risk free rate of 3% = market risk premium: 8%

iii Adjust for Beta 8% × 0.75 = 6%; add risk free rate: 6% + 3% = 9%

Chapter 15

1 A budget may be defined as:

> ***A plan, quantified in monetary terms, prepared and approved prior to a defined period of time, usually showing planned income to be generated and/or expenditure to be incurred during that period, and the capital to be employed to attaining a given objective.***

Important parts of the definition are that a budget is a *plan* designed to attain a given *objective* and that it should be *approved* prior to a defined period of time.

2 A fixed budget is based on a planned level of output. A flexible budget (distinguishing between fixed and variable costs) has different versions that vary according to different levels of output.

3 Many advantages are claimed for operating a system of budgetary control, as shown in **Section 13.4**. In such a small business the amount of work to operate a detailed budgetary control system would probably not be worthwhile. As the organization is too small to have a management structure (there would be just one boss) issues of authorizing expenditure, delegation of responsibility, communication and co-ordination would scarcely arise: it would all be in one person's head. However, even in such a small organization, it would be worth defining objectives (perhaps a given sales and profit level for the year, or even for each month), and keeping an eye on actual results on a regular basis (control). It might not be necessary to produce monthly income statements. Monitoring receipts from sales, and payments of expenses (using bank statements) might provide sufficient control information.

4

	Budget August Year 6 £000	Flexed budget August Year 6 £000	Actual results August Year 6 £000	Workings for flexed budget
Sales	600	690	690	
Direct materials	120	138	140	120 + 15%
Direct labour	100	115	117	100 + 15%
Production overheads	200	215	223	100 + (100 + 15%)
Distribution costs	80	89	95	20 + (60 + 15%)
Administrative overheads	60	51.5	70	50 + (10 + 15%)
Total costs	560	608.5	645	
Profit	40	81.5	45	

The fixed budget showed that sales increased from £600,000 to £690,000 and profits increased from £40,000 to £45,000. Some people might be satisfied with an increase in profits of more than 10 per cent when sales increase by 15 per cent. However, as many costs tend to be 'fixed', profits should have increased by significantly more than 15 per cent. The flexed budget shows that profits should have more than doubled.

As there was a 15 per cent increase in sales, a 15 per cent increase in variable costs is expected in the flexed budget. But direct material and direct labour costs increased by £4,000 more than expected. Moreover, all overhead costs increased by more than the flexed budget specified. Overall, costs increased by £85,000 when they should have increased by only £48,500. It seems that, in the effort to increase output by 15 per cent, insufficient attention was paid to the control of costs.

5 A very successful business will have serious cash shortages if its profits are poured into additional assets. This may be a healthy expansion of inventories and receivables in line with sales; and investment in additional non-current assets, and buying shares in other companies. It may be unhealthy if poor control

results in too many assets being bought, excessive inventory levels and fixed assets that are not profitably utilized.

The situation could also arise if substantial loans are repaid, and if the company pays out more as dividends than it earns as profits.

6 Rachel

a **Budgeted income statement**

	Jan	Feb	Mar	Apr	May	Jun	Jul	Aug	Sep	Oct	Nov	Dec	Total
Sales	5,000	5,000	10,000	10,000	10,000	10,000	6,000	6,000	10,000	10,000	10,000	2,500	94,500
Expenses													
Operating expenses	1,000	1,000	2,000	2,000	2,000	2,000	1,200	1,200	2,000	2,000	2,000	500	18,900
Fixed overheads	3,000	3,000	3,000	3,000	3,000	3,000	3,000	3,000	3,000	3,000	3,000	3,000	36,000
	4,000	4,000	5,000	5,000	5,000	5,000	4,200	4,200	5,000	5,000	5,000	3,500	54,900
Profit	1,000	1,000	5,000	5,000	5,000	5,000	1,800	1,800	5,000	5,000	5,000	(1,000)	39,600

b **Cash budget**

	£	£	£	£	£	£	£	£	£	£	£	£	£
	Jan	Feb	Mar	Apr	May	Jun	Jul	Aug	Sep	Oct	Nov	Dec	Total
Receipts													
From receivables	2,500	2,500	5,000	5,000	10,000	10,000	10,000	10,000	6,000	6,000	10,000	10,000	87,000
Payments													
Operating expenses	1,000	1,000	2,000	2,000	2,000	2,000	1,200	1,200	2,000	2,000	2,000	500	18,900
Fixed overheads	1,000	1,000	1,000	1,000	1,000	1,000	1,000	1,000	1,000	1,000	1,000	1,000	12,000
	2,000	2,000	3,000	3,000	3,000	3,000	2,200	2,200	3,000	3,000	3,000	1,500	30,900
Net receipts or deficits	500	500	2,000	2,000	7,000	7,000	7,800	7,800	3,000	3,000	7,000	8,500	56,100
Opening balance	1,000	1,500	2,000	4,000	6,000	13,000	20,000	27,800	35,600	38,600	41,600	48,600	1,000
Closing balance	1,500	2,000	4,000	6,000	13,000	20,000	27,800	35,600	38,600	41,600	48,600	57,100	57,100

c

	£
Profit	39,600
Depreciation	24,000
	63,600
Increase in receivables	
(£12,500 − £5,000)	7,500
Increase in cash	56,100

d Drawings should not exceed profit of £39,600

Chapter 16

1 Most wood, metal and components and sub-assemblies would be treated as direct materials. Cleaning materials, lubricants, and many widely used items of low value such as glue, screws and nails would be treated as indirect materials. Anything that becomes part of the finished item is really a direct material, but with items of low value it is often not worth the trouble of charging them to different jobs. Materials used in the factory which do not become part of the finished item are part of production overheads.

2 a £23m ÷ 1.4m = £16.42867, or £16.43 per hour

b £23m ÷ 1.4m = £16.42867, or £16.43 per hour

The budgeted production overheads for the year are the same as the budgeted wages for the year, so the answers to (a) and (b) are the same.

c 100%

i Dept A £1m ÷ 500,000 hrs = £2 per hour

Dept B £2m ÷ 500,000 hrs = £4 per hour

Dept C £20m ÷ 400,000 hrs = £50 per hour

ii Dept A £5m ÷ 500,000 hrs = £10 per hour

Dept B £8m ÷ 500,000 hrs = £16 per hour

Dept C £10m ÷ 400,000 hrs = £25 per hour

iii Dept A £2 ÷ £10 = 20%

Dept B £4 ÷ £16 = 25%

Dept C £50 ÷ £25 = 200%

d 13 hrs × £16.43 = £213.59

e Labour cost 13 hrs × £16.43 = £213.59 × 100% = £213.59

f Dept A 3 hrs @ £2 = £6

Dept B 6 hrs @ £4 = £24

Dept C 4 hrs @ £50 = £200 £230

g Labour cost

Dept A 3 hrs @ £10 = £ 30 × 20% = £ 6

Dept B 6 hrs @ £16 = £ 96 × 25% = £ 24

Dept C 4 hrs @ £25 = £100 × 200% = £200 £230

In this example, it is assumed that the same wage rate is paid to all operatives within a department; using percentage on direct labour cost therefore gives the same answer as using a direct labour hour rate. If different operatives within a department were paid different hourly rates, the two methods would give different answers.

3

	Contract 1	Contract 2
a	FIFO 1,0001 @ £12 = £12,000	1,500 @ £11 = £16,500
	500 @ £11 = £5,500	
	£17,500	
b	LIFO 500 @ £14 = £7,000	1,000 @ £11 = £11,000
	1,000 @ £11 = £11,000	500 @ £12 = £6,000
	£18,000	£17,000

c Average weighted average = £41,000 ÷ 3,500 = £11.714285

1,500 @ £11.71 = £17,565[2]   1,500 @ £11.71 = £17,565

4 Production overheads are directly allocated to particular cost centres where this is possible; for example, where a machine or a member of staff exclusively belongs to one cost centre. Production overheads are apportioned to cost centres where this is not possible, perhaps on the basis of the number of square metres occupied, or the number of employees. After total production overheads have been calculated they are charged to particular jobs or products, which are said to absorb them.

2 The answer is inaccurate due to rounding. The correct answer would be £17,571.43.

5 Administrative expenses and selling and distribution costs are not absorbed by products. They are not part of product costs; they are not included in closing inventory; they are charged against profits in the period in which they are incurred.

6 a Overhead absorption rate = total overheads £288,000/total number of staff hours 7,200* = £40 per hour*

*(25 × 40) + (3,000 × 2) + (100 × 2) = 7,200 staff hours.

Cost per course:

Pony trekking 25 × 40 = £1,000

General lesson 2 × 40 = £ 80

Advanced riding skills 2 × 40 = £ 80

(Check: 40 pony trekking courses cost £40,000, 3,000 general lessons cost £240,000, 100 advanced riding skills cost 8,000, total £288,000.)

b Staff costs driven by total number of staff hours (40 × 25) + (3,000 × 2) + (100 × 2) = 7,200 hours.

£108,000/7,200 = £15 per hour

Number of brochures (40 × 30) + (3,000 × 1) + (100 × 5) = 4,700. £7,050/4,700 = £1.50 per brochure.

Admin costs driven by number of events (40 × 10) + (3,000 × 4) + (100 × 6) = 13,000 events. £33,800/13,000 = £2.60 per event.

Insurance driven by number of clauses (40 × 14.15) + (3,000 × 1.5) + (100 × 5) = 5,566.

£139,150/5,566 = £25 per clause.

c Reallocation of overheads using ABC:

Pony trekking: (25 staff hours × £15) + (30 brochures × £1.50) + (10 admin events × £2.60) + (14.15 insurance clauses × £25) = £375 + £45 + £26 + £353.75 = £799.75

General lessons: (2 staff hours × £15) + (1 brochure × £1.50) + (4 admin events × £2.60 + (1.5 insurance clauses × £25) = £30 + £1.50 + £10.40 + £37.50 = £79.40

Advanced riding skills: (2 staff hours × £15) + (5 brochures × £1.50) + (6 admin events × £2.60 + (5 insurance clauses × £25) = £30 + £7.50 + £15.6 + £125 = £178.10

Check (£799.75 × 40 courses) + (£79.40 × 3,000 courses) + (£172.90 × 100 courses) = £31,990 + £238,200 + £17,810 = £288,000

d *General advantages*

- More accurate and meaningful product cost information can be determined.
- There is an improvement in management's understanding of costs and their causes.
- Improved management information in terms of performance measurement prevails in budgeting, new products/processes and general cost reduction.

Specific advantages

- Provides quality service at low cost.
- Horizontal view, quality chains.
- Activity-based budgeting can result from this.
- Develop into activity-based management.

Disadvantages

- Behavioural issues, for example, resistance to change.
- Selling benefits to managers.
- Willingness to participate.
- Effect of new performance measures.

7 a Traditional volume based absorption costing

Absorption costing method

This method uses a single volume basis that is the number of holidays sold.

Overhead absorption rate = Total Overheads/Total number of holidays sold

Overhead absorption rate = £800,000/(2,000 + 1,200)

Overhead absorption rate = £250 per holiday

b Activity based costing

Cost centre

i Enquiries
ii Brochure
iii Courier trips

c Advantages and disadvantages of activity based costing

Advantages

- More meaningful product costs
- Improves understanding of overhead costs
- Helps development of non-financial performance
- Targets cost reduction
- Assists in the design of new products and services

Disadvantages

- It is just another method of cost absorption
- Selection of cost drivers may be problematical
- The time and cost of implementation may be prohibitive

Chapter 17

1 Contribution is: sales less variable costs.

Contribution per unit is: selling price less variable costs per unit.

Break-even point is: fixed costs/contribution per unit.

Margin of safety is: expected (or budgeted) sales less break-even point.

2 Fixed costs can be separated from variable costs according to:

a whether they vary with output;

b a given range of output or time.

For example, to manufacture up to 100,000 machines a company might need one supervisor, but beyond 100,000 they might need two supervisors. Hence, the fixed costs will rise in steps as output exceeds expected boundaries.

3 Dannidoon's contribution is (£60 − £35) = £25 per unit; need enough contribution to cover fixed costs of £700,000.

£700,000 ÷ £25 = 28,000 units to break even

4

	September	October	Change
	£000	£000	£000
Sales	600	650	50
Profit	100	120	
Total costs	500	530	30
Variable costs 60% of sales	360	390	
Fixed cost	140	140	
Contribution	240	260	

Contribution/sales ratio September 240 ÷ 600 = 40% or 0.4
October 260 ÷ 650 = 40% or 0.4

Break-even point 140 ÷ 0.4 = £350,000

a With 30,000 hours

		Holiday chalets	Terraced houses		Luxury villas
		£000	£000		£000
Selling price		100	200		800
Variables costs		70	120		420
Contribution per unit		30	80		380
Hours to build a unit		300	600		3,000
Contribution per labour hour		100.00	133.33		126.67
Ranking	3rd	1st	2nd		
Maximum sales	20	30	10		
Optimal production	0	30	4		
Labour hour required	-	18,000	12,000		30,000
Contribution	0	2,400	1,520	Total	3920
					i.e. £3,920,000

If it built 10 luxury villas it would use 30,000 labour hours, which is all that are available. The contribution would be £3,920,000.

b With 51,000 hours

	Holiday chalets	Terraced houses	Luxury villas
	£000	£000	£000
Selling price	100	200	800
Variables costs	70	120	420
Contribution per unit	30	80	380
Hours to build a unit	300	600	3,000
Contribution per labour hour	100.00	133.33	126.67

	Holiday chalets £000	Terraced houses £000	Luxury villas £000	
Ranking	**3rd**	**1st**	**2nd**	
Maximum sales	20	30	10	
Optimal production	10	30	10	
Labour hour required	3,000	18,000	30,000	51,000
Contribution	300	2,400	3,800	Total 6500
				i.e. £6,500,000

With 51,000 hours it would build 30 terraced houses, 10 luxury villas and 10 holiday chalets. The contribution would be £6.5m.

This analysis assumes that there is no interrelated demand and also that, with only 30,000 labour hours, the company believes that it is prepared to cut production of what hitherto it has considered its key product, luxury villas.

c If it built 10 luxury villas it would use 30,000 labour hours, which is all that are available. The contribution would be £3,920,000.

d It would build 30 terraced houses producing a contribution of £2,400,000, and 4 luxury villas producing a contribution of £1,520,000. The total contribution would be £3,920,000.

5

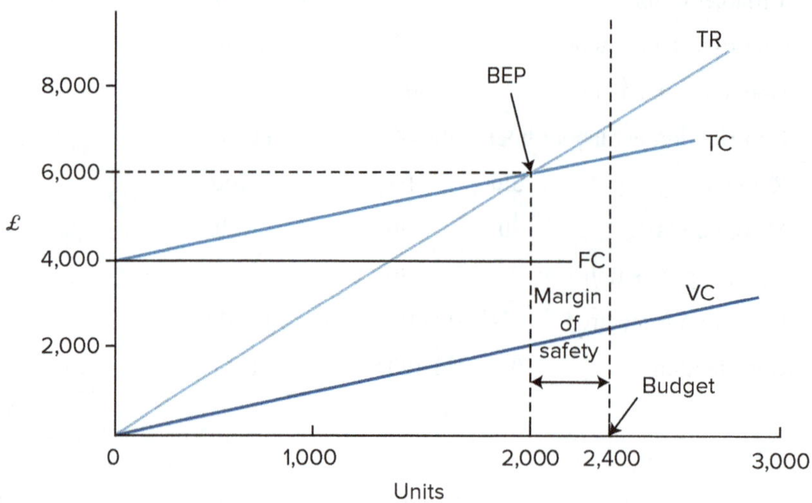

$$\text{BEP} = \frac{\text{Fixed costs}}{\text{Contribution per unit}}$$

Fixed costs = £4,000

Contribution per unit = £2

BEP = 2,000 units

= £6,000

Margin of safety = Budget − BEP

= 2,400 − 2,000

= 400 units

= £1,200

= 16.7%

Chapter 18

1 Corrina made 11 loaves instead of 10, and so it is not surprising that the cost of her materials was more than the £10 she had planned. But her material cost variance was *favourable*. This is because she spent only £10.50 to make 11 loaves whereas the standard cost of making 11 loaves would be £11.

a Direct materials cost variance

Actual cost	Standard cost
	11 loaves @ £1
£10.50	£11

Direct material cost variance

b Direct materials price and usage variances

Actual cost		Actual quantities at standard (or cost budgeted) cost per kg		Standard cost
		10.4 kg @ £1 per kg		11 loaves @ £1
£10.50		£10.40		£11
	Direct material price variance 10p adverse		Direct material usage variance 60p favourable	
		Direct material cost variance 50p favourable		

The price of dough was higher than expected, but this was more than offset by efficient usage. Perhaps she made smaller loaves.

2 Anomelg

Actual cost		Actual hours at standard (or budgeted) rate per hour		Standard cost
		84 hours @		7 @ £300
		£30		£2.50
£2,400		£2,520		£2,100
	Direct labour rate variance £120 favourable		Direct labour efficiency variance £420 adverse	
		Total direct labour cost variance £300 adverse		

a There was an adverse labour cost variance of £300 because it cost more to do seven conveyances than it should have done.

b The adverse cost variance was due to inefficiency. She took 84 hours to do seven conveyances that should have taken only 70 hours. This was partly offset by a reduction in her rate of pay per hour.

3 Wee Lee Cycle Company

a Budget

	£
Sales 10,000 bicycles at £100 each	1,000,000
Costs 10,000 bicycles at £80 each	800,000
Profit	£ 200,000

b Actual

Sales 11,000 bicycles	979,000
Costs 11,000 bicycles	902,000
Profit	£ 77,000

c Budgeted profit margin £100 − £80 = £20

Actual profit margin £979,000 ÷ 11,000 = 89. £89 − £80 = £9. Assumes standard cost of production. Cost variances are separately identified.

Actual volume of sales at actual margin per unit	Actual volume of sales at budgeted margin per unit	Budgeted volume of sales at budgeted margin per unit
11,000 units	11,000 units	10,000 units
@ £9 per unit	@ £20 per unit	@ £20 per unit
£99,000	£220,000	£200,000
Sales margin price variance £121,000 adverse	Sales margin volume variance £20,000 favourable	
Total sales margin variance £101,000 adverse		

Actual cost of producing the actual number that were produced	Standard cost of producing the actual number that were produced
£902,000	11,000 × £80 = 880,000
Total cost variance £22,000 adverse	

d Difference between budgeted and actual profit £200,000 − £77,000 = £123,000

Total of variances	Sales margin variances	£101,000 Adverse
	Cost variances	£ 22,000 Adverse
		£123,000

The most striking features of the results are:

i a lot more bicycles were sold than planned (11,000 instead of 10,000); and

ii profit was a lot lower than planned (£77,000 instead of £200,000).

The problem with sales was not the *volume* of sales, but the *price* of the units sold. The sales revenue was £979,000 for 11,000 bicycles: that is £89 per bicycle instead of £100 per bicycle. The *volume variance* was favourable, but the price variance was unfavourable.

It was planned that each bicycle would generate a profit (or 'margin') of £20. If nothing had changed other than the volume of sales, the additional profit generated would have been 1,000 extra bicycles at £20 each, which is £20,000: there was a favourable sales margin volume variance of £20,000.

Unfortunately, there was also an unfavourable variance because of the average price being reduced from £100 to £89. Instead of making a profit of £20 per bicycle, they made only (£89 − £80 =) £9 per bicycle, or £11 less than planned. The result of the price reduction was that each bicycle sold (11,000) made £11 less than expected. In other words, there was an adverse sales margin price variance of (11,000 × £11=) £121,000.

There was also a problem with costs. Each bicycle was expected to cost £80 to produce. As 11,000 units were produced, total costs should have been (11,000 × 80 =) £880,000. But the actual costs for the month amounted to £902,000.[3] There was an adverse total cost variance of £22,000.[4]

4 Wool Witch Company

			£	£
a	Budgeted profit	5,000 @ £13		65,000
b	Actual profit	Sales	108,000	
	DM	12,200		
	DL	39,500		
	O	9,500	61,200	46,800
	Total variance			18,200

c Direct materials

Actual cost		Actual quantities @ planned price		Standard cost
		3,900 kg		4,000 @ £3
		@ £3 per kg		
£12,200		£11,700		£12,000
	Direct material price variance £500 adverse		Direct material usage variance £300 favourable	
		Direct material cost variance £200 favourable		
Direct labour				

[3] Normally, we expect costs per unit to decrease as the volume of production increases (because fixed costs are spread among more units – what economists call 'economies of scale'). In this example costs per unit have increased even though the volume of production has increased.

[4] It cost £902,000 to produce 11,000 units, that is, £82 per unit, or £2 per unit more than planned. As 11,000 units were produced; the total adverse cost variance was 11,000 × £2 = £22,000.

Actual cost		Actual hours @ planned rate		Standard cost
		3,850 hrs		4,000 @ £10
		@ £10 per hr		
£39,500	Direct labour rate variance £1,000 adverse	38,500	Direct labour efficiency variance £1,500 favourable	£40,000

Direct labour cost variance £500 favourable

Overheads Actual cost		Budgeted hours @ planned rate		Actual hours @ planned rate		Standard cost
		5,000 @ £2 per hr		3,850 @ £2 per hr		4,000 @ £2
£9,500		£10,000		£7,700		£8,000
	Overhead expenditure variance £500 favourable		Overhead capacity utilization variance £2,300 adverse		Overhead efficiency variance £300 favourable	

Overhead volume variance £2,000 adverse

Overhead cost variance £1,500 adverse

Sales margin variances

Selling price	£28
Standard cost DM + DL + 0: £3 + £10 + £2 =	£15
Planned margin	£13

Actual selling price £108,000 ÷ 4,000 = £27

Margin (assuming standard cost)

£27 − £15 = £12

Actual sales		Actual sales @ planned margin		Budgeted sales @ budgeted margin
4,000 @ £12		4,000 @ £13		5,000 @ £13
£48,000		£52,000		£65,000
	Sales margin variance £4,000 adverse		Sales margin volume variance £13,000 adverse	

Direct material cost variance £17,000

d Summary of variances

	£		£	
Direct material price variance	500	adverse		
Direct material usage variance	300	favourable		
Direct material cost variance			200	adverse
Direct labour rate variance	1,000	adverse		
Direct labour efficiency variance	1,500	favourable		
Direct labour cost variance			500	favoured
Overhead expenditure variance	500	favourable		
Overhead capacity utilization variance	2,300	adverse		
Overhead efficiency variance	300	favourable		
Overhead cost variance			1,500	adverse
Sales margin price variance	4,000	adverse		
Sales margin volume variance	13,000	adverse	17,000	adverse
Total variances			18,200	adverse

Efficiency and usage variances were all favourable, which suggests good cost control. There were adverse price variances for materials and labour, which may have been outside the company's control. The main problems were with not producing and selling enough. There was a substantial adverse capacity utilization variance, and also an adverse selling price variance. But the largest adverse variance was in sales volume. Even price reductions failed to produce sales at the planned level.

5 Poleg Limited

	Unit	Original budget	Flexed budget	Actual	Fav	Adv	
Units		1,000	1,400	1,400			
Sales	150	150,000	210,000	212,800			
Materials	67.5	67,500	94,500	121,000			
Labour	30	30,000	42,000	34,000			
VO	15	15,000	21,000	15,000			
Total VCs	112.5	112,500	157,500	170,000			
		-	-				
Contribution	37.5	37,500	52,500	42,800			
FO	7.5	7,500	7,500	6,000			
Profit (i.e. margin)	**30**	**30,000**	**45,000**	**36,800**			
					Fav	**Adv**	
Budgeted profit							30,000
Sales price variance	AQ(AP − SP)	1,400(152 − 150)	1,400 × 2		2,800		
Sales volume contribution variance	SC(AQ − SQ)	37.50 (1,400 − 1,000)	37.50 × 400		15,000		
Standard contribution for actual sales							47,800
Materials							

	Unit	Original budget	Flexed budget	Actual		
price	AQ(AP - SP)	121,000 - (22,000 × 4.50)	121,000 - 99,000		22,000	
efficiency	SP(AQ - SQ)	4.50 (22,000 - 1,400 × 15)	4.50 × (22,000 - 21000)		4,500	
Labour						
rate	AH(AR - SR)	34,000 - (6,800 × 6))	34,000 - 40,800	6,800		
efficiency	SP(AH - SH)	6((6,800 - 1,400 × 5))	6(6,800 - 7,000)	1,200		
Variable overheads		245 - (250 × 1.25)				
rate	AH(AR - SR)	15,000 - (6,800 × 3)	15,000 - 20,400	5,400		
efficiency	SR(AH - SH)	3((6,800 - (1,400*5))	3 × (6,800 - 7,000)	600		
Fixed overheads						
expenditure	Actual - Budget	7,500 - 6,000		1,500		
				15,500	**26,500**	(11,000)
Actual profit						**36,800**

Chapter 19

1 Various definitions are available. A few are reproduced below:

- In 1987, the United Nations Brundtland Commission* defined sustainability as 'meeting the needs of the present without compromising the ability of future generations to meet their own needs'.
- The United States Environmental Protection Agency defines sustainability as: 'Everything that we need for our survival and well-being depends, either directly or indirectly, on our natural environment. To pursue sustainability is to create and maintain the conditions under which humans and nature can exist in productive harmony to support present and future generations.'
- The *Cambridge Dictionary* has a very short definition, 'the quality of being able to continue over a period of time', suggesting a long-term sustainability.

2 Integrated reporting (IR) provides a conceptual framework for understanding how organizations conduct their operations and how to effectively communicate an organization's long-term value proposition to the market. It aims to foster trust in business, encourage long-term investment, promote strong corporate governance, and advocate for responsible capitalism, all of which are high priorities for businesses and governments.

IR aims to empower and motivate businesses to transparently articulate how they generate, preserve or diminish value. This is crucial for the reasons mentioned above, and also because the quality of a business's information influences investors' assessments of management quality.

At the core of the IR concept lies integrated thinking: the active consideration by an organization of the interdependencies between its different operating and functional units and the resources and relationships (i.e., its various forms of capital) that the organization uses or impacts. Integrated thinking leads to integrated decision-making and actions that take into account the creation of value over the short, medium and long term.

3 There is no right answer here, as it will depend on the situation and the business.

- Policy and legal risks relate to emission reporting obligations and exposure to litigation.

  Financial impact: increased operating costs, increased insurance premiums and higher compliance costs.

* www.un-documents.net/our-common-future.pdf

- Technology risk relates to the production of new products with lower emissions and new technology.

  Financial impact: write-offs of existing assets, reduced revenue due to reduced demand of existing products/services, additional R&D expenses, purchase of new technology and equipment, training costs.
- Market risk is related to changing customer behaviour, increased costs of raw material.

  Financial impact: reduced demand due to changes in consumer preferences; increased input and output costs and repricing of assets, e.g. fossil fuel reserves and land valuations.
- Reputation risk is related to changing customer behaviour; stakeholder concerns are higher

  Financial impact: reduced demand and reduced revenue.
- Acute risk is related to the severity of extreme weather.

  Financial impact: increased costs related to supply chain interruptions, write-off of assets, staff absenteeism and health and safety.
- Chronic risk is related to higher temperatures and rising sea levels.

  Financial impact: increased costs related to supply chain interruptions, write-off of assets, staff absenteeism and health and safety costs, increased operating costs due to lack of water, increased capital costs related to damage to facilities, increased insurance premiums.

Chapter 20

1 Assets : 22,450 + 5,400 + 250 + 1,700 = £29,800
Liabilities : 3,450 + 400 = £3,850
Assets = liabilities + capital, so capital = 29,800 − 3,850 = £25,950

2 a

	£	%
Cost price	×	100%
+ mark-up		60%
= sales price	22,500	160%

Cost price, X = 22,500/1.60 = £14,063

b

	£	%
Cost price	×	40%
+ mark-up		60%
= sales price	22,500	160%

Cost price, X = 22,500 × 40% = £9,000

3

Trade receivables

Opening balance	11,400	95,600	*Bank receipt*
so sales	89,870		
(the missing figure)		5,670	*Closing balance*
	101,270	101,270	
Opening balance	5,670		

Sales

to income statement	89,870	89,870	*Trade receivables*
	89,870	89,870	

Trade payables

Bank payments	45,100	9,450	*Opening balance*
Closing balance	10,100	45,750	*so, purchases*
			(the missing figure)
	55,200	55,200	
		10,100	*Opening balance*

Purchases/Cost of sales

Trade payables	45,750	45,750	*to income statement*
	45,750	45,750	
so: sales	89,870		
purchases	45,750		

4 Shai

Income statement for year ended 31 December Year 3

Sales			
Receipts from customers		120,000	
Less: from previous year		(10,000)	
Plus: this year's trade		12,000	
Cash sales		60,000	182,000
Cost of sales			
Opening inventories		14,000	
Payments to suppliers	125,000		

Less: from previous year	(15,000)		
Plus: this year's trade payables	17,000		
Purchases		127,000	
		141,000	
Deduct Closing inventory		16,000	125,000
Gross profit			57,000
Wages	25,000		
Expenses	20,000		
Depreciation	1,800		46,800
Net profit			10,200

Balance sheet as at 31 December Year 3

Fixtures and fittings	
(18,000 - 1,800)	16,200
Premises	187,000
Inventories	16,000
Receivables	12,000
Cash	13,000
Total assets	244,200
Payables	17,000
Loan	170,000
Capital	47,000
Retained earnings	10,200
	244,200

Balance sheet at beginning of Year 3

Fixtures and fittings	18,000
Inventories	14,000
Receivables	10,000
Cash	20,000
Total assets	62,000
Creditors	15,000
Capital	47,000
	62,000

Shai made a profit of £10,200 during the year, but his cash balance fell from £20,000 to £13,000. The business did much better than the cash figures suggest. Indeed, he managed to pay a deposit of £17,000 and buy new premises.

Cash flow statement for Shai		£
Cash generated from operations		
Operating profit		10,200
Depreciation		1,800
		12,000
Increase in inventories	(2,000)	
Increase in receivables	(2,000)	
Increase in payables	2,000	(2,000)
Cash flow from operations		10,000
Cash used in investing activities		
Purchase of premises		(187,000)
Cash generated from financing activities		
Loan		170,000
Decrease in cash		£7,000
Opening cash balance	20,000	
Closing cash balance	13,000	

Notes:

1 Interest payable was £168m. Borrowings were (£1,030m long term plus £654m short term = £1,684m), suggesting an average interest rate of 10 per cent which seems high in a period of low interest rates.

2 The answer is inaccurate due to roundings. The correct answer would be £17,571.43.

3 Normally we expect costs per unit to decrease as the volume of production increases (because fixed costs are spread amongst more units - what economists call 'economies of scale'). In this example costs per unit have increased although the volume of production has increased.

4 It cost £902,000 to produce 11,000 units, that is £82 per unit, or £2 per unit more than planned. As 11,000 units were produced, the total adverse cost variance was 11,000 × £2 = £22,000.

5 Van at cost £32,000, minus provision for depreciation at 31 December Year 7, £14,000, gives a net book value of £18,000 at the beginning of the year. The depreciation charge is 25 per cent of £18,000 = £4,500.

Answers to Chapter 4 Activities

4.1 Druisdale plc

Ratio	Year 5		Year 6		Comment
1 Current ratio	120 : 60	2 : 1	120 : 80	1.5 : 1	Looks weaker because of increased current liabilities
2 Liquidity ratio	60 : 60	1 : 1	60 : 80	0.75 : 1	Looks weaker because of increased current liabilities
3 Gearing ratio	60/240	25%	40/240	16.7%	Lower, less risky, because of reduced borrowings
4 Interest cover	60/5	12 times	69/4	17¼ times	Higher, less risky, because of reduced borrowings, reduced interest and increased operating profit

4.2 Druisdale plc

Ratio	Year 5		Year 6		Comment
5 Return on shareholders' capital employed	40/180	22.2%	50/200	25%	Profitability for shareholders has increased because profits have increased more than the increase in shareholders' capital employed
6 Return on total long-term capital employed	60/240	25%	69/240	28.75%	Overall profitability in the use of assets has increased
7 Operating profit as a percentage of sales	60/300	20%	69/350	19.7%	Profit as a percentage has declined, indicating an increase in costs as a percentage of sales
8 Asset turnover	300/240	1.25 times	350/240	1.46 times	Overall increase in profitability is due to improved utilization of assets (sales have increased; assets have not)

Relationship between ratios 6, 7 and 8

Year 5 25 ÷ 20 = 1.25

Year 6 28.75 ÷ 19.7 = 1.46

4.3 Druisdale plc

Ratio	Year 5		Year 6		Comment
9 Gross profit ratio	100/300	33⅓	120/350	34.3%	The margin between buying prices has improved by increasing selling prices and/or reducing the cost of purchase
10 Distribution costs as a % of sales	15/300	5%	20/350	5.7%	Distribution costs have increased by a bigger proportion than sales
11 Administrative expenses as a % of sales	25/300	8⅓	31/350	8.9%	Administrative expenses have increased by a bigger proportion than sales

4.4 Druisdale plc

Ratio	Year 5		Year 6		Comment
12 Sales/non-current assets	300/180	1.67 times	350/200	1.75 times	Sales have increased by a bigger proportion than fixed assets, thus improving the utilization of fixed assets
13 Sales/current assets	300/120	2.5 times	350/120	2.92 times	Sales have increased, current assets have not, thus improving the utilization of current assets
14 Inventory turnover ratio	60 ÷ 200 × 365	109.5 days	60 ÷ 230 × 365	95.2 days	Stock levels have remained constant while turnover has increased
15 Receivables ratio	40 ÷ 300 × 365	48.7 days	50 ÷ 350 × 365	52 days	Debtors have increased by a bigger proportion than sales, indicating that it is taking a few days longer to get money in from debtors
16 Payables ratio	60 ÷ 200 × 365	109.5 days	80 ÷ 230 × 365	127 days	Creditors have increased by a bigger proportion than cost of sales, and it is taking even longer than an already long period to pay them

Comments on profitability

Overall profitability (measured as return on capital employed, ratios 5 and 6) increased from year 5 to year 6. This was not due to an improvement in the profitability of sales, which declined (ratio 7). It was due to improved utilization of assets (asset turnover, ratio 8, increased).

The problems with the profitability of sales were due to an increase in distribution costs and administrative expenses; the gross profit ratio increased, suggesting that there was not a problem with the cost of sales or selling prices.

The improved utilization of assets applied to both non-current assets and current assets. Inventory turnover increased, although this was offset by a slowing down in the collection of receivables. The period taken to pay creditors is excessive, and increased; but this increasing reliance on funding by receivables contributed to the increase in profitability.

4.5 Druisdale plc

Ratio		Year 5		Year 6		Comment
17	Price/earnings (P/E) ratio	£5.60 ÷ 40p	14	£7.50 ÷ 50p	15	Share price has increased by an even bigger proportion than earnings per share (EPS)
18	Dividend yield	25p ÷ £5.60 × 100	4.5%	30p ÷ £7.50 × 100	4%	Dividend has increased by a significant proportion, but the share price has increased by an even bigger proportion so that dividend is a smaller proportion of the share price
19	Dividend cover	40/25	1.60 times	50/30	1.67 times	Dividends have increased almost in line with profits, but there is a slight increase in cover
20	Net assets per share	£180/100	£1.80	£200/100	£2.00	Net assets per share have increased as profits have been retained; but the market price is much higher than the underlying asset value

4.6 Garwick Ltd

Ratio		Year 7	Year 8
1	Current ratio	2.47 : 1	1.5 : 1
2	Liquidity ratio	1.88 : 1	0.85 : 1
3	Capital gearing ratio	53.3%	42.9%

Ratio		Year 7	Year 8
4	Interest times cover	4.75 times	7.67 times
5	Return on shareholders' funds	31.4%	37.5%
6	Return on total long-term capital employed	25.3%	32.9%
7	Operating profit as a % of sales	18.8%	21%
8	Asset turnover	1.35 times	1.57 times
9	Gross profit ratio	30.7%	32.7%
10	Distribution costs as a % of sales	6.9%	6.4%
11	Administrative expenses as a % of sales	5%	5.5%
12	Sales/non-current assets	2.02 times	1.83 times
13	Sales/current assets	2.4 times	3.67 times
14	Inventory turnover ratio	52.1 days	64.1 days
15	Receivables ratio	50.6 days	53.1 days
16	Payables ratio	88.6 days	98.6 days
17	(P/E) ratio	17	19
18	Dividend yield	4.3%	3.5%
19	Dividend cover	1.4 times	1.5 times
20	Net assets per share	£0.35	£0.40

Comments

In year 7 the current and liquidity ratios were strong, but they had declined to worrying levels in year 8.

In year 7 the gearing ratio was high, and the interest times cover was low, indicating heavy reliance on long-term borrowing. The level of gearing was lower (safer), and the interest cover was stronger in year 8.

The company had reduced its reliance on long-term borrowing mainly by reducing the amount of cash held.

The level of overall profitability was high, and increased in year 8 (ratios 5 and 6). The increase was due both to an increase in the profitability of sales (ratio 7) and in the utilization of assets (ratio 8).

The increase in the profitability of sales was due both to an increase in the gross profit ratio, and to a decrease in distribution costs as a percentage of sales; this was offset by an increase in administrative expenses as a percentage of sales.

The improvement in the utilization of assets was due entirely to an increase in the turnover of current assets; the utilization of non-current assets declined (because the amount of non-current assets increased by a bigger proportion (20 per cent)[1] than the increase in sales (just less than 10 per cent).[2]

The improvement in the utilization of current assets was due partly to the reduction in the amount of cash, and partly to the increase in stock turnover; these were offset by the deterioration in the debtors ratio. The amount of net assets was also reduced (and so capital employed was reduced)[3] by the increase in creditors.

[1] From £50,000 to £60,000.

[2] From £101,000 to £110,000.

[3] And so return on capital employed was increased.

Overall, there was a good improvement in profitability, but some concern about solvency and excessive liabilities remains.

The share price increased substantially, and the increase in the P/E ratio indicates investors' optimism about the company. The amount of dividend paid by the company increased substantially (by 25 per cent), but the share price increased by a greater proportion, and so the dividend yield declined; a reduction in dividend yield may be seen as an indicator of the market's confidence in the company. There may be questions about the sustainability of dividends (cover was only 1.4 times in year 7), but this improved a little in year 8.

The market value of the company is much higher than the statement of financial position value of it (the share price is much higher than the net assets per share).

Glossary

The word 'company' is used in this glossary although most of the definitions apply to other businesses and entities.

A

Absorption costing A traditional costing method in which individual products bear their share of both fixed and variable production costs.

Accounting policies The specific bases, conventions, rules and practices applied by an entity in preparing and presenting financial statements.

Accounting rate of return (ARR) The average accounting profit divided by the initial (or average) investment, expressed as a percentage (also called return on investment (ROI)).

Accounting standards Quasi-legal regulations defining terms and explaining how figures are to be calculated or disclosed in external financial accounts. These have been issued as ***SSAPs***, ***FRSs*** (UK and Ireland) ***IASs*** and ***IFRSs*** (international).

Accrual An accrual is an expense that has been incurred but not yet recorded at the year end; the trial balance has to be adjusted to include accruals as an adjustment to the expense and as a current liability. Accruals are only a small part of the accruals concept.

Accruals concept On an income statement revenue is recorded in the period when it is earned and not when the cash is received; expenses are recorded in the period in which they are incurred and not when they are paid; expenses are matched against revenues. This is distinct from the cash (or receipts and payments) basis of accounting. Additionally, costs are matched with revenues.

Acid test *See **liquidity ratio.***

Activity-based costing (ABC) A method of costing in which the fixed costs are allocated to products or other cost objects on the basis of the activities that drive them.

Articles of association The internal constitution of a company including the rights of shareholders.

Asset A resource controlled by the enterprise as a result of past transactions or events and from which future economic benefits are expected to flow to the enterprise.

Associate An associate company is not a subsidiary company but it is one over which an investing company has significant influence, usually by owning between 20–50 per cent of its shares.

Auditor's report A report appearing in a company's annual report, written and signed by the independent auditor and addressed to the shareholders expressing their opinion on whether the accounts show a 'true and fair view' and comply with the Companies Act and other specified regulations such as IFRSs.

Auditing An external annual process whereby all but small companies are subject to independent and expert assessment of their financial records and statements and systems of internal control, to express an opinion on whether the accounts have been prepared in accordance with the Companies Act and relevant accounting standards and regulations, and show a true and fair view.

B

Balance sheet A statement of ***assets***, ***liabilities*** and ***equity*** as at a given date, typically at the end of a year, or a month. Often now called the statement of financial position.

Bank reconciliation A statement in which bank receipts and payments which have not yet cleared the banking system are added and subtracted from the balance per the bank statement in order to confirm the cash book balance is correct.

Bonus (or scrip) issue An issue of shares to existing shareholders in proportion to their existing shareholding. No money changes hands. Reserves or retained earnings are redesignated as share capital and the market value per share reduces in proportion to the proportionate increase in the number of shares.

Break-even point Number of units sold, or sales revenue whereby total revenue equals total cost and where profit is zero.

Budget A quantitative plan showing forecast sales and costs such as direct materials, direct labour and overheads, purchases, inventory and cash for a future period which is used for planning, co-ordination, control and motivation.

Business entity concept Financial accounts report the activities, assets and liability of the business and not those of the owner.

C

Capital expenditure Expenditure incurred in buying, creating or adding to non-current assets.

Cash A current asset; it includes petty cash and bank. It can be negative, usually shown as an overdraft, a ***current liability***.

Cash book A book of prime entry in which the bank receipts and bank payments are listed by date and analysed with details of the name of payer or payee and the bank balance is shown. This will be reconciled to the bank statement from time to time on a ***bank reconciliation***.

Cash flow The term has no precise meaning but is sometimes used as if it means profit plus depreciation. Cash flow statements show separately cash flows from operating activities, investing activities and financing activities.

Cash flow statement One of the principal statements in a published set of accounts, it shows cash inflows and outflows in operating activities, investing activities and financing activities, the net result of these three categories being the increase or decrease in the cash balances.

Company A separate legal entity, owned by shareholders and managed by directors. The shareholders usually have limited liability and the company is required to produce annual accounts which must be sent to the shareholders and are filed at Companies House where they are available for public scrutiny.

Concepts The ideas and conventions which underpin the financial accounting process. The idea of four fundamental accounting concepts (prudence, consistency, accruals and going concern) has been superseded by emphasis on qualitative characteristics, relevance and reliability, comparability and understandability.

Consistency Consistent accounting policies or treatment is applied to similar items within a given year and from year to year.

Consolidated financial statements Financial statements of a group of companies that includes 100 per cent of the assets, liabilities, revenues and expenditure of all subsidiary companies, even if they are only, say, 60 per cent owned. The amounts in respect of ***minority interests*** are separately shown on the financial statements. The consolidated statement of financial position shows all the assets and liabilities controlled by the parent company.

Consolidated (or group) accounts This is a report of a parent company and its subsidiaries, as if it was one reporting entity, showing all the assets and liabilities and profits controlled by the parent company.

Consolidated profits The parent's own profits together with the group share of the post-acquisition profits of the subsidiary less impairment of goodwill on consolidation.

Contingent liability A possible obligation from past events or transactions, which will be confirmed by the occurrence or non-occurrence of a future uncertain event, that are not within the control of the company (e.g. a pending court case).

Contribution Sales revenue less variables costs.

Control accounts A statement including the day book totals for invoices and payments in which the total arising agrees with the total of the individual balances in the sales ledger and purchase ledger, thereby proving the accuracy and completeness of the two ledgers.

Corporate governance The system by which companies are directed and controlled, involving law and other regulation and convention, and the roles and relationships between a company's directors, management and shareholders and other stakeholders, and the company's objectives.

Cost centre A unit to which only costs are charged and apportioned and are considered the responsibility of the manager (e.g. a department, a process, a service).

Cost driver A factor which causes a change in the cost of a cost object.

Cost object Anything we wish to know the cost of (e.g. a product, an activity, a process, a department).

Cost of capital The rate used to discount the project cash flows in a net present value computation.

Cost of sales In a retailing organization, this is opening inventory plus purchases minus closing inventory. In a manufacturing organization, it is opening inventories plus costs of production, minus closing inventories. Also known as cost of goods sold. It is deducted from sales revenue to arrive at ***gross profit***.

Costs Costs may be classified as ***fixed costs*** and ***variable costs***; or as ***production costs*** (which include ***production overheads***) and other ***overheads***, which include distribution costs (selling and distribution overheads), and administration overheads. Production costs may be classified as ***direct materials***, ***direct labour*** and production overheads. ***Prime cost of production*** comprises direct materials and direct labour (and ***direct expenses***, if any). *See also* ***opportunity cost***.

Creditors *See* ***payables***. Future financial obligations arising from past transactions or events.

Creditors: amounts falling due after more than one year These are now called ***non-current liabilities***.

Creditors: amounts falling due within one year These are now called ***current liabilities***.

Creditors' ratio The relationship between trade payables (creditors) and purchases (or cost of sales) usually expressed as a number of days.

Current assets ***Assets*** such as ***inventories***, ***receivables*** and ***cash***, which are held short term (less than one year) and expected to be converted into cash within a year.

Current cost accounting (CCA) A system of accounting that adjusts for changing values following SSAP 16.

Current liabilities Amounts expected to be paid within a year.

Current purchasing power accounting (CPP) A system of accounting that adjusts for inflation following (P)SSAP 7.

Current ratio The ratio of ***current assets*** to ***current liabilities*** that indicates a company's ability to meet its current liabilities as they fall due.

D

Day books Books in which the financial transactions are first recorded in the accounting records. Day books include the sales day book, the purchase day book, the cash book and the petty cash book.

Debenture Long-term loan, usually with a fixed rate of interest and often secured on fixed property or the floating assets such as inventory and trade receivables.

Debtors (receivables) period The relationship between trade receivables (debtors) and sales, usually expressed as a number of days.

Depreciation The systematic allocation or writing-down of the carrying amount (cost or revaluation) of a non-current asset, as an expense, over its expected economic life as the economic benefits arise. The depreciation expense for the year is shown in the income statement, while the accumulated depreciation is deducted from the carrying amount to show the asset's net book value in the statement of financial position.

Direct expenses (Much less frequently encountered than direct labour and direct materials.) Costs of the type that would normally be treated as part of ***production overheads***, but instead are treated as part of ***prime cost of production*** because they are directly attributable to a particular job, product or service. For example, a car repair business would normally treat machinery costs as being part of production overheads; but if a special-purpose machine has to be hired to repair a specialist car, the cost of hiring that machine would be treated as part of the cost of repairing that car, and not included in general production overheads.

Direct labour The costs of remunerating employees who work directly on a product or service to be sold; these labour costs are separately identified and charged to particular products or services (as opposed to being treated as part of ***production overheads***). Part of ***prime cost of production*** which, when production overheads are added, make up total ***production cost***.

Direct materials The cost of direct materials and components that are separately identifiable and enter into and become constituent elements of a product or service to be sold. Part of ***prime cost of production*** which, when ***production overheads*** are added, make up total ***production cost***.

Director A person appointed by the shareholders to manage a company.

Director's remuneration Compensation of a director comprising a salary, fees, bonus or use of a company's property.

Discounted cash flow (DCF) A method of capital investment appraisal in which the relevant expected cash inflows and outflows of a project are discounted to their present value using the time value of money. DCF techniques include net present value (NPV) and internal rate of return (IRR).

Dividend Amount distributed (or paid out as a scrip dividend) to shareholders from distributable profits, usually twice a year (interim dividend, final dividend). Sometimes companies pay more dividends than they have earned as profits in the year, in which case retained profits from previous years are being distributed.

Dividend cover Net profit after tax (or profit available to pay dividends) divided by dividends payable for the year.

Dividend yield The most recent annual dividend per share as a percentage of share price.

Double entry The system whereby accounting transactions and adjustments are recorded in the ledger, both as a debit and as a credit entry. Debits are increases to assets and expenses while credits are increases to liabilities and revenues.

E

Economic order quantity (EOQ) A technique in which the optimal reorder quantity is computed using ordering and holding costs of inventory.

Equity The total of shareholders' funds including ordinary share capital, share ***premium***, and other reserves and retained earnings.

Exceptional items The term now has no precise definition, but there is usually separate disclosure of unusual or non-recurring items, such as write-downs of inventories, impairment of property, plant and equipment, restructuring, profits or losses on disposal of investments or tangible non-current assets. They must be separately disclosed because of their abnormal incidence or size. All these affect earnings per share.

Expectations gap The difference between what many seem to expect of auditors and what they actually do.

Extraordinary items A material item possessing a high degree of abnormality which arises from events or transactions that fall outside the ordinary activities of the reporting entity and which is not expected to recur. Note that disclosure of extraordinary items is no longer permitted (*FRS 102: The Financial Reporting Standard applicable in the UK and Republic of Ireland)*.

F

Fair value of a non-current asset This is the amount for which it could be exchanged in an arm's length transaction.

Finance cost Interest payable.

Finance income Interest receivable.

Financial Reporting Standards (FRSs) These were issued by the Accounting Standards Board, but have now been superseded by ***IASs***.

Fixed assets Now normally known as ***non-current assets***.

Fixed costs Costs (such as rent for the premises, or most salaries) that tend to remain at the same level when there are changes in the volume of production or sales. In ***marginal costing*** fixed costs are separated from ***variable costs***. (Some costs are semi-variable.)

G

Gearing The extent to which a company's long-term finance relies upon debt (such as debentures) as compared to equity. The first of these is often represented as D; and the second as E. It may be calculated showing D as a percentage of D plus E; or, more simply, showing D as a percentage of E. Also known as capital gearing or ***leverage***.

Going concern The assumption that the business will continue in operational existence for the foreseeable future and, as a result, it is assumed, in the financial accounts, that the non-current assets will be used and the inventory sold in a relaxed manner and not sold in a liquidation.

Goodwill The amount paid to acquire a business over and above the fair value of its net separable assets. It is an intangible asset and subject to annual impairment reviews.

Goodwill on consolidation This is the consideration given by the parent company for the controlling interest in the shares of the subsidiary, in excess of the fair value of the separable net assets underlying those shares. It must be revalued each year and any impairment of its value will be written off against group reserves.

Gross profit Sales revenue minus ***cost of sales***.

Gross profit ratio Gross profit as a percentage of sales.

Group accounts *See* ***consolidated financial statements***.

I

Impairment Goodwill is not now systematically amortized; it is subject to an annual impairment review.

Income statement A statement of sales revenue, costs and net profit for a period (e.g. one year). Used to be known as a profit and loss account.

Incomplete records Some small businesses do not keep proper double-entry accounting records and accountants need to construct statements of financial position and income statements from incomplete records that usually comprise bank statements and a variety of documents such as invoices, and unpaid receivables and payables and inventory at the statement of financial position date.

Indirect costs These are costs which cannot be identified with the individual cost unit.

Intangible asset An asset with no physical substance.

Interest cover Operating profit (or profit available to pay interest) divided by interest payable.

Interest times cover Profit available for paying interest (usually operating profit) divided by the amount of interest payable (finance costs).

Internal rate of return (IRR) The discount rate at which the net present value of expected outflows and inflows from a project are zero.

International Accounting Standards (IASs) These have been superseded by ***IFRSs***.

International Financial Reporting Standards (IFRSs) These are issued by the International Accounting Standards Board.

Inventories Raw materials, components, work in progress, finished goods and goods held for resale. Formerly known as ***stocks***.

Investment centre Much like a cost centre or profit centre but here, the manager is responsible for and answerable for costs, revenues and investments.

J

Joint venture A business jointly owned by several other businesses, none of whom has a controlling interest.

L

Leverage *See* ***gearing***.

Liability A present financial obligation arising from past events, the settlement of which is expected to result in an outflow from the enterprise embodying economic benefits.

Limited liability The liability of the company's shareholders is limited to any sum they have not paid into the company for the purchase of shares. In the event of a liquidation, if the shareholders have fully paid for their shares, they have no further liability for any debts of the company.

Limiting factor An input factor which is temporarily unavailable.

Liquidity The ease and speed with which assets can be turned into cash to pay imminent liabilities.

Liquidity (or quick, or acid-test) ratio The ratio of current assets excluding inventories to ***current liabilities*** that indicates a company's immediate ability to meet its current liabilities as they fall due. Liquid assets include cash and receivables, but exclude inventories.

M

Margin of safety Expected sales less break-even point.

Marginal costing A costing system in which individual products are charged with variable but not fixed production overheads; useful in decision-making and break-even analysis.

Mark-up Percentage added to cost price to arrive at selling price. This is not the same as gross profit (or margin) ratio.

Memorandum of association A document setting out a company's name, its objects and its registered share capital.

Minority interest The share of the net assets (or capital and reserves) of a subsidiary at the statement of financial position date, attributable to the non-group shareholders.

N

Nominal value *See **par value**.*

Non-current assets Formerly known as ***fixed assets***. Assets that are held for long-term use (more than one year) including tangible assets such as property, plant and equipment; intangible assets, such as ***goodwill***, patents and trademarks: and financial assets that are investments such as shares and debentures. The non-current assets were not purchased in order to sell them.

Non-current liabilities Formerly known as ***creditors: amounts falling due after more than one year***. These are liabilities which are due for repayment in the long term (more than one year after the statement of financial position date, and include long-term bank loans and debentures.

O

Operating costs These are the main difference between gross profit and profit before tax. These operating costs are usually designated and disclosed as distribution costs and administrative expenses.

Opportunity cost The value of a benefit sacrificed in favour of an alternative course of action. If a business owns premises that are currently unoccupied, the cost of using them for a particular purpose should not be regarded as zero; the 'opportunity cost' of using them for that purpose is the amount that they could have earned from the best alternative use (e.g. renting them out).

Overheads All costs other than ***direct materials***, ***direct labour*** (and ***direct expenses***, if any). There are ***production overheads***, distribution costs (which comprise selling and distribution overheads) and administration overheads.

Overtrading A rapid expansion in business activity with insufficient long-term capital to finance it, which often leads to difficulty in paying liabilities as they fall due.

P

Par value Each share has a theoretical, or par, or nominal value that is of little importance other than it appears on the statement of financial position.

Partnership A business owned and controlled by a number of people in partnership with a view to profit. It is not incorporated and so not subject to Companies Act requirements in terms of formation, limited liability or public accounting disclosure.

Payables Amounts that a business owes and is required to pay, for example trade payables (creditors).

Payback period Capital investment appraisal technique which measures how long it will take to recover the initial investment; that is, when the cash inflows will equal the cash outflows.

Preference shares Shares with a predetermined rate of dividend which must be fully paid before any dividend is paid to ordinary shareholders and the par value of which will be paid to its shareholders before any ordinary shareholder receives any distribution in the event of a liquidation. Now usually classified as non-current liabilities.

Premium Shares are often issued at a premium above their nominal or par value. For example, a 20 pence share might be issued for 30 pence, which means the premium is 10 pence. On a balance sheet, share premium is very much like share capital.

Prepayment A current asset representing the amount to which an expense has been paid in advance at the statement of financial position date.

Price/earnings ratio (P/E ratio) This is share price divided by earnings per share.

Prime cost of production The total of ***direct materials***, ***direct labour*** (and ***direct expenses***, if any). It excludes production and other overheads.

Production cost This includes ***prime cost of production*** and ***production overheads***.

Production overheads The costs of providing a production or manufacturing facility that are not directly attributable to individual products or services. It includes rent and rates for the factory premises, depreciation and repairs for machinery, and wages and salaries for people in the factory who are not part *of* ***direct labour***. These costs are allocated and apportioned to individual products in an ***absorption costing*** system.

Profit and loss account Now usually known as an income statement. The term 'profit and loss account' may still be used in conversation, as part of the double-entry bookkeeping system, and in the process of producing the final statement that is called an ***income statement***.

Profit centre Much the same as a cost centre except here, both costs and revenues are charged and allocated and are considered the responsibility of the manager.

Provision A liability of uncertain timing or amount.

Prudence Prudence was regarded as a fundamental accounting concept. Profits should not be recognized until realized, while expenses must be recognized as soon as they can be anticipated with a reasonable degree of probability. It no longer has the same degree of force.

Q

Quick assets ratio *See* ***liquidity ratio***.

R

Receivables Money expected to be received from customers who may be referred to as trade debtors. Part of current assets.

Relevant costs Expected future incremental cash costs arising from a project.

Return on shareholders' funds (ROSF) or return on equity (ROE) Net profit after tax as a percentage of equity.

Return on total long-term capital employed Operating profit as a percentage of long-term funding (equity plus long-term borrowings).

Revenue expenditure Costs incurred in earning revenues during the period; it excludes ***capital expenditure***.

Rights issue An issue of shares to existing shareholders at a price below the current market price. These rights can be sold by the existing shareholder to a third party.

S

Segmental reporting Diversified companies report separate figures for sales, operating profit and net assets for each of their business and geographic segments.

Sensitivity analysis An assessment of those variables in a project which will have the most profound impact on its suitability. Those variables to which the project is most sensitive will then be given most focus in further analysis (e.g. 'What if labour rates increase by 10 per cent?).

Share capital The part of the company's equity that has been sold to shareholders for cash or an equivalent item of capital value. The share capital appears in the statement of financial position at its par/nominal/authorized value. The shares can be sold by the existing shareholder to another person.

Share premium *See* ***premium***.

Sole trader A business owned and controlled by one person. It is unincorporated and so not subject to Companies Act requirements in terms of formation, limited liability and public accounting disclosure.

Statement of changes in equity Statement showing the changes during the year in each of the elements in equity shown on the statement of financial position. This includes increases and decreases in share capital and share premium, movements in revaluations reserves and movements in the retained profits such as profits and dividends paid as well as unrealized gains.

Statement of financial position A statement of assets, liabilities and equity as at a given date, typically at the end of a year, or a month. Formerly and still sometimes called the balance sheet.

Statements of Standard Accounting Practice (SSAPs) These were issued by the Accounting Standards Committee, but have now been superseded by ***FRSs***.

Stewardship Directors are assumed to be stewards of shareholders' funds and so directors are accountable to shareholders.

Stocks *See* ***inventories***.

Stock turnover ratio The relationship between inventories (stocks) and cost of sales (or purchases) usually expressed as a number of days.

Subsidiary company A company controlled by another company (a parent company), which usually owns (or controls in another way) more than 50 per cent of its shares.

Sunk costs Past costs which are irrelevant in a net present value calculation since they will not be affected whether or not the project proceeds.

Suspense account A t-account used to correct errors such as trial balance differences and when it is not known to which t-account a transaction should be posted. In due course, these errors and 'unknowns' must be corrected by journal entries which post the entries to the correct t-account and remove all the postings into the suspense account. The suspense account balance will then be zero.

T

Time value of money The value of money, not in absolute terms, but taking into consideration when it flows and the interest rate expected to prevail in the meantime. A sum received now is worth more than the same sum received at some future time.

Trial balance A list of balances extracted from each ledger account, some of which will be debits (the assets and expenses) and some credits (liabilities and revenues) in which the total of the debit balances and the credit balances will agree. The trial balance can be *extended* to include adjustments, such as depreciation and bad debt provisions, to produce the figures which will appear in the final statement of financial position and income statement.

V

Variable costs These costs (e.g. ***direct material*** costs) tend to vary in proportion to the level of production or sales. In ***marginal costing***, variable costs are separated from ***fixed costs***. Some costs may be regarded as semi-variable, or semi-fixed.

Variance The difference between the budgeted figures and the actual figures.

W

Working capital The excess of ***current assets*** over ***current liabilities***. It can be negative.

Working capital ratio *See* ***current ratio***.

Z

Z-score A combination of ratios that can predict financial distress.

Index

A

ABC (activity-based costing), 414-16
absorption costing
  absorption of costs, 412-13
  accounting in context, 421-2
  allocation of costs, 412-13
  apportionment of costs, 412-13
  assessment questions, 419-21
  averaging system for prices, 409
  changes in price, dealing with, 408-9
  closing inventories, establishment of cost of, 406
  costing systems, 'cost-plus' approach to, 406
  costing systems, role and origins of, 406-7
  costs, classification of, 407
  direct expenses, 410
  direct labour, 409
  direct labour cost, percentage on, 410-11
  direct labour hour rate, 411-12
  direct materials, pricing and, 408-9
  evaluation of, 413-14
  FIFO (first-in-first-out), 408-9
  indirect materials, pricing and, 408
  key points review, 417
  learning objectives, 405
  LIFO (last-in-first out), 409
  machine hour rate, 412
  management accounting, 337-8, 342-3
  marginal costing, decision-making and, 423-4, 426
  production overheads, 410-12
  production overheads, other methods for charging, 412
  replacement cost system, 409
  self-testing questions, 417-19
  standard cost system, 409
  UK drug shortages aggravated due to Brexit, 422
accountancy and power, 206
accounting choices, reduction of, 197
accounting defined, 1-2
accounting in context, 187
  absorption costing, 421-2
  bookkeeping to trial balance, 250-51
  budgerary planning and control, 403-4
  cash flow statements, 160
  financial reporting, current issues in, 217-18
  financial reporting, development of, 76-7
  financing a business, 312-13
  income statement, 52-3
  investment appraisal, 380-82
  management accounting, 348-9
  marginal costing, decision-making and, 440-41
  ratios, interpretation and, 104-5
  standard costing and variance analysis, 458-60
  statement of financial position, 29-30
  stock market assessment of company performance, 126-7
  sustainability and accounting, 472-4
  trial balance to final accounts, 289-91
  working capital, management of, 333
accounting information, users of, 3-5
accounting process, 1-2
accounting standards
  creative accounting and, 202
  financial reporting and, 58-9
Accounting Standards Steering Committee, 58-9
accruals
  cash flow statements and application of, 131-2
  cash flow statements and concept of, 130-32
  prepayments and, 235-7
  principle of, 60
acquisitions. income statements and, 44
advantages of
  budgerary control systems, 392-3
  marginal costing, 431-6
  rolling budgets, 397-8
  SDGs (UN Sustainable Development Goals), 470
AICPA (American Institute of Certified Public
    Accountants), 462
allocation of costs, 412-13
Altman Z-scores, 175-7
APMs (alternative performance measures), 196
apportionment of costs, 412-13
ASB (Accounting Standards Board), 58-9
assessment questions
  absorption costing, 419-21
  bookkeeping to trial balance, 247-50
  budgetary planning and control, 402-3
  cash flow statements, 154-9
  financial reporting, current issues in, 217
  financial reporting, development of, 76
  financing a business, 309-12
  income statement, 49-52
  interpretation of accounts, 185-6
  investment appraisal, 377-9
  management accounting, 346-7
  marginal costing, decision-making and, 439-40
  ratios, interpretation and, 102-3
  standard costing and variance analysis, 456-8
  statement of financial position, 26-8
  stock market assessment of company performance, 124-5
  trial balance to final accounts, 285-9
  working capital, management of, 330-32
assets
  asset utilization ratios, 97-8
  classification of, 11-12
  definition of, 63
  measurement of, 63-4
  utilization of, 87-9
  warnings from, 175
associates, 44
Auditchain Protocol, 76-7
auditing
  audit opinion, formation of, 182-3
  auditor's report, 182-3
  creative accounting and, 202-3
authorization, control systems and, 393
averaging system for prices, 409

B

balance sheet
  wide use of term, 6-7
  see also statement of financial position
balancing accounts, 232
bank reconciliations, 242-3
Benevolent AI, 160
biodiversity depletion, 467
Black Rock rolls out first generative AI tools, 440-41
blockchain and accounting, 250-51
bonus issues of shares, 297-8
bookkeeping in practice, 231-9
bookkeeping systems, 239-44
bookkeeping to trial balance, 221-51
  accounting in context, 250-51
  accruals, prepayments and, 235-7
  assessment questions, 247-50
  balancing accounts, 232
  bank reconciliations, 242-3
  blockchain and accounting, 250-51
  carriage inwards and outwards, 237
  cash account, 223-4
  cash and bank, 233
  control accounts, 241
  crediting, 229-31
  day books, 240
  debiting, 229-31
  depreciation of non-current assets, 237-8
  discount allowed and received, 233
  group activities, discussion questions and, 250
  journals, 240
  key points review, 245
  learning objectives, 221
  ledgers, 240
  non-current assets, depreciation of, 237-8
  non-current assets, sale of, 238-9
  prepayments, 236-7
  purchase account, 225
  recording transactions, 224-5
  returns inwards and outwards, 233-5
  sale of non-current assets, 238-9
  sales account, 226-9
  self-testing questions, 245-7
  suspense accounts, 243-4
  transactions, double-entry bookkeeping and, 222-31
borrowing
  attractions of, 301, 302
  debentures, 301-2
  financing a business and, 294, 299-303
  overdrafts, 301
BP CEOs, 126-7
break-even analysis, 427-9, 435
break-even charts, 430
break-even formula, 428-9
Brundtland Commission (UN, 1987), 461-2
budgerary planning and control, 383-404
  accounting in context, 403-4
  assessment questions, 402-3
  authorization, control systems and, 393
  cash budgets, 390-92
  communication and co-ordination, control systems and, 393
  delegation, control systems and, 393
  fixed budget, 388
  flexible budget, 388-9
  group activities, discussion questions and, 403
  incremental budgets, budgetary control and, 394-5
  key points review, 400
  learning objectives, 383
  limiting factors, control systems and, 392-3
  management by exception, control systems and, 393
  master budget, 387-8
  motivation, control systems and, 393
  objectives, budgetary control and definition of, 395
  objectives, control systems and, 392
  paperwork exercise, budgetary control and, 395
  participation, budgetary control and, 394
  performance evaluation, control systems and, 393
  performance levels, budgetary control and, 394
  PPBS (Planning and Programming Budgeting System), 399-400
  resources, budgetary control and competition for, 394
  responsibility, control systems and, 393
  reward schemes, budgetary control and, 394
  rolling budgets, 397-9
  self-testing questions, 400-402
  spending up to budget, budgetary control and, 395
  summary budget, 387-8
  ZBB (zero-based budgeting), 396-7
  ZBB (zero-based budgeting), transferable to zero-based
    management, 403-6
budgetary control
  data required for master budget, 387
  definition of, 386
  effectiveness of, 396
  game between managers, 395-6
  implementation of, 387-9
  management accounting and, 339
  problems in practice, 394-6
  systems of, advantages of, 392-3
budgets
  budgetary control and, 384-7
  definition of, keywords in, 385
  draft budgets, realism in, 386
business finance, publication of, 17

C

capital expenditure, 21, 45, 48, 193, 326, 387
  capitalization of interest and, 66, 71-2
  development costs and, 65
  revenue expenditure and, 45
capitalized interest, 66, 71-2
CAPM (capital asset pricing model), 371, 372
carriage inwards and outwards, 237
cash account, 223-4, 225, 230
cash and bank, 39, 233
cash budgets, 390-92
cash flow
  categories of, 120
  investment appraisal, profit and, 351-2
  stock market assessments and, 112, 120
cash flow per share, 139
cash flow ratios, 138-9
cash flow statements, 129-61
  accounting in context, 160
  accruals concept, 130-32
  accruals concept, application of, 131-2
  assessment questions, 154-9
  Benevolent AI, 160
  cash flow per share, 139

cash flow ratios, 138-9
cash flow statements, 132-7
cash return on capital employed, 139
cash used in financing activities, 147
cash used in investing activities, 146, 148
cash used in operating activities, 145-6
depreciation, 134, 148
dividends paid, 135
Financial Reporting, Conceptual Framework for (2018), 130
financing activities, 136
financing activities, cash generated from, 147, 148
format of, 141-7
free cash flow, 137-8
group activities, discussion questions and, 159-60
IAS 7 classification for cash flows, 143
interest and dividend cover, 138-9
interest expense, 135, 149
interest paid, 135
interpretation of, 137-41
interpretation of statements, 140-41
investing activities, 136
investing activities, cash generated from, 146, 148
key points review, 151
learning objectives, 129
non-current assets, 143, 146, 148-50
operating activities, 134-7
operating activities, cash generated from, 145-6, 147-8
preparation of, 147-50
profit before taxation, 134, 148
published statements, 139-40
self-testing questions, 151-4
taxation paid, 135
working capital increase, 135, 147-8
cash flows
relevant costs for investment appraisal, 365-8
warnings in, 175
cash generated, profit measurement as indication of, 55-6
cash management, 326-7
cash return on capital employed, 139
cash used
in investing activities, 146, 148
in operating activities, 145-6
cash used in
financing activities, 147
CDP (Carbon Disclosure Project), 463
CDSB (Climate Disclosure Standards Board), 463
changes in price, dealing with, 408-9
CIMA (Chartered Institute of Management Accountants), 388
climate change risks and implications, 466-7
climate patterns, TCFD and risks in, 468
climate-related risks, TCFD and, 467
closing inventories, establishment of cost of, 406
collapse of companies, 13
collecting due payments, 320-22
communication, control systems and, 393
companies, 264-74
accrued charges adjustments for, 267
adjustments to financial statements, summary of, 266-7
bad debt provision, 267
bad debt write-offs, 267
corporation tax, 264
corporation tax adjustments, 267
dealing with extended trial balance question, 269-74
depreciation adjustments, 267
differences from sole traders, 264-6
dividends, 264
expenses, 264
extended trial balance, 268-74
income statement for, 43
interest payments, 265
inventory adjustments, 267
land revaluations, 267
management of, accounting information and, 3-4
non-current assets adjustments, 267
prepayments adjustments, 267
published statements by, 41-3
share capital, 264
shareholders' funds, 264
statement of financial position, 8-11
statement of financial position, publication of, 17-19
Companies Act (1969), 58
Companies House, 2-3
comparability
comparing costs over periods, 426-7
objective of, 61
ratios, comparisons of, 92-3
Competitive Advantage (Porter, M.), 466
competitors, accounting information and, 4
concepts
accruals, 130-32
duality, 61
financial reporting, development of, 60-62
sustainability, 462
consistency, principle of, 60
consolidated (group)
accounts, rules for, 171-2
financial statements, 169-73
contingent liabilities, 67
control accounts, 241
co-ordination, control systems and, 393
Corporate Report (1975)
financial reporting, current issues in, 206-7
financial reporting, development of, 60, 61
corporate reporting, sustainability and, 464-5
corporate social responsibility (CSR), 208
cost behaviour, 340-42
cost of capital, 358-73
evaluation of approaches to, 372-3
cost of sales
interpretation of accounts, 168-9
management accounting, 338
costing systems
'cost-plus' approach to, 406
role and origins of, 406-7
costs, classification of, 407
COVID-19 pandemic
accounting considerations for, 196
hospitals need to change costings methods, 458-60
creative accounting, 190-94
bad techniques, 194
curtailment of, 202-6
development of, 191-2
effects of, 192-3
judgement becoming creative, 193-4
problem areas for, 195-201
creativity problems, subjective measurement of, 45-6
credit allowances, 320
credit customers, 320
crediting, bookkeeping and, 229-31
creditors

accounting information and, 3
profit measurement as guide for, 57
CSR (corporate social reporting)
accountancy, 210-11
current issues in, 207
practice of, 212-14
current assets, 13
current liabilities, 18-19
current ratio, 167
customers, accounting information and, 3

D

day books, 240
debiting, bookkeeping and, 229-31
decision making
AI (artificial intelligence) and, 460
costs and, 343, 424, 427
directors' reports and, 181
internal decision making, 424
management accounting and, 22
marginal costing and, 431
reliability and, 61
deferred taxation, 68
delegation, control systems and, 393
depreciation
cash flow statements, 134, 148
income statement, 39-40, 45
of non-current assets, 237-8
problem with, 71
'values' and, 14-15
deprival value, idea of, 64
detailed items in income statements, 43-5
development costs and other intangibles, 65
development expenditure, 198
developments in management accounting, 343
Diploma plc, 104-5
direct costs, 342
direct expenses, 410
direct labour, 409
cost of, percentage on, 410-11
hour rate for, 411-12
variances in, 445-7
direct materials
costs of, 340
pricing for, 408-9
variances in, 444-5
directors' report, 181-2
disadvantages
of fixed budgets, 389
of internal rate of return, 363
of payback periods, 356
of rolling budgets, 307-8
discontinued and continuing operations, 44
discount allowed and received, 233
discounted cash flow, 361-8
method of, 356-61
dividend cover
interpretation of accounts, 169
ratios, interpretation and, 90
stock market assessment of company performance, 111, 118
dividend decisions, profit measurement as guide to, 55
dividend growth model, 371-2
dividend paid, 135, 169
dividend receivable, 44
dividend yield, 90
calculation of, 116-17
information from, 117-18
stock market and, 111, 116-18
dividends, 34, 110-11
duality, concept of, 61

E

EBITDA (earnings before interest, taxes, depreciation and amortization), 121-2
economic efficiency, profit measurement as indicator of, 57-8
EDS (Exposure Drafts), 58
employees
accounting information and, 3
social reporting and, 208-9
enhancing characteristics, 62
environment
environmental accounting, 210
social reporting and, 209-10
EOQ (economic order quantity), 325-8
equity
classification of, 12
statement of changes in, 70
ERT (European Round Table for Industry), 465
evaluation
of absorption costing, 413-14
standard costing and variance analysis, 453-4
event-driven risks, TCFD and, 468
exceptional items
income statement and, 44-5
problem of, 195
excessive debt, 174
expenses
classification and disclosure of, 41
financial reporting, development of, 70
income statement, 37-41
statement of financial position, 15-16
extraordinary items, problem of, 195

F

factoring, 307
invoice discounting and, 323-4
fair value, idea of, 64, 74-5
faithful representation, fundamental characteristic of, 62
FASB (Financial Accounting Standards Board, US), 59
FIFO (first-in-first-out), 408-9
financial accounting
management accounting and, 22, 337-9
financial analysts and advisers, 4
financial distress, prediction of, 174-7
financial impacts of climate risks, 468
financial instruments, 198
financial planning, 336
financial position
assessment of, 20-21
interpreting statements of, 299
Financial Reporting, Conceptual Framework for (2018), 130
financial reporting, current issues in, 189-220
accountancy and power, 206

accounting choices, reduction of, 197
accounting in context, 217-18
accounting standards, creative accounting and, 202
APMs (alternative performance measures), 196
assessment questions, 217
auditing, creative accounting and, 202-3
Corporate Report (1975), 206-7
corporate social reporting (CSR), 207
corporate social reporting (CSR), accountancy and, 210-11
corporate social reporting (CSR), practice of, 212-14
COVID-19 pandemic, accounting considerations for, 196
creative accounting, 190-94
creative accounting, bad techniques, 194
creative accounting, curtailment of, 202-6
creative accounting, development of, 191-2
creative accounting, effects of, 192-3
creative accounting, judgement becoming creative, 193-4
creative accounting, problem areas for, 195-201
CSR (corporate social responsibility), 208
development expenditure, 198
employees, social reporting and, 208-9
environment, social reporting and, 209-10
environmental accounting, 210
exceptional items, problem of, 195
extraordinary items, problem of, 195
financial instruments, 198
fuzzy rules, 201
goodwill, 197
group activities, discussion questions and, 217
HMRC rules OK, 205
information, freedom of access to, 204-5
interest, capitalization of, 198
key points review, 206-14
laissez-faire approach, 204
learning objectives, 189
left wing proposals, 205
non-recurring items, problem of, 195
offenders, punishment of, 203-4
provisions, 196-9
radical proposals, 204-5
responsible investment, winners and losers, 218
revenue recognition, 199
right wing proposals, 204-5
self-testing questions, 216
share options, 199-200
social and environmental reporting, 206-14
State Auditing Board, 205
suspicious treatments, 200-201
sustainability report, 211
UK disclosure obligations, 211
UK sustainability disclosure standards, 211-12
financial reporting, development of, 54-77
accounting in context, 76-7
accounting standards, 58-9
Accounting Standards Steering Committee, 58-9
accruals, principle of, 60
ASB (Accounting Standards Board), 58-9
assessment questions, 76
assets, definition of, 63
assets, measurement of, 63-4
Auditchain Protocol, 76-7
capitalized interest, 66
cash generated, profit measurement as indication of, 55-6
Companies Act (1969), 58
comparability, objective of, 61
concepts, 60-62
consistency, principle of, 60
contingent liabilities, 67
Corporate Report (1975), 60, 61
creditors, profit measurement as guide for, 57
deferred taxation, 68
depreciation, problem with, 71
deprival value, idea of, 64
development costs and other intangibles, 65
dividend decisions, profit measurement as guide to, 55
duality, concept of, 61
economic efficiency, profit measurement as indicator, 57-8
EDS (Exposure Drafts), 58
enhancing characteristics, 62
equity, statement of changes in, 70
expenses, 70
fair value, idea of, 64, 74-5
faithful representation, fundamental characteristic of, 62
FASB (Financial Accounting Standards Board, US), 59
Framework for the Preparation and Presentation of Financial Statements (1989), 60
FREDs (Financial Reporting Exposure Drafts), 58
FRRP (Financial Reporting Review Panel), 58-9
FRSs (Financial Reporting Standards), 58-9
going concern, principle of, 60
goodwill, 64-5
goodwill, problem with impairment of, 71
group activities, discussion questions and, 76
human assets, 65-6
IASB (International Accounting Standards Board), 59
IFRSs (International Financial Reporting Standards), 59
income statement approach, 68-72
interest, problem with capitalization of, 71-2
investment decisions, profit measurement as guide to, 57
key points review, 75
learning objectives, 54
liabilities, definition of, 66
liabilities, measurement of, 66
management performance, profit measurement as indication of, 56
price changes, adjustment of financial statements for, 72-5
price changes, dealing with, 73-4
principles, 60-62
problem areas, 71-2
problem assets, 64-8
problem liabilities, 66-8
profit figures, wide-ranging quotation of, 58
profit measurement, functions of, 55-8
provisions, 67
prudence, principle of, 60-61, 62
relevance, fundamental characteristic of, 62
relevance, objective of, 61
reliability, objective of, 61
revenue recognition, 70
revenues, income and gains, 69-72
self-testing questions, 75-6
separate value, principle of, 61
setting accounting standards, 58-9
share options, problem with, 72
SSAPs (Statements of Standard Accounting Practice), 58-9
statement of financial position approach, 62-8
Statement of Principles for Financial Reporting (ASB, December 1999), 61
taxation basis, profit measurement as, 57
understandability, objective of, 61, 62

warranties, 67
Financial Stability Board, 465
financial statements, 183
financial strengths and weaknesses, 12-14
Financial Times, 112-14, 115, 119
financing a business, 293-313
accounting in context, 312-13
assessment questions, 309-12
bonus issues of shares, 297-8
borrowing, 294, 299-303
borrowing, attractions of, 301, 302
borrowing, debentures, 301-2
borrowing, overdrafts, 301
factoring, 307
financial position, interpreting statements of, 299
group activities, discussion questions and, 312
key points review, 308
KKR, financing Asian infrastructure fund, 312-13
learning objectives, 293
minimizing need to raise finance, 306-7
non-current assets, lease of, 306-7
ordinary shares, 295-8
outsourcing, 307
preference shares, 298-9
retained profits, 294, 303-6
retained profits, dividend policy, 303-6
rights issues of shares, 296-7
sale and leaseback, 306
self-testing questions, 308-9
share capital, 293, 295-9
sources of finance, 293-5
financing activities
cash flow statements and, 136
cash generated from, 147, 148
finished goods costs, 340
fixed budget
budgetary planning and control, 388
disadvantages of, 389
fixed costs
management accounting and, 341
marginal costing, decision-making and, 424
separation from variable costs, 426-7
fixed overhead variances, 448-9
flexible budgets, 388-9
format
of cash flow statements, 141-7
income statement, 32-4
Framework for the Preparation and Presentation of Financial Statements (1989), 60
FREDs (Financial Reporting Exposure Drafts), 58
free cash flow, 137-8
FRRP (Financial Rrporting Review Panel), 58-9
FRSs (Financial Reporting Standards), 58-9
FTSE 100 Index, 108
fuzzy rules, 201

G

gearing, 14
financial structure and, 92
gearing ratio, 167-8
going concern, principle of, 60
goodwill, 64-5
financial reporting, current issues in, 197
impairment of, 40-41
problem with impairment of, 71
government, accounting information and, 3
GRI (Global Reporting Initiative), 463
gross profit
income statement, 33
interpretation of accounts, 168
gross profit ratio, 38
group accounts in practice, 173
group activities, discussion questions and
bookkeeping to trial balance and, 250
budgetary planning and control and, 403
cash flow statements and, 159-60
financial reporting, current issues in and, 217
financial reporting, development of and, 76
financing a business and, 312
income statement and, 52
interpretation of accounts and, 186-7
investment appraisal and, 379
management accounting and, 347-8
marginal costing, decision-making and, 440
ratios, interpretation and, 103
standard costing and variance analysis and, 458
statement of financial position and, 29
stock market assessment of company performance and, 125-6
sustainability and accounting and, 472
trial balance to final accounts and, 289
working capital, management of and, 332

H

HMRC (HM Revenue and Customs, UK), 3, 4
accounting information and, 3
HMRC rules OK, 205
human assets, 65-6

I

IASB (International Accounting Standards Board), 59
IASs (International Accounting Standards)
IAS 1, 9, 32-4, 69-70, 195-6
IAS 7, 129-51
IAS 11, 199
IAS 12, 68
IAS 14, 44
IAS 17, 93
IAS 18, 199
IAS 23, 66, 72, 198
IAS 32, 201, 298-9
IAS 33, 178
IAS 36, 71, 197
IAS 37, 67, 197
IAS 38, 65-6, 198
IAS 39, 201
IFRSs (International Financial Reporting Standards), 59
S1 and S2, 465
IIRC (International Integrated Reporting Council), 463
income statement (profit and loss account), 31-53
accounting in context, 52-3
acquisitions, 44
assessment questions, 49-52
associates, 44
capital expenditure, 45

for company or group, 43
company's published statement, 41-3
creativity problems, subjective measurement and, 45-6
depreciation, 39-40, 45
detailed items, 43-5
discontinued and continuing operations, 44
dividend, 34
dividends receivable, 44
exceptional items, 44-5
expenses, 37-41
expenses, classification and disclosure of, 41
financial reporting, income statement approach to, 68-72
format, 32-4
goodwill, impairment of, 40-41
gross profit, 33
gross profit ratio, 38
group activities, discussion questions and, 52
inventory value, 45-6
joint ventures, 44
key points review, 47
learning objectives, 31
limitations of, 46-7
mark-up, 38
non-controlling interests, 43-4
operating profit, 34
profit as efficiency measure, 35
profit as performance measure, 35
profit as taxation basis, 35
profit before and after tax, 34
profit reporting, need for explicitness in, 35-6
profits, reasons for measurement of, 34-6
revenue expenditure, 45
revenues (or income), 32, 36
sales, cost of, 37-8
sales, revenues and, 36
segmental reporting, 44
self-testing questions, 47-9
terminology, 32-4
timing, 46
Watches of Switzerland, 52-3
incremental budgets, budgetary control and, 394-5
indirect costs, 342
indirect materials, pricing and, 408
individual's statement of financial position, 7-8
information
freedom of access to, 204-5
information presentation, 424-6
installation costs, 365
Integrated Thinking and Strategy Group, 464
interest
capitalization of, 198
dividend cover and, 138-9
interest cover, interpretation of accounts and, 168
interest expense, 135, 149
interest paid, 135
problem with capitalization of, 71-2
interpretation of accounts, 162-88
Altman Z-scores, 175-7
assessment questions, 185-6
assets, warnings from, 175
audit opinion, formation of, 182-3
auditor's report, 182-3
cash flows, warnings in, 175
consolidated (group) accounts, rules for, 171-2
consolidated (group) financial statements, 169-73
cost of sales, 168-9
current ratio, 167
directors' report, 181-2
dividend cover, 169
dividend paid, 169
excessive debt, 174
financial distress, prediction of, 174-7
financial statements, 183
gearing ratio, 167-8
gross profit, 168
group accounts in practice, 173
group activities, discussion questions and, 186-7
interest cover, 168
investments, selective performance of, 180
key points review, 184
learning objectives, 162
liquidity ratio, 167
losses (or falling profits), 174
Marks & Spencer plc, comments on published accounts, 167-9
Marks & Spencer plc, published accounts of, 163-9
negative goodwill, 173
net assets per share, 169
operating expenses, 168
operating profit, 168
P/E ratio, 169
profit after tax, 168
published accounts, calculation of ratios from, 163-9
sales revenue, 168
segments, selective performance of, 178-80
selective performance, 177-80
self-testing questions, 184-5
share price, warnings from, 175
shareholders' equity per share, 169
solvency, 174-7
warning signs, 174-5
interpretation of cash flow statements, 137-41
interpretation of variances, 451
contribution approach to, 452-3
inventory
management, 324-5
turnover ratio, 88
value, 45-6
investing activities, 136
cash generated from, 146, 148
investing in shares, 107
investment analysis, 109, 110
investment appraisal, 351-2
investment decisions, profit measurement as guide to, 57
investment appraisal, 350-82
accounting in context, 380-82
assessment questions, 377-9
CAPM (capital asset pricing model), 371, 372
cash flow, profit and, 351-2
cash flows, relevant costs for, 365-8
cost of capital, 358-73
cost of capital, evaluation of approaches to, 372-3
discounted cash flow, 361-8
discounted cash flow method, 356-61
dividend growth model, 371-2
group activities, discussion questions and, 379
installation costs, 365
investment, 351-2
IRR (internal rate of return), 361-8
IRR (internal rate of return), calculation of, 364-5
key points review, 375

learning objectives, 350
methods for, 352-68
NPV (net present value), 356-61
NPV (net present value), calculation of, 364-5
opportunity cost, 368-9
payback period, 355-6
P/E ratio, 371
profit, cash flow and, 351-2
risk uncertainty and, 373-4
ROCE (return on capital employed), 352, 354, 371
ROI (Return on Investment), 352-4, 355
scrap values, 365
self-testing questions, 375-7
taxation, 365-6
taxation, discounted cash flow and, 366-8
UK water vs banking sector failures, 380-82
uncertainty, risk and, 373-4
weighted average cost of capital, 369-71
working capital, cash flow and, 365
investments, selective performance of, 180
investors, accounting information and, 5
invoice discounting, 323-4
IOSCO (International Organization of Securities Commissions), 465
IR (Integrated Reporting)
aims of, 464
framework for, 463-5
IRR (internal rate of return), 361-8
calculation of, 364-5
ISSB (International Sustainability Standards Board), 465
iXBRL final accounts program, VT launch of, 290

J

joint ventures, 44
journals, 240
just-in-time, 325-6

K

key points review
absorption costing, 417
bookkeeping to trial balance, 245
budgetary planning and control, 400
cash flow statements, 151
financial reporting, current issues in, 206-14
financial reporting, development of, 75
financing a business, 308
income statement, 47
interpretation of accounts, 184
investment appraisal, 375
management accounting, 344
marginal costing, decision-making and, 437-8
ratios, interpretation and, 99-100
standard costing and variance analysis, 455
statement of financial position, 22-3
stock market assessment of company performance, 123
sustainability and accounting, 471
trial balance to final accounts, 279
working capital, management of, 328
KKR, financing Asian infrastructure fund, 312-13

L

laissez-faire approach, 204
learning objectives
absorption costing, 405
bookkeeping to trial balance, 221
budgetary planning and control, 383
cash flow statements, 129
financial reporting, current issues in, 189
financial reporting, development of, 54
financing a business, 293
income statement, 31
interpretation of accounts, 162
investment appraisal, 350
management accounting, 335
marginal costing, decision-making and, 423
ratios, interpretation and, 78
standard costing and variance analysis, 442
statement of financial position, 6
stock market assessment of company performance, 106
sustainability and accounting, 461
trial balance to final accounts, 252
working capital, management of, 314
ledgers, 240
left wing proposals, 205
legal risks, TCFD and, 467
lenders, accounting information and, 3
liabilities
classification of, 12
definition of, 66
measurement of, 66
LIFO (last-in-first out), 409
limitations
of income statement, 46-7
limiting factors, control systems and, 392-3
of marginal costing, 436-7
ratios, interpretation and, 93-4
of standard costing, 453-4
of statement of financial position, 21-2
limited liability companies, 2
limited liability partnerships (LLPs), 3
line by line inspection of costs, 426
liquidity ratio, 167
long term financial strength, 80-82
long term liabilities, 12, 13-14
long-term classification, 11-12
losses (or falling profits), 174

M

machine hour rate, 412
management accounting, 335-49
absorption costing and, 337-8, 342-3
accounting in context, 348-9
assessment questions, 346-7
budgetary control, 339
cost behaviour, 340-42
cost of sales, 338
developments in, 343
direct costs, 342
direct materials costs, 340
financial accounting and, 337-9
financial planning, 336

finished goods costs, 340
fixed costs, 341
group activities, discussion questions and, 347-8
indirect costs, 342
key points review, 344
learning objectives, 335
manufacturing accounts, 340-42
marginal costing, 342-3
operating expenses, 340
origins of, 336
prime costs, 340
production costs, 340
self-testing questions, 344-6
semi-variable costs, 341
standard costing, variance analysis and, 343
Superdry, de-listing from LSE, 348-9
terminology for manufacturing accounts, 340
variable costs, 341
work in progress, 340
management by exception, control systems and, 393
management performance, profit measurement as indication of, 56
manufacturing accounts, 340-42
margin of safety, 429
marginal costing, decision-making and, 423-41
absorption costing, 423-4, 426
accounting in context, 440-41
advantages of marginal costing, 431-6
assessment questions, 439-40
Black Rock rolls out first generative AI tools, 440-41
break-even analysis, 427-9, 435
break-even charts, 430
break-even formula, 428-9
comparing costs over several periods, 427
comparing costs over two periods, 426
'contribution' towards fixed costs, 424-5
decision making, 431
fixed costs, 424
fixed costs, separation from variable costs, 426-7
group activities, discussion questions and, 440
information presentation, 424-6
key points review, 437-8
learning objectives, 423
limitations of marginal costing, 436-7
line by line inspection of costs, 426
margin of safety, 429
marginal costing presentation, points emerging from, 425
profit/volume charts, 430
self-testing questions, 438-9
variable costs, 424
variable costs, separation from fixed costs, 426-7
marginal costing, management accounting and, 342-3
market capitalization, 114
market risk, TCFD and, 468
Marks & Spencer plc
comments on published accounts, 167-9
published accounts of, 163-9
mark-up, 38
master budget, 387-8
MDGs (UN Millennium Development Goals), 469
methods
COVID-19: hospitals need to change costings methods, 458-60
for discounted cash flow, 356-61
for investment appraisal, 352-68
production overheads, other methods for charging, 412
minimizing need to raise finance, 306-7
motivation, control systems and, 393

N

negative goodwill, 173
net asset value, 111, 119-20
net assets, profit and, 16
net assets per share
interpretation of accounts, 169
ratios, interpretation and, 90-91
non-controlling interests, 43-4
non-current assets, 143, 146, 148-50
depreciation of, 237-8
lease of, 306-7
sale of, 238-9
non-current liabilities, 19
non-recurring items, problem of, 195
NPV (net present value)
calculation of, 364-5
investment appraisal and, 356-61

O

objectives
budgetary control and definition of, 395
control systems and, 392
offenders, punishment of, 203-4
operating activities
cash flow statements and, 134-7
cash generated from, 145-6, 147-8
operating expenses
interpretation of accounts, 168
management accounting, 340
operating profit
income statement and, 34
interpretation of accounts and, 168
opportunity cost, 368-9
ordinary shares, 295-8
origins of management accounting, 336
outsourcing, 307
overtrading, 318-19

P

paperwork exercise, budgetary control as, 395
Paris Agreement (COP 21), 466
participation, budgetary control and, 394
partnerships, 2
partnership accounts, issues in, 277-9
trial balance to final accounts for, 274-9
payables management, 327-8
payback period, 355-6
P/E (price/earnings) ratio
calculation of, 114
information from, 114-16
interpretation of, 89-90, 115-16
interpretation of accounts, 169
investment appraisal and, 371
stock market assessment of company performance and, 114-16
performance, predictors of, 114-20, 121-2
performance evaluation, control systems and, 393

performance levels, budgetary control and, 394
policy risks, TCFD and, 467
Porter, Michael, 466
power, accountancy and, 206
PPBS (Planning and Programming Budgeting System), 399-400
preference shares, 298-9
preparation of cash flow statements, 147-50
prepayments, 236-7
presentation of 'ratios,' 79
price changes
  adjustment of financial statements for, 72-5
  dealing with, financial reporting and, 73-4
prices, averaging system for, 409
prime costs, 340
principles
  financial reporting, development of, 60-62
  Statement of Principles for Financial Reporting (ASB, December 1999), 61
private business, accountability in, 2-3
problem areas for financial reporting, 71-2
problem assets, 64-8
problem liabilities, 66-8
problems with standard costing, 453-4
production costs, 340
production overheads
  absorption costing and, 410-12
  methods for charging for, 412
profit
  after tax, 168
  cash flow and, 351-2
  statement of financial position and, 15-16
profit and loss account see income statement
profitability of sales, 87
profitability overall, 84-6
profitability ratios, 84-9, 97
profits
  before and after tax, 34
  as efficiency measure, 35
  as performance measure, 35
  profit figures, wide-ranging quotation of, 58
  profit measurement, functions of, 55-8
  profit pressure, new CEO and, 187
  profit reporting, need for explicitness in, 35-6
  profit/volume charts, 430
  publication of, 17
  reasons for measurement of, 34-6
  stock market assessment of company performance, 110
  before taxation, cash flow statements and, 134, 148
  as taxation basis, 35
provisions
  financial reporting, current issues in, 196-9
  financial reporting, development of, 67
prudence, principle, 60-61, 62
public groups and individuals, accounting information and, 4
public sector bodies, accounting information and, 3
published accounts, calculation of ratios from, 163-9
published statements, 139-40
purchase account, bookkeeping and, 225

R

radical proposals, 204-5
ratios, interpretation and, 78-105
  accounting in context, 104-5
  assessment questions, 102-3
  asset utilization ratios, 97-8
  assets, utilization of, 87-9
  comparisons, 92-3
  Diploma plc, 104-5
  dividend cover, 90
  dividend yield, 90
  gearing, financial structure and, 92
  group activities, discussion questions and, 103
  inventory turnover ratio, 88
  key points review, 99-100
  learning objectives, 78
  limitations, 93-4
  long term financial strength, 80-82
  net assets per share, 90-91
  presentation of 'ratios,' 79
  price/earnings (PE) ratio, 89-90
  profitability, 84-9
  profitability of sales, 87
  profitability overall, 84-6
  profitability ratios, 97
  ready reference for ratios, 94-9
  sales profitability ratios, 97
  sales/current assets ratio, 88
  sales/non-current assets ratio, 87-8
  self-testing questions, 100-101
  short term financial strength, 80
  solvency, financial strength and, 80-84
  stock market ratios, 89-91, 98
  strength/solvency ratios, 96-7
  trade payables ratio, 88-9
  trade receivables ratio, 88
  working capital management, 91-2
receivables management, 319-22
recording transactions, 224-5
refinancing after post-pandemic liquidity crunch, 333
relevance
  fundamental characteristic of, 62
  objective of, 61
reliability, objective, 61
replacement cost system, 409
reputation risk, TCFD and, 468
resources, budgetary control and competition for, 394
responsibility
  control systems and, 393
  responsible investment, winners and losers in, 218
retained profits
  dividend policy and, 303-6
  financing a business, 294, 303-6
returns inwards and outwards, 233-5
revenue expenditure, 45
revenue recognition
  financial reporting, current issues in, 199
  financial reporting, development of, 70
revenues (or income)
  income and gains, 69-72
  income statement, 32, 36
  statement of financial position, 16
reward schemes, budgetary control and, 394
right wing proposals, 204-5
rights issues of shares, 296-7
risk in investing in shares, 109
risk uncertainty and, 373-4
ROCE (return on capital employed), 352, 354, 371
ROI (return on investment), 352-4, 355

roles
- standard costing and variance analysis, 453
- statement of financial position, 20-21

rolling budgets
- advantages and disadvantages of, 397-8
- budgetary planning and control, 397-9

S

sale and leaseback, 306
sale of non-current assets, 238-9
sales
- contribution variances, 450-52
- cost of, 37-8
- margin variances, 449-50
- profitability ratios, 97
- revenue from, 168
- revenues and, 36
- sales account, 226-9
- sales/current assets ratio, 88
- sales/non-current assets ratio, 87-8

SASB (Sustainability Accounting Standards Board), 463
scrap values, 365
SDGs (UN Sustainable Development Goals)
- drawbacks of, 470-71
- significance for organizations, 469-71

segmental reporting, 44
segments, selective performance of, 178-80
selective performance, 177-80
self-testing questions
- absorption costing, 417-19
- bookkeeping to trial balance, 245-7
- budgetary planning and control, 400-402
- cash flow statements, 151-4
- financial reporting, current issues in, 216
- financial reporting, development of, 75-6
- financing a business, 308-9
- income statement, 47-9
- interpretation of accounts, 184-5
- investment appraisal, 375-7
- management accounting, 344-6
- marginal costing, decision-making and, 438-9
- ratios, interpretation and, 100-101
- standard costing and variance analysis, 455-6
- statement of financial position, 23-6
- stock market assessment of company performance, 123-4
- sustainability and accounting, 472
- trial balance to final accounts, 280-85
- working capital, management of, 329-30

semi-variable costs, 341
separate value, principle of, 61
setting accounting standards, 58-9
share capital, 293, 295-9
share options, 199-200
- problem of, 72

share price, warnings from, 175
share prices
- accounting information and, 110-12
- influences on, 108-9

shareholders
- accounting information and, 3
- equity per share of, 169

shares, lack of 'true value' in, 109
short term financial strength, 80
short-term classification, 11-12
size and growth, publication of, 17
social and environmental data, quality and scope of, 462
social and environmental reporting, 206-14
sole traders, 2
- accruals adjustments for, 260
- adjustments to accounts for, 257-64
- bad debt provision, 261-4
- bad debt write-offs, 261
- closing inventory adjustments, 257-8
- current assets, 255
- depreciation adjustments, 258-9
- drawings adjustments, 260
- equity of, 255
- error corrections, 264
- expenses, 256
- long-term liabilities, 255
- non-current assets, 255
- prepayment adjustments, 260
- revenue (turnover), 256
- short-term liabilities, 255
- trial balance question, dealing with, 256
- trial balance to final accounts for, 253-64

solvency
- financial strength and, 80-84
- interpretation of accounts, 174-7
- publication of, 17

sources of finance, 293-5
spending up to budget, budgetary control and, 395
SSAPs (Statements of Standard Accounting Practice), 58-9
standard cost system, 409
standard costing and variance analysis, 343, 442-60
- accounting in context, 458-60
- assessment questions, 456-8
- COVID-19: Hospitals need to change costings methods, 458-60
- direct labour variances, 445-7
- direct material variances, 444-5
- evaluation, 453-4
- fixed overhead variances, 448-9
- group activities, discussion questions and, 458
- interpretation of variances, 451
- interpretation of variances, contribution approach, 452-3
- key points review, 455
- learning objectives, 442
- limitations of standard costing, 453-4
- problems with standard costing, 453-4
- role and functions, 453
- sales contribution variances, 450-52
- sales margin variances, 449-50
- self-testing questions, 455-6
- 'standard hours' calculation using, 447
- summary of variances, 450-51
- summary of variances, contribution approach, 452
- variable overhead variances, 447-8
- variance analysis, 442-4

'standard hours' calculation using, 447
State Auditing Board, 205
statement of financial position, 6-30
- accounting in context, 29-30
- assessment questions, 26-8
- assets, classification of, 11-12
- balance sheet, wide use of term, 6-7
- business finance, publication of, 17
- collapse of companies, 13
- company's published statement of, 17-19

company's statement, 8-11
current assets, 13
current liabilities, 18-19
depreciation, 'values' and, 14-15
equity, classification of, 12
expenses, 15-16
financial accounting, management accounting and, 22
financial position, assessment of, 20-21
financial reporting and, 62-8
financial strengths and weaknesses, 12-14
gearing, 14
group activities, discussion questions and, 29
individual's statement, 7-8
key points review, 22-3
learning objectives, 6
liabilities, classification of, 12
limitations of, 21-2
long term liabilities, 12, 13-14
long-term classification, 11-12
net assets, profit and, 16
non-current liabilities, 19
profit and, 15-16
profits, publication of, 17
revenues, 16
role of, 20-21
self-testing questions, 23-6
short-term classification, 11-12
size and growth, publication of, 17
solvency, publication of, 17
Sutton & East Surrey Water, Pennon Group plc and, 29-30
terminology used in, 9-11
worth, problems in establishing, 8

Statement of Principles for Financial Reporting (ASB, December 1999), 61

stock market assessment of company performance, 106-28
accounting in context, 126-7
assessment questions, 124-5
BP CEOs, 126-7
cash flow, 112, 120
cash flow, categories of, 120
dividend cover, 111, 118
dividend yield, 111, 116-18
dividend yield, calculation of, 116-17
dividend yield, information from, 117-18
dividends, 110-11
EBITDA (earnings before interest, taxes, depreciation and amortization), 121-2
Financial Times and, 112-14, 115, 119
FTSE 100 Index, 108
group activities, discussion questions and, 125-6
investing in shares, 107
investment analysis, 109, 110
key points review, 123
learning objectives, 106
market capitalization, 114
net asset value, 111, 119-20
performance, predictors of, 114-20, 121-2
price/earnings (P/E) ratios, 114-16
price/earnings (P/E) ratios, calculation of, 114
price/earnings (P/E) ratios, information from, 114-16
price/earnings (P/E) ratios, interpretation of, 115-16
profits, 110
risk in investing in shares, 109
self-testing questions, 123-4
share prices, accounting information and, 110-12
share prices, influences on, 108-9
shares, lack of 'true value' of, 109
stock market ratios, 122

stock market ratios, 89-91, 98
assessment of company performance and, 122

strength/solvency ratios, 96-7

summary budget, 387-8

summary of variances, 450-51
contribution approach and, 452

Superdry, de-listing from LSE, 348-9

suppliers, accounting information and, 3

suspense accounts, 243-4

suspicious treatments, 200-201

sustainability and accounting, 461-75
accounting in context, 472-4
AICPA (American Institute of Certified Public Accountants), 462
biodiversity depletion, challenge of climate change and, 467
Brundtland Commission (UN, 1987), 461-2
CDP (Carbon Disclosure Project), 463
CDSB (Climate Disclosure Standards Board), 463
climate change risks and implications, 466-7
climate patterns, TCFD and risks in, 468
climate-related risks, TCFD and, 467
concept of sustainability, 462
corporate reporting, 464-5
ERT (European Round Table for Industry), 465
event-driven risks, TCFD and, 468
financial impacts of climate risks, 468
Financial Stability Board, 465
GRI (Global Reporting Initiative), 463
group activities, discussion questions and, 472
IFRS (International Financial Reporting Standards) S1, 465
IFRS (International Financial Reporting Standards) S2, 465
IIRC (International Integrated Reporting Council), 463
importance of sustainability, reasons for, 462-3
Integrated Thinking and Strategy Group, 464
IOSCO (International Organization of Securities Commissions), 465
IR (Integrated Reporting), aims of, 464
IR (Integrated Reporting) framework, 463-5
ISSB (International Sustainability Standards Board), 465
key points review, 471
learning objectives, 461
legal risks, TCFD and, 467
market risk, TCFD and, 468
MDGs (UN Millennium Development Goals), 469
Paris Agreement (COP 21), 466
policy risks, TCFD and, 467
reputation risk, TCFD and, 468
SASB (Sustainability Accounting Standards Board), 463
SDGs (UN Sustainable Development Goals), advantages of, 470
SDGs (UN Sustainable Development Goals), drawbacks of, 470-71
SDGs (UN Sustainable Development Goals), significance for organizations, 469-71
self-testing questions, 472
social and environmental data, quality and scope of, 462
sustainability, 461-2
sustainable fashion, 472-4
TBL (triple bottom line), 462
TCFD (Task Force on Climate-related Financial Disclosures), 465

TCFD (Task Force on Climate-related Financial Disclosures), recommendations of, 467-8
technology risk, TCFD and, 468
transition risks, TCFD and, 467
value chain, competition, companies and, 466
value chain, sustainable businesses and, 466
sustainability report, 211
sustainable fashion
ESG (environmental, social and governance) concerns and, 472-4
fashion problems in developing countries, 473
fast-fashion, sustainability and, 473-4
media reports, adverse impact of ESG controversies on investment, 472-3
sustainability and accounting, 472-4
Sutton & East Surrey Water, Pennon Group plc, 29-30

T

taxation
corporation tax, 264, 267
deferred taxation, 68
discounted cash flow and, 366-8
investment appraisal and, 365-6
profit before and after tax, 34
profit before taxation, 134, 148
profit measurement as basis for, 57
taxation paid, 135
TaxCalc expands FRS 103 capabilities to include limited liability partnerships, 291
TBL (triple bottom line), 462
TCFD (Task Force on Climate-related Financial Disclosures)
recommendations, 467-8
sustainability and accounting, 465
technology risk, TCFD and, 468
terminology
income statement and, 32-4
for manufacturing accounts, 340
in statement of financial position, 9-11
timing of income statement, 46
trade payables ratio, 88-9
trade receivables ratio, 88
transactions, double-entry bookkeeping and, 222-31
transition risks, TCFD and, 467
trial balance to final accounts, 252-91
accounting in context, 289-91
assessment questions, 285-9
companies, 264-74
companies, accrued charges adjustments, 267
companies, adjustments, 266-7
companies, bad debt provision, 267
companies, bad debt write-offs, 267
companies, corporation tax, 264
companies, corporation tax adjustments, 267
companies, dealing with extended trial balance question, 269-74
companies, depreciation adjustments, 267
companies, differences from sole traders, 264-6
companies, dividends, 264
companies, expenses, 264
companies, extended trial balance, 268-74
companies, interest payments, 265
companies, inventory adjustments, 267
companies, land revaluations, 267
companies, non-current assets adjustments, 267
companies, prepayments adjustments, 267
companies, share capital, 264
companies, shareholders' funds, 264
group activities, discussion questions and, 289
iXBRL final accounts program, VT launch of, 290
key points review, 279
learning objectives, 252
partnerships, 274-9
partnerships, partnership accounts, issues in, 277-9
self-testing questions, 280-85
sole traders, 253-64
sole traders, accruals adjustments, 260
sole traders, adjustments, 257-64
sole traders, bad debt provision, 261-4
sole traders, bad debt write-offs, 261
sole traders, closing inventory adjustments, 257-8
sole traders, current assets, 255
sole traders, dealing with trial balance question, 256
sole traders, depreciation adjustments, 258-9
sole traders, drawings adjustments, 260
sole traders, equity, 255
sole traders, error corrections, 264
sole traders, expenses, 256
sole traders, long-term liabilities, 255
sole traders, non-current assets, 255
sole traders, prepayment adjustments, 260
sole traders, revenue (turnover), 256
sole traders, short-term liabilities, 255
TaxCalc expands FRS 103 capabilities to include limited liability partnerships, 291
trial balance, 253
VT Software, info from company website, 289-90

U

UK disclosure obligations, 211
UK drug shortages aggravated due to Brexit, 422
UK sustainability disclosure standards, 211-12
UK water vs banking sector failures, 380-82
inadequate regulation, 381
investment appraisal, 380-82
parallels with banking industry, 380-81
uncertainty, risk and, 373-4
understandability, objective of, 61, 62

V

value chain
competition, companies and, 466
sustainable businesses and, 466
Value Reporting Foundation, 463
variable costs
management accounting, 341
marginal costing, decision-making and, 424
separation from fixed costs, 426-7
variable overhead variances, 447-8
variance analysis, 442-4
VT Software, info from company website, 289-90

W

warning signs, 174-5
warranties, 67
Watches of Switzerland, 52-3
weighted average cost of capital, 369-71
work in progress, 340
working capital, management of, 314-33
  accounting in context, 333
  assessment questions, 330-32
  cash flow, investment appraisal and, 365
  cash flow statements and working capital increase, 135, 147-8
  cash management, 326-7
  collecting due payments, 320-22
  costs and benefits of different approaches, 322-3
  credit allowances, 320
  credit customers, 320
  EOQ (economic order quantity), 325-8
  factoring, invoice discounting and, 323-4
  group activities, discussion questions and, 332
  inventory management, 324-5
  invoice discounting, 323-4
  just-in-time, 325-6
  key points review, 328
  learning objectives, 314
  overtrading, 318-19
  payables management, 327-8
  ratios, interpretation and, 91-2
  receivables management, 319-22
  refinancing after post-pandemic liquidity crunch, 333
  self-testing questions, 329-30
  working capital, 315-25
  working capital, how much?, 316
  working capital, objectives of management of, 316-18
worth, problems in establishment of, 8

Z

ZBB (zero-based budgeting)
  budgetary planning and control, 396-7
  transferable to zero-based management, 403-6